Troubleshooting and Supporting Windows 11

Creating Robust, Reliable, Sustainable, and Secure Systems

Mike Halsey

Apress®

Troubleshooting and Supporting Windows 11: Creating Robust, Reliable, Sustainable, and Secure Systems

Mike Halsey
Genouillac, France

ISBN-13 (pbk): 978-1-4842-8727-9
https://doi.org/10.1007/978-1-4842-8728-6

ISBN-13 (electronic): 978-1-4842-8728-6

Managing Director, Apress Media LLC: Welmoed Spahr
Acquisitions Editor: Smriti Srivastava
Development Editor: Laura Berendson
Coordinating Editor: Mark Powers

Cover designed by eStudioCalamar

Cover image designed by Freepik (www.freepik.com)

Distributed to the book trade worldwide by Springer Science+Business Media New York, 1 New York Plaza, Suite 4600, New York, NY 10004-1562, USA. Phone 1-800-SPRINGER, fax (201) 348-4505, e-mail orders-ny@springer-sbm.com, or visit www.springeronline.com. Apress Media, LLC is a California LLC and the sole member (owner) is Springer Science + Business Media Finance Inc (SSBM Finance Inc). SSBM Finance Inc is a **Delaware** corporation.

For information on translations, please e-mail booktranslations@springernature.com; for reprint, paperback, or audio rights, please e-mail bookpermissions@springernature.com.

Apress titles may be purchased in bulk for academic, corporate, or promotional use. eBook versions and licenses are also available for most titles. For more information, reference our Print and eBook Bulk Sales web page at http://www.apress.com/bulk-sales.

Any source code or other supplementary material referenced by the author in this book is available to readers on GitHub via the book's product page, located at www.apress.com/. For more detailed information, please visit http://www.apress.com/source-code.

Printed on acid-free paper

For Jake and Rory Webster, who took care of everything else for me this summer, so I could take care of writing this book.

Table of Contents

About the Author

Mike Halsey is the author of more than 20 books and is a recognized technical expert. He has been a Microsoft Most Valuable Professional (MVP) awardee since 2011. He is the author of *The Green IT Guide* and *Windows 10 Troubleshooting, Second Edition* (Apress, 2021).

He understands that some subjects can be intimidating, so he approaches each subject area in straightforward and easy-to-understand ways.

Mike is originally from the UK, but now lives in the south of France with his rescue border collies, Evan and Robbie. You can contact Mike on Twitter at **@MikeHalsey** and find more hints, tips, and support at his website: `www.Windows.do`.

Introduction

If you're looking for a career in IT administration or support, or have already been working in IT for some time, you will know that the world you work in has changed considerably. The pandemic of 2020 rewrote the guidebook for supporting end users and maintaining computers, and what was the exception just a few short years ago, of people working from home and from coffee shops at all manner of strange hours, has now become the norm.

I've been writing Windows troubleshooting books since Windows 7 launched, but knew that this new approach to work would require a new approach to training and to the books that I write. For this book then, I took a completely different approach, keeping subjects tight and concise and making sure that remote support and the new challenges it presents are covered.

For everything else, if I don't reference it directly, then you will find links to further information within this book to help you get the information you need. I've put all my years of experience as an author and an IT professional into making sure that you get the information you need quickly, because supporting end users quickly and maintaining high productivity is the order of the day.

I sincerely hope you enjoy this book too, not as a dry technical guide but as a fun read with anecdotes, stories, and fun snippets, and everything you need to keep you entertained as you learn new and updated skills.

PART I

Troubleshooting Fundamentals

CHAPTER 1

Introducing Troubleshooting in Windows 11

We're living in interesting times when it comes to working in IT and providing support for end users in the business space. Having now emerged from the global pandemic of 2020 (if only there was a phrase we could have used to describe seeing it coming), many if not most companies and organizations have workforces that, to a certain extent anyway, have rather enjoyed working from home.

It certainly hasn't been without its challenges. Many were holed up throughout repeated lockdowns in small apartments, many without even a small balcony to step out onto. Many more had children at home all day, every day, becoming more and more frustrated with being unable to see their friends, and with home workers also having to double as unqualified and unprepared teachers, using whatever resources they could lay their hands on.

Despite all of this, people found great value in working from home. Days were longer for people, and more could be done without the time spent, from half an hour to sometimes six hours a day travelling to and from the workplace. Not having to spend vast sums of money, sometimes thousands of dollars, on fuel or public transport also brought its own benefits.

When you have more time to spend with your family, or on your hobbies and interests, the reasons to return entirely to the way life was before can begin to appear unreasonable. It's no coincidence that during the lockdown periods Microsoft saw huge spikes in the numbers of people playing games on Xbox.

© Mike Halsey 2023
M. Halsey, *Troubleshooting and Supporting Windows 11*, https://doi.org/10.1007/978-1-4842-8728-6_1

So when 2022 came around and I began writing this book, many companies were finding themselves having to tactfully and diplomatically negotiate with their employees. Apple is a good example of this. Having just spent around five billion dollars on their new California headquarters, some employees threatened legal action if the company forced them to return to the office full time, no matter how nice the new premises were. Other companies such as Google sought to cut costs by withdrawing some employee benefits such as on-site laundry and dry cleaning and tried to make it more difficult for employees to claim free evening meals.

None of that acted as an incentive to return to the office full time. It may happen eventually, but there will forever be an aspect of hybrid work that you will be supporting.

Then there's the cloud aspect of the change. In 2021, Microsoft released its Cloud PC offering as part of the Microsoft 365 Enterprise suite of services. Initially expensive, we can fully expect prices to drop, and no doubt for the feature to make its way to consumer subscriptions in the fullness of time.

Cloud PC enables people to run a full streamed Windows 11 desktop to any device they own, from a PC to an iPad and a Chromebook. With Microsoft's push under CEO Satya Nadella to transition to a services company and support every operating system platform out there, you can access business services from any device again, and you'll no doubt find yourself supporting end users, working from home, on their Google Chromebook from time to time.

How Windows 11 Came About

There's still good reason to support and troubleshoot Windows 11 desktop PCs and laptops though, and a large part of this is the story of how Windows 11 came about in the first place. There had long been a story that Microsoft had publicly stated Windows 10 was to be the last version of Windows. This story is actually apocryphal, and the company never made a formal statement to that effect.

It was actually a Microsoft senior technical evangelist, a guy called Jerry Nixon, who at the Microsoft Ignite conference in 2015 said, "Right now we're releasing Windows 10, and because Windows 10 is the last version of Windows, we're all still working on Windows 10."

It could be that this *was* an official Microsoft policy at the time, because it tallies with something I was told the same year by a senior Microsoft marketing official at the 2015 Microsoft MVP (Most Valuable Professional) Summit. He was talking about the naming for Windows 10, being a little odd coming as it came after Windows 8.1 (some Microsoft staffers joked the point was actually a tiny plus [+] sign).

He told the assembled MVPs in the room that there were two reasons for the Windows 10 name. Firstly, Microsoft had taken the name Windows 9 to focus groups (and Microsoft love using focus groups) who fed back that 9 didn't make it sound like the big release that it was.

Then came the interesting bit, Microsoft had planned to just call it "Windows" and be done with it. Windows 7 was out of support and nobody was using Windows 8, so why the hell not? This is when, he said, the lawyers had got involved. Twice in recent years, they'd been sued over a name: first by Rupert Murdoch's Sky Television network in the UK over the name "SkyDrive" and then by a German cash-and-carry company over the use of the word "Metro" to describe their design language for Windows 10.

In both instances, the names had to be changed; SkyDrive became OneDrive (which is a better name anyway if you want my opinion), and Metro became Fluent. The lawyers pointed out that if a double-glazing company in Finland (to give one random example) sued over possible confusion caused by the name "Windows," then Microsoft would be completely unable to change the name.

The plan then became, so he told us, to call it "Windows 10," and then when Windows 8.1 was falling out of support and Windows 10 was the only version of Windows in use, to just start calling it "Windows." Because it would still officially be called "Windows 10," that ought to be enough to placate the lawyers if anybody were to sue over the name (I know, it's ridiculous when you think about it, but this apparently is what lawyers go to bed thinking about at night).

Then came Windows 10X. Microsoft's Surface hardware group were planning to release two new dual-screen devices that they announced in late 2019. In the end, only one of the devices came to market, the Surface Duo, and by the time it had, the OS choice had changed to Google's Android.

Windows 10X was supposed to be the next huge leap in Windows architecture and very likely would have made this book entirely unnecessary overnight had it succeeded.

When Windows 10 was being developed, Microsoft had changed the underlying architecture so that they could componentize the OS. There would be "Windows 10 Core" which included the kernel files, and then all other aspects of the OS from the desktop interface to server features could be plugged in as needed.

The overall effect was that Microsoft could produce many different "flavors" of Windows 10, from Windows 10 IoT (Internet of Things) to Windows 10 Server, Windows 10 Azure Server, Windows 10 standard (the Home, Pro, and Enterprise editions), and so on.

This componentization work continued with Windows 10X which was to take it to the next stage. For some years, Microsoft had supported completely virtualized apps and software in Windows. Microsoft Virtual Desktop Infrastructure (VDI), which later transitioned into Windows Azure Virtual Desktop and then to Windows 365 Cloud PC, has been around for some years and allows anything from an individual app to an entire desktop to be run on a client machine in a virtualized environment.

The trick with all this is that the end user would never know the difference between a virtualized and streamed app and a locally installed one, as they would both be launched from the Start Menu or Taskbar and operate identically. You might remember "Windows XP Mode" for Windows 7 that operated in exactly the same way, and this is also the same way that the Xbox game console works, with one VM for the Xbox shell and another for games.

The upshot of Windows 10X would be that everything from the desktop to installed apps and software would be containerized and run its own, distinct virtual machine (VM). Even the currently running Windows kernel would have apparently run in a VM, meaning the actual kernel could be updated and upgraded "on the fly" without the need to reboot the PC.

This would have transformed Windows forever. Completely banished would have been instabilities and incompatibilities caused by the need to support legacy software dating all the way back to DOS and Windows 95. Any app, service, or driver that crashed wouldn't be able to take the entire operating system or other apps and services with it. The Blue Screen of Death (BSOD) would have been relegated to the dustbin of history, and yours truly would have been put well and truly out of a job.

The problem came with performance, and Microsoft eventually scrapped Windows 10X, admitting they couldn't get it to work reliably and with decent enough performance to release it. This is a shame as (and especially as I'm heading into early retirement anyway) I truly hope they find a way to make this work as hardware performance improves over time, perhaps releasing this as Windows 12 around 2024.

Microsoft had talked extensively about Windows 10X, however, and shown many demos and screenshots of the new interface they had designed for it. This new interface garnered many positive reviews and plaudits, so when PC Makers, also called Original Equipment Manufacturers (OEMs), came to Microsoft during 2021 bemoaning a slump in PC sales and asked if Microsoft could release something new and shiny to reinvigorate the market for them, the decision was made to fold the new componentized interface into Windows 10 and create a new OS called Windows 11.

How Windows 11 Differs from Windows 10

It's this componentization that means that underneath, Windows 10 and Windows 11 are the same core OS. They share the same kernel with each other and with Windows Server. This componentization was done primarily for reasons of cost, making it much cheaper to support one Windows core, rather than several different ones, and as the kernel was separate from all the other plug-in components, support and maintenance for them would also become cheaper.

There are some distinct differences between Windows 10 and Windows 11 though that go deeper than a slick new interface (and the interface is a subject I'll come back to later on). These changes though are mostly focused on which PCs Microsoft deemed suitable for Windows 11 to be installed on, and they were controversial indeed.

The most controversial decision was to enforce the need for a Trusted Platform Module (TPM) 2.0 chip or support for a Firmware Trusted Platform Module (fTPM) in the UEFI firmware. Microsoft wanted to make Windows 11 much more secure than previous versions and also encourage people to use biometric security more, such as their Windows Hello features, in their drive to banish the need for passwords.

TPM chips had been mandatory for new Windows PCs since the release of Windows 8+1 (sorry, Windows 8.1) in 2013. This only applied to new PCs sold through OEMs however. It didn't apply to PCs that gamers, pro users, and enthusiasts built for themselves, nor did it apply to new motherboards that were sold individually, though a few did come with a socket for a TPM chip anyway.

It also didn't apply to all the older Windows 7 desktop and laptop PCs that businesses and organizations around the world upgraded to Windows 10 or purchased new for Windows 10 from manufacturers that agreed to produce older-specified machines so as to maintain full compatibility with an organization's software and hardware peripherals.

fTPMs though were still in the planning stage in 2015 when Windows 10 was released and weren't widely available until shortly before the release of Windows 11.

So while many businesses and organizations and even consumers had Windows 8.1 era PCs that included a TPM, this was often a TPM 1.0 chip, and Microsoft deemed this lacked important security they were requiring for Windows 11 because boot keys could be intercepted and hacked as they were transmitted unencrypted between the chip and the boot loader.

The theory, Microsoft thought, was that any PC with a TPM 1.0 chip would be very old by the time Windows 11 was released (TPM 1.0 became available in 2011, with TPM 2.0 replacing it in 2014, the year before Windows 10's release), and everybody from consumers to corporations would be purchasing new PCs anyway.

Sadly, what Microsoft failed to factor in was the overall reliability of modern computers. Back in the days of Windows 95, computer hardware could be flaky and often expire after just three to five years, forcing people to upgrade.

Only yesterday though as I write this, a friend who works in IT and one of his colleagues found an old Dell laptop running Windows XP that booted to the desktop and worked perfectly when they tested it (see Figure 1-1).

Figure 1-1. *Stephen Coombes and Laith Al-Wasity at Bournemouth School (UK)*

It's therefore possible for a modern desktop or laptop PC to work for 15 years or perhaps even longer. I've recently upgraded my older Surface Laptop 2, which I purchased in 2018 (so four years old by this point) with a Surface Laptop Studio. Not wanting a perfectly good laptop to go to landfill, I offered it to another friend who had previously had my cast-off Dell XPS 13 laptop (circa 2015 and now seven years old), but he told me the XPS was still perfectly good, that he really liked it, and that he felt no need to upgrade.

A few months before writing this, I wrote *The Green IT Guide* (Apress, 2022) in which I talk a lot about the problems of ewaste. Some 50 million tons of ewaste are created globally each year, but as I write this, only around 20% of it is recycled, with the rest of it going into landfill.

The problem with modern electronics is that they contain many metals and minerals that can heavily pollute the environment; pose health risks to people, animals, and plant life; and even be carcinogenic. In India, where ewaste recycling is in its infancy, experts say that some 80% of the country's surface water is polluted. I won't go on about this here, I would rather encourage you to purchase the book, but it's a huge problem that's not going away any time soon.

The other controversial change was that Windows 11 would require an eighth-generation Intel processor (and equivalent generation AMD processors). This was primarily for reasons of security, with the seventh-generation Intel chips being hit by some serious malware when flaws were discovered in 2017.

These seventh-generation chips though were sold with PCs and laptops between 2016 and 2020 (the eighth-gen chips being sold from 2017 through to 2021), meaning that many Windows 10 PCs would be ineligible to run Windows 11 despite being only two or three years old themselves.

With Windows 10 ending support on October 14, 2025, though we can likely expect paid-for extended support as happened with Windows 7, this means these PCs could be as little as five or six years old when Microsoft makes them completely obsolete and insecure. From an environmental standpoint, this is intolerable, though Microsoft made a very good case for security overall.

These changes and the new interface aside, that's pretty much it for the differences between Windows 11 and Windows 10. The old Administrative Tools have been renamed Windows Tools (we'll look at this in Chapter 2) which will be important for you as an IT Pro and troubleshooter, the Windows 11 Start Menu no longer supports Live Tiles (we won't miss them), and Windows 10 can't run Android apps from the Amazon Appstore, but that's about all.

How Windows 11 Will Change During Its Life

What is of importance though is how Windows 11 itself will change over the coming years until we get that completely virtualized Windows 12 I'm still holding out hope for around 2026 or so.

Take a look at Figure 1-2, and you'll see the Settings panel as it appeared in Windows 10 when it was launched in 2015 and how it looked at the end of 2021 around the time of the launch of Windows 11.

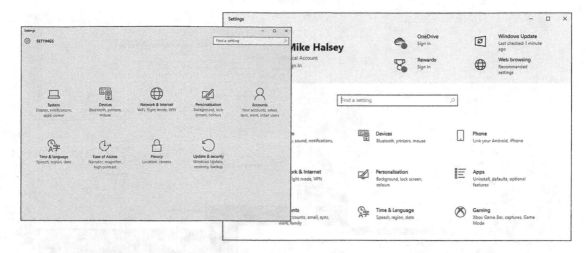

Figure 1-2. *Windows 10 changed considerably during its life*

This was just one aspect of the operating system that changed. When Microsoft first introduced Settings in Windows 8, it was a very basic affair and didn't even offer all the desktop personalization options of the OS. Microsoft has been on a mission though to remove the venerable Control Panel and replace it with a much more modern, and more suitable for a modern OS, Settings interface.

There are many reasons for this, and part of it is making the main interface for Windows look and operate much more like that found in Apple's Mac OS operating system or on an iPad or Android smartphone, or even a Google Chromebook, all of which are leagues ahead of Windows for the simplicity of their settings.

This isn't a bad thing, but it's slow going. The primary reason for this is that there are legacy components in Windows that are still required by some businesses and organizations that date back to Windows 3.1. In Figure 1-3, you can indeed see that you don't have to dig very hard in Windows 11 to find interface elements that date back to the early 1990s.

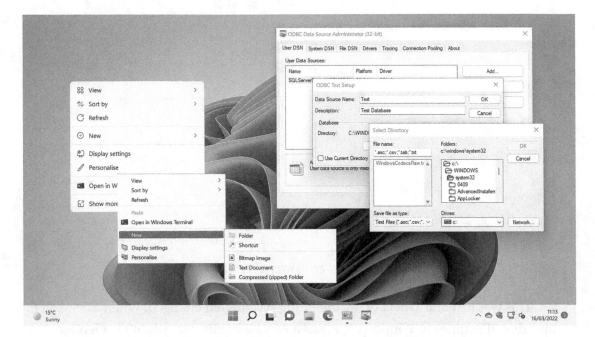

Figure 1-3. *Some interface elements in Windows 11 date back to Windows 3.1*

So what's the reason for this, as surely Microsoft should have replaced all these interface elements with modern ones already, based on their fluent design language I mentioned earlier? The problem stems from several places. Firstly, these old interface elements have to look and work just as they did before, sometimes on mission-critical hardware that's quite old itself (but of course isolated from the Internet for reasons of basic security).

These interface elements also have to work with scripting tools just as they did before. The second problem is that these were all written in different languages. Much of the earliest versions of Windows were written in C or 8086 assembly language. Later versions of Windows and elements of their interfaces went on to be written in C+, C++, C#, WinForms, and .NET. All in, there's a bit of a mess with the legacy code, some of which may not even be accurately documented. Chewing through all of this to update it for a modern UI is a mammoth task that requires completely rewriting all the old code while maintaining compatibility for all the businesses and organizations that still require them.

Whereas companies such as Apple have a "clean slate" policy every few years, and Linux users can install completely different interfaces and versions of the OS, Windows PC just don't have that luxury or flexibility.

Regardless of the scale of the challenge, Microsoft is plodding on, and this brings me to an extremely important point about the content of this book.

Where Will All the Little Applets Go?

Over the life of Windows 10 as I said, many Control Panel items were removed and folded into Settings. The Control Panel itself had 42 applets when it launched in 2015 compared to 36 in 2021, while the number of Settings categories grew during that time from 9 to 13.

Windows 11 launched with the same 36 Control Panel applets, and we can be certain that this number will decrease, and likely the number of categories in Settings will increase during the coming years.

I'll take you through all the different control and other settings and tool panels you'll need to troubleshoot problems in Windows 11 in Chapter 2, but I want first to address what these changes will mean for using this book and finding what you need in the OS as it evolves.

If I'm at any point talking about a Control Panel or other settings or options that you can't find, there will be two places to look for them. Some of these applets will be folded into Settings. They could be straightforward to find, but failing that, the Settings panel does contain a search box you can type in to find exactly what you're looking for.

The other place where Control Panel applets can be moved is Windows Tools, and this is where the administrator-focused applets are likely to wind up. I very much doubt that by the time Windows 12 is released, the Control Panel will be gone entirely, but it's likely another ten applets would have been removed entirely (I'll detail this in a moment) or moved to Settings or Windows Tools.

Now I just mentioned that some features of Windows could be removed entirely. It's actually very likely with some of them, as there are Windows features that are old and no longer in development, and whether they stay or go will depend entirely on metrics Microsoft receive about how many people and businesses are still using them.

Among the features I fully expect to be removed from Windows 11 over the years though are

- Backup and Restore, which is the old Windows 7 file backup system

- File History, another deprecated file backup system

- Creating a System backup image, which is perhaps slightly less likely to be removed but has been replaced by Reset anyway

- Internet Options, as this is related entirely to the now defunct Internet Explorer web browser

- Mail (Microsoft Outlook), as it duplicates functionality in Outlook anyway

- Phone and Modem, as fewer and fewer people need dial-up Internet access

- Sync center, as it's only for much older business file sync systems

- Storage spaces, which has been deprecated for a while now

- Work Folders, as this has already been moved into Settings

Then there are the Control Panel applets I expect to see moved into Windows Tools:

- Bitlocker Drive Encryption

- Credential Manager

- Device Manager

- RemoteApp and Desktop Connections

- Turn Windows Features On or Off (currently in Programs and Features)

- Windows Defender Firewall

Lastly, there are the Control Panel applets I expect to see removed completely as they are folder further and further into Settings:

- Autoplay

- Color Management

- Date and Time

- Default Programs

- Devices and Printers

- Ease of Access Center

- File Explorer Options

- Fonts

- Indexing Options

- Keyboard

- Mouse

- Network and Sharing Center

- Power Options

- Programs and Features

- Recovery

- Region

- Security and Maintenance (likely moved into Windows Security)

- Sound

- Speech Recognition

- Taskbar and Navigation

- Troubleshooting

- User Accounts

This overall is a lot to get rid of, but during the lifetime of Windows 10, much of that work had already been done.

Windows 11 Editions

I mentioned earlier that Microsoft componentized Windows to make it easier to create specialist versions of the OS and to make those versions cheaper to support. Indeed, there are many more versions of Windows 11 than you might think, but while some might lack a user interface, they will all be supportable using scripting such as Command Line and PowerShell or remote access tools such as Remote Desktop Services.

The list of Windows 11 editions includes

- Windows 11 Home

- Windows 11 Pro

- Windows 11 Enterprise

- Windows 11 Education (a variation on Enterprise)

- Windows 11 Pro Education

- Windows 11 SE (a Google Chromebook competitor for low-power PCs in the education market)

- Windows 11 Pro for Workstations

- Windows 11 Mixed Reality

- Windows 11 IoT (Internet of Things)

- Windows 11 IoT Enterprise

- Windows 11 Team (used in Surface Hub)

Indeed, there are probably other specialist editions out there too for cars, medical and industrial appliances, and such, though these are likely to be based on the IoT edition anyway.

There are differences between them too above the cosmetic. You might find yourself supporting PCs running Windows 11 Home for hybrid workers who are using their own laptop or desktop; indeed, the $3000 Surface Laptop Studio I purchased for myself recently comes with Windows 11 Home (grumble, grumble).

So what's missing in the Home edition that could affect how you troubleshoot problems and provide support? Features that are not included in the Home edition of Windows 11 are as follows:

- Bitlocker Device Encryption, though a full disk encryption feature does exist in settings in some (but for some bizarre reason, not all) PCs with a TPM, something I hope Microsoft address in the future

- Windows Information Protection (WIP)

- Assigned Access

- Dynamic Provisioning

- Enterprise State Roaming with Azure

- Group Policy

- Kiosk Mode Setup

- Microsoft Store for Business (though this is being deprecated anyway)

- Mobile Device Management (MDM)

- Support for Active Directory (including Domain Join)

- Support for Azure Active Directory

- Windows Update for Business

All of the other editions are roughly the same with the exceptions of Windows 11 SE not supporting win32 desktop software installation and the IoT editions excluding the desktop interface components.

Windows 11 Update Channels

This reference to Windows Update for Business brings me to the subject of Windows Update Channels. The version of Windows you use will determine how frequently you receive updates, how long you can defer updates for, and how long a particular "Feature Pack" is supported.

Feature Packs are what we used to call Service Packs and are the big update Microsoft releases once a year that include a roll-up of bug and security fixes and new features for the operating system.

Microsoft changed all this with Windows 10, removing to some extent the update roll-up aspect of the Feature Pack and moving to a six-month release. This increased frequency of releases didn't sit well with many IT Pros and companies that needed time to test new features with their own software and systems and didn't want the additional training and support expense of teaching employees how to use a new Windows feature or taking a huge number of support calls from people all asking, "What the hell is this thing that's just appeared on my desktop?" With Windows 11, we're back to an annual Feature Pack, released each fall (autumn), usually sometime in October.

Note   Patch Tuesday has become the name for the day each month when Microsoft ships updates. The second Tuesday of each month is usually the day when updates are released for Windows.

So what are the differences between Windows versions with regard to Feature Packs and updates, and how long can you defer updates? First, it's important to understand the different types of updates that Microsoft releases for Windows 11:

- **Feature Updates**, as I have already mentioned, are delivered once a year. These contain update roll-ups and also significant feature additions to the operating system. Note that some features are shipped at other times of the year, usually because they're an update to an app that's delivered through the Microsoft Store rather than Windows Update itself.

- **Quality Updates** are what you might think of the more traditional Windows Updates. These include security and stability updates, critical updates, and driver updates. Updates for Microsoft software that can be managed by Windows Update, such as Office or Visual Studio, are also considered Quality Updates.

Windows 11 Home

This is the most strictly enforced version of Windows, with updates being able to be paused for up to five weeks and that's about it. This doesn't include important stability and security updates which will be installed anyway.

Windows 11 Pro (Stand-Alone PC)

In a non-Enterprise, stand-alone environment, updating Windows 11 Pro works identically to how it does in the Home version, with updates being able to be paused in Windows Update for up to five weeks, but important security and stability updates being pushed to the PC by Microsoft regardless.

Windows 11 Pro and Enterprise

In the Enterprise environment, PCs running Windows 11 Pro, Pro for Workstation, Enterprise, or Education versions and their offshoot versions can take advantage of Windows Update for Business. This offers system administrators additional flexibility when updates are managed centrally from a service such as Mobile Device Management (MDM) or Microsoft Intune.

When using Windows Update for Business, the different types of updates can be deferred for the following periods:

- Feature Updates for 365 days

- Quality Updates for 30 days

- Other updates, nondeferrable

You can find out more about managing Windows Update for Business on the Microsoft Docs website at https://pcs.tv/3qfmOPo.

Windows 11 LTSC

This brings us to the Long-Term Servicing Channel (LTSC) version of Windows 11.[1] This is a special edition of Windows designed to be used with specialist equipment such as automatic teller machines (ATMs) and medical and industrial machinery. These are all devices that the end user doesn't interact with and that doesn't really have or need a desktop experience, but where stability and longevity are absolutely crucial.

Microsoft's LTSC editions of Windows have a five-year lifecycle from the time a Feature Pack is released, with those packs typically being released every two years.

Note   Microsoft has been known to move the goalposts on updates for both business and LTSC. When Windows 10 first launched, the LTSC lifecycle was ten years, with the change to five years being made later.

---

[1] When Windows 10 launched, I was asked by an IT company in the United States to advise a major corporation in Florida about their rollout. This company wanted to use the LTSC edition on all their desktops. I explained this wouldn't work and was a terrible idea, but they wouldn't budge. Eventually, I got so frustrated I told them to "suck it up" only later discovering the company was Lockheed Martin, one of the world's biggest arms manufacturers, which, by then, probably also knew where I lived. 😳

Windows 11 IoT Editions

Lastly, we come to the Internet of Things (IoT) editions of Windows 11 where the support lifecycles can vary, but largely follow the LTSC channel. This is because an IoT implementation of Windows will almost always be used in a specific device, such as a home automation system or an automobile. Full details about the IoT editions of Windows and their support lifecycles can be found online at `https://pcs.tv/3qd3r9x`.

Windows 11 Lifecycle

Every operating system has an end-of-life date, with the date all support ends for Windows 10 being October 14 2025. This was approximately ten years after the operating system launched, so assuming Windows 11 will follow the same lifecycle, we can reasonably expect all support to end sometime in 2031 or 2032.

Each Feature Pack however has its own end-of-support date, after which it will receive no more security and stability updates. Before this happens, you should always make certain you have upgraded your systems to a more recent Feature Pack.

These end-of-life dates for Feature Packs vary depending on what edition of Windows 11 you are using. For the non-Enterprise editions, including Home, Pro, and Pro for Workstation when used in a stand-alone environment, each Feature Pack will be supported for 18 months from the release date.

In the enterprise environment, each Feature Pack will be supported for up to 36 months from the release date, though remember what I said that Microsoft has been known to move the goalposts on updating in the past.

Useful Windows 11 Features

This is a troubleshooting book, so there's no need here for me to detail what's new and improved in the operating system; I would encourage you to purchase my book *Windows 11 Made Easy* (Apress, 2022) if you want to know about that. There are some new features in Windows 11 though that could come in handy when you're troubleshooting problems.

Snap Layouts

You might be familiar with a Windows feature called "Snap." This was first introduced with Windows 7 and allowed you to drag a window all the way to the left or right side of the screen where it would automatically fill all of that side of the desktop space. This was later expanded to allow the four corners of the screen to be used.

With Windows 11, Microsoft acknowledges that people are now using larger screens and screens with more horizontal space as well (my own screen is an ultrawide 21:9 ratio monitor). With Windows 11 then, they introduced snap layouts, not only allowing for more and more varied snap options but making the feature more discoverable as well.

You can use snap layouts by hovering your mouse cursor over the *Maximize* button in the top-right corner of a window, where a selection of snap layout options will appear (see Figure 1-4). As I write this, Microsoft is testing new snap layout functionality where the layout options will also appear when you resize a window.

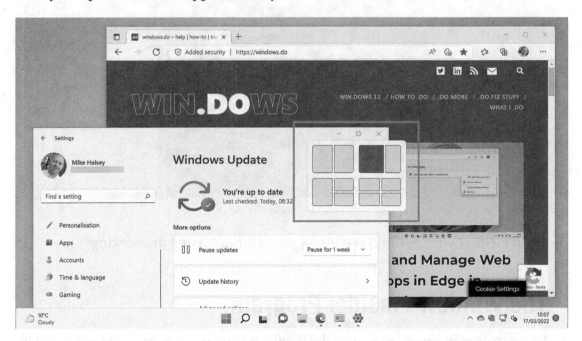

Figure 1-4. *Snap layouts can make window management simple*

Quick Settings

We'll look in detail at other new features of Windows 11 like the Windows Terminal and the revamped Settings panel in Chapter 2, but *Quick Settings*, see Figure 1-5 can be a useful way to get access to services and features you might need, including Wi-Fi and network connections and power settings.

You access it by clicking the *Network / Sound icon*, and if you're using a laptop, *Battery* icons and a customizable panel will pop up with quick link buttons to turn Windows features on or off.

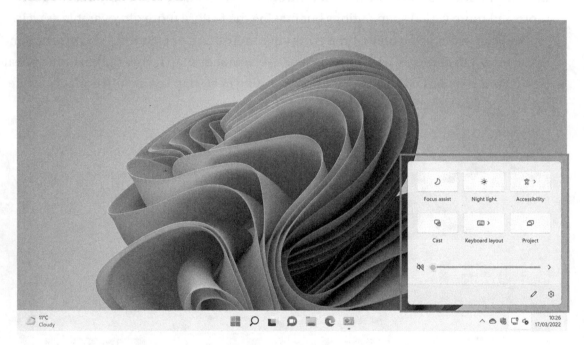

Figure 1-5. *Quick Settings is a useful panel for accessing networking*

The Windows Insider Program

I want to drop in a note here about the Windows Insider Program and how it might be relevant to you when troubleshooting problems on PCs. Essentially, the Insider Program is a public alpha and beta channel in Windows Update. It allows anybody that's not had it blocked by Group Policy anyway to download and install early builds of the next Feature Update and to help Microsoft test features that might come to Windows at a later date.

The flip side of it being a public feature and of being built into Windows 11 is that you might find yourself supporting PCs that are on the Insider Program, so if somebody is having a problem with their PC, it's always a good idea to check if they are using an Insider build.

You can check in Windows Update in Settings where *Windows Inside Program* is listed as an option. If the PC is enrolled in the program, then you will see it clearly detailed there (see Figure 1-6).

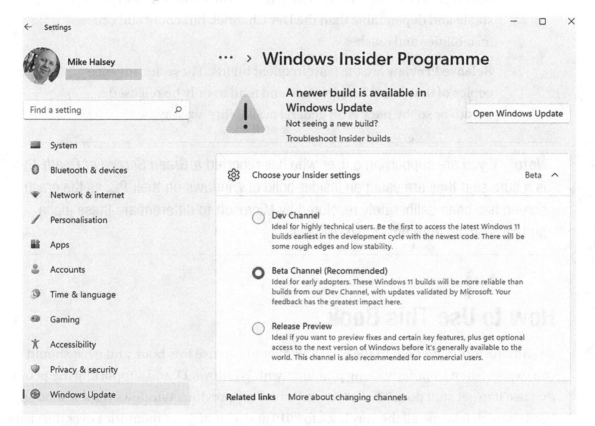

Figure 1-6. *Windows Update will tell you if the PC is enrolled in the Insider Program*

There are three different channels in the Insider Program, with each one delivering a different experience and more risk to the end user and that PC. Bear in mind though that Microsoft has changed the channel names and their content before, so this could happen again, and it's not beyond the realms of possibility that the Insider Program as a whole could be withdrawn at some point in the future.

- **Dev (Developer) Channel** is for the most technical users only and should definitely not be used on a PC where you actually need to "get stuff done." These builds will be the most frequent and will include the newest test features, but they will also be the least stable and least reliable.

- **Beta Channel** is where early adopters can get their fix of what's coming next to Windows 11. These builds will be much more stable and dependable than the Dev Channel, but could still cause instabilities and crashes.

- **Release Preview** are the least frequent builds. These are advance copies of that year's Feature Pack and tend to only be released a month or so the pack is on general availability anyway.

Note   If you are supporting a user who has reported a *Green Screen of Death*, this is a sure sign they are using an Insider build of Windows on their PC, as the crash screen has been deliberately recolored by Microsoft to differentiate these alpha and beta builds from the stable releases.

How to Use This Book

So with the formalities out of the way, how should you use this book and what should you expect when troubleshooting problems with Windows 11 and supporting the people that use it to get stuff done? If you've read any of my previous Windows troubleshooting books, which take me all the way back to 2010 and a lot of great memories over the years, you'll already have noticed from flicking through the table of contents that I'm doing things slightly differently this time around.

In the past, I've split these books into three distinct sections, beginner, intermediate, and advanced. This time, I'm throwing you all in at the deep end (with great help and support along the way of course) and treating each subject as its own distinct thing. This avoids the repetition that crept into the previous books and, for such a large subject, will help you find and digest the information you need more quickly.

Let's face it, speed is the name of the game now as a loss of productivity very quickly equals a loss of money for your business or organization, and there will be a lot of pressure on you to keep people working and to keep both their and your own productivity high.

In Chapter 2 then, we'll look at all the places where there are tools you'll need for troubleshooting and configuring Windows, such as the Control Panel, Settings, Windows Tools, the Windows Terminal, Recovery Console, and a few additional tools that can be downloaded in Microsoft's Sysinternals Suite. You might then want to refer back to Chapter 2 occasionally if I later mention something that you can't find.

Speaking of things you can't find, it's important to bear in mind how Windows 11 is going to change over its life. I have detailed all the places where I expect changes to happen, such as the Control Panel being stripped out and its applets being moved either to Settings or Windows Tools.

Linux on Windows

There will also be changes over the years with third-party software and tools, most likely with new ones becoming available. One of the major changes Microsoft brought with Windows 11 was the ability for third-party app stores to be plugged into the Microsoft Store.

The first examples of this were the Epic Games Store and the Amazon Appstore, the latter of which brought a paltry and pretty rubbish selection of Android apps to the Windows desktop for the first time (hey, you've got to take your victories where you can find them!).

In the future, however, we could see more useful tools being brought to the store, such as support for Linux apps. There is already a Windows Subsystem for Linux (WSL) built into the Pro and Enterprise editions of both Windows 11 and Windows 10. This allows you to install both scripting and GUI installations of Linux that run virtualized on the Windows' desktop and that enable you to use Linux scripting tools such as BASH (seemingly the only short code name for a tech product to not be an acronym for anything).

This is worth keeping an eye on then, as WSL has proven hugely popular with Windows app developers, and it's possible in the future that the subsystem could be used to port more Linux apps to Windows. Given that Linux is generally a much more "techiefied" (that's a word, okay) operating system than Windows has ever been, you might find some of your favorite Linux tools becoming available in the future.

The Fundamentals of Providing High-Quality Support

I've already mentioned throughout this chapter that you're not only supporting Windows 11 PCs but the people that use them. These people might work in your own office or remotely anywhere in the world. They could work from home, perhaps even on their own PC that's shared with their family and used by their children.

There will be chapters in this book devoted to how you go about supporting users, especially when you want to take them with you to help ensure problems don't recur further down the line. In Chapters 5 and 7 then, I'll take you through how to become an effective trainer; how to recognize and work with diversity in education, background, and language; and how to manage the accessibility needs of users when providing support.

Being an educator though is a skill in itself, so in Chapters 16 and 21 we'll look at the wider implications of our uses of technology and how the connected world we live in can cause problems all on its own.

Summary

So there we have it; hopefully, this chapter has given you a heads-up about what Windows 11 is and how it is inevitably going to change over the years. You need to keep your skills relevant as the years pass, and I too need to make sure this book is as useful to you years from now as it is today.

With that in mind, we'll jump right in, and in the next chapter, we'll examine all the tools you'll need to configure and troubleshoot Windows. We'll see where you can find everything and where things that move are likely to end up, and we'll look at some of the cool tools and utilities available to make your job simpler.

CHAPTER 2

Tools and Utilities Used Throughout This Book

The tools and utilities that you will need and use are scattered around Windows 11, and some of the most useful are pretty well hidden such as the System File Checker and the Deployment Image Servicing and Management (DISM) tool, both of which we'll look at in depth in Chapter 9, and the Problem Steps Recorder which we'll demonstrate in Chapter 6.

Some of the most useful tools aren't even part of Windows but are available from the Microsoft website or the Microsoft Store to download. There are a complete wealth of useful tools and utilities however which I've always found odd.

The reason for this is that the number of problems you tend to get in Windows is the inverse of the number of tools available to diagnose and fix them. Windows XP, for example, had many stability and reliability problems and yet didn't come with half of the tools available in the much more stable Windows 7.

With Windows 11 though, things will be subject to change. I detailed in Chapter 1 how Windows 10 changed throughout its life and how Windows 11 will inevitably follow the same path. This means that some of the tools I detail in this chapter will very likely move in the future, but I will always detail if this is likely at the appropriate time.

Settings

It was back with Windows 8 that Microsoft first introduced a *Settings* panel. This was largely a joke as even some of the desktop personalization options weren't available there at the time. This, of course, was in response to absolutely every other operating system having moved to a more friendly settings interface for users, with even Linux having had a more friendly settings interface than Windows for many years. Steven

27

© Mike Halsey 2023
M. Halsey, *Troubleshooting and Supporting Windows 11*, https://doi.org/10.1007/978-1-4842-8728-6_2

Sinofsky, who was the man running the Windows division at Microsoft during the years of Windows 7 and Windows 8, wanted to make the Windows experience work and feel more like we were used to on a smartphone and tablet.

In some ways, the ideas he and his team introduced were not just revolutionary but widely praised, such as the sideways-scrolling panels that could aggregate all your messaging or social media feeds into a single place in Windows Phone (see Figure 2-1).

Figure 2-1. *Windows Phone's scrolling panels were considered revolutionary*

Alas, there were problems with this as the big social media companies objected to Microsoft baking support for their platforms directly into the OS. They wanted more control over pushing advertising to their users and thus wanted everybody using their own apps. Microsoft caved and before very long Windows Phone became a shadow of the great OS it had been at launch.

Things didn't go so well with the port to the desktop either, with the Windows Phone interface being inadequate for large PC monitors, and the push toward full screen, and if I'm honest, woefully badly written apps, just wasn't the way PC users wanted to work.

By the time Windows XP and Windows 7 came to the ends of their supported lives, there were still around 20% or more of PCs running the older OS. I have given talks to user and other groups about end of support, and on my website **windows.do**, I had many articles advising people what to do about the end of support for Windows 7, just as I will do with Windows 10 when that reaches the end of its life in 2025. With the end of support for Windows 8.1 though in January 2023, I doubt I'll bother, as there's just nobody still using it.

Settings has expanded greatly though since it was refined for the launch of Windows 10 in 2015. In Chapter 1, I detailed by just how much it had been expanded, and this will continue to happen with Windows 11.

Tip   Settings includes a search box in its top-left corner which can be helpful as some settings are buried and can be quite difficult to find.

Settings is available from the Start Menu All Apps list, and it's automatically pinned to the Start Menu when Windows 11 is installed. It's straightforward to use with main categories on the left side and options for the currently selected category on the right (see Figure 2-2).

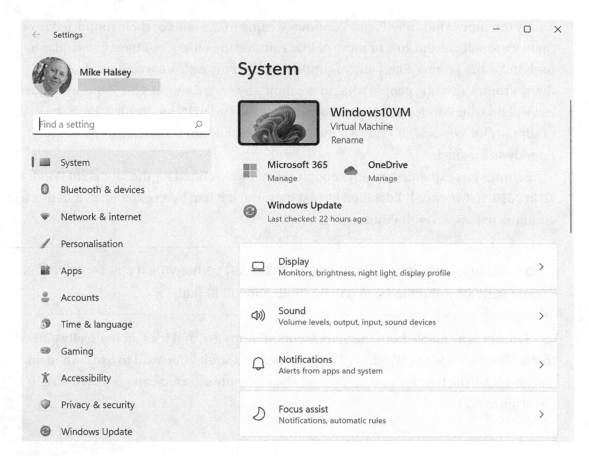

Figure 2-2. *The Settings panel in Windows 11*

There are, at least when I write this, 11 main categories available in Settings:

- **System** is where the main end user–focused configuration options for the PC are to be found, including display, sound, battery, and notifications. It is also where some troubleshooting tools can be found, such as Recovery (which we'll look at later in this chapter and in Chapters 6 and 22) and Remote Desktop (see Chapter 6 for details on this).

- **Bluetooth & devices** is something we'll cover in Chapter 15 and is where you'll find configuration and connection settings for wired and wireless peripherals, but also where privacy settings for devices such as cameras and microphones can be found.

- **Network & internet** is one of the Settings areas that will be expanded into the future, with more Control Panel applets being brought to it. This contains options for managing wired and wireless networks, as well as configuring Virtual Private Networks (VPNs), cellular hotspots, flight mode, and proxy servers, as well as being where data usage can be monitored.

- **Personalization** is where the end user will go to change the look and feel of Windows 11, from dark mode, and desktop wallpapers, to the lock screen, themes, and some accessibility features including the mouse cursor.

- **Apps** is also going to see more Control Panel applets folded into it and currently is where you can set default apps for files, add and manage optional features for Windows, and manage what programs run at startup, but I fully expect additional functionality including turning Windows features on or off to be added at a later date.

- **Accounts** is where end users can add and manage personal, family, child, and work or school (Microsoft 365 and Azure AD) accounts and also where Windows Hello biometric security is configured and managed.

- **Time & language** is a fairly generic settings panel for setting localization and region options. There are still a few Control Panel applets left to be folded into these settings.

- **Gaming** contains features used with Xbox gaming on the PC, including the Game Bar and Game Mode options. These will likely be extended over time as we see further integration with Xbox Cloud Gaming, and we see more technology including high dynamic range (HDR) displays and high refresh rate displays becoming commonplace on PCs.

- **Accessibility** is where the bulk of all the accessibility and ease of access settings in Windows 11 can be found. To find out how these can help everybody from young children, the elderly, and even people that work in noisy environments, you should read my book *Windows 11 Made Easy* (Apress, 2022).

- **Privacy & security** is where all of the privacy settings not already in *Bluetooth & devices* can be found, along with permissions for installed software and apps on the PC.

- **Windows Update** is quite obviously where you'll find the update features for Windows 11, along with the update history log, configuration options for updating, and details of how to enroll the PC in the Windows Insider Program.

Control Panel

The Control Panel has been in Windows since its very first version in 1985 (see Figure 2-3), but at some point in the future, it will be disappearing completely. As I detailed in Chapter 1, the number of applets available in the Control Panel diminished significantly during the lifetime of Windows 10, and there are plenty of other applets that are prime candidates to be moved either to Settings or into Windows Tools, which I'll detail shortly.

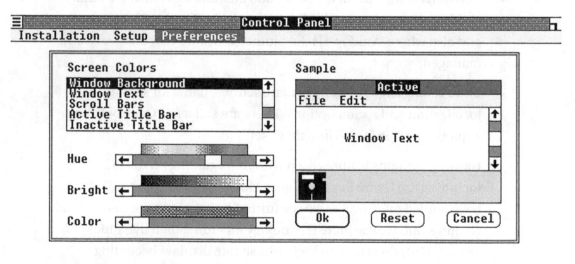

Figure 2-3. *The Control Panel was first introduced in Windows 1 in 1985*

There's not much in Control Panel for Troubleshooting, though some of the applets will be very useful for you indeed for as long as they're there. In Figure 2-4, you can see the full list of all the available Control Panel applets that were included at the time Windows 11 launched, though you will also see that many are already partly folded into Settings, and others are prime candidates for joining them.

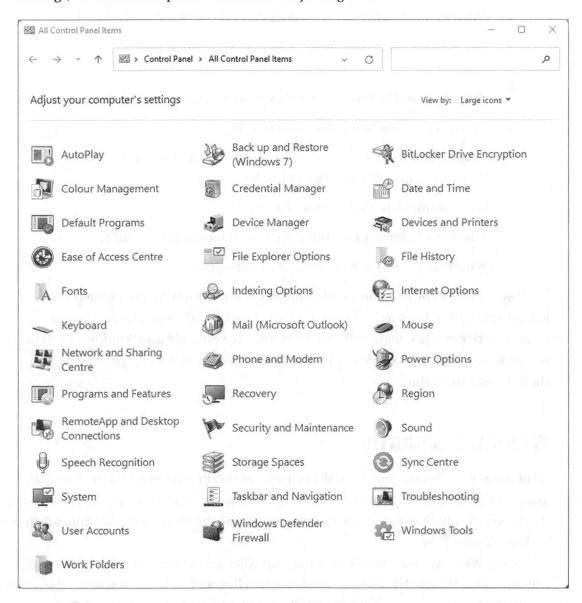

Figure 2-4. *The Control Panel should disappear during Windows 11's lifetime*

Of the Control Panel applets that are useful for troubleshooting, and that we will cover in this book, these are the ones you will need:

- **Bitlocker Drive Encryption**, which we will cover in Chapter 17.

- **Device Manager** is something we will look at in depth in Chapter 15.

- **Devices and Printers** is also something to be covered in Chapter 15.

- **Network and Sharing Center**, which we will look at in depth in Chapter 14.

- **Programs and Features** will be covered to an extent in Chapter 12.

- **Recovery** is something we'll cover in Chapter 3.

- **Troubleshooting** is where the automatic troubleshooting tools can be found, and we'll look at these in Chapter 6.

- **User Accounts** is a subject for Chapter 10.

- **Windows Defender Firewall** is what we'll look at in Chapter 3.

- **Windows Tools** is to be covered later in this chapter.

If at any point you can't find something in Control Panel that I've pointed you toward, it will have been moved to one or two places. For the more technical and administrative applets, these will have been moved wholesale into Windows Tools and will invariably work exactly as they had in the Control Panel; for everything else, you should check in Settings.

Windows Security

All of the anti-malware, main firewall (as there are two interfaces for this in Windows 11) and other security settings can be found in the *Windows Security* panel. This is found in the *All Apps* list in the Start Menu, but also by clicking the Shield icon that appears in the Taskbar System Tray.

Again, Windows Security is something that will change over time, partly because it will be given a "Fluent UI" makeover to bring it in line with Settings (what you'll see here is still Windows Security sporting its Windows 10 look and feel; see Figure 2-5), but also because security does change over time.

Figure 2-5.   *Windows Security is where you will find most, but not all, security options*

Over the last few years, Microsoft has been porting more and more of its enterprise-grade security features to Windows, such as Microsoft Defender Application Guard. The security options are largely out of the scope of this book, though I will discuss many of them in Chapters 3, 17, and 18. You can also find out about all the security features of Windows 11 in my book *Windows 11 Made Easy* (Apress, 2022).

Windows Tools

For those of you that have been working with and administrating Windows for a few years, you will probably recognize this as *Administrative Tools*. Indeed, it's the same panel that's been rebranded to better reflect its use and position in Windows going forward. This is because many tools that might not be considered strictly "administrative" are being moved here, such as *Windows Fax and Scan* and *Hyper-V*. You can see the full list of currently available tools in Figure 2-6, and if something can't be found in Settings or Control Panel, this is where it will be.

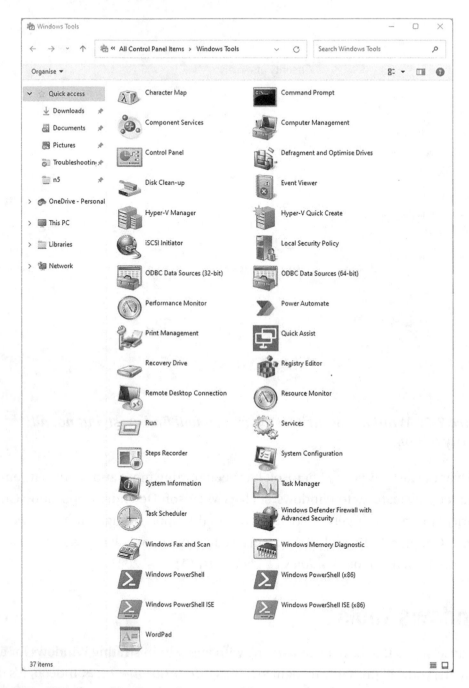

Figure 2-6. *Windows Tools is where everything not in Control Panel or Settings can be found*

There are a lot of tools here that we'll use throughout this book and in various chapters. These include

- **Command Prompt** which has largely been replaced by *Windows Terminal*, which I'll detail shortly, but it can also be used and accessed from the Recovery Console, which will also be covered in this chapter. This can be useful if you have a PC that won't start to the desktop or if you need to edit the main Registry on a nonbootable PC, or the Registry for a specific user, and I'll talk about these use cases in much more detail in Chapters 20 and 19, respectively.

- **Computer Management** is less of a utility we'll need directly, but it is a centralized place from which you can access other utilities we do need, including Event Viewer, Device Manager, and Disk Management.

- **Control Panel** is something I detailed a little while ago, but this is just to let you know this is the best place to find it outside of a search in the Start Menu.

- **Event Viewer** is something I will detail in some depth in Chapter 8. Almost everything that happens on a PC (Blue Screens of Death excluded) is recorded here.

- **Local Security Policy** and **Group Policy** will be covered in Chapter 3.

- **Performance Monitor** and **Reliability Monitor** will be covered in Chapter 8, along with a hidden tool that really should be here and might find itself included in the future, called **Reliability History**.

- **Quick Assist** is a highly effective remote assistance tool and, along with **Remote Desktop Connection**, will be covered in Chapter 6, along with the **Steps Recorder**.

- **Recovery Drive** is a useful little tool that I'll show you how to use in Chapter 3.

- **Registry Editor** is by far one of the most useful and most important tools in Windows. Chapter 19 is dedicated to this subject.

- **Services** will be covered in Chapter 12 when we discuss apps.

- **System Configuration** is something we'll cover in Chapter 18, though its use these days is pretty limited.

- **System Information** is a utility that can provide all manner of detailed information about a PC. We'll look at it in Chapter 8.

- **Task Manager** is also available by right-clicking the Start button (hopefully anywhere on the Taskbar by the time you read this), and it is highly useful. We'll see what it can do in Chapter 12.

- **Windows Defender Firewall with Advanced Security** is the second firewall interface I mentioned, and this will be covered in Chapter 18.

- **Windows Memory Diagnostic** is a useful little utility we'll examine in Chapter 15.

- **Windows PowerShell** is something that has largely been replaced by the Windows Terminal, which we'll look at next, but the Integrated Scripting Environment (PowerShell ISE) is very useful for writing PowerShell scripts.

Windows Terminal

Microsoft first introduced the Windows Terminal (see Figure 2-7) in 2019 to almost universally positive reviews. It was an integrated environment for Command Prompt, PowerShell, and the Azure Cloud Shell, but came with the additional benefit that third-party scripting tools could be plugged into it, such as BASH which is used by a lot of Linux programmers.

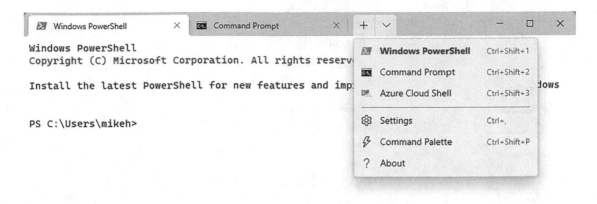

Figure 2-7. *Windows Terminal is a great scripting tool in Windows 11*

Available from the Microsoft Store at the following links or as a download from Microsoft for Windows 10, Windows Terminal is built into Windows 11 and can be found in the *All Apps* list in the Start Menu. Perhaps most easily though you can access Terminal from right-clicking the Start button or pressing the *Windows key + X* from the desktop to open the Administration menu.

Windows Terminal download from Microsoft.com – `https://pcs.tv/36M9Lhv`

Windows Terminal in the Microsoft Store – `https://pcs.tv/3JB8pVh`

You click the down arrow (▼) icon on the title bar in Terminal to open new tabs for specific scripting environments, but you can also configure those environments and add more by selecting *Settings* from the drop-down menu that appears. There are a great many settings for Terminal, including being able to copy HTML-formatted text (see Figure 2-8).

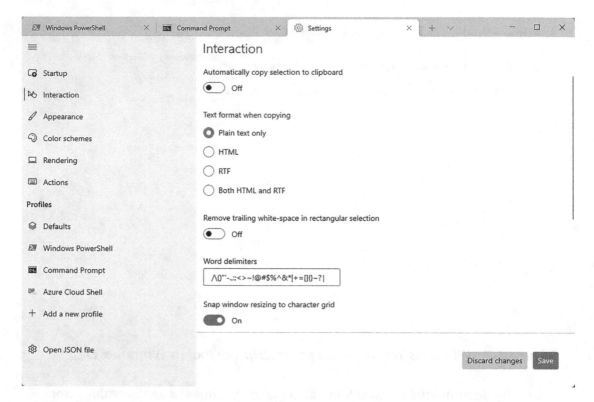

Figure 2-8. *Windows Terminal is highly configurable*

There are a few options that are well worth highlighting however, such as the *Appearance* and *Color schemes* options, which allow you to change the colors of everything from different command and argument types to the background of the Terminal itself. This can be especially useful if you have difficulty reading what's on screen, perhaps because you have poor eyesight or maybe due to color blindness.

The *Actions* options allow you to assign keyboard shortcuts to Terminal operations, and whenever you make a change, you can save this new configuration to a JavaScript Object Notation (JSON) file. This file is stored as a %LOCALAPPDATA%\Packages\ Microsoft.WindowsTerminalPreview_8wekyb3d8bbwe\LocalState\settings.json file on the PC. Additionally, the Terminal settings have an *Open JSON file* option so that you can import a JSON file created on another PC.

JSON files are plain text scripts that can be opened in Notepad on a PC (see Figure 2-9), if you want to edit the settings for Terminal manually.

```
settings.json - Notepad                                                    —    □    ×

File    Edit    View                                                                  ⚙

{
    "$schema": "https://aka.ms/terminal-profiles-schema",
    "actions":
    [
        {
            "command":
            {
                "action": "copy",
                "singleLine": false
            },
            "keys": "ctrl+c"
        },
        {
            "command": "find",
            "keys": "ctrl+shift+f"
        },
        {
            "command": "paste",
            "keys": "ctrl+v"
        },
        {
            "command":
            {
                "action": "splitPane",
                "split": "auto",
                "splitMode": "duplicate"
            },
            "keys": "alt+shift+d"
        }
    ],
    "copyFormatting": "none",
    "copyOnSelect": false,
    "defaultProfile": "{61c54bbd-c2c6-5271-96e7-009a87ff44bf}",
    "profiles":
    {
        "defaults": {},
        "list":
        [
            {
                "commandline": "powershell.exe",
                "guid": "{61c54bbd-c2c6-5271-96e7-009a87ff44bf}",
                "hidden": false,
                "name": "Windows PowerShell"

Ln 1, Col 1                              100%        Unix (LF)              UTF-8
```

Figure 2-9. *You can edit the settings file for Terminal in Notepad*

To add a new scripting environment to Terminal, click *Add a new profile* in settings and browse to the location on your hard disk of the appropriate executable (see Figure 2-10).

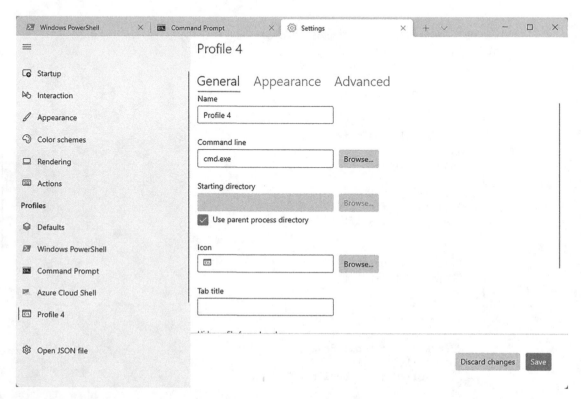

Figure 2-10. *You can plug third-party scripting environments into Windows Terminal*

There is much more information and documentation for how you can use and get the best benefit from Windows Terminal on the Microsoft Docs website at `https:// docs.microsoft.com/en-gb/windows/terminal`.

Windows Subsystem for Linux

As I mentioned in Chapter 1, BASH is already available through the Windows Subsystem for Linux which is installable in the Pro and Enterprise versions of Windows 11. This useful subsystem and the newly included Windows System for Android might also see the inclusion of additional scripting environments becoming available in the future.

You can activate the Windows Subsystem for Linux by searching in the Start Menu for *Turn Windows features on or off*, where it will appear in the list of options (see Figure 2-11). It is possible that the Windows Subsystem for Android might also be available here, but as I write this, it is still undergoing testing and is installed directly from the Microsoft Store.

Figure 2-11. *You can activate the Windows Subsystem for Linux easily*

With the Windows Subsystem for Linux installed, you can install specific Linux distros from the Microsoft Store, where there are many to be found including SUSE, Kali, Oracle, Ubuntu, Debian, and Fedora (see Figure 2-12).

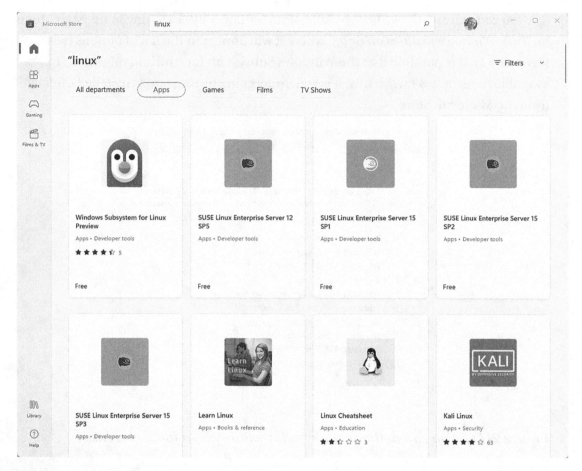

Figure 2-12. *You install Linux distros from the Microsoft Store*

Recovery Console

The Recovery Console contains tools to help you get up and running if Windows encounters a problem and can't start to the desktop. There are several different ways to access the Recovery Console:

- If the PC is unable to boot two or three times, it will automatically start to the Recovery Console and start running the *Startup Repair* tool, which I will detail shortly.

- You can boot the PC from a USB Recovery Drive, and I will show you how to create one of these in Chapter 3.

- Hold down the *Shift* key when selecting *Restart* from the Start Menu or Lock Screen.

- Start the PC from Windows 11 installation media and click the *Repair your Computer* option when it appears near the bottom-left corner on screen.

When the Recovery Console loads, you will see four main options for continuing and booting Windows normally, *Use a device* if you want to boot from a USB Flash Drive containing recovery or installation media or that contains an offline anti-malware scanner, *Troubleshoot* which we'll look at shortly, and *Turn off your PC* which is fairly self-explanatory (see Figure 2-13).

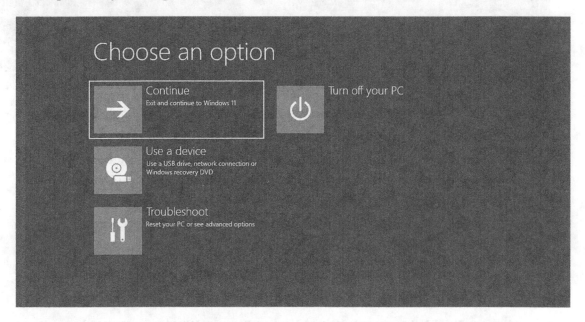

Figure 2-13. *The Recovery Console is a useful troubleshooting environment*

Clicking *Troubleshooting* will then present options to *Rest this PC*, which is something we'll look at in Chapter 22, or more *Advanced options*. This takes you to a screen that has the options you're likely to want to use (see Figure 2-14).

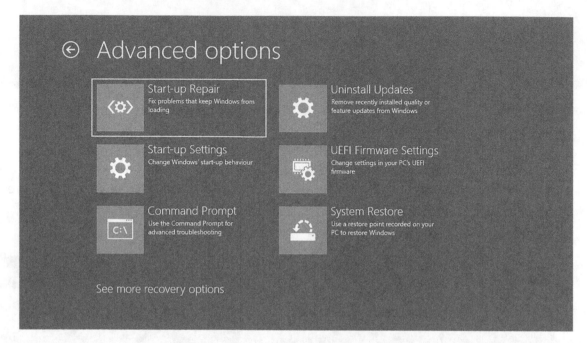

Figure 2-14.   *There are useful troubleshooting tools in the Recovery Console*

- **Start-up Repair** is a tool that resets Windows boot components to
  their default state in an attempt to get a nonbooting PC to start to the
  desktop again. It will run automatically if the PC fails to start two or
  three times, and if it doesn't find that it can fix the problem, it will
  bring you to the *Advanced options* screen.

- **Start-up Settings** will restart the PC to display the boot menu you
  would have been familiar with in Windows versions prior to Vista:

  - **Enable low-resolution video mode** starts Windows to a 640 by
    480 low video mode.

  - **Enable debugging mode** turns on kernel debugging in Windows
    that can be sent to a different network-connected PC that's
    running a debugger. The data is sent over the COM1 Serial port at
    15,200 baud.

  - **Enable boot logging**, which saves a text file containing details of
    everything that happened during startup. The file is saved to
    c:\Windows\ntbtlog.txt, and I'll show you how to access this in

the Recovery Console shortly. You can also enable boot logging in the *System Configuration* panel from the desktop, and I'll show you how to use this in Chapter 18.

- **Enable safe mode** is also something I'll discuss in Chapter 18.

- **Disable driver signature enforcement** will disable the requirement for all boot drivers to be digitally signed. This can allow older and unsigned third-party drivers to be loaded. We will look at drivers in much more detail in Chapter 15.

- **Disable early-launch anti-malware protection** stops Windows from loading its built-in or installed third-party anti-malware driver. This can be useful if anti-malware software is causing a problem where the PC is unable to boot to the desktop.

- **Disable automatic restart on system failure** will prevent the PC from automatically restarting after a Blue Screen of Death (BSOD) event. This gives you more time to read the error message displayed. I will detail the BSOD in Chapter 8.

- **Command Prompt** is something I'll detail shortly as it can be extremely useful.

- **Uninstall Updates** can be used to remove a Windows Update that has caused a problem preventing the PC from booting to the desktop.

- **UEFI Firmware Settings** loads the UEFI firmware on the PC so you can make changes. This exists here because some PCs start so quickly, there is literally no time to press the Esc or F2 keys, or because the PC is a tablet and no such option exists for you.

- **System Restore** can roll back changes that have made the PC unbootable. I will talk more about this in Chapter 3.

- **System Image Recovery** *might* be removed from Windows 11 at some point in the future. It is a system that allows the creation of a backup disk image for the installed OS. I will show you how this works in Chapter 3.

Command Prompt

Having the Command Prompt available from the Recovery Console can be extraordinarily helpful, and I will detail just how useful it can be in Chapter 20.

Command Prompt doesn't support PowerShell commands, though I most sincerely hope these are added at some point in the future, but many commands are available to you. Some of the useful commands to use from the Recovery Console are as follows:

- **Regedit** to open the Registry editor. From here, open the File menu and click *Import* to open a local Registry file on the PC which is available on the *X:* drive. You can also click *HKEY_LOCAL_MACHINE* and from the File menu select *Load Hive*, to load a registry file from the PC, again on the *X:* drive. I will detail the Registry in depth in Chapter 19.

- **Notepad** will open the Notepad text editor; in this environment, you can open and read many Windows log files, including the *ntbtlog.txt* boot log file I mentioned a little while ago. I will detail the Windows log files in full in Chapter 11.

- **Diskpart** opens the Windows disk management and partitioning tool. I will detail how to use this in Chapter 10.

- **Rstrui** will launch System Restore, which is also available as a main menu item in the Recovery Console.

All the other commands that can be run from the Command Prompt in the Recovery Console are detailed on the Microsoft Docs website at this link: `https://pcs.tv/3NhJWq4`.

Microsoft Sysinternals Suite

The last suite of tools we'll use throughout this book to troubleshoot and repair problems with Windows 11 is by far the most significant. Microsoft Sysinternals suite began life as a pet project in 1996 for software developers Bryce Cogswell and Mark Russinovich.

Sysinternals was a suite of freeware tools for administering and monitoring Windows installations and the software, drivers, services, and hardware running on them.

In 2006, the product was bought by Microsoft with Cogswell and Russinovich moving to the company to maintain it. You can download Sysinternals from the Microsoft website at `https://pcs.tv/2vJ7K2m` or from the Microsoft Store at `https://pcs.tv/3IOMkBz`.

Russinovich has thrived at Microsoft, rising to the position of Technical Fellow, Microsoft's most senior technical position, and Chief Technology Officer for Azure cloud services. He's also the author of several successful tech-based thriller novels, in addition to many technical books.

I won't detail the specific tools within Sysinternals that we'll use throughout this book as each one will be detailed in full in the relevant chapters, but it consists of 74 utilities across the subject areas of file and disk, networking, process, security, system, and other miscellaneous tools.

Other Third-Party Tools

While we won't specifically be using any of the following tools throughout this book, these are the ones that my colleagues and I have always found useful. They cover a broad range of subjects including security, gathering system information, and providing remote access. I always find these are useful bookmarks to keep:

Aida64 – `www.aida64.com`

CCleaner – `www.piriform.com/ccleaner`

Disk Digger – `www.diskdigger.org`

GRC – `www.grc.com`

Hiren's Boot CD – `www.hiren.info/pages/bootcd`

Sandra Utilities – `www.sisoftware.eu`

TeamViewer – `www.teamviewer.com`

Ultimate Boot CD – `www.ultimatebootcd.com`

WhoCrashed – `www.resplendence.com/whocrashed`

Support Websites

There are also useful support and driver websites that are worth bookmarking. These fall into different categories depending on whether they're for OEM (Original Equipment Manufacturer) hardware or cloud and online service status pages.

Hardware Driver and Support Websites

Acer – www.acer.com/support

Asus – www.asus.com/support

AMD – support.amd.com

Dell – www.dell.com/support

HP – support.hp.com

Intel – downloadcenter.intel.com

Lenovo – support.lenovo.com

Microsoft Surface Support – www.microsoft.com/surface/support

Nvidia – www.nvidia.com/page/support.html

Samsung – www.samsung.com/support

Cloud and Online Service Status Websites

Microsoft Azure – status.azure.com

Amazon Web Services (AWS) – health.aws.amazon.com

Google Cloud – status.cloud.google.com

These last two links can be most useful as they both monitor hundreds of online services from messaging chat and communications to hosting providers:

www.downdetector.com

www.isitdownrightnow.com

Summary

There are a lot of tools and utilities built into Windows 11 that you can use to troubleshoot and repair problems and issues, and more besides when you then factor in the Command Prompt and PowerShell commands and scripts that you can run, and we'll cover all of the most useful and relevant throughout this book.

There are so many useful Microsoft and third-party tools available as downloads however, and Microsoft's Sysinternals suite definitely stands at the top of the tree. You may use your own preferred tools and utilities for troubleshooting and monitoring PCs, and if that's what you're happy using, you should definitely carry on doing so.

It's all about what makes you most comfortable and what you find you're most productive using. For most of the guides throughout this book, I will detail at least two ways of doing things, normally one using a tool in the Windows interface and another using scripting.

In the next chapter, we're going to look at how we can prevent problems from occurring in the first instance though, by examining how to create a robust and secure PC ecosystem.

CHAPTER 3

Building a Robust and Secure PC Ecosystem

You may have heard the term "prevention is better than cure," which is mostly attributed to the Dutch philosopher Erasmus around the year 1500. Over the years, the phrase has been widely adopted by healthcare but also has significance when it comes to Windows 11 troubleshooting… hear me out on this one.

When problems occur with PCs, you generally have two options, to reimage the PC or to try and find and fix whatever is the cause. If you choose the former option, then you'll get a quick initial fix, perhaps just 20 minutes reimaging the PC, but then you'll have a far longer period of either, depending on which reimaging route you take, downloading a ton of Windows and app updates or reinstalling all of your apps and software from scratch. We'll talk about these options in detail in Chapter 22.

If you go down the troubleshooting route, which of course is what this book exists to help you with, then the initial fix period will be longer, but the overall process of getting the PC back in full service should be less than the reimaging route. There are no guarantees with this depending on the type of problem you're facing, as it could turn out to be a real head-scratcher, but you're up for a challenge, right?

Where prevention is better than cure comes into play is in trying to mitigate the problems to begin with and make sure that nothing ever goes wrong with the PC in the first instance so you don't need to troubleshoot problems at all. Of course, this is an oxymoron as the very nature of PCs with their near infinite combinations of installed software, hardware, peripherals, and connections mean you can never fully mitigate every problem that will occur, and frankly it would be folly to assume that you can.

Setting up your PCs though in a robust way is always good practice though, and it would be remiss of me to not discuss how to avoid problems in the first instance as part of a troubleshooting book.

© Mike Halsey 2023
M. Halsey, *Troubleshooting and Supporting Windows 11*, https://doi.org/10.1007/978-1-4842-8728-6_3

Understanding System Restore

Back in the earliest days of my life as an author, I was attached to a book about Windows 8 that I soon afterward was booted off. There were problems here from the beginning, largely because the book was to be written with a specific "voice" that was used in the series that I had difficulty conforming to (you might have already guessed I'm fond of going off on tangents and slipping in jokes, quotes, and anecdotes like this one whenever I can).

The other issue for me though was the co-author I had been assigned. This author was insisting the book start with a section called "Safety First with System Restore." This stuck in my mind afterward as it started one unholy argument.

In essence, my co-author was quite right; making sure System Restore was working on a PC is a great idea. Where I believed they were wrong however was that (A) the book wasn't about troubleshooting, rather being a beginner's guide, and (B) that they wanted us to tell the reader that the very first thing they should do was to create a System Restore point they could go back to if they ever encountered a problem.

System Restore was of course (as he slips gently into another anecdote) first introduced with Windows Me which was released in the fall of 2000. It was widely derided in the days before Windows Vista as a place where viruses and malware would go to hide, ready to pounce again the moment the system was restored, which back in the days of Windows Me was frankly a lot.

Windows Vista was of course the operating system that introduced User Account Control (UAC) which was horrendously intrusive in its first guise, but successfully blocked malware from making changes to a PC that could affect anything other than just the currently signed-in user's desktop experience. Until this point, the first thing I did on any PC was to turn System Restore *off*, but with Vista and UAC, it at long last became useful.

So where does this bring us to with the argument over the Windows 8 book and why does it matter? What System Restore does is that it creates a snapshot of critical system files such as the Registry and parts of the Windows kernel whenever a change is made that could cause the PC to become unstable. This includes installing a new piece of win32 desktop software (it doesn't kick in with Microsoft Store apps) or when a Windows Update is installed.

System Restore reserves a small percentage of the disk, usually between 2% and 5% in which it keeps its backups. This means that if a lot of activity takes place on a PC, such as downloading a lot of updates and installing a lot of software, previously captured restore points are deleted in order to make space for a new one. The installing of software and downloading of updates are, of course, things that happen rather a lot with a new PC, and so I think you can guess why I got so agitated over how pointless it would have been to tell the owner of a shiny new Windows 8 PC to create a Restore Point first.

Configuring System Restore

You should always have System Restore activated on a PC though, and it can be quite common with Windows 11 installations to find that it isn't activated by default. You can find System Restore most easily by searching for it in the Start Menu and clicking *Create a restore point* when it appears in the search results. You can also find it in *Settings* under *System* ➤ *About* and labelled as *System protection* in the related links section.

Tip   System Restore can be run from the Command Prompt or from a PowerShell window by using the command **SystemPropertiesProtection** and pressing Enter.

With the System Protection panel open on your desktop, you will be able to see if System Restore is configured for each drive or partition you have in your PC. Click the *Configure* button to set and change its options (see Figure 3-1).

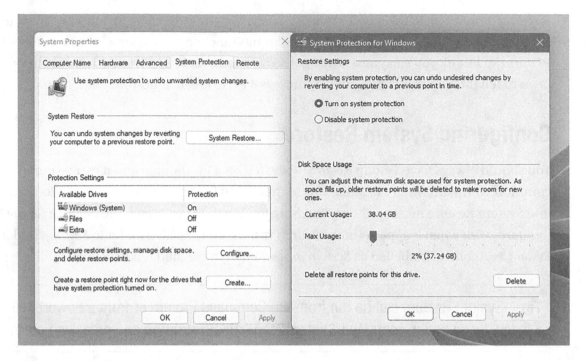

Figure 3-1. *System Restore is simple to configure*

The options need to be changed individually for each disk or partition and include turning System Restore on or off for that disk and assigning how much space on that disk is allocated to the feature. The reason you can configure System Restore for disks other than the one on which Windows is installed dates back to a file versioning feature that was available to Windows File Server administrators back in the days before cloud computing was a thing, and that was later hooked directly into Windows with the File History document and file backup feature; things that in the days of Azure, OneDrive and superfast broadband all now seem incredibly quaint. Suffice to say that System Restore on anything other than your Windows drive serves no purpose these days and isn't worth activating.

Configuring System Restore Using Scripting

You can also configure System Restore using PowerShell. Open the Windows Terminal and use the following commands: Enable-ComputerRestore to enable System Restore for a drive with the following switches.

`-Drive <String[]>` to specify the drive to activate System Restore on, for example, `Enable-ComputerRestore -Drive "C:\"`

`-Confirm` to force prompting for confirmation before implementing the change

`-WhatIf` to show what would happen if the cmdlet runs

Additionally, you can deactivate System Restore for a drive with the `Disable-ComputerRestore` command. You can also use `Get-ComputerRestorePoint` to list the available Restore Points that can be restored and `Checkpoint-Computer` to manually create a new Restore Point.

If you need to restore a previous backup, use `Restore-Computer` with the switch `-RestorePoint <Int32>` where the integer corresponds to the *Sequence number* of the Restore Point you require and that was displayed using the `Get-ComputerRestorePoint` command.

Restoring System Restore Backups

There are several ways to restore your Windows 11 installation to a previous point using System Restore, the first of which uses PowerShell and that I detailed in the previous section. From the desktop, search in the Start Menu for **System Restore** and click *Create a Restore Point* when it appears in the search results.

This will display the dialog we saw earlier, and you can click the *System Restore* button to start the System Restore operation.

If the PC is unable to start to the desktop, you can run System Restore from the Recovery Console. Click *Troubleshoot* and then *Advanced options*, and you will see a *System Restore* option displayed that will operate just as it does on the desktop.

Tip   System Restore can be run from the Command Prompt or from a PowerShell window by typing **rstrui** and pressing Enter.

You will be offered a *Recommended restore* which will usually be the most recent restore point, but you will also see an option to *Choose a different restore point* (see Figure 3-2).

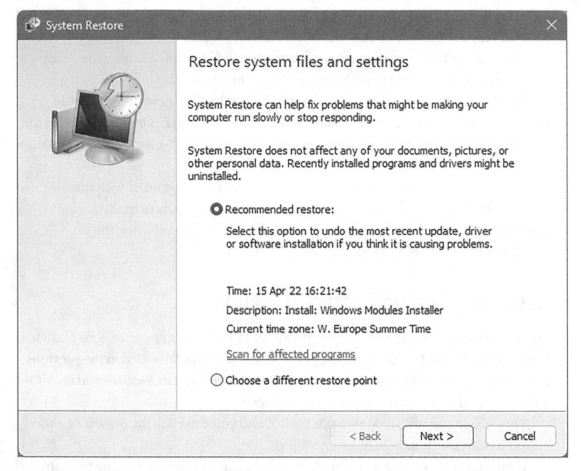

Figure 3-2. *The most recent restore point will be displayed as recommended*

When you see the list of available restore points, you might be surprised if there are just one or two available (see Figure 3-3). This is because Windows 11 is, annoyingly, trying to be helpful by giving you the most recent and what it believes are the most relevant points. You might find though that the issue is being caused by software that was installed a few days or even a week or so before. To display all the available restore points, check the *Show more restore points* box.

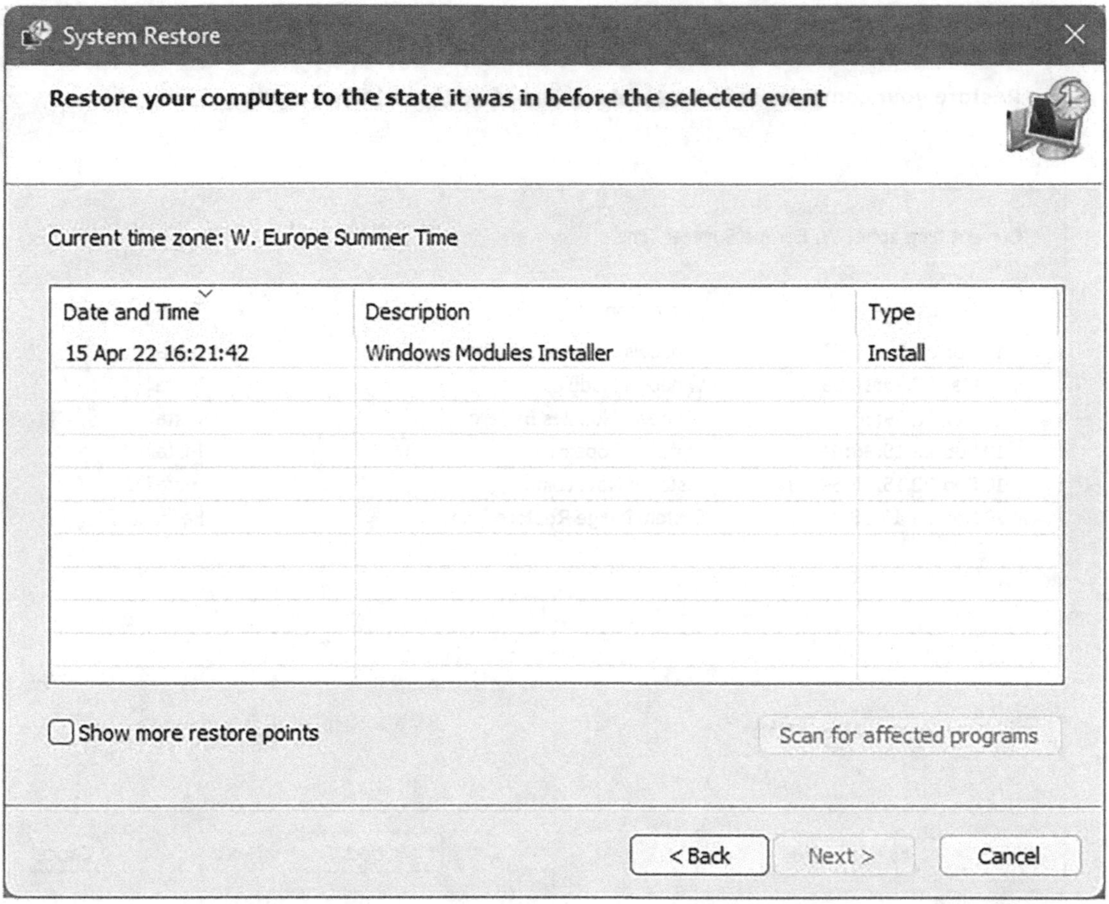

Figure 3-3. *Not all available restore points will be displayed*

Now you will see a list of all available restore points. Many are deleted when the space available for them is full and needs to be reused. If there is not a lot of general activity on your PC though with updates and software installs, you can find, as seen in Figure 3-4, that the available restore points can helpfully date back a few months.

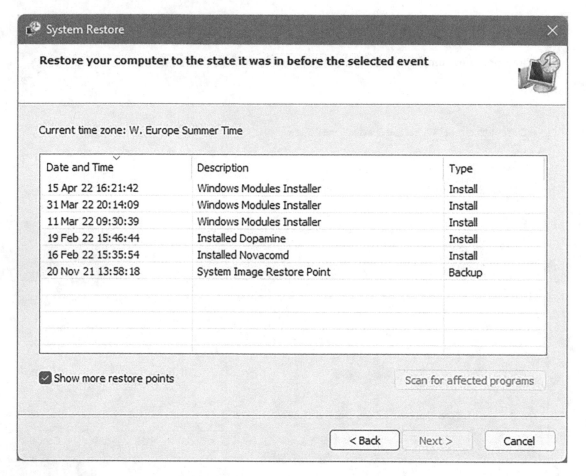

Figure 3-4. *You can display all available restore points*

Check the restore point you are interested in using, and then you can click the *Scan for affected programs* button. Doing so will present a list of all the Win32 programs and drivers installed on your PC that have been installed or updated since that restore point was captured (see Figure 3-5).

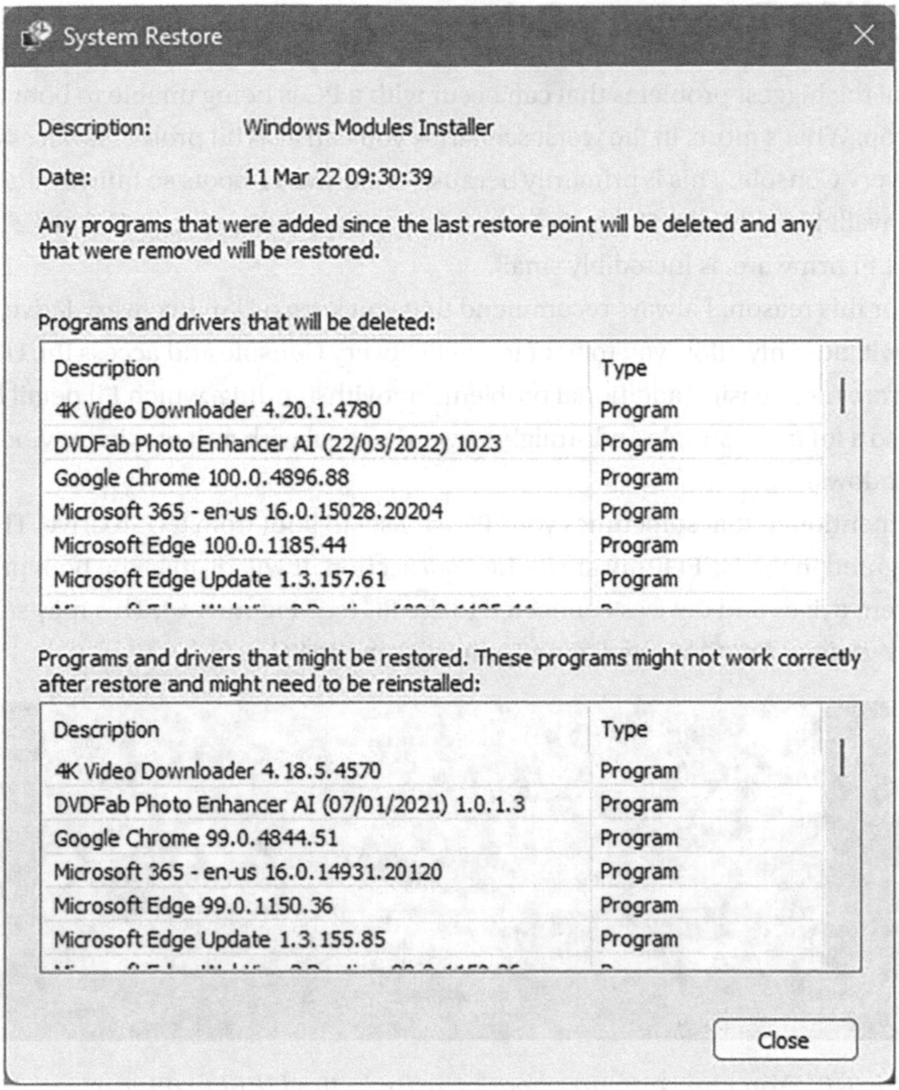

System Restore   ×

Description: Windows Modules Installer

Date: 11 Mar 22 09:30:39

Any programs that were added since the last restore point will be deleted and any
that were removed will be restored.

Programs and drivers that will be deleted:

Description	Type
4K Video Downloader 4.20.1.4780	Program
DVDFab Photo Enhancer AI (22/03/2022) 1023	Program
Google Chrome 100.0.4896.88	Program
Microsoft 365 - en-us 16.0.15028.20204	Program
Microsoft Edge 100.0.1185.44	Program
Microsoft Edge Update 1.3.157.61	Program

Programs and drivers that might be restored. These programs might not work correctly
after restore and might need to be reinstalled:

Description	Type
4K Video Downloader 4.18.5.4570	Program
DVDFab Photo Enhancer AI (07/01/2021) 1.0.1.3	Program
Google Chrome 99.0.4844.51	Program
Microsoft 365 - en-us 16.0.14931.20120	Program
Microsoft Edge 99.0.1150.36	Program
Microsoft Edge Update 1.3.155.85	Program

Close

Figure 3-5. You can check what programs will be affected

Note here that apps installed from the Microsoft Store or from a third-party store will
not be included in this list. What is helpfully included though is the version number of
the program or driver. This can be especially useful if you are troubleshooting a Windows
update and want to roll a specific driver back to a point before an update to that driver
made the PC unstable.

With the correct restore point selected, click the *Next* button to roll the system back
to that point. The PC will need to restart to complete this process.

The USB Recovery Drive

One of the biggest problems that can occur with a PC is being unable to boot to the desktop. What's more, in the worst scenarios you can also hit problems accessing the Recovery Console. This is primarily because Windows 11 boots so quickly; the time you have available to hit the F8 key to access the boot options menu, or Del or F2 to access the UEFI firmware, is incredibly small.

For this reason, I always recommend that you keep a USB Recovery Drive handy. This will not only allow you to boot to the Recovery Console and access the UEFI firmware more easily (additional problems notwithstanding, which I'll detail later), but it's also a lot more simple and straightforward to deal with as it was in previous versions of Windows.

I mentioned that sometimes your PC isn't set to boot from a USB drive. This can be configured in the UEFI firmware in the *Boot* section. It will display the boot priority for different drives and devices connected to the PC (see Figure 3-6). This may start with your *Windows Boot Manager* or a specific disk in the PC.

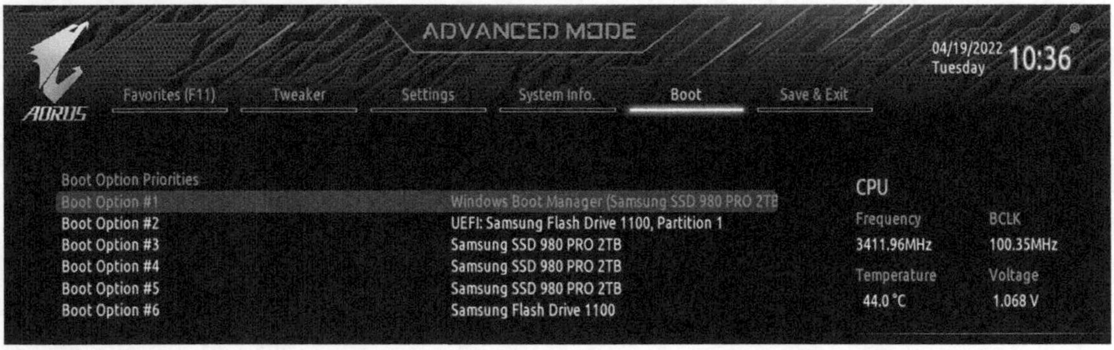

Figure 3-6.   You can configure boot priority in the UEFI firmware

You can change this boot priority however so that ahead of the Windows Boot Manager is a USB Flash Drive option (see Figure 3-7). This means that if you ever encounter a problem and the PC won't boot to the desktop, you can very easily start it to a USB Recovery Drive.

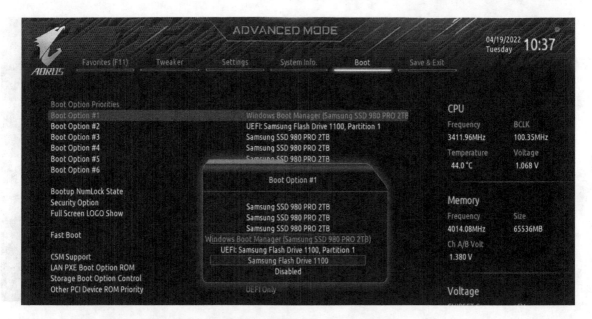

Figure 3-7. *You can choose which are the first, second, and third choice boot devices*

USB Drives and Fast Boot

One of the features of modern UEFI motherboards is called *Fast Boot*, see Figure 3-8. This is a system that lets your PC start much faster than it would normally by initializing all of your hardware at the same time, rather than one device at a time in the way older BIOS systems did it.

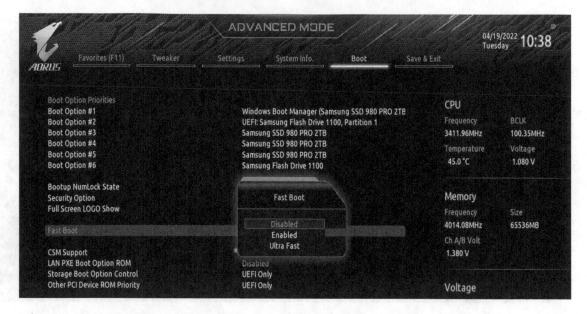

Figure 3-8. *Disabling Fast Boot can sometimes be wise*

In order for Fast Boot to work, you need a graphics card that supports UEFI GOP (Graphics Output Protocol). One of the disadvantages of Fast Boot however is that it disables the ability to boot the PC from a USB Drive. On my own PCs, I disable Fast Boot as, let's face it, they boot quickly enough these days anyway, and you might wish to also disable the Fast Boot feature, which can be done from the Boot options if you have a motherboard that supports it.

Creating a USB Recovery Drive

Creating a USB Recovery Drive in Windows 11 is straightforward and takes just a few minutes. It's also considerably less complicated than with previous Windows versions as I mentioned earlier. The reason for this is that the boot systems of Windows 8, in which the feature first appeared, and earlier versions of Windows 10, had to support BIOS-only motherboards and 32-bit Windows editions.

This meant that the Recovery Drive created would only ever work on that specification, and trying to use a 64-bit Recovery Drive on a 32-bit Windows installation, or a BIOS Recovery Drive on a UEFI system, or the other way around, would result in a PC that wouldn't start. Fortunately, Microsoft ceased production of 32-bit versions of Windows 10 in May 2020, and Windows 11 won't install on older BIOS motherboards anyway due to its requirement for TPM 2.0 encryption support.

To create a USB Recovery Drive, search in the Start Menu for **recovery** and click *Recovery Drive* when it appears in the search results. The process is simple: plug in a USB Flash Drive (that will be formatted so make sure you don't need anything on it) of at least 512MB in size and click the *Next* button (see Figure 3-9).

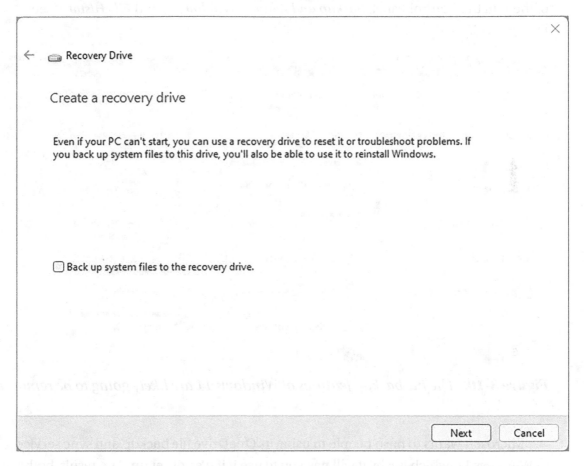

Figure 3-9. *It is very easy to create a USB Recovery Drive in Windows 11*

You will see an option to *Back up system files to the recovery drive*. This will create a copy of the Windows *Reset* image, which is a feature we'll look at in Chapter 22. For this backup image to be copied to the drive, you will need a much larger USB Flash Drive, at least 4GB at a minimum.

The reason you might not want to create this image though is that it will date very quickly. In the same way, a *System Image Backup*, which I will also detail in Chapter 22, will date quickly due to updates and Feature Packs being installed on your PC. You might find that by the time you need to reinstall this image, it's two or more years old.

File Backup and Restore

I want to put in a note about File Backup and Restore in Windows 11 as it's still there, but for how long is anybody's guess. There are two file backup features available, both of them in the Control Panel, *Backup and Restore (Windows 7)* and *File History* (see Figure 3-10).

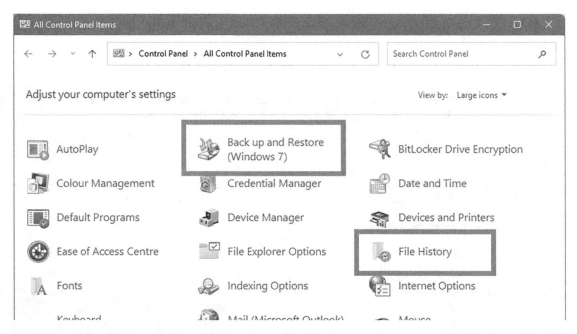

Figure 3-10. *The file backup features of Windows 11 are likely going to be removed*

Microsoft wants to push people to using its OneDrive file backup and sync service in Windows 11, which is why it will nag you to use it if it's not set up. As a result, both of these older features have been deprecated for a while and are prime candidates for removal in a future update to the operating system.

It's not worth therefore showing you how to use these as I feel it would be unwise to encourage you to use a backup system you might later find you're unable to recover your files from.

OneDrive can be configured to use both a personal and a business account simultaneously. There's no need in a troubleshooting book to show you how to configure them, but it's very simple and you can find a whole suite of easy-to-follow guides on my website at https://pcs.tv/3OhwBPn.

Group Policy

If you use Windows 11 in a workplace environment, then it would be unwise to not set Group Policy for your users. If you're not aware, Group Policy allows you to set approve or deny permissions and specific configuration options for every aspect of the Windows user experience, from accessing Windows Update and installing drivers to changing the default desktop wallpaper and denying write and copy operations from external media such as USB Flash Drives.

The easiest way to access Group Policy is by typing **gpedit** at the Start Menu and clicking *Edit Group Policy* when it appears in the search results. The main Group Policy Editor window is standard Microsoft Management Console (MMC) fare and is unlikely to change during the lifetime of Windows 11 (see Figure 3-11).

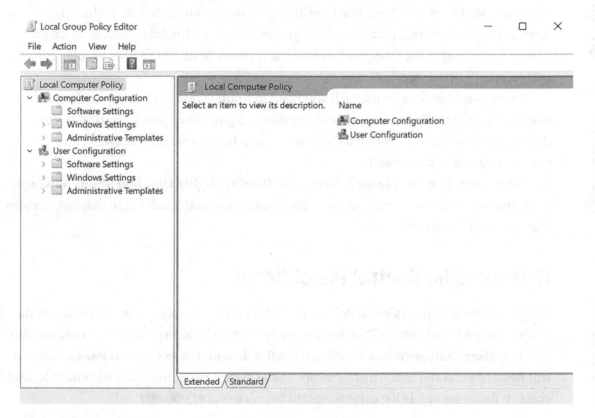

Figure 3-11. *The Group Policy Editor in Windows 11*

Policies are split into two separate areas. Computer configuration will set policies that apply to every user on the PC, and User configuration specifies policies that only apply to the currently logged-in user. At the bottom of the windows are *Extended* and *Standard* tabs. The Extended view will display a panel containing a verbose description of the policy currently selected, to aid you in setting policies that are correct and appropriate for the user and the PC.

While, as I have said, there are Group Policy options for every single aspect of the PC and user experience, there are some that are particularly helpful when it comes to building a resilient system, and for troubleshooting PCs, and for this I want to give a shout-out to the Microsoft MVP community for submitting their top Group Policy suggestions.

Displaying Detailed Status Messages

If you're a Windows old-timer like I am, then you might remember that when the operating system started and shut down you would see technical information about what it was doing at the time, such as starting services, loading the user profile, and so on.

These messages can be useful if you need to troubleshoot a problem with startup, shutdown, or with the loading of a user profile and given they don't slow the system during those operations, and will likely be ignored by the end user anyway you can reactivate them in Windows 11.

Administrative Templates ➤ System ➤ Display Highly Detailed Status Messages is the policy you need to activate to enable this feature, and it will begin displaying them after the next restart of the PC.

Hide Specific Control Panel Items

This is a fairly well-used Group Policy option for corporations and can be used to hide all of the Control Panel applets you don't want the user to be able to see or access. You can find it in **User Configuration ➤ Administrative Templates ➤ Control Panel**, and you will need to enter the canonical name for each Control Panel item you wish to hide, and you can find a complete list on this link: https://pcs.tv/3KmyM07.

Configure Remote Desktop Access

In Chapter 6, we'll look at how we can use remote access tools to support users in remote locations, and one of the main tools is Remote Desktop. This needs to be activated on PCs and can be done so using Group Policy. Navigate to **Computer Configuration ➤ Administrative Templates ➤ Windows Components ➤ Remote Desktop Services ➤ Remote Desktop Session Host ➤ Connections** where you can enable remote access of the PC.

Block Inbound Connections for Public Networks

Security can be tightened significantly on a PC by blocking all inbound connections when the computer is connected to a public network, such as a coffee shop or when on a train. Open **Computer Configuration ➤ Windows Settings ➤ Security Settings ➤ Windows Defender Firewall with Advanced Security ➤ Windows Defender Firewall with Advanced Security** and then click the **Windows Defender Firewall Properties** link.

This will display a dialog in which you can click the *Public Profile* tab and block all incoming connections (see Figure 3-12).

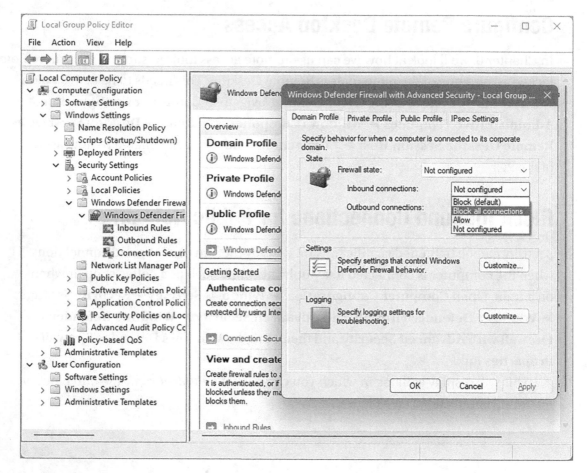

Figure 3-12. *Blocking incoming connections for public networks can make a PC more secure*

Enable Firewall Logging

Additionally in the Windows Defender with Advanced Firewall policies, you can enable logging for the firewall (see Figure 3-13). This will save a log of firewall activity to a %systemroot%\system32\logfiles\firewall\pfirewall.log file which might be useful later when troubleshooting network issues.

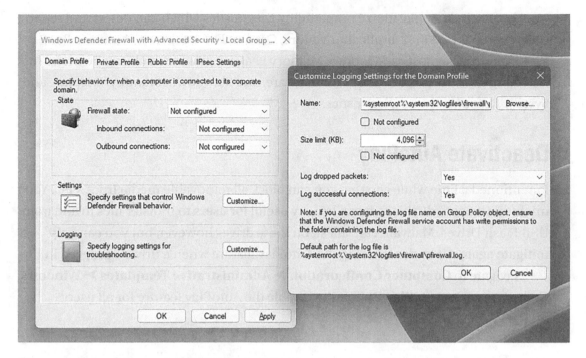

Figure 3-13. *You can enable logging for the Windows Firewall*

Disable Removable Storage

One of the main ways for malware to find its way into a corporate network is for it to be brought in by users on a USB Flash Drive. You can disable all removable storage use in Windows 11, and this is also a recommended policy if your servers contain data that might be sensitive to theft.

Computer Configuration ➤ Administrative Templates ➤ System ➤ Removable Storage Access is where you will find the policies for disabling read and write access to a variety of removable storage types including USB Flash Drives, which fall into the *Removable Disks* category.

Troubleshooting and Diagnostics

This selection of policies, which can be found in **Computer Configuration ➤ Administrative Templates ➤ System ➤ Troubleshooting and Diagnostics**, contains many policies you might find are useful to implement on your PCs.

They include Application Compatibility Diagnostics which can detect and report different types of Win32 application failure, Corrupt File Recovery, Windows Boot Performance Diagnostics, Windows Memory Leak Diagnosis which can be useful in detecting possible route of attack for malware, and Shutdown, Standby/Resume, and System Responsiveness Diagnostics.

Deactivate AutoPlay

I mentioned a little while ago that you can block all removable media from a PC. You might not want to do this as it can be very useful for users to transfer files to and from USB Flash Drives. Malware can still sit on these drives however, but you can help mitigate against it by deactivating the AutoPlay feature when a drive is plugged in.

Navigate to **Computer Configuration ➤ Administrative Templates ➤ Windows Components ➤ AutoPlay Policies** to disable the AutoPlay feature for all users on the PC.

Managing Event Logging and Error Reporting

Computer Configuration ➤ Administrative Templates ➤ Windows Components ➤ Event Log Service is where you will find policies for managing the Windows Event Log. We'll look at the Event Log in detail in Chapter 8, but it's an incredibly useful tool for diagnosing problems on a PC. You can manage the Event Log in Group Policy including automatically making backup copies of the event log when it is full.

There are additional error reporting policies to be found in **Computer Configuration ➤ Administrative Templates ➤ Windows Components ➤ Windows Error Reporting.**

Additional Group Policy Settings

Some of the additional policies you might want to implement can make the PC more secure and less vulnerable to attack by hackers and malware. You can find these in the following locations: **Computer Configuration ➤ Administrative Templates ➤ Windows Components**, and then select the sub-options for…

- ActiveX Installer Service
- Add Features to Windows 11

- App Package Deployment

- Biometrics

- Bitlocker Drive Encryption

- Microsoft Defender Antivirus

- Microsoft Defender Application Guard

- Microsoft Defender Exploit Guard

- Microsoft Secondary Authentication Factor

- Remote Desktop Services

- Windows Installer

- Windows Logon Options

- Windows Remote Management (WinRM)

- Windows Security

- Windows Update

Local Security Policy

In addition to all the control offered by the Group Policy Editor, the Local Security Policy panel provides additional options and control. Most easily accessed from the Start Menu by searching for **secpol**, the Local Security Policy panel is separated into different easy-to-understand categories (see Figure 3-14).

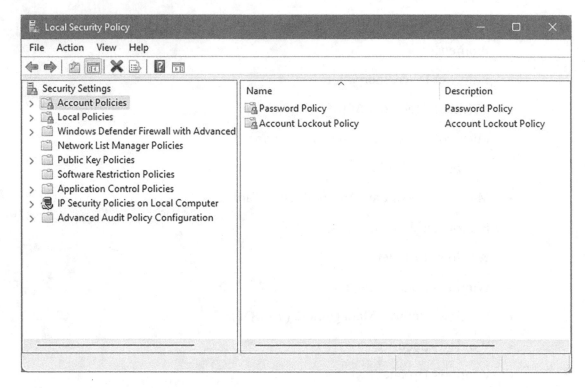

Figure 3-14. *You can specify security policies for the PC*

These security policies cover all aspects of using and operating the PC. The most useful security policy areas are the following:

- **Account Policies** is where you can specify minimum password, age, length, and complexity requirements, as well as determine after how many failed login attempts the account is locked on the PC.

- **Local Policies** contains options for auditing (keeping event logs) account events, as well as specifying security policies for the rights and accesses different users and user groups have on the PC and what types of accounts can be configured.

- **Public Key Policies** allows you to specify security policies for encryption/decryption keys and data recovery associated with the Encrypting File System (EFS), Data Protection, and Bitlocker, and we'll look at EFS and Bitlocker more in Chapter 17.

- **Software Restriction Policies** allows you to strictly control access to installed software and apps on the PC.

- **Application Control Policies** is where you can set policies for Microsoft's AppLocker service; this gives system administrators great control over what apps and files can be run and opened and how executable files, scripts, installers, and dynamic-link libraries (DLLs) can open and operate on the PC.

Biometrics and Two-Factor Authentication

While we're on the subject of security, I want to take a little while to talk about the importance of biometrics and two-factor authentication (TFA) as both are absolutely crucial in maintaining the data security of businesses and organizations and also the privacy and financial security of absolutely everybody.

There are big differences between the two, and not every method is perfect. You'll no doubt be aware of what both biometrics and TFA (sometimes referred to as multifactor authentication) are, so I won't bore you with those details, but I want to highlight some of the real-world problems that we face with these systems and what some of the solutions can be. This is because you might want to take these into account when deciding on what policies to implement for your PCs and systems.

I want to deal with two-factor authentication first as this one drives me absolutely nuts. I live in rural France as I've already mentioned earlier in this book. My house has a secondary outbuilding common to France called a gîte. Gîtes are considered holiday homes for visiting guests, but are usually old farm worker accommodation or converted outbuildings. My own gîte used to be a small barn.

Anyway, without wishing to bore you too much with my personal living arrangements, my gîte is where I have put my home office (see Figure 3-15). I did this for two reasons, firstly to keep some kind of separation between my home and work lives and also because (for reasons of it just being healthier this way) I wanted to keep my desktop PC out of the house.

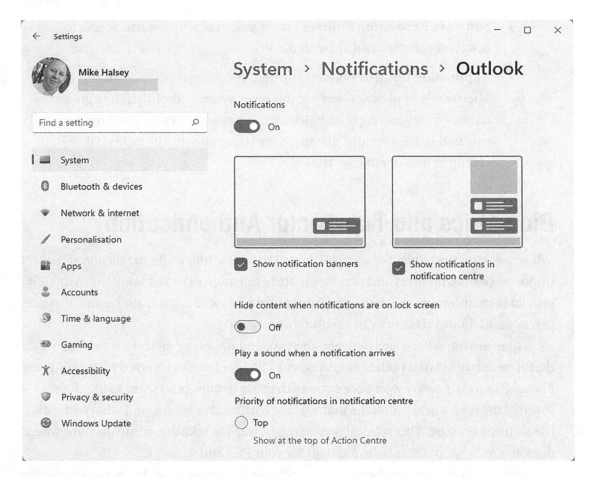

Figure 3-15. *My home office is in my gîte*

So how does this relate to two-factor authentication I hear you ask? The simple fact is that the notifications for TFA alerts almost always come in the form of SMS text messages or pop-ups on my smartphone. "This is perfectly normal, so I'm still not getting it," you say. I don't like phones, especially ones that constantly ping, beep, and cry out for my attention. I switch off all notifications and even the call ringer on my smartphones because there's no message or call that could ever come through that would be so important it couldn't wait for an hour.

This switching off from my phone means that I don't habitually carry it around. Thus, and you're probably guessing now where this is going, it means that whenever I get a TFA alert, the phone is either in a completely different building to me or is buried away somewhere, forcing me to have to go hunting for it.

A few companies are getting much better at managing TFA alerts. My American Express card is a good example where AMEX gives me a choice of receiving my TFA code by SMS or email. It's nice, frankly, to have the choice as the number of times I've been on my PC in the gîte and had to go stomping back to the house in a bad mood to find my damn phone is too great to count.

So, you say, given that more and more people are switching off from their smartphones and trying to live healthier lives where they're not constantly connected to the Internet and social media, the answer lies in providing more than one way to receive a TFA alert? Well, yes but with caveats.

The problem here comes with the sending of these alerts by email. Email is the very definition of unsecured communication. It's unencrypted, easily intercepted, and readable on just about every device we have. Do you have any devices where, once the device is unlocked, you need to enter a password or scan your fingerprint to read your email? Because I don't, nor do I know anybody that does.

This means that, to take one example, somebody steals your laptop and is able to get to the desktop because you were signed in at the time. They want to perform an action that requires a TFA alert, but rather than also needing access to your smartphone, which is still sitting in your pocket, they can just open your email and get the security code there. Alternatively, the laptop is locked, but they can still get the code as a little preview of the arriving email will appear on the Lock Screen, probably displaying the code in plain text.

Of course, you can prevent the display of email and other incoming messages on the PC's Lock Screen in *Settings* ➤ *Notifications*, and this, frankly, is always a sensible thing to do (see Figure 3-16).

Figure 3-16. *You can hide content from notifications on the Lock Screen*

The solution comes in the form of biometrics. This can be done in one of two ways. The first is that you have a smartphone set up so that you must use a fingerprint or facial recognition to unlock it every time it's used, though this can quickly become wearing for the end user and runs the risk of being turned off or reduced to after five or so minutes. The other is to use the Windows Hello biometrics system built into Windows 11.

Biometrics in Windows currently comes in three different flavors, fingerprint, facial recognition, and smart card, and you can configure Windows Hello in *Settings ➤ Accounts ➤ Sign-in options*.

Tip   It is widely acknowledged that fingerprint sign-in is more secure than facial recognition, which can often be fooled by twins or people that look alike and even on occasion by a photograph depending on the system used.

One of the biggest benefits of using Windows Hello is that Microsoft is heavily pushing a passwordless future and is encouraging third-party companies to hook into the biometric systems of your PC. One of the first to hop on board was Google, and you may already have noticed that you can use Windows Hello to authenticate your access to your Google and Google Workspace accounts.

Microsoft also have extensive documentation for how you can use Windows Hello biometrics in your own business or organization, and this goes far beyond what's available to sign in to an Azure AD or a Microsoft 365 account.

Microsoft's biometrics system has been adopted by other companies and organizations too, including the Fido (Fast IDentity Online) Alliance, which includes hundreds of other members including Apple, Intel, Samsung, and VMware and financial institutions like Visa, American Express, Mastercard, and PayPal. You can find out more about Fido on `https://fidoalliance.org`, and the future of Windows Hello biometrics being supported by other companies and organizations will only grow as the years progress.

You can read technical and configuration documentation about using Windows Hello biometrics in your own organization on the Microsoft Docs website at this link: `https://pcs.tv/3Mw2UIq`.

The Windows Security Center

You'll have probably guessed from reading this chapter, but I have always felt that a significant part of maintaining a robust and resilient PC ecosystem is in setting and maintaining good security, and Windows 11 does indeed include some pretty great security features. In Chapter 18, I'll show you how to manually remove malware infections from a PC, but even with the main antivirus features switched off and working with live viruses, I was completely unable to infect my test virtual machine. This is clearly a testament to the hard work Microsoft has put in over the last few years.

The *Windows Security* center is accessible in a few ways. You can search for it in the Start Menu, click the *shield* icon in the Taskbar System Tray, or open it from *Privacy & Security* in Settings. I want to make a note here that what you see and what I describe in this section will change over the years. This is both because at the time of writing, Windows Security hasn't yet had a Windows 11 visual makeover and also because Microsoft is occasionally adding new features and functionality to address the latest threats posed to our PCs.

The main Windows Security center layout though is very unlikely to change, with the main categories for protection listed in a panel on the left side and sub-items for the currently selected panel on the right (see Figure 3-17).

Figure 3-17. *Windows Security is managed from a central panel*

Note   Microsoft does annoyingly use Windows Security to try and push you into using its services, and so you might see some alerts if you don't have something like OneDrive configured on the PC or if a local account is being used. Hopefully, this is something the company will rectify in the coming years.

Virus and Threat Protection

The main section is where all the anti-malware tools can be found and where you can control the antivirus scanner. There are the usual options available such as quick scan, full scan, custom scan (e.g., for removable media), and also *Microsoft Defender Offline Scan* which will restart the PC and run a malware scan in the Recovery Environment where no malware can be loaded.

I'm not going to run through all of the anti-malware features, but there are some that are especially noteworthy I want to draw attention to.

Excluded Items

One of the challenges with troubleshooting virus and malware issues can be the problem of false-positives. These can come from a variety of sources. You might, as an example, have older visual basic or other macro scripts that you need to use in your workflow, where those workflows haven't been transitioned to newer methods yet or where it's simply not feasible to do so.

You will likely know that scripts and macros are a great place for malware to hide, and for many years, Word, Excel, PowerPoint, and Adobe Portable Document Format (PDF) files were targeted by malware writers or distributed by them via email to try and spread infection.

As a result, the companies combating malware, Microsoft included, built safeguards into their software which, naturally, greatly increased the likelihood of getting a false-positive result on a nonmalware-infected file that you need or use in your daily workflow.

In the main Windows Security panel, under the *Virus & threat protection* section, you can add (and remove) exclusions for a PC (see Figure 3-18). This means you can tell Windows Security *not* to scan files it is flagging as infected incorrectly.

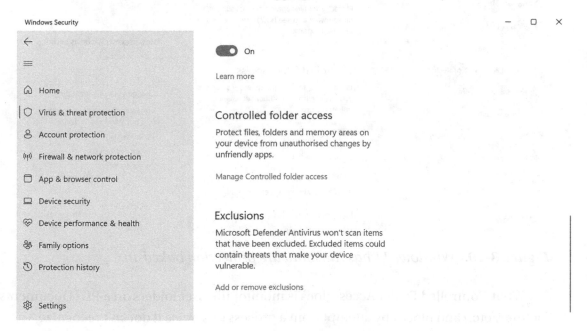

Figure 3-18. *You can exclude false-positive files from malware scans*

Tip You can roll out global configuration for Windows Security across your organization, including adding file exclusions, by using the Group Policy Editor. You will find all the available options under *Computer Configuration* ➤ *Administrative Templates* ➤ *Windows Components* ➤ *Microsoft Defender Antivirus*.

Controlled Folder Access

Just above Excluded items in the Virus & threat protection center is a feature called *Controlled Folder Access* (see Figure 3-19). This is a highly useful and highly effective feature for combatting ransomware, and if you use Windows Security antivirus on your PCs as opposed to a third-party solution, then I thoroughly recommend you activate it.

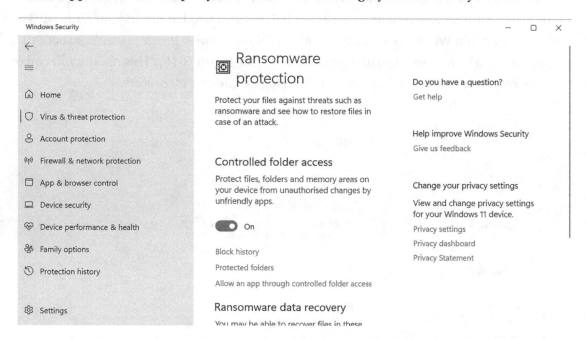

Figure 3-19. *Windows 11 has ransomware protection baked-in*

What Controlled Folder Access does is monitor the user folders on a PC (Documents, Pictures, etc.) and block any attempt from a process or service it doesn't recognize that tries to make a change. These changes include modifying a file to inject malware, encrypting or changing it, or deleting it.

Where Controlled Folder Access can cause problems is where you have third-party software that legitimately needs to access the protected folders, but that isn't recognized by the feature, or where you need an additional folder or folders on the PC protected by the feature, such as a file store on a second internal hard disk or SSD.

The first problem is very common for gaming PCs, where the games need access to the file stores. If an app is blocked from making changes to the protected folders, a pop-up alert will appear in the bottom-right corner of the desktop, telling you that "unwanted changes were blocked." This, fortunately, is both very easy to fix and only has to be fixed once.

In the Controlled Folder Access settings in Windows Security, there are four options available to you. The first is a simple on/off toggle switch for the feature. Below this, you will see links to display your *Block history*, to set your *Protected folders*, and to *Allow an app through controlled folder access* (see Figure 3-20).

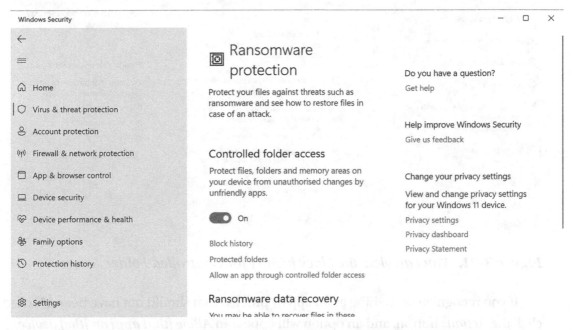

Figure 3-20. *You can manage Controlled Folder Access in Windows Security*

To add a folder or indeed a full drive to Controlled Folder Access, click the *Protected folders* link where you will be able to add (or remove) folders from monitoring. If you need to allow an app through, then click the *Allow an app through...* link where you will be able to add it.

On many occasions however, an app will be blocked, you won't really know what it is, and perhaps the pop-up notification telling you (or another user you are supporting) disappeared from the desktop before they could properly read it.

This is where the *Block history* comes in useful. Click this and you will see a list of events that were blocked by Controlled Folder Access. Click one to expand it and view more information, and you will see details about the date and time the event occurred, as well as the name of the app or process that was blocked, and the protected folder it tried to access (see Figure 3-21).

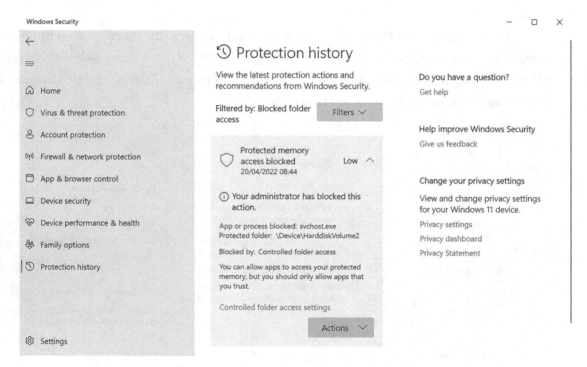

Figure 3-21. *You can view the block history for Controlled Folder Access*

If you recognize something as an app or process that should not have been blocked, click the *Actions* button, and an option will appear to *Allow [that app] on [the] device*. Just clicking this once will set the exclusion globally, and you won't have to worry about it again on that PC.

Bear in mind however that some apps have several different processes that need to access. It can be wise to keep a list of which apps need to be allowed through. You can then configure this globally for your organization using Group Policy. Navigate in the Group Policy Editor to *Computer Configuration* ➤ *Administrative Templates* ➤ *Windows Components* ➤ *Microsoft Defender Antivirus* ➤ *Microsoft Defender Exploit Guard* ➤

Controlled Folder Access, and you will see an option to *Configure allowed applications* along with other global controls for the feature (see Figure 3-22).

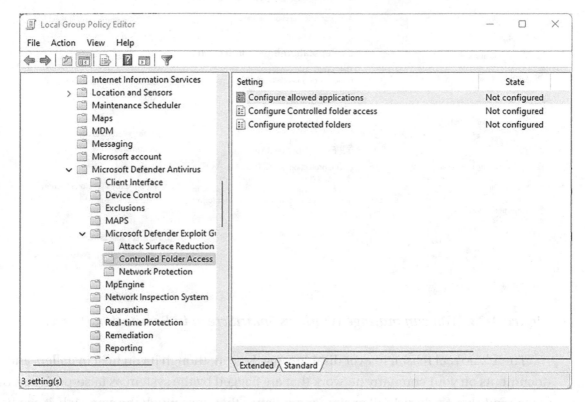

***Figure 3-22.** You can configure Controlled Folder Access using Group Policy*

Reputation-Based Protection

Microsoft has for a few years now included in Windows a cloud protection feature called *SmartScreen*. What this does is check downloaded files and apps against white and black lists held by Microsoft. These lists are compiled collaboratively between Microsoft and many other operating system and security firms. If a file or an app is being downloaded that appears suspicious, then it will be automatically blocked by the system.

Again, this can be problematic in business where you might occasionally or even regularly need to share older apps and files that aren't on the white list. To fix this, open *Windows Security* and navigate to *App & browser control*, where you will see a *Reputation-based protection settings* link (see Figure 3-23).

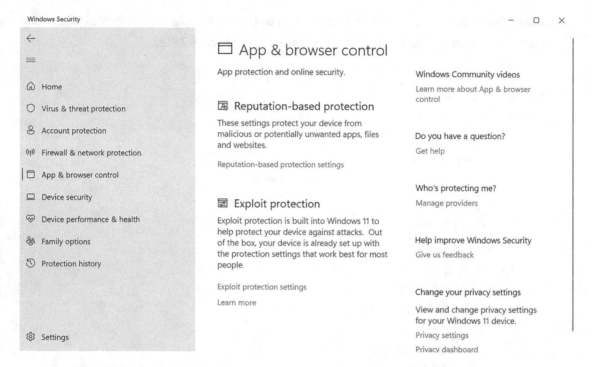

Figure 3-23. *You can manage Windows SmartScreen in Reputation Protection*

There's no real reason to ever disable SmartScreen, though if you host installers and documents on your company network that are flagged by the system as false-positives, or you already have a SonicWall or similar appliance that does much the same job, it can be disabled.

Microsoft has a facility where you can submit files that are being incorrectly reported, so they can be added globally to the SmartScreen white list. You can find this at `www.microsoft.com/en-us/wdsi/filesubmission`.

Additionally, if you need to check what files have been blocked by SmartScreen, you can use the PowerShell command `wevtutil sl Microsoft-Windows-SmartScreen/ Debug /e:true` to display the full SmartScreen log for a PC.

Exploit Protection

The other security settings I want to highlight are under *App & browser control* and *Exploit protection* (see Figure 3-24). These include settings that are more closely linked to your PC's hardware, such as the processor and memory, and they exist to prevent events like memory buffer overflows that can be used to inject malware into a system.

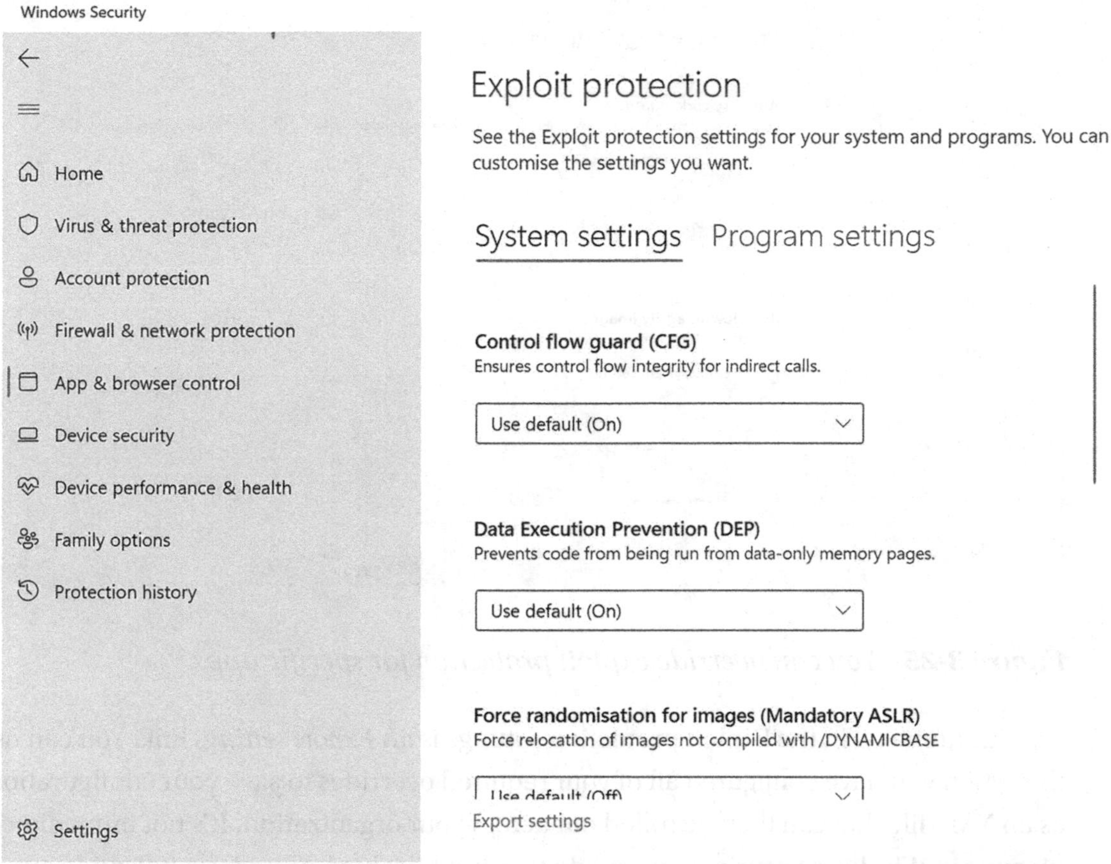

Windows Security

←

≡

⌂   Home

🛡   Virus & threat protection

👤   Account protection

((•))   Firewall & network protection

🗔   App & browser control

🖵   Device security

💗   Device performance & health

👪   Family options

🕚   Protection history

⚙   Settings

Exploit protection

See the Exploit protection settings for your system and programs. You can customise the settings you want.

System settings   Program settings

Control flow guard (CFG)
Ensures control flow integrity for indirect calls.

| Use default (On) | ⌄ |

Data Execution Prevention (DEP)
Prevents code from being run from data-only memory pages.

| Use default (On) | ⌄ |

Force randomisation for images (Mandatory ASLR)
Force relocation of images not compiled with /DYNAMICBASE

| Use default (Off) | ⌄ |

Export settings

Figure 3-24. *Exploit protection settings are more closely linked to your processor and physical memory*

Where you might need to configure this is if you are using older, custom software written for a specific purpose at your organization. This can frequently use programming techniques that are frowned upon today, such as always requiring administrator privileges to work, which was common back in the days before Vista.

Click *Program setting* and you can add and edit override settings for specific applications that are blocked by Windows 11's security or do not function correctly (see Figure 3-25).

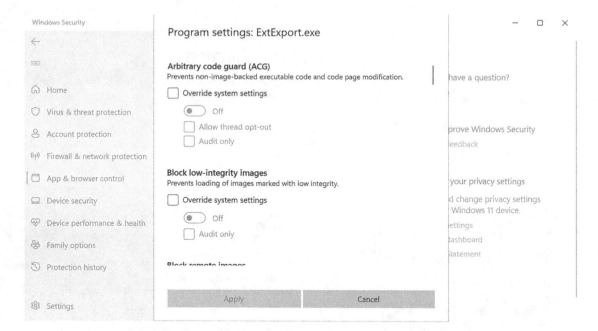

Figure 3-25. *You can override exploit protection for specific apps*

Additionally, in the Exploit protection settings is an *Export settings* link. You can use this when you have configured all of your required overrides to save your configuration as an XML file that can then be rolled out across your organization. It's not immediately obvious in Windows Security how you do this, but Microsoft provides a full guide on its Doc website at `https://pcs.tv/3FPJT1q` including how you can use PowerShell to automate the export and deployment process.

Device Security

An additional memory integrity option exists in *Device security* ➤ *Core isolation* though this is disabled by default because it can interfere with the operation of some older apps. Core isolation helps prevent malware from inserting code into high-security memory processes by virtualizing some parts of the Windows and app operation on the PC.

This is, of course, a highly useful security feature, though you will need to thoroughly test all of your bespoke and mainstream apps to make sure they won't be broken by its security. There is a *Learn more* link in the Core isolation settings page that takes you directly to a Microsoft website that provides more in-depth and up-to-date information about this feature.

Protection History

The last part of Windows Security I want to highlight is the *Protection history* link at the bottom of the main menu list (see Figure 3-26). This is an easy-to-access panel that will display all the security events that have been blocked by Windows Security, and it's a useful "quick find" location if you want to determine if settings need to be tweaked or an app allowed through a security feature.

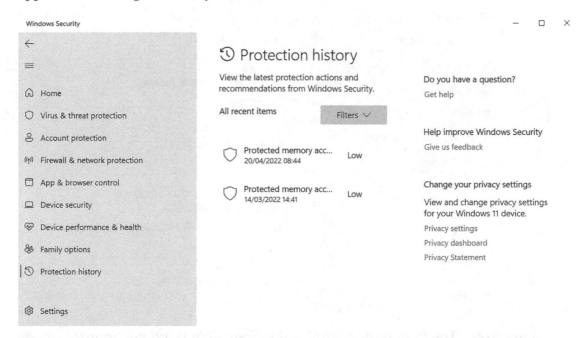

Figure 3-26. *You can easily access your Protection History in Windows Security*

The Windows Advanced Firewall

Windows 11 includes two different firewall interfaces. The main firewall is available in Windows Security under *Firewall and network protection*. This is a fairly basic interface all told as the Windows Firewall rarely needs any real configuration; it's just something that sits quietly in the background and that works so effectively that many third-party antivirus companies have long since abandoned their own bundled firewalls.

At the bottom of the *Firewall & network protection* panel however are some useful links (see Figure 3-27). The most useful of these is to *Allow an app through the firewall*.

This currently takes you to a Control Panel applet, but it's something that will be folded completely into settings at a future time.

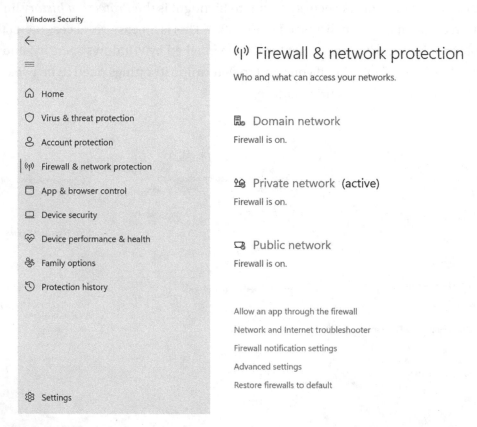

Figure 3-27. *You have basic control of the Firewall in Windows Security*

If you click the *Advanced settings* link, then *Windows Defender Firewall with Advanced Security*, otherwise known as the Advanced Firewall interface, will open (see Figure 3-28). Note that you can also find the Advanced Firewall in Windows Tools.

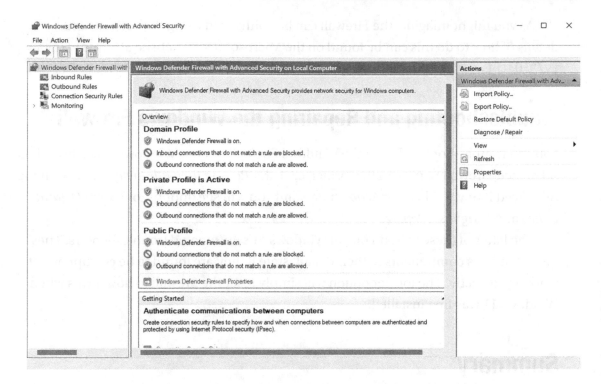

Figure 3-28. *The Advanced Firewall offers full firewall control and configuration*

It is in this interface that you can configure custom rules such as allowing or blocking specific ports on the PC or specifying that network and Internet connections of certain types must always be encrypted.

Note   Windows Defender Firewall with Advanced Security is also available in the Group Policy Editor under *Computer Configuration ➤ Windows Settings ➤ Security Settings ➤ Windows Defender Firewall with Advanced Security.*

Under the *Action* menu in the Advanced Firewall, you will find *Import* and *Export* options which will use *.wfw files which are binary Registry Hive files. These can be opened using the Registry Editor in Windows. Make certain though that you first create a new Registry key to import the Hive into; otherwise, you might find yourself overwriting rules on the PC you would rather not be touched. You should delete your temporary Registry key when you are finished.

As you might imagine, the Firewall can be configured using PowerShell, and details of how to do this can be found on the Microsoft Docs website at `https://pcs.tv/3FQ4tPt`.

Troubleshooting and Repairing the Windows Firewall

You can troubleshoot and reset the Windows Firewall in both Windows Security and the Advanced Firewall panels. In the former, click the *Restore firewalls to default* link. In the Advanced Firewall, click the *Action* menu and you will see options to *Restore Default Policy* and *Diagnose/Repair*.

The latter of these will run one of Windows 11's automated troubleshooters. These reset Windows components to their default state if they are found to be corrupt or not working correctly. The former option will simply reset the firewall to how it was when Windows 11 was first installed.

Summary

There are a lot of features available in Windows 11 to help safeguard against problems occurring in the future, and the security features are indeed extensive. We can expect these security options to be changed and expanded on over time as new types of threat emerge, so it's possible that what I have described in this chapter could be different a few years down the line.

What is clear however is that correctly configuring Windows 11 is key to a happy and productive time using your PCs, so in the next chapter we'll examine how to do this from managing user accounts and shell user folders to helping hybrid workers and creating sustainable PC systems.

CHAPTER 4

Configuring Windows 11

A hugely important part of configuring a PC so as to make it as bombproof as possible is in the initial setup and making sure that your user accounts and overall configuration are managed in such a way so as to help avoid problems occurring later on.

In the previous chapter, we looked at some of this, such as using the Group Policy and Security Policy editors to set appropriate restrictions for users, such as hiding specific Control Panel items you don't want them to have access to. There are other parts of the Windows installation though that you should know about, if only so that you can find them quickly if you suspect a problem with one has arisen.

Using Group Policy to Manage Configuration and Settings

When Microsoft first created the *Settings* panel with Windows 8, the aim was to have an area where nontechnical users could access and tweak options for how their desktop looks and operates, without exposing them to anything else that an administrator might not want them to change or risking their accidentally changing something that could interfere with the smooth operation of the PC or their software.

While Settings in Windows 8 was pretty basic, with just a small handful of options that still required end users to need to delve into the Control Panel for many things, the feature was expanded over the lifetime of Windows 10, and in Windows 11 it is pretty full-featured.

Slowly but surely, all the items in the Control Panel are being moved either into Settings or into the Windows Tools folder (previously known as Administrative Tools). Settings therefore is becoming a place where any end user can change configuration options to their heart's content, with no risk of causing problems with the OS... or so you might believe.

93

© Mike Halsey 2023
M. Halsey, *Troubleshooting and Supporting Windows 11*, https://doi.org/10.1007/978-1-4842-8728-6_4

The truth is somewhat different, as there are actually a great many options that can cause issues with the PC. Let's take the example of an end user I'll call "the Tinkerer." We've all met this person; you may have even been one yourself in the past. This is a nontechnical user who believes that they can fix problems because *they're easy, it's not a complicated job*" when all they're really going to do is make matters worse.

Two of the best examples of how this can happen are with printers and Bluetooth devices, both of which are controlled entirely from Settings. Let's say the Tinkerer isn't able to print a document from their laptop and they decide that the printer is misconfigured, so all they need to do is remove the printer in Settings and reinstall it.

This could have the desired effect, especially if the print queue is snarled with a failed job, but it's very likely to make matters worse overall. The name, IP address, or sharing assignment of the printer on the network would be reset, and every other user who then needs to use that printer can suddenly find that it's not available to them.

Then we come to a Tinkerer who uses a Bluetooth headset as part of their workflow for online meetings. One day, they discover the headset isn't working, so the obvious, to them anyway, solution is to remove it in settings and reinstall it. Bluetooth devices can often be problematic, and for as much as the solution can largely be restarting the device or the laptop, or just checking the Bluetooth device is charged in the first place, removing a Bluetooth device doesn't guarantee that it'll successfully install again afterward, such is the nature of the technology and the fact that Windows has always had a problem with Bluetooth devices.

Clearly then you'll want to disable changes to some items using Group Policy. The options for Settings in Group Policy are still labelled as Control Panel. Whether this will change in the future is anybody's guess, but I would assume not.

Hiding Settings

There are two areas where policies can be found for Settings, *Computer Configuration* ➤ *Administrative Templates* ➤ *Control Panel* and *User Configuration* ➤ *Administrative Templates* ➤ *Control Panel*.

To be honest, it's pretty much everything in these policy areas you'll want to consider changing, perhaps with the exception of the *Personalization* policies, as you'll only want to enforce those if your organization insists its own desktop wallpaper is used (something I've also found a bit totalitarian personally).

In Figure 4-1, you'll see the policies pertaining to printers, including being able to block the deletion and installation of printers on the PC

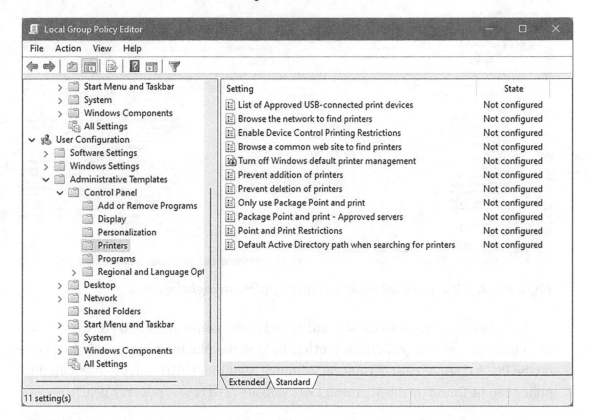

Figure 4-1. *Group Policy options for Settings are still named Control Panel*

In both *Computer Configuration* ➤ *Administrative Templates* ➤ *Control Panel* and *User Configuration* ➤ *Administrative Templates* ➤ *Control Panel*, you will see a policy called *Setting Page Visibility*. This enables you to hide whole areas of the Settings panel, such as hiding the Bluetooth options completely (see Figure 4-2).

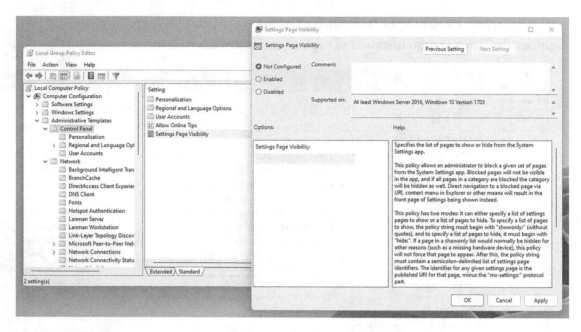

Figure 4-2. *Group Policy makes hiding applets straightforward*

You use this policy with the `showonly:` and `hide:` commands, and you can choose what to display such as `hide:bluetooth` to hide all the Bluetooth controls from all users on the PC. A complete list of Uniform Resource Identifier (URI) codes to use with this policy can be found on the Microsoft Docs website at `https://pcs.tv/3PsCTw1`.

Hiding Control Panel Items and Windows Tools

Similarly, and using the same URI list, you can hide specific Control Panel items. The policy for this can be found in *User Configuration* ➤ *Administrative Templates* ➤ *Control Panel* and is configured in the same way as that for the Settings panel. You do have two separate policies here however, *Hide specified Control Panel items* and *Show only specified Control Panel items*.

Tip   If you want to completely block all access to the Control Panel and Settings for a specified user, use the policy *User Configuration* ➤ *Administrative Templates* ➤ *Control Panel* ➤ *Prohibit access to Control Panel and PC settings*. Do note however that this will remove all access users might want to accessibility, and time, date, and region options they may require.

What you might also want to hide from the end user is the *Windows Tools* panel, as this clearly includes administrator-level tools the user does not need to be accessing. In *User Configuration* ➤ *Administrative Templates* ➤ *Control Panel*, you need to open the *Hide specified Control Panel items* policy and add `Microsoft.AdministrativeTools` to the list of hidden items.

Using the Registry to Restrict Windows Tools Access

You can also achieve this with a Registry change, by navigating to *HKEY_CURRENT_USER\Software\Microsoft\Windows\CurrentVersion\Explorer\Advanced* and adding a DWORD called `StartMenuAdminTools` to which you assign a value of 0 (zero).

There are additional options here that mirror those in Group Policy, such as being able to hide specific drives in Explorer and setting overrides for desktop and Taskbar animations and configuration.

Managing Programs and Apps

In addition to hiding Settings and Control Panel items, you will also want to manage what users can do with apps. If we go back to our Tinkerer, they could decide that an app doesn't need to be installed or that one of their favorite apps from home should definitely be on the PC.

Computer Configuration ➤ *Administrative Templates* ➤ *Start Menu and Taskbar* and *User Configuration* ➤ *Administrative Templates* ➤ *Start Menu and Taskbar* are where you will find the main options for policies such as hiding the *All Apps* list and preventing users from customizing the Start Menu (useful for a dedicated PC that is to be used by different people).

In *User Configuration* ➤ *Administrative Templates* ➤ *Control Panel* ➤ *Add or Remove Programs*, you can *Prevent uses from uninstalling applications from Start* which is certainly a good policy to enable. It is also possible here to remove specific items from the Start Menu power options, such as preventing a user from shutting down the PC, which is useful if you undertake updating and auditing overnight.

In both *Computer Configuration* ➤ *Administrative Templates* ➤ *Windows Components* ➤ *Store* and *User Configuration* ➤ *Administrative Templates* ➤ *Windows Components* ➤ *Store*, you can disable the use and installation of apps from the Microsoft Store (which is where your users might want to install some games from) or even disable the Microsoft Store entirely on the PC.

You will also see a policy here where you can *Turn off the offer to update to the latest version of Windows*, which you will certainly want to do if you strictly test and control the deployment of Windows Updates, Feature Packs, and new versions of the operating system.

Managing User Accounts

In *Computer Configuration* ➤ *Administrative Templates* ➤ *System* ➤ *User Profiles* and *User Configuration* ➤ *Administrative Templates* ➤ *System* ➤ *User Profiles*, you will find options to manage user accounts, such as forcing the implementation of local or roaming profiles.

There are other ways of managing users on a PC however, and one of these is to assign users on a PC or a network to "groups." These groups of users can have different access to files and shares, and different privileges on the PC, and because the permissions are assigned to the group, any user that you later add to that group will automatically inherit the same permissions.

You use the Local User Manager (search for **lusrmgr.msc** in the Start Menu) to create and manage both users and groups on the PC (see Figure 4-3). This is standard Microsoft Management Console fare, with main categories in the left panel, context-sensitive menu options in the right panel, and the meat and potatoes information in the center.

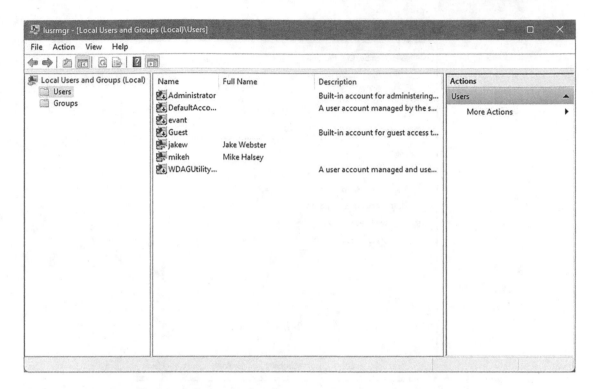

Figure 4-3. *Local User Manager is where you can manage user groups*

The main view shows a list of all the user accounts configured on the PC. This includes some that are hidden by default, including *Guest*, which is a legacy hangover from earlier versions of Windows that supported a Guest account, and *DefaultAccount*, which is used by the operating system as the template for new accounts when they are created.

Double-clicking an account displays additional options for it (see Figure 4-4), including password policies, which user group(s) the account is a member of, and specifying that a script must be run on the PC each time that user signs in.

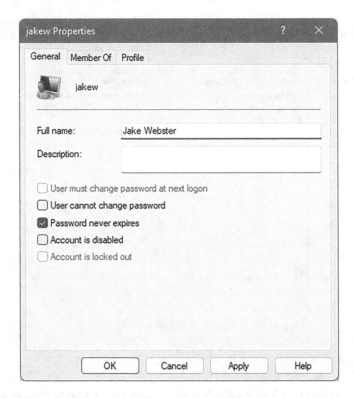

Figure 4-4. *You can set specific options for individual user accounts*

Clicking *Groups* in the left panel displays a list of all the user groups defined on the PC, and there are a lot of them in the default setup (see Figure 4-5). This panel is really only useful for adding users to specific groups, as there are no configurable permissions defined here.

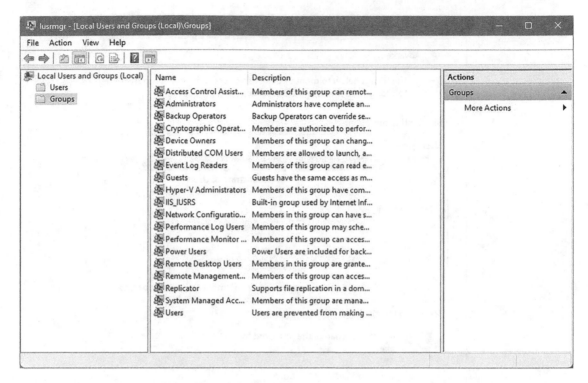

Figure 4-5. *You can modify permissions for user groups and create new groups*

Permissions in Windows are defined on different objects, these being files, folders, and disks, and we'll look at these permissions in detail in Chapter 10.

Another useful tool for managing user accounts is the Network Places Wizard (search for **netplwiz** in the Start Menu). This provides additional options for the user accounts configured on a PC (see Figure 4-6).

Figure 4-6. *You can manage user accounts further using netplwiz*

Click the *Advanced* tab at the top of the Network Places Wizard, and you'll get more options such as *Advanced user management* which takes you to the Local User Manager window. Perhaps the most useful option here for organizations is a simple check box requiring users on the PC to use a more secure sign-in method, by having to press Ctrl + Alt + Del at sign-in (see Figure 4-7).

Figure 4-7. *You can force users to sign in using Ctrl + Alt + Del*

Click the *Manage Passwords* button, and the Windows Credential Manager will open. It is here you can create and manage locally stored passwords and security certificates for network resources, installed software, and web and intranet sites (see Figure 4-8).

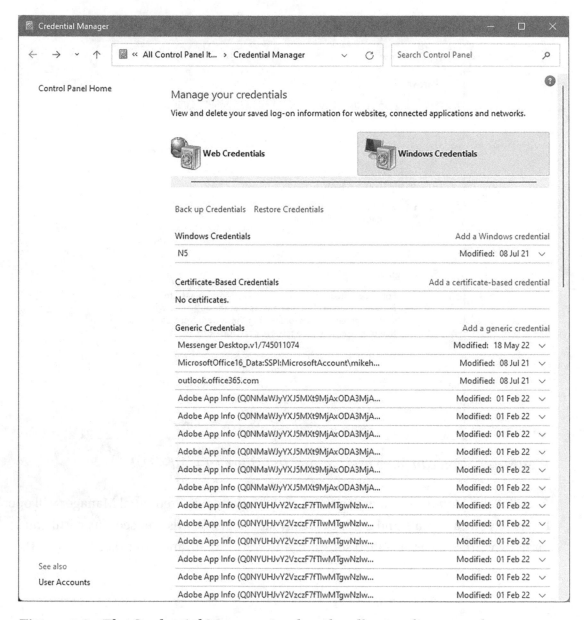

Figure 4-8. *The Credential Manager is where locally stored passwords can be managed*

It is here that you can make backups of or restore the password and certificate database and also where you can add organization-specific passwords and security certificates. To the right of each item in the list is a small down arrow. Click this to manage the password or certificate.

Local vs. Roaming

If you have your user accounts connected to a domain, then the user profile will be stored on a server, or in Azure AD in the cloud, and pulled to the PC at the time of sign-in. This enables users to be able to work from any PC with the same profile being used.

These *roaming profiles* can be extremely helpful in business, but there are times too when you might need, or it might just be preferable, to have the user account held locally on the PC, perhaps because it's a dedicated workstation for video production or engineering design, and you only have one or two of these machines.

The setting to switch a user account between local and roaming profiles still resides in the Control Panel. It's difficult to judge at this stage whether it will ultimately move to Settings or Windows Tools, but the latter perhaps seems more likely.

In Control Panel, open *User accounts* and you will see links on the left side of the window to *Configure advanced user profile properties* and to *Change my environment variables*. Click the former link and you will be presented with a dialog in which you can change the account profile type for the currently signed-in user (see Figure 4-9).

Figure 4-9. *You can switch accounts between local and roaming profiles*

User Environment Variables

Sometimes, though, you need far more granular control of a user profile, such as change the default shell user folders. This is where you click the *Change my environment variables* link. You are then presented with a dialog containing settings for the user account's user and system variables (see Figure 4-10).

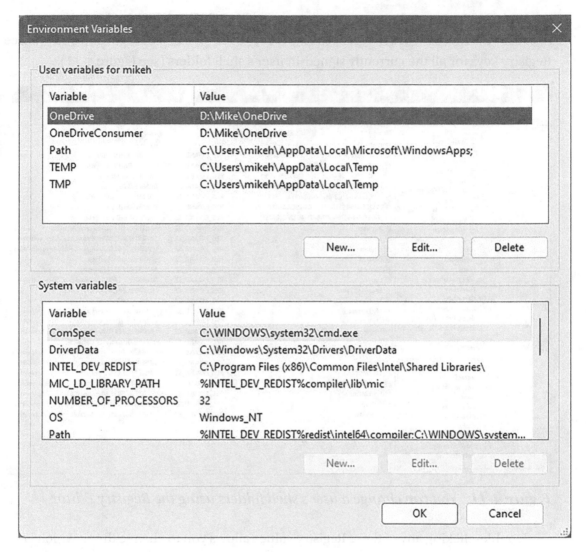

Figure 4-10. *Some user environment variables can be changed from Control Panel*

Moving the Shell User Folders

Not all environment variables can be changed here however, and the system variables cannot be changed at all for many accounts. To change all the shell user folders (Documents, Pictures, etc.), you need to use the Registry Editor, type **regedit** in the Start Menu, or run *Registry Editor* from Windows Tools.

With the Registry Editor open, navigate to HKEY_CURRENT_USER\Software\
Microsoft\Windows\CurrentVersion\Explorer\User Shell Folders, and you will see
Registry keys for all the currently signed-in user's shell folders (see Figure 4-11).

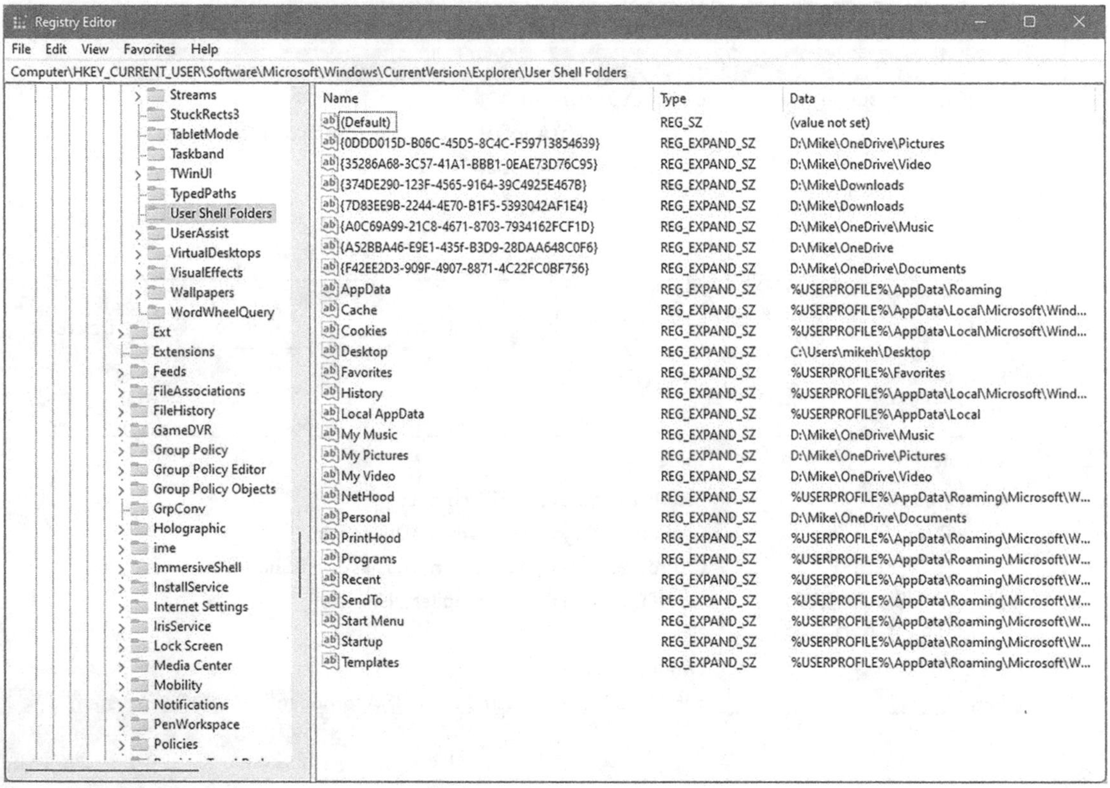

Figure 4-11. *You can change a user's shell folders using the Registry Editor*

Double-clicking any of these Registry values allows you to change them, which is
useful for the currently signed-in user, but what about other users on the PC? We'll look
in depth at the Windows Registry in Chapter 19, but if you have HKEY_USERS selected in
the left panel, a *Load Hive* option becomes available from the *File* menu. This will allow
you to temporarily load Registry files for other users on the PC.

You will need to have *Show hidden files, folders and drives* selected, which you can
do in File Explorer by clicking the menu icon in the toolbar and then clicking *Options*
from the menu that appears, which will display a dialog in which you can select the
appropriate *Hidden files and folders* option.

When you click *Load Hive*, you should navigate to the %USERPROFILE% folder for the
user you want the Registry hive for, which can be found in the *C:\Users* folder on the

PC. It is the **NTuser.dat** file you should open. You will be prompted for a key name. This will help you identify that Registry file in the Registry Editor, so perhaps name it after the user account name you're editing.

With that done, under HKEY_USERS you will now see Registry entries for the name you have just specified, **Jake** in Figure 4-12, and you can navigate to the *User Shell Folders* keys to make the necessary changes.

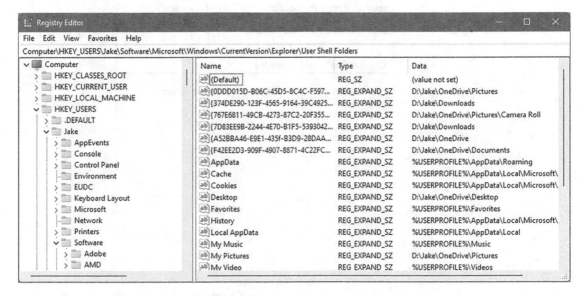

Figure 4-12. *You can edit the Registries of other users on the PC*

There are a couple of other ways for changing the locations of the Shell User Folders, but the relevant account must be signed in at the time. Right-clicking one of the folders in File Explorer, I have chosen *Documents* in Figure 4-13, presents a dialog in which you have a *Location* tab.

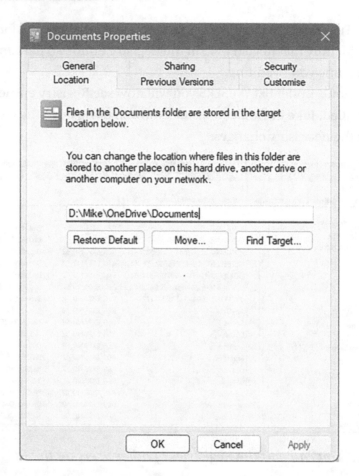

Figure 4-13. *You can change a user folder location in File Explorer*

If you then click the *Move* button, you can select a new location on the disk for the user folder. With this done, Windows 11 will ask if you want to move all the files and folders in the old location to the new one, and unless you have already moved them manually, it will do the job for you.

One of the downsides to this approach, apart from the fact that the user has to be signed in at the time, is that you have to do it one user folder at a time. It is possible however to use File Explorer to move multiple shell user folders at once, and it's so devilishly simple and straightforward you'll wonder why it's not more obvious.

This method involves selecting the shell user folders you want to move and using a simple *cut* and *paste* operation to move them to the new location. Windows knows what you're doing when this happens, and it will automatically update all the appropriate Registry keys for you on the fly.

Managing Home and Hybrid Workers

Everything I've detailed so far is great for workers at your own premises, or where they use company-provisioned laptops when out and about, but what about hybrid and home workers using their own PCs?

These workers can present a challenge as not only do you have no real control over the computer they use, it could be shared with their children who use it for playing games as an example, you don't have any real control over what type of operating system it runs in the first instance.

This is where Mobile Device Management (MDM) and Microsoft Endpoint Manager come into play. You can find all manner of excellent resources about this on the Microsoft website at `https://docs.microsoft.com/mem/intune`, but suffice to say that most modern operating systems support MDM, including Mac OS, iPad OS (see Figure 4-14), ChromeOS, and Android, and it's most helpful because if your employee is happiest using a keyboard with their iPad Pro when that's what they should be able to use, rather than forcing them to buy a laptop they'll probably hate, or for your organization to provision a laptop for them that they'll probably hate too.

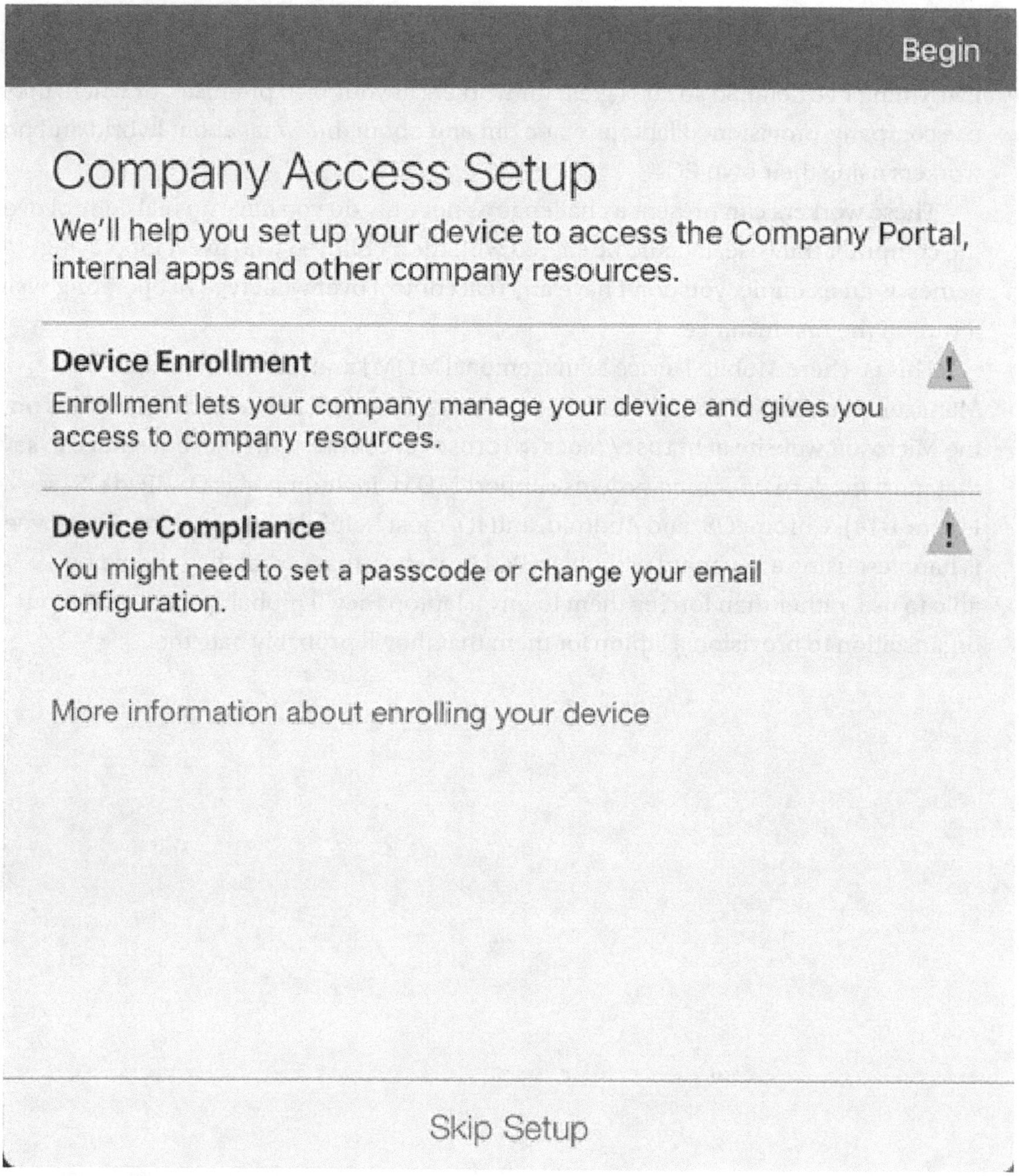

Begin

Company Access Setup

We'll help you set up your device to access the Company Portal, internal apps and other company resources.

Device Enrollment   ⚠

Enrollment lets your company manage your device and gives you access to company resources.

Device Compliance   ⚠

You might need to set a passcode or change your email configuration.

More information about enrolling your device

Skip Setup

Figure 4-14. MDM is supported on many devices, seen here on an iPad

What MDM does is it allows your organization to set and manage certain security and privacy policies for any type of personal device, from a Windows 10 PC to a Chromebook. These policies include minimum security requirements, that is, that the computer must have up-to-date anti-malware and security provisioned and that if the person leaves your organization, any files and documents of yours they still have residing on their personal device can be remotely wiped.

With Intune and MDM correctly provisioned, the hybrid or home worker can use their own personal device while still having full access to company cloud services, documents, and shared resources, such as Teams chats and company calendars. It is frankly an essential set of tools for any business that supports remote workers, even if they're using company-provisioned laptops.

Creating Sustainable PC Systems

In my book *The Green IT Guide* (Apress, 2021), I wrote A LOT about sustainable computing, from our smartphones and laptops to powerful desktop systems, and cloud and online hosted services, and how you can make smarter purchasing decisions in all of these areas with a little bit of help and research. It's a good book, genuinely, and I'm not just saying that because I wrote it!

When you are provisioning computers for any of your workers, sustainability ought to be high on your priority list. Currently, the amount of ewaste produced is estimated to be around 50 million tons annually, of which only 20% is currently recycled.

In the book, I detail a whole host of ways in which still working IT equipment can be reused when it's retired, from donating it to projects helping the school-age children of low-income families to veterans and schools in the developing world.

One of the biggest challenges at the moment though is around a subject you might have heard of called "Right to Repair." This is a movement that's gaining significant traction around the world and covers everything from our laptops and smartphones to John Deere tractors and McDonald's ice cream flurry machines.

For a device to meet Right to Repair standards, it should comply with four basic principles:

1. The device should be constructed and designed in a manner that allows repairs to be made easily.

2. End users and independent repair providers should be able to access original spare parts and tools (software as well as physical tools) needed to repair the device at fair market conditions.

3. Repairs should be possible by design and not hindered by software programming.

4. The repairability of a device should be clearly communicated by the manufacturer.

This means that computers where the memory and SSD (solid-state disk) are soldered to the motherboard and not removable without breaking the whole thing should not be purchased, with businesses and consumers instead favoring devices where components can be swapped out and where batteries and screens can be easily replaced in smartphones.

The problem has been caused in recent years by the trend of devices getting thinner and thinner, whereby traditional screws to hold them together have been replaced entirely by strong glue, making a great many devices completely unrepairable. You can check the repairability scores for thousands of laptops, smartphones, and other devices online at `www.ifixit.com`.

So when choosing new IT equipment, it's a good idea to keep Right to Repair in mind as this is not only good for the environment and reducing the amount of ewaste that ends up in landfill, with all the resultant chemical pollution that brings and there are some very nasty chemical and metals in our devices, but it means that the device will have a much longer potential lifespan in your organization, which brings with it the happy coincidence of reducing your overall costs.

Summary

Clearly, there's a lot you can do to correctly provision Windows 11 PCs for your workforce, and a lot of choices to be made, especially with Group Policy, balancing security and user experience. There are whole books on Group Policy and Mobile Device Management in the Apress catalogue and more resources still available on the Microsoft Docs website.

In the next chapter, we'll look more at hybrid workers and the processes of actually supporting local and remote users. You'll learn how you can take the end user with you on the journey to help reduce repeat problems occurring and how you can establish appropriate and effective IT training.

CHAPTER 5

Training Local and Remote PC Users

When you are troubleshooting and repairing a Windows PC, or any other type of electronics and computing device, it's not the computer you're supporting, it's the end user, a person. Now we'll skip lightly over the fact that in some cases it will have been that person who caused or contributed to the problem in the first place. It's not their job to be perfect, that's yours.

Supporting end users is considerably more complicated than it used to be. When I began writing Windows troubleshooting books, when Windows 7 was new out of the gate in 2009, things were very different in the business space. Back then, remote workers tended to be sales reps or marketing and executive types jetting off around the planet for meetings.

These people all needed their laptops to be working properly on the journey and when they arrived. After all, they needed to put the final polish to that PowerPoint presentation they were so proud of. Most end users though worked in offices, factories, and buildings that if they didn't have their own IT support engineer, they certainly had one available within a few hours travel.

Look at the situation now though, and it's astonishing that the world of the modern workplace has changed so dramatically. We can say it's the pandemic that's responsible for such a seismic shift of huge volumes of people now working from home, or from their local coffee shop, but with the rise of cloud computing services like Microsoft Azure (which launched just a year after Windows 7) and Google Workspace, it was fairly inevitable that work/life balance would change things and that people just didn't want to spend four hours, five days a week sitting in heavy traffic.

Companies have tried to get workers back to the office, but they're not doing very well as, aided by a period of employment prosperity, workers are voting with their feet

© Mike Halsey 2023
M. Halsey, *Troubleshooting and Supporting Windows 11*, https://doi.org/10.1007/978-1-4842-8728-6_5

and their open letters, quitting their jobs for different firms, or coming out en masse to say "No!" in a way that would have just got them all fired a few years before.

Even Apple, which tried *really* hard to get people back to the office, and who can blame them after spending five billion dollars on the place, has had to admit defeat and soften its stance to home and remote working.

As I write this, I'm currently planning my first trip to Microsoft's headquarters in Redmond (WA) just outside Seattle for the first time since 2019, three years ago. It's about a week and a half away, and while many of my Microsoft Most Valuable Professional (MVP) awardee peers are quite envious that I get to visit the mothership again, I'm not sure what to expect. There's a very good chance that when I arrive, the enormous Microsoft campus, which covers 502 acres and is normally home to more than 50,000 employees, will feel quite empty.

Couple all these fresh changes with the fact that you're not sure what type of computer the individual is going to be using, from a Chromebook to an iPad Pro to a Windows 10 machine, and you certainly know you're going to face a challenge. Indeed, this time my *Windows 10 Troubleshooting Second Edition* (Apress, 2021) and this book will be happily coexisting on sale, such is the nature of the workplace changes we've seen.

This all means that you're probably experiencing some challenges in your role as a miracle worker, so let's have a look and see if we can't alleviate some of the stress by taking the idea of support back to its core principles.

Understanding User Diversity

Who are your users? Do you know who they are and understand them? *Do you really*? One of the biggest challenges I've found when providing IT support is the sheer diversity of the workforce. If you work for a small, local organization, then there's a better than average chance that the workforce will all be from the local area, meaning there's a good chance they're of similar backgrounds, all went to the same schools, and therefore are of similar educational and competency levels.

Even that's dumbing it down though as the human species is a very diverse bunch, despite our often seemingly limited gene pool. If you work for a larger organization, then you'll likely have both offices in other countries around the world, but also employ people who have migrated from their country of origin to your own (to take one personal example, I'm a Brit who moved to France for a better quality of life a few years ago).

If your business operates in the "global supply chain," then you'll be working with other businesses, organizations, and even academic and governmental institutions in different countries around the world.

Every single one of the people working in your or other organizations that you encounter will be different. These people may speak different first languages or have different levels of comprehension and conversational skills in your language. Hell, you might not speak English as your first language and might have difficulty translating some of the more esoteric language that I use in this book.

Then there are the different educational and experiential backgrounds for the workforce. Not everybody will have had a college- or university-level education. I know it's common for governments (especially the one in the UK) to try and push everybody to achieve their best and undertake an academic education, but it's really not feasible, as an academic education isn't for everybody and, to quote that sage of good advice Peter Griffin from *Family Guy* (FOX Television), "It really grinds my gears" to see governments letting children and young adults down by pushing them in a direction they're simply not suited for.

In your own organization, you will have people of all manner of different educational backgrounds. Some will have been to university; a few of those may even have taken a master or a doctorate. Others will have a college education, and yet more will have stopped their education at high school. Of those people, some will have excelled, and others will have stumbled and been let down by the system.

Then we have differing levels of understanding and competency with technology. Not everybody is good with technology, and this is a good thing because it's why both you and I have a job. Some people are really great and technically minded (as I am), while others have their skills in different areas, like cooking or horticulture (I can just about get by with the former, but while I appreciate plants and flowers I have absolutely no idea how they work).

It's a misnomer too to assume that the higher the level of achievement in a person's life, the higher their understanding of technology must be. Some of the cleverest people on the planet will have absolutely no idea how to set up a printer and will still point at their desktop monitor and call that the computer.

In all then, the best assumption to make when approaching the support of any end user is not to make any assumptions. Go into every situation completely fresh, don't dumb things down (in case you upset them), but don't get too technical either (in case you lose them). You're probably thinking at this point that this seems terribly complicated and you'd never be able to manage it, so without making any assumptions about yourself, let's look to rectify this.

Teaching Fundamentals

When you provide IT support to another person, you're as much of a teacher as you are an engineer and a computer expert. This is because it's your job to help the person understand what it is that went wrong, so as to avoid getting the same call from the same person somewhere down the road.

I am, for those of you that haven't read some of my other books where I talk about this, a fully qualified teacher with specialisms in English and Mathematics. This means I can get quite hot under the collar when people misuse apostrophes or don't use brackets correctly in a sum. Aside from the personal foibles (I think I'm a bit too far gone for counseling), it does come in very useful when IT support is involved, so let's cover some teaching theory and give you a bit of a primer.

There are four main styles of learning, sometimes called VARK. It's common in some classrooms and colleges for students to be handed a short VARK questionnaire to complete, as it's a great way for the teacher to determine how people best learn. VARK stands for four different ways a person best absorbs information:

- **Visual** – They learn by watching, either a demonstration or a video.

- **Auditory** – They learn by listening to a person, such as a TED talk.

- **Read/write** – They learn by reading text and books and then writing what they have learned to consolidate it in their own mind.

- **Kinesthetic** – They learn through practical experience, such as building models and performing actions.

In the real world, you'll find that the vast majority of people, some 70% or more, will be predominantly kinesthetic learners, while the next largest group will be read/write learners as writing down notes about what you've learned can really help clarify things for a person.

How does this help when it comes to IT support? Well, actually, it doesn't because people are either going to be watching you fix something or listen to your explanation of how it all went wrong in the first place. Where it does come in helpful is in staff training, and if you can get the training right, then you can probably mitigate against a lot of the problems that'll occur, certainly the smaller, more common mistakes anyway.

Before we come to training and other subjects of that ilk though, let's stick for a moment with the one-to-one end-user support experience. There are things you can do to make the process easier for you and to help educate the end user at the same time.

In Chapter 6, I'll take you through the remote support tools available in Windows 11 and some of the utilities that an end user can use to demonstrate the problem they are facing or to fix things themselves. While there is a natural tendency for the sake of expediency and because of high workloads for the average IT support technician or IT Pro to take full remote control of a PC and implement changes themselves, there are also times when it's worth taking a step back and guiding the end user through the process so they are fixing their own PC directly.

The primary reason for doing this is that if it's a problem that tends to come up a lot, as many of the simpler problems do, then you're saving time overall by hopefully reducing the number of repeat calls, both from that user and perhaps from other users in their immediate workspace they can help.

The secondary reason is that the end user will get their own sense of achievement, and the customary endorphin hit that comes with it, having learned something. This makes them happy and in return gives them a better impression of you (end users frequently just think of IT departments as the people that just say "No" all the time), which can never be a bad thing.

No KISSing

Given everything I've said in this chapter so far about not making assumptions, and about how everybody's understanding of and use of technology is different, and how some people that use computers every day just work from muscle memory in one or two programs, you might assume that you just need to dumb things down and start with the basics. This is the approach often exemplified by the phrase "Keep It Simple, Stupid" (KISS).

I would argue the opposite; it's perfectly acceptable to ask the end user how comfortable they are being guided through the repair process. Some will be more than happy to hand the whole thing over to you, while others might be genuinely surprised that you've asked and ready to take on the challenge.

You don't need to be intimidated by the end user either. Asking this of a senior executive can often get the same response as you'd have from somebody working in logistics. The phrase "it's lonely at the top" might be an oxymoron, but a change of pace for a short while can often brighten somebody's day.

Assessment and Evaluation

This brings me to one of the core principles of education theory, that of "checking learning." This is the process of checking in with the learner periodically to see that they actually understand what's been taught to them, because if it's just gone over their head, all that's happened is everybody's time has been wasted.

So at the beginning of a teaching session, you will assess the level at which a person understands the basics of the subject, and at the end of the session, you will evaluate them to determine the degree to which the stated goals have been attained.

You can do this in several ways, but in a one-to-one scenario, either in person or via a phone or video call, it's likely best through questioning and conversation. Ask the user what their experiences are of technology, what they generally use away from work, and how comfortable they feel around computers. This is useful information to help gauge their overall competency.

At the end of the session, you can ask them to recap what's been done. For longer fixes, it's a good idea to stop periodically, perhaps at the end of each main area of action, to evaluate the person. This way, you can determine what they've understood about the process so far, or overall, and it gives you a good idea of how competently they might be able to avoid a repetition of the problem in the future.

Lastly, you might find it helpful to suggest the person make some notes on what's been done. This, as I mentioned earlier, is a great way for people to consolidate in their own minds what they've learned, and it also gives them something to refer back to later as a refresher should they forget it.

Don't Get Too Technical

One of the problems people can face when receiving IT support, or even just talking to somebody about computers and technology such as purchasing a smartphone or a laptop in a store, is getting bogged down with jargon and technical terminology.

If you talk to somebody about a Core i3, Core i5, Core i7, and Core i9, or about a 512Gb SSD as opposed to a 2Tb one, people will likely only hear and be able to process the numbers. They'll think that the bigger the number, the better the "thing" must be, which, while true after a fashion, doesn't equate in the real world as somebody buying a laptop for their child to use at school should probably not get anything more powerful than a Core i5.

With memory and storage, it's equally confusing for people. Talk to an end user about terabytes, and they might think that was just a rubbish Gerry Anderson puppet TV show from the 1980s.

Then there's overall terminology. I've already mentioned that it's very common for nontechnical people to point to a desktop monitor and call that the computer. If it's an all-in-one, then fine, but somebody telling you "the computer won't come on" when there's actually nothing wrong with the PC itself, but rather the HDMI cable has come loose, isn't helpful in quickly solving their problem.

The best approach then is to use terminology and language the person *will* understand, such as referring to the screen, or the fan noise, or the big box on the floor. This way, you are both much more likely to be on the same page, and you'll be able to help solve the problem with much less frustration for them and much more expediency for yourself.

Ask Questions with Yes or No Answers

This brings me on to the subject of questions, specifically the questions you ask of the end user to get information about the problem. Setting aside for a moment the technical level of understanding for the end user, I want to jump back to what I said earlier in this chapter about language and about never making assumptions.

You don't know where the person was born or what their first language was; their staff record might say they're from Canada, but you might not know they were brought up in Quebec where French was "langue de préférence." Or they might obviously have been born abroad and have perfectly good conversational and business language skills, but struggle with some of the less common words and phrases used in your own language.

You might have experienced this yourself when on a foreign holiday where you perfectly understand the question you're asking the waiter, but have absolutely no idea what they're saying in reply.

The way around this is to try and focus your questions to elicit "yes" or "no" answers. If the person can just answer simply, then (A) there's no chance they'll get their own terminology wrong, and (B) it's likely they'll have clearly understood you and certainly know how to reply.

Not every question can be asked this way, but some of the tools I'll detail in Chapter 6 can also help by highlighting on a PC's screen what it is a user is talking about and doing at the time. Any advantage you can get though to help cut through complexity and have both you and the person you are trying to help get onto the same page will give you a huge advantage in both understanding and time taken to get the problem solved.

Establishing Effective IT Training

Many IT professionals are required to run training sessions periodically or perhaps would like to have periodic training to help bring the workforce up to speed on software, operating systems, and IT practices in the organization. You might have done this when you were rolling out Windows 11, so as to familiarize people with the new Start Menu, desktop, and some of the productivity features including snap layouts, or you might have just bought a few copies of a book to pass around the office such as the excellent *Windows 11 Made Easy* (Apress, 2021) by Mike Halsey, whoever the hell he is.

Training is a chore however. Anybody that has attended a staff training day will know that, unless you consider it a great way to get out of work and have a change of pace for a day, they are often dull and ineffectual, and the "professional trainer" they get in either doesn't properly understand the subject, can't find a way to make it engaging, or very clearly loves themselves much more than they love you. I can't help with the latter unfortunately, but with the other two let's have a crack at it and see what we can come up with.

The best way to deliver IT training is to do it yourself. You may not be a natural at presenting, or you may not even know how to put together a lesson plan, but these are things that can eventually come naturally with a little bit of practice.

Lesson Planning

The first thing you need to ask yourself is "what am I trying to achieve?" With this, we need to examine what the outcome of the day's training is to be and what goals you want. These can be set out in such a way as to help you better plan the training.

Let's take a troubleshooting example. We want to teach people the basics of good PC management, so they're less angry at yourselves in the IT department and more understanding of the role you play and why you have to say no to them a lot. If we look at the set of objectives, we might set it out as such:

- What is and isn't permitted on a workplace PC

- What everything is and what it all does

- Simple ways to avoid problems

We'll leave it as just these three items, as having too many goals in a single six-hour training session runs the risk of the learners becoming confused as they're unable to take it all in.

So we have three different subjects and six hours of training (excluding lunch and breaks), and we can devote two hours to each one. That seems reasonable, so how do we set out our training?

The first two hours will be about "What is and isn't permitted on a workplace PC." For this, we could just stand and recite a long list of rules and why they're important, but let's be honest, nobody cares. Rules were made to be broken as the saying goes, and people are only being told rules because it makes life easier for the person dishing them out, so why bother paying attention to them?

We need an outcome where each person in the room understands why those rules are important and feels invested in them, and so we should probably make *them* the rule makers, rather than the rule takers. So we already have a plan for our session. We're going to break everybody into small groups, and they can plan their own set of rules for the IT systems.

You might want to give each group a different type of rule sets to come up with, one for workers in the office, one for remote workers, one for home workers, one for senior management (that's always fun), and so on. Next, we need to give these groups a set of parameters they have to consider.

These parameters could be that they need to keep the workforce productive, reduce downtime, reduce the volume of calls made to the IT department (so they can remain productive as there's not a lot of people working there), and then throw in something that's perhaps a little more interesting and specific to their group task, such as managing data security for laptops on the move that could be lost or stolen, planning how to accommodate computers at home that might also be used by children for playing games and the potential consequences thereof, and also perhaps preventing senior management and company executive from getting delusions of grandeur and believing they can do whatever the hell they want all the time as they run the company.

You will probably find, having set all this out, that the rules your workforce come up with are (A) very similar to the rules imposed by the other groups in the exercise and (B) broadly in line with the rules they have to abide by anyway. Who knows, they might even come up with an idea you've not thought of.

Using Mixed Peer Group Learning

This brings me neatly onto the subject of mixed peer group learning and how you can use it to your advantage. When people come into your group training session, you might want to start them with a short questionnaire so that you can gather some basic information about them.

This might best be multiple choice, for reasons I'll come to shortly, and would start with their name (obviously not multiple choice that one unless you're a Man in Black) and which department at the organization they work in.

You will want to ask them three to five short questions so that you can learn something about them. VARK, which I mentioned earlier in this chapter, is probably less important here as the training session will be too short and has already been written anyway. You will want to know about their understanding of IT systems however, so you could ask questions like the following:

1. How do you feel about your own level of computer literacy?

    a. Computers scare me.

    b. I know how to do what I need to do.

    c. I'm fairly confident using computers.

    d. I'm very good with computers.

2. What type of computer do you use outside of work?

    a. A desktop PC or laptop running Windows.

    b. An iPad and an iPhone.

    c. A Chromebook.

    d. I have absolutely no idea, it just works for me.

Armed with this information, we can decide who will go in each of our groups. We want to mix things up as much as possible. This is because in addition to learning from you, these people can learn from each other. We also don't want one person taking too much of a lead so that the quieter, less confident people don't get their voice heard and feel isolated and left out of discussions.

Achieving the first of these is simple, as all you need to do is mix together people who are technically literate with other people that aren't. For the latter, you might suggest that every person create one rule, but this will place an artificial pressure on the quiet ones and make them uncomfortable, which is ultimately self-defeating as they won't learn anything or get any benefit from the training.

Instead, you might want to mix people from different departments together. This brings two benefits. Firstly, the people are less likely to know each other well and therefore perhaps more likely to all interact. The biggest benefit however is that as each department has its own unique requirements and ways of working, people in one department might suggest ideas that would be completely overlooked by people in another department.

The end result of using these mixed-ability groups is that we achieve some very important aims:

- We create an environment in which everybody can be encouraged to participate.

- People can learn from the differences between working practices and what's important across the whole organization.

- Those who are more technically literate can assist those who are less confident, taking some of your own workload away from you.

This ultimately frees you up to wander quietly around the room, listening to the discussions, offering the odd word of advice or suggesting something a group might have missed, and asking the odd question of a quieter group member as a gentle prod of encouragement.

All of this brings us back to the subject of assessment and evaluation, as what you're actually doing as you wander is assessing how well they're understanding the subject and evaluating when it might be good to bring the exercise to a close (I've never been a fan of the arbitrary ten-minute rule).

With each group feeding back on their proposed rules, and the walls of the room hopefully filling up with flip-chart paper, you can use the rest of the session to discuss each group's ideas more broadly; remember that in order to keep people engaged, no suggestion can ever be a bad suggestion, it just might be more difficult to implement, leading to further discussion.

Eventually, you'll narrow things down to a tight set of rules everybody can agree on. If you have additional policies for people to follow, these too can be discussed, but it's always good to provide context. If you have tight rules about data privacy and encryption and the groups haven't suggested these (or perhaps not suggested them strongly enough), you can ask the groups what they know about the government and international data protection law and how different governments and companies such as Google and Meta treat personal data, that sort of thing.

Data privacy is a good example as you'll inevitably have strict rules governing it anyway. People might not consider their own data important, as what can it be used for they might ask. If you were to ask the same person how they feel about the privacy of their children, you might get a very different response. This can be expanded to ask how the privacy of children should or could be any different from that of themselves, or the company's employees, customers, and stakeholders, and what the potential consequences of a breach might be (from customers departing to money being stolen), then you'll possibly have a very engaged audience by the end of the session.

Mixing Activities

For the next part of the session, we're covering "What everything is and what it all does." How might you approach this and why is it important to do something completely different from what you did in the first part of the day's training? Well, the reason for the latter is clear, to mix things up a bit so as to keep people engaged and interested. If things become too repetitive, then people will quickly become disinterested, at which point you've probably lost them.

This part of the training could be handled in different ways. You could, for example, have pictures of lots of different computer and IT components (desktop PC box, monitor, USB cable, Ethernet switch, smartphone, Wi-Fi access point, etc.), and again in groups people can put these together, again using peer support, to figure out how IT systems are structured and why things are the way they are.

Alternatively, and if you think it might work, we could return to the flip-chart paper, and people could write and draw pictures of different pieces of IT equipment, making the necessary connections between them as they go.

How this helps, apart from being a very kinesthetic exercise, is that it clarifies in people's minds what they should be aware of when using their workplace IT equipment. It's common for people to trip over power cables, pull Ethernet cables and damage sockets, and desktop PCs and monitors confused.

You might follow this up by throwing in a few hazards, some very clear as threats to computers and others a little more esoteric. Images of a virus symbol, a photo of a hacker, a USB Flash Drive, and a cluttered mess of cables would be obvious, but you can use the opportunity to raise awareness of other problems such as a thick stone wall (which can affect a Wi-Fi signal) or sand and dog hair (both of which can cause havoc with any electrics they encounter).

Consolidating Learning

The last part of our training session is called "Simple ways to avoid problems," and we can use this to bring everything together as something called consolidating learning. What this means is that everything that's been covered throughout the day's training is brought together into a cohesive whole, both to wrap it all up with people understanding what are good and bad practices for IT use and also to help clarify things in people's minds to help them remember it in the longer term. This last part is tremendously important as there's nothing worse than people forgetting what it is you've taught them five minutes outside of the room.

Evaluation here is very important, as this is your chance to ensure people have actually taken in what you've been teaching and crucially that they can make sense of it and place it inside of the context of their own home and working lives.

There are different ways of achieving this. And there's nothing wrong with you choosing several of the following methods and using them together:

- Encouraging people to make notes can help them understand and make sense of things; it also gives them something that they can refer back to later that's in a language they can relate to, if they need any reminders.

- Asking everybody in the room to identify one thing they consider important about the subjects covered in the session.

- Perhaps asking people if they can think of anything additionally that
  could also be considered (people might still think of good rule ideas
  after the first part of the training is over).

You could even take the session subject matter further through the use of something like a Post-It wall, where people can post sticky notes suggesting things they consider important for IT use or ideas about why privacy and security are important. Maybe a few would even want to post a short story about something that affected them or someone they know, like a virus infection, someone getting access to their credit card details, or the day they suddenly discovered why two-factor authentication is important.

Training Outcomes

With all of this done, you could find that not only have you achieved your stated aims with the training session, and not just that people will remember the subject later, but that they might want to discuss it with colleagues, friends, and family (spreading the love as it were) and that... shock horror, they might have actually enjoyed themselves!

This is where you should never ruin the session with the wrong type of evaluation form. In fact, I would argue that if you can get away with it, you shouldn't have a training evaluation form at all, though human resources departments do seem very fond of their paperwork trail.

If you must have a training evaluation form, there are a couple of things you absolutely must not do and a few things that can be a good idea. Of the things you mustn't do, when you ask people to rate something, never give them a choice from one to five. In fact, you should always make it an even number that they can choose from, as this prevents them from arbitrarily picking the number in the middle. That type of feedback isn't useful to anybody, and you certainly won't be able to get any useful data from it.

The second is something I find particularly hateful, and it's very common with third-party "professional" trainers that businesses and organizations bring in from outside the company. This is the "How do you rate the trainer" question. There's one reason and one reason only to ask this question, and that's because the trainer wants to get a good ego-stroking.

If you want to get some useful data from the feedback, ask people what they feel was the part of the training they got the most benefit from or something they learned that they hadn't been aware of before. These are useful as they can help you to identify what worked and, by omission of subjects on the form, what didn't work so well, but it also helps consolidate things in the minds of the learners.

Training Home and Remote Workers

Everything we've covered so far is great for people who work full time in an office, or who can come to an office periodically for a training refresher, but how do you train people remotely, either those on the move in a hotel room somewhere in the world or those people working from home?

This is where you can play into your IT strengths and use the videoconferencing tools that you'll already have set up for those workers. You'll be using something like Zoom for basic videoconferencing or a more full-featured package like Teams where you can structure all manner of side activities and even plug-in dedicated questionnaires and training modules.

These online training events will, by their very nature, need to be different to in-person training. You can't, for example, place people in mixed groups as that simply won't work. So the training does become slightly harder and more problematic overall.

Having smaller groups in the session is one way to overcome this, as you can still work through all the activities of the in-person session, but with just one peer group instead of several. You can also use collaboration apps such as a Microsoft Whiteboard to allow people to perform tasks such as making lists and putting together their maps of how IT systems work.

An alternative to Teams and Zoom is that some companies will pay for third-party video courseware from companies such as Pluralsight or LinkedIn Learning. I have a library of 12 courses of my own on Pluralsight, which you can find at `https://app.pluralsight.com/profile/author/mike-halsey` should you so wish, but finding IT and business courses for any subject and at every level is straightforward on these services. Additionally, a corporate account makes it easy to track what training individuals have watched, and many include evaluation you can use to see how helpful people found them and how much they learned.

These video services became very popular during the pandemic lockdowns of 2020, with my own courses seeing a huge spike in viewing hours as people were asked by their employers to make the best use they could of their time stuck at home.

Top Tips for Tip Top Training

Hopefully, in this chapter, I've instilled in you some of the best training techniques and the reasons for doing so, but clearly I'm also the one here doing the training, so it would be remiss of me to not follow my own rules and finish with some consolidation and perhaps a few additional notes that didn't make their way into the main content.

Classroom Management

We tend to think of classroom management in the context of making the naughty children sit at the front of the class where they can be properly supervised. Classroom (or training room) management is equally important in further, higher, and in-workplace education as well, and it's primarily for the reasons I detailed earlier about encouraging mixed-ability peer groups.

Sitting people in mixed-ability groups at the start of the session helps in several ways. Firstly, you don't have everybody upending themselves throughout the training; people don't enjoy this as they like to pick a spot they will feel comfortable in.

Also, the problem of people sitting with their friends so they can chat to them doesn't end when people leave high school. Adults of any age will do exactly the same thing, and, while individuals might not see any harm in doing so, it's a distraction any day of the week, as any idle banter between friends is time not spent paying attention to the subject or task at hand.

Lastly, keeping friends away from one another helps with the mixed-ability peer groups in that you don't end up with just a few people dominating proceedings when group activities are taking place.

Then there's the seating arrangements to consider. You might have a preference, such as round tables or chairs that can be positioned so that groups sit around the same table. You might prefer rows of long tables (though this can make people feel intimidated if they've been out of education for a long period, or who didn't have a happy educational experience in childhood).

Whatever you choose for seating and tables, try to make sure that people can be where they need for activities with the minimum of fuss and upheaval and without too many chairs and tables having to be heaved about the room.

Never Use the Word "Understand"

It's a big no, no in education to use the word "understand" in the context of what a learner has learned and the subject matter you cover. If one of your stated aims is that "The learners will understand what basic problems can arise with computers in the workplace," then what does this actually mean? Different people will understand things in different ways and have different levels of understanding.

What's more, it's impossible to have somebody show you understanding. What you need to do is choose more relevant vocabulary, both for the learners and for yourself. Demonstrate and explain are always good examples as it helps with evaluation and consolidation. "The learners will be able to explain why a rule for IT use is important," not all the rules, just one will do. Each different person will have their favorite, and they'll be able to explain it to you and why they consider it to be valuable to the business. Alternatively, you could use "Learners will be able to demonstrate how to set up two-factor authentication."

Never Make Assumptions

This ties back to what I said at the very beginning of this chapter, but it really is the *most* important consideration when delivering training. One group of learners will never be the same as another group, and everybody will be at different levels of comprehension and ability with the subject matter, while some will be more eloquent and confident than others.

Managing this comes with experience, but it's something you can learn if you concentrate on it. Assessing people as they're working and mixed peer practical and discussion activities can give you a great opportunity to observe. This helps you to see what's working, who's falling behind or looking confused, and if there's anybody running away with the subject or just plain disinterested.

It's Not Them... It's You

People are never, as an aside, disinterested because they don't like the subject, not with education anyway. People are disinterested because the training is being pitched to them either in a way they can't comprehend as it's too technical, in a way that's too dumbed down for them, or in a way that they can't relate to their own personal or professional lives.

It's no shame to admit you're doing it wrong. The learners aren't the only people in the room learning, as you are too. You're learning how to deliver training, how to relate subjects to individuals, how to engage people, and how to make often dry subjects interesting and fun.

You won't always get it right, you will sometimes stumble, and perhaps you'll even come away from a session angry at yourself for having completely ballsed it all up. I've done that, many times even as an experienced teacher. Sometimes, it's an off day, sometimes my planning was wrong, and sometimes I needed more information about the group that I hadn't been given or had more likely forgot to ask for.

Being a successful trainer is not just about being a good trainer, it's about learning how to improve as you go, and an evaluation on what worked, what didn't work, and what you can change or improve for next time is a valuable piece of personal reflection that can help you in the long term.

Summary

Not everybody has the personality or the confidence to present or train. Some people, no matter how often they may be forced to do so, cannot get over their fear of presenting a PowerPoint slide deck to a room of people. Some, by extension, will never feel comfortable delivering training to a group, small or large.

With the guides in this chapter though, you will hopefully have a good chance of keeping people engaged and letting them all have some fun along the way. Don't worry about appearing nervous, so are they. All you need to do is prove that you know and understand the subject matter.

In the next chapter, we'll make a change in our subject matter and look at the tools and utilities that already exist within Windows 11 that you can use to help troubleshoot and repair problems with both networked and remote PCs and what exists to help the user help you in return.

CHAPTER 6

Windows 11's Support Tools

In Chapter 8, we are going to start looking in depth at the various utilities and tools within Windows 11 for diagnosing, troubleshooting, and repairing specific problems and problem areas, and there is indeed a lot to show! Having spent a little time discussing the end user however, I wanted to show you the support tools available in Windows 11, as there are more than you might think.

The best part of using the built-in tools is that some of them can be used by the end user, quite simply and easily, to help them demonstrate what the problem they're facing is. This can often mean you can give them advice on how to rectify their situation in a quick message or email, rather than having to dive into a full and perhaps lengthy discussion and online or in-person support session.

Taking Screenshots in Windows 11

One of the easiest, and probably by far the most familiar, ways for an end user to show you what's happening on their PC is for them to take a screenshot they can email to you. There are several ways to achieve this in Windows 11. There are a few different ways to do this.

Method 1: Using Print Screen

The oldest and likely most familiar way for somebody to take a screenshot is to use the Print Screen (**PrtScrn**) button on their keyboard. This will save a screenshot to the clipboard, and it can then be pasted into a graphics program, such as Paint, and saved as a JPG or other image file or pasted directly into an email or messaging app like Teams.

© Mike Halsey 2023
M. Halsey, *Troubleshooting and Supporting Windows 11*, https://doi.org/10.1007/978-1-4842-8728-6_6

There are two downsides to using Print Screen. The first is that while it's fine for keyboard warriors who are used to using shortcuts such as Ctrl + C (copy) and Ctrl + V (paste), the lack of an actual *thing* they can see might confuse them.

The other problem comes down to the different types of PC and computer the user might have. They could have a laptop that doesn't have a PrtScrn button, or it could be mixed with the function keys row, and they need to press or to hold the **Fn** key to get it to work. This is something that can easily confuse a nontechnical user.

Then we have to consider if they're using a PC at all. You could be troubleshooting a problem with a Windows 11 Cloud PC installation running from the Windows 365 service on a Chromebook or an iPad (see Figure 6-1). These computers will very likely not have a Print Screen button at all and will probably illicit memories of Homer Simpson desperately trying to find the "Any" key he was asked to press in the classic television cartoon series.

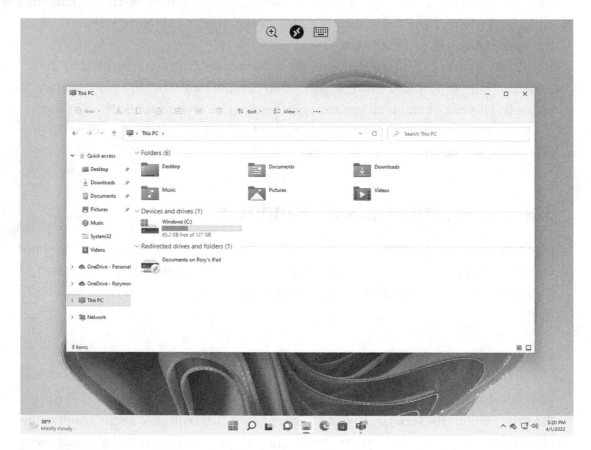

Figure 6-1. *You could be asked to support a Windows 11 Cloud PC running on an iPad*

Method 2: Windows Key + Print Screen

If the computer is a PC though and it does have a **PrtScrn** button, then you can ask the user to press the keyboard combination *Windows key + PrtScrn* which will capture a screenshot and save it as a PNG image file to the user's *Pictures\Screenshots* folder. The folder will be automatically created if it does not already exist.

This allows a completely nontechnical user to easily find the screenshot and send it to you in an email or Teams chat message, which is something they damn well ought to be able to do by that point anyway.

Method 3: Alt + Print Screen

These days, we have really large PC monitors, mine is an ultrawide affair with a resolution of 3840 by 1600 pixels, and finding screens with even greater pixel density is becoming more and more common. You might then just want the user to capture the current open window.

They can do this by, making sure the window they want to capture is selected, pressing **Alt + PrtScrn** on their keyboard. This works in exactly the same way as with just PrtScrn in that it saves an image to the clipboard that can then be pasted into Paint or directly into an email or Teams chat message.

However, Alt + PrtScrn only captures the currently selected window, which can make it much easier to quickly see what the end user is talking to you about.

Tip   If the user is using a tablet such as a Microsoft Surface Pro or Surface Go that doesn't have a keyboard, perhaps because they're a first-line worker, a screenshot will need to be captured using the physical buttons on the device. This will vary from one manufacturer's tablet to another, but for a Surface, it is to press **Power + Volume up** at the same time. This will save the screenshot to the *Pictures\Screenshots* folder on the device. Bear in mind however that such a tablet is likely going to be locked to "Kiosk mode" in which only a single app can be run, and the desktop cannot be accessed. In this scenario, they can capture the screenshot but would be completely unable to send it to you.

Method 4: Xbox Game Bar

Okay, so this one is a little more strange. If you want the user to use Alt + PrtScrn but for the image to be automatically saved for them, you can ask them to use the **Windows key + Alt + PrtScrn**. This will save the image but will prompt the user to view it using the Xbox Game Bar (see Figure 6-2).

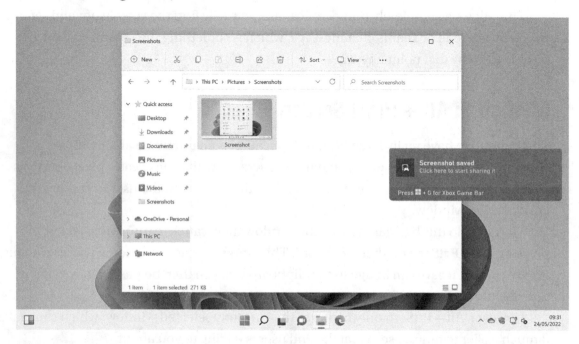

Figure 6-2. *Xbox Game Bar can be used to capture screenshots*

The user can, if they're an Xbox gamer familiar with such things, press the Windows key + G if they like to open the Xbox Game Bar, where they will be shown their captured screenshot. What's easier though is to tell the user to navigate in File Explorer to *Video* (yes, really) and then *Captures* where their screenshot will be stored.

Method 5: Snipping Tool

The Snipping Tool has been built into Windows since XP Tablet Edition in 2005 and has been expanded in functionality and usefulness over time, with Microsoft adding features such as pen support for annotating screenshots. You can find the Snipping Tool in the Start Menu.

The user should select what *Windows mode* to use (see Figure 6-3) from rectangle, window, full screen, or free form, where the user can select an area with a pen or mouse.

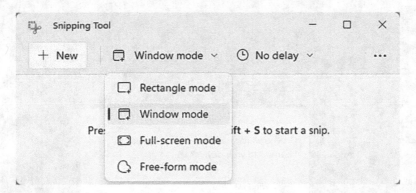

Figure 6-3. *The Snipping Tool is a more flexible way to capture screenshots*

Perhaps what is more useful however is the *Delay* mode. This allows the screenshot capture to be delayed by up to ten seconds and is very useful for capturing screenshots at times when it is otherwise very difficult or even seemingly impossible to do so, such as when the Lock Screen is active or a User Account Control (UAC) prompt is displayed (see Figure 6-4).

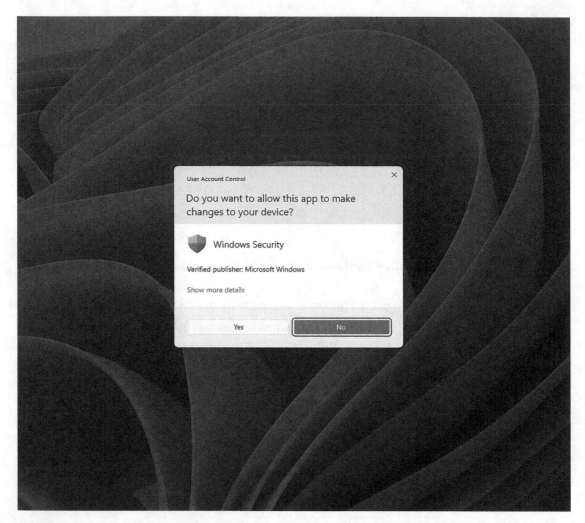

Figure 6-4. *Delay mode can be used to capture otherwise impossible screenshots*

When the user is ready to capture their screenshot, they should press the **+ New** button in the Snipping Tool window. If they have chosen a window, rectangle, or free-form screenshot, the screen will darken, enabling them to select the area to capture, and the screenshot will then appear in the Snipping Tool window.

Tip   You can quick launch the Snipping Tool and go straight into capturing a screenshot with the keyboard shortcut **Windows key + Shift + S**.

Problem Steps Recorder

Back in 2008 and early 2009, I was a member of Microsoft's closed beta program for Windows 7, long before the company introduced the Insider Program. A small but significant part of this beta was something called the Problem Steps Recorder (or just Steps Recorder when you search for it in the Start Menu).

This was a tool created specifically for the beta that could be used by testers to demonstrate problems they encountered with the various OS builds that Microsoft released. So popular though was the Steps Recorder that it was kept in the final release of Windows 7 and still resides in Windows 11 today.

Tip   You can most easily find the Problem Steps Recorder by searching for **PSR** in the Start Menu.

With the Problem Steps Recorder open on the desktop, the user will see a small toolbar containing just four buttons (see Figure 6-5). These are *Start Record*, *Stop Record*, *Add Comment*, and *Help* which on a drop-down menu where you will find the Settings for the Steps Recorder, including the maximum number of images to capture in a recording session, the default is 25.

Figure 6-5. *The Problem Steps Recorder has a simple toolbar*

When the user is ready to record what they do, they can click the *Start Record* button. You can tell them that they don't need to rush as this isn't recording a long video, just a series of images and some text.

The user should then run through the series of clicks and tasks that result in the error they are encountering. At any point during the proceedings, they can click the *Add Comment* button. This will display a text dialog in which they can type a message for you (see Figure 6-6) that will be saved in the appropriate place in the final file.

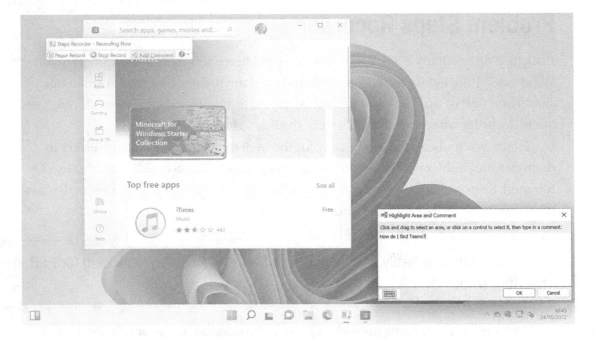

Figure 6-6. *The user can add text comments at any time*

When they are finished, they should click *Stop Record*, and the Steps Recorder window will expand to display the full session of what they have captured (see Figure 6-7).

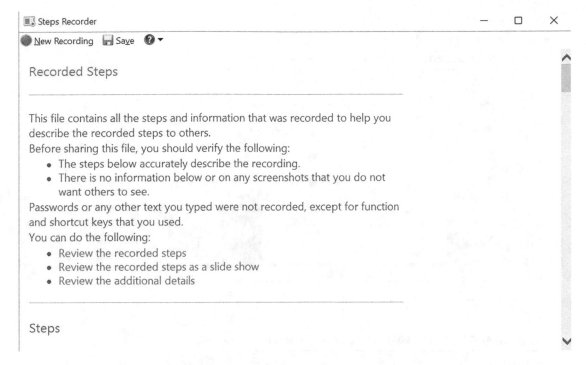

Figure 6-7. *The user should save the output Steps Recorder document*

At this point, the user should either click the *New Recording* button if they feel they've made an error and wish to redo things or click *Save* and save the output file to their PC; by default, it will ask to save to the desktop.

This output file, which is in the ZIP format, should then by sent to yourself by email or messaging after which you can open it to view what the user experienced. You will see that every time something happened on the PC, or whenever the user clicked something or interacted with the desktop or an app, the appropriate item is highlighted with a green border (see Figure 6-8). You will also see any *User Comments* they made along the way.

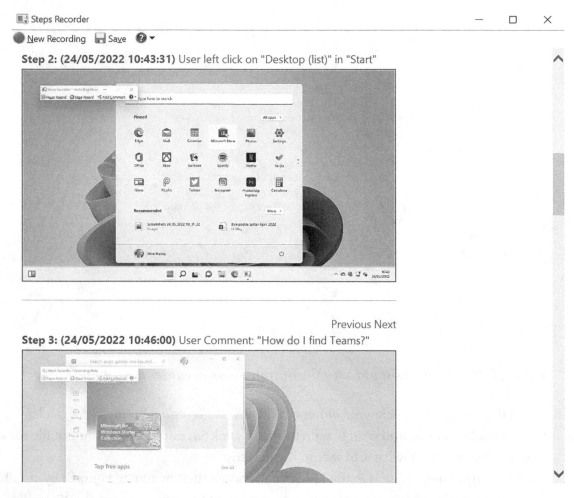

Figure 6-8. *Screenshots are all annotated in the Steps Recorder*

At the very bottom of the output file, you will find technical information about the session. This includes the filenames of programs, apps, and services being used and accessed by the user during the recording, along with version numbers (very useful for checking compatibility in a workplace) and verbose descriptions of what the user was doing for each step (see Figure 6-9).

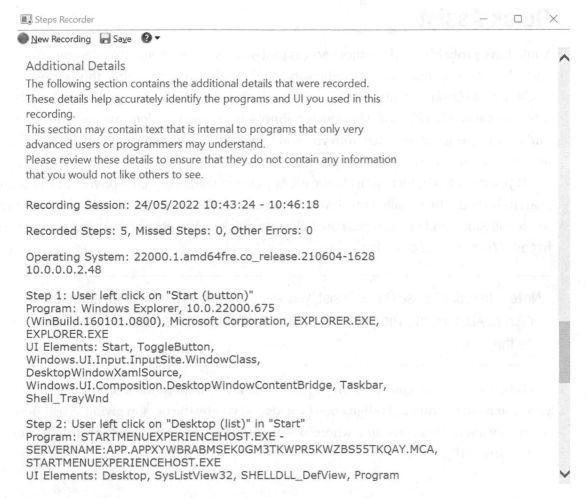

Figure 6-9. *Technical details are provided for steps recorded*

The Problem Steps Recorder is a truly great way for an end user to be able to demonstrate what it is they're doing wrong, erm... sorry, for them to be able to demonstrate what it is that's going wrong on their PC. It can be a great time saver for you, and it can also significantly alleviate the problems that can occur with a nontechnical user trying and failing to accurately describe what they're doing, what they're seeing, and what else is happening on their PC.

Quick Assist

You'll have probably used a remote access tool on PCs at some point to take control of a user's system so that you can troubleshoot and repair problems. While this is most likely *Remote Desktop*, which we'll detail later in this chapter, Windows 10 introduced a new tool called *Quick Assist*. This tool is a simple-to-use and straightforward way for an end user to request assistance from you and for you to take full control of their PC, even allowing you to reboot it during a support session.

If you can't find Quick Assist in the All Apps list of the Start Menu, or via a Start Menu search (it should be installed on all Windows 11 PCs), then you can download it from the Microsoft Store, and you can pass the following quick link to people you need to support: `https://pcs.tv/quickassist`.

Note   In order to use Quick Assist, you will be asked to sign in with a Microsoft or Azure AD account. The person receiving assistance does not need an account to use the app.

When you launch Quick Assist, you are asked if you want to *Get assistance*, in which case you need to enter a six-digit code provided to you by the person giving assistance, or if you want to *Give assistance* where, unsurprisingly, you'll be given the six-digit code (see Figure 6-10).

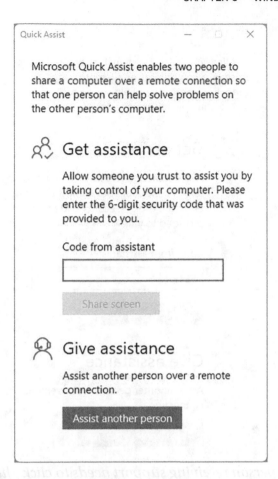

Figure 6-10. *Quick Assist has a straightforward and easy-to-use starting interface*

Once the person receiving support has typed the six-digit code into their Quick Assist app, they should click the *Share screen* button (see Figure 6-11).

Figure 6-11. *The person receiving support needs to click Share screen*

The next stage is very important as you will be asked if you want to *Take control* of the remote PC, and the person receiving support will need to accept (see Figure 6-12).

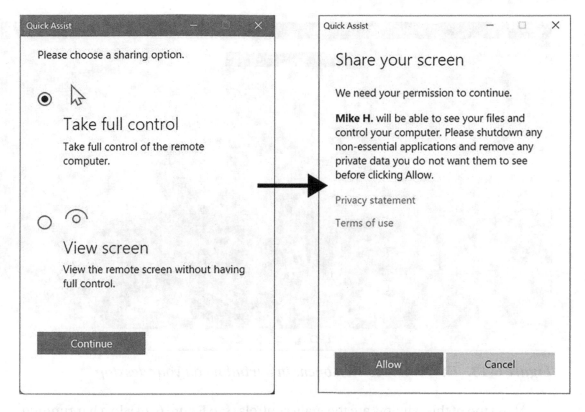

Figure 6-12. *You need to take control of the remote PC*

With this done, a window will open on your desktop showing the full desktop, either full size or scaled to fit depending on the resolution and scaling on your own screen (see Figure 6-13).

Figure 6-13. *The remote session opens in a window on your desktop*

At the top of this window are the main controls (see Figure 6-14). In a bar running along the top of the window, you will find controls for switching between multiple remote monitors, if the remote PC has more than one screen attached, annotating the screen to show or highlight something to the remote user, fitting and scaling the screen to the current support window, opening the instruction channel (more on this in a moment), restarting the remote PC while keeping the support session active, opening Task Manager on the remote PC, and finally refreshing the session, pausing the session, and ending the session.

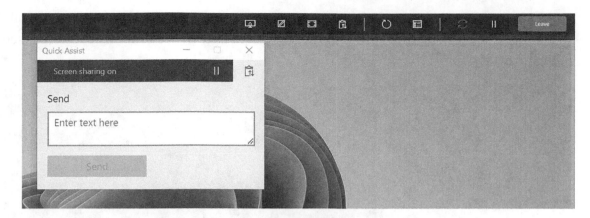

Figure 6-14. *Controls for managing the session are at the top of the window*

The remote PC also has a command box that appears at the top center of their screen, which includes a pause button, an exit (end session) button, and a button to open the instruction channel (see Figure 6-15). This allows live chat to take place between both parties if you do not have a phone or other voice lines open at the time.

Figure 6-15. *You can open a chat window for both participants*

If you restart the remote PC at any time during the support session, Quick Assist will automatically resume when the remote user signs in and the session will be restored (see Figure 6-16).

Figure 6-16. *The remote session will be restored after restarting the remote PC*

Windows Remote Assistance

Windows Remote Assistance is less useful than Quick Assist overall, as it's more limited in functionality and dates all the way back to Windows XP. It's also possible, though unlikely, that this feature will be completely removed from Windows 11 at some point in the future.

There are a few minor advantages that Remote Assistance has over Quick Assist in the corporate space. Microsoft charges a fee for using Quick Assist to corporations, something which caused a right stink when it was first announced. Remote Assistance on the other hand is free.

Remote Assistance also doesn't require you to be using a Microsoft or Azure AD account, making it slightly more flexible for people who use local accounts on their PC.

You need to make sure that Remote Assistance is activated on the PC that is being supported, and often it is disabled by default simply for reasons of maintaining good security. Search for **Remote Assistance** in the Start Menu, and an option to *Allow Remote Assistance invitations to be sent from this computer* will appear. Here, you can make sure there is a check in the *Remote Assistance* option (see Figure 6-17).

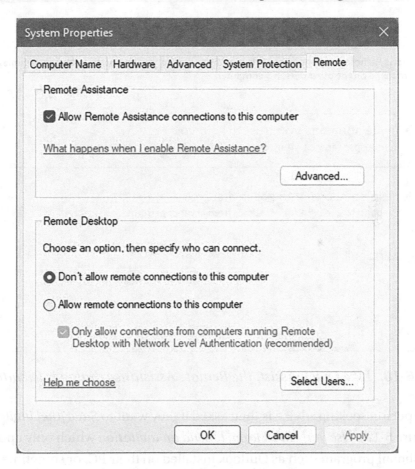

Figure 6-17. *You need to make sure Remote Assistance is enabled on the remote PC*

You can also find this option in Group Policy via *Computer Configuration* ➤ *Administrative Templates* ➤ *System* ➤ *Remote Assistance*.

Like Quick Assist, Remote Assistance needs to be run on both PCs, and you are asked if you want to invite someone to help you or to help someone that has invited you (see Figure 6-18).

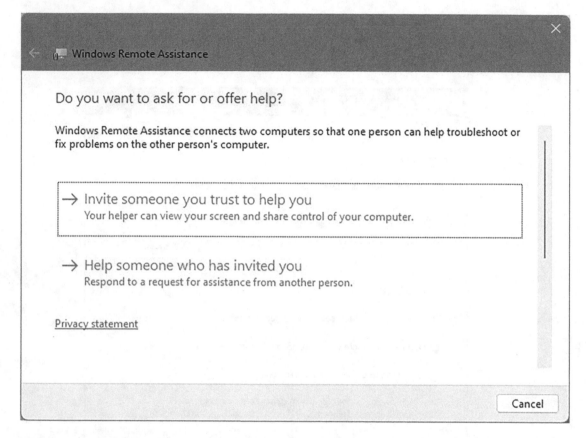

Figure 6-18. *Like Quick Assist, the Remote Assistance dialog is friendly*

The person seeking advice is then asked if they want to *Save [the] invitation as a file* (see Figure 6-19), *Use [an] email [app] to send an invitation* which only appears if they have an email program such as Outlook installed on their PC, or sometimes to *Use Easy Connect*, which is a peer-to-peer system that is sometimes available if both parties are using a Microsoft or an Azure AD account.

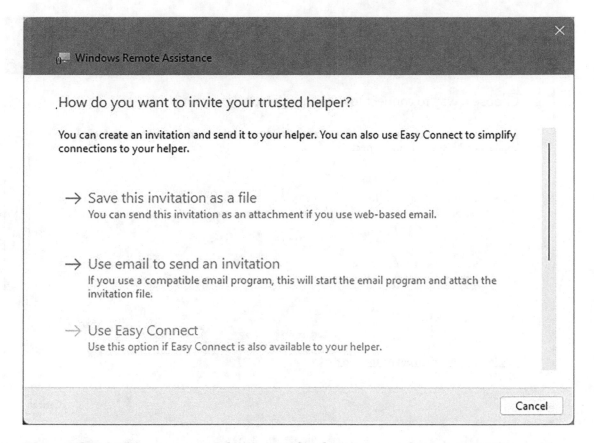

Figure 6-19. *There are up to three ways for the person seeking support to request it*

If you are the person providing support, you are prompted to either open an invitation file you have already received or to use Easy Connect if it is available (see Figure 6-20). Honestly though, it's simpler to just open the invitation file when you receive it.

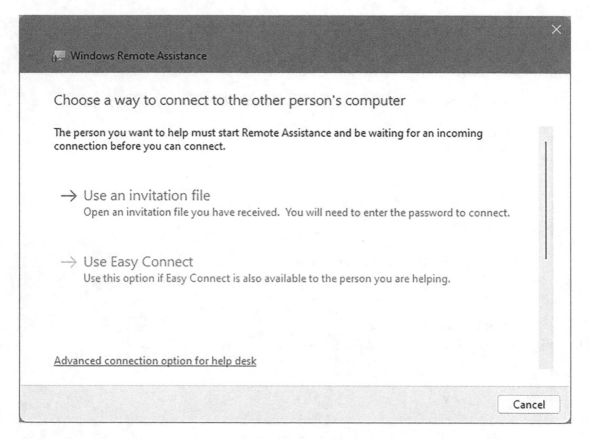

Figure 6-20. *It is simpler for the person providing support to wait for the invitation file*

With the invitation file open, you will be connected to the remote session and prompted to enter a password. This password appears on the screen of the remote PC (see Figure 6-21).

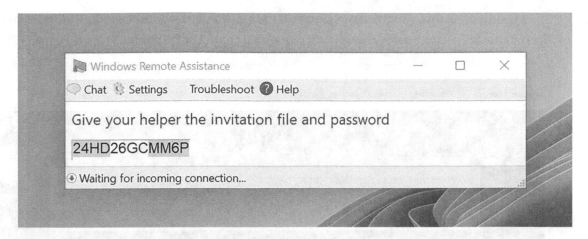

Figure 6-21. *The password appears on the screen of the Remote PC*

Remote Assistance isn't as friendly as Quick Assist where all permissions are obtained up front. The remote user must stay at their desktop for a while, as they have to permit the session once the password has been entered (see Figure 6-22).

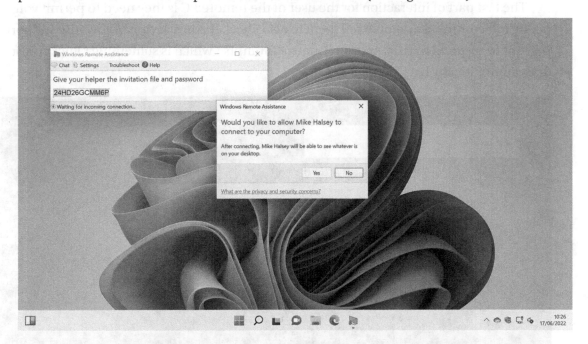

Figure 6-22. *The person seeking control must give permission for the session*

With the session now active, you will both see a toolbar on the remote PC containing options such as stopping and pausing the session, opening a chat window, and changing settings for the session.

In addition to this, you will have options in the top left of the support window for rescaling the remote desktop and, fairly crucially, for requesting control of the remote PC (see Figure 6-23).

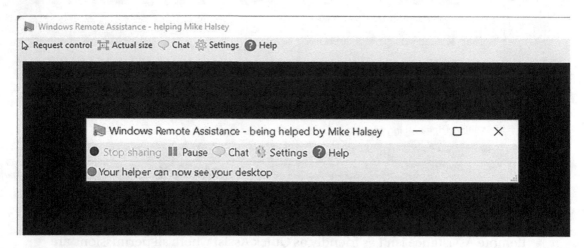

Figure 6-23. *Once in the session, you must Request Control*

The last part of interaction for the user of the remote PC is they need to permit you taking full control. You should tell them to also check the box saying "Allow [the support person] to respond to User Account Control Prompts," which is something Quick Assist does automatically (see Figure 6-24).

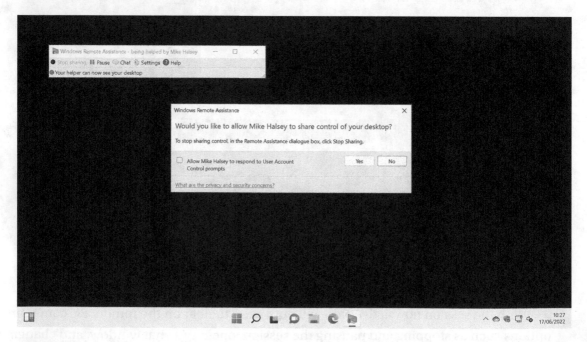

Figure 6-24. *Control must be granted at the remote PC*

Remote Desktop

The daddy of remote support tools in the enterprise is Remote Desktop, which has been a part of Windows desktop editions since Windows 2000, a version of the operating system for which I'll always have fond memories. Remote Desktop needs to be activated on any PC receiving support, and you can do this in Settings under *System* and then *Remote Desktop* (see Figure 6-25). You can also enable Remote Desktop via Group Policy or Mobile Device Management (MDM).

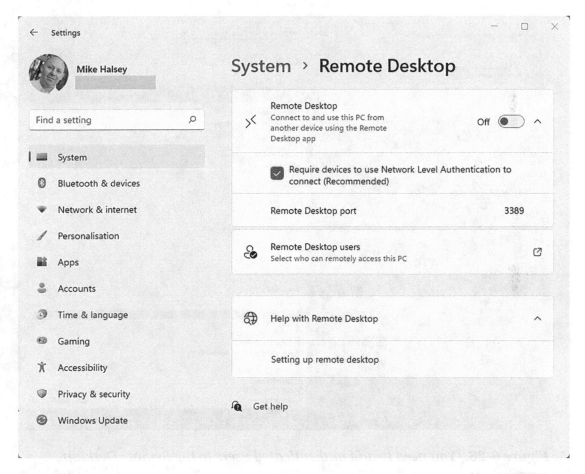

Figure 6-25. *Remote Desktop needs to be enabled in Settings or via Group Policy and MDM*

Clicking the *Remote Desktop users* link will display a dialog in which you can choose which users are allowed to connect to a PC remotely, and again this can be achieved using tools such as MDM. If you click the *Advanced* button when searching for users, you can then click *Find now* to display a list of all users on the PC and crucially all user groups such as Administrators, which can make configuring the feature simpler (see Figure 6-26).

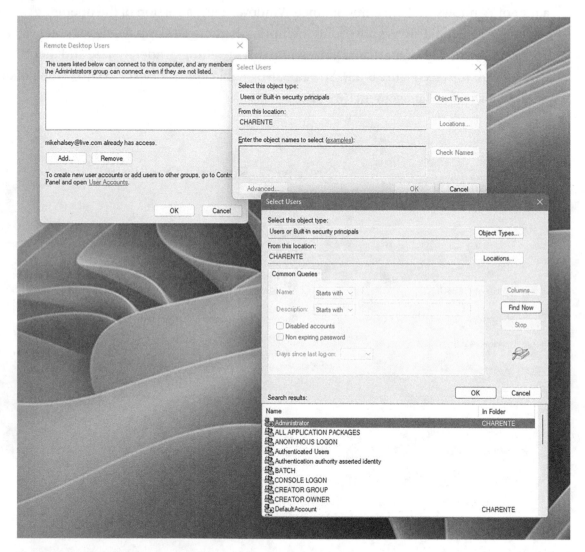

***Figure 6-26.** You need to add authenticated users to the Remote Desktop permissions*

With Remote Desktop activated on the PC you will be supporting, you will be given the name of that PC. This will be needed when you seek support (see Figure 6-27).

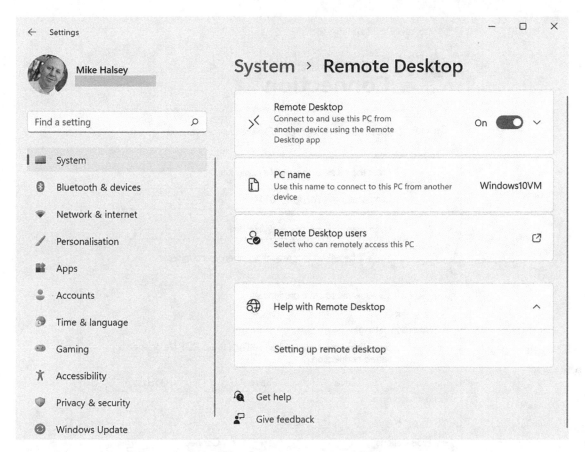

Figure 6-27. *You will need the name of the Remote PC to gain access*

When you want to gain access to a remote PC, search in the Start Menu for *Remote Desktop,* and you will see *Remote Desktop Connection* appear in the search results. Here, you can type the name of the remote PC, along with the username of the user you wish to connect as (see Figure 6-28). Checking the *Allow me to save credentials* check box can also prove useful.

Figure 6-28. *You can enter and save login credentials for a remote PC*

There are tabs along the top of the Remote Desktop Connection dialog that allow you to customize your remote experience. *Display* lets you set the display resolution you will connect at, and you might want to set this to be the same as the resolution of your own PC, unless you specifically want to open the session in a window on your desktop.

The *Local Resources* tab is by far the most useful; this allows you to configure audio settings and determine what happens when you press key combinations such as Alt + Tab and Ctrl + Alt + Del. In the *Local devices and resources* section however, you can choose which drives and resources, such as USB Flash Drives and printers, on your own machine will also be accessible from the remote PC (see Figure 6-29). This can be incredibly useful if you need to copy files to and from the remote PC.

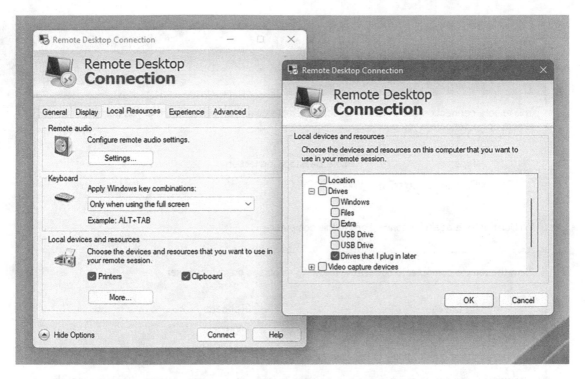

Figure 6-29. *You can access local drives and resources from the remote PC*

The *Experience* tab allows you to choose bandwidth options for the connection, but this is really a legacy feature and most useful now if a low-bandwidth connection such as cellular is being used. Lastly, the *Advanced* tab contains options for setting security and other connection options.

When you are ready to connect to the remote PC, click the *Connect* button, and you will be asked to trust the remote connection. A drop-down option will display what is permitted to be shared, and a *Don't ask me again for connections to this computer* will save your preferences (see Figure 6-30).

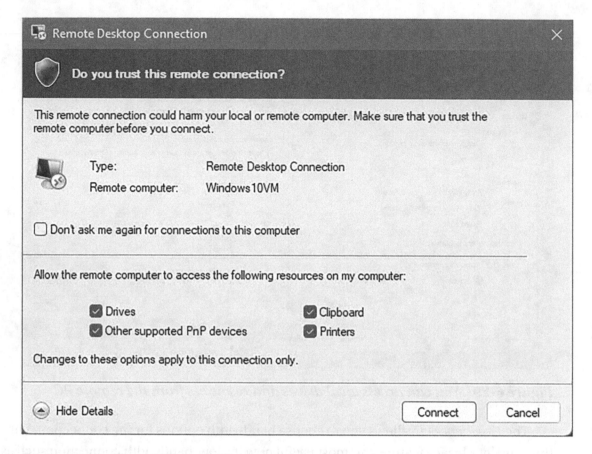

Figure 6-30. *You will be asked to trust the connection to the remote PC*

After entering the password for the remote account (you cannot connect to accounts that do not have a password), one more security dialog will appear displaying details of any security certificate attached to the remote PC (see Figure 6-31).

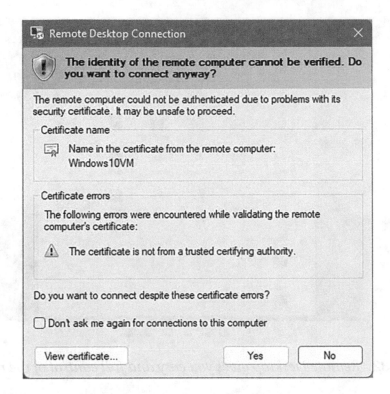

Figure 6-31. *You are shown the security certificate from the remote PC*

With the connection to the remote PC established, in this case a virtual machine running in Hyper-V, you have full control including being able to restart the remote PC and maintain the connection (see Figure 6-32).

Figure 6-32. *Remote Desktop gives you easy and full control of the remote PC*

Because you are already authenticated by the system, there is no involvement required by the remote user, though if they are using the PC at the time, you should let them know you are taking control of their account as they will be signed out on their own screen.

If you are using Remote Desktop full screen, you will see a toolbar at the top center of your screen containing options to check the connection quality, to minimize window, and to exit the remote desktop session (see Figure 6-33).

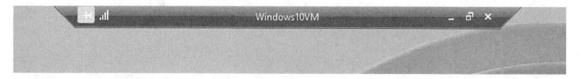

Figure 6-33. *A toolbar appears if you use Remote Desktop full screen*

The Microsoft Remote Desktop App

I want to put in a note about the Remote Desktop app that is available for all platforms in appropriate app stores for Windows 10 and Windows 11, Mac OS, iOS, ChromeOS, and Android. This app is really for connecting to remote desktop and remote PC environments such as Microsoft Azure and Windows 365 (see Figure 6-34).

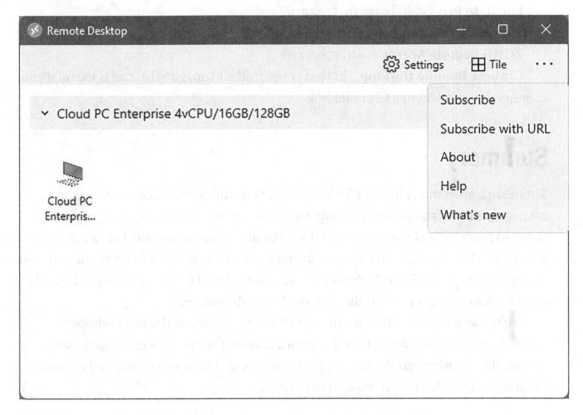

Figure 6-34. *Microsoft has a Remote Desktop app for cloud VMs*

To connect to a remote PC or VM using this app, click the three dots menu icon in the top-right corner of the window, and click either *Subscribe*, which will allow you to connect to Azure or a similar service with your account credentials and often a QR code, or *Subscribe with URL* if you have been given a full web address for the VM you wish to connect to.

Third-Party Remote Support Tools

There are a huge variety of third-party remote tools, and you are by no means tied to the ones that are supplied with Windows 11. You may already have a subscription and a favorite tool or suite of tools to use. If you are unfamiliar with what is available, some of the best tools available include

LogMeIn Pro – `www.logmein.com/pro`

TeamViewer – `www.teamviewer.com`

ZOHO Remote Access – `www.zoho.com`

Chrome Remote Desktop – `https://remotedesktop.google.com` is useful if you ever need to connect to a Chromebook.

Summary

There are a great many highly effective and very useful remote access and remote management tools available in Windows 11, but for providing support, it really comes down to Remote Desktop (most useful for PCs on the same network) or Quick Assist (for remote PCs). If the user can walk you through the steps required to reproduce an error though, the Problem Steps Recorder can save you a lot of time, especially if the end user is doing something on the PC that you might not do yourself.

We'll take support further in the next chapter and look at the methodology of providing high-quality technical support, covering subjects as managing user accessibility, setting up effective support systems, and how you create and manage reporting and auditing systems and paperwork.

CHAPTER 7

The Methodology of Supporting Users

Who do you work for and what do you do? It's all too common to think of ourselves when working in IT support as working for the big company, Fujitsu Siemens was my first big support role, and just working for them. I would argue the reality is quite different. I would say that we actually work for the end users, and our role is to make them all look good.

So what do I mean by this? Well, the role of IT support is one that's generally considered unimportant by company bosses, and this is because, when it's done well, it disappears into the background and becomes something that they don't ever need to think about.

Company and organization bosses want to think about the things that are important to them, such as profitability, turnover, and productivity. We cost them money, we're a huge money sink, and that's not good for them. What's worse, because we're the ones that are technically minded and not them, they really have absolutely no idea what it is we do anyway; therefore, what we do is of little value to them, and anything that's of little value to them is of little value to the business and should therefore have its budget slashed.

I'm pretty sure this is a scenario that you've faced in the past and present and that you will continue to face into the future, and if so, then that's great as it means you're doing a good job.

Your role is to keep productivity high, operating costs low, and morale on an even keel. This is quite a responsibility overall, and it's not that often that people who work in IT support think of it in these holistic terms.

So, now you've sat down with a headache and a nice hot cup of tea, how do you go about being the morale officer, the drill sergeant, and the auditor while at the same time doing all the tech and support stuff too? The answer, and I'm sure you figured this out already, is to keep doing what you're doing, but be even better at it than you already are.

© Mike Halsey 2023
M. Halsey, *Troubleshooting and Supporting Windows 11*, https://doi.org/10.1007/978-1-4842-8728-6_7

Understanding the Support Ecosystem

Back in Chapter 5, I talked about the many different types of people you need to support and what a hugely diverse bunch they all are. In this chapter though, we're going to look at you and your team, because even if you work entirely on your own, you have to think of yourself as a team. Let me explain.

Everything about providing IT support revolves around being able to quickly respond to both new and existing support queries. This means that your reporting and documentation has to be good, and we'll look at exactly how you can do this later in this chapter.

People

So let's take a few examples of the corporation, the medium-sized business, and the small business. In the latter, you are the only person providing support. This puts a lot of strain on you and your time. You'll likely always have your laptop on you as, unless your business has a strict Monday to Friday, 9 to 5 mentality, you never know when the next support call will come in or what its and your circumstances might be.

What happens though when you're on vacation or perhaps off sick with the lurg.[1] In this circumstance, one of three things will happen. First, you'll have no choice but to answer the call anyway, which is unfair to you. Second, the support call will go unanswered until you're back at work, which is bad for the business. Third, somebody else will temporarily stand in for you. This could be a temp, this could be a friend that's temporarily out of work and looking for some extra cash, or it could be Martin from the warehouse who's a bit tech savvy and has been shadowing you for a few months on Tuesday afternoons.

In all three of these circumstances, you need to make sure that your documentation and tracking are perfect. In the first instance, you frankly have more important things to think about and might need a reminder; in the second, something huge might come up and an external tech might be required; and in the third, you don't need the temp having to start again from the very beginning for all support inquiries.

When it comes to the medium-sized business, there will be several of you in the department. People will go on vacation, people will go off work sick, but all of you are busy and so don't need to be having to start from scratch on any support inquiry.

---

[1] "Lurg," urban slang for a virus, cold, or other nasty ailment it's difficult to shake off.

With the corporation, you will have multiple offices, perhaps multiple support teams or perhaps more likely a single support engineer in the larger remote offices, plus a series of mobile engineers. Here, time is precious because you not only have the time spent responding to the query but also often the time spent for an engineer to get there and back.

Places

Then we come to the buildings you all inhabit. This clearly has changed over the last few years with huge numbers of the everyday workforce now working from home on a semiregular, regular, or on a full-time basis. All of this just makes your job harder, but the need for good reporting much stronger.

Some of the larger businesses have now spread out over campuses, a move popularized by the big tech companies including Microsoft, whose campus is getting a major overhaul as I write this with much more office and lab space being created at its heart, as I saw for myself when I visited a couple of months ago (see Figure 7-1).

Figure 7-1. *Microsoft's 2022 campus expansion is on its own, the size of a large city business park*

You need to factor in the time taken to get from point A to point B or for an engineer to drive to point C where there could be all manner of additional barriers, such as strict security screening, slow and heavy traffic, or perhaps even a flight being involved if it's a very small, very remote office.

PCs

Lastly, we need to consider what equipment you're using or what equipment your workforce is using. You might still have a traditional setup of every desk having a PC and those workers that require one having a laptop. In this setup, you're probably supporting at least two versions of the Windows operating system at any one time and perhaps even some Apple or Linux machines too.

You'll likely by now also be supporting home workers' own devices, be that anything from an iPad with an attached keyboard to a Chromebook to a gaming PC shared with a son or daughter.

You'll probably be very keen to move to the cloud at this point because of the benefits it brings to your own role. When somebody is using a cloud service, such as Microsoft 365, not only does where they are in the world or on what device they are working become less relevant, but management becomes much simpler as you can do it on your desktop PC or laptop from wherever you happen to be at the time.

You're probably keen to move people to Windows 365 where the full desktop runs in a virtual machine the user connects to using Remote Desktop, something I detailed in Chapter 6. At the time of writing, this service is still hugely expensive and also quite limited in the diverse number of variants available, but I know this is due to change over time, and it will make the support role for the largest businesses much simpler when they not only have access to the whole desktop available from any device, but where they only really need to support security, encryption, and the Remote Desktop client on many of the work computers; mobile laptops will of course always need to be stand-alone due to the nature and availability of mobile Internet around the world and when travelling.

You also have to consider if you're still using your own servers, or other critical infrastructure such as Network Attached Storage (NAS) drives, and what else you have to support such as switch panels, security and firewall appliances, third-party online telephony, and other services and all the extra peripherals and hardware the business will need including printers (which have always been a pain in the butt), keyboards, mice, monitors, yadda yadda.

These all make good reporting important too, because as I'll detail in Chapter 16, "the hip bone is connected to the leg bone," and the leg bone is connected to a satellite somewhere in low Earth orbit.

Managing Accessibility with IT Support

When I talked about users and user diversity in Chapter 5, I discussed how ability comes into play when not making any assumptions about people's use of computers. This is where accessibility is important, and you might be surprised just how many people in the business can benefit from accessibility, so it's always worth considering when setting up new PCs, systems, and services for end users and when supporting those users.

So who can benefit from accessibility on their PCs and in Windows 11? You'll obviously think of people with a "disability," a term I personally dislike as it implies they are unable in some way to perform the tasks achieved by others. This might have been the case even a hundred years ago, but "less able" is perhaps a better choice of phrase today.

But what about everybody else? Well, here are a few examples of where accessibility tools, features, and hardware can help people in the everyday world:

- People that wear glasses like myself can benefit from display scaling, with some perhaps benefitting from high-contrast color schemes.

- People who are color blind can benefit from the specific color blindness settings in all operating systems, including Windows 10 and Windows 11, and perhaps also from display scaling and high-contrast color schemes.

- People who have shaky hands, perhaps because they are older, or have in the past suffered an injury can benefit from larger keyboards and features such as sticky keys and mouse controls.

- People who suffer a common physical ailment including repetitive strain injury (RSI) can benefit from accessible mice and also from the benefits for people with shaky hands.

- People who find it difficult to concentrate, perhaps because they're recovering from a heavy cold, perhaps because they work in a noisy or distracting environment, or perhaps because of a previous injury, can benefit from desktop accessibility tools such as keeping pop-up notifications displayed for longer and flashing the desktop to announce an alert.

- People who have busy working lives can benefit from simple visual clues such as colored stickers on a keyboard.

These are just a few of the types of people that can benefit from the accessibility tools and utilities built into Windows 11 and other operating systems and from basic and affordable accessibility hardware. I write about accessibility in some depth in my book *Windows 11 Made Easy* (Apress, 2022), and naturally my book *The Windows 10 Accessibility Handbook* (Apress, 2015) is all about accessibility for anybody still using that operating system.

When you're providing support, then it's always a good idea to consider accessibility, especially when you're seeking the support and help of the end user in determining what the problem is that they're facing. This doesn't mean keeping a document on each user detailing what cognitive, motor, auditory, and visual needs they have as, frankly, that one could come back and bite you on the arse, but being aware that the people you are supporting might benefit from taking things slightly more slowly or scaled upward so they can follow you can be broadly welcomed.

Keeping notes about what individual accessibility tools and settings make a PC easier to use for someone though is a good idea, as this can help both you and them get up to speed again quickly if they get a new PC or their current one needs to be reimaged.

Lastly, it's worthwhile making the workforce aware of what accessibility tools and utilities are available to them in the first instance and allowing them to play around to find something that makes them more comfortable. Most people will know there are accessibility tools available on their PC, but they'd be unlikely to know what to look for or even where to find them.

Setting Up Effective Support Systems

Here's where we really start to think outside of the box as the traditional top-down methods of providing IT support don't really apply in the modern world as they might have done when you or I began working in the industry. This all comes down to just how much the world of IT has changed over the last decade or so and how huge and varied it is today.

So do you have a manager, first-line, second-line, and third-line support personnel and some engineers? Well, yes, you can still use this approach, and later in this chapter when I talk about setting up your reporting, this is exactly the approach I'll take as it's still highly effective. Whereas everybody in the past might have been expected to be a jack of all trades however, you might want to consider including specialisms within your team as well.

Tip   Never have just one person solely responsible for X or Y, as you can guarantee a crisis will emerge at the very time they've settled down on a beach in Cuba for a week. Besides, encouraging new specialisms in your team is great for the business and great for their own careers.

Back in the day long before I became an author and wrote my first Windows troubleshooting book, I worked as a second-line IT support tech for Fujitsu Siemens. We were expected to respond to any tech query, no matter what it was, and call the user back after first-line support had failed to resolve it for them, more on how you can improve this later.

The tech we were expected to support included desktop and laptop PCs running Windows XP, printers, and specialist equipment that included everything from scientific instruments to checkout cash registers. The problem for me was that I was a PC guy. The cash registers I could deal with as they were effectively sealed IoT devices with not much going on, but printers I hated with a passion.

Hardware just wasn't my thing, and so I actively avoided printers like the plague. This wasn't because I wasn't prepared to learn about the specific printers we supported or because I didn't think I was capable of fixing problems with them. I recognized that for my own skills, and the workload we had to plow through each week, the team as a whole could be much more effective if the people that *really* knew that hardware took those calls, and I didn't slow myself down with them.

This of course is where training comes into play. We did receive occasional training on new hardware, but it was delivered by techs, not by qualified teachers. The inevitable consequence of this is something I talked about in Chapter 5, and it's essential to make training effective and to make damn sure the people you are training understand the subject afterward; otherwise, as was all too frequently the case with the training I received at the time, you're wasting both your time and theirs.

Shadowing people can be helpful here. Very often in a support role, this is where somebody new to the business or organization will start. It can also be highly useful in an ongoing basis though as continuing professional development (CPD). This is where people who are already expert in their own field can broaden their skills.

Some people will be expert in the desktop, as I am. Some people will be expert in hardware or in cloud services and administration. Some people will be expert with virtualization or coding and scripting with PowerShell, Command Line, BASH, or C##. Some people will know how to fix problems with websites and intranet sites easily; others won't have a clue.

Tech is *such* a diverse field these days that it's simply impossible to expect one person to go into an office or a workplace and expect them to be a master of all. Online services such as Microsoft 365 and Google Workspace help here to a certain extent, as it's a lot easier to administer settings in an online portal than it is to write a script to administer a file server, but the average if not every IT support person and administrator will find they have skills gaps.

In a large part, that is why you're reading this book and why I wrote it. This is CPD itself. I have other books available from **Apress** that are also CPD, and if you use Pluralsight for online video training, you can find me there too at `www.pluralsight.com/authors/mike-halsey`.

Keep an eye out for offers on Apress too for discounts on books and eBooks, as they come around frequently as this too is great CPD. Having a physical book or a searchable eBook is also a great reference for those things you're learning but not yet expert at, as they give you something you can quickly grab off the shelf and refer to.

But shadowing still performs an important role. There are things a book can't teach you; in fact, this is the whole reason why Chapter 21 exists. Those things might be specific to your own custom hardware, software, and services setup. They might be coding and scripting tips and techniques that existing admins have found useful. Frankly, the list of areas where even an experienced tech can learn new skills from shadowing a colleague for a few hours a week is enormous.

Is Setting Up Support Systems As Easy As One, Two, Three?

Earlier in this chapter, I mentioned the traditional first-line, second-line, and third-line support structure. This is where the first-line support people are nontechnical, call center workers that will read from a script. Most problems they'll receive calls from are fairly straightforward anyway, or at the very least common and repetitive, and can be quickly identified and fixed from notes written earlier by the people in third-line support or from notes on a device manufacturer's website.

Second-line support, which is where I used to work, are the people who return the calls of the people first-line support couldn't help. There's pressure on second-line support personnel, of which there are far fewer people than for first-line, to know their stuff, fix the problem, and close the case. This is partly because the number of people in third-line support will likely be very small (as these people are expensive if nothing else) but also because the truly knotty problems they have to deal with can sometimes tie them up for days.

This isn't even taking into account that the people working in third-line support will also commonly be the system administrators, testing new software, patches, and OS builds, rolling these out across the organization, and then praying that nothing goes horribly wrong.

We've all encountered times though when we're forced to call first-line support and have tried to preempt the most obvious questions with phrases such as "I'm an IT engineer so have already tried the obvious things like turning it off and on again" and "No, resetting it won't fix the problem, as fixing the problem involves changing a VPN setting and not starting again from scratch with the whole damn device."

If you're setting up or managing a first-line support team, then I have a simple piece of advice. Employ better able and more knowledgeable staff with fewer constraints placed on them. This generally turns out to be better overall for the companies that provide it already. I can think of a couple of ISPs in the UK, Plusnet and Zen, both of which consistently win awards for their support because they've either ditched the first-line support personnel entirely or have hired and correctly trained the appropriate people in the first instance.

With an effective team in place, with specialisms where you need to have them, no single person solely responsible for anything, and people able to respond appropriately to queries, you'll likely find that not only will costs fall over time but the volume of support requests you get will also drop.

Creating and Managing Support Reporting

So now we've tackled the subject of staffing, how about the reporting itself? Well, the first crucial area, there are several of these, is the source of the call. There's absolutely no point in recording a support query if you can't call the person back afterward or send an engineer to the correct piece of equipment.

For this reason, it's also essential to record the asset tag or serial number of the device (see Figure 7-2), as for all you know, the person who made the original support call might be going on vacation the following day or could even be leaving the company or moving to a different role or department.

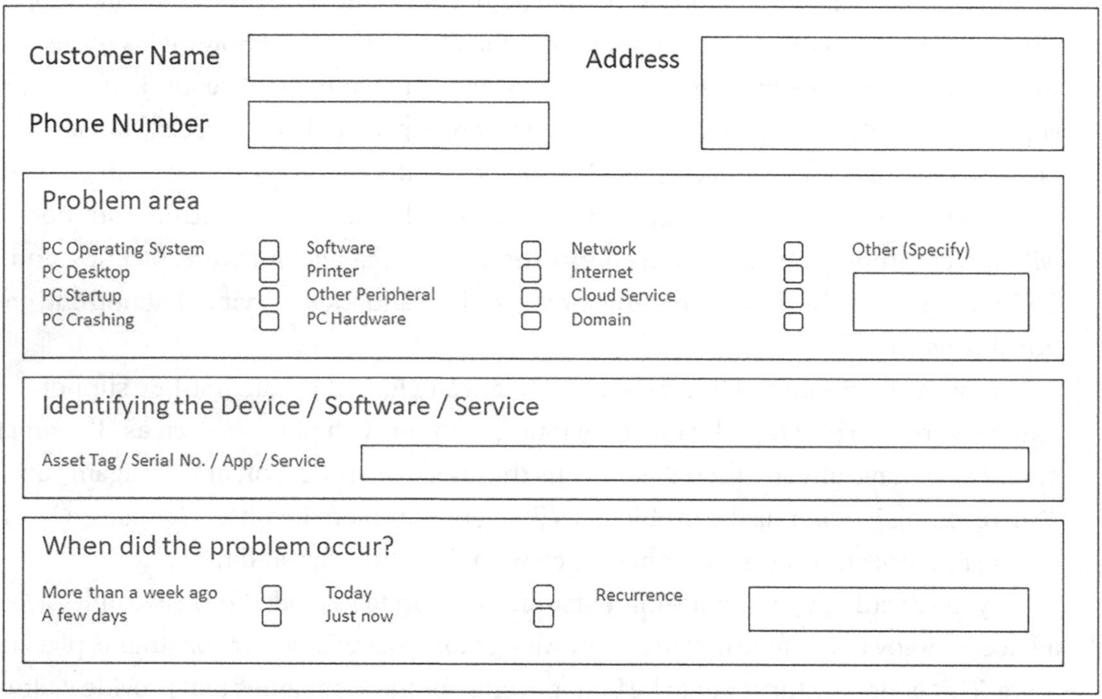

| Customer Name | | Address | |
| Phone Number | | | |

Problem area

PC Operating System	☐	Software	☐	Network	☐	Other (Specify)
PC Desktop	☐	Printer	☐	Internet	☐	
PC Startup	☐	Other Peripheral	☐	Cloud Service	☐	
PC Crashing	☐	PC Hardware	☐	Domain	☐	

Identifying the Device / Software / Service

Asset Tag / Serial No. / App / Service

When did the problem occur?

More than a week ago	☐	Today	☐	Recurrence	
A few days	☐	Just now	☐		

Figure 7-2. *Starting with clear information about the source of the query is essential*

There will always be main areas where problems can begin. Remember that nothing ever goes wrong with an IT system without *something* changing, be it an update, power outage, or user intervention (see Figure 7-3). Reporting what has already been tried and that has failed to work can also prevent repetition. I'm sure you've been asked to repeat something you've already done as many times as I have, and it can be hugely frustrating for the person receiving the support.

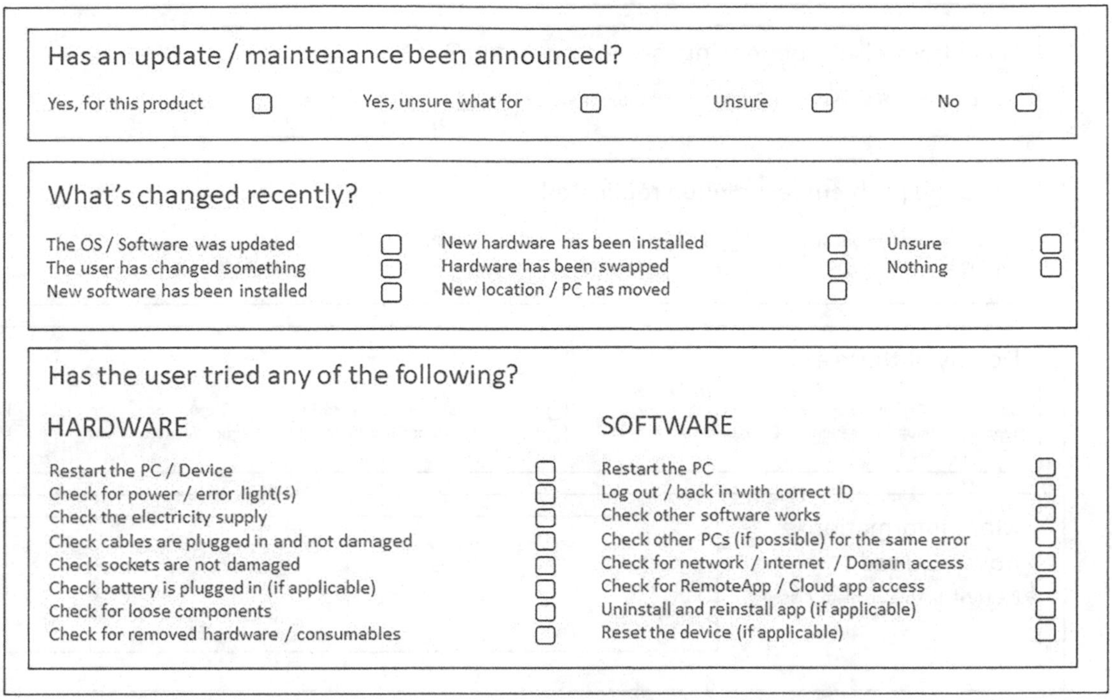

Has an update / maintenance been announced?

| Yes, for this product ☐ | Yes, unsure what for ☐ | Unsure ☐ | No ☐ |

What's changed recently?

The OS / Software was updated ☐	New hardware has been installed ☐	Unsure ☐
The user has changed something ☐	Hardware has been swapped ☐	Nothing ☐
New software has been installed ☐	New location / PC has moved ☐	

Has the user tried any of the following?

HARDWARE

Restart the PC / Device ☐
Check for power / error light(s) ☐
Check the electricity supply ☐
Check cables are plugged in and not damaged ☐
Check sockets are not damaged ☐
Check battery is plugged in (if applicable) ☐
Check for loose components ☐
Check for removed hardware / consumables ☐

SOFTWARE

Restart the PC ☐
Log out / back in with correct ID ☐
Check other software works ☐
Check other PCs (if possible) for the same error ☐
Check for network / internet / Domain access ☐
Check for RemoteApp / Cloud app access ☐
Uninstall and reinstall app (if applicable) ☐
Reset the device (if applicable) ☐

Figure 7-3. *Clear information about the main possible problem areas and what's been tried are also essential*

Now we need to start thinking outside of the box and realizing that this device doesn't operate completely in isolation. I'll speak about this in much more depth in Chapter 16, but asking if the problem is occurring to anybody else can really help narrow down the cause (see Figure 7-4). You should also ask the person calling for support if there's anything they can try such as replicating the error or problem so that you can see it for yourself or maybe even just taking a photograph and emailing it to you.

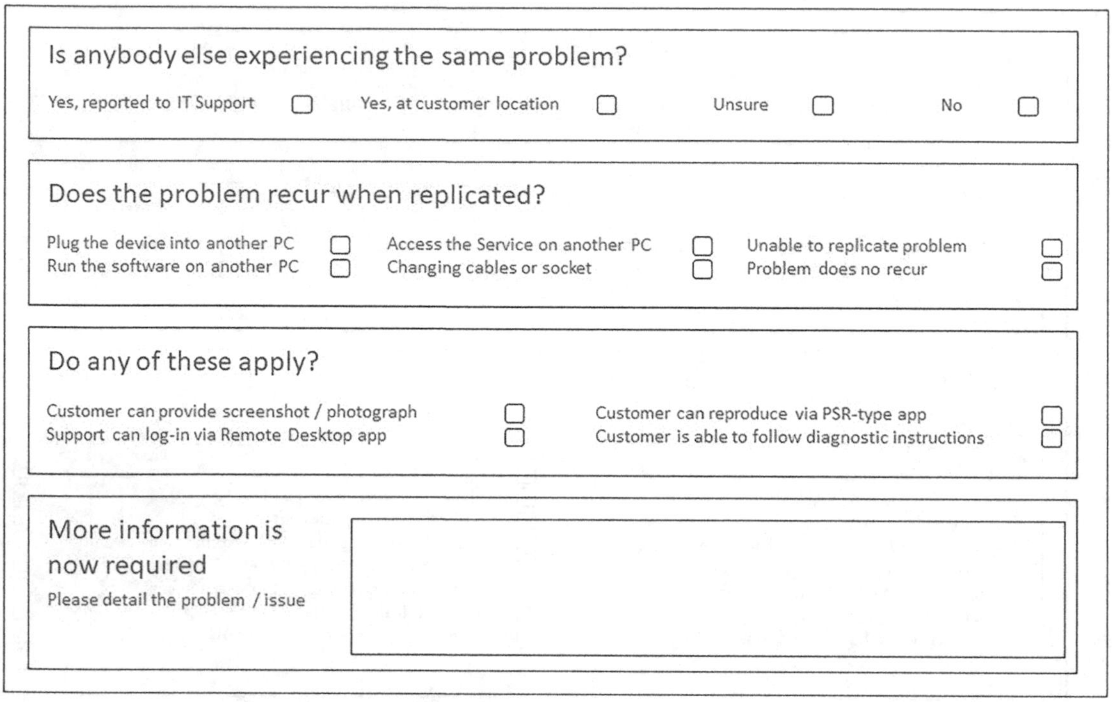

Is anybody else experiencing the same problem?

Yes, reported to IT Support ☐   Yes, at customer location ☐   Unsure ☐   No ☐

Does the problem recur when replicated?

Plug the device into another PC ☐   Access the Service on another PC ☐   Unable to replicate problem ☐
Run the software on another PC ☐   Changing cables or socket ☐   Problem does no recur ☐

Do any of these apply?

Customer can provide screenshot / photograph ☐   Customer can reproduce via PSR-type app ☐
Support can log-in via Remote Desktop app ☐   Customer is able to follow diagnostic instructions ☐

More information is now required

Please detail the problem / issue

Figure 7-4. *Thinking outside of the box should be replicated in the reporting*

You will then have some common fixes that you will apply, and common methods of trying to repair the problem, such as accessing the PC via Remote Desktop or asking the end user to see if they can replicate the problem on a different PC. Appropriately logging each thing that's been tried and done can reduce duplication later, resulting in less frustration for the end user and less time spent on the query for you (see Figure 7-5).

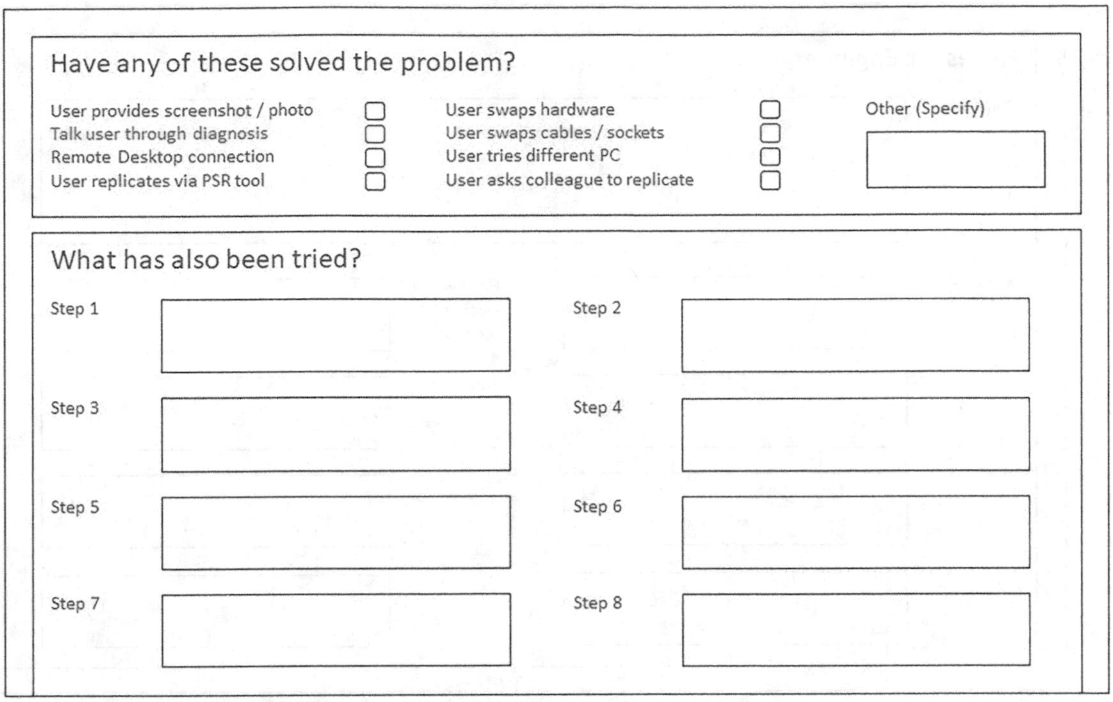

Have any of these solved the problem?

User provides screenshot / photo	☐	User swaps hardware	☐	Other (Specify)
Talk user through diagnosis	☐	User swaps cables / sockets	☐	
Remote Desktop connection	☐	User tries different PC	☐	
User replicates via PSR tool	☐	User asks colleague to replicate	☐	

What has also been tried?

Step 1

Step 2

Step 3

Step 4

Step 5

Step 6

Step 7

Step 8

Figure 7-5. *Let people add things your reporting may not have anticipated, it will make for better support in the future*

If you need to send an engineer to look at and repair the problem personally, the quality of the notes you provide for them is crucial (see Figure 7-6). Remember that the engineer will likely be entirely on their own. They likely won't be able to call you or one of your colleagues for that information as you'll be busy and they'll be short on time with lots of other stops to make. The more information you can provide to them, the faster everything will get resolved, and the less chance there will be of the engineer having to visit the site on a second occasion for the same problem.

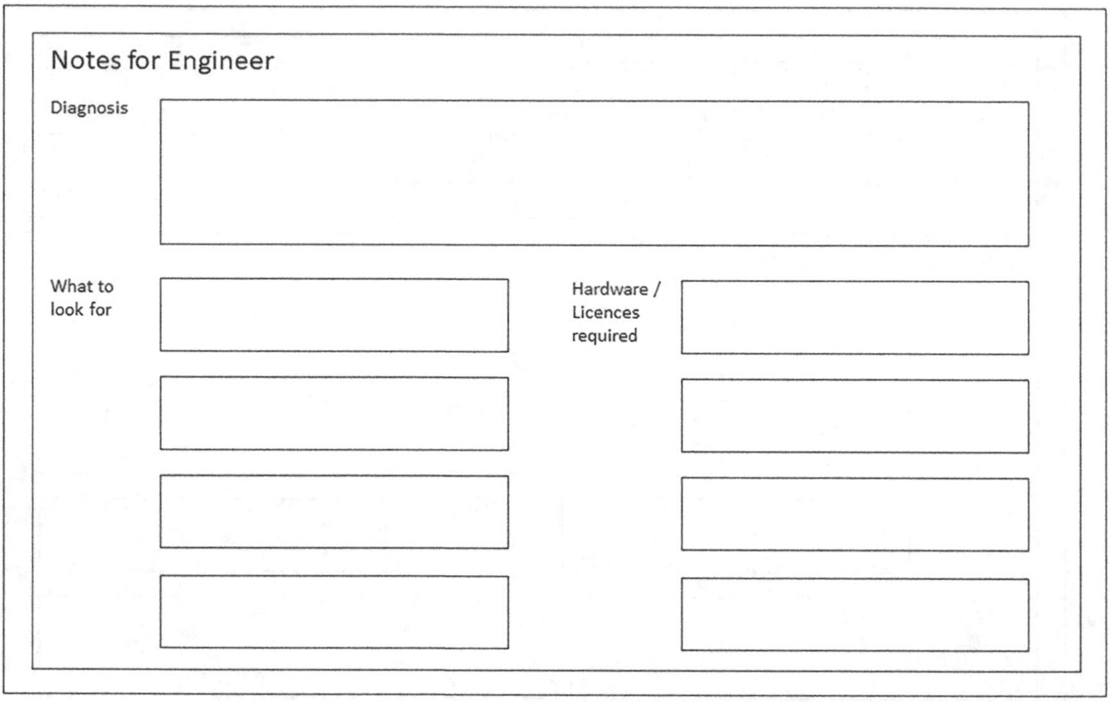

Figure 7-6. *Engineers need clear notes and instructions as they'll be entirely on their own*

Lastly, we get the final report (see Figure 7-7). This again needs to be as detailed as possible, but don't go on for pages and pages as nobody wants to read anything that long. Be concise but clear where lessons can be learned, policies and practices implemented or changed, or questions and steps added to first-line support documentation where this is a problem that might occur again on other IT equipment or services, and where an easy fix can be implemented.

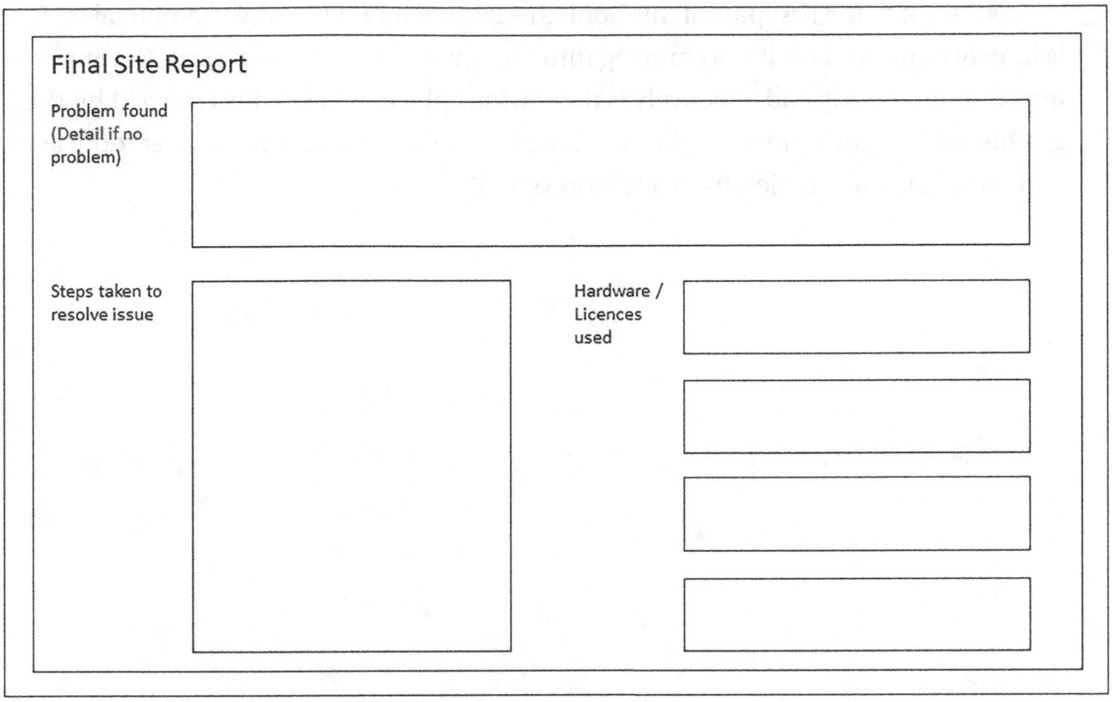

Final Site Report

Problem found (Detail if no problem)	

Steps taken to resolve issue	Hardware / Licences used	

Figure 7-7. *A final report that can be seen and audited by third-line support can help update reporting for future issues*

With all of this in place, you will find that the whole support operation, from the first call to the final report, becomes much more effective, swift, and cheaper. Having a system that's not too rigid also helps because this is where easy changes and fixes can be implemented and made available to help quickly fix the problem in the future.

Did somebody write a script that fixed the problem? That person should be encouraged to document the script and add a link to it, or a copy of it, with the final report. Did somebody find that a specific driver version fixed the problem? What was that driver version and can a copy of it be held locally?

Summary

This, in short, is how you can set up, manage, and run an effective, productive, and cheap-to-run IT support system. There's much more to it than just this however, and I would encourage you, for a bit more CPD, to also obtain a physical or eBook copy of my book *The IT Support Handbook* (Apress, 2019), where this chapter is expanded into almost 200 pages of training and support materials.

As we get to the first part of this book though, we'll find that the theoretical stuff is largely done, and we'll start moving into the actual meat of the subject. Getting information quickly and effectively is the obvious place to begin, and so we'll hit the ground running by examining the Windows Event Viewer and how you get more event and reliability information from a Windows 11 PC.

PART II

Troubleshooting Windows 11

CHAPTER 8

Events and Reliability Troubleshooting

When you want to diagnose a problem or an issue in Windows, there's good news, as there's almost nothing that happens on a PC without being logged and recorded. No, I'm not talking about the National Security Agency (NSA) or the Chinese Ministry of State Security (MSS) spying on your online activities as if I'm honest I doubt the Chinese government is really that concerned about how many cat videos you search for on YouTube or the cookery tutorials you subscribe to on TikTok (let's see how well this book ages with the TikTok reference; Ed).

Windows doesn't spy on you either, so you don't need to worry about the operating system keeping records of your private correspondence. If you are concerned about your online privacy though, I can highly recommend the book *Windows 11 Made Easy* (Apress, 2022) which has a great resource on maintaining your online safety and privacy. I know this because I wrote it.

It's not just recording events and other activities on the PC though so you can refer back to them later and find the cause of a problem, the real-time reporting of what is happening on a PC is just superb, and you can drill down into the smallest process or activity to see in great detail what's going on. This can be especially useful when diagnosing something like a malware infection or a piece of software that's chewing all of your available bandwidth (Adobe Creative Cloud updater, I'm looking at you).

The tools available in Windows to be able to see all this information are many and varied, but they're by far the most important tools for any IT Pro or troubleshooter, so in this chapter we're going to look at them in great detail and see just how they can be harnessed.

© Mike Halsey 2023
M. Halsey, *Troubleshooting and Supporting Windows 11*, https://doi.org/10.1007/978-1-4842-8728-6_8

Reliability History

We'll begin with one of the most basic yet one of the most useful, the Reliability History. This tool is also one of the best hidden as you won't find it in either Settings or Windows Tools, and it can be found as a link under *Security and Maintenance* in the Control Panel, but a Start Menu search will display it quickly enough.

The Reliability History contains two panels: one is a timeline of days over the last few weeks, and in the bottom is information about events in the currently highlighted day (see Figure 8-1).

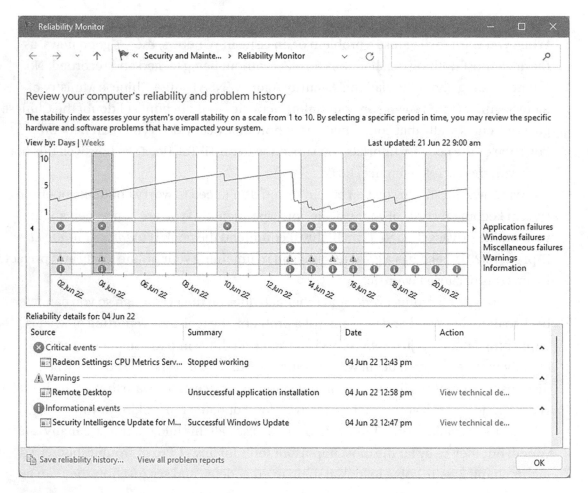

Figure 8-1. *The Reliability History highlights event types in color*

You can move back and forward dates by clicking the back and forward arrows to the left and right of the dates panel, though remember that Windows typically keeps its event data for only 30 days to avoid filling your hard drive with files you don't need.

Each event is highlighted with a different type of icon. The red circular icon with an X in its center is for the critical events; these include things such as driver and service crashes. The yellow warning triangle is for warnings when something has failed, but it's not going to affect the PC critically, such as an unsuccessful Windows Update installation which can later be retried. Lastly, there are informational events which are indicated by a blue circular information icon, the type of which you might see at a roadside on a sign giving tourist advice.

For many events, but not always all critical events, there is a *View technical details* link to their right in the information panel. Clicking this will display technical information about the event. In Figure 8-2, we can see that on my own PC a game I have played for years and love dearly, *Elite Dangerous*, has crashed.

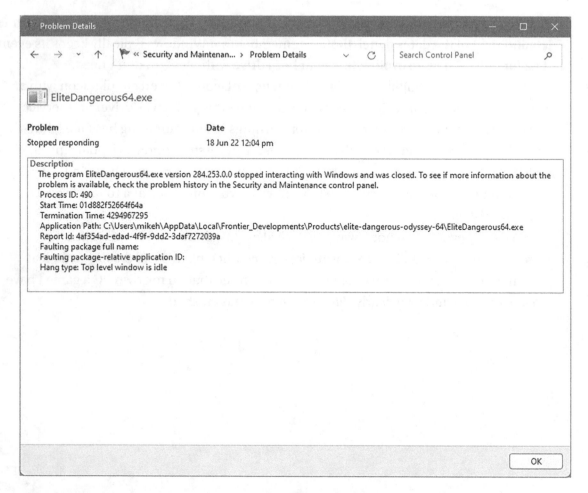

Figure 8-2. *You can get highly useful technical details about events*

We can see the date and time the game crashed; there is a verbose description of the event along with the name of the offending file *EliteDangerous64.exe*, though this could also display the name of a Windows or third-party service or driver depending on the error. We can see the full path of the file, and you might see other information such as a Windows error code.

Tip Windows error codes always come in the format 0x00… which makes them unique and easy to search for online. There are a great many error code categories, and the full list can be found on the Microsoft Docs website at `https://pcs.`
`tv/3HIaAGA`.

Windows 11 will automatically report many errors directly to Microsoft so that they can perhaps be fixed in an upcoming patch or new driver release. If you click the *View all problem reports* link at the bottom of the Reliability Monitor window, you will see all the reports that have been submitted (see Figure 8-3).

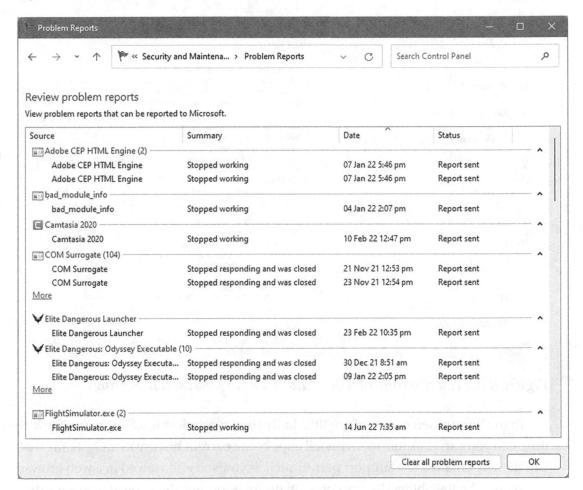

Figure 8-3. *Windows auto-submits problem reports to Microsoft*

It is not possible to disable all diagnostic feedback to Microsoft as much of it used to determine the operating system, software, and driver state so that the correct Windows Updates can be downloaded and installed, but there is some control you can get in *Settings ➤ Privacy & security ➤ Diagnostics & feedback* (see Figure 8-4), such as the sending of "optional" diagnostic data.

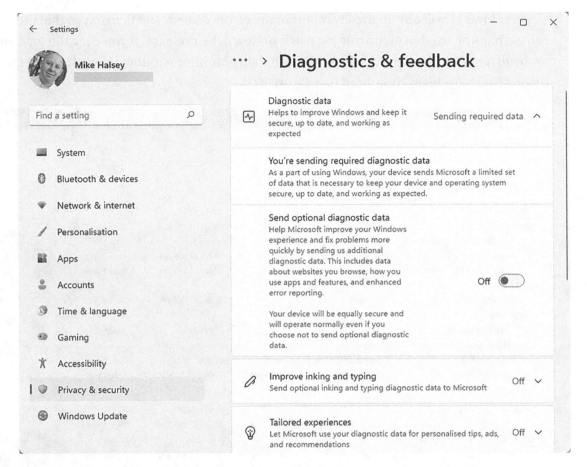

Figure 8-4. *You can control what data is sent to Microsoft in Settings*

In the bottom-left corner of the Reliability History window is a *Save reliability history* link, and you can click this to save a full copy of the current history as an XML file that can then be emailed to a support person such as yourself and viewed in a web browser.

Where the Reliability History comes in useful is for quickly being able to view the major events on a PC, such as when Windows Updates or antivirus definitions were downloaded and installed or when drivers, services, or applications crash or fail to work as intended. It's possible for an end user to open this panel, if they know on what day a problem occurred and read the basic information to you over the phone or by message, which can be considerably more effective than trying to get a nontechnical person to describe what they saw and experienced.

Getting Reliability Information with PowerShell

If you want to use scripting to manage your PCs, you can use PowerShell commands to get reliability information. This script can be used to generate basic reliability information:

```
Get-Ciminstance Win32_ReliabilityStabilityMetrics |
Measure-Object -Average -Maximum  -Minimum -Property systemStabilityIndex
```

There is also a very interesting developer blog on the Microsoft website showing how you can harness the Get-Ciminstance PowerShell command to obtain all manner of useful reliability information about a PC. You can find the article online at https://pcs.tv/3bGcOoS.

Performance Monitor

Where the Reliability History is useful for seeing reports on what's happened on the PC in the past, the Performance Monitor is great for seeing what's going on at that exact moment, and while it's not the only tool in town, its graphing capabilities are useful for seeing where some resource on the PC is being hogged or maxed out by a process or service.

You can run the Performance Monitor either from Windows Tools, by searching for it in the Start Menu, or by typing **perfmon /rel** from the Command Line.

In the main Performance Monitor view, you get overview information about the memory, network, disk, and processor use on the PC (see Figure 8-5), but you can drill down much further.

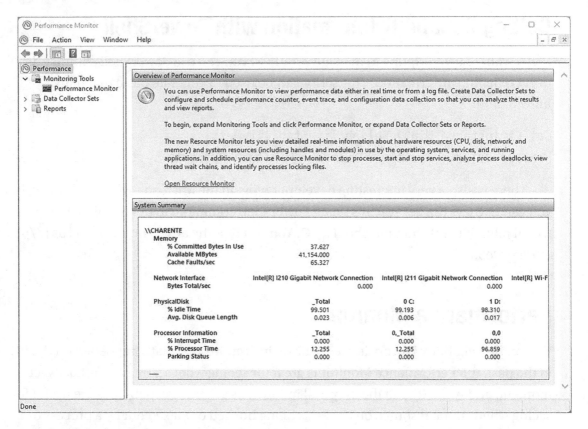

Figure 8-5. Performance Monitor provides useful information on the current status of the PC

Clicking *Performance Monitor* under *Monitoring Tools* in the left panel will display a real-time graph that will display the current processor usage (see Figure 8-6). At the top of the graph though is a toolbar that allows you to customize the view, and the real-time data that it can provide can be incredibly useful.

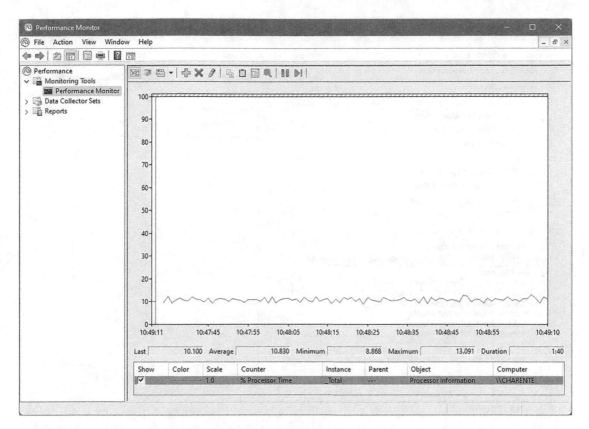

Figure 8-6. *Real-time data about the PC can be viewed as a graph*

If you click the green plus (+) icon at the top of the graph, you can choose from hundreds of additional graphs to display (see Figure 8-7). These cover all aspects of the hardware including networking, memory, disk, and processor.

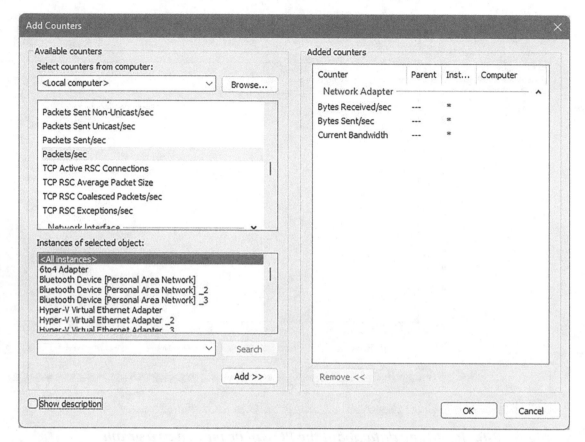

Figure 8-7. *You can add hundreds of additional graphs to the live view*

If you are unsure about what any of the options are you can add, click the *Show description* check box in the bottom-left corner of the window, and a verbose description will appear about the currently highlighted item.

With your other graphs added, they will display as color-coded lines in the main graph view (see Figure 8-8). At the bottom of the Performance Monitor window are descriptions of what each graph line represents.

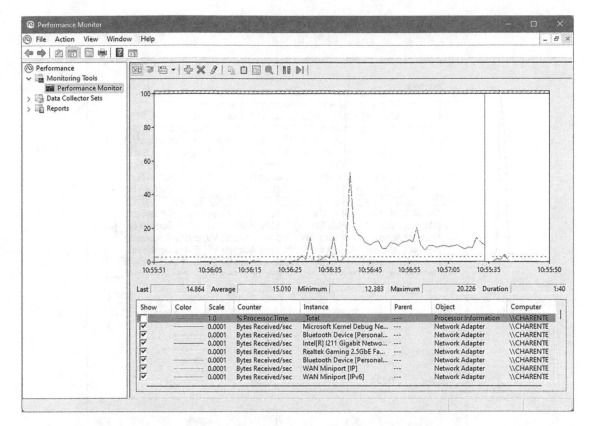

Figure 8-8. *Graphs are color-coded so you can tell them apart*

You may find that some of the graphs are difficult to see, such as in Figure 8-8 where one of the networking graphs appears in yellow on a white background. If you double-click the item in the bottom panel, you can choose other options for that graph, such as changing its color, line thickness, and style (see Figure 8-9).

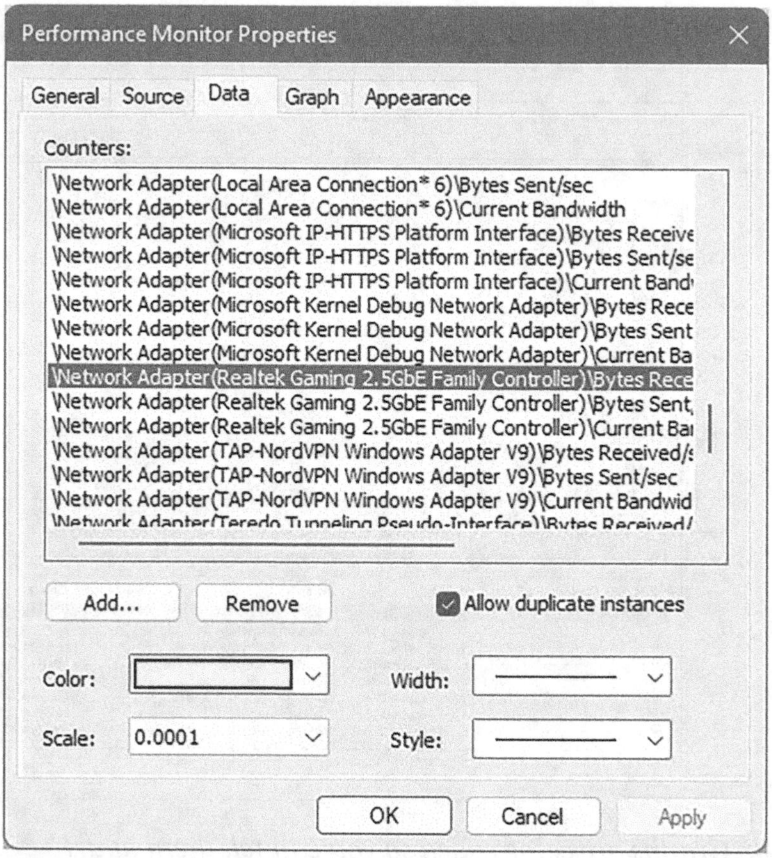

Figure 8-9. *You can change the color and style of graphs*

When you want to remove or hide a graph line, there are two ways to do so. You can either uncheck the box next to the item in the bottom panel, which will cause it to no longer be displayed, but will give you the option of reactivating it later, or you can click the red cross (X) icon in the toolbar to remove the currently selected graph item.

If you want to quickly highlight a specific graph, then select it in the bottom panel and then click the pen icon in the toolbar. This will highlight that graph, making it much easier for you to see (see Figure 8-10).

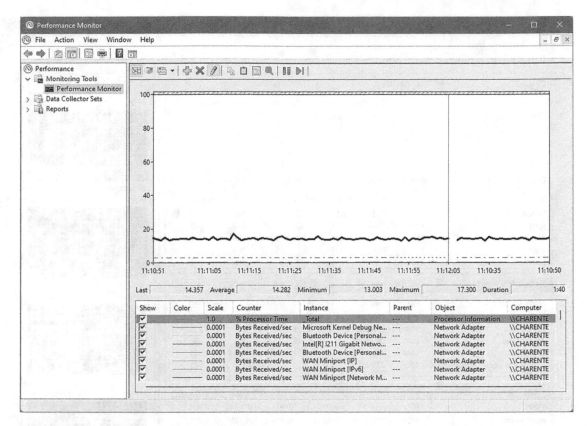

Figure 8-10. *You can quickly highlight a specific graph*

Another useful tool in the Performance Monitor is the *Freeze Display* button which you will see represented by a pause icon in the toolbar. This will freeze the graph at that point so you can see in more detail what's going on.

Resource Monitor

While the Performance Monitor is great for giving you a general overview of aspects of your PC's hardware where you might be hitting a bottleneck, if you need to really drill down into what's going on the Resource Monitor has all the information you need.

You can open it from Windows Tools, or from a search in the Start Menu, and the Resource Monitor really does give you fine and granular information on everything happening on the PC at the time. The default view is based around collapsible panels on the left side and live graphs on the right (see Figure 8-11).

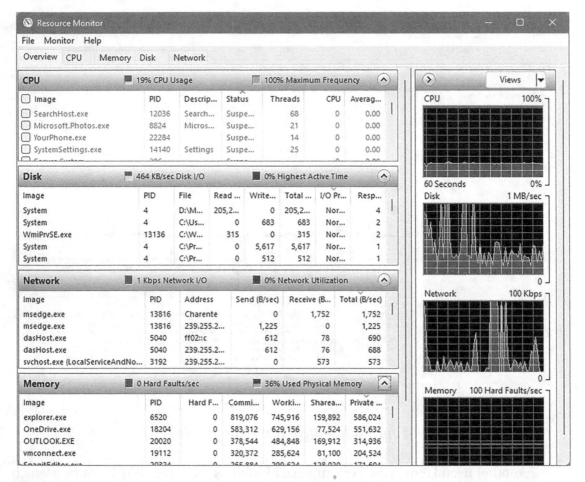

Figure 8-11. *The Resource Monitor is based around collapsible*
information panels

Along the top of the window are tabs for *Overview, CPU, Memory, Disk,* and *Network.*
The main overview panel will show you general information about running processes,
disk read and write operations, overall network activity, and what processes are currently
using what and how much memory each of the running processes is using.

Similarly, the graphs on the right side of the window will show you CPU, Disk,
Network, and Memory usage and make it simple to see where there is a lot of activity or
none at all.

Click the CPU tab, and all the running processes and services on the PC are listed in
their own panels (see Figure 8-12). You can check the box to the left of any process to see
any associated Handles (an integer that identifies the process to Windows) or Modules

associated with it, which is a dynamic link library (.dll) or executable (.exe) file that has been opened by the process.

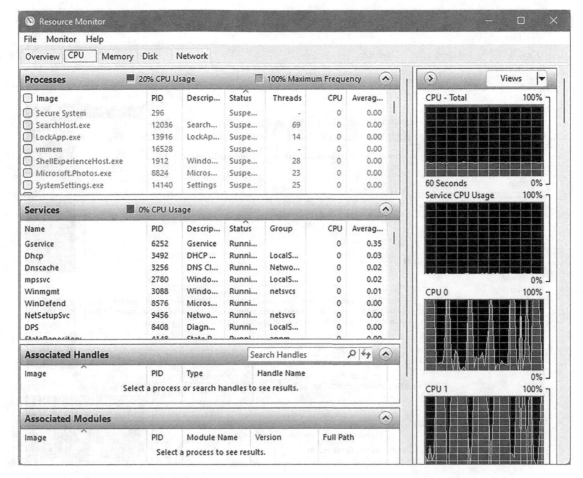

Figure 8-12. *The CPU tab provides information on processes and services*

For each process and service, additional information is listed, such as its long-form description, how much CPU time it is using, and the current status of the process or service, such as if it is currently suspended (highlighted in blue), running, or stopped.

When you right-click a process, you will see options to *End [the] process*, *End [the] process tree* which will also close any dependencies that have been opened by that process, and to *Suspend [the] process* which will pause it.

If you have a process that has hung or crashed and want to find out which other process might have called it, you can select *Analyze wait chain* from a right-click. This will display a tree view of the process and any processes that have called it or that it has called (see Figure 8-13). You can select one or more of the processes that appear in the dialog and click *End process* to terminate them.

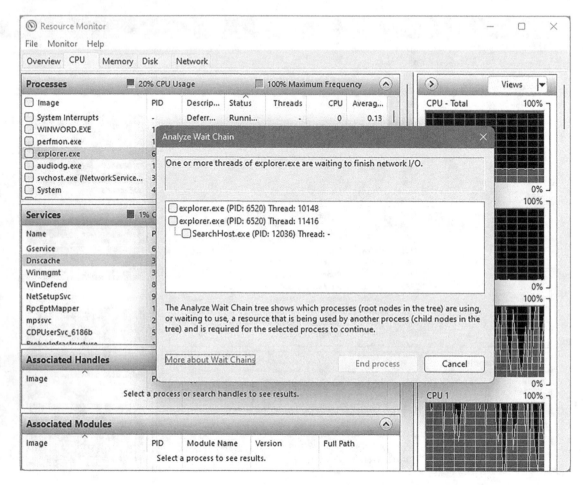

Figure 8-13. *You can determine what processes have called others*

When you click the *Memory* tab, you will see a long list of all the processes and services using memory, how much memory they are using, and whether they are using their own private memory address space, or if they are using a shred memory space, which can be useful for determining when processes have a memory leak occurring (see Figure 8-14).

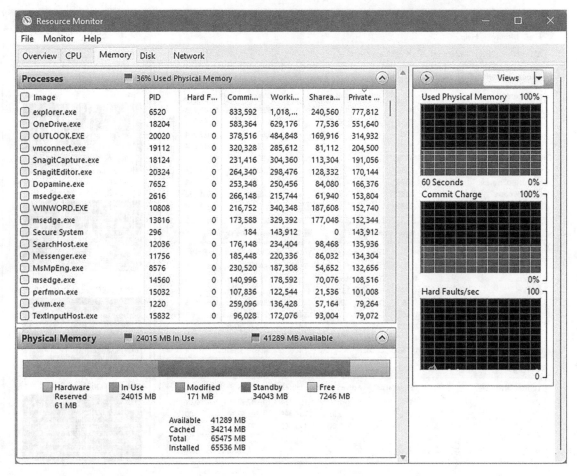

Figure 8-14. *You can see what processes are using memory and how much*

At the bottom of the panel is a simple graphic showing the proportions of memory in use and for different purposes, such as that reserved for the operating system and hardware, and how much is currently free.

The *Disk* tab will display information on which processes are read and writing to or performing other operations on disks and what disk they are using (see Figure 8-15).

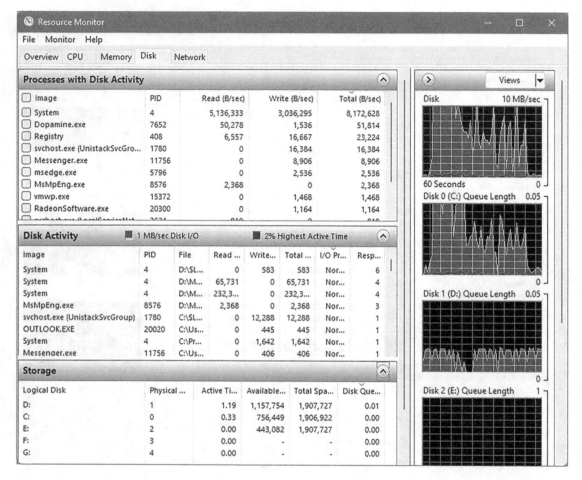

Figure 8-15. *You can see detailed disk activity by process*

Additionally, in the *Disk Activity* section, you can get information on specific files that are being written or read. Note though that this section won't give you details about network shared disks, unless those disks have previously been mapped to the PC as a local drive.

Perhaps the most useful panel however is the *Network* tab where you can see what processes and services are using networking and how much of your bandwidth they are using (see Figure 8-16).

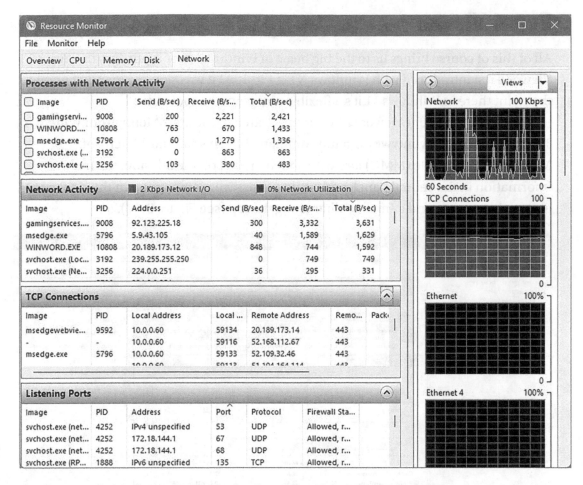

Figure 8-16. *The Network tab displays details of network activity*

Additionally, you can see details about both local and remote *TCP Connections* and identify the remote IP addresses that processes are connected to, such as websites and servers, and this can be useful for identifying malware that is trying to "call home."

Lastly, the *Listening Ports* panel is where you can see what networking ports are being accessed and by what. If you have ports locked down on the PC for security reasons, you might find that a process is trying to access a port, and then its *Firewall status* will be displayed as "Blocked."

Tip   If you want to pause the display so you can spend time drilling down into what is happening at a specific moment, select *Stop Monitoring* from the *Monitor* drop-down menu at the top of the window. This will pause all readings, giving you ample time to investigate an issue.

Event Viewer

All of this of course brings us to the big beast of Windows error reporting, the Event Viewer. First introduced with Windows NT 3.1 in 1993 it was slowly expanded upon to the point there in Windows 11 it's a flexible and powerful tool indeed.

You open the Event Viewer either from a search in the Start Menu, from Windows Tools, or by typing **eventvwr** from the command line. It's standard Microsoft Management Console (MMC) fare with a menu panel on the left side, the main information in the central panel, and context sensitive menu option in the right panel, along with a menu and a small toolbar along the top (see Figure 8-17).

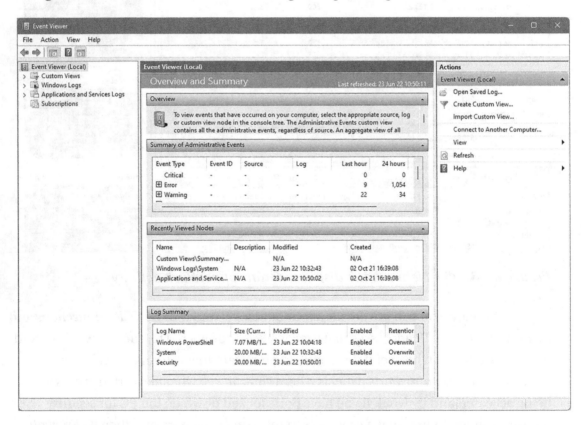

Figure 8-17. *The Event Viewer is standard Microsoft Management Console fare*

In the main information panel, you have three collapsible sections. *Summary of Administrative events* separates the event logs into type. *Critical* is for crashes such as Blue Screens of Death, *Errors* are when failures occur such as a process or service stopping or an update failing to install, *Warnings* are for less critical events such as a USB device failing to initiate when you plug it in, *Information* is for general everyday activities such as an update being installed, and *Audit Success* and *Audit Failure* cover events such as signing in to and out of the PC (see Figure 8-18). Each log type tells you how many events have been recorded in the last hour, last 24 hours, and in the last 7 days. Logs will be kept for a full 30 days though before being deleted.

Overview and Summary					Last refreshed: 23 Jun 22 11:26:39	
Overview						▲

To view events that have occurred on your computer, select the appropriate source, log or custom view node in the console tree. The Administrative Events custom view contains all the administrative events, regardless of source. An aggregate view of all the logs is shown below.

Summary of Administrative Events						▲
Event Type	Event ID	Source	Log	Last hour	24 hours	7 days
Critical	-	-	-	0	0	0
⊞ Error	-	-	-	0	1,054	3,307
⊞ Warning	-	-	-	0	34	280
⊞ Information	-	-	-	54	668	3,971
⊞ Audit Success	-	-	-	325	6,545	28,155
⊞ Audit Failure	-	-	-	0	0	8

Figure 8-18. *The Event Viewer splits logs by severity*

The *Recently Viewed Nodes* section displays a list of event log areas you have recently viewed, and the *Log Summary* section displays common log areas.

When you expand a log category and double-click an entry, the view will change to give you all the data available for that specific log, including the total number of recorded events, with their times and dates, and a verbose description of the log (see Figure 8-19).

Level	Date and Time	Source	Event ID	Task Category
Error	18 Jun 22 12:06:41	VSS	13	None
Error	14 Jun 22 12:43:07	VSS	13	None
Error	13 Jun 22 15:26:24	VSS	13	None
Error	26 May 22 11:24:07	VSS	13	None
Error	15 May 22 09:58:43	VSS	13	None
Error	15 May 22 09:58:43	VSS	13	None

Number of events: 6

Event 13, VSS   ✕

General   Details

Volume Shadow Copy Service information: The COM Server with CLSID {4e14fba2-2e22-11d1-9964-00c04fbbb345} and name CEventSystem cannot be started. [0x8007045b, A system shutdown is in progress.]

Log Name:	Application		
Source:	VSS	Logged:	18 Jun 22 12:06:41
Event ID:	13	Task Category:	None
Level:	Error	Keywords:	Classic
User:	N/A	Computer:	Charente
OpCode:	Info		

More Information: Event Log Online Help

Figure 8-19. *Double-clicking an entry will display technical information about it*

The information included will clearly vary from one entry to another, but can include the filename and disk location of the process, application, or service the log is relevant to, the user account assigned to that process or service, and a Windows error code (you can see the code 0x8007045b in Figure 8-19). There will also be an *Event ID* which is something we'll need in the next section.

Creating Custom Event Views

Sometimes, you need to drill down into the event log to find specific information, such as errors associated with networking or Active Directory (AD) connections. You can do this by clicking *Create custom view* in the right-side panel. Doing so will open a dialog in which you can choose what you want displayed (see Figure 8-20).

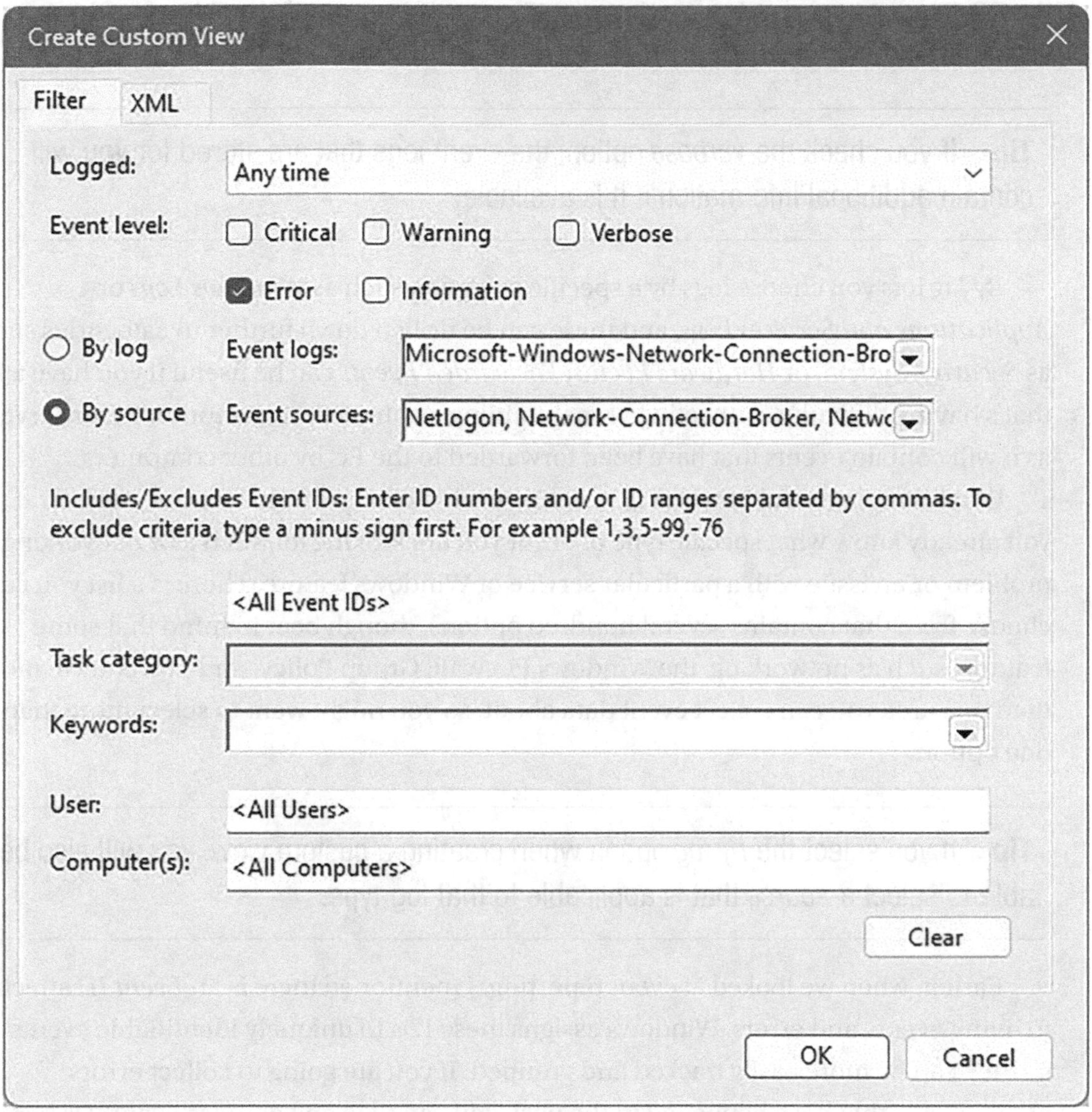

Create Custom View   ✕

Filter   XML

Logged: Any time   ⌄

Event level: ☐ Critical   ☐ Warning   ☐ Verbose

                 ☑ Error   ☐ Information

○ By log   Event logs: Microsoft-Windows-Network-Connection-Bro ▼

◉ By source   Event sources: Netlogon, Network-Connection-Broker, Netwc ▼

Includes/Excludes Event IDs: Enter ID numbers and/or ID ranges separated by commas. To
exclude criteria, type a minus sign first. For example 1,3,5-99,-76

                 <All Event IDs>

Task category: [▼]

Keywords: [▼]

User: <All Users>

Computer(s):   <All Computers>

                                                               Clear

                                              OK   Cancel

Figure 8-20. *You can create custom views to filter events*

It's possible to be very specific about the data you want to collect. At the top of
the dialog, you are asked when you want to collect logs from. This is used if you are
collecting logs from events that have already happened in the past on the PC. Remember
that logs are typically kept on a PC for a period of 30 days before being automatically
deleted.

The *Event level* options allow you to select the severity of the events to store logs
about. You may decide that you only want logs about "Critical" events or "Errors" on

the PC. Then you get to choose what specific type of event you're looking for; this is separated into two sections.

Tip   If you check the *verbose* option, the event logs that are stored for you will contain additional information if it is available.

By log lets you choose logs by a specific category, such as *Windows Logs* or *Applications and Services Logs,* and these can be drilled down further in categories such as *Security, System,* or *Hardware Events. Forwarded Events* can be useful if you have a PC that's having difficulty connecting or maintaining a connection to another PC or server, as it will contain events that have been forwarded to the PC by other computers.

What is more useful however is selecting events *by source.* This is most useful if you already know what specific type of event you are looking for, such as a networking problem or an issue with a particular service or Windows feature. There is a list you can choose from that contains several hundred options, though bear in mind that some features such as networking, the Windows Firewall, Group Policy, and power have more than one area you can collect event data about, so you might want to select more than one option.

Tip   If you select the *by log* option when creating a custom view, you will also be able to select a *source* that is applicable to that log type.

Earlier, when we looked at event reporting, I mentioned there is an *Event ID* attached to many events and errors. Windows assigns these IDs to uniquely identifiable events so they can be more easily tracked and grouped. If you are going to collect errors about events that have happened in the past, you can type one or more event IDs here, separated by a comma (2,9). You can also include a range of IDs using a dash (2-9). If you want to exclude specific IDs, place a minus sign (dash) before its number (-6).

Next, we have the *Task category*. This will not always be selectable as it only contains options that exist within the event source you have chosen, and many contain no subcategories.

You can also specify keywords to help you narrow down your event reporting further. This doesn't mean you can type your own keywords however, as a drop-down menu will present the available options to you, such as *Audit Failure* and *Audit Success*.

Lastly, there are options for selecting a user and a computer. The *User* field is for when there is more than one user account on the PC, and you are trying to determine when a specific user encounters an event. *Computer* is for where the computer is acting as a server and sharing resources such as folders, a printer, or storage.

When you have selected the options you need, you will be asked to give your custom view a name before saving it. The custom view will then appear in the *Custom Views* panel in the left side of the Event Viewer window.

With the custom view created, there are different things you can do with it. Right-click the custom view (see Figure 8-21), and a menu of options will appear.

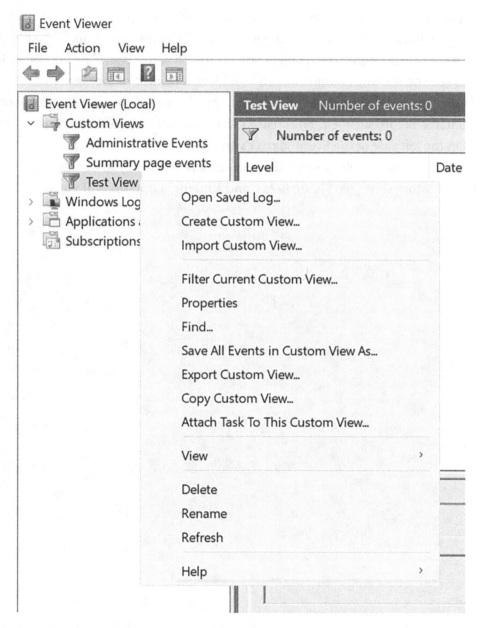

Figure 8-21. *You can work with and amend a custom view*

If you want to amend the custom view, select *Properties* where you will have an option to rename it, or click the *Edit Filter* button to further amend what it captures.

Other useful options include *Filter Current Custom View* which will let you view a subset of the collected events that you define. *Save All Events in Custom View As...* will save the event log for that view as an .evtx file. This can be sent to a third party or support person as required and opened in the Event Viewer on their own PC.

Attaching a Task to an Event

Then you will find options to open, save, import, and copy the custom view or to *Attached [a] Task to this Custom View....* Note that you can also right-click any event in the Event Viewer and attach a task to it. This can be very useful as it allows you to tell the PC to automatically perform an action when the event (this is more useful for an *Error* or *Critical* event) takes place (see Figure 8-22).

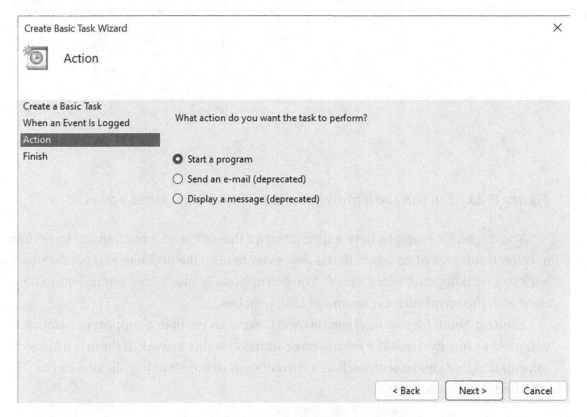

Figure 8-22. *You can attach one of three task types to an event*

The three options available to you include *Start[ing] a program* which allows you to either run a win32 or other compatible program types, such as Windows Troubleshooter, or to run a script such as a batch file or a PowerShell cmdlet (see Figure 8-23).

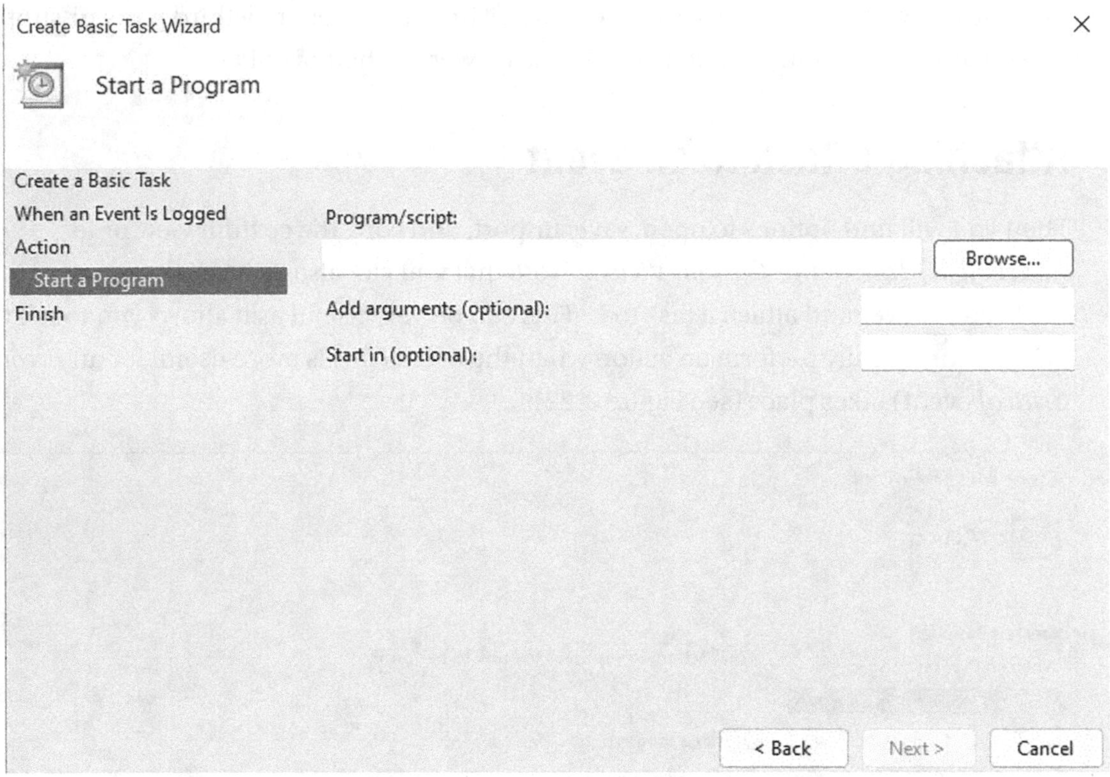

Figure 8-23. *You can run a program or a script when an event occurs*

You might, for example, have a specific script that will reset a component or perform another troubleshooting action that is necessary to reset the problem and get the user back to a working state with their PC. You can optionally specify any arguments to be used with the script such as Command Line switches.

Send an Email (deprecated) can be used to send an email to a support person, and you need to specify the SMTP email server address for this to work. If there is a file with information that can be sent, such as a current copy of the event log file, this can be attached (see Figure 8-24).

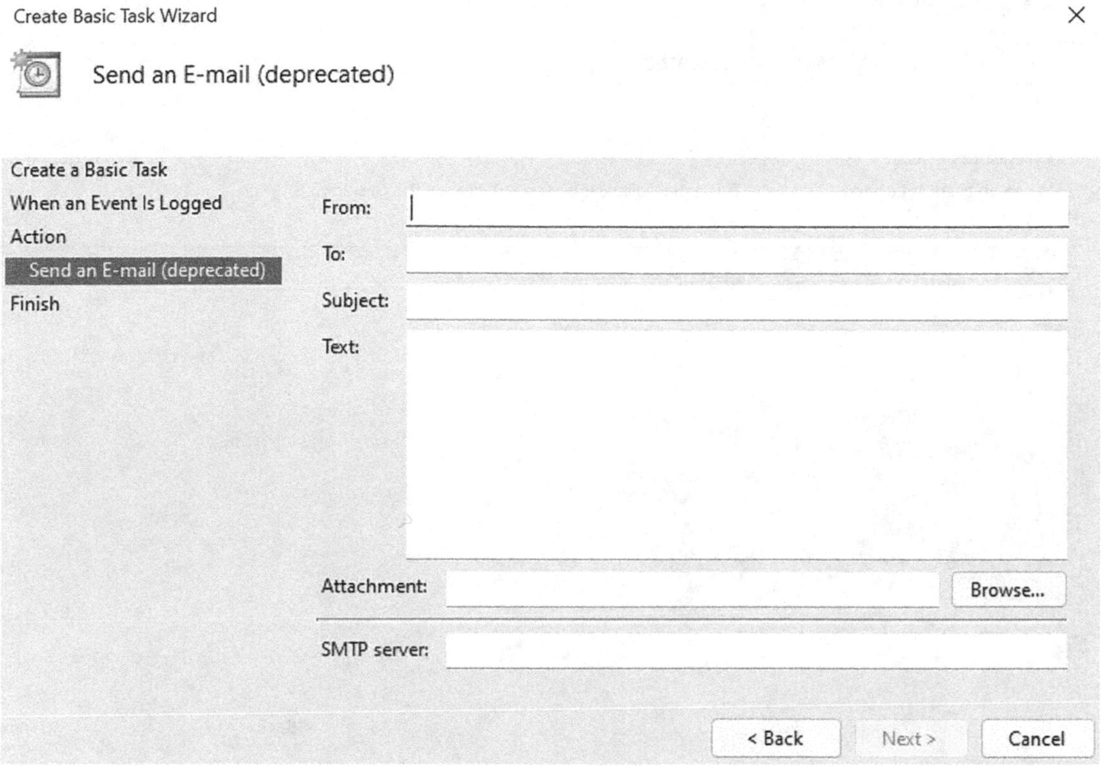

Create Basic Task Wizard   ✕

Send an E-mail (deprecated)

Create a Basic Task		
When an Event Is Logged	From:	
Action	To:	
Send an E-mail (deprecated)	Subject:	
Finish	Text:	
	Attachment:	Browse...
	SMTP server:	

< Back   Next >   Cancel

Figure 8-24. *You can send an email when an event occurs*

What might be more useful however when an event occurs is to *Display a message (deprecated)* which can be used to display a pop-up message on the user's screen, such as "It's happened again, please stop what you're doing and call Tony in support." (see Figure 8-25).

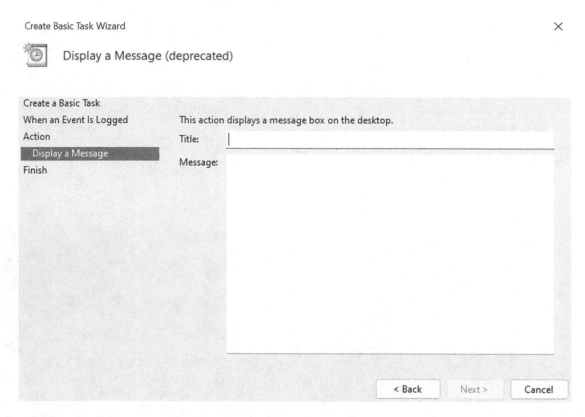

Figure 8-25. *You can display a message on the user's screen when an event occurs*

Note   I want to make a note about what *deprecated* means in the context of sending an email or displaying a message. This doesn't mean the feature is being removed from Windows (though it could still disappear in a future version of the operating system). What it means though is that the feature is no longer being supported or developed further, so you should not expect new features or functionality to be added to it.

When you get to the last page of the task dialog, you will see an option at the bottom of the window to *Open the Properties dialog for this task when I click Finish*. Doing so will give you considerably more control over the task (see Figure 8-26).

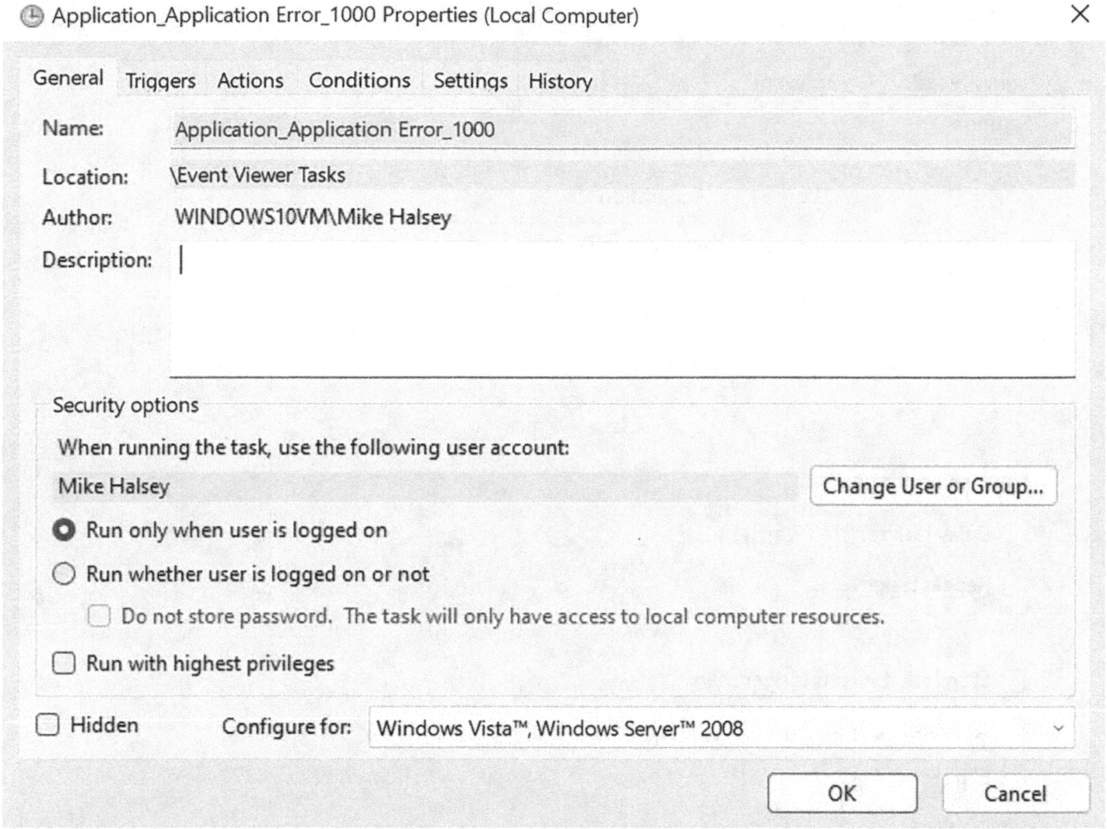

Figure 8-26. *You can get more control over tasks with its "Properties" dialog*

There are a great many options available in the task properties dialog, such as being able to specify the task should run even if the user isn't signed in to the PC at that time, useful for events that can occur randomly in the background and for which you still need to run a program or script.

This *General* tab also allows you to set which user or user group the task is to be set for and whether the task needs to be run with Administrative privileges.

The *Trigger* tab allows you to set parameters for how and when the task will run (see Figure 8-27). You can delay the task for up to one day, repeat it if necessary after a period, stop it if it runs longer than a specified period, or set date when it should first activate or expire.

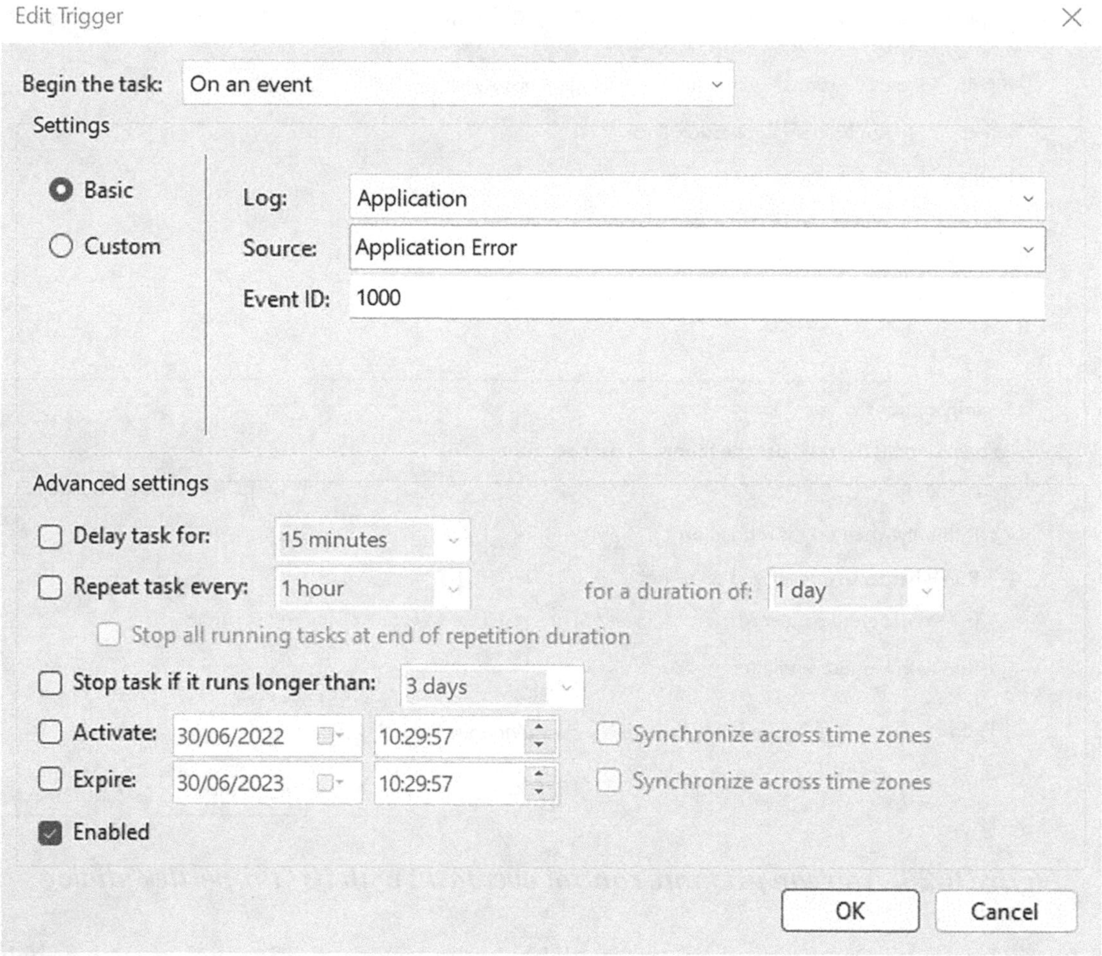

Figure 8-27. *You can set trigger parameters for a task*

While the *Actions* tab only allows you to modify parameters you have set previously, while adding nothing new, the *Conditions* tab has useful options such as only running the task if the computer is plugged into the main electricity or starting running the task only when the PC has been idle for a few minutes, meaning the user is away and won't be disturbed (see Figure 8-28).

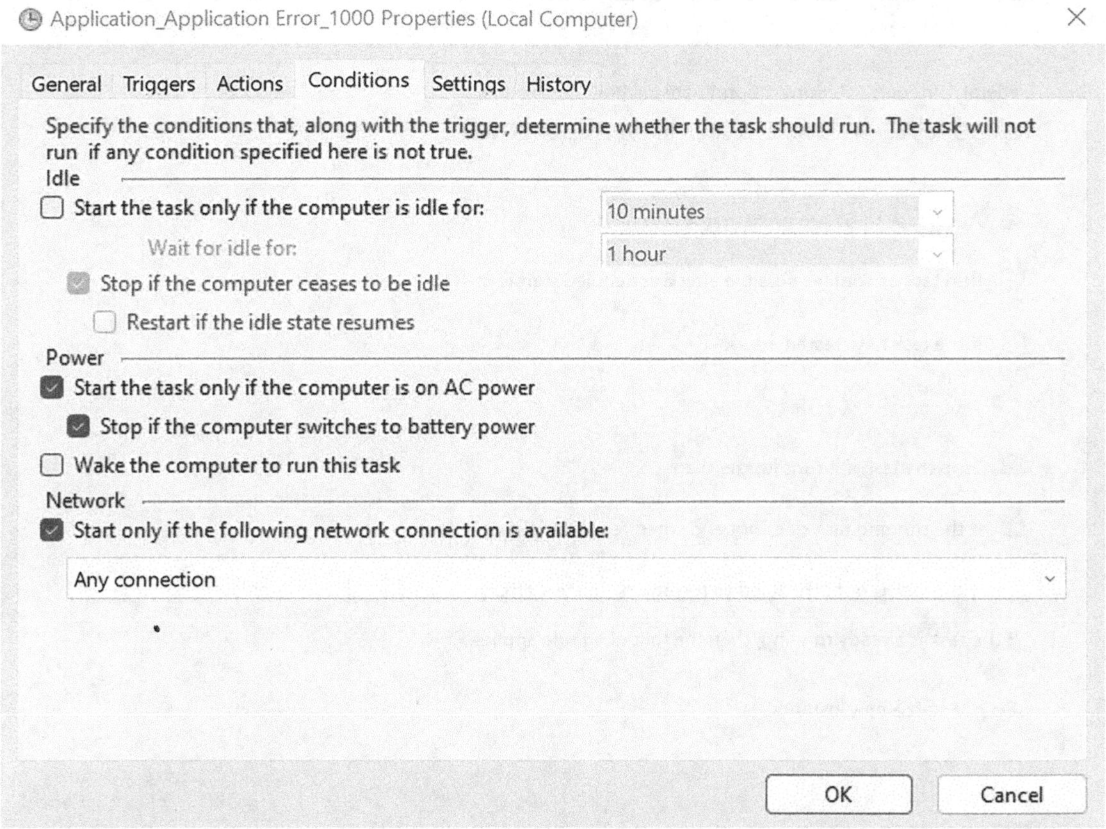

🕐 Application_Application Error_1000 Properties (Local Computer)   ✕

| General | Triggers | Actions | **Conditions** | Settings | History |

Specify the conditions that, along with the trigger, determine whether the task should run. The task will not run if any condition specified here is not true.

Idle ───

☐ Start the task only if the computer is idle for: 10 minutes   ⌄

    Wait for idle for: 1 hour   ⌄

  ☑ Stop if the computer ceases to be idle

    ☐ Restart if the idle state resumes

Power ──

☑ Start the task only if the computer is on AC power

  ☑ Stop if the computer switches to battery power

☐ Wake the computer to run this task

Network ───

☑ Start only if the following network connection is available:

Any connection   ⌄

   ·

                                                                                                                                    [OK]   [Cancel]

Figure 8-28. *Tasks can be set to run when they won't interrupt the user*

There are additional *Settings* available such as restarting the task should it fail to run and forcing the task to stop if it itself hangs (see Figure 8-29). Lastly, the *History* tab will display a list of the times the task has already been run, which is useful for logging.

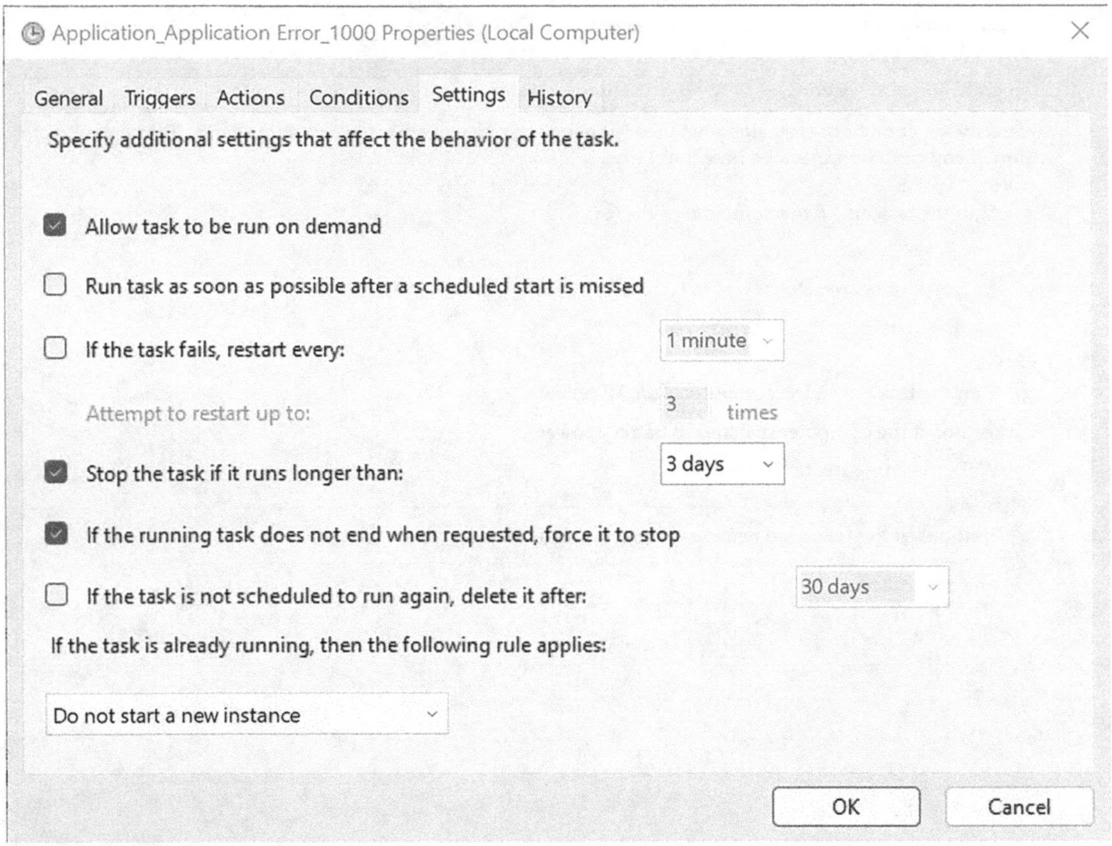

Figure 8-29. *Settings exist to manage hung processes in response to an event*

If you later want to further edit or to delete this task, perhaps when it is no longer needed, then open the *Task Scheduler* from a search in the Start Menu or *Windows Tools*, and in the left panel, expand *Task Scheduler Library* before clicking *Event Viewer Tasks*. Here, you will see all of your custom tasks listed, and you can edit them or delete them as needed (see Figure 8-30).

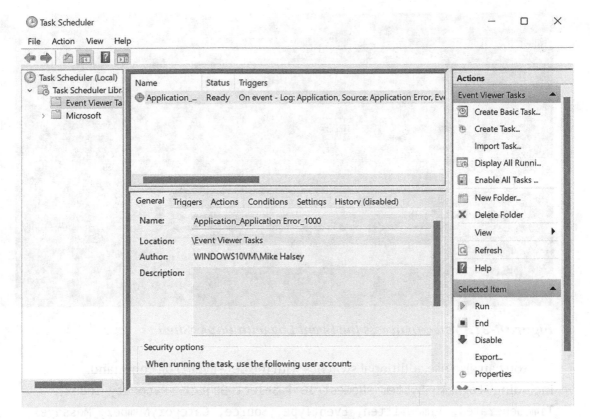

Figure 8-30. *You can manage Event Tasks in the Windows Task Scheduler*

Using PowerShell with Events

If you use PowerShell scripting to manage your PCs, you can do so with the Event Log. Information can be gathered from the Event Log in Windows 11 with the command `Get-EventLog -LogName System | Where-Object {$_.Eventid -eq 1074}` which will display, in this example, shutdown events for the PC.

If you use the `-Newest X` switch, you can display the most recent (X) number of events in the log, such as `Get-EventLog -LogName System -Newest 10` which, when run, displays the ten most recent system events (see Figure 8-31).

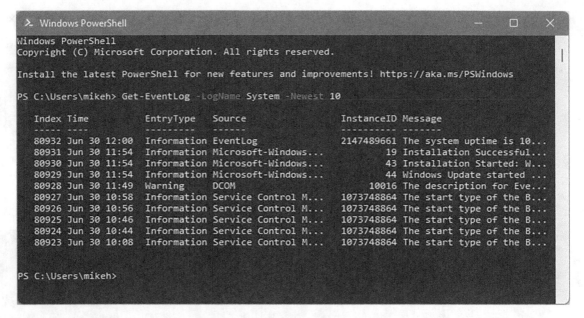

Figure 8-31. You can access the Event Log with PowerShell

You can also use additional switches with the Get-EventLog command, including -LogName System -Newest 10 | Select-Object -Property Index, TimeGenerated, TimeWritten, EventType, Source, CategoryNumber, Message.

Useful additional commands are

- Get-EventLog -List to view event logs on the local PC

- Get-EventLog -LogName System -EntryType Error to see all error events for a specific log

- Get-EventLog -ComputerName <PCName> -LogName System to gather logs from a remote PC

- Get-EventLog -LogName System -ComputerName <PC1>, <PC2>, <PC3> to gather event data from multiple PCs

You can read more about the Get-EventLog command on the Microsoft Docs website at this link: https://pcs.tv/2WtF4J5.

The Get-WinEvent command works in a similar way to Get-EventLog but displays information differently. You can find detailed information on how it is used at the Microsoft Docs website on the following link: https://pcs.tv/3kHFkfN.

While the Get-EventLog command is useful, displaying this data in the PowerShell window is far from ideal. You can export the results as a CSV file however that can be opened and read in Excel. For this, you will use the additional command | Export-Csv -Path "Path and File Name". For example, in Figure 8-32, I have used the command Get-EventLog -LogName System -Newest 10 | Export-Csv -Path "E:\systemlog.csv" to export a file with details of the ten most recent system events.

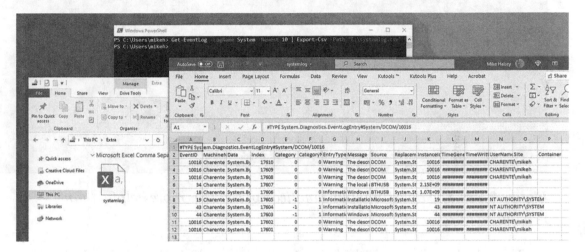

Figure 8-32. *You can export Event Log data at CSV files using PowerShell*

The Blue Screen of Death

When it comes to getting information from Windows, there's nothing quite like the legendary Blue Screen of Death (BSOD), or the Blue Unhappy Emoticon of Death as I like to call it these days (see Figure 8-33). This is because this unhappy blue smiley, with just a single error message and occasionally a QR code you'd never scan before it vanished, is actually more helpful than you might think.

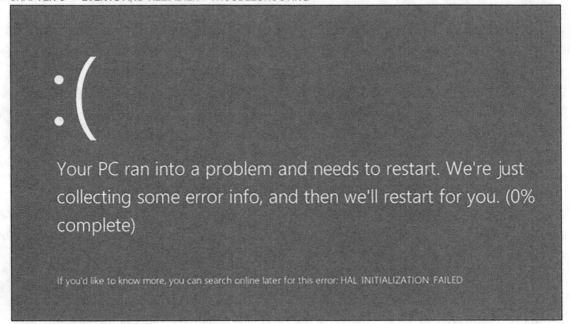

:(

Your PC ran into a problem and needs to restart. We're just collecting some error info, and then we'll restart for you. (0% complete)

If you'd like to know more, you can search online later for this error: HAL_INITIALIZATION_FAILED

Figure 8-33. *The Blue Unhappy Emoticon of Death is more helpful than you think*

The help doesn't come in the form of the screen itself, that's probably the least helpful part of the operating system (aside from the inclusion of *Candy Crush* obviously; Ed); it's in the information it saves to the hard disk for you.

Open the *Start-up and Recovery* options which is most easily accessed by choosing *System* from the *Windows key + X* menu, then clicking the *Advanced system settings* link, and finally the *Settings* button in the Start-up and Recovery section (what can I say, Windows still needs some streamlining), and you will see some useful options (see Figure 8-34).

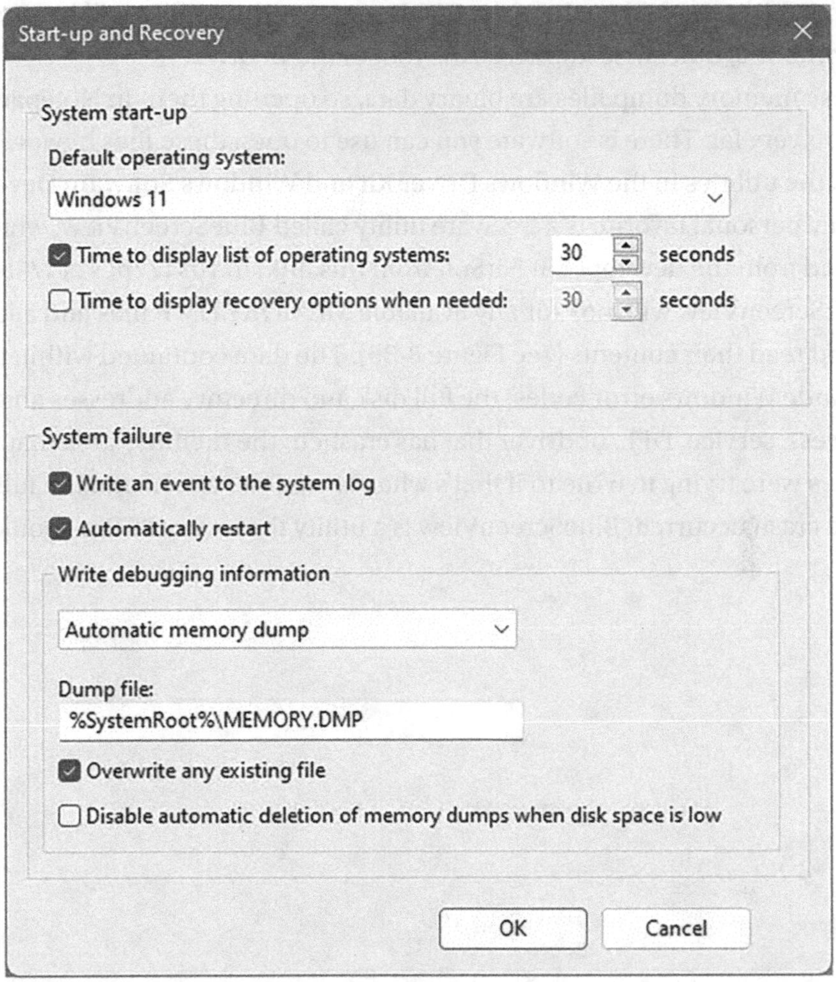

Figure 8-34. Start-up and Recovery contains useful options

This is the dialog you might have traditionally gone to if you had a dual-boot setup on your PC, but it's also where you'll find the *System failure* options. These are all checked by default, but the *Write debugging information* section is worthy of note.

By default, it is set to *Automatic memory dump* which is perfectly fine, and I've never known anybody that ever wanted to change it. Other options do exist in its drop-down though, including *Complete memory dump*, so if you're one of those people that likes "all" of the information, you can have it on a blue screen, though you might find this is information overload.

The standard option will detail all the information you need to diagnose the actual error without including a load of other information that's not relevant.

Below this is the folder where the BSOD memory dump files will be stored, in %SystemRoot%, otherwise known as the root of the C: drive.

These memory dump files are binary data, so opening them in Notepad isn't going to get you very far. There is software you can use to open these files however, such as some of the utilities in the Windows Driver Kit and Windows Software Development Kit. By far, my personal favorite is a freeware utility called BlueScreenView, which you can download from the developer at NirSoft from this link: `https://pcs.tv/3bvSFGQ`.

BlueScreenView will look for any available MEMORY.DMP files and allow you to open and read their contents (see Figure 8-35). The data contained within these files can include Windows error codes; the full disk and directory addresses and names of the process, service, DLL, or driver that has crashed; the memory area that two different processes were trying to write to if that's what caused the crash; and the full date and time the crash occurred. BlueScreenView is a utility that every IT Pro should keep to hand.

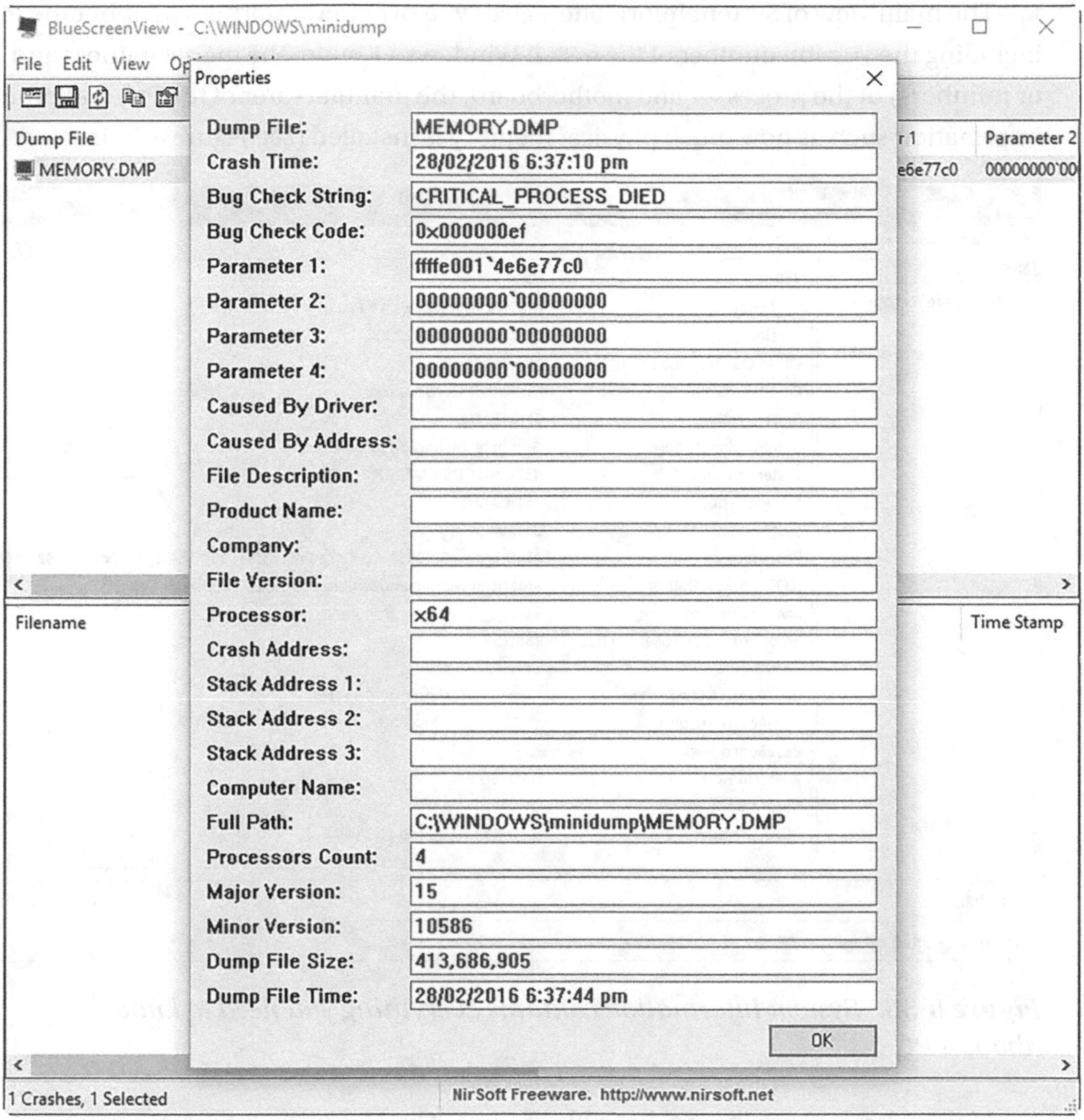

BlueScreenView - C:\WINDOWS\minidump		— □ ×

File   Edit   View   Op

Dump File			r 1	Parameter 2
MEMORY.DMP			e6e77c0	00000000`00

Properties   ×

Dump File:	MEMORY.DMP
Crash Time:	28/02/2016 6:37:10 pm
Bug Check String:	CRITICAL_PROCESS_DIED
Bug Check Code:	0x000000ef
Parameter 1:	ffffe001`4e6e77c0
Parameter 2:	00000000`00000000
Parameter 3:	00000000`00000000
Parameter 4:	00000000`00000000
Caused By Driver:	
Caused By Address:	
File Description:	
Product Name:	
Company:	
File Version:	
Processor:	x64
Crash Address:	
Stack Address 1:	
Stack Address 2:	
Stack Address 3:	
Computer Name:	
Full Path:	C:\WINDOWS\minidump\MEMORY.DMP
Processors Count:	4
Major Version:	15
Minor Version:	10586
Dump File Size:	413,686,905
Dump File Time:	28/02/2016 6:37:44 pm

Filename   Time Stamp

OK

1 Crashes, 1 Selected   NirSoft Freeware. http://www.nirsoft.net

Figure 8-35. *BlueScreenView lets you read the contents of Memory.dmp files*

System Information

If you need more detailed and technical information about the PC and its configuration, then the *System Information* panel is where you want to be. Most easily found from a search in the Start Menu but it can also be run from Windows Tools.

The main view of System Information gives you overview information about the PC, including the version number of the install Windows 11 build, the model names (and or numbers) of the processor and motherboard, the manufacturer of the PC, and other information such as how much physical memory is installed (see Figure 8-36).

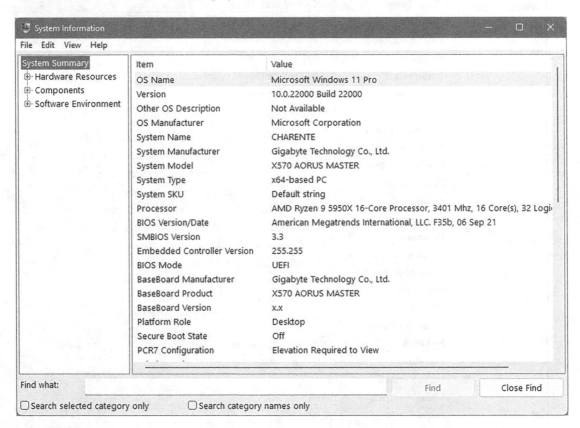

Figure 8-36. *System Information contains everything you need to know about a PC*

In the left panel are three collapsible options. The *Hardware resources* section provides information about memory and any known IRQ (processor Interrupt Request) conflicts. *Components* strip the hardware down into its component sections, such as network, sound, printing, USB, and display, and provide technical information on each (see Figure 8-37).

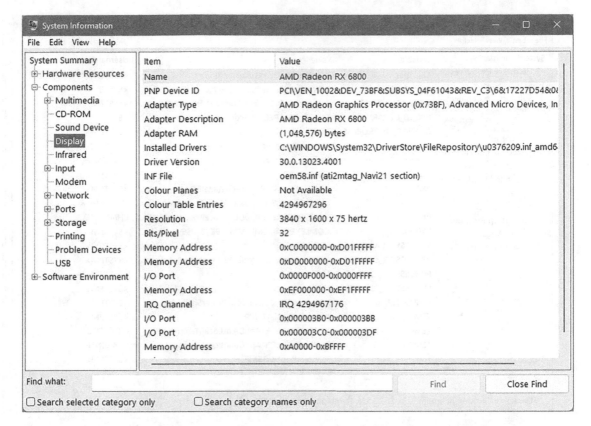

Figure 8-37. *You can get technical information on hardware and drivers*

This information can include memory allocated to running drivers and services, the full names and file addresses of drivers, current operating status, and even the VEN_ (vendor) and DEV_ (device) codes needed to identify USB hardware, something we'll look at more in Chapter 15.

The *Software Environment* section contains everything you need to know about the current Windows 11 installation, from loaded drivers to environment variables, installed services, and startup programs to running tasks and anything currently sitting in a print queue (see Figure 8-38).

Variable	Value	Username
ComSpec	%SystemRoot%\system32\cmd.exe	<SYSTEM>
DriverData	C:\Windows\System32\Drivers\DriverData	<SYSTEM>
INTEL_DEV_REDIST	C:\Program Files (x86)\Common Files\Intel\Shar...	<SYSTEM>
MIC_LD_LIBRARY_PATH	%INTEL_DEV_REDIST%compiler\lib\mic	<SYSTEM>
NUMBER_OF_PROCESS...	32	<SYSTEM>
OneDrive	D:\Mike\OneDrive	CHARENTE\...
OneDriveConsumer	D:\Mike\OneDrive	CHARENTE\...
OS	Windows_NT	<SYSTEM>
Path	%INTEL_DEV_REDIST%redist\intel64\compiler;%...	<SYSTEM>
Path	%USERPROFILE%\AppData\Local\Microsoft\Win...	NT AUTHORI...
Path	%USERPROFILE%\AppData\Local\Microsoft\Win...	CHARENTE\...
PATHEXT	.COM;.EXE;.BAT;.CMD;.VBS;.VBE;.JS;.JSE;.WSF;.WS...	<SYSTEM>
PROCESSOR_ARCHITE...	AMD64	<SYSTEM>
PROCESSOR_IDENTIFIER	AMD64 Family 25 Model 33 Stepping 0, Authent...	<SYSTEM>
PROCESSOR_LEVEL	25	<SYSTEM>
PROCESSOR_REVISION	2100	<SYSTEM>
PSModulePath	%ProgramFiles%\WindowsPowerShell\Modules;...	<SYSTEM>
TEMP	%SystemRoot%\TEMP	<SYSTEM>
TEMP	%USERPROFILE%\AppData\Local\Temp	NT AUTHORI...
TEMP	%USERPROFILE%\AppData\Local\Temp	CHARENTE\...
TMP	%SystemRoot%\TEMP	<SYSTEM>

Figure 8-38. *System Information provides data on the status of the current Windows 11 installation*

At the bottom of the System Information panel is a search box you can use to find specific information, but the drop-down menus contain more useful options. The *View* menu, for example, has a *Remote computer* option which you can use to view the system information of another PC on the network.

If you need to save system information data though to either read later or to send to a support person, then the *File* menu has an *Export* option. This will save the data as a text (.txt) file. The *Save* option alternatively will allow you to save the data as an .nfo file instead. These files will be opened directly by System Information, making it much simpler to see the data contained within.

Using PowerShell to Get System Information

If you use scripting to manage your PCs, it is possible to gather detailed information about all aspects of a PC, local or remote. Indeed, the amount of information you can gather with PowerShell and the number of commands available would fill an entire book. You should consider this section then as an introduction, and I will provide links to additional information and resources on the Microsoft Docs website where appropriate.

File and Disk Information

If you want information on the file and disk structure and for a PC, use the `Get-Disk` and `Get-PhysicalDisk` commands. The data provided by these reports can be exported to both CSV and HTML files with the additional commands `| ConvertTo-Html -Title 'Disk Information' | Set-Content E:\DiskReport.htm` and `| Export-Csv -No TypeInformation -Path E:\DiskReport.csv`.

If you want data on the partition structures on the local disks, use the `Get-WmiObject` command in the format `Get-WinObject -Class Win32_LogicalDisk` with the optional command `| ft -AutoSize` (see Figure 8-39).

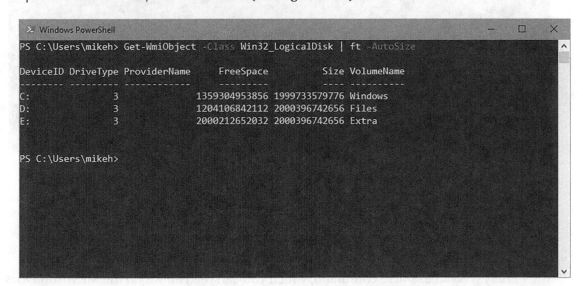

Figure 8-39. *You can display partition information with the Get-WmiObject command*

To see information on files, you can use the command `Get-WmiObject -List -Namespace ROOT\CIMV2 | Where-Object Name -Match 'share' | Sort-Object Name`.

This command will display all shared resources on the PC. This includes disks, printers, devices, folders, and files. It is possible to get more concise information, however, and also obtain additional information on when shares were created and the maximum number of users permitted to access the share and to modify share parameters for both local and networked computers. You can read about the `Win32_Share` command on the Microsoft Docs website at the following link: `https://pcs.tv/3sQOY4M`.

In the same way you can view information about shares, you can also get information about file, folder, and disk permissions. The command `Get-Acl -Path C:\Windows`, for example, can be used to see the Owner and Access permissions for the Windows folder on the local PC.

If we want more detailed information however, we can use the format `Get-Acl -Path D:\Mike\OneDrive\Documents | Select-Object -ExpandProperty Access | Format-Table -AutoSize`, as seen in Figure 8-40.

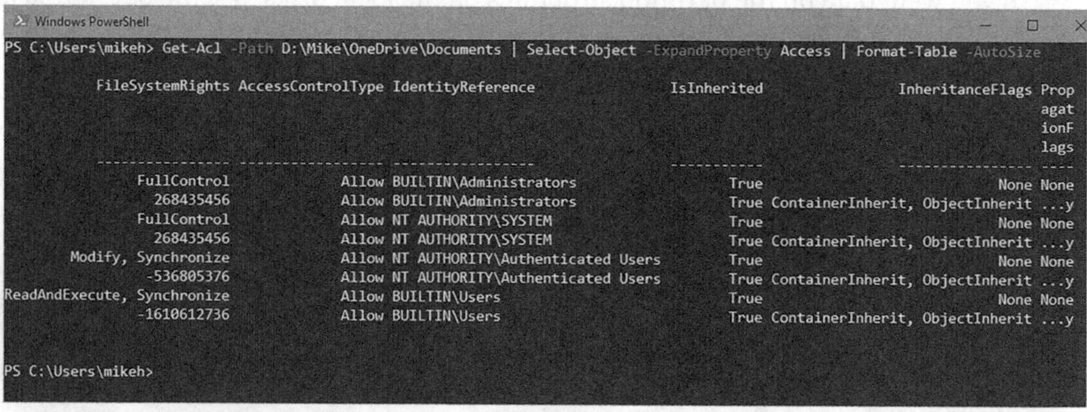

Figure 8-40. *You can get detailed information about ownership and access permissions*

You will most commonly need to view this information because some permission or inheritance will be misconfigured and you'll need to rectify it. For this, we can use the `FileSystemAccessRule` command, which you can read about on the Microsoft Docs website at `https://pcs.tv/38hBofE`, and the `Set-Acl` command, which again you can read about on the Microsoft Docs website at `https://pcs.tv/2XYsK3Y`.

Set-Acl can be used in a variety of ways and on many things from files to Registry keys. You can, for example, copy the security permissions from one file to another using the following commands:

```
$FirstFile = Get-Acl -Path "D:\MasterFiles.txt"
Set-Acl -Path "D:\SubordinateFile.txt" -AclObject $FirstFile
```

If you need to apply permissions to multiple files, you can do this with the following command:

```
$NewAcl = Get-Acl MasterFile.txt
Get-ChildItem -Path "D:\Folder" -Recurse -Include "*.txt" -Force | Set-Acl -Acl
Object $NewAcl
```

There are additional scripts available on the Microsoft Docs website I linked earlier for enabling and disabling inheritance and granting full access permissions for files and folders.

Hardware and System Information

Detailed information about hardware can be gathered using PowerShell, from the command Get-CimInstance -ClassName Win32_BIOS which can be used to display information about the UEFI (BIOS) system on a PC. This and other commands can also be used with the switches | Export-Csv -NoTypeInformation -Path D:\BiosReport. csv to save the information to a file you can then open in Excel. You can also use the switch -ComputerName <PCName> to connect to another remote PC on the network so that you can gather data on it. To gather data on multiple remote PCs you should separate their names with a comma (,) or space. You can read more about the Win32_BIOS command on the Microsoft Docs website at https://pcs.tv/38cPzTg.

The command Get-CimInstance -ClassName Win32_ComputerSystem | Format-List -Property * will display information about the PC (see Figure 8-41), which includes technical information about the hardware. Again, and as with all the commands listed here, it can be used with the switches -ComputerName <PCName> and | Export-Csv to gather information on multiple computers on the network and to export the results to a file.

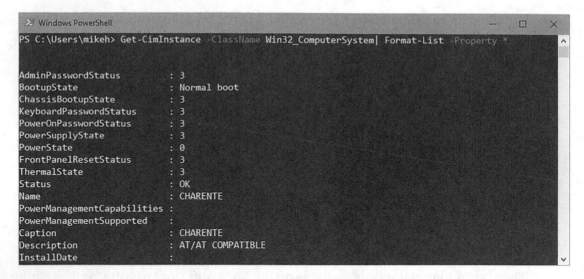

Figure 8-41. *You can view detailed information about a PC's hardware in PowerShell*

If you need information about the processor(s) in one or more PCs, you can use the commands Get-CimInstance -ClassName Win32_ComputerSystem | Format-List -Property * and Get-CimClass -Namespace Root\CimV2 -ClassName win32*processor*.

Processes and Services Information

When it comes to software, it can be useful to see what applications are installed on PCs across the network. For this, you can use the command Get-CimInstance -ClassName Win32_Product | Format-List. This displays a list of all the applications installed on the local PC (see Figure 8-42). When used with the -ComputerName <PCName> and | Export-Csv switches however, it comes into its own for diagnosing issues caused by different versions of software causing problems on specific computers.

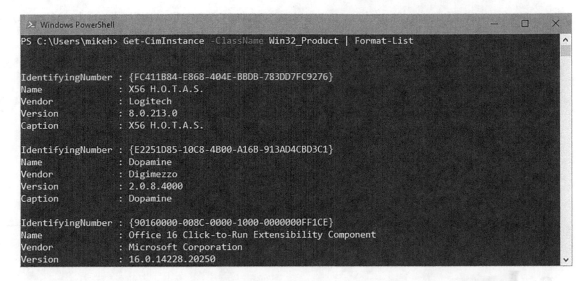

Figure 8-42. *You can view installed software information including version numbers*

We'll look in much more detail at processes and services in Windows in Chapter 13, but as we're talking about getting information using PowerShell, you can find information about running processes on a local or remote PC(s) with the Get-Process command. There are additional options and subcommands you can use this with to drill down into specific processes on the PC to get data about them, and you can read about these subcommands on the Microsoft Docs website at the following link: https://pcs. tv/2Wnbzbr.

Windows and third-party services can be interrogated the same way with the Get-Service command. You can use this command on its own to see the status of all installed services or in one of the following formats:

- Get-Service "net*" will list services that begin with set characters but continue using a wildcard.

- Get-Service -Displayname "*network*" will display services that have a specific word or term in their descriptive name.

- Get-Service -Name "net*" -Exclude "Netlogon" will search for services but exclude specific ones from the results.

- Get-Service | Where-Object {$_.Status -eq "Running"} will display a list of current running services. This can also be used with the subcommands "Stopped" and "Suspended".

You can read more about how to manage services using PowerShell on the Microsoft Docs website at the following link: `https://pcs.tv/3kszYF0`.

Tip Some very useful commands for managing processes and services on a PC include `Stop-Process`, `Start-Process`, `Stop-Service`, `Start-Service`, and, perhaps one of the most useful, especially with troublesome third-party services, `Suspend-Service` and `Restart-Service`. More information on how these useful and simple commands work can be found on the Microsoft Docs website at `https://pcs.tv/3ynX9Fp`.

Summary

There is a huge amount of information you can gather about Windows 11 from the tools and utilities provided as part of the operating system, to log and dump files created by Blue Screen events, and by interrogating both local and remote PCs using PowerShell.

In the next chapter, we'll start looking at how we utilize this information and how we troubleshoot and repair problems with the Windows operating system files and the Windows core OS (kernel) files, and we'll look more at how to troubleshoot and manage Windows Update.

CHAPTER 9

Integrity and Updating Troubleshooting

How many times had you had or heard of a Windows Update causing problems on a PC, from instabilities to causing the system to completely fail to boot? To be honest, if I had a dollar for each time I'd heard this, I'd be enjoying a fair few more nights in fancy restaurants than I currently do.

If you look at the system holistically though, it's a wonder that Microsoft manage to keep Windows PCs stable at all. I've been to Microsoft's Redmond campus outside Seattle many times (see Figure 9-1), and I've met many times with engineers and senior figures in the Windows team. These are just ordinary people with ordinary lives. They go to the gym, struggle to find a home they can afford, raise families, and play Xbox games.

M. Halsey, *Troubleshooting and Supporting Windows 11*, https://doi.org/10.1007/978-1-4842-8728-6_9

Figure 9-1. *The large Microsoft sign is on the corner of NE 40th St and 156th Ave NE in Redmond and is popular for photos*

So when you consider the somewhat superhuman effort required in making sure that billions of different combinations of hardware, software, services, and drivers all work happily with each other in a stable and reliable way, it's a wonder they're able to achieve this at all. Certainly, my own PC is unique. I can guarantee there's not a single other computer anywhere on the planet with its own combination of hardware, peripherals, and installed software. Unless you're using a laptop with no peripherals, configured the same as other laptops in your business or organization, your own PC will likely be unique too.

That said, these people and Windows itself are fallible, and occasionally a borked update does get delivered, or an update is delivered that then goes on to bork something else. This is complicated further when you consider that not everything that comes through Windows Update comes direct from Microsoft. There are a great many driver updates that are written by third-party companies, such as Nvidia, Intel, and AMD, and firmware updates for UEFI systems provided by Dell, Lenovo, HP, and so on.

So when something does go wrong, how can you troubleshoot and repair the problem quickly and simply? Fortunately, this is actually fairly straightforward, and there are different approaches you can use.

Built-In System Repair Utilities

Windows 11 includes several built-in repair utilities, some of which you might have heard of and some of which you might not. These are very good at repairing problems with a corrupt version of the operating system, and one or more should likely be your first port of call when a corruption occurs.

ChkDsk

Microsoft's ChkDsk (Check Disk) utility can be traced all the way back to Seattle Computer Products' 86-DOS, the product that was bought by a fledgling Microsoft for $50,000 and that became MS-DOS; it's been around since the very first days of the personal computer. However, just as you wouldn't tell an aging Oscar-winning actor that they're no longer useful because of their age, ChkDsk can still perform useful tasks on a modern PC.

You run ChkDsk from an Administrator-elevated Command Prompt in the format **CHKDSK C:**, and there are plenty of switches you can use with it:

- **/F** is used to tell ChkDsk to attempt to fix any disk errors it finds.

- **/V** uses verbose logging, where the name of every file and folder checked is displayed.

- **/R** locates bad sectors on a hard disk and attempts to recover unreadable information.

- **/X** forces the volume to dismount first, which can be useful if the disk is locked by an application, preventing ChkDsk from working.

- **/I** performs a less vigorous check only of data index entries and reduces the time taken to perform the check.

- **/C** does not check cycles in the folder structure and reduces the time taken to perform a check.

- **/L[:<size>]** changes the log file size to that size you specify; if you omit **[:<size>]**, then **/L** displays the size of the log file.

- **/B** clears the list of bad clusters on a disk and then rescans the disk for errors; this also includes the functionality of **/R**.

- **/Scan** runs an online scan of the volume.

- **/Forceofflinefix** must be used with **/Scan** and bypasses all online repairs; all defects found are then queued for offline repair, which we will cover shortly.

- **/Perf** must be used with **/Scan** and uses more system resources to complete the scan as quickly as possible.

- **/Spotfix** repairs the volume at the next reboot.

- **/Sdcleanup** runs a memory cleanup for unwanted security descriptor data.

- **/Offlinescanandfix** runs an offline scan and fix on the volume.

- **/Freeorphanedchains** frees any orphaned cluster chains instead of recovering their contents.

- **/Markclean** marks the volume as clean if no problems are detected.

SFC

There are a few hidden gems in Windows, such as the Problem Steps Recorder I detailed in Chapter 6, and the System File Checker (SFC) certainly ranks highly in the useful hidden tools list. This tool was first introduced with Windows 98 as a GUI (Graphical User Interface) utility, but was moved to the Command Line with Windows 2000.

Again, it is run from an Administrator-elevated Command Prompt, and it checks all the files that make up the core operating system to try and find any that are missing or corrupt. If it does find them, it can attempt to repair the problem. You use the System File Checker in the format **SFC** with the following switches:

- **/SCANNOW** scans all protected OS files and repairs problems when possible.

- **/VERIFYONLY** scans all the OS files but does not attempt repairs if it finds a problem; instead, it will report any problems found.

- **/SCANFILE=<file>** can be used to verify the integrity of a specific OS file and repair it if possible.

- **/VERIFYFILE=<file>** scans a specific file but does not attempt to repair it.

- **/OFFBOOTDIR=<offline boot directory>** will attempt to scan and repair an offline boot directory; this is useful if you are running SFC from the Recovery Console where you will likely find the Windows installation on drive **X:**.

- **/OFFWINDIR=<offline Windows directory>** will scan an offline Windows directory, again useful if you are running SFC from the Recovery Console where you will likely find the Windows installation on drive **X:**.

- **/OFFLOGFILE=<log file path>** will create a log file for offline scanning and repair.

DISM

The Deployment Image Servicing and Management (DISM) tool is also run from an Administrator-elevated Command Prompt. It was first introduced with Windows Vista as part of the Windows Assessment and Deployment Toolkit. DISM is a tool for querying, configuring, installing, and uninstalling Windows features for enterprise installations.

Now being built into Windows however, it can also be used to repair corruptions with the installed OS files. You use it in the format **DISM /Online /Cleanup-Image / RestoreHealth** to launch its ScanHealth feature which will scan the core OS files and attempt to repair any problems it finds.

DISM uses the Reset image that Windows 11 keeps, which I will detail later in this chapter, as its backup file repository, but occasionally you might receive a *cannot find source files* message. This happens because DISM has found a file or files to repair, but cannot find the correct file or the correct version of the file in the backup repository.

When this happens, use DISM with the additional switches **/source:WIM:[X:]\ Sources\Install.wim /LimitAccess** where X: is the location of a mounted disk image file (.ISO) for the currently installed version of Windows; note that the versions have to match.

I am going to assume at this point that your Windows 11 PC is up to date with the latest feature update. You will be able to download an up-to-date Windows image (or an older one if that's what's required) from your Volume Licensing Service Center or from the Visual Studio Subscriptions portal. If you don't have access to these however, you can download an up-to-date ISO disk image file of the Windows installer from www. microsoft.com/en-us/software-download/windows11.

With the ISO file downloaded, you can right-click it and select *Mount* from the options that appear. It will then appear as a normal drive in File Explorer (see Figure 9-2).

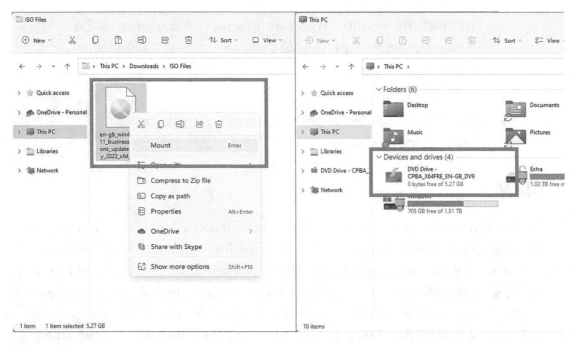

Figure 9-2. *You need to mount a disk image file for DISM to access its contents*

A useful time-saving tip, as you might not know immediately what drive letter Windows has assigned to the mounted image, when you have located the *install.wim* file in the *Sources* folder, click the file icon to the left of the File Explorer address bar, and the folder address on your PC will be revealed (see Figure 9-3).

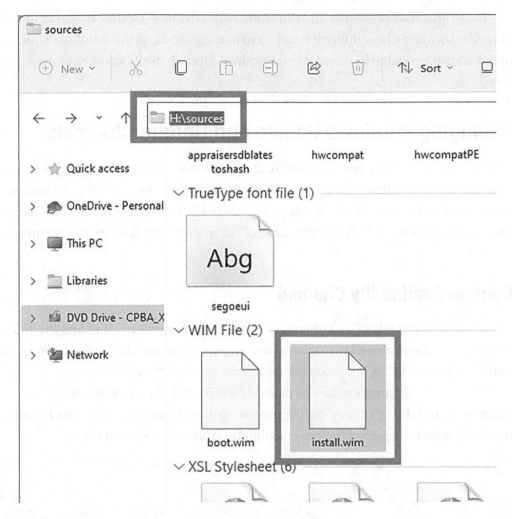

Figure 9-3. *There is an easy way to find the folder location of a file on your PC*

Windows Update

At the beginning of this chapter, I talked about how Windows Update can cause problems on a PC, especially when updates are delivered that, either because they've not undergone enough testing or just because of unforeseeable incompatibilities with other software, services, or drivers, bork a perfectly good and well running PC.

There are other problems that can come with Windows Update however that I want to tackle, including how difficult it can be to manage and control Windows Update in the first instance and what happens when Windows Update itself becomes corrupt and stops working.

Managing Windows Update and Update Channels

There are different "channels" for delivering Windows Updates. They are known to change these from time to time and to vary the deferment periods you can choose from, and indeed throughout the life of Windows 10, these channels did change quite a bit, even beginning with a different name of "branches." For now, at least we just have the three.

General Availability Channel

The General Availability (GA) Channel is what all Windows 11 Home and Pro machines running in a stand-alone environment will be part of. In this channel, all updates are downloaded to a PC as Microsoft releases them through Windows Update.

In this channel, updates can be paused for a period of up to five weeks (see Figure 9-4), but doing so requires the user to open *Settings*, click *Windows Update*, and manually select the period for pausing updates from a drop-down menu.

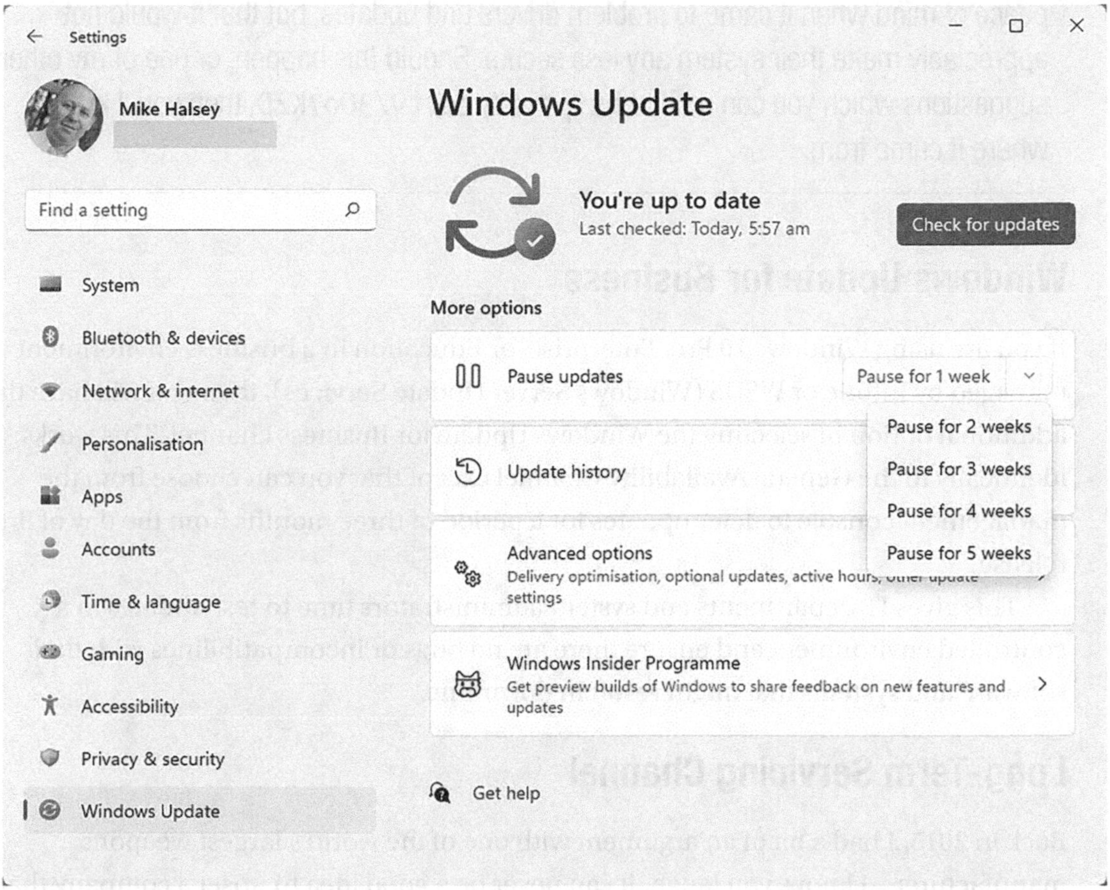

Figure 9-4. *Updates can be paused for up to five weeks in the General Availability Channel*

The reason for pausing updates in this way is because some people might be working on an important project, such as writing a book about Windows Update, and not want to be disturbed by the PC needing to restart the PC. This is especially true if the PC really can't be restarted such as when it's performing a complex video or graphical rendering process.

Note   The month before writing this chapter, I was invited to Microsoft's Redmond (WA) headquarters as part of a small delegation to meet and feed back directly to senior Windows engineers about future builds of the operating system. One of the many suggestions I made was that deferring updates on a PC for a week or two should be an option you can *lock* in place. The reason is that it would give end users much more peace of mind when it came to problem drivers and updates, but that it would not appreciably make their system any less secure. Should this happen, or one of my other suggestions which you can read at `https://pcs.tv/3Oo7KZD`, then you'll know where it came from.

Windows Update for Business

If you are using Windows 10 Pro, Enterprise, or Education in a business environment managed by Intune or WSUS (Windows Server Update Services), then you will have the additional option of selecting the Windows Update for Business channel. This works identically to the General Availability Channel except that you can choose from the management console to defer updates for a period of three months from the day of first release.

This gives IT departments and system administrators time to test updates in a controlled environment and ensure there are no bugs or incompatibilities with their software and systems that might result in downtime.

Long-Term Servicing Channel

Back in 2015, I had a bit of an argument with one of the world's largest weapons manufacturers. I know, you laugh, it can never be a good idea to upset a company that (A) makes battlefield missiles and (B) knows where you live. Anyway, this company was getting ready to roll out Windows 10 across their PCs and wanted each desktop PC to be running the Long-Term Servicing Branch (LTSB), as it was called then, version of the operating system.

On the face of things, this seemed perfectly sensible. The long-term servicing version of Windows only needed to receive updates once every year and a half, and each individual installation would still be supported with security and stability updates (these still were pushed out in the same way as they are for business PCs).

The company said they had some older custom software that might not work properly under Windows 10 as it changed and evolved, and they needed stability for the business. Thus, the LTSB version of Windows 10 was the perfect fit for them.

I politely explained that this is not what the LTSB edition of Windows 10 was for. It had been designed to run on static machines such as ATMs, hospital scanners, and factory robots. Not only was it unsuitable for desktop PCs, and potentially much more vulnerable as it wouldn't be getting the twice-yearly update roll-up, Microsoft had configured it in such a way as to prevent people installing Microsoft Office on it as a deterrent against this very behavior.

This went back forth for a few days until I eventually had enough of them and told them in no uncertain terms to "Suck it up!" They had to update their old custom software, it's not as though they couldn't afford it, and as a weapons manufacturer, they ought to understand a thing or two about security anyway.

Suffice to say, I won the argument, and there were no news stories in the intervening years about this company having a major security breach or any productivity downtime, so we can assume they got on fine with Windows 10 Enterprise. It is a good lesson though about what the long-term servicing versions are and what they're for.

So as I have already said, the Long-Term Servicing Channel (LTSC) version of Windows 11 is for specific static hardware that runs Windows. This includes medical equipment and scanners, ATMs, factory robot production systems, and of course some systems that directly control weaponry for the armed forces, such as a battleship.

These systems differ from desktop PCs in one very important respect. They must never ever fail to work or, to be blunt, the consequences could be severe. A hospital patient might be misdiagnosed or perhaps even die, a factory producing machinery that will save us from climate change might shut down, or Joe might not be able to pay for the last train home after his pop concert.

There is only one version of Windows 11 that can be enrolled in LTSC and that's a specific *Windows 11 Enterprise LTSC* edition. Microsoft has engineered this version in such a way as to make it impossible (or at least extremely difficult) to install desktop and office software, and they have perhaps understandably removed *Candy Crush* (surely reason enough for all of us to use it; Ed).

The LTSC version of Windows 11 will still, as I mentioned, get critical security and stability updates that will inevitably be deferred and tested by IT managers and will get a general update every two to three years.

How Long Is a Windows Feature Update Supported For?

Where LTSC differs from the Home, Pro, Enterprise, and Education versions of Windows 11 is that for the main editions, each major update, called Feature Update, is supported for a period of 24 months for personal and stand-alone machines and 36 months for managed installations in enterprise environments.

The LTSC version of Windows 11 however will have a five-year support lifecycle, meaning that while feature updates will still be released for it every two to three years (not including any new features I might add as the computers running it don't need them), system administrators can wait the full five years before deploying one, and this will give them all the time they need to make sure the update won't interrupt the smooth operation of the machine.

Taming Windows Update

I don't know if you watched it, but back in 2020 and running just for two seasons before being cancelled was an excellent Netflix comedy series called *Space Force*. This starred Steve Carell and John Malkovich as part of the hapless team running the US Military's new space command.

Series 2 episode 7, "The Hack," is the one to watch if you're a fan of Windows Update causing chaos. The facility is hacked, the power is cut, and their computer systems are disabled. This has the result of sending one of their satellites out of orbit. Our intrepid heroes work together to get their systems back online, but when they try to reprogram the satellite, their computer restarts to install a Windows Update.

Windows 11 does include some features to help alleviate the pain, just in case you are managing a satellite that begins to fall out of orbit or are binge-watching *Space Force* on your Surface tablet. Open *Setting* and click *Windows Update*, and you will see an *Advanced options* button.

Clicking this displays the options you have available to you (see Figure 9-5), two of which I want to highlight. *Active hours* lets you specify when you're typically using the PC. This tells the operating system not to restart the PC during those hours.

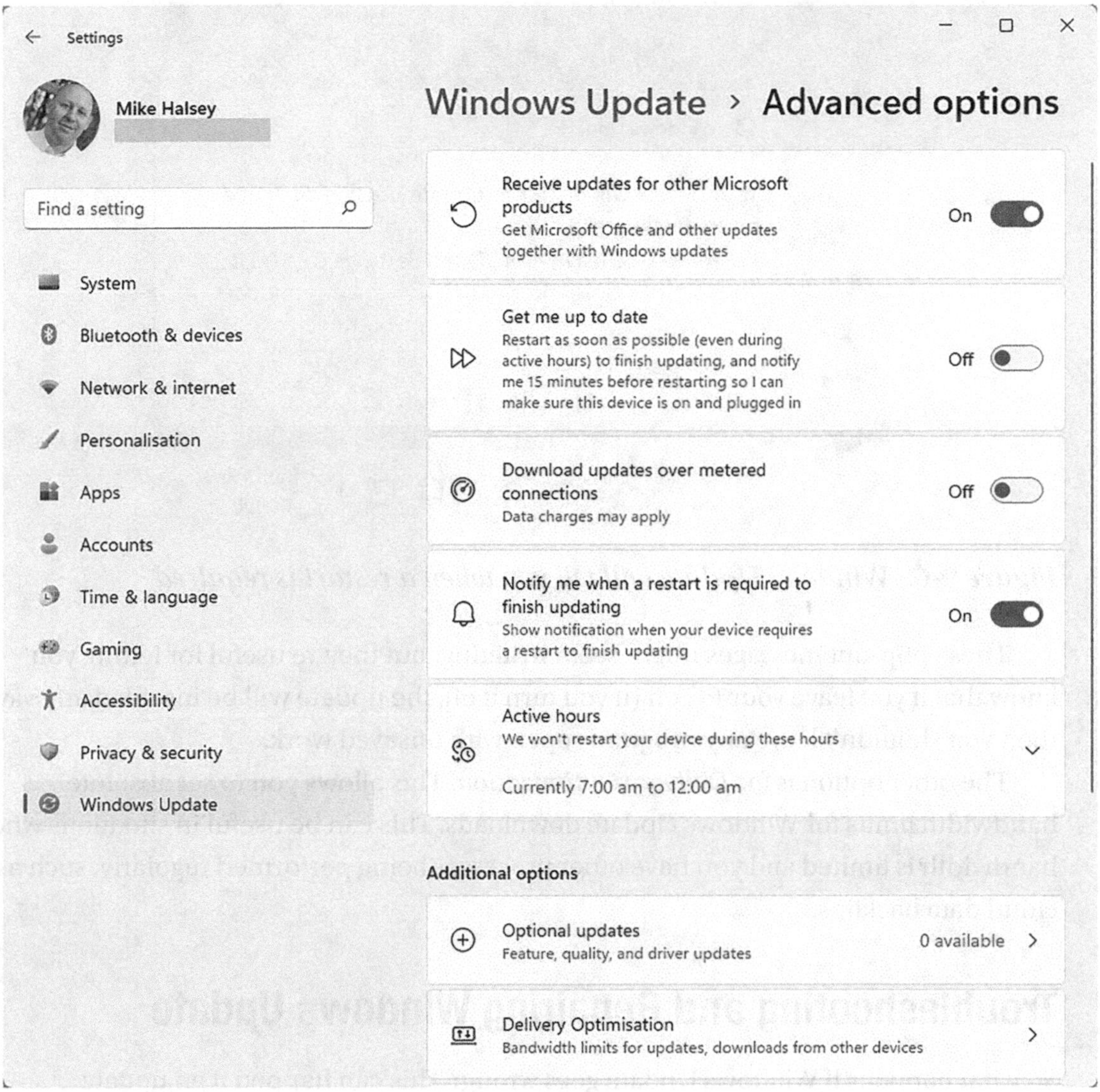

Figure 9-5. *Windows 11 lets you control Windows Update to some degree*

If you then get an update that will require restarting the PC in order for it to install, you will be notified by a pop-out message (see Figure 9-6). This will tell you roughly how long the restart and install will take and give you an option to restart the PC then should you want to.

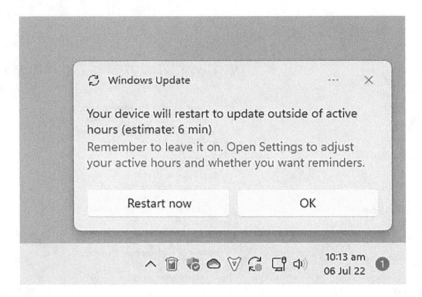

Figure 9-6. *Windows Update will tell you when a restart is required*

These pop-out messages might seem irritating, but they're useful for letting you know that if you leave your PC on (if you turn it off, the update will be installed anyway), then you shouldn't leave any programs open with unsaved work.

The other option is for *Delivery Optimization*. This allows you to set absolute bandwidth limits for Windows Update downloads. This can be useful in situations where bandwidth is limited and you have other processes being performed regularly, such as cloud data backups.

Troubleshooting and Repairing Windows Update

So what happens if Windows Update goes wrong? This can happen if an update download becomes corrupt, and it can cause the whole update system to break, preventing any updates from being downloaded or installed. There are two things you can do here, depending really on whether you are supporting a user remotely or locally.

If the end user needs to fix the problem themselves, ask them to open *Settings* and, in the *System* section, scroll down to *Troubleshoot*. Then click *Other trouble-shooters* before running the one called *Windows Update* (see Figure 9-7). These troubleshooters reset Windows components to their default state and can often fix problems.

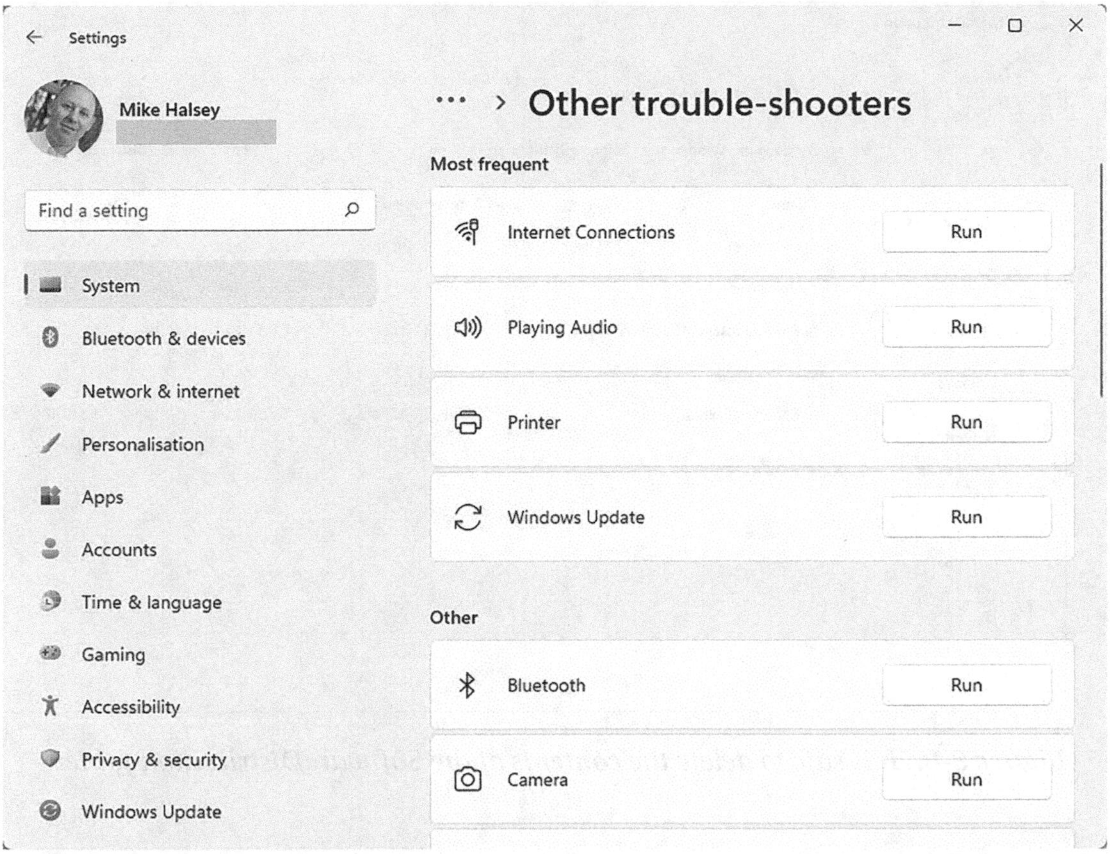

Figure 9-7. Windows 11 includes a troubleshooter to reset Windows Update

If this doesn't work, we need to get our hands dirty. Open *Services* from a Start Menu search or from Windows Tools, and scroll down the list until you find two services, **Windows Update** and **Windows Update Medic Service**. If these are running, you need to right-click each and select *Stop*.

Next, and you only have a limited amount of time to do this before Windows Update will automatically restart those services, open File Explorer and navigate to **C:\Windows\SoftwareDistribution**. This is the main repository of Windows Update files, including all downloads.

You can safely select all of the files and subfolders in this folder and delete them (see Figure 9-8). The next time you run Windows Update on the PC, they will all be recreated, but any corrupt file(s) will be gone.

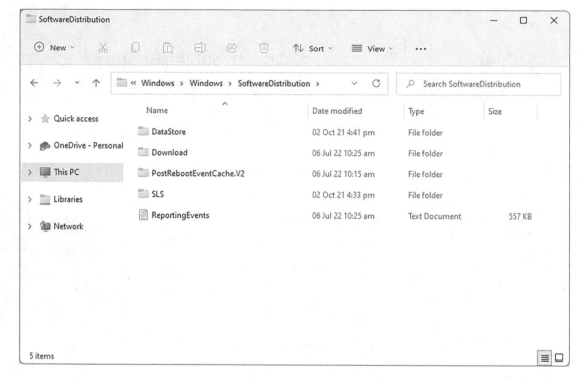

Figure 9-8. *It is safe to delete the contents of the SoftwareDistribution folder*

Rolling Back and Uninstalling Updates

If you get an update on a PC that does cause problems, you will need to get rid of it.
There are three different ways to achieve this depending on what type of update it was.
If an annual *Feature Update* is causing problems on the PC, then this can be rolled back
for a period of 30 days, as a folder called **Windows.old** is kept on the hard disk with the
previous installation files (see Figure 9-9).

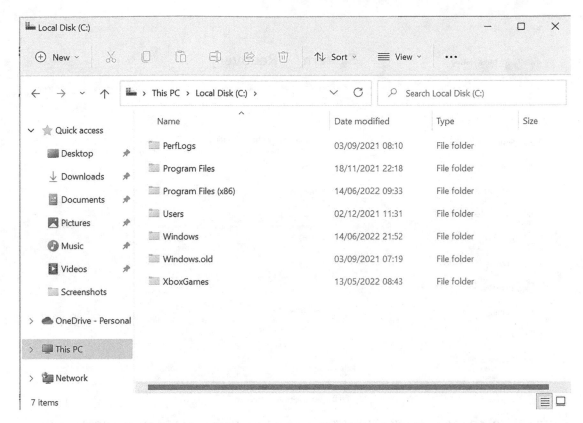

Figure 9-9. *The Windows.old folder is kept for 30 days by the system*

To roll back, in *Settings* click *Recovery* in the *System* section, and you will see a *Go back* option. Click this unless it is grayed out as it will then no longer be available for you to use (see Figure 9-10).

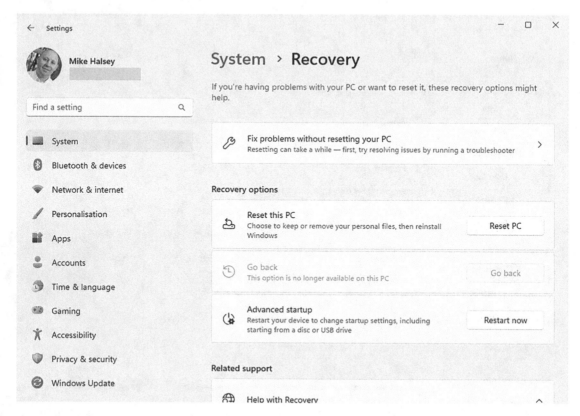

Figure 9-10. *You can "Go back" to a previous Feature Update for 30 days*

If this option isn't available to you, there are other things you can do. In *Settings*, click *Windows Update* and then *Update history*. Scroll to the bottom of the page, and you will see an *Uninstall updates* option (see Figure 9-11).

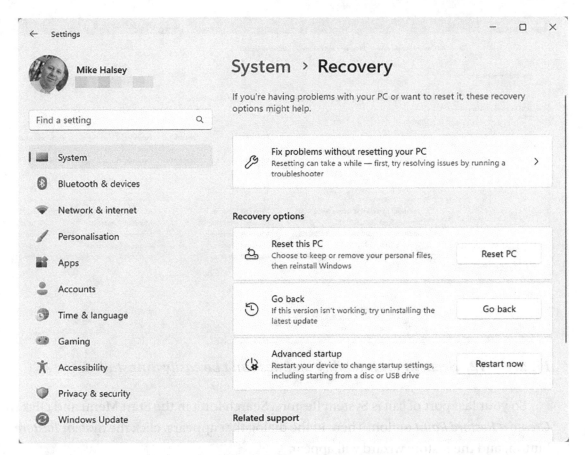

Figure 9-11. *You can uninstall some Windows Updates*

This currently opens in the old Windows Update Control Panel applet, though we can likely expect it to be completely folded into Settings at some point in the future, as Windows Update is one of the applets that's been marked for complete removal.

You will notice however that while the list of installed updates in Settings is long, the list of updates you can actually remove is short (see Figure 9-12). This is because Microsoft deems security and stability updates as being too important to remove. If it's one of those you need to get rid of, then you'll see a different route for doing so.

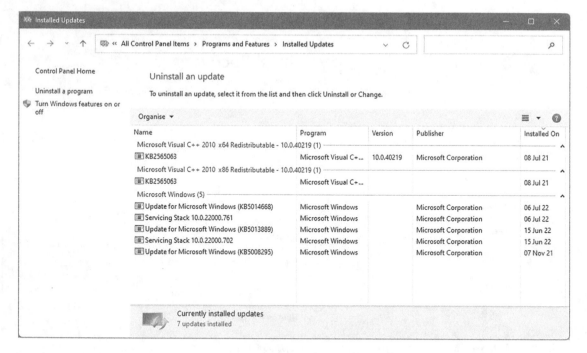

Figure 9-12. *Security and stability updates can't be easily uninstalled*

So your last port of call is System Restore. Search for it in the Start Menu and click the *Create a Restore Point* option. Then, in the dialog that appears, click the *System Restore* button, and the restore wizard will appear.

You will be offered a *Recommended Restore Point* to recover to, which will be the most recent, but you can choose a different one. There may not be many that appear in the list, but check the *Show more restore points* check box in the bottom-left corner of the dialog, and more will likely appear (see Figure 9-13).

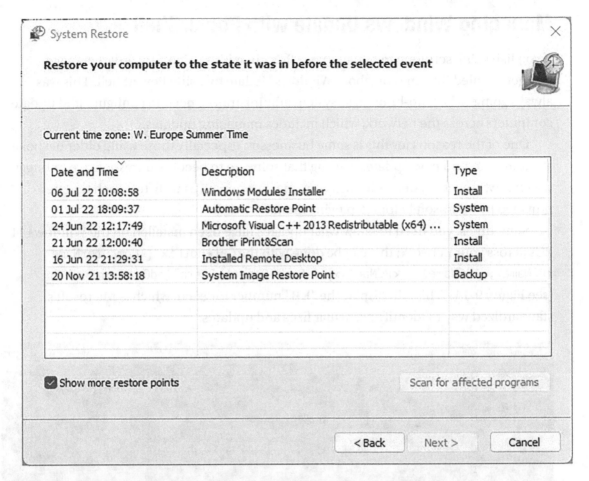

Figure 9-13. *You can roll back updates with System Restore*

Choose the Restore Point that correlates to the time and date the problem occurred, that is, the time of the Windows Update that caused the issue, and click *Next*.

The last thing you need to do after the restore is complete is to go back into *Settings* and *Windows Update* and pause updates for a few weeks, as I described earlier in this chapter. This is because the offending update will inevitably come down to you again, and pausing updates will give Microsoft or the third-party vendor time to identify and either fix the update or pull it completely so that it doesn't cause people any more headaches.

Managing Windows Update with PowerShell

If you like using scripting to manage your PCs, then it's straightforward to manage and get detailed information about Windows Update by using PowerShell. This was always going to be a no-brainer, as system administrators need to configure and update computers across the network, which includes managing updates.

One of the reasons for this is some businesses, especially those using older bespoke software, can find new updates causing that software to become unresponsive or buggy, which is why every system administrator, maybe yourself as well, test each update provided by Microsoft before deploying them.

Sometimes, you need to know what updates have been installed on the Windows 11 PCs across your network; this can be done with the Get-HotFix {-ComputerName <PCName>, <PCName2>, <PCName3>} | Sort-Object InstalledOn command (see Figure 9-14). This will display the "**KB**" number for each, which is Microsoft's standardized way to identify particular fixes and updates.

```
Administrator: Windows PowerShell
PS C:\Windows\system32> Get-HotFix | Sort-Object InstalledOn

Source        Description      HotFixID      InstalledBy            InstalledOn
------        -----------      --------      -----------            -----------
CHARENTE      Update           KB5000736                            09/04/2021 00:00:00
CHARENTE      Security Update  KB5005260     NT AUTHORITY\SYSTEM    12/08/2021 00:00:00
CHARENTE      Update           KB5004331     NT AUTHORITY\SYSTEM    13/08/2021 00:00:00
CHARENTE      Security Update  KB5005033     NT AUTHORITY\SYSTEM    13/08/2021 00:00:00


PS C:\Windows\system32>
```

Figure 9-14. *You can check which updates have recently been installed on local or remote PCs*

If you want more detailed information about what updates have been installed on a PC or PCs over time, use the command Get-WindowsUpdateLog, which will export the full event logs from Windows Update, including error and failure events, and write them to a *WindowsUpdate.txt* file placed on your desktop (see Figure 9-15).

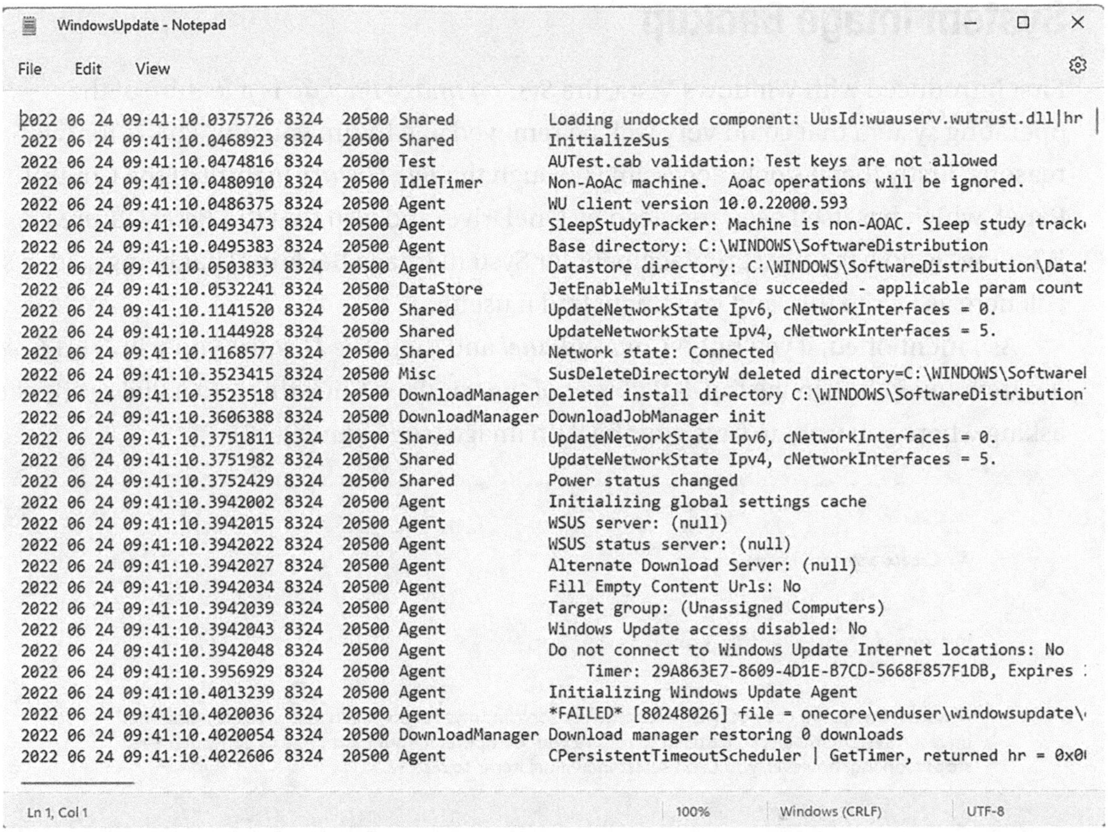


```
2022 06 24 09:41:10.0375726 8324  20500 Shared          Loading undocked component: UusId:wuauserv.wutrust.dll|hr
2022 06 24 09:41:10.0468923 8324  20500 Shared          InitializeSus
2022 06 24 09:41:10.0474816 8324  20500 Test            AUTest.cab validation: Test keys are not allowed
2022 06 24 09:41:10.0480910 8324  20500 IdleTimer       Non-AoAc machine.  Aoac operations will be ignored.
2022 06 24 09:41:10.0486375 8324  20500 Agent           WU client version 10.0.22000.593
2022 06 24 09:41:10.0493473 8324  20500 Agent           SleepStudyTracker: Machine is non-AOAC. Sleep study track
2022 06 24 09:41:10.0495383 8324  20500 Agent           Base directory: C:\WINDOWS\SoftwareDistribution
2022 06 24 09:41:10.0503833 8324  20500 Agent           Datastore directory: C:\WINDOWS\SoftwareDistribution\Data
2022 06 24 09:41:10.0532241 8324  20500 DataStore       JetEnableMultiInstance succeeded - applicable param count
2022 06 24 09:41:10.1141520 8324  20500 Shared          UpdateNetworkState Ipv6, cNetworkInterfaces = 0.
2022 06 24 09:41:10.1144928 8324  20500 Shared          UpdateNetworkState Ipv4, cNetworkInterfaces = 5.
2022 06 24 09:41:10.1168577 8324  20500 Shared          Network state: Connected
2022 06 24 09:41:10.3523415 8324  20500 Misc            SusDeleteDirectoryW deleted directory=C:\WINDOWS\Softwarel
2022 06 24 09:41:10.3523518 8324  20500 DownloadManager Deleted install directory C:\WINDOWS\SoftwareDistribution
2022 06 24 09:41:10.3606388 8324  20500 DownloadManager DownloadJobManager init
2022 06 24 09:41:10.3751811 8324  20500 Shared          UpdateNetworkState Ipv6, cNetworkInterfaces = 0.
2022 06 24 09:41:10.3751982 8324  20500 Shared          UpdateNetworkState Ipv4, cNetworkInterfaces = 5.
2022 06 24 09:41:10.3752429 8324  20500 Shared          Power status changed
2022 06 24 09:41:10.3942002 8324  20500 Agent           Initializing global settings cache
2022 06 24 09:41:10.3942015 8324  20500 Agent           WSUS server: (null)
2022 06 24 09:41:10.3942022 8324  20500 Agent           WSUS status server: (null)
2022 06 24 09:41:10.3942027 8324  20500 Agent           Alternate Download Server: (null)
2022 06 24 09:41:10.3942034 8324  20500 Agent           Fill Empty Content Urls: No
2022 06 24 09:41:10.3942039 8324  20500 Agent           Target group: (Unassigned Computers)
2022 06 24 09:41:10.3942043 8324  20500 Agent           Windows Update access disabled: No
2022 06 24 09:41:10.3942048 8324  20500 Agent           Do not connect to Windows Update Internet locations: No
2022 06 24 09:41:10.3956929 8324  20500 Agent              Timer: 29A863E7-8609-4D1E-B7CD-5668F857F1DB, Expires
2022 06 24 09:41:10.4013239 8324  20500 Agent           Initializing Windows Update Agent
2022 06 24 09:41:10.4020036 8324  20500 Agent           *FAILED* [80248026] file = onecore\enduser\windowsupdate\
2022 06 24 09:41:10.4020054 8324  20500 DownloadManager Download manager restoring 0 downloads
2022 06 24 09:41:10.4022606 8324  20500 Agent           CPersistentTimeoutScheduler | GetTimer, returned hr = 0x0
```


Figure 9-15. *You can view full event logs for Windows Update with PowerShell*

More information on the PowerShell commands you can use with Windows Update on PCs across a network can be found on the Microsoft Docs website at the following link: `https://pcs.tv/3mHleEP`.

Resetting and Reinstalling Windows 11

Sometimes, you need to reset Windows 11 completely because things have gotten so bad that's really the only option available to you. There are a couple of different ways to do this in Windows, and both produce different results.

System Image Backup

First introduced with Windows Vista, the *System Image Backup* is a feature of the operating system that could very well be removed in a future version. This is for two reasons, firstly that it's only accessible through the *File History* feature of the Control Panel, which has itself been replaced by OneDrive, and also that the *Reset* feature in Windows is now the direct replacement for System Image Backup. That being said, it's still here as I write this, and you might find it useful.

As I mentioned, if you open *Control Panel* and then *File History*, you will see a *Create a system image* link in the top-left corner of the window. Click this and a dialog appears asking where you want to save your backup image (see Figure 9-16).

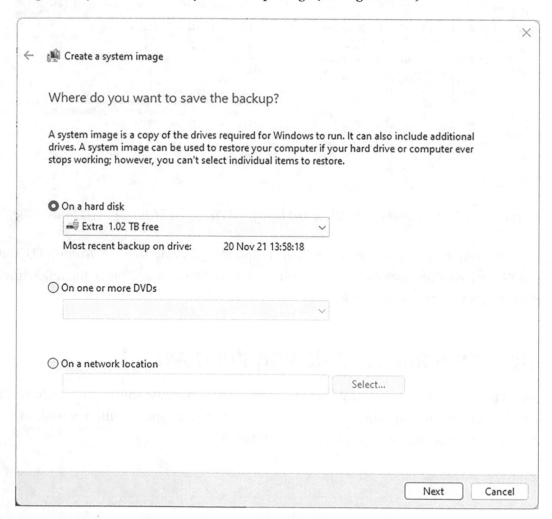

Figure 9-16. *Windows allows you to save a backup install image*

You can choose between saving it on a different partition or hard disk in the PC, on one or more DVDs (if you find any at the back of a drawer), or on a network location.

Caution   Do not save a System Image Backup on a network location the PC can only connect to by Wi-Fi or it will be unavailable if you need to restore it.

Clearly, the only option here is a separate partition or disk in the PC, which will already rule out this feature for many people. When you save the image, it creates a snapshot image of your Windows 11 installation at that time, including all your settings, installed programs, and also all your files and documents if they're stored on the same disk as your Windows installation.

This creates another problem, in that to use this feature you will also need to have all your files and documents stored on a separate partition or disk to Windows, or you will find that all your new and updated files will be completely wiped out and replaced with older ones when you come to do a restore. Be warned!

The benefit of a System Image Backup though is that, while you'll still need to download a ton of Windows Updates after restoring it, all your software and installed apps will be right where you left them, and, arguably, installing and configuring these again is the bigger job out of the two.

You restore a System Image Backup from the Recovery Console. Either boot the PC from a USB Recovery Drive, which I detailed in Chapter 3, or hold down the *Shift* key when restarting the PC from the Start Menu or Lock Screen.

When in the Recovery Console, click *Troubleshooting* and then *Advanced Options*. You will see a *See more recovery options* link, and clicking this will reveal an option to restore the PC using *System Image Recovery* (see Figure 9-17).

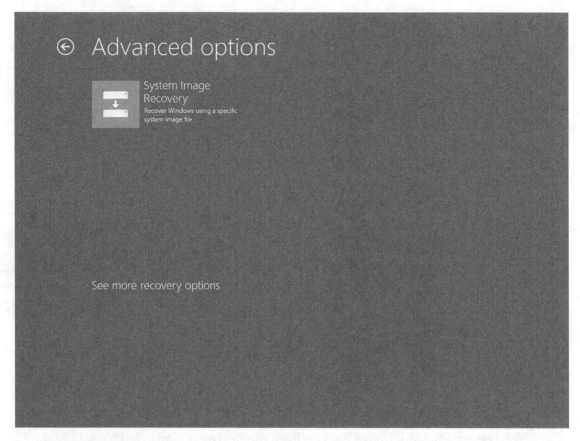

Figure 9-17. *You can restore a System Image from the Recovery Console*

The system will look for a System Image on the local PC and report if it can't find one. Select the *Select a system image* option and click *Next*. At the next screen, click *Advanced* and you will be asked if you want to *Search for a system image on the network*, and remember this will only work for hardwired networked PCs, or if you want to *Install a driver* such as one needed for the system to access a local RAID array (see Figure 9-18).

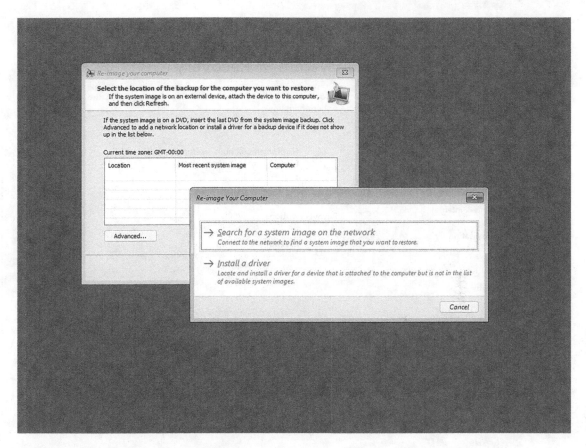

Figure 9-18. *You can only restore a System Image from a wired network*

Reset This PC

Windows Reset is the option that has effectively replaced the System Image Backup, and it's superior in some ways and vastly inferior in others. Windows keeps a backup copy of itself at all times that is 30 days old. The logic of this is that if your PC worked reliably 30 days ago, that's a backup image you can use to restore it in the event of a failure.

You don't need to do anything to create this backup, Windows does it automatically. You can restore it at any time in *Settings* under *System* and *Recovery* where you will see a *Reset this PC* option (see Figure 9-19).

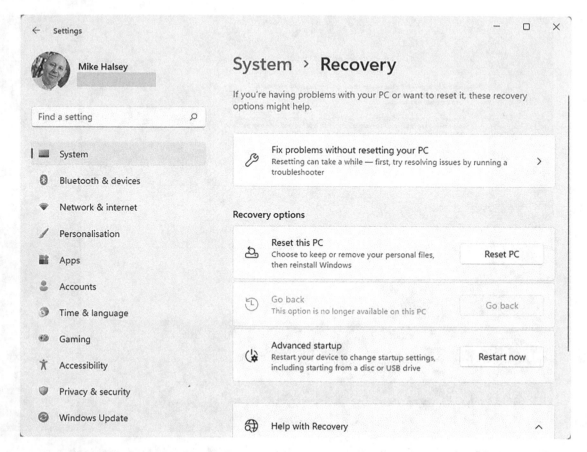

Figure 9-19. *You can reset the PC from Settings*

You will then be asked what type of Reset you wish to perform. You can choose *Keep my files* which will keep your files and accounts intact or *Remove everything* which is the option to choose if you're selling or giving away the PC.

Caution   Resetting a PC will offer to securely wipe data from the drive, but this is not as secure as the double- and multiple-wipe options offered by some software including the excellent and free CCleaner that you can download from `www.ccleaner.com`.

You are then asked if you want to download a fresh copy of Windows or use the local backup (see Figure 9-20).

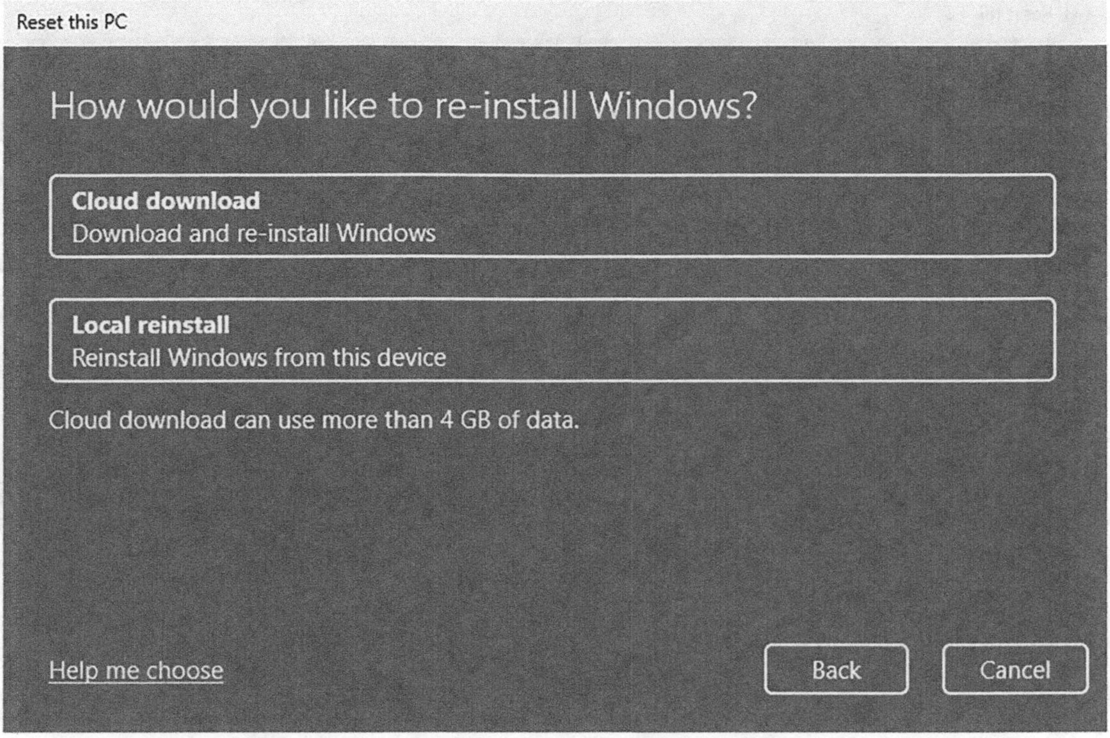

Reset this PC

How would you like to re-install Windows?

Cloud download
Download and re-install Windows

Local reinstall
Reinstall Windows from this device

Cloud download can use more than 4 GB of data.

Help me choose   Back   Cancel

Figure 9-20. *You can choose from a cloud download or local reinstall*

You can use the *Cloud download* option if you suspect the backup Reset image on the PC is perhaps corrupt and won't work for you. Downloading a copy is a good way to ensure you have a fresh, crisp installation that's up to date.

Lastly, and only if you are removing everything, you are asked if you want to *Clean the drive* (see Figure 9-21). I mentioned in the caution earlier that this is nowhere near as secure as other multiple-wipe options, so you should always securely wipe files on a PC that has contained personal files. I have an article on my website telling you how you can securely wipe a PC to sell or donate it, which you can find at https://pcs.tv/3RhD7qz.

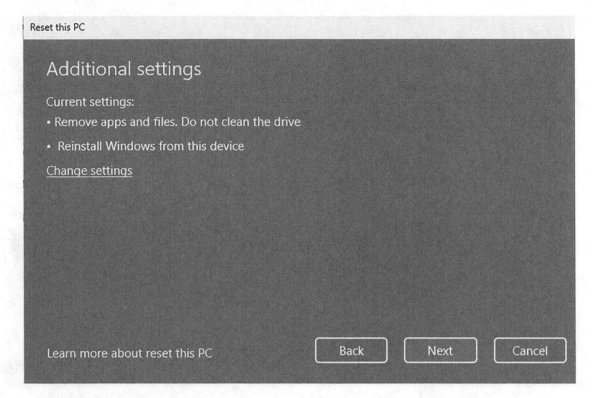

Figure 9-21. *You can wipe the drive for a full reset but use caution*

You can also reset a PC from the Recovery Console, if you can't get it to boot to the desktop. From the main Recovery Console screen, click *Troubleshoot* and you will then see a *Reset this PC* option (see Figure 9-22). This works in the same way as I have described earlier.

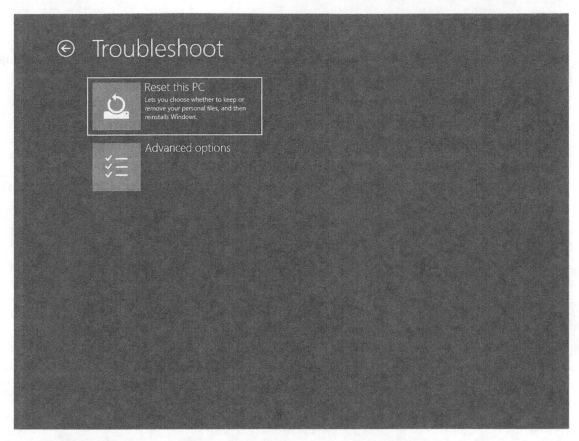

Figure 9-22. *You can reset a PC from the Recovery Console*

The benefit of Reset is threefold. The first is that you don't need to set it up, it's just always working in the background. The second is that you will have a PC afterward that has all your files, documents, and accounts intact and up to date, even if they're stored on the same disk or partition as your Windows installation. This restored PC will also be completely up to date with security and stability patches and the most recent feature update too. You could even slip in a fourth benefit that it won't face removal from Windows 11 in the future.

The downside of Reset however is that it won't keep *any* of your installed software, not win32 desktop apps and not Microsoft Store apps. You will have to reinstall and configure *all* of them after resetting the PC. This makes it a swings and roundabouts option when compared to System Image Backup.

Summary

Clearly, there's quite a bit you can do to repair the operating system itself if it starts going screwy, not to mention just performing a System Restore at any time should you need to. The choice between Reset and System Image Backup can be tricky though, and you might already have and prefer your own system backup software from a third party.

One of the biggest problems facing PC users though is issues with user accounts, documents, files, and drives and what happens when you get a corruption there that prevents you or an end user from signing in or accessing any files. This is what we'll look at in the next chapter.

CHAPTER 10

User Account and File Troubleshooting

There are two things that are always a certainty with PCs. The first is that they'll be used by a person (or people), and the second is that these people will be working on files and documents in order to get stuff done. You can just imagine then the chaos that can befall the land when one of these important services is unavailable.

Windows 11 does include powerful features though for managing user accounts, and account problems, but especially for managing disk, folder, and file access and permissions.

Note   In Chapter 3, I detailed how you can use Group Policy to manage security and access permissions for user accounts. Many IT Pros now though prefer to use Mobile Device Management (MDM) instead of Group Policy for this task. You can read more about MDM on the Microsoft Docs website at `https://pcs.tv/3OWSa7K`.

Configuring User Accounts

The configuration and management of user accounts in Windows 11 now takes place entirely in *Settings*. There are a couple of important aspects of this though that relate directly to business and enterprise usage. These offer options for somebody signing into a PC using their workplace credentials or for when they sign in using their own Microsoft Account and want to add their workplace account as a second set of credentials to the PC.

© Mike Halsey 2023
M. Halsey, *Troubleshooting and Supporting Windows 11*, https://doi.org/10.1007/978-1-4842-8728-6_10

For the latter, open *Settings* and then click *Accounts*, and in the right-hand pane, click *Email & accounts*. Here, you will see an option to *Add a workplace or school account* (see Figure 10-1).

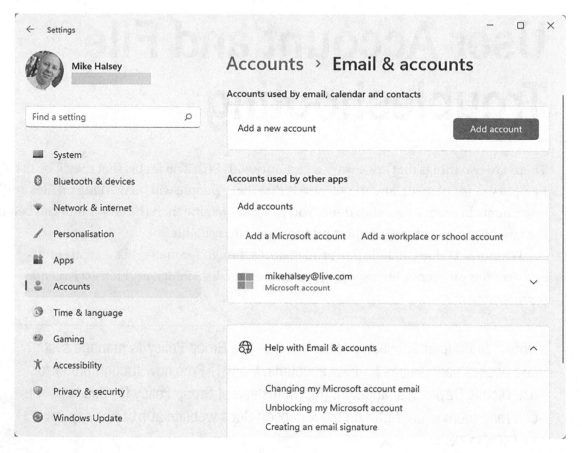

Figure 10-1. *You can add a workplace account as a supplementary account*

This will give the end user three different options for signing in to their workplace account: either through using their username and password, by using a company-supplied security key, or by searching for the organization if it has its accounts and user configuration set up on Azure (see Figure 10-2).

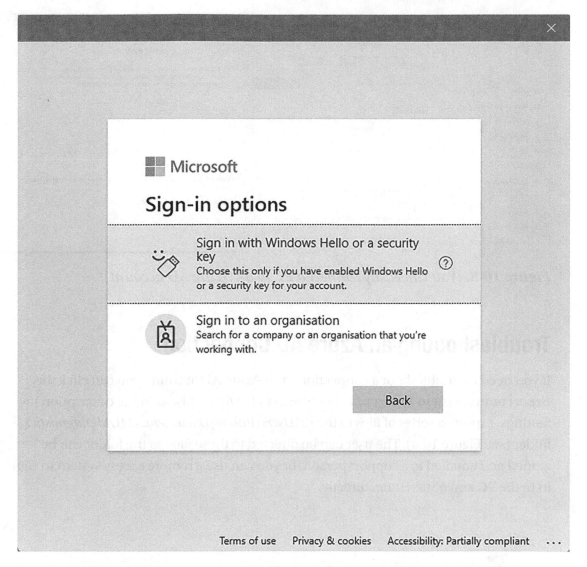

Figure 10-2. *Microsoft makes it easy for people to sign in using a workplace account*

The other method is for people that want to create a whole separate sign-in on the PC for their workplace account. Again, go to *Settings* and *Accounts*, and then in the right-side panel, click *Access work or school*. Here, you can easily connect the PC to a workplace Azure AD account (or a Domain if the user is connecting using their own laptop in the office); see Figure 10-3.

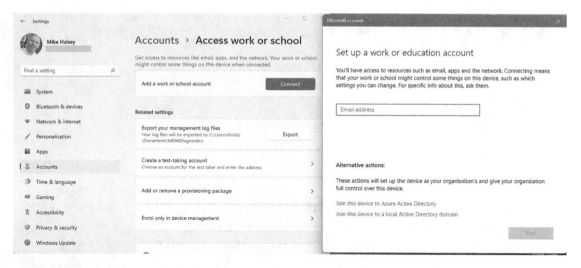

Figure 10-3. *You can easily connect a PC to an Azure AD account*

Troubleshooting an Azure AD Connection

If you need to troubleshoot a connection to an Azure AD account, you can click the *Export* button next to *Export your management log files*. This, as in the description in Settings, exports a series of files to the *C:\Users\Public\Documents\MDMDiagnostics* folder (see Figure 10-4). The user can be directed to these files so the folder can be zipped and emailed to a support person, or you can use a remote access system to sign in to the PC and obtain them directly.

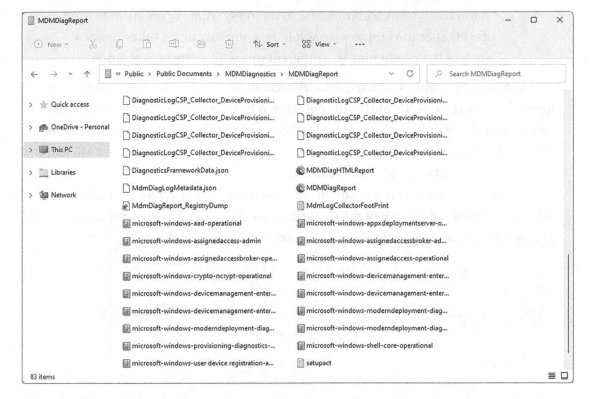

Figure 10-4. *You can export connection telemetry data about an Azure AD connection*

Managing Provisioning and Device Management

In Microsoft's Mobile Device Management (MDM) system, the company provides device management and provisioning systems. This enables a PC that connects to company servers to have certain security managed from a corporate level. None of this affects the end user, but it allows the system administrator to do some important things.

- Specify a minimum level of security for the PC to meet in order for a connection to the company systems to be established. For example, antivirus protection and Windows Updates must be up to date.

- Specify that the user account on the PC must have a password or be protected by Windows Hello biometric sign-in to keep corporate data safe.

- Allow the system administrator to remotely wipe corporate data from the PC after the employee has left the company or for other reasons such as their switching to a different role within the organization.

Additionally, businesses can create *Provisioning Packages* for remote PCs. These allow the PC to be quickly and easily configured by downloading and configuring required business software and policy settings without the need for reimaging the PC. You can read more about how to create a provisioning package on the Microsoft Docs website at `https://pcs.tv/3Cn1CuX`.

Both these systems can be configured in Settings. Go to *Accounts* and *Access work or school,* and near the bottom of the right panel are links to *Add or remove a provisioning package* and *Enrol only in device management* (see Figure 10-5).

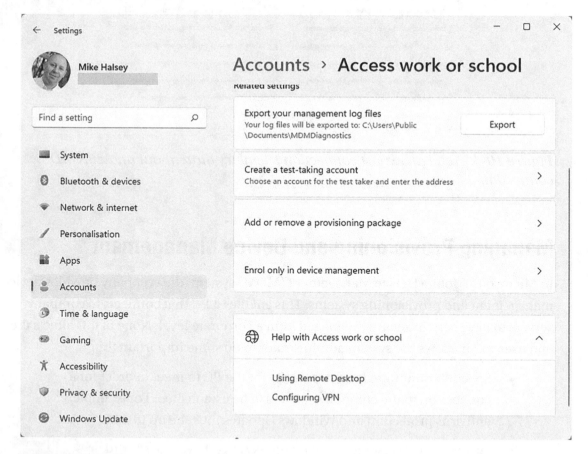

Figure 10-5. *You can manage provisioning packages and device enrollment in Settings*

The first is used if you have provided a provisioning package, either on a USB Flash Drive or by another method such as by emailing it to the user, and the latter can be used if you're happy for the end user to use their own Microsoft Account on the PC, but you still need control over corporate data they access and store on the PC.

Managing Local Accounts

Then we come to local accounts on the PC. These are both created and managed in Settings under *Accounts* and *Family & other users*. In the *Add other user* section, you can click the *Add account* button to add somebody's account to the PC. Also, here, you can then click that account to change the account type (between Administrator and Standard User) or to remove the account and (optionally) its documents and files from the computer (see Figure 10-6).

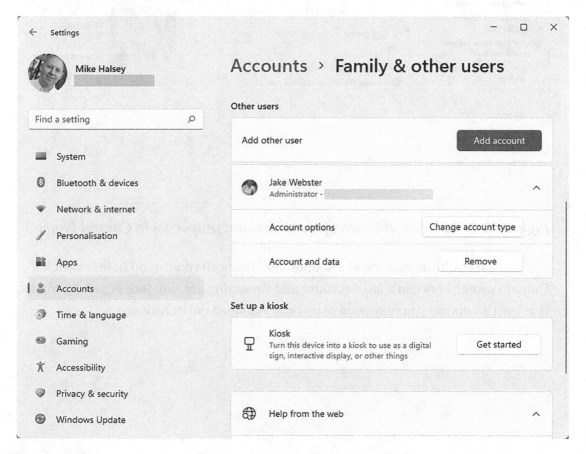

Figure 10-6. *You can add local accounts in Settings*

Other than this, there isn't much you can do in Windows to "troubleshoot and repair" user accounts, and it's often much simpler to delete the account, create a new one, and port over any settings and files needed. If you open *Control Panel* though (and again we can expect this to all be folded into either Windows Tools or Settings at some point in the future), you have options to manage file encryption certificates for the user, something we'll look at in Chapter 17; to manage environment variables, which we'll discuss in Chapter 11; and to *Configure advanced user profile properties* (see Figure 10-7).

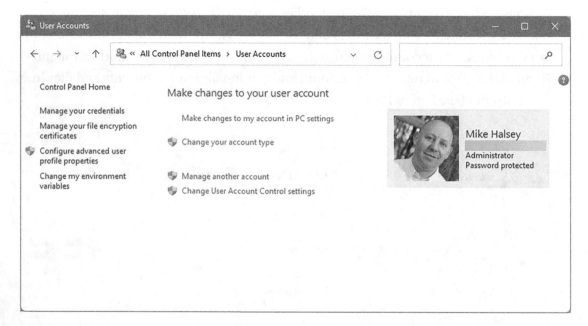

Figure 10-7. *You can still manage some account properties in Control Panel*

This isn't quite as exciting as it sounds, and really all you can do here is switch a Domain profile between a *local* account and a *roaming* account (see Figure 10-8), but it is at least an option you may need to use in a managed environment.

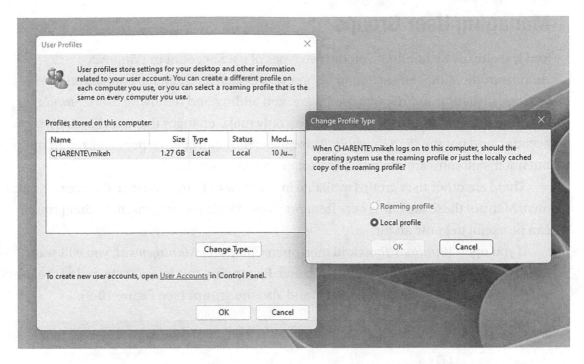

Figure 10-8. *If you use a Domain, options exist to change the account profile type*

Managing User Groups and Accounts

There are many circumstances in which a user could find themselves locked out of files, folders, and even whole disks in a PC. These include a file or disk corruption, working with or from a drive or device on which NTFS permissions aren't supported, which can sometimes be the case with Network Attached Storage (NAS) drives, reinstalling Windows on the PC, transferring files and documents to a different user, having a user switch from one user "group" to another (we'll look at these), and using recovered files after a malware or ransomware attack.

The result can be frustrating at best and pretty catastrophic at worst. Being unable to access a file, folder, or even a whole disk is a problem and a huge barrier to productivity. So how do permissions work in Windows 11, what is inheritance, and how do user groups affect how we can access and work with files?

Managing User Groups

You will already be familiar with the two types of user account in Windows. *Administrator* allows any action to be performed such as changing configuration settings, installing and removing software, and adding and removing users. *Standard* users are different because these users can only make changes that affect their own account, and not the PC as a whole. This means they can change personalization options but not install software except for Store apps, as an example.

There are other user groups available in Windows 11, and you can also create your own. Many of these are hangovers from previous Windows versions, but other groups can be useful to know about.

If you open *Windows Tools* and then open *Computer Management*, you will see a *Local Users and Groups* link in the left panel. Expanding this lets you view all of the users' currently assigned accounts on the PC and also the groups (see Figure 10-9).

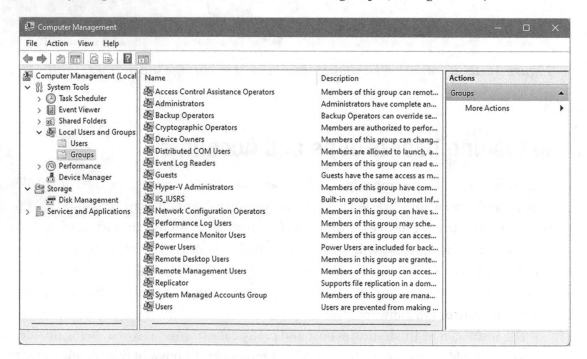

Figure 10-9. *You can manage users and user groups in Computer Management*

Some of these groups you will want to work with for PCs on your network, such as Hyper-V Administrators and Remote Desktop Users. If you double-click a group, a dialog will open displaying details of any users assigned to that group, with *Add* and *Remove* buttons. Click *Add* and you can search for users on the PC, clicking the *Check Names* button to have the system identify the user so they can be added (see Figure 10-10).

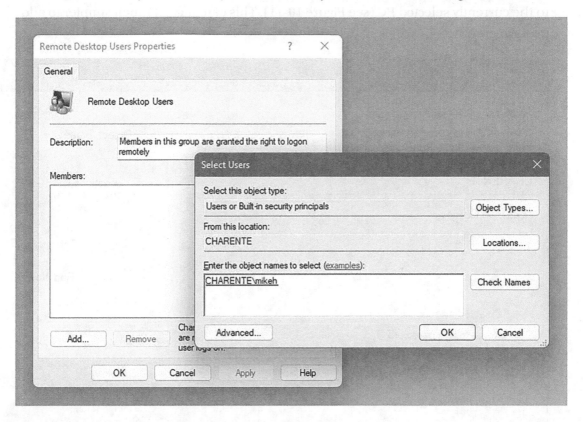

Figure 10-10. *You can add users to user groups*

Using the Select Users Dialog

I want to put in a note about the best way to use the *Select Users* dialog in Windows, as when you're searching for a user you won't always find them when you click the *Check Names* button.

By default, the dialog will search for users on the current PC; in this example, the PC is named *Charente*. Click the *Locations* button to see other network-connected PCs on your network that you have access to, as it might be that a server administrator needs to be added to a group on a PC without having an account on that PC themselves.

If you then click the *Advanced* button, a more detailed search dialog will be displayed. Clicking the *Find Now* button will display a list of every user account assigned to the currently selected PC (see Figure 10-11). This can make it much simpler to add users to groups.

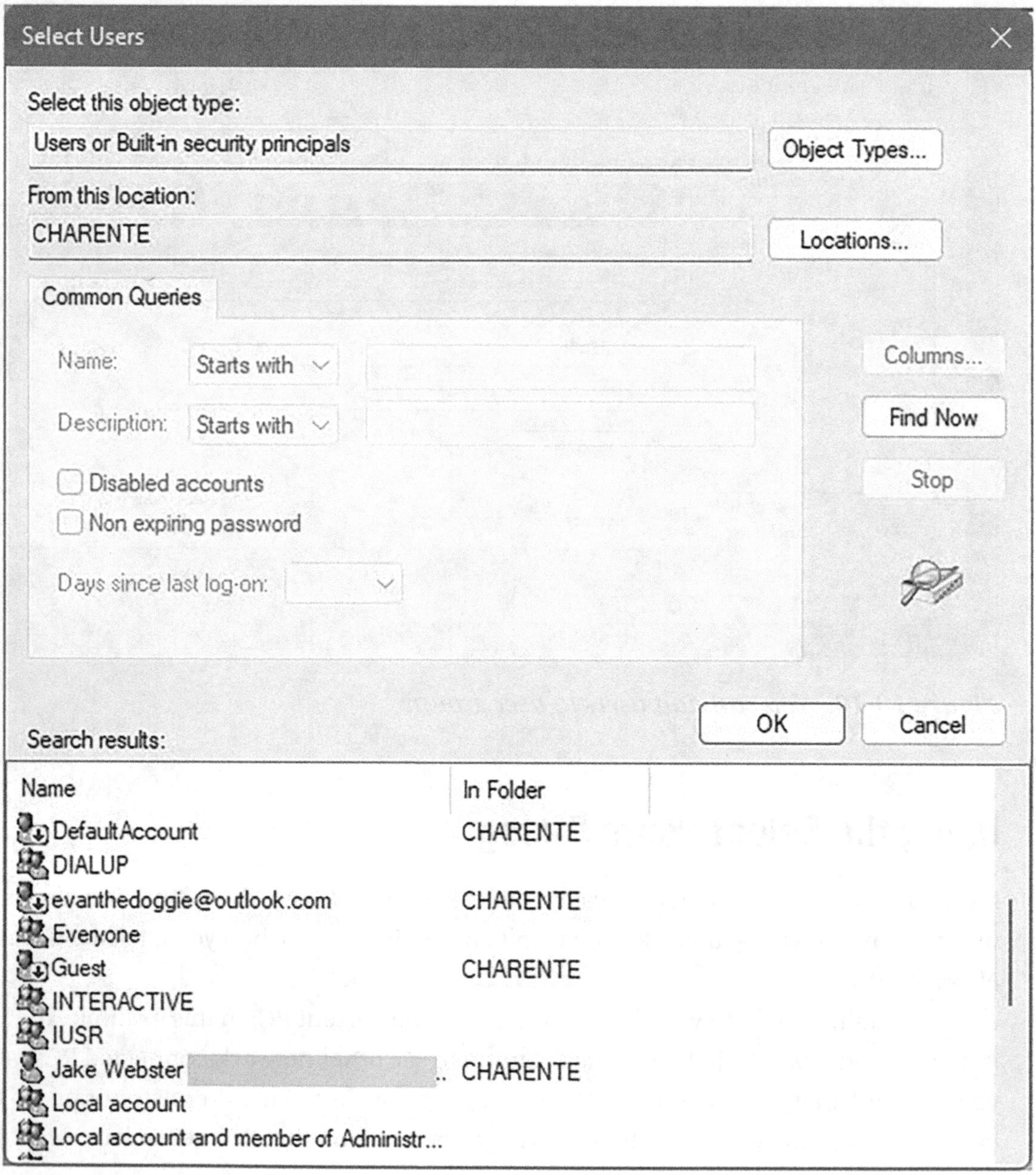

Figure 10-11. *The Select Users dialog can be made to display all users on the PC*

Managing User Accounts on the PC

When it comes to user accounts on the PC, again in *Computer Management*, available from *Windows Tools*, and by clicking *Local Users and Groups* in the left panel, you will see a full list of all the user accounts on the PC (see Figure 10-12). These are listed with the user's full name, if available and applicable, and a description of the account, which is for the default accounts for the Windows system.

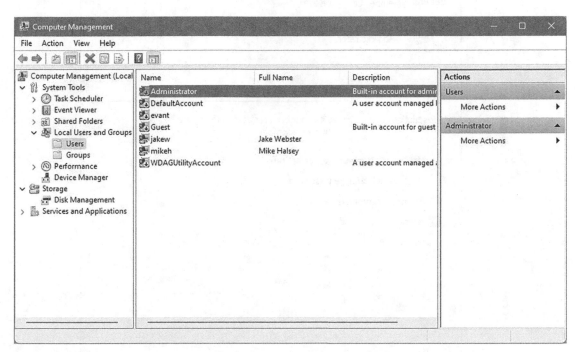

Figure 10-12. *User accounts are managed from the Computer Management Console*

Double-clicking an account will open a dialog with additional details of that account (see Figure 10-13), including whether the account is disabled (and hidden) on the PC and whether the password never expires, if the user must change the password on the next sign-in or if the user cannot change the password.

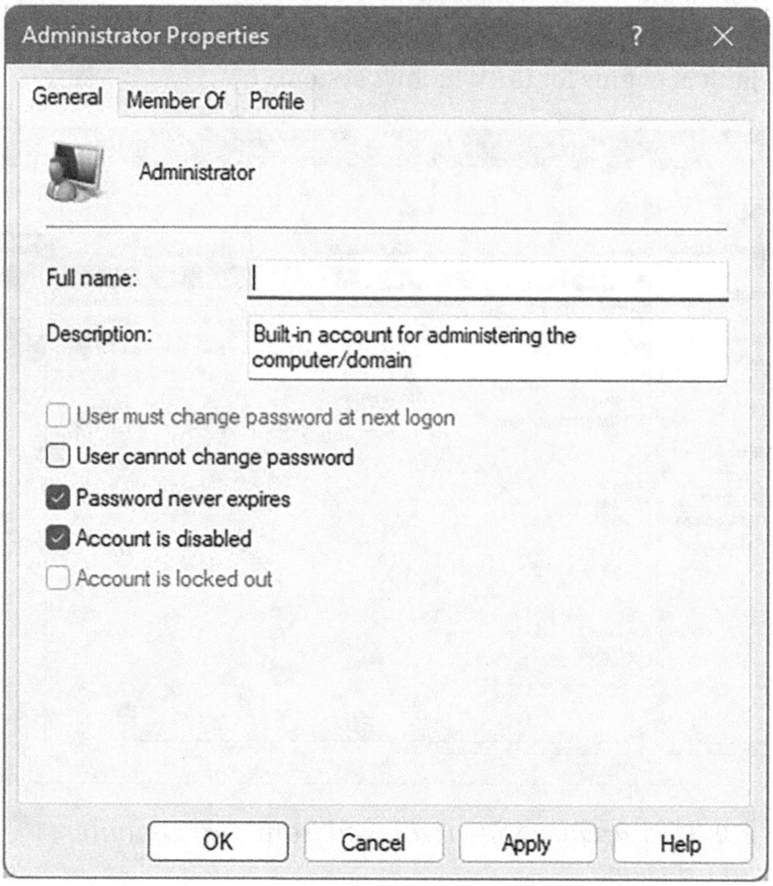

Figure 10-13. *You can manage password settings for accounts*

If you click the *Member Of* tab at the top of this dialog, you will see what, if any, groups that user is assigned to (see Figure 10-14). You will see *Administrator* or *Users* for most users, though some, such as *DefaultAccount*, have their own group. This is because DefaultAccount is the account used as a template when new user accounts are created on the PC.

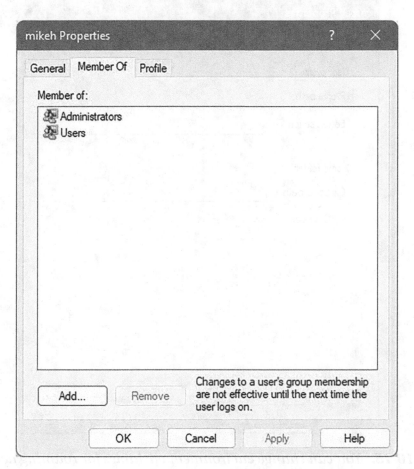

Figure 10-14. *You can see what group(s) a user is assigned to*

If the user has a roaming profile on the PC, such as they connect through a Domain or Azure AD, then the *Profile* tab will allow you to view and change the path to the location of their profile on the server and optionally define a script to be run when the user signs in (see Figure 10-15).

Figure 10-15. *You can change environment variables for roaming account types*

Managing Permissions for Disks, Folders, and Files

Each object in a PC, be it a disk, folder, or file, has permissions assigned to it. These permissions determine what users and what user groups can do with it and if and how they can access it. There are different permission types you can assign to objects, as seen in Table 10-1.

Table 10-1. *NTFS file and folder permission types*

Basic Permission	Description: When Applied to a Folder or Disk	Description: When Applied to a File
Full Control	Allows for the creation, reading, modification, and deletion of folders and the contents of subfolders and for applications to be run	Allows for the creation, reading, modification, and deletion of files and for applications to be run
Modify	Allows for the creation, reading, and modification of folder contents and for them to be run, but not for the subfolders or contents to be deleted	Allows for the creation, reading, and modification of file contents and for applications to be run, but not for the files to be deleted
Read and Execute	Allows the contents of a folder to be accessed and applications to be run	Allows files to be viewed and applications to be run
List Folder Contents	Allows the contents of the folder to be viewed	N/A
Read	Allows content to be accessed	Allows file contents to be accessed but not for applications to be run
Write	Allows adding of files and subfolders	Allows a user to modify, but not to delete a file

You can view and modify the permissions for an object by right-clicking it and selecting *Properties* from the menu that appears. Clicking the *Security* tab in the Properties dialog will display the different user groups that have permissions on the object, and you can click a user group to check what those permissions are (see Figure 10-16).

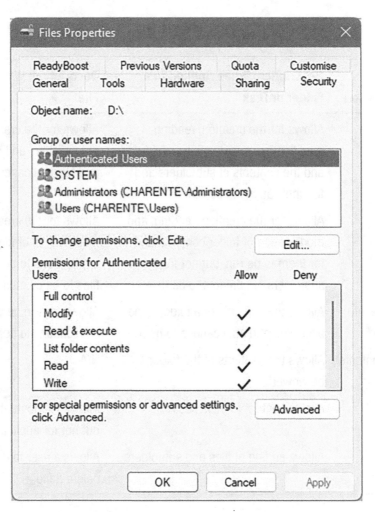

Figure 10-16. *You can check permissions for any object*

To modify the permissions for an object, first make sure you are signed in as an Administrator, and then with the user group you want to change permissions for selected, click the *Edit* button.

This will display a dialog in which you can choose a user group to change the permissions for (see Figure 10-17). You can click the *Add* or *Remove* buttons to add group permissions, and when you are finished, click *Apply* to set the new permissions; note this may take a few minutes if permissions have to be set on multiple items.

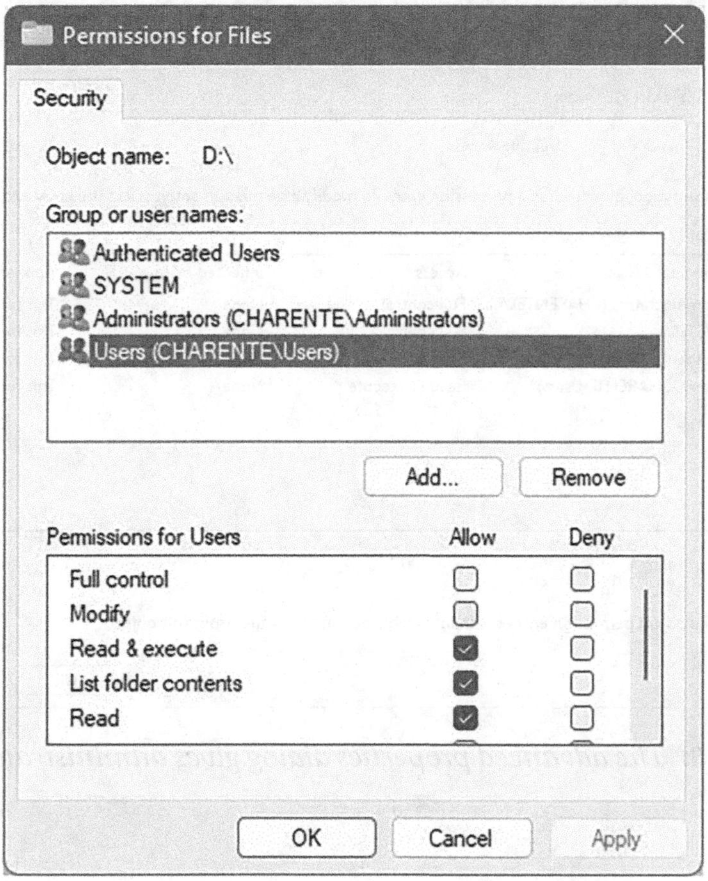

Figure 10-17. *You can edit, add, and remove permissions for objects*

If you want more advanced control than the Permissions dialog provides, from the Properties dialog you can click the *Advanced* button. This will display a different dialog with more available options (see Figure 10-18).

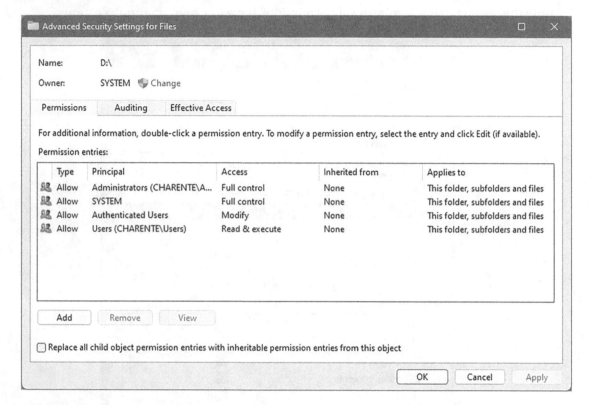

Figure 10-18. *The advanced properties dialog gives administrators more control*

When you select a user group, you will be shown a list of the current permissions that are set (see Figure 10-19). This is very similar to the standard permissions dialog, though additional options are available to you. For example, at the top of the dialog is an option to *Allow* or to *Deny* the permissions you set on the object(s).

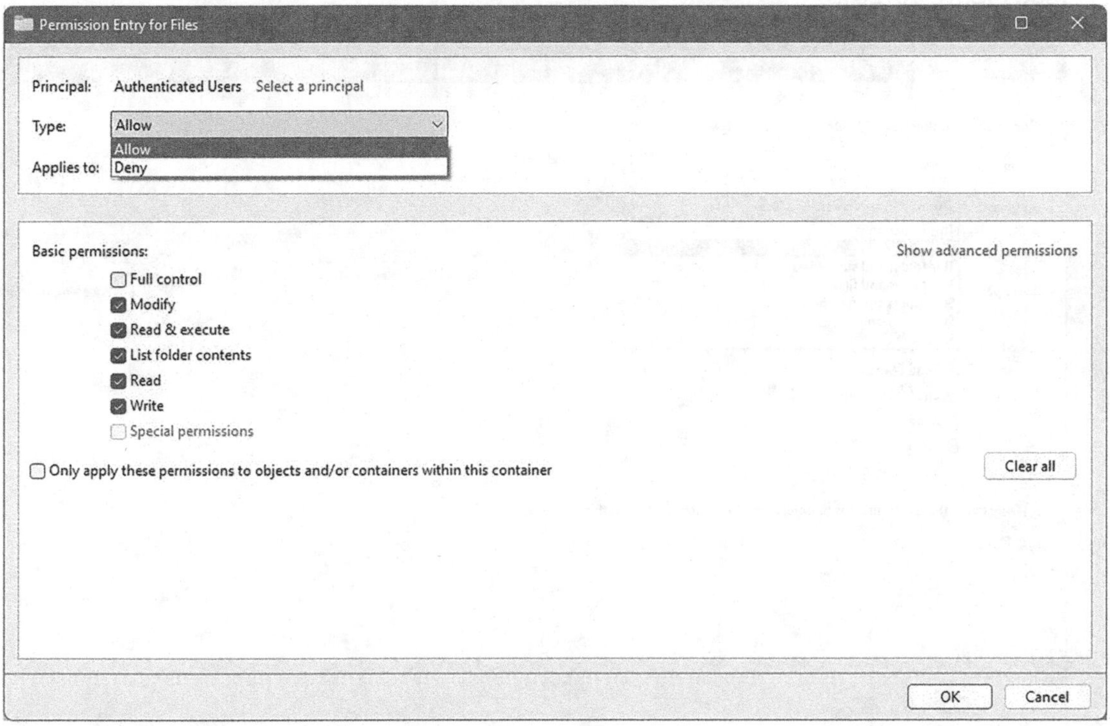

Figure 10-19. *You can manage permissions for objects*

Below this is a drop-down menu where you can have much finer control over what the permissions will be set for, and this is where inheritance comes into play which I will detail shortly. You can choose to set the new permissions only for the current folder, for the folder and everything underneath it, or in a more granular way, such as only for files (see Figure 10-20).

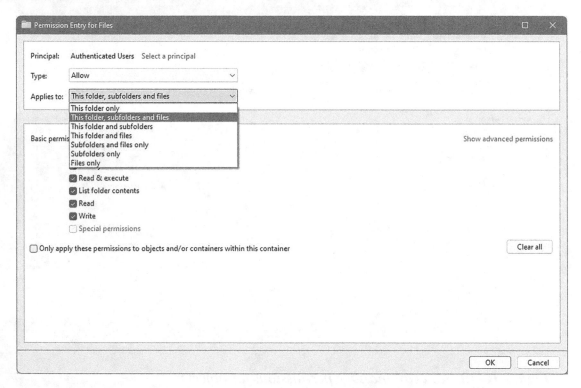

Figure 10-20.   *The dialog allows you to specify what permissions are set for*

Lastly, on the right of the dialog is a *Show advanced permissions* link. Clicking this will display additional permission options that aren't available in the standard permissions dialog (see Figure 10-21). In fairness though, you should never need these extended permissions.

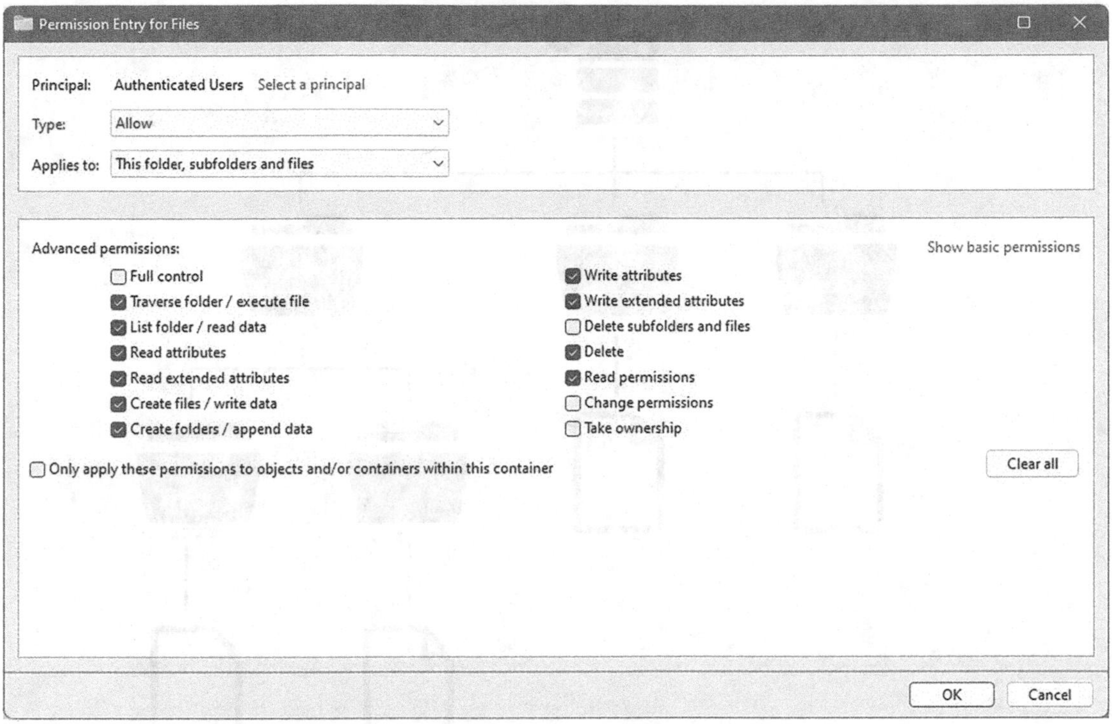

Figure 10-21. You can view and set advanced permissions

Understanding Inheritance

Inheritance isn't when a version of Windows dies and leaves you a ton of money in its will, though they do say "*Where there's a will, there's a wa'hay!*"; rather, it's an easy way to manage permissions on a PC. In short, it means that any object that is created on a disk or in a folder will gain the same permissions as the object it was created from.

Let's say you have a disk that has certain permissions set; this is the principal object, and anything created underneath it will "inherit" the same permissions that the principal has. In Figure 10-22, we can see an example of this with a disk, on which a series of folders, subfolders, and files has been created. All of these folders and files will have the same permissions as the main disk.

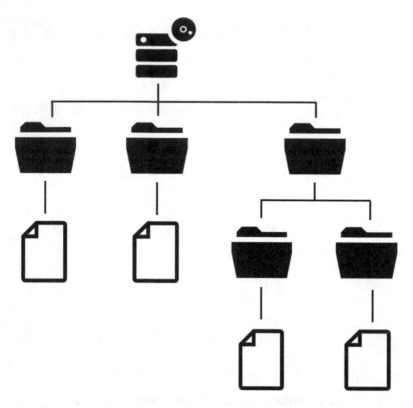

Figure 10-22. *Inheritance is when objects gain their permissions from the objects above them in the tree*

Where this becomes an issue is when files or folders are copied from one source to another, and the permissions for those objects are copied with them and aren't automatically updated by Windows to match the permissions currently set on the destination drive or in the destination folder. This can occasionally occur when copying objects to or from a NAS drive that has its own proprietary file system, copying files from a non-Windows computer across the network, or copying files that are encrypted.

Under this circumstance, you will want to change the permissions on the copied items so that they match the permissions for the principal, or so they have different permissions that you define.

Note   If a folder beneath the Principal has different permissions set, it will then become its own Principal for anything created within it.

Let's say you change the permissions on a folder. You also want to make certain that all the subfolders and files underneath or contained within this folder also have their permissions changed; otherwise, the permissions for those items will remain as they are.

In the advanced permissions dialog, when you change permissions on an object you should therefore make sure in this circumstance to check the box *Replace all child object permission entries with inheritable permission entries from this object* (see Figure 10-23). This will ensure that the permissions are set, not only for the currently selected object but also for all the objects beneath it in the folder tree.

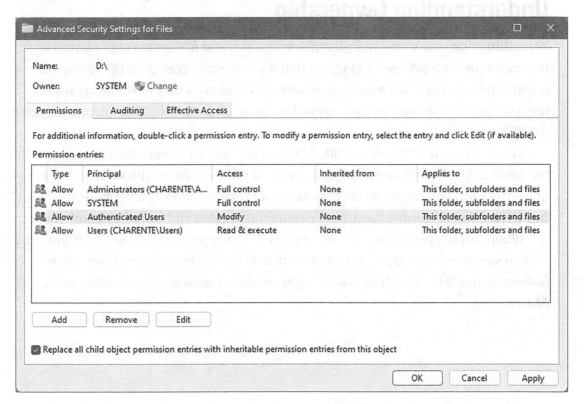

Figure 10-23. *You need to be careful to tell Windows to set permissions for all child items*

Note   For some folders on a PC, you will see a *Disable inheritance* button in the advanced permissions dialog. You can click this to disable the automatic inheritance for new objects created under the folder, though you will later need to check and set their own permissions appropriately.

Understanding Ownership

Something that can occasionally happen when files and folders are copied from a network store, or from another PC, but that is very common after an operating system reinstall on a PC, or when a faulty user account is deleted and a new one created, is that you can find yourself completely locked out of all access for files, folders, or even a full disk.

This is a feature of Windows called Ownership, and it is where the user account that has been defined by the operating system as the owner of those objects denies access to any other user. This happens for reasons of user security and to prevent one user on a PC from accessing or viewing the private documents created and stored by another user.

When this happens, you need to change the owner for the object(s). In Figure 10-24, we can see the advanced properties for both a disk and a folder. They have different owners, with the owner of the disk being *System* and the owner of the folder being *Mike Halsey*.

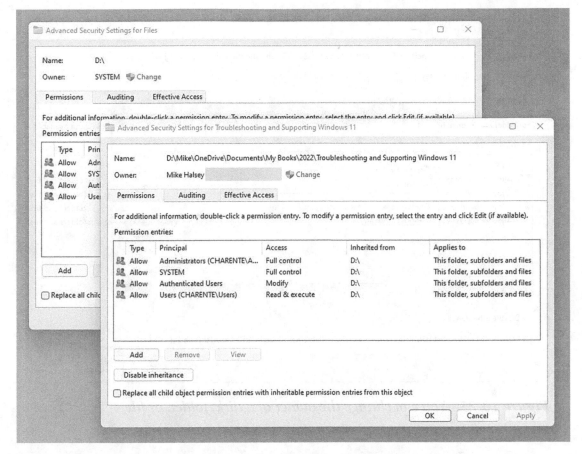

Figure 10-24. *Different objects on a PC can have different owners*

Caution   It is vital that the root of any disk has *System* set as its owner; otherwise, the operating system will not have the permissions it needs to perform vital operations such as virus and malware scans and file backups.

At the top of the advanced permissions dialog, you can click the *Change* link next to the owner details. In the dialog that appears, you can then select a new owner from the accounts set on the PC (see Figure 10-25). Make certain though you check the *Replace all child object permission entries with inheritable permission entries from this object* check box, so that all objects under the folder you have selected also have their ownership changed.

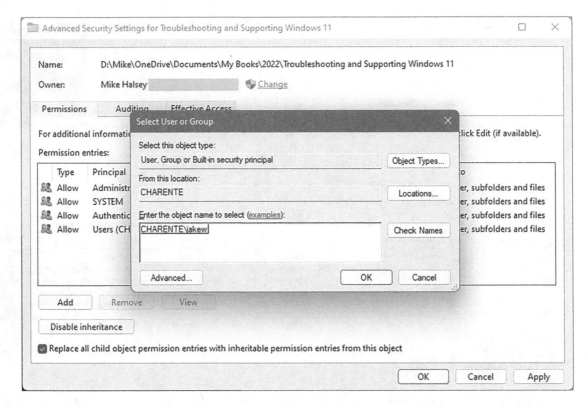

Figure 10-25. *You can change the owner of a disk, folder, or file*

Managing Permissions Using Scripting

If you prefer to use scripting to manage your PCs, you can use the Command Line tool *icacls* which displays and allows you to modify parameters on what's called the *Access Control Lists* for a PC. The operations are performed on *Discretionary Access Control Lists* (DACLs) on the files, folders, or disks specified.

There are a great many switches you can use to display, create, and modify permissions and ownership using icacls, which is used in the format `icacls <filename> [/grant[:r] <sid>:<perm>[...]] [/deny <sid>:<perm>[...]] [/remove[:g|:d]] <sid>[...]] [/t] [/c] [/l] [/q] [/setintegritylevel <Level>:<policy>[...]]`. The full list of switches available to use with icacls can be seen in Table 10-2.

Table 10-2. *Icacls command line switches*

Parameter	Description
<filename>	Specifies the filename for which to display or modify the DACL
<directory>	Specifies the folder for which to display or modify the DACL
/t	Performs the operation on all files in the current folder and in all subfolders
/c	Continues the operation if error messages occur
/l	Performs the operation on a symbolic link instead of the destination drive or folder
/q	Suppresses success messages
[/save <ACLfile> [/t] [/c] [/l] [/q]]	Stores DACLs for all matching files in a backup ACL file for use later with the /restore switch
[/setowner <username> [/t] [/c] [/l] [/q]]	Changes the owner of an object
[/findsid <sid> [/t] [/c] [/l] [/q]]	Finds all files that contain a DACL explicitly mentioning the Security Identifier (SID)
[/verify [/t] [/c] [/l] [/q]]	Finds all files with ACLs that are not canonical or have lengths inconsistent with access control entry (ACE) counts
[/reset [/t] [/c] [/l] [/q]]	Replaces ACLs with default inherited ACLs for all matching files
[/grant[:r] <sid>:<perm>[...]]	Replaces specific permissions on objects; not specifying :r means that permissions are added to any previously specified permissions
[/deny <sid>:<perm>[...]]	Denies permissions for the objects specified
[/remove[:g | :d]] <sid>[...] [/t] [/c] [/l] [/q]	Removes all occurrences of a specified SID from the DACL, use with :g to remove all occurrences of granted rights to the specified SID and :d to remove all occurrences of denied rights to the specified SID

(continued)

Table 10-2. (*continued*)

Parameter	Description
[/setintegritylevel [(CI)(OI)] <Level>:<Policy>[...]]	Explicitly adds an integrity access control entry (ACE) to all matching files, used as l (low), m (medium), or h (high)
[/substitute <sidold><sidnew> [...]]	Replaces an SID (sidold) with a new SID (sidnew), requires the <directory> parameter
/restore <ACLfile> [/c] [/l] [/q]	Applies stored DACLs from <ACLfile> to files in the specified <directory>
/inheritancelevel: [e l d l r]	Sets an inheritance level which can be e (enables), d (disables), or r (disables and removes only inherited ACEs)

Security is obviously very important when it comes to our PCs and especially our files and documents, so you can find detailed information on Security Identifiers (SIDs) on the Microsoft Docs website at https://pcs.tv/3c0goiB.

You can also use PowerShell to manage permissions with the Get-ACL and Set-ACL commands. These are straightforward in the way icacls is, but have many options. Detailed documentation on how this command is used can be found on the Microsoft website at https://pcs.tv/3lKn8UO.

Checking Effective Access for a Disk, Folder, or File

Sometimes, you want to check if a specific user or user group has the correct permissions for a disk or folder, which allows you to determine if those permissions need to be modified. This can be done from the *Advanced Permissions* dialog by clicking the *Effective Access* tab.

Click the *Select a user* link and search for the user or user group you wish to check the access permissions for. When you click the *View effective access* button, the permissions for that user or that user group on the currently selected object will be displayed (see Figure 10-26).

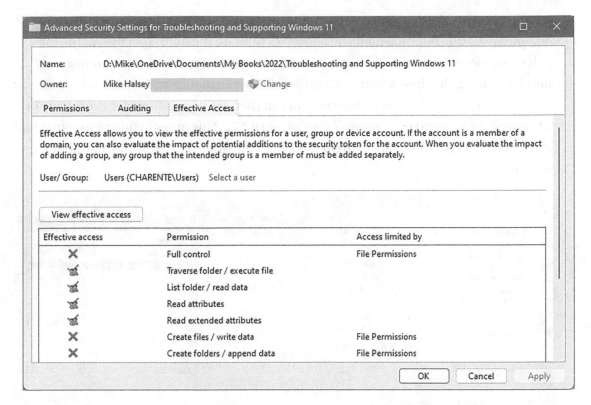

Figure 10-26. *You can check what permissions other users and user groups have on an object*

Managing Object Sharing on a PC

Sometimes, you will have a disk, folder, or perhaps an external drive such as a USB hard disk or optical drive that you want to share from a PC. This can be managed from the object's properties by right-clicking it and selecting *Properties* from the menu that appears.

Tip   Sharing an optical drive, such as a DVD or Blu-ray drive, is a good way for a laptop or tablet to gain access to data or software it requires that's only on an optical disk, but where the optical disk drive is physically installed in another desktop computer.

Clicking the *Sharing* tab reveals options to share the object, but there is also an *Advanced sharing* button which will allow you to share the item, specify a name for it so it can be found easily on a private or domain network, and to limit the number of simultaneous users that can access it (purely for performance reasons).

If you click the *Permissions* button, you can then set permissions for everybody or add specific users and user groups (see Figure 10-27). This means you can assign people read permissions, but not allow them to write to the drive or modify any files that are contained on it.

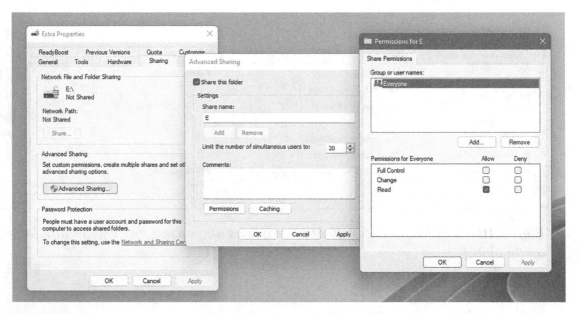

Figure 10-27. *You can configure permissions for shared drives*

Summary

Disk, folder, and file access and permissions can be a headache for system administrators, power users, and home users alike, especially when something has gone wrong that requires either a reinstall while keeping files and documents intact or deleting and creating a new local profile for a user. Fortunately, Windows has for years now included some excellent and fully featured tools for managing those permissions.

We'll take this a step further in the next chapter and look in detail at the file and folder structure of Windows itself. We'll examine what everything is, why it's important, and why the installed operating system on your hard disk is always significantly larger than the 4GB installer you used to put Windows 11 on the PC in the first instance.

CHAPTER 11

Windows 11 File and Folder Structure in Depth

I've just done a count of how many files I have on the C: drive of my PC where Windows 11 is installed. It's not a small number being 689,246 files in 139.196 folders, taking up a not insignificant 1.06TB of my 2TB SSD. This isn't including my documents and files either, which I always store on a separate SSD and which consume 638GB on their own.

This is a lot of files then, but if we focus just on the C:\Windows folder where the bulk of the operating system resides, and that's 277,286 files in 97,319 folders, taking up 27.6GB of space. This is pretty unwieldy given we're always told a Windows installer will occupy a 4GB USB Flash Drive and that Windows can be installed on devices with only a small amount of storage.

Indeed, you may remember that back in the days of Windows 8, there were quite a few tablets released to the market that came with as little as 32GB of eMMC storage (eMMC essentially being a plug-in memory card that's so slow you should always upgrade to the SSD model of any low-end PC or Chromebook that you're looking to purchase).

I still have one of these devices, an HP Stream 7 tablet, and it's stuck on Windows 8.1 not because it won't run Windows 10 (it certainly doesn't meet the security requirements to run Windows 11) but because with just a few apps installed, there's not enough free space for the Windows installer to use. Microsoft had to release a workaround for upgrades to Windows 8.1 for these devices, which I myself had to use, where an OTG (On-the-Go) USB adapter had to be purchased so a Flash Drive could act as temporary storage for the installer.

© Mike Halsey 2023
M. Halsey, *Troubleshooting and Supporting Windows 11*, https://doi.org/10.1007/978-1-4842-8728-6_11

This storage limitation effectively made the operating system, and ultimately the device, completely unusable unless you only ever used the built-in apps like Mail and lived in the web browser for everything else.

Fortunately, 32GB Windows devices are a thing of a past as OEMs (Original Equipment Manufacturers) quickly realized they were, effectively, rubbish. It's not uncommon for devices to come with just 128GB of storage though, and eMMC disks too, such as the Microsoft Surface Go which, as I write this, comes with both for its basic configuration.

When you think that the Windows installer is and has for years now only been around 4GB in size, what do I have installed to have enabled that to balloon to 27.6GB? Well, this isn't software, as I didn't even count the Program Files and Users folders in that figure; it's Windows, or, rather, the multiple copies of Windows that reside on your PC. Let me explain.

Windows Files and Folders

Windows comprises four different types of files: files that are available to view and open/manipulate on the PC, files that are *Hidden* from the user but otherwise available to view in File Explorer, files that are marked as *System* which really is a sort of "You can't find me!" double-hidden, and files that are locked by the operating system because frankly they're very important.

You can view the first two categories of hidden files in File Explorer by clicking the three horizontal dots icon for the menu, selecting *Options*, and from the dialog that appears, clicking the *View* tab and changing the options for *Show hidden files, folders and drives* and *Hide protected operating system files (Recommended)* (see Figure 11-1). Honestly though, there's no real reason to do either.

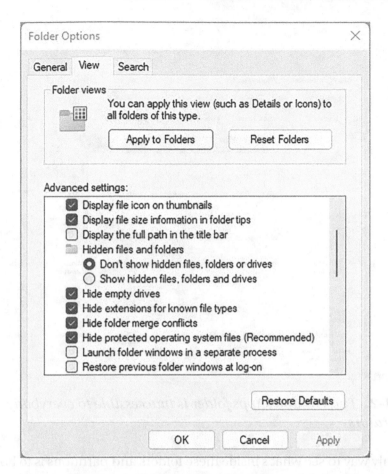

Figure 11-1. *You can display hidden and system files in File Explorer*

The third category of hidden files and folders are ones that are truly locked by the operating system and inaccessible for reasons of maintaining good security on the PC. This means that even as an Administrator, you cannot access these files and folders because if malware were to gain Administrator privileges, as can happen, then all manner of merry hell could be unleashed on your PC and across your network.

There are only a few of these which include the UEFI system boot partitions, something we'll look at in depth in Chapter 20 when we cover troubleshooting problems with the Windows boot system. The other is the hidden **C:\Program Files\ WindowsApps** folder (see Figure 11-2). This contains configuration and security files for apps installed through the Microsoft Store which, now win32 and other types of more traditional programs can be installed from there can make a PC much more secure overall.

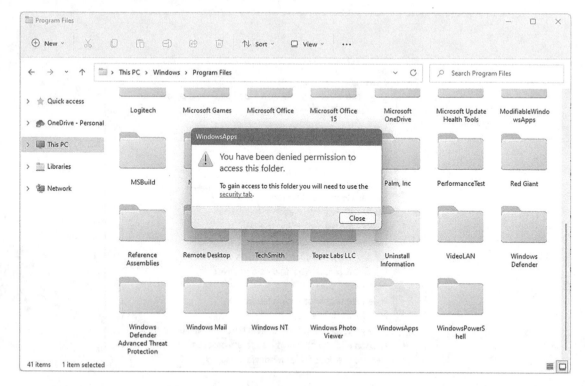

Figure 11-2. *The WindowsApps folder is inaccessible to everybody, including Administrators*

The only way to see what's inside these folders and partitions is to boot the PC from a compatible portable OS, such as GNU/Linux.

Why Are Operating System Files Visible to the User?

This asks the question: Why is most of the operating system visible to the user and why are just a few folders and partitions truly protected? Surely, after all, the whole OS should be like this? You'd be right if Windows 11 was a modern operating system, which of course it isn't.

You don't have to dig very deep in Windows 11 to find interface elements that date all the way back to Windows 95 (see Figure 11-3) and even earlier in some cases.

Figure 11-3. *Is Windows 11 still Windows 95 in a party dress?*

If you look at who uses Windows, then home or prosumer users are a very small percentage of the overall user base. Most users these days want the simplicity of an iPad or a Chromebook. I have Windows PCs, but I need the full desktop environment and software for my job; let's be honest, it would be difficult for me to write authoritatively about an operating system I no longer used. I'm also a PC gamer, something I'll come onto again in a while, as I prefer the full keyboard and mouse control a PC gives you, and the only other platform that provides that, Mac OS, has almost no serious games and certainly not the ones I enjoy such as *Elite Dangerous*.

A year after Windows 11 was released, Windows overall was still Microsoft's biggest cash cow. This is despite the company's cloud services, Azure, still growing exponentially year on year now for more than a decade.

I asked a senior figure at Microsoft just a month before writing this why the traditional file and folder structure still existed, as clearly Microsoft was keen to move to a much more secure future for desktop computing; see my comments about Windows 10X in Chapter 1.

Clearly, I already knew what the answer was, but I wanted to hear it from them. The answer was clear, "We will not do anything that breaks any functionality for corporates." Microsoft gets an awful lot of telemetry about how people use Windows, what features they use, how often they're used, and so on. Now don't panic about this as all the data is anonymized. Microsoft only needs to know that nobody is using X or Y feature anymore, so it can be marked for removal.

What this does mean though is that Microsoft can see that among desktop PCs running Windows 11 Enterprise, there are still B% of machines where program compatibility settings, something I'll talk about in Chapter 12, are being used for one or more programs, and that C% of older, custom programs still need Administrator privileges to run.

Why is this? Well, there are two reasons. The first is that many businesses and corporations have older software they've been using for years, perhaps much longer than a decade, and they don't want to replace it with a new, modern app because (A) it still works, (B) the staff would all need to be retrained on the new app which costs time and money, and (C) because most corporate executives wouldn't recognize the value of spending money on upgrading something if they stepped in it.

The other reason, certainly the reason for older software requiring Administrative privileges, is that before the days of Windows Vista, lots of programs were very poorly, very sloppily written. This is simply a case of programmers being lazy and not bothering to code anything properly.

Microsoft then sees all the telemetry saying that D% of older win32 programs need direct access to R and S in the Windows file system, and they know that if they try and make the core OS any more secure by hiding those folders and files, they'll break those programs completely. For as long as major corporations are Microsoft's bread and butter, and for as long as they're refusing to replace those older programs with modern apps, the situation will sadly never change.

This was the reason for Windows 10X, where apps would run in a virtualized environment that simulated a traditional PC, but where the actual file system was inaccessible to the user. Sadly, that OS model was cancelled at the time because on lower-end hardware it had horrible performance and programs all ran really slowly.

When it comes to the folders that are protected, these are all things that came into existence with or after the advent of Windows Vista and User Account Control. Any programmer writing a program for a PC after that time would know they'd have to code things properly, and, as such, Microsoft could afford to be more strict with the file system and operating system files.

What Are the Root Files and Folders on a PC

The folders on the C:\ drive of a PC will actually vary depending on what software and features you have installed, as some PCs will have a Bluetooth folder or one related to specific hardware of software such as an AMD or an Xbox Games folder. There are folders though that are the same across all PCs.

Root Windows Folders

- **MSOCache** will be seen only on systems with Microsoft Office 2007 or a later version installed. It contains installation files for the Office suite that are used if the installed apps need to be repaired; it is not needed for the most recent editions of Office.

- **ProgramData** contains win32 app data that applies to all users on the PC. This includes configuration and other files necessary for the apps to run. It can be a very large folder but should never be deleted.

- **System Volume Information** is seen on all of your hard disks and is used by the System Restore and File History features, the latter likely to be removed in a future build of Windows 11. It contains archived and encrypted versions of critical system files, such as the Registry, and files that change on app installations. It does this with versioning control, so that System Restore can roll back to previous versions if needed. It is also used in a limited way by the File History feature for version control of your documents.

Win32 Program and Store App Folders

- **Program Files** and **Program Files (x86)** are the folders in which win32 desktop apps are installed. The Program Files (x86) folder is only seen in the 64-bit versions or Windows, and of course Windows 11 only comes in a 64-bit version. This is a hangover from earlier versions of the OS. It is where 32-bit software is installed, though some 64-bit software does end up being installed here, presumably because of decisions made by the publishers including Adobe.

- **Program Files\WindowsApps** is the install location for all Microsoft Store apps. This folder is heavily protected by the OS, to the point where even the local Administrator account cannot gain access to it.

- **Packages** is a folder found in the **Users\[UserName]\AppData\ Local** folder. This is where Microsoft Store apps are installed. If you have a very large Store app, you can copy an installation folder from here to another PC, as I did with an installation of the 320GB game, *Microsoft Flight Simulator*. This folder can also be accessed by using the address **%localappdata%\Packages**.

Windows Operating System Folders

- **Windows\AppPatch** contains application compatibility files.

- **Windows\Boot** contains files necessary for starting the OS; I detailed these in Chapter 13.

- **Windows\CSC** contains offline files and documents, used for caching.

- **Windows\Cursors** contains cursor and icon files for the OS.

- **Windows\Debug** contains Windows error logs. I'll talk more about the log files shortly.

- **Windows\Fonts** where all the installed typefaces on your PC are installed.

- **Windows\Globalization** where language packs, dictionary files, and other files relating to location are stored.

- **Windows\IME** contains language files used by the OS and apps, also IME (x86) on 32-bit systems.

- **Windows\ImmersiveControlPanel** contains the files that constitute the Settings panel.

- **Windows\INF** contains device driver installation files.

- **Windows\Media** contains audio and video files that are used by the OS, such as sound packs.

- **Windows\Prefetch** the system Windows uses to load commonly used files before you open them. The OS tries to anticipate what you want to use and open. Sometimes, this cache can become corrupt, and if so, it is safe to delete the contents of this folder.

- **Windows\Resources** contains ease-of-access themes, accessibility themes, and other themes for Windows.

- **Windows\Security** contains security files and logs used by Management Console snap-ins.

- **Windows\SoftwareDistribution** is the folder used by Windows Update. Should you find that Windows Update is unable to download or install any updates, you can completely delete the contents of this folder. I detailed the process of how to do this in Chapter 9.

- **Windows\System** exists to maintain compatibility with legacy apps that do not look for the System32 folder.

- **Windows\System32** is the main repository of all files that constitute the Windows operating system.

- **Windows\System32\Config** contains the main Registry files used by the OS. Additional Registry files can be found in the %userprofile% and %userprofile%\AppData\Local\Microsoft\Windows folders.

- **Windows\System32\Drivers** contains installed driver files.

- **Windows\System32\Divers\etc** contains configuration text files such as the Hosts file, which can be used to modify the mapping of host names to IP addresses.

- **Windows\System32\GroupPolicy** contains Group Policy script and template files.

- **Windows\System32\icsxml** contains files used by the Universal Plug-and-Play feature for hardware.

- **Windows\System32\Microsoft** contains cryptography files.

- **Windows\System32\oobe** contains files that are used by the Windows Out-of-Box Experience when setting up new users on the PC.

- **Windows\System32\ras** contains remote access encryption files for Windows server connections.

- **Windows\System32\Recovery** contains files used by the Windows Reset feature.

- **Windows\System32\restore** contains files used by the System Restore feature.

- **Windows\System32\spool** contains files associated with your installed printers and the print spool queue.

- **Windows\SysWOW64** used to store files necessary to maintain app and driver compatibility between 32- and 64-bit code.

- **Windows\Tasks** contains scheduled task files.

- **Windows\WinSxS** called the Windows Side-by-Side folder. It contains multiple copies of dynamic link libraries (DLLs) and other files that are crucial to your app and OS operation, but where different versions of the same file may be required to be loaded by different apps simultaneously. This folder can grow to an enormous size but is crucial to the operation of Windows 11.

- **Windows\Web** contains images used by the lock screen and for Windows wallpapers.

User Account Folders

- **Users\[UserName]\AppData\Local** is also known by the shortcut **%localappdata%**; this folder contains the data and settings that are necessary for installed apps and for your user profile to operate correctly. Internet temporary files are also stored in this folder.

- **Users\[UserName]\AppData\LocalLow** contains data that cannot be moved and has lower-level access on your PC, such as when a web browser is used in privacy mode.

- **Users\[UserName]\AppData\Roaming** can be accessed by the shortcut **%appdata%**. It contains data and settings that can move with your user account, such as when you are connected to a domain.

Windows Log Folders

- **PerfLogs** is where custom Data Collector Sets that are created in the Performance Monitor are stored.

- **Windows\Debug** is where log files are created when an app or service crashes or when certain audit processes are performed, such as installing Windows Updates. These logs are stored in plain text format and can be read in Notepad.

- **Windows\Logs** is the main log folder for the Windows OS. It contains many log files such as WindowsUpdate.log. These files are sometimes stored as Extensible Markup Language (XML) files that can be opened in a web browser. Many files, however, are stored as Event Trace Log (ETL) files. You can read these files in the *Event Viewer* by clicking the *Action* menu and then the *Open saved log* option.

- **Windows\Minidump** contains crash reports that are created by applications and Blue Screens of Death (BSOD). They have the file extension .dmp. You cannot read these files in Notepad and will need the Windows Driver Kit (WDK) or Windows Software Development Kit (SDK), both of which are available as part of Microsoft Visual Studio.

- **Users\[UserName]\AppData\Local\CrashDumps** contains crash dump files that are pertinent to the specific user account. They can also be accessed through the address **%localappdata%\CrashDumps**.

Windows Temporary File Folders

- **Users\[UserName]\AppData\Local\Temp** is the main temporary file storage, stored on a per-user basis. It is used for multiple purposes, including downloaded files and web pages that are viewed in your browser. You can most easily access it by navigating to **%temp%**.

- **Users\[UserName]\AppData\Local\Microsoft\Windows\ INetCache** is used for storing temporary Internet files.

- **Users\[UserName]\AppData\Local\Microsoft\Windows\ Temporary Internet Files\Low** is another Internet files temporary folder.

- **Windows\Temp** is a protected temporary file store used by the OS and apps.

Windows File Types

- **Bootmgr** is a critical file required at PC startup.

- **Desktop.ini** is a file found in every folder on your PC. It contains configuration data about how that folder and its contents should be viewed in File Explorer.

- **DLL** files, dynamic link library files, contain code shared by many different apps and services. These apps and services can call upon DLLs to perform tasks that may be required by different apps, such as managing the print queue and displaying window furniture.

- **EXE** files, win32 apps that can be run on a double-click of the mouse.

- **Hiberfil.sys** is the Hibernation file that stores the PC's memory state.

- **INF** files are device driver installation files.

- **INI** files are configuration and option files for apps and Windows features.

- **Thumbs.db** contains thumbnail images of files and documents within a folder. You may also have some **ehThumbs.db** files, which were used by Windows Media Center from Windows XP to Windows 7.

- **Pagefile.sys** and **Swapfile.sys** are used by the virtual memory feature in Windows 10.

- **SYS** files contain system settings used by the OS and both software and hardware drivers on the PC.

Managing the Shell User Folders

In Chapter 9, I talked about how when I set up my desktop PCs, I always have a second SSD on which I store all of my documents and files. This is for several reasons, some of which no longer apply really. I used to always create and maintain System Image Backups of my Windows installation, something else I discussed in Chapter 9, so that when a problem arose with the operating system I could simply reimage the machine without affecting any of those files.

These days, Windows 11 is very stable overall and the need the I and many people had to reimage Windows once a year to refresh it doesn't really apply anymore.

The other reason though, and it's more pertinent these days, is that I have a huge amount of files, over 600GB, but I also use a large amount of very large software. Just the packages I use with Adobe Creative Suite come in at 22GB, then there are a series of virtual machines running in Hyper-V that take up 240GB of disk space.

I'm also a gamer, and rather than wanting a powerful desktop for work plus another powerful PC for gaming, I have a single machine that can do both. I mentioned before that I'm an *Elite Dangerous* player, well, that's 50GB, then there's 320GB for *Microsoft Flight Simulator*. I also have friends using my PC for gaming when they come to visit, and that's another 310GB.

All in it's more than a terabyte just for Windows 11, software, apps, and games. It makes sense then to store my best part of a terabyte of documents and files somewhere else.

There are a few ways to move the Shell User Folders (Documents, Pictures, Music, Video, and Downloads) to a different location. By far, the simplest is to use cut and paste in File Explorer from the current location to the new one. When you do this, Windows 11 knows what you're doing and automatically updates all the OS references for you.

Alternatively, if you right-click any of these folders and select its *Properties* from the menu that appears, a dialog will open in which you can manually change the location of the folder in the *Location* tab (see Figure 11-4).

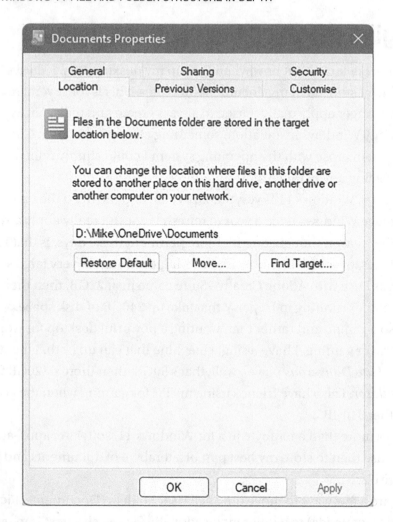

Figure 11-4. *Windows makes it easy to move the Shell User Folders*

If you want more control, you can move folders in the Registry Editor. Navigate to the following keys to find all of the shell user folders and many additional folders such as the location of local and roaming profile stores:

- HKCU\Software\Microsoft\Windows\CurrentVersion\Explorer\ User Shell Folders

- HKCU\Software\Microsoft\Windows\CurrentVersion\Explorer\ Shell Folders

You can see in Figure 11-5 that the Registry gives you much more control over the locations of user folders on the PC, though you need to restart the machine for any changes to take effect. I will show you in Chapter 19 how to connect to the Registries of other users on the PC and how to connect to the Registries of remote PCs to make changes on a wider scale.

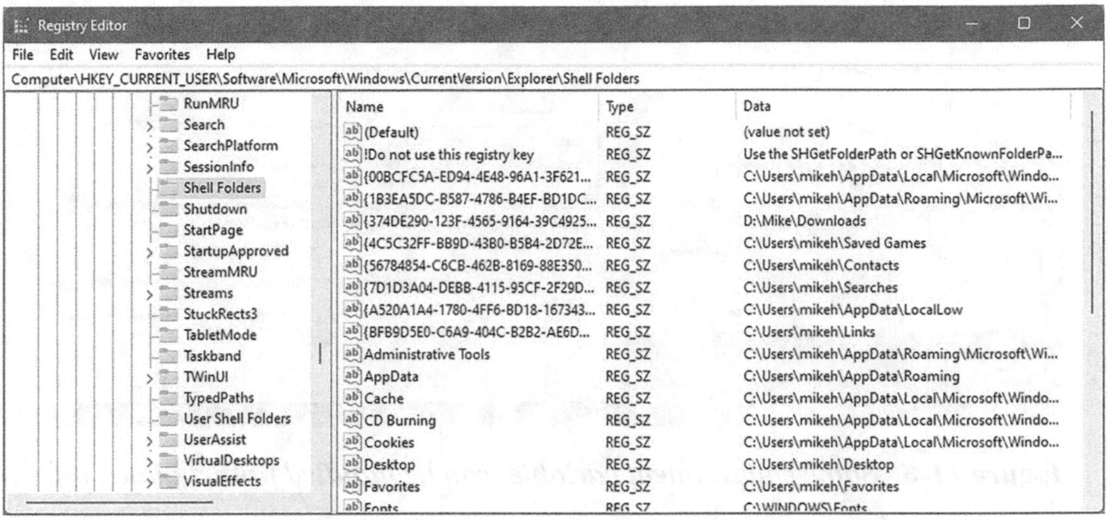

Figure 11-5. *The Registry gives you full control of shell user folders*

Some additional controls can be found by searching in the Start Menu for **Advanced System Settings** and clicking the *Environment Variables* button in the dialog that opens (see Figure 11-6). These controls are much more limited however but can offer a friendlier interface than the Registry Editor for some folders.

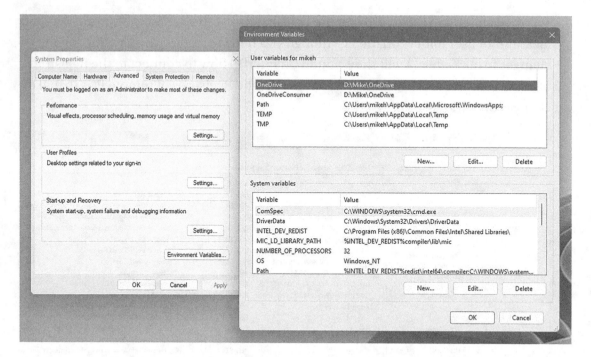

Figure 11-6. *Some environment variables can be handled from a dialog interface*

Creating Symbolic Links

A symbolic link is a virtual file or folder, appearing to be in one location where the actual file or folder is stored elsewhere, such as on a network share. Windows has supported symbolic links since Vista, and they can be useful for giving people quick access to files that are not stored on their own computer.

The best example of a symbolic link is a shortcut icon that you might drag (sometimes accidentally) onto your desktop or into a folder (see Figure 11-7). It's a quick way to access files elsewhere, but if you delete the symbolic link, the original files remain untouched.

Figure 11-7. *An example of a symbolic link is a folder shortcut*

There are two types of symbolic link in Windows. A **soft link** is one that works in a similar way to a shortcut, and it can be created for anything from a file to a disk. It's useful for creating an easy way for someone to access a network share, but if the name or location of the destination file or folder changes, the link will break.

Hard links on the other hand are pointers not to the item but to the storage space holding it. This means that any changes to the destination are always and immediately reflected at the other end of the link. Hard links are mostly used to provide a secondary access address to something and have the disadvantage that if you delete the hard link, you will also delete whatever is at the other end of it.

With a soft link though, you can delete the link without deleting whatever is at the destination, as the link and destination are different things. All of this makes hard links only really useful for specialist purposes for backups and programming, and soft links good for everything else.

To create a symbolic link, you use the Command Line tool **MKLINK**. Let's say I want to create a symbolic soft link to the folder \\N5\n2\Virtual Machines on my NAS drive and link it to a folder called "VMs" on the E: drive on my PC. I would use the command MKLINK /D E:\VMs \\N5\n5\Virtual Machines.

The **MKLINK** command is used with the following syntax: MKLINK [[/D] | [/H] [/J]] [Link] [Target] where

- **/D** creates a link to a directory.

- **/H** creates a hard link which makes it look as though the file or folder actually exists in the target destination and can be useful for times where software is having compatibility issues with standard soft links.

- **/J** is used to create a directory junction, which is a hard link that acts like a hard disk, partition, or disk volume.

- **[Link]** is the new symbolic link location and name.

- **[Target]** is the file or folder you want to link from.

Disks and Partitions

The files, folders, and documents we have all reside on our physical disks and on partitions on those disks. At the beginning of this chapter, I detailed why Windows 11 supports so many legacy options and features, and it's no different with disk and partition types and formats.

Windows 11 does try and limit what you can do with disks and partitions however. If you open the *Computer Management* console from Windows Tools and click *Disk Management* in the left panel, or just search in the Start Menu and launch *Create and format disk partitions*, then you get very limited options for formatting disks and removal drives.

Hard disks and SSDs installed in the PC can only be formatted in the NTFS file system, more on this shortly (see Figure 11-8), and USB Flash Drives can only be formatted as NTFS or exFAT.

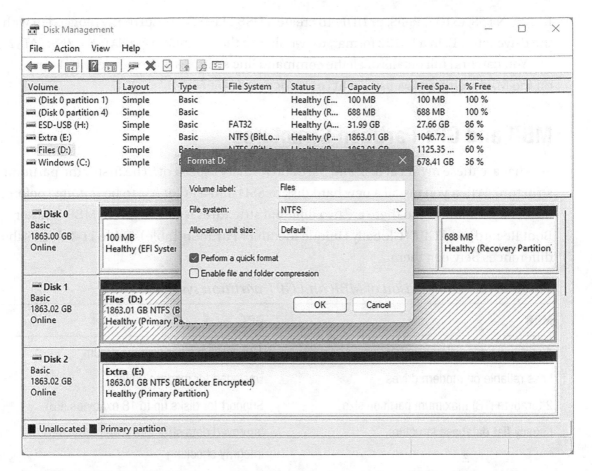

Figure 11-8. *The Disk Management Console tries to limit how you can format disks*

Sometimes though, you might need a different format. One of the oldest is FAT32 (File Allocation Table, 32-bit), and if like me you have a UEFI firmware on your motherboard that supports taking screenshots (some of which I have needed throughout this book), only a FAT32 formatted drive will work.

To get greater control, we need to use the **FORMAT** command from the Command Line. This is used with the syntax

```
Format <volume> [/FS:file-system] [/V:label] [/Q] [/L[:state]] [/A:size]
[/C] [/I:state] [/X] [/P:passes] [/S:state]
```

There are many switches you can use with the Format command, but the most relevant to this example is **/FS:filesystem**. You can specify different options here: FAT,

FAT32, NTFS, exFAT, ReFS, or UDF. To create a USB Flash Drive currently plugged in with the drive letter E: in a FAT32 format, we would use the command FORMAT E: /FS:FAT32.

You can find full details of all the command line switches you can use with Format on the Microsoft Docs website at https://pcs.tv/3AAPF6x.

MBR and GPT Partition Structures

So what are these mythical disk and partition formats I speak of? The first is the partition structure. When you install a new hard disk or SSD into a PC, it has to be *initiated* before it can be formatted, and there are two different structures it can be given, MBR (Master Boot Record) and GPT (Globally Unique Identifier Partition Table). Table 11-1 details the differences between them.

Table 11-1. *Comparison of MBR and GPT partition systems*

MBR	GPT
4 partitions per disk maximum	128 partitions per disk maximum
Less reliable on modern drives	Designed for modern drives
2 terabyte (TB) maximum partition size	Support for disks up to 18 exabytes (EB)
Legacy flat database structure	Improved data structure with parity and integrity checking
No built-in redundancy	Creates primary and backup partition tables
Bootable from BIOS, or legacy BIOS mode on EFI firmware systems	Bootable only from an EFI firmware interface
Available to all removable media types	Not available for removable media
MBR disk can be converted to GPT disk	Conversion to MBR only available with all partitions removed

Windows File Systems

Once a disk has been initiated, it can be formatted in a variety of ways. The default is NTFS (New Technology File System), which was first introduced with Windows NT 3.1, but the others include CDFS (for Compact Disks and DVDs), UDF (Universal Disk

Format), FAT12, FAT16, FAT32 which dates from the time of DOS, exFAT which is a modern version of FAT designed for USB Flash Drives and that supports large disk and file capacities, NTFS, and ReFS which is a relational database structure used by Windows Server. The differences between these and their uses are detailed in Table 11-2.

Table 11-2. *The different file systems available in Windows 10 for formatting*

File System	Characteristics
FAT (FAT16)	First introduced in 1981 and supported by DOS, OS/2, Linux, and Windows 3.1 onward
	Only available through the **Format** command at the Command Prompt. Use with the switches Format X: /FS:FAT
FAT32	Supported by Windows 95 SP2 and later, file size limit of 4GB, volume size limit of 32GB
	Only available through the **Format** command at the Command Prompt. Use with the switches Format X: /FS:FAT32
	Used for taking UEFI screenshots in supported firmware
exFAT	64-bit support with extended file allocation table, introduced with Windows Vista and designed specifically for Flash Storage Devices
	Volume size limit of 256TB and supports more than 1000 files per directory
	Widely supported, can be used from the Format option in File Explorer or from the Disk Management Console
	Has no native file encryption or compression, does not support Bitlocker To Go
	In-place conversion from exFAT to NTFS drives using the command CONVERT F: /fs:NTFS

(continued)

Table 11-2. (*continued*)

File System	Characteristics
NTFS	*New Technology File System*. Default file system in Windows since Vista, supports Bitlocker drive encryption and 64-bit file tables with redundancy
	Volume sizes up to 256TB with file sizes up to 16TB
	Proprietary so not supported by all non-Windows devices and operating systems
	Can be used from the Format option in File Explorer or from the Disk Management Console
ReFS	*Resilient File System*. First introduced with Windows Server 2012, designed for data storage with a relational database-type file system
	Has dependability, redundancy, and stability baked into the design
	Has no support for compression or encryption. Not available for use on bootable drives
	Only available through the **Format** command at the Command Prompt. Use with the switches `Format X: /FS:ReFS`

Summary

The Windows disk, folder, and file structure can at best be described as "complex," and this is why security features such as User Account Control (UAC) exist to help prevent the end user or malware from deleting or changing anything they shouldn't.

On my own PC, the WinSxS (Windows Side-by-Side) folder that contains multiple different versions of DLL (dynamic link library) files that are required by both the OS and installed software on the PC is a whopping 10GB. I have known people in the past to wonder what this is, assume they don't need it, and delete it, only to discover afterward that Windows won't work and none of their software will load.

Speaking of software, that's where we're going to take this next, as it's only logical at this point to discuss how to troubleshoot software and app compatibility and how you can repair apps that aren't working on a PC, not to mention looking at how the addition of Android apps in Windows 11 might complicate things further.

CHAPTER 12

Apps and Software Troubleshooting

Software is probably one of the most complex and convoluted aspects of a modern PC as there's just so much variety now supported. You can run a DOS script from 1981, a 32-bit application from Windows 95, a 64-bit program that was written a week ago, or a Windows Store app that was introduced with Windows 8. Now it's even more complex with the addition of Android apps installed from the Amazon Appstore. If we add the ability to run programs and scripts designed for GNU/Linux and the BASH command line, then things get more complex still.

Why Windows is so cross-compatible is an easy question to answer, and that answer comes in two parts. With regard to the legacy software, Microsoft collects telemetry (completely anonymously) that tells it what aspects of the operating system are being used, how often, and on how many PCs. Much of this telemetry will come from corporate customers, many of whom still have older, legacy software that in many if not most cases was written specifically for them to perform a role crucial to the business. Microsoft will simply not remove anything from the operating system that breaks functionality still being used by customers.

The people that wrote that code however will have long since moved on and left the company or even retired in some cases. In other cases, the original source code will no longer be available, won't be complete, will be undocumented, and will be messy and difficult to discern (delete as applicable). The third reason is that executive boards will just not see the benefit in investing money into replacing this software when what they already have still works. These aren't technically minded folks, and so they don't see the challenges it all throws up for the system administrators that have to keep things running smoothly.

© Mike Halsey 2023
M. Halsey, *Troubleshooting and Supporting Windows 11*, https://doi.org/10.1007/978-1-4842-8728-6_12

With regard to the more modern code, such as the addition to Windows of the Subsystem for Linux and the Subsystem for Android, these aren't just things that Microsoft chucked in because they wanted to. The Subsystem for Linux was first introduced to encourage more software development on Windows. Microsoft learned the hard way with Windows 8 and Windows Phone that an operating system lives or dies on the volume and quality of apps and software that is available for it, and they could see a large number of developers abandoning the platform and buying Apple Mac computers so they could instead develop for iOS, which was seen by many as being more lucrative for them.

With the additions that Apple made to iPadOS in 2019 that allowed for multitasking and windowed apps, there was now a much more credible competitor to Windows laptops and the Microsoft Surface Pro devices. Microsoft had to do something and embraced software development in a big way. Bringing the BASH shell, a scripting environment favored by many software developers, to Windows was just the start, and they followed this up with the ability to run Linux GUI (Graphical User Interface) apps and then with the purchase of the online developer platform GitHub.

Android apps on Windows came out of a development project for Windows Phone. Microsoft had tried, unsuccessfully, to launch their new app development platform UWP (Universal Windows Platform) with its own app store with Windows 8 and Windows Phone, and it turned into an unmitigated disaster for them. Firstly, developers were simply not interested in redeveloping apps they'd already written for iOS and Android for a third platform, and especially when Windows Phone was so late to the market and consequently had such small market share. Secondly, Microsoft shot themselves squarely in the foot with the apps they released for Windows 8 which looked like they'd been programmed by a complete novice with zero user interface knowledge.

So Microsoft spent a while looking into bringing Android apps to Windows Phone instead to try and revive the platform. Nobody knows the real reason why it never happened. The best known story is that it worked too well, and from this one of two things could have happened. Most people believe that Microsoft's higher-ups thought it would damage development of Windows apps even more, but there's a chain of thought that Google objected to the idea.

This is given more credence when you consider that the original sliding panel design of Windows Phone in its first iteration, which brought all your social media, contacts, messaging, and photos from different platforms into sideways-scrolling aggregated panels, and which was utterly brilliant, was later removed from the OS after complaints from companies, including Google and Facebook, that wanted people using their own apps instead so they could collect tracking and usage data and push advertising to them.

Microsoft is known though for not completely abandoning good technologies, and even though they may sit on them for some years, development is often picked up again somewhere down the line. When Microsoft thought about opening their app store to third parties, with the Epic Games Store being first in line, Android seemed like a good fit. Microsoft couldn't come to terms with Google, but Amazon stepped in with its own, somewhat limited but still useful Android app store.

With the addition in Windows 11 of Microsoft allowing not just UWP apps to be distributed through the Microsoft [App] Store but also Win32 apps, and those made using other technologies such as PWAs (Progressive Web Apps), Microsoft sought to reestablish itself as the platform to develop apps for once again.

And so we end up with this slightly complex, slightly messy application environment that is Windows 11. For the most part though, the new app platforms, with apps delivered through the store, take care of themselves. However, this doesn't help the beleaguered system administrator that has to make sure a program written before they were born still operates as it was intended.

Managing Legacy App Compatibility

Which brings us neatly onto the subject of software compatibility as Windows 11 will not run 16-bit apps that were designed for Windows 3.1, but it will still run apps designed for Windows 95, and that operating system was released 26 years before Windows 11 was announced.

Program compatibility begins with installation, and this is where we start to see some of the legacy issues with Windows itself. You might remember me mentioning earlier that for custom apps developed by companies and corporations, the original code might be messy, undocumented, or simply unavailable; well it's a similar case with Windows.

In order to make sure that legacy features still work in the operating system, many of them have been left as-is. Sometimes, this is because the code really is undocumented, sometimes it's because the code is messy, sometimes it's because the original developer has long since left the company/retired/passed away (etc.), but often it's because as different programming languages have been developed over the years, different Windows features have been written in different languages, and sometimes it's best to just leave well enough alone.

When you install a program in legacy compatibility mode, then you have a hoop to jump through. The first step is to right-click the installer to bring up a menu of options. Then however, whereas you might normally select *Properties* from the menu, you instead need to click *Show more options* (see Figure 12-1).

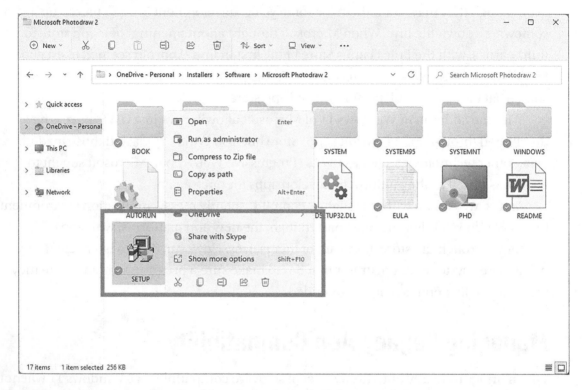

Figure 12-1. *Some see the "dumbing down" of the Windows 11 interface as a retrograde step*

This will reveal a second menu that looks completely different from the Windows 11 interface, because it's an older Windows component that was written in a different programming language in a different time (the desktop interface of menus, Start Menu, and Taskbar in Windows 11 is all new code). You have two options with this menu, either click *Troubleshoot compatibility* (see Figure 12-2) or click *Properties*.

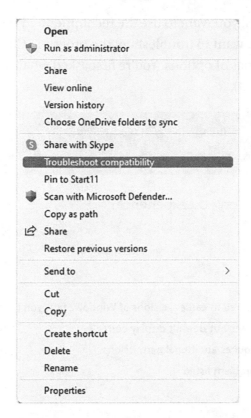

Figure 12-2. *There are two ways to install a legacy program in Windows 11*

The Program Compatibility Troubleshooter

So let's start with the first of these, the Program Compatibility Troubleshooter. This is something that can be run at any time for even an installed program, I'll show you how in a while, and that can help you solve compatibility issues if you're unsure what are the best settings to use.

You're first asked if you want to use the recommended settings (which likely won't fix the problem) or if you want to troubleshoot the program. Choosing this option will then talk you through a series of options. You're first asked what type of issue it is that you're having (see Figure 12-3).

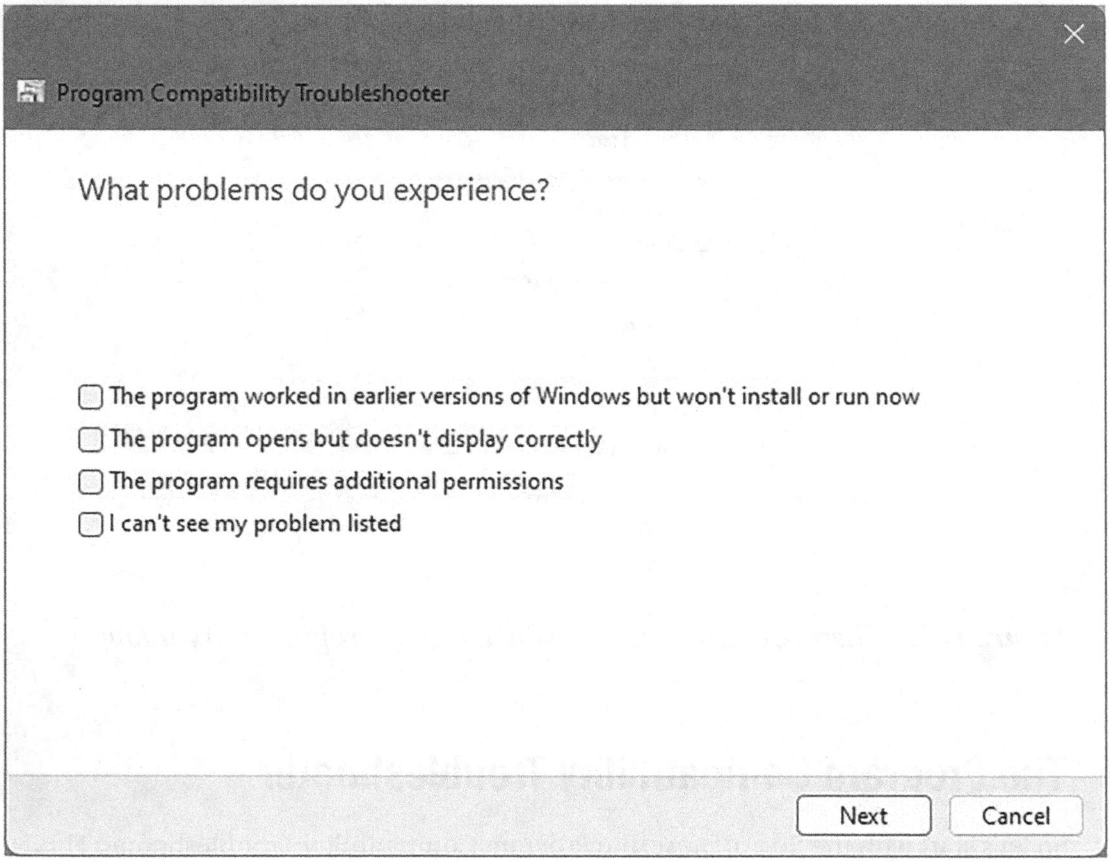

Program Compatibility Troubleshooter

What problems do you experience?

☐ The program worked in earlier versions of Windows but won't install or run now
☐ The program opens but doesn't display correctly
☐ The program requires additional permissions
☐ I can't see my problem listed

Next   Cancel

Figure 12-3. *The Program Compatibility Troubleshooter asks a series of questions*

It asks if the program worked in earlier versions of Windows but doesn't work now, if it opens but won't display correctly, or if it requires administrator privileges to run.

If you select the first option, you are then asked in which version of Windows did the program work perfectly before (see Figure 12-4). For the Program Compatibility Troubleshooter however, this only goes back to Windows XP.

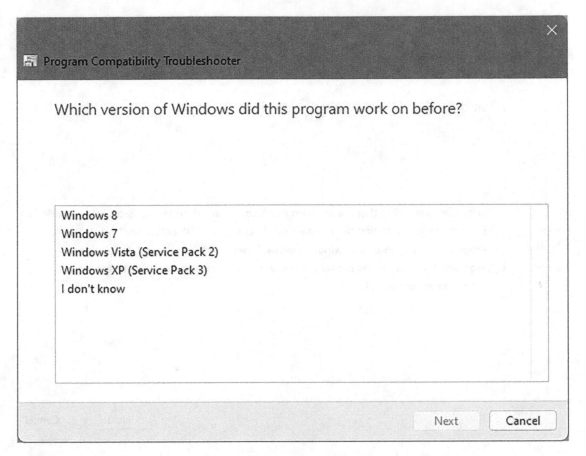

Figure 12-4. *You are asked in which version of Windows the program worked before*

If the problem is how about the program not displaying properly when it is run, you are asked if you get an error message or if the program just doesn't display correctly (see Figure 12-5).

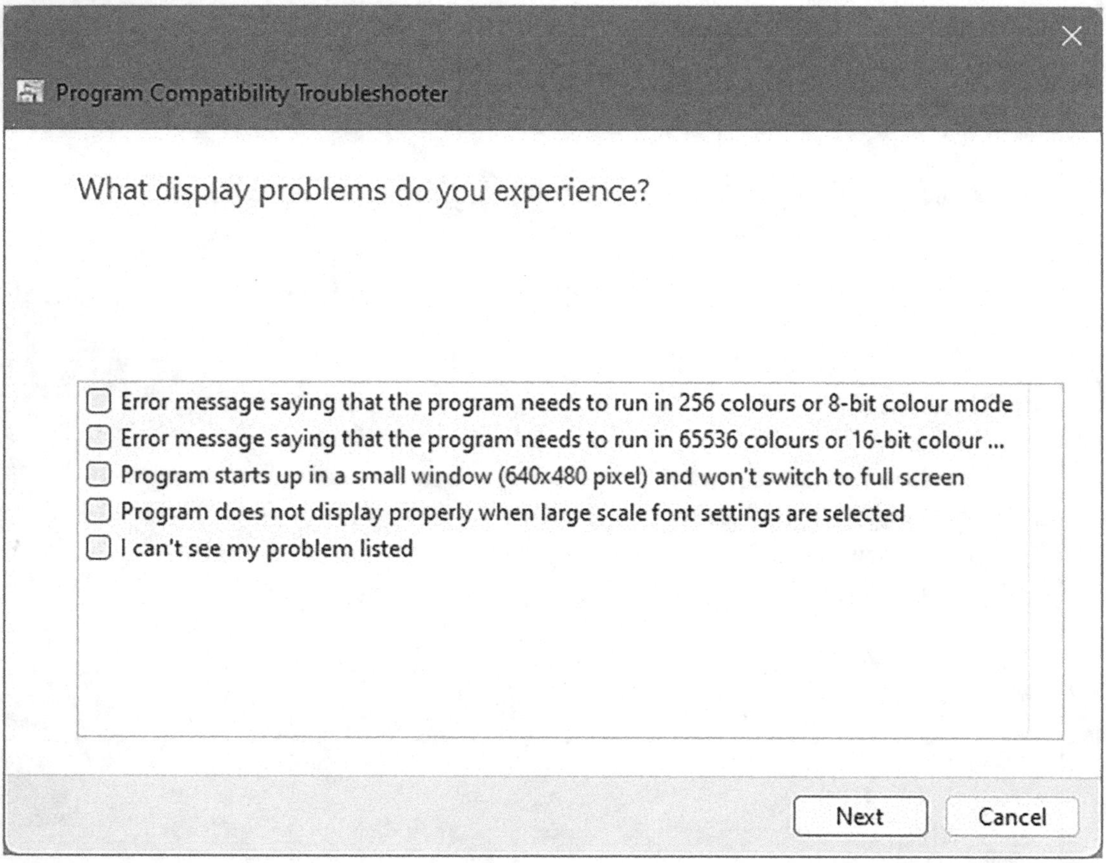

Figure 12-5. *Windows asks what happens when a program won't display correctly*

With the questions answered, Windows will set what it thinks are the best compatibility settings and then ask you to test the program (see Figure 12-6), before asking again if things worked.

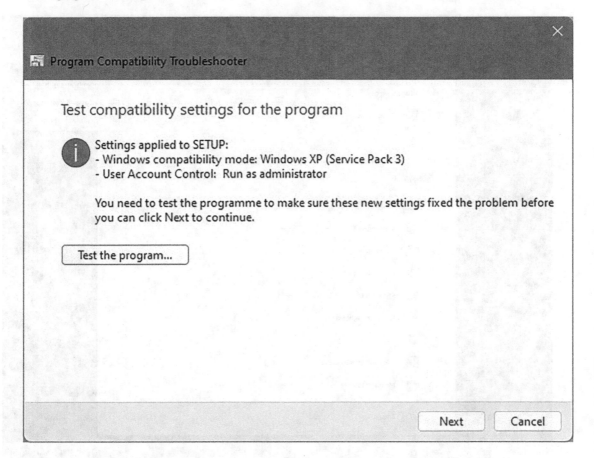

Figure 12-6. *The Troubleshooter asks you to test the program to see if it now works*

Manually Configuring Compatibility

If you need to set compatibility for a program manually, you first need to get access to its *Properties* panel. If the program's icon is on the desktop or is pinned to the Taskbar, then right-click it and select *Properties* from the menu that appears.

This option doesn't appear though for anything pinned to the Start Menu or in the All Apps list. Here, you should right-click the program, then from the menu that appears, select the *More* option and finally *Open file location* (see Figure 12-7).

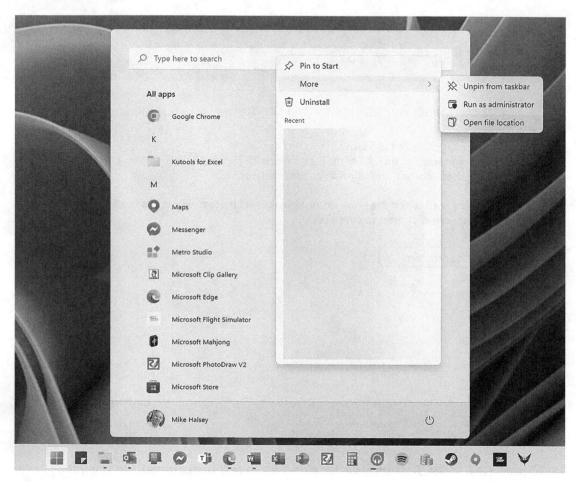

Figure 12-7. *Accessing the Properties panel for a program in the Start Menu is complex*

The next step is either going to work for you, or it won't as the results can vary depending on what software it is you are troubleshooting. File Explorer opens with a link to the "shortcuts" for the program in the Start Menu. You can then right-click the program and select Properties to get to the compatibility options (see Figure 12-8).

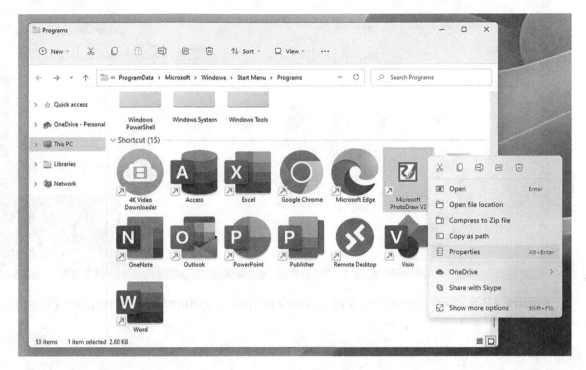

Figure 12-8. *You can right-click a program's shortcut icon*

If this doesn't work, then you'll need to navigate in File Explorer to the actual location on the disk, most likely in the C:\Program Files (x86) folder where the program resides. The Properties panel for the shortcut might tell you where this is if you won't know.

From the Program Files (x86) folder, you can then right-click the program icon and select *Properties* to get to the compatibility options (see Figure 12-9).

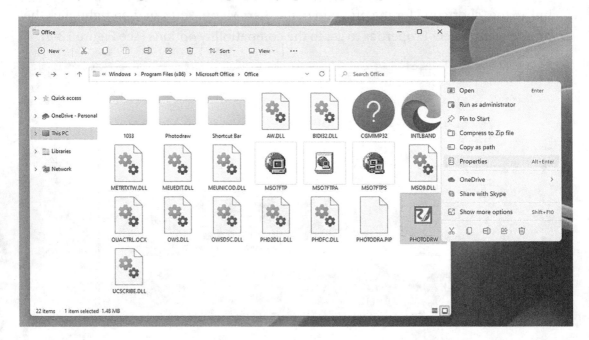

Figure 12-9. *You can access a program's properties from the C:\Program Files (x86) folder*

When you have the program's *Properties* panel open, click the *Compatibility* tab, and you will see various options (see Figure 12-10).

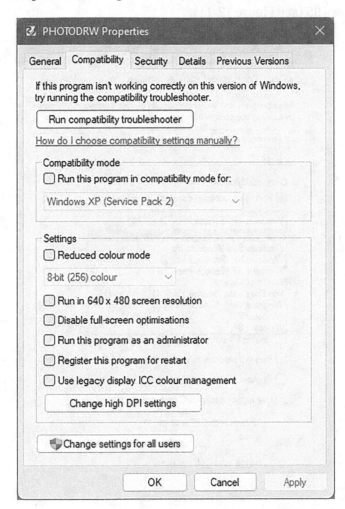

Figure 12-10. *The program compatibility properties contains more options than the troubleshooter offers*

The first of these options is to select which version of Windows the program previously worked in, and it is here that you can select an OS version going all the way back to Windows 95 (see Figure 12-11).

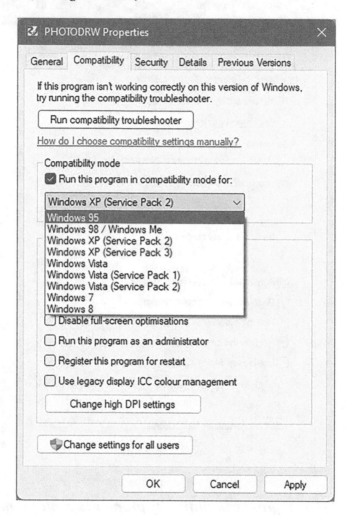

Figure 12-11.   *You can select an OS the program worked under all the way back to Windows 95*

Additionally, and if the program is not displaying correctly on the screen, you can select a different color mode for it to be displayed in such as 8-bit (256 colors) and 16-bit (65,536 colors) (see Figure 12-12). By default, Windows displays in 32-bit or sometimes 48-bit color depending on your graphics capabilities and monitor.

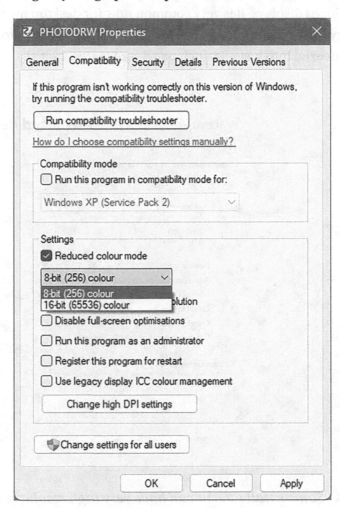

Figure 12-12. *You can select a color mode for the program to run in*

Then you will see additional settings and options such as locking the program to a 640 by 480 pixel resolution, disabling the ability to run the program full screen, and always running it as an administrator, which will require authorizing a User Account Control (UAC) prompt whenever the program is run, something to consider if an administrator password has to be entered.

Register this program for restart will autostart the program after restarting or starting the PC and signing in to an account, and ICC color management might be required by some older photo and video programs.

Something new with Windows 11 is support to manage legacy programs for high DPI (dots per inch) displays. It is very common now for desktop monitors and laptops to come with very high-resolution screens. My Microsoft Surface Laptop Studio has 2400 by 1600 pixels squeezed into just a 14-inch panel (see Figure 12-13).

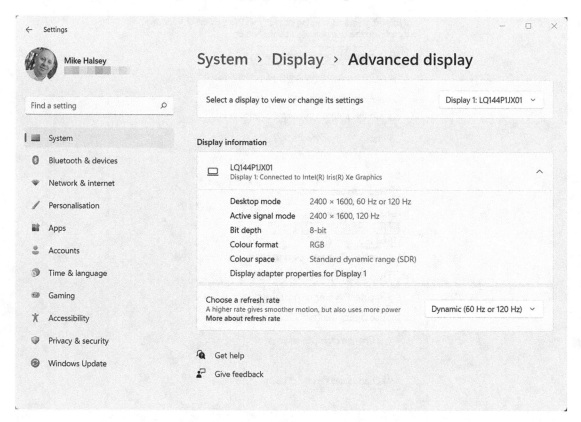

Figure 12-13. *Some small screens can have very high resolutions*

Thus, I have to run this screen at 125% scaling, effectively making the perceived resolution smaller; otherwise, everything is too small to see and read for me, even with my glasses on.

Some legacy programs will misbehave when desktop scaling is used, and so in the compatibility options, you will see a *Change high DPI settings* button. Clicking this will display (if you'll excuse the pun) options for managing the legacy program when desktop scaling is being used (see Figure 12-14).

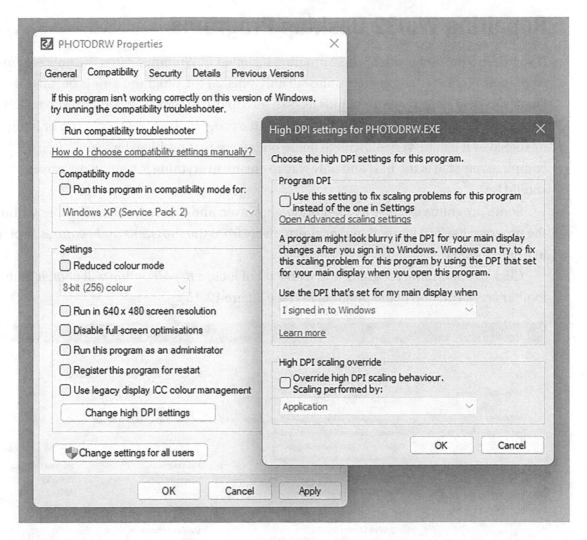

Figure 12-14. *You can manage compatibility when desktop scaling is used in Windows 11*

Lastly at the bottom of the dialog is a *Change settings for all users* button. Compatibility settings for an app are stored in the Windows Registry and loaded when the program runs. If you have more than one user account on the PC and they also need to use this program, clicking this button will also set the compatibility options in their own Registry files, and in Chapter 19, we'll look at how and why each user on the PC has their own Registry files.

Repairing Win32 Desktop Programs

If you have a problem with a win32 program installed in Windows, often the only way to fix that problem is to completely uninstall and reinstall the program. This is because it creates its own Registry entries, adds its own files to the *Program Files* folder, and installs its own services and dynamic link library files. If a program flatly refuses to run or badly misbehaves it can be very difficult to figure out where that problem lays, and often a complete reinstall is the best and only way to ensure everything is reset to the way it should be.

Some programs do have a repair option however, and this can be found either within the program itself (if it's working) or alternatively from the *Programs and Features* applet in *Control Panel*.

Click the offending program, and with a bit of luck, a *Repair* option will appear in the toolbar across the top of the program list (see Figure 12-15).

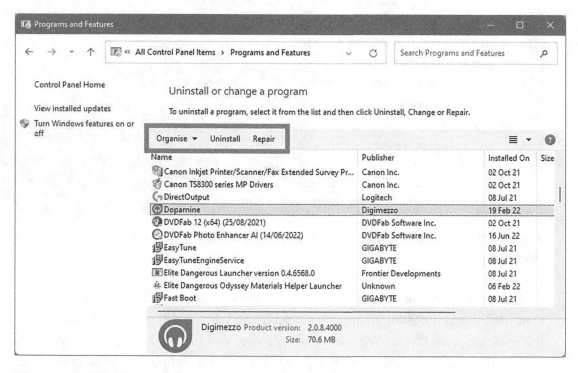

Figure 12-15. *The excellent Dopamine music player comes with a self-repair option*

If a repair option doesn't appear, you may see one called *Change*. This exists to allow you to install and uninstall optional features for the program, but in some cases, such as with Microsoft Office, it will allow you to repair the installation, either from a local backup or from an online source (see Figure 12-16).

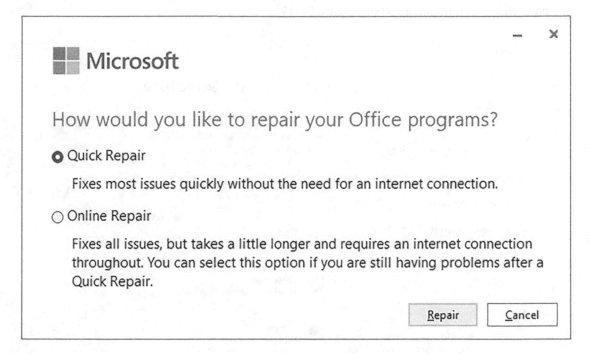

Figure 12-16. Microsoft Office comes with a self-repair option

Managing Microsoft Store and Third-Party Store Apps

Microsoft Store apps can also be repaired, and there are a few ways to achieve this, depending on whether it's just the app malfunctioning or if it's a problem that's being caused by the store itself such as preventing the app from auto-updating.

If it's an app itself you need to repair, open *Settings* and then *Apps* and *Apps & features*. Here, you will see a long list of every app and program installed on the PC. Scroll down the list until you find the offending store app and click the three dots icon to its right. This will reveal a menu that includes an *Advanced options* link that you can click to repair the app (see Figure 12-17).

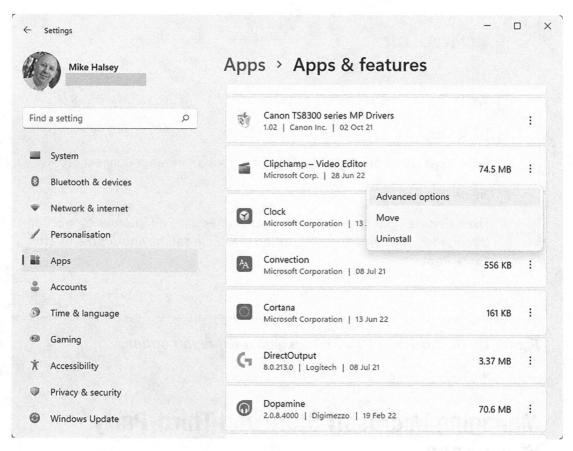

Figure 12-17. *You can repair Microsoft Store apps from Settings*

At the next screen, you will see the information Windows has about the app, from its version number to the amount of space it consumes on the PC and how much Internet data it has used. At the bottom of this page are four options you can use to manage and repair the app (see Figure 12-18).

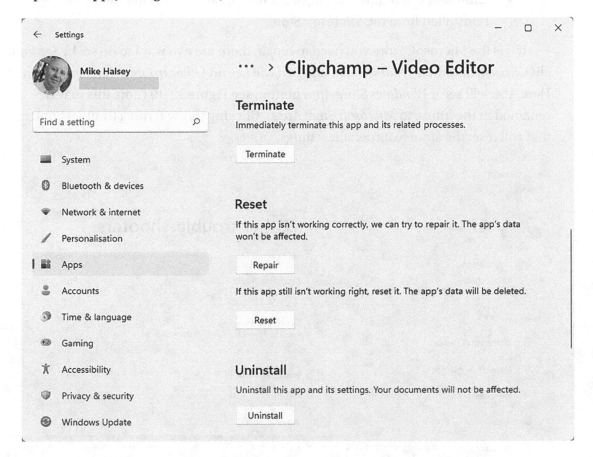

Figure 12-18. Settings offers different options for repairing store apps

- **Terminate** can be used if the app has hung and isn't responding. You can also terminate apps from the Task Manager, and I'll show you how to do this later in the chapter.

- **Repair** will attempt to repair the app without deleting any of your user and configuration data. This should be the first thing you try to get an app working again.

- **Reset** will completely reset the app, effectively reinstalling it. This will however delete all of your user and configuration data for the app, including any sign-ins and preferences.

- **Uninstall** will remove the app from the PC, and it can later be reinstalled from the Microsoft Store.

If it is the Microsoft Store you need to repair, there are two ways to do so. In *Settings*, click *System* and then *Troubleshoot*, and you will see an *Other trouble-shooters* button. Here, you will see a *Windows Store Apps* button, see Figure 12-19 (note this may be renamed in the future to *Microsoft Store Apps*). Clicking this will run a troubleshooter that will reset the store to its default settings.

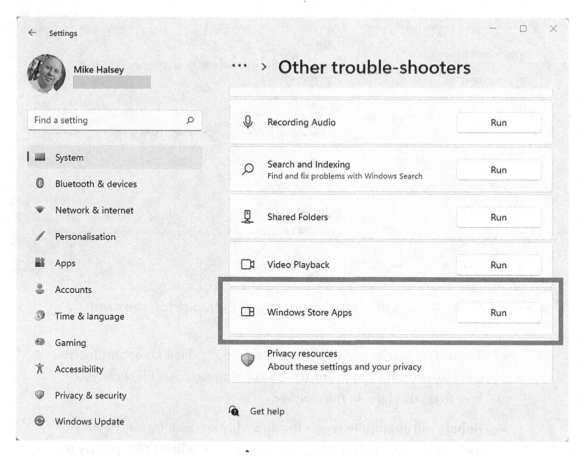

Figure 12-19. *You can reset the Microsoft Store from Settings*

To reset the Microsoft Store using scripting, open a Command Prompt window, you do not need to do this as an Administrator for this task though you will need to be signed in as an Administrator, and type the command wsreset. This will reset the Microsoft Store and then open a Store window for you (see Figure 12-20).

Figure 12-20. *You can reset the Microsoft Store from the Command Line*

Note   With third-party stores such as those from Amazon and Epic, you can reset those stores in the same way I described resetting Microsoft Store Apps, as they are effectively installed apps themselves. The apps they install *may* also appear in the *Apps & features* panel, though depending on the store they may not. These stores may, or again may not, have their own mechanisms for repairing and resetting apps, and this will vary from one store to another.

Managing Apps with Task Manager

The Task Manager in Windows 11 is incredibly useful and full-featured, and we have and will continue to look at different aspects of it throughout this book. You can manage programs and apps using it however. The easiest way to open Task Manager is to right-click the Start Button and click it when it appears in the pop-up menu. You can also open it from pressing the *Windows key + X* to open the administration menu, or from a *Ctrl + Alt + Del* key press. You need to be running the full Task Manager, so make sure you click the *More details* button in the bottom-left corner if there is one.

Note   It's possible by the time you read this that Microsoft will have reversed their decision to remove running Task Manager from a right-click anywhere in a blank space on the Taskbar. To be honest, this is something I don't care about at all, but it certainly seemed to be the number one complaint from IT Pros and power users after Windows 11 launched in 2021.

We'll begin with Microsoft Store apps. Click the *App history* tab in Task Manager, and you will see recorded usage data for installed store apps from the last 30 days (see Figure 12-21).

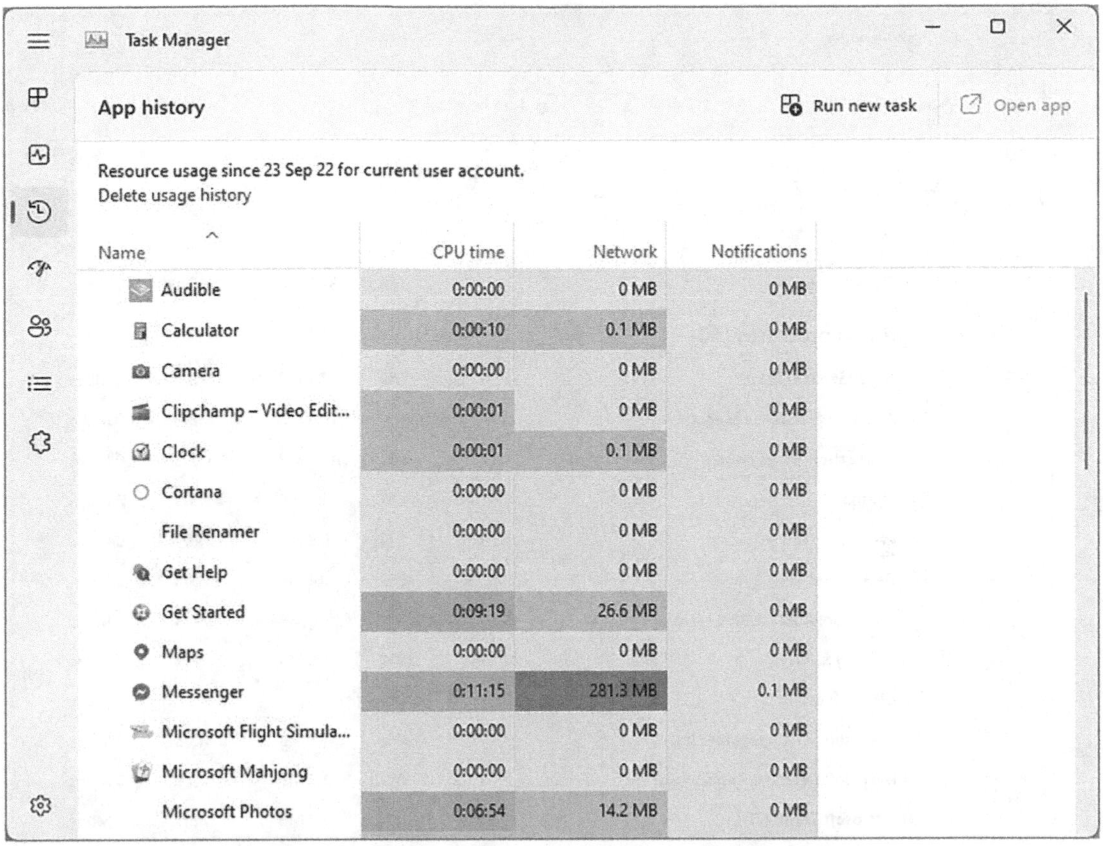

Figure 12-21. Windows records store app data for 30 days

This data includes information on how long the app has been running, how much network and Internet bandwidth it has used, and how much of that has been used on a metered (cellular) network. We can ignore the *Tile updates* column as Windows 11 doesn't support live tiles, and this will inevitably be removed in the future.

The data this panel provides is heat-mapped, with any especially high usage appearing as either an orange or a red highlight. If you have a store app that you feel is monopolizing your processor time or bandwidth, this can be a useful place to find it.

For all programs and apps, navigate to the *Processes* tab. Here, and again all heat-mapped so you can easily see high CPU, memory, disk, and network usage, is a list of all the running processes on the PC. This will include any currently running apps and also any background processes that are running (see Figure 12-22).

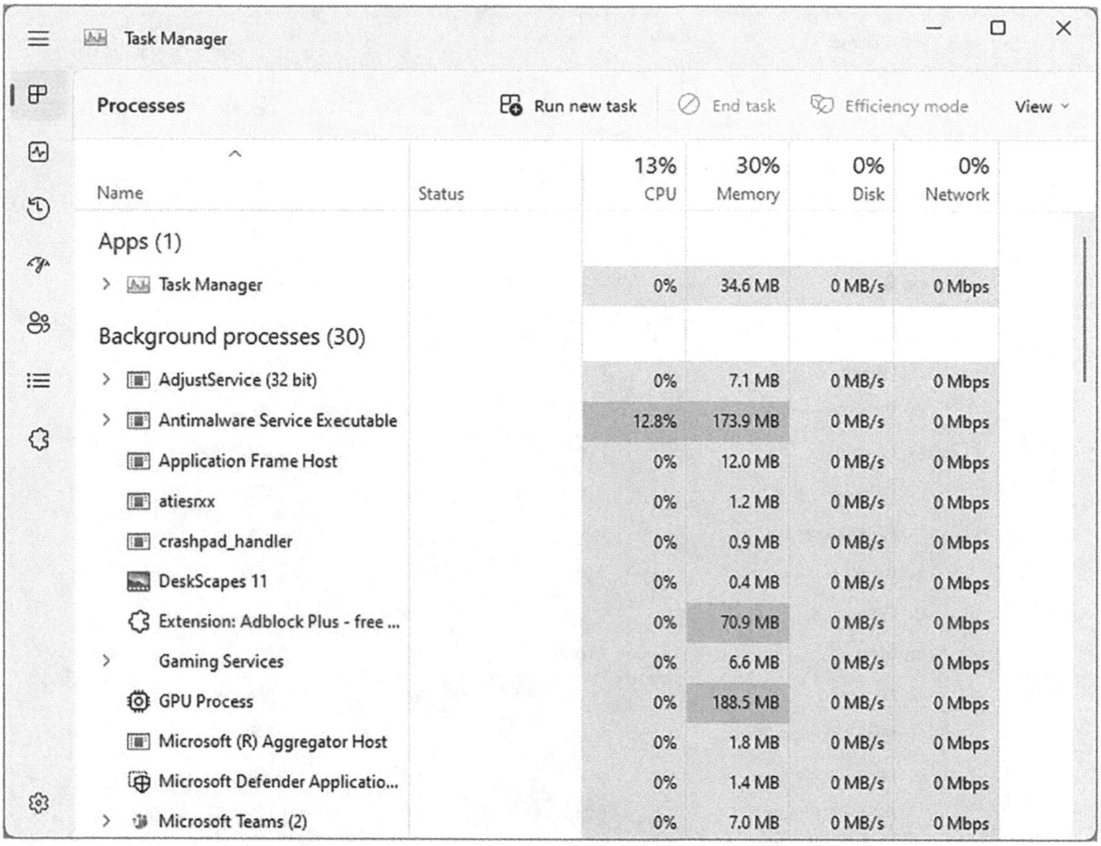
Task Manager
Processes
Run new task
End task
Efficiency mode
View
Name
Status
13% CPU
30% Memory
0% Disk
0% Network
Apps (1)
Task Manager 0% 34.6 MB 0 MB/s 0 Mbps
Background processes (30)
AdjustService (32 bit) 0% 7.1 MB 0 MB/s 0 Mbps
Antimalware Service Executable 12.8% 173.9 MB 0 MB/s 0 Mbps
Application Frame Host 0% 12.0 MB 0 MB/s 0 Mbps
atiesrxx 0% 1.2 MB 0 MB/s 0 Mbps
crashpad_handler 0% 0.9 MB 0 MB/s 0 Mbps
DeskScapes 11 0% 0.4 MB 0 MB/s 0 Mbps
Extension: Adblock Plus - free ... 0% 70.9 MB 0 MB/s 0 Mbps
Gaming Services 0% 6.6 MB 0 MB/s 0 Mbps
GPU Process 0% 188.5 MB 0 MB/s 0 Mbps
Microsoft (R) Aggregator Host 0% 1.8 MB 0 MB/s 0 Mbps
Microsoft Defender Applicatio... 0% 1.4 MB 0 MB/s 0 Mbps
Microsoft Teams (2) 0% 7.0 MB 0 MB/s 0 Mbps

***Figure 12-22.** You can view a list of all running processes on the PC*

To the left of each app is an arrow, and clicking it will reveal a sublist of all the dependent processes for that app (see Figure 12-23). This includes any open file(s) and, in the case of the following example, any plug-ins and extensions that are running.

☰ Task Manager						
Processes		🔲 Run new task	⊘ End task	⟳ Efficiency mode		View ˅
		5%	**31%**	**0%**	**0%**	
Name	Status	CPU	Memory	Disk	Network	
Apps (8)						
> 💬 Messenger (2)		0%	144.5 MB	0 MB/s	0.1 Mbps	
> 🌐 Microsoft Edge (14)	🍃	0%	780.5 MB	0 MB/s	0.1 Mbps	
> 📧 Microsoft Outlook		0%	149.0 MB	0 MB/s	0 Mbps	
˅ Ⅱ Microsoft Teams (8)		0%	369.5 MB	0 MB/s	0 Mbps	
Ⅱ Microsoft Edge WebView2		0%	1.3 MB	0 MB/s	0 Mbps	
Ⅱ Microsoft Teams		0%	46.0 MB	0 MB/s	0 Mbps	
Ⅱ WebView2 GPU Process		0%	94.8 MB	0 MB/s	0 Mbps	
Ⅱ WebView2 Manager		0%	35.3 MB	0 MB/s	0 Mbps	
Ⅱ WebView2 Utility: Audio S...		0%	3.3 MB	0 MB/s	0 Mbps	
Ⅱ WebView2 Utility: Networ...		0%	5.7 MB	0 MB/s	0 Mbps	
Ⅱ WebView2 Utility: Storage...		0%	5.1 MB	0 MB/s	0 Mbps	
> Ⅱ WebView2: Recent chats |...		0%	178.0 MB	0 MB/s	0 Mbps	
> W Microsoft Word		0%	84.1 MB	0 MB/s	0.1 Mbps	
> 🖼 Photos		0%	136.9 MB	0 MB/s	0 Mbps	
> 📊 Task Manager		0.1%	73.1 MB	0 MB/s	0 Mbps	
> 📁 Windows Explorer (2)		0.1%	316.5 MB	0 MB/s	0 Mbps	

Figure 12-23. *You can view any dependent processes for running apps*

Again, you have CPU, memory, disk, and network usage for these subprocesses, helping you to determine if, for example, a DLL has crashed or if an extension is using too much disk time.

There are other useful features for managing and troubleshooting processes in Task Manager, and we will look at this in detail in Chapter 13.

Managing Startup Apps and Programs

One more aspect of managing apps and programs is keeping a lid on everything that wants to start automatically when you start or sign in to your PC. This used to be managed, in years gone by, from the **msconfig** panel, which we'll look at in Chapter 18, but in Windows 11, it's managed in Task Manager.

Clicking the *Startup* tab in Task Manager reveals all the apps and programs that are currently running at Startup or that have previously run at startup and that have since been disabled (see Figure 12-24).

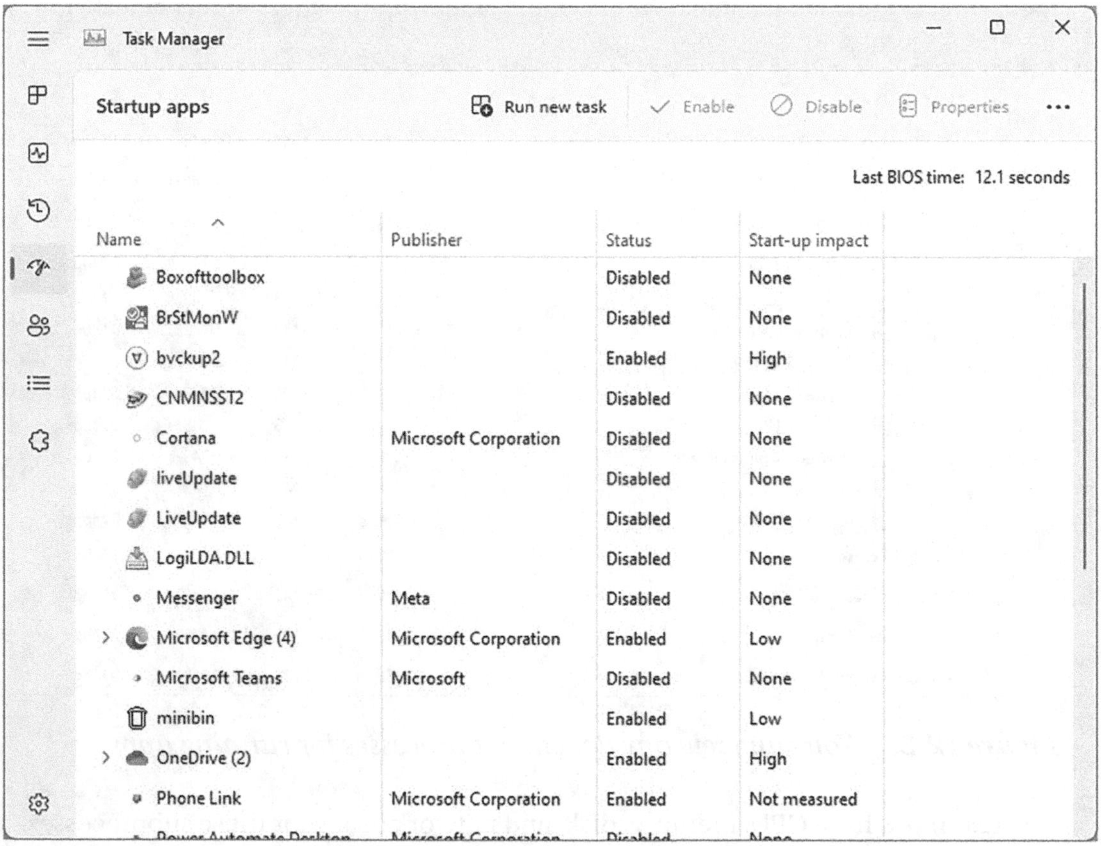

Name	Publisher	Status	Start-up impact
Boxofttoolbox		Disabled	None
BrStMonW		Disabled	None
bvckup2		Enabled	High
CNMNSST2		Disabled	None
Cortana	Microsoft Corporation	Disabled	None
liveUpdate		Disabled	None
LiveUpdate		Disabled	None
LogiLDA.DLL		Disabled	None
Messenger	Meta	Disabled	None
> Microsoft Edge (4)	Microsoft Corporation	Enabled	Low
Microsoft Teams	Microsoft	Disabled	None
minibin		Enabled	Low
> OneDrive (2)		Enabled	High
Phone Link	Microsoft Corporation	Enabled	Not measured
Power Automate Desktop	Microsoft Corporation	Disabled	None

Task Manager — Startup apps — Run new task — Enable — Disable — Properties — Last BIOS time: 12.1 seconds

Figure 12-24. *You manage startup apps and programs in Task Manager*

To set an app or program to automatically run, or not run at startup, all you need to do is select the item and then click the *Enable* or *Disable* button that appears in the bottom-right corner of the Task Manager window.

You will see though that each item has a *Start-up impact* score. This is a measure of how long it takes the app to start and how much it might slow the PC. For a fast, high-end desktop like my own, with a 16-Core AMD Ryzen and 64GB RAM, I don't worry about such things, but for a low-end laptop, a high score here can make the difference between a quick startup time to the desktop and a slow one.

Summary

If you think there's a lot in Windows 11 to help you manage processes and running programs, we haven't even got started yet. In the next chapter, we'll look at the more advanced tools in Task Manager for managing running processes and how processes interact with and are dependent on Windows services (and of course we'll examine what services are).

You can also manage and troubleshoot processes and services with PowerShell just in case you were disappointed that I missed scripting tools in this chapter. The best tools for managing and troubleshooting processes and services though come as part of the Microsoft Sysinternals suite, which I first mentioned in Chapter 2. We'll look at what's available to help with processes and services and how to get the best from those tools.

CHAPTER 13

Processes and Services Troubleshooting

At the end of Chapter 12, I teased you that we hadn't even got started on managing and troubleshooting Windows applications, processes, and services. This is because maintaining compatibility for older (legacy) programs and software and managing the Microsoft Store and third-party store apps is just a small part of what's on offer.

Let's face it, while there are a great many millions of people very happy to live exclusively within a web browser for banking, shopping, messaging, email, and work, there is no substitute for a full desktop PC or laptop. My main mobile device as I write this is called the Astro Slide, available from `www.planetcom.co.uk`. It's a handheld device with a slide-out 6.39-inch screen and a full keyboard (see Figure 13-1).

Figure 13-1. *The Astro Slide from Planet Computers*

© Mike Halsey 2023

M. Halsey, *Troubleshooting and Supporting Windows 11*, https://doi.org/10.1007/978-1-4842-8728-6_13

As mobile devices go, this is a fantastic device for "getting stuff done" while on the move, and it's popular with everybody from people that need to write longer messages, and emails, to coders that want to work on the move. The device, and this is one of the reasons I mention it here, is also popular with IT system administrators and datacenter technicians that need access to a scripting environment (the Astro runs both Android and Linux) for server-side configuration and troubleshooting. This can happen at just about any time, and having a device on which this can be done, right in your pocket, means both that the response can be faster and that the technician doesn't have to carry a bulky laptop with them all the time.

As great as the Astro is however, this book is around 600 or more pages long (difficult to be precise at this point in writing it as my last book ran over by more than 100 pages there was so much great information to include), and I simply couldn't write this or any other of its chapters on a handheld keyboard, no matter how good it was.

For this, I need a full PC; I don't get on with laptops either for "real work," much preferring the ergonomics that come with a full keyboard, mouse, and a good-sized monitor at a distance that my desktop PC provides. But this also brings me to software. I could, you might argue, be able to write this book perfectly well in Microsoft Word online, the stripped down web-based version of the web browser.

To this, there are three answers. Firstly, the features and functionality of the web-based version of Word don't provide all of the features and functionality I need to write, edit, and review a book with my editors. Secondly, I have purchased a Microsoft 365 subscription which comes with the full desktop version of Office anyway, and lastly why would I buy a powerful desktop PC and then just use stuff in a browser?

So, for my long-winded way at getting to the point, we all need software, be this Microsoft Office, customer relationship managers, HR, accounts, and logistics packages, custom (bespoke) packages written especially for the business, or large suites of audio, video, or photo editing software, computer-aided design (CAD), computer graphics design and rendering, programming environments, and so on. The list of tasks for which we still need a proper software package isn't going to get shorter in the next decade or so.

However, you could feel one of those coming, didn't you? The increasing use of online apps and Progressive Web Apps (PWAs) and people wanting to live in their web browsers do mean we need to maintain compatibility, so let's begin there.

Internet Explorer Is Dead... Long Live Internet Explorer!

Microsoft's Internet Explorer (IE) web browser, which was first introduced in the optional "Plus!" pack for Windows 95 and not even bundled with the operating system at that time, is officially dead... sort of.

All support for the browser ended on June 15, 2022, with no more security or stability patches being issued... which again isn't true as it's still included with Windows 10, and Microsoft have committed to supporting it for enterprise customers only for as long as the operating system also gets support.

Internet Explorer though, you might ask, has never been included with Windows 11, so why even mention it here? Well, there are many organizations and corporations that, in the same way they have legacy programs to install, also use legacy intranet and website systems that don't play nice with modern web browsers.

This support, provided in Microsoft's Edge web browser, will be supported until "at least 2029" according to Microsoft. So what is this support and how can you take advantage of it?

You can find Internet Explorer compatibility mode in Edge's *Settings*, under *Default browser* (see Figure 13-2).

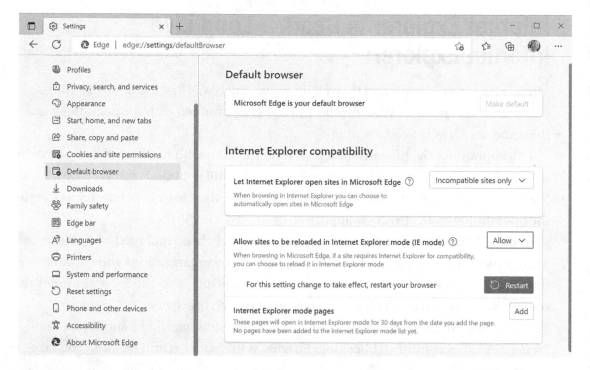

Figure 13-2. *You can manage Internet Explorer compatibility in Edge*

There are three options available to you. The first is to allow IT to open website and intranet sites in Edge. The choices are *Never, Incompatible sites only*, and *Always (recommended)*. Below this is an option to choose which web and intranet sites you want to open in IE compatibility mode; the options are *Default, Allow*, and *Don't allow.*

Lastly, you can add specific websites and intranet sites to the feature using the *Add* button. Type or cut and paste the address from your browser to add it. One downside though is that this expires after one month and needs to be refreshed (see Figure 13-3), so it's better to manage this feature through Group Policy or server-side configuration if you can.

Internet Explorer mode pages   Add

These pages will open in Internet Explorer mode for 30 days from the date you add the page.
You have 1 page that'll automatically open in Internet Explorer mode.

Page	Date added	Expires	
☐ http://contoso.com/	18/07/2022	17/08/2022	🗑

Figure 13-3. *You can add web and intranet sites to IE compatibility mode*

To set these policies, open *Group Policy* by searching for **gpedit** in the Start Menu
and navigate to *Computer Configuration* ➤ *Administrative Templates* ➤ *Windows
Components* ➤ *Microsoft Edge*. Here, you will find several IE 11 policies including "Send
all intranet sites to Internet Explorer 11" (see Figure 13-4).

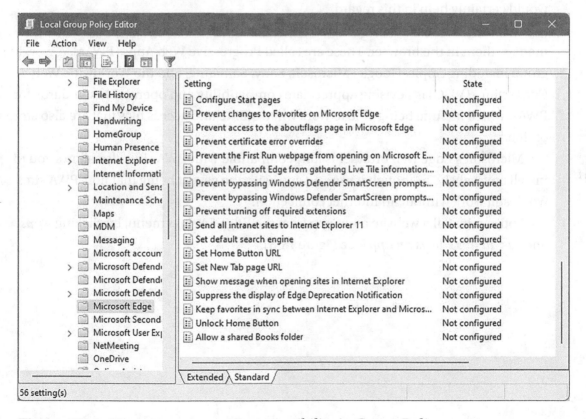

Figure 13-4. *You can manage IE compatibility in Group Policy*

Using Installed Web Apps and Edge OS?

Microsoft has been losing out to Google in the education market now for years, with the rival's Chrome OS having made strong inroads due to being lightweight enough to run on low-end hardware and not requiring restarts for large updates. In more recent times, Google has begun making impressive inroads into the business sector, and this is a real and credible threat to Microsoft, not just for Windows but for sales of Microsoft 365, Office, and their Azure Cloud services, all of which Google has a (not as good admittedly) competitor to.

In recent months, there have been rumors circulating about Edge OS, a super-lightweight version of Windows 11 that contains only the Edge web browser (which is now based on Google's Chromium browser engine anyway) and the Microsoft Store.

This new OS, if it even exists and is released, could compete much more readily with Chrome OS, and the addition of Android apps through the Amazon Appstore plug-in would certainly help in this regard.

In Windows 11 you can use Edge to install websites as though they were apps and manage them in the browser. These are called Progressive Web Apps (PWAs). A working group including Apple, Google, Microsoft, Sony, Samsung, and the Worldwide Web Consortium (W3C) is devising appropriate compatibility and operability standards for PWAs, which include being able to work while offline and access files that are also stored offline.

Microsoft's Edge web browser is fully compatible with PWAs but also allows you to install any website as though it were an app, with the caveat being that non-PWA sites won't still work without an Internet connection.

You can install a website as an app from the Edge *Settings* menu, by clicking *Apps* and *Install this site as an app* (see Figure 13-5).

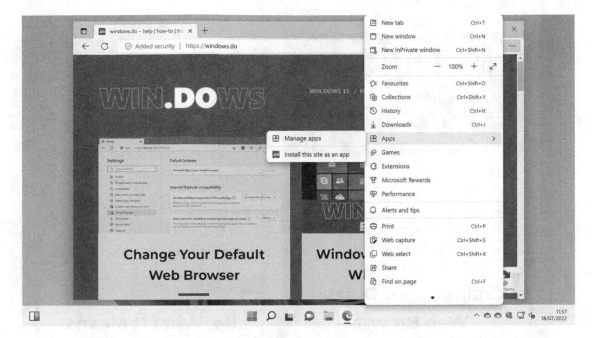

Figure 13-5. *Any website can be installed as an app in Edge*

With the app installed, you are asked if you want to pin its icon to the Start Menu or Taskbar or to add a link to the desktop and even start the "app" when you sign in to Windows (see Figure 13-6).

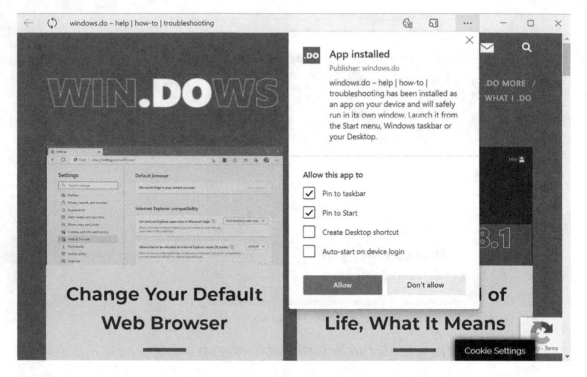

Figure 13-6. *You can pin web apps to the Start Menu and Taskbar*

With the app installed, you can then run it as though it were any other app (see Figure 13-7), and it will appear in its own window on the desktop.

Figure 13-7. *You can run installed websites as though they were a normal app*

When you need to manage or to remove a web app, you do this from within Edge. Again, from the browser *Settings*, click *Apps* and then click *Manage apps*. This will open a browser tab displaying all the apps you have installed (see Figure 13-8). From here, you can get *Details* of the app such as any permissions that are set for it.

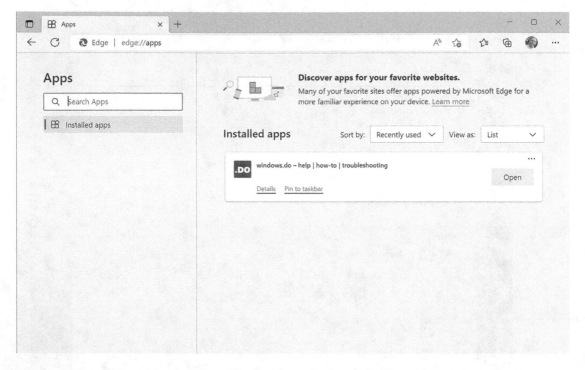

Figure 13-8. *You manage installed web apps from the browser*

Also, either from the *Details* panel or from the three dots icon in the top-right corner of the app information, you can find an *Uninstall* option.

Using the Browser Task Manager

Just as Windows 11 has its own Task Manager for managing running processes and services, so too does Edge, and this is one of the reasons why some people suspect Edge OS to be a real thing. From the Edge *Settings* menu, click *More Tools* and then *Browser Task Manager*. This opens a fairly basic Task Manager in which you can see tabs and processes running inside the browser (see Figure 13-9).

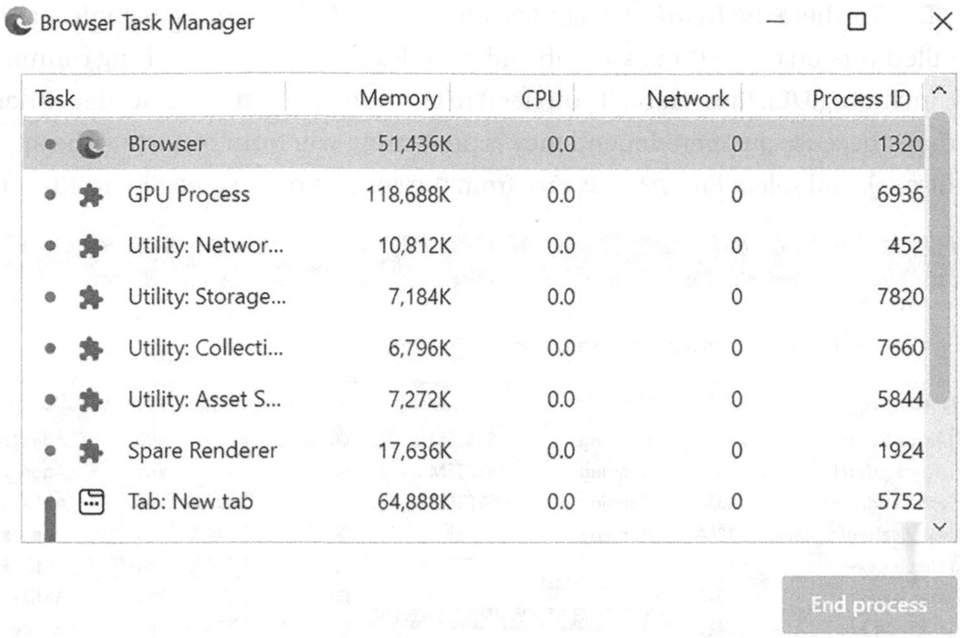
Browser Task Manager
Task
Memory
CPU
Network
Process ID
Browser 51,436K 0.0 0 1320
GPU Process 118,688K 0.0 0 6936
Utility: Networ... 10,812K 0.0 0 452
Utility: Storage... 7,184K 0.0 0 7820
Utility: Collecti... 6,796K 0.0 0 7660
Utility: Asset S... 7,272K 0.0 0 5844
Spare Renderer 17,636K 0.0 0 1924
Tab: New tab 64,888K 0.0 0 5752
End process

Figure 13-9. *You can manage hung processes direct from the browser*

Right-clicking anywhere inside the Browser Task Manager will display a menu of available metrics, such as CPU Time, Start Time, GPU Memory, and Process Priority.

If you need to close a process that has hung or is misbehaving, you can do this by clicking the process and then clicking the *End process* button in the bottom-right corner of the window.

Advanced Management of Windows Processes and Services

While we're on the subject of Task Manager, you'll remember that in Chapter 12 I detailed how you can use the Windows 11 Task Manager to manage running processes. It's actually more powerful than this still as there are advanced controls available under the *Details* tab.

If you need to close any process on the PC that has hung, then just as you can with the *Processes* tab, you can right-click any process and select *End Task* from the context menu that appears to close it; sometimes, though, you need more control, especially if several dependent processes are also running that you need to shut down.

This is where the *Details* tab comes into its own. This is a more technical and more detailed version of the Processes tab and includes absolutely everything running on the PC, including DLL files. Here, if you need to close an app with *all* of its dependencies, perhaps because an open dependency is preventing you from restarting the app, you can right-click and select *End Process Tree* from the context menu (see Figure 13-10).

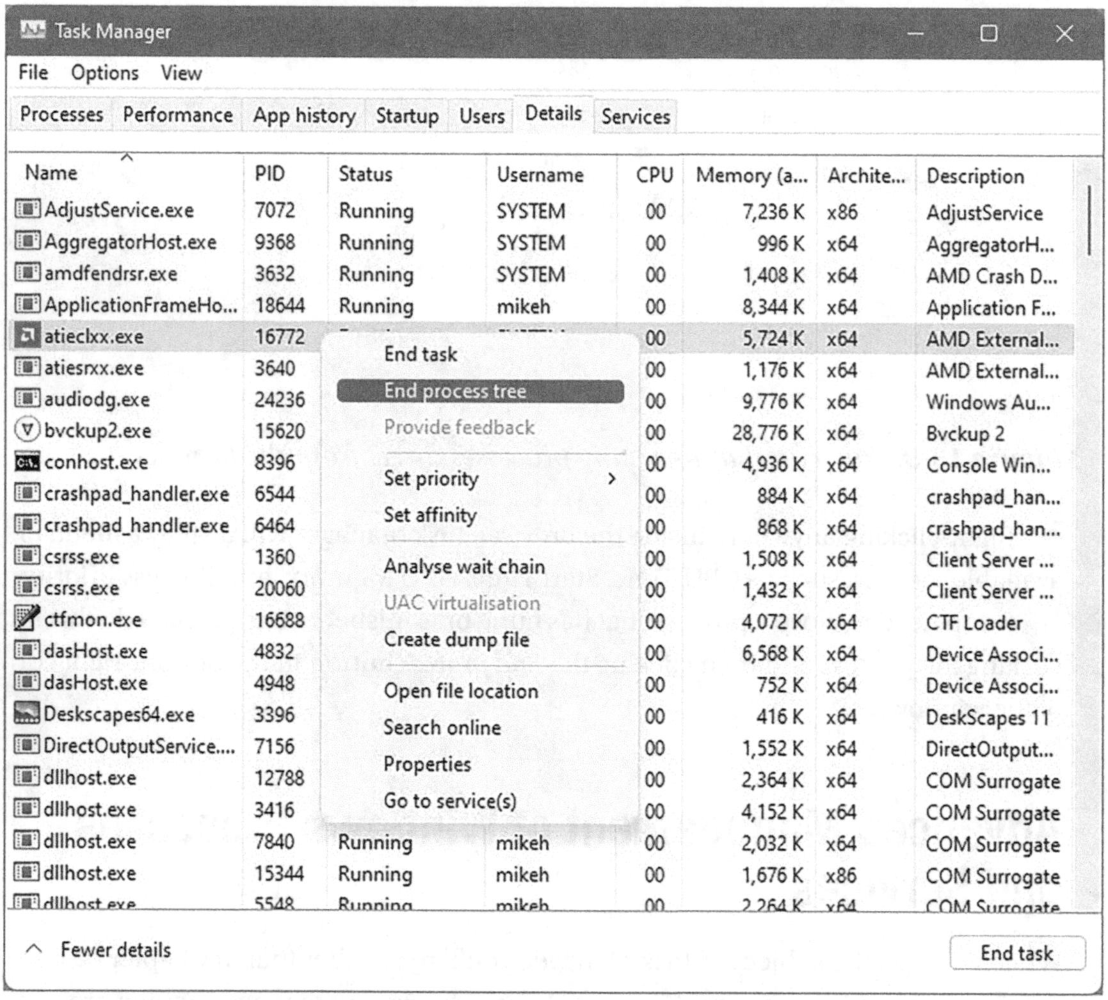

Figure 13-10. *You can close a process and all its dependencies from the Details tab*

It is by right-clicking a process in the Details tab that you can also choose additional options:

- **Set priority** allows you to set a processing priority for the process, from *low* to *Real time*. This is useful if you need or want to give the process more processing power, such as when rendering video.

- **Set affinity** lets you choose which physical and virtual processor cores will be used by the process.

- **Analyze wait chain** displays which processes are using or are waiting to use a resource that is currently in use or locked by another process.

- **UAC virtualization** obfuscates the path for a target folder the process needs to write to and instead presents it with a virtualized container, a sort of symbolic link to that path. This can be used when an older program needs permissions that are normally blocked by User Account Control.

- **Create dump file** will create a binary .DMP file with data on what the process is doing at that moment and save the file to the %LocalAppData%\Temp folder on your hard disk. This can later be read using a compatible program such as the Windows Software Development Kit to see what was going on with the app and its PC resource usage at that moment.

- **Open file location** will open a File Explorer window at the install location of that process executable or DLL.

- **Search online** will open a search window looking for details on the process.

- **Properties** will open a properties inspector panel for that process.

- **Go to services** will switch to the Services tab, and we'll look at these later in this chapter.

Managing and Troubleshooting Services

Services are programs that run in the background on your PC and that perform specific duties, such as managing print queues, implementing security, and handling network traffic. Essentially, they're programs that enable software to utilize hardware and features of your PC and of Windows and that are called by and shared by different apps on the PC simultaneously.

This is in stark contrast to how things were done in the early days of PCs. In my home office, I have created my own computer museum (available at `https://windows.do/my-computer-museum` for those who are interested). In among the many palmtop and handheld devices that I've always been a fan of, as I'm sure you guessed at the beginning of this chapter, and such classics as an original Apple Macintosh and a first-generation IBM 5150 PC with a copy of WordPerfect 5.1.

I loved this word processor and achieved so much with it. One of its idiosyncrasies though was that among the many 5¼-inch floppy disks it came on were disks containing drivers for the most common printers available at the time. As WordPerfect 5.1 was a DOS program, there were no such things as print services; you needed to load the correct printer driver into the program when you needed to print a document.

These days, services are just something we take for granted. They can cause problems though, especially when you have services that are shared between different running apps on the PC, and doubly so when you consider these are not just written by Microsoft but also come from third-party software companies.

Task Manager in Windows 11 contains its own *Services* tab from which you can manage services, but it's only truly useful for being able to search online on a right-click for a service if you're unsure of what it is (see Figure 13-11).

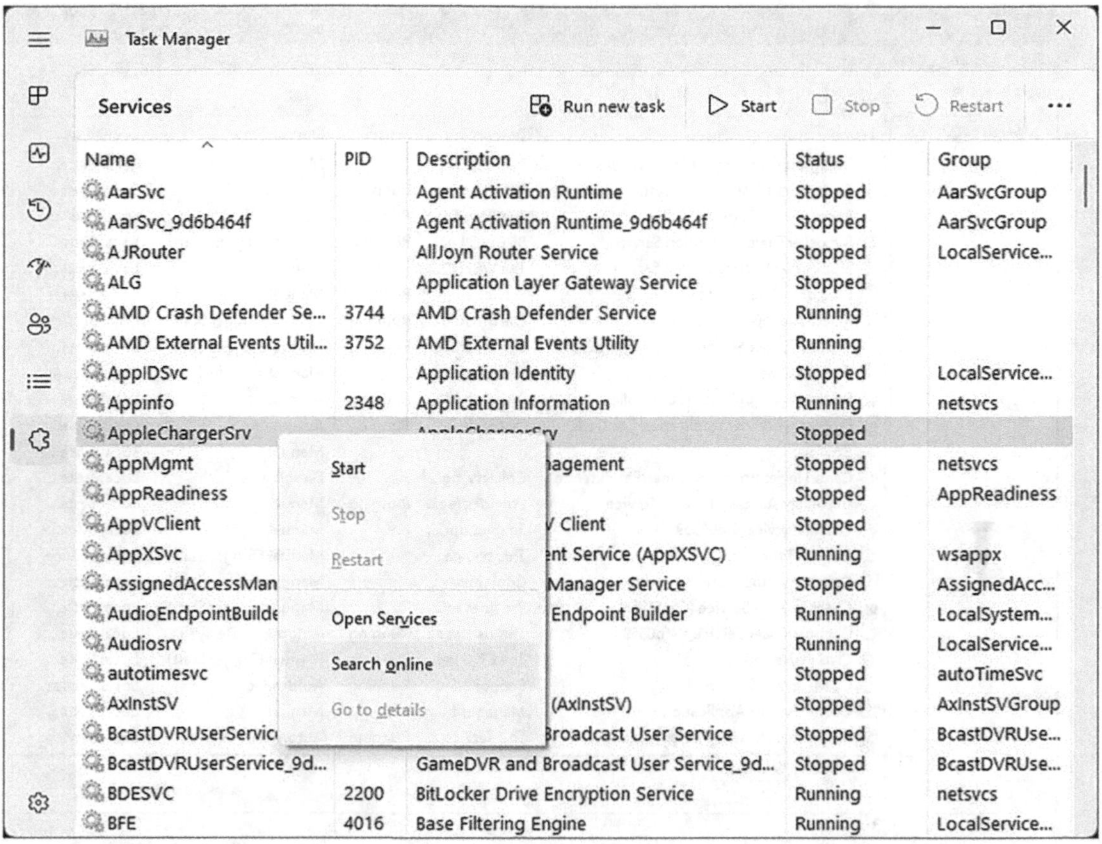

Figure 13-11. *Task Manager allows you to search online for details of services*

The best place to manage and troubleshoot services is directly from the *Services* panel. You can access this from Windows Tools or from a Start Menu search. When it opens, you will see it's standard Microsoft Management Console (MMC) fare and contains a full list of all the installed services on the PC, along with their current status (Stopped, Running, Suspended) and their startup type (Disabled, Manual, Automatic) (see Figure 13-12).

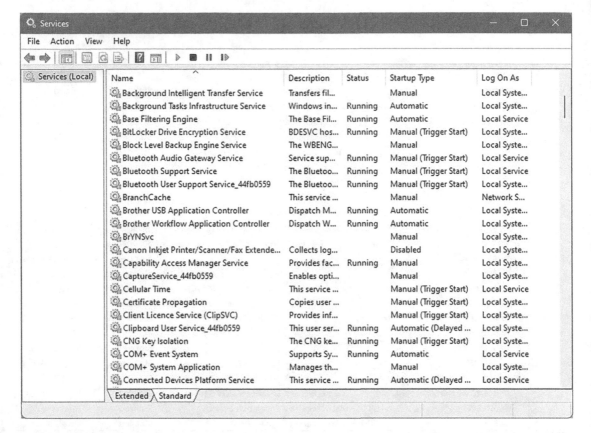

Figure 13-12. *The Services MMC is the best place to manage and troubleshoot services*

Tip   One advantage Task Manager has over the Services MMC is that it lists the PID (Process Identifier) for running services. This is useful if you need to match a PID in an Event Viewer report to a service on the PC to identify it.

Clicking the column headers in Services will enable you to sort them by that column type, so you can, for example, group them by *Status* to make it easier to see all the running and stopped services.

If you suspect a service has crashed or is misbehaving, you can restart it, stop it, or start it from a right-click (see Figure 13-13).

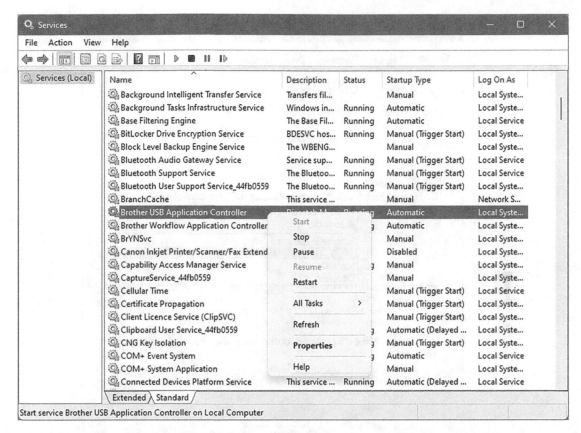

Figure 13-13. *You can start, stop, and restart services from a right-click*

Tip   The *Pause* option for Services is useful when stopping a service will result in an error being generated and perhaps a program crashing. It is also useful when diagnosing malware infections, which we will look at in Chapter 18, when stopping a service may cause the malware to start a new instance of that service.

When you need finer control over a service, right-click it and select *Properties* from the menu that appears. This will display a dialog with four tabs (see Figure 13-14).

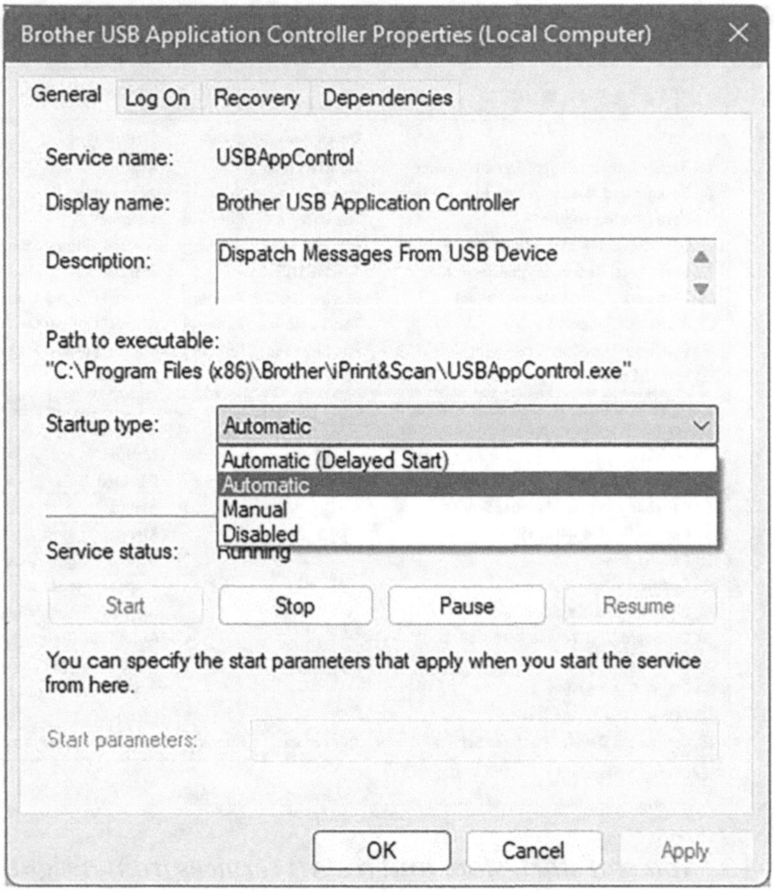

Figure 13-14. *You can get fine control over services in Windows*

The first tab, *General*, contains buttons to Start, Stop, Pause, and Resume the service in addition to being able to change its "Startup type." The way services start in Windows is determined by the service author, and they will determine the best way to start services.

You may find though, for one example, that a service is causing a PC to start slowly or take a long while to get to the desktop after sign-in. This can happen on lower-end hardware if a lot of services are set to run when a user signs in. If you identify services that won't be needed for the first couple of minutes, perhaps a printer service, you can set them for a *Delayed Start* which will start then quietly in the background after the user is already at the desktop and can start work.

Under the *Log On* tab, you will see that the service will almost certainly be set to sign in as the Local System Account (see Figure 13-15). This enables the system to be properly managed by Windows. You may have a custom service running in your organization however that requires specific sign-in credentials, either for security or permission reasons.

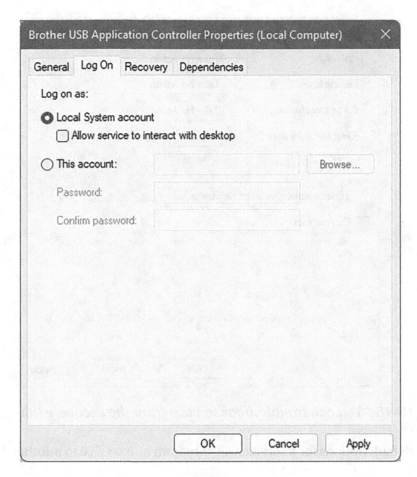

Figure 13-15. *You can set sign-in credentials for a service*

While this situation is rare, it can be useful. To give just one example, you might have a running security service that needs elevated privileges that the user does not have, so that it can access a secure folder store on the network. Here, you can give the service access to the secure environment without also needing to pass those permissions to the end user.

It's under the *Recovery* tab that you'll find all the troubleshooting tools for services (see Figure 13-16). Here, you can tell the PC what it should do if and when a service fails or crashes.

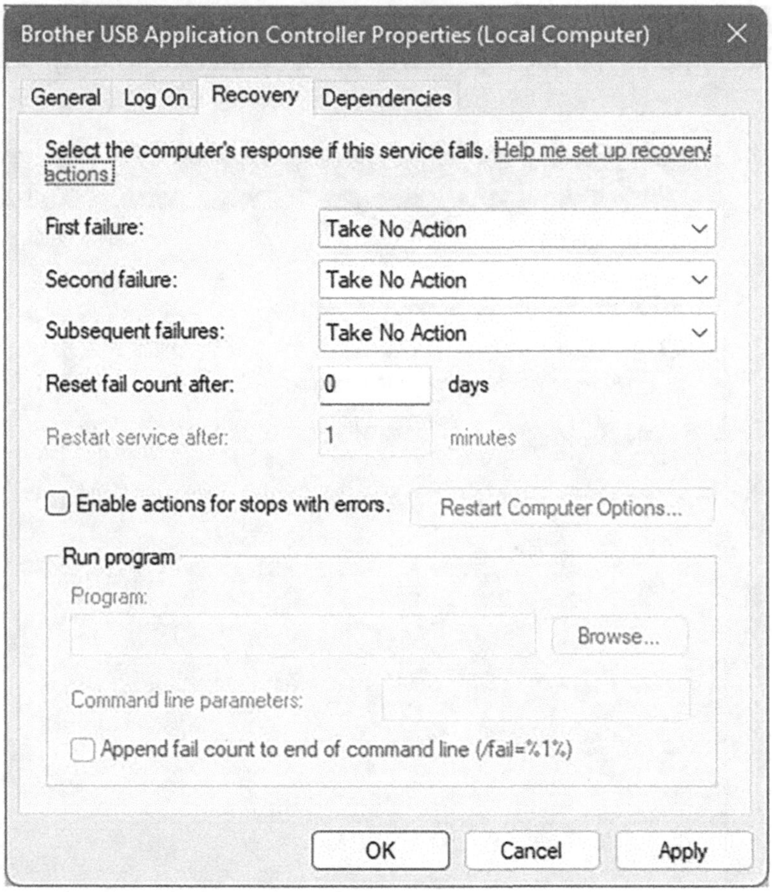

Figure 13-16. *You can troubleshoot services from the Recovery tab*

The default options for a service will vary from one service to another, but they are as follows:

- **Take no action** so that when the service crashes, it will just stop.

- **Restart the service** which will start the service again or at least attempt to restart it. You can optionally specify a delay in minutes for the service to be restarted after.

- **Run a program** which will enable you to specify a program or script to run, with optional command line parameters. This can be used to report errors, reinstall or restart the service, or run a diagnostic tool.

- **Restart the computer** which is best used only for stand-alone machines that do not have a user interacting with them, as they might get upset. If you have a dedicated PC running as an ATM, a manufacturing controller, or a medical device, then having Windows automatically restart the PC can often be a good way to keep the system running.

These options are available for the first, second, and subsequent failures, and you can *Reset [the] fail count* after a specified number of days.

Lastly, the *Dependencies* tab will tell you if any other Windows services are dependent on this one (see Figure 13-17). It is most common for a service to stand entirely on its own, but you might find that some services call and require the use of others. These can also crash and be affected when a service fails, and you might need to also restart or troubleshoot them.

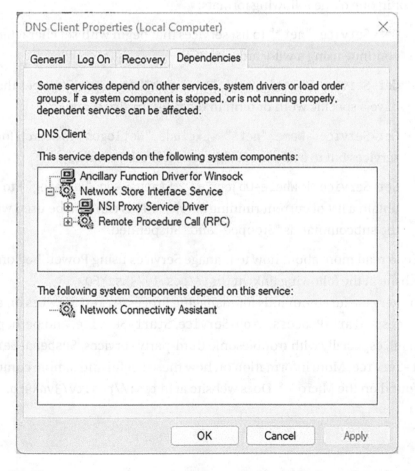

Figure 13-17. *You can see any services that are dependent on the selected one*

Managing and Troubleshooting Processes and Services with PowerShell

As you might expect, PowerShell comes with a range of commands for managing and troubleshooting processes and services. You can get information about running processes on a local or remote PC(s) with the `Get-Process` command. There are also different options and subcommands you can use this with to drill down into specific processes on the PC to get data about them, and you can read about these subcommands on the Microsoft Docs website at the following link: `https://pcs.tv/2Wnbzbr`.

Windows and third-party services can be interrogated the same way with the Get-Service command. You can use this command on its own to see the status of all installed Services or in one of the following formats:

- `Get-Service "net*"` to list services that begin with set characters but continue using a wildcard.

- `Get-Service -Displayname "*network*"` to display services that have a specific word or term in their descriptive name.

- `Get-Service -Name "net*" -Exclude "Netlogon"` to search for services but to exclude specific ones from the results.

- `Get-Service | Where-Object {$_.Status -eq "Running"}` to obtain a list of current running Services. This can also be used with the subcommands "Stopped" and "Suspended."

You can read more about how to manage Services using PowerShell on the Microsoft Docs website at the following link: `https://pcs.tv/3kszYFO`.

Some very useful commands for managing Processes and Services on a PC include `Stop-Process`, `Start-Process`, `Stop-Service`, `Start-Service`, and perhaps one of the most useful, especially with troublesome third-party services, `Suspend-Service` and `Restart-Service`. More information on how these useful and simple commands work can be found on the Microsoft Docs website at `https://pcs.tv/3ynX9Fp`.

Troubleshooting Processes and Services with Microsoft Sysinternals

Microsoft's Sysinternals suite contains a wealth of tools and utilities for managing processes and services on a PC, both locally and for remote PCs across a network. You can download Sysinternals from `https://docs.microsoft.com/sysinternals`.

PsTools

PsTools isn't a single utility, but it is a full suite of utilities for administering PC systems remotely. It includes utilities that can remotely execute apps, display information about files and users, kill processes, get detailed information about processes, and shut down and restart the PC. Full details of the tools available and their switches can be found on the Sysinternals website.

PsExec

This command is used to execute processes on a remote PC. Use this in the format **PsExec \\RemotePC "C:\\long app name.exe"**.

PsFile

PsFile, also detailed earlier in this chapter, will display a list of files that are currently open on a remote PC. Use this in the format **PsFile [\\RemotePC [-u OptionalUsername [-p UserPassword]]] [[id | PathAndNameOfFile] [-c** ToCloseFile].

PsGetSid

This tool is used to display the Security Identifier (SID) of a remote computer or user. Use it in the format **psgetsid [\\RemotePC[,RemotePC[,...]] | @file\] [-u OptionalUsername [-p UserPassword]]] [account|SID]**.

PsInfo

PsInfo can display information about a remote computer. You can use this with the switch **\\RemotePC** for a specific PC or * to run it on all networked PCs. You can also use it with these switches to get detailed information on **[-h]** installed hotfixes, **[-s]** installed applications, and **[-d]** disk information and use **[-c]** to export the data as a CSV file.

PsPing

PsPing does exactly what you might expect it to: it displays detailed ping information to test network connections. It is a Command Line utility that is much more configurable than Windows 10's standard Ping command. PsPing is used with one of four main switches and then a series of subswitches to test for ICMP (the main protocol used by routers for reporting errors), TCP, latency, and bandwidth. Full details of the switches are available on the Sysinternals website.

PsKill

If you need to kill a running process on a remote PC, then PsKill is the tool to use. Use it in the format **pskill [-] [-t] [\\RemotePC [-OptionalUsername [-p UserPassword]]] <processname | process id>** where **[-]** displays a list of supported options, and **[-t]** kills not just the process but all its dependent processes as well.

PsList

PsList will display detailed information about the processes running on a remote PC. Use it with the switches **[-d]** to display additional details, **[-m]** to show memory usage information, and **[-t]** to show process trees.

PsLoggedOn

This tool will display details of each user currently logged on (signed in) to a remote PC. This can be used with the switch **[-l]** to only show accounts logged in to the PC locally, and not across the network.

PsLogList

This is used to create a dump of event log records from a remote PC. There are quite a few switches and commands for this utility, which you can see in Table 13-1. You use it in the format psloglist [-] **[\\RemotePC[,RemotePC[,...]] | @file [-u OptionalUsername [-p UserPassword]]] [-s [-t delimiter]] [-m #|-n #|-h #|-d #|-w][-c][-x][-r][-a mm/dd/ yy][-b mm/dd/yy][-f filter] [-i ID[,ID[,...] | -e ID[,ID[,...]]] [-o event source[,event source][,..]]] [-q event source[,event source][,..]]] [-l event log file] <eventlog>.**

Table 13-1. *Available switches for PsLogList*

Switch	Description
@file	Executes the command on each of the PCs specified
-a	Exports the records timestamped after the specified date
-b	Exports the records timestamped before the specified date
-c	Clears the event log after displaying its contents
-d	Only displays records from previous *n* days
-e	Excludes events with the specified ID or IDs (up to 10)
-f	Filters event types with a string (e.g., **[-f w]** to filter warnings)
-h	Only displays records from previous *n* hours
-i	Shows only events with the specified ID or IDs (up to 10)
-l	Exports records from the specified event log file
-m	Only displays records from previous *n* minutes
-n	Only displays the number of most recent entries (e.g., **[-n 6]**)
-o	Shows only records from the specified event source
-p	Specifies an optional password for a username. You will be prompted for a password if you omit this
-q	Omits records from the specified event source or sources
-r	SDump log from least recent to most recent
-s	Displays Event Log records one per line, with comma-delimited fields
-t	Changes the delimiter to a specified character
-u	Specifies an optional username for login to a remote computer
-w	Tells PsLogList to wait for new events, exporting them as they generate (on the local PC only)
-x	Dumps extended data
eventlog	Open the event log

PsPasswd

This security tool can be used to change account passwords on a remote PC. Use it in the format pspasswd [[\\RemotePC[,RemotePC[,..] | @file [-u Username [-p Password]]] Username [NewPassword].

PsService

This lets you view and control services on a remote PC. Use it in the format **psservice [\\RemotePC [-u OptionalUsername] [-p UserPassword]] <command> <options>** where the options include those listed in Table 13-2.

Table 13-2. *Switches for the PsService command*

Switch	Description
query	Displays the status of a specified service
config	Displays the configuration of a specified service
setconfig	Sets the start type for a specified service (disabled, auto, on-demand)
start	Starts the specified service
stop	Stops the specified service
restart	Stops and then restarts a specified service
pause	Pauses the specified service
cont	Resumes a paused specified service
depend	Lists all of the the services that are dependent on the one specified
security	Dumps the specified service's security descriptor
find	Searches the network for the specified service

PsShutdown

PsShutdown can be used to either shut down or restart a remote PC. This can be used with the following useful switches: **[-f]** to force all applications to close immediately rather than giving them time to close on their own; **[-l]** to lock the remote PC; **[-m]** to display a message to appear on the screen for anybody using the PC when the shutdown countdown commences, which can be set with the **[-t xx]** switch, the default being 20 seconds; **[-r]** to restart the PC; and **[-c]** to allow the shutdown to be aborted by somebody still using the remote PC.

PsSuspend

If you need to suspend a process on a remote PC, then this tool will do the job. Use it in the format **pssuspend [-] [-r] [\\RemotePC [-u OptionalUsername] [-p UserPassword]] <process name | process id>** where **[-r]** resumes the suspended processes after they have been previously suspended.

AutoRuns

In Chapter 12, I showed you how to manage startup programs and apps in Windows 11, but there's actually considerably more that starts with the operating system that you might not know about. These include audio and video codecs, dynamic link libraries (DLLs), scheduled tasks, drivers, services, and more.

AutoRuns lets you examine absolutely everything that starts with the PC so that if you are getting an error on startup or when a user signs in, you can find and disable the offending item (see Figure 13-18). This can often happen when a program is uninstalled incorrectly, perhaps because of an error or perhaps because it's an older or poorly written uninstaller.

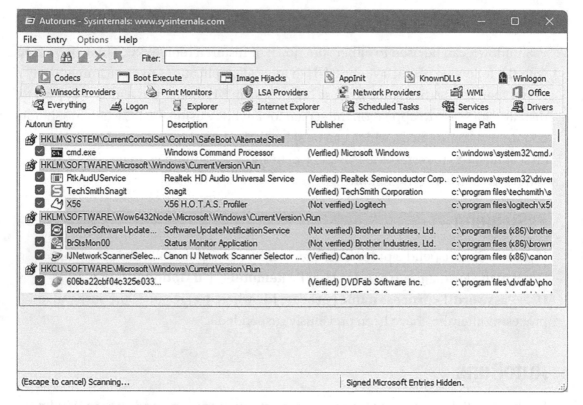

Figure 13-18. *AutoRuns lets you manage every startup item on a PC*

In the *Options* menu, you can show or hide empty locations and also Microsoft entries, as you don't want to be disabling a part of Windows 11 when it starts up. Additionally, some useful features sit in the *File* menu:

- **Analyze Offline System** lets you examine the Windows startup entries for an attached hard disk that's been removed from another PC. This can be useful if you are diagnosing a PC that won't start or that has a malware infection.

- **Save/Open** lets you save the startup entries as a file that can be emailed to a support person or read and examined on another PC.

- **Compare** is an option that allows you to compare the current startup entries on the PC with the saved entries from another PC.

- **Scan Options** is found under the *Options* menu and allows you to check the VirusTotal.com database to see if any matches with known malware are found in the startup entries.

You can disable and reenable entries in the startup list by unchecking or checking their box in AutoRuns. This can be useful as opposed to deleting the entry completely. You disable and re-enable entries from the *Entry* menu, in case you accidentally delete a startup entry that later proves to be necessary to the smooth operation of Windows and your installed software.

Each entry in the main list is also color-coded to help you identify them more easily:

- **Yellow** where a startup entry exists, but AutoRuns cannot find the installed program on your PC.

- **Green** where the entry was added recently since the last time you used AutoRuns.

- **Pink** where no known publisher information exists, either because the entry is not digitally signed or because no publisher information has been included with the process.

- **Purple** is the Registry address of the entry.

Handle

Earlier in this chapter, I showed you some Sysinternals utilities for dealing with locked files. Handle is a Command Line utility that can provide details of which app has opened and locked a particular file or director on your PC. Use it in the format **Handle <filename>** with additional switches, which are detailed on the Sysinternals website being useful, such as **[-u]** to show the username of the person with the open file.

ListDLLs

DLLs are files that are an essential part of Windows 10, or provided by third-party software companies, which enable apps to share functions on the PC. Back in the days of DOS, every running program had to provide its own way of managing everything, and I remember the excellent WordPerfect 5.1 word processor coming with a battery of disks that contained its own printer drivers.

DLLs took all this pain away, but knowing what's running can be impossible without the use of a utility such as ListDLLs. This is a Command Line utility (with switches available on the Sysinternals website) that can list all the DLLs that have been loaded by an app or process or list all the processes that are accessing a particular DLL. Should you find, for example, that an app, process, or DLL is crashing, you can use this tool to see if the DLLs in use have any other dependencies which may be causing the problem.

You can use it in the format **ListDLLs [processname]** to see what DLLs are in use by a specific process or in the format **ListDLLs [-d DLLname]** to see what running processes are using a specific DLL. Other useful switches, which are available on the Sysinternals website, include **[-u]** which will display only unsigned DLLs and **[-v]** which will display DLL version information.

Portmon

If you are using a PC system to which Serial or Parallel devices are attached, and they're still more common than you might think, then the Portmon utility can display all the activity for those ports. This includes successful and failed communications and the process using each port. This information can be useful in tracking down communication problems between the PC and attached devices.

ProcDump

ProcDump is a Command Line utility with two uses. The first of these is for monitoring an app for CPU processor spikes and reporting when a spike occurs. If you have an app that is periodically, or even regularly, using huge amounts of processor time, then ProcDump can provide valuable information about what it's doing at the time.

The second use for ProcDump is to monitor apps when they are hung. Sometimes, you may encounter an app for which the window appears to temporarily crash. This is because the app is doing or trying to do something in the background and cannot proceed until that task is complete. In this circumstance, ProcDump can provide information on what is occurring with that app at the time. Full details of the very many switches available to use with ProcDump are available on the Sysinternals website.

In its basic format however, use it as **ProcDump winword.exe** (see Figure 13-19), and it will produce its output in a .DMP file. This can be read using Microsoft Visual Studio, the Windows Driver Kit (WDK), or Windows Software Development Kit (SDK), but a search online will reveal other free .dmp file readers.

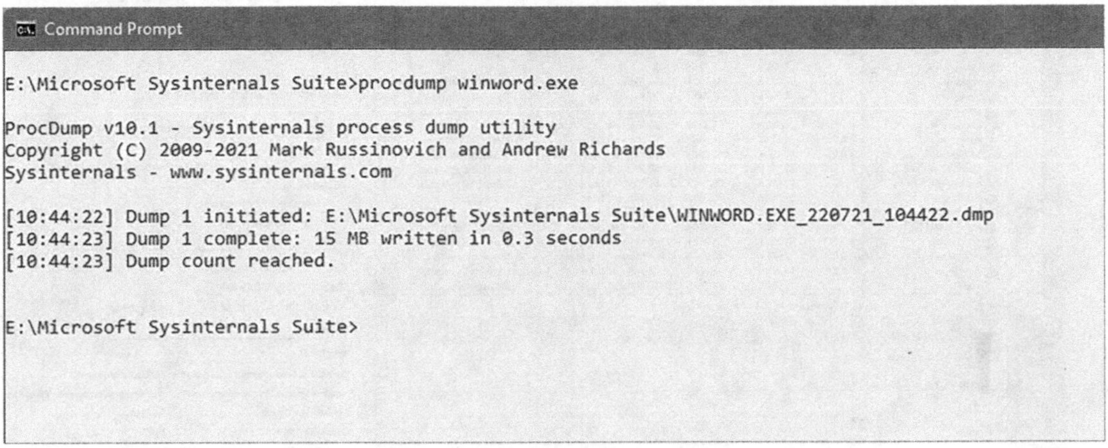

```
Command Prompt

E:\Microsoft Sysinternals Suite>procdump winword.exe

ProcDump v10.1 - Sysinternals process dump utility
Copyright (C) 2009-2021 Mark Russinovich and Andrew Richards
Sysinternals - www.sysinternals.com

[10:44:22] Dump 1 initiated: E:\Microsoft Sysinternals Suite\WINWORD.EXE_220721_104422.dmp
[10:44:23] Dump 1 complete: 15 MB written in 0.3 seconds
[10:44:23] Dump count reached.

E:\Microsoft Sysinternals Suite>
```

Figure 13-19. *ProcDump produces reports about crashed programs*

Process Explorer

A Sysinternals suite contains a few highly useful tools that should be in any IT Pro's toolkit. One of these is AutoRuns as I detailed earlier, and another is Process Explorer.

Process Explorer will tell you absolutely everything going on with running and hung processes on the PC, including their CPU, memory, and network usage, which DLLs are being used by the apps, if it's secure or being run in a virtualized environment, the permissions different users and user groups have with the app, and more (see Figure 13-20).

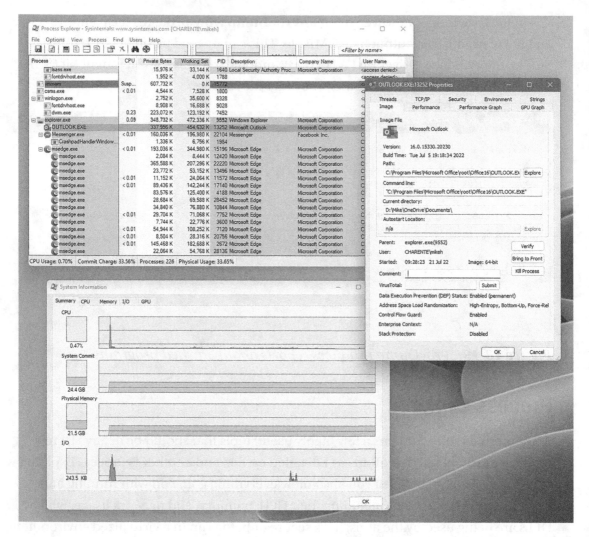

Figure 13-20. *Process Explorer provides a huge amount of detail on running processes*

The main view of Process Explorer lists all the running processes on the PC, along with details of any subprocesses. These items are all color-coded to make them easier to identify.

Tip   Sometimes, Process Explorer can fail to run, reporting an "*Unable to extract 64-bit image. Run Process Explorer from a writeable directory*" error. Should you encounter this, navigate to your AppData\Local\Temp folder by typing **%tmp%** into the Start Menu or the breadcrumb bar in File Explorer, right-click the `procexp64` app, and run it as an Administrator from there.

- **Purple** processes, which in our case include the malware, are files that may be compressed (also called packed), which for legitimate applications can help them to use less memory, but in the case of malware can also help to hide the code from your anti-malware scanner. Looking at the purple-colored files should be your first step.

- **Red** processes are ones that are currently existing (being stopped).

- **Green** processes have been freshly run (also known as spawned).

- **Light blue** processes are those run by the same account that started Process Explorer.

- **Dark blue** processes are ones that have currently been selected by yourself in Process Explorer.

- **Pink** processes are running Services on the PC, such as the common *svchost.exe*, which is a Windows system process that can host one or more other services where they share a process to reduce overall resource usage on a PC.

You can perform actions on processes such as killing them; killing the process tree, which will also shut down any dependent processes; restarting the process; and suspending it. This last option is useful where you are troubleshooting a process, and shutting it down will generate an error or cause something else to stop working.

Additionally, you can set the affinity of the process, meaning you can determine what physical and virtual processor cores are available to it, and its processing priority.

Under both the *Process* and the *Options* menus, you can check processes against the database at the virustotal.com website if you suspect a running process might be malware.

You can double-click a process to open its properties panel where a great deal of information and control can be found. Under the *Image* tab, for example, you can see the path and, if appropriate, the autostart entry for the process, which could be a Registry entry (see Figure 13-21).

Figure 13-21. *Detailed information about processes is available*

Additionally, under the Security and Environment tabs, you can see technical information about the process, including which users and user groups have permissions to access and run the process.

The remaining properties tabs will provide live information about the process, such as its CPU, memory, GPU (Graphics Processor), and networking activities and usage.

Process Monitor

Another of the highly useful tools in the Sysinternals suite is Process Monitor. This utility is incredibly useful when diagnosing and troubleshooting many types of problems on a PC, including hung apps and app dependencies, malware infections, misconfigured software, deleted files and Registry keys, and more besides (see Figure 13-22).

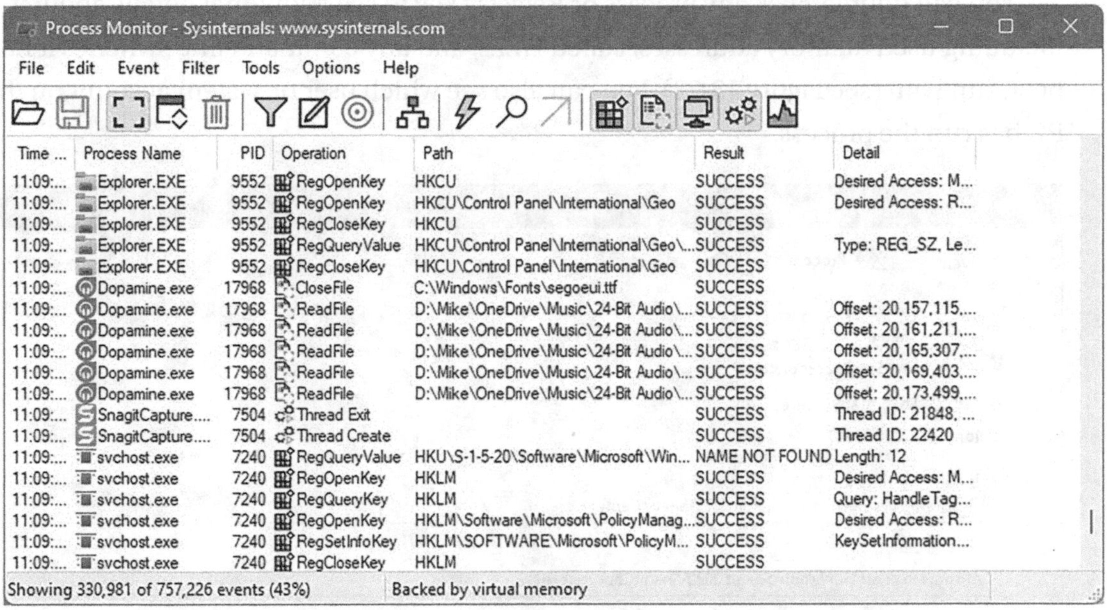

Figure 13-22.   *Process Monitor is highly useful for seeing what's happening on a PC*

Process Monitor details, in real time, every running process and service on the PC, with information about every operation they are performing, every Registry key they have open or have access to, and whether the actions they are taking are successful or are reporting an error.

Perhaps you are looking for the dependencies for malware that has infected a PC. You can use Process Monitor to identify all of the Services, DLLs, and Registry keys associated with the core malware app. You can also use Process Monitor to check the dependencies for any running app on the PC, to see what files and keys are associated with it. All of this information can come in handy when diagnosing problems with apps and Windows features, because you can see at a glance what's happening, if the tasks performed have been successful or not, or if essential Registry keys, DLLs, or Services are missing or reporting an error.

Additionally, you can filter the view to narrow the information displayed to a subset of the full available information. If a file is locked on the PC and unable to be deleted, moved, copied, or even opened, you can also see what process is currently using and has locked the file, so that the process can be closed or terminated. Perhaps most usefully, you can set Process Monitor to record every operation at boot time, and this data can then be exported to be read later in a variety of formats, including CSV and XML files.

You can double-click any process or Registry key to see additional details about it including used memory addresses, called DLLs, and any command line switches it has been run with (see Figure 13-23). You can also see which user or system account on the PC has run the process.

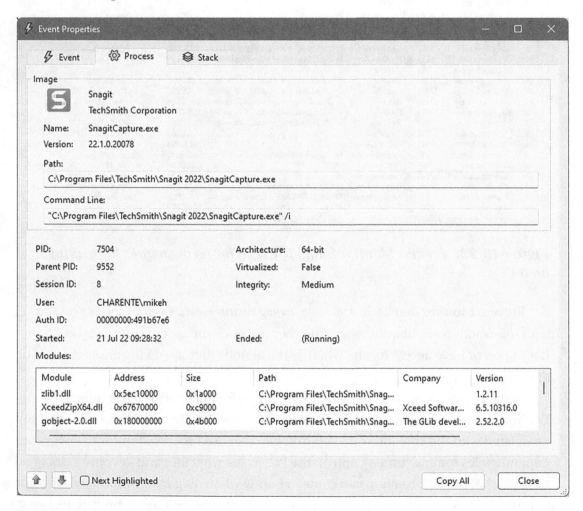

Figure 13-23. *Process Monitor provides extensive information*

When you are troubleshooting and diagnosing a process activity that has failed, such as the memory buffer overflow error seen in Figure 13-24, you can get the exact time and day of the failure and see technical details about it.

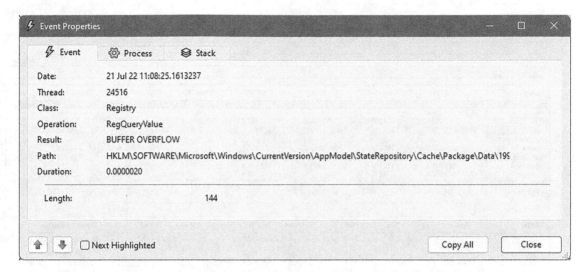

Figure 13-24. You can get technical details on process failures

ShellRunas

ShellRunas is another Command Line utility, but one that allows you to launch an app or process under the sign-in credentials of a user other than the one who is already signed in to the PC. Use it in the format **ShellRunAs /reg** to add this functionality to the *right-click* context menu in File Explorer with more switches available on the Sysinternals website.

VMMap

PCs don't just hold running apps and processes in memory; they also save some memory to disk in the form of virtual memory, known as the Paging File in Windows. VMMap allows you to view the physical and virtual memory usage of a specific process (see Figure 13-25). If an app or process is hogging memory, this utility can provide detailed information on how much memory and what memory types are being used.

Type	Size	Committed	Private	Total WS	Private WS	Shareable WS	Shared WS	Locked
Total	2,220,142,080 K	889,272 K	189,600 K	346,196 K	167,688 K	178,508 K	178,508 K	
Free	135,218,811,328 K							
Heap	17,792 K	9,208 K	9,144 K	8,788 K	8,784 K	4 K	4 K	
Image	364,184 K	364,184 K	7,464 K	108,308 K	3,656 K	104,652 K	104,652 K	
Managed Heap								
Mapped File	264,024 K	264,024 K		64,832 K		64,832 K	64,832 K	
Page Table								
Private Data	71,642,888 K	172,104 K	171,816 K	154,520 K	154,496 K	24 K	24 K	
Shareable	2,147,541,532 K	78,576 K		9,036 K	40 K	8,996 K	8,996 K	
Stack	286,720 K	1,176 K	1,176 K	712 K	712 K			
Unusable	24,940 K							

Address	Type	Size	Committed	Private	Total WS	Private ...	Sharea...	Share...	Lock...	Blocks	Protection
⊞ 000000007FFE0000	Private Data	4 K	4 K	4 K	4 K		4 K	4 K		1	Read
⊞ 000000007FFEC000	Private Data	4 K	4 K	4 K	4 K		4 K	4 K		1	Read
⊞ 000000BB13000000	Private Data	2,048 K	284 K	284 K	284 K	284 K				35	Read/Write
⊞ 000000BB13200000	Thread Stack	8,192 K	180 K	180 K	168 K	168 K				3	Read/Write/Guard
⊞ 000000BB13A00000	Private Data	8,192 K	8 K	8 K	4 K	4 K				4	Read/Guard
⊞ 000000BB15200000	Thread Stack	8,192 K	20 K	20 K	8 K	8 K				3	Read/Write/Guard
⊞ 000000BB15A00000	Private Data	8,192 K	8 K	8 K	4 K	4 K				4	Read/Guard

Figure 13-25. VMMap allows you to view Page File use for a process

Summary

After two chapters about troubleshooting and diagnosing problems with processes and services, it's fairly clear that there's an awful lot that can be done to keep programs and software running smoothly on a PC and to keep the PC stable in the event of a program crashing or being incorrectly uninstalled.

Microsoft's Sysinternals suite in particular is extraordinarily useful in this regard, especially with AutoRuns, Process Explorer, and Process Monitor, all of which we'll look at in more detail when we examine how to remove malware infections in Chapter 18.

In the next chapter, we'll look at more Sysinternals tools as part of how to configure, diagnose, and troubleshoot networking problems on a PC as, let's face it, our PCs are pretty much a piece of junk if they can't get access to network shares, cloud services, and the Internet.

CHAPTER 14

Network and Internet Troubleshooting

So far in this book, we've covered how to troubleshoot problems with the core Windows OS and Windows Updates. We've looked at how problems with user accounts and file and document access can be diagnosed and repaired. We've also looked at how legacy software can be supported, and troublesome apps and programs can be restored or removed.

None of that though compares to my solemn duty in this chapter, as I have genuinely met and worked with people who forget how to stand upright and feed themselves when they lose access to the Internet, and I'm fairly certain you will know some of these people as well.

Of course, it's not just Internet access that can cause major problems for businesses, organizations, and individuals, as local network access problems can act as a huge barrier to productivity and even bring entire workflows to a grinding halt. Not being able to access your local Network Attached Storage (NAS) drive or even a network printer can result in traipsing back and forth with a USB Flash Drive (after you've spent half an hour trying to find one; Ed) or just reaching into your desk drawer and pulling out that pack of playing cards you keep there for times just like this.

Prevention Is Better Than Cure

You may have heard the phrase "prevention is better than cure," a British saying attributed to Dutch humanist scholar Desiderius Erasmus around 1500AD. The philosophy behind this is straightforward. If you set up a system so as to prevent a

© Mike Halsey 2023
M. Halsey, *Troubleshooting and Supporting Windows 11*, https://doi.org/10.1007/978-1-4842-8728-6_14

problem from occurring in the first instance, then your life will be much more simple and uncomplicated than trying to fix the problems that could occur from it later on.

So it is with network settings in Windows. It's very often the case that you plug in a network cable or install a Wi-Fi driver and everything just works as it should and continues to work indefinitely. Sadly, things are often not that simple, as you might need to configure a Virtual Private Network (VPN) and connect someone via a cellular modem or even a dial-up modem in some parts of the world, and then there's the problem of international travel.

Let's start with this as it's often something that catches people by surprise. When people from the United States of America or Canada travel to Europe or the Middle East, they can frequently be caught out by the stable and reliable Wi-Fi they're used to at home suddenly not working any more.

This has a simple cause. In the United States and Canada, houses and workplace buildings are commonly made from fairly thin wood or breeze block construction. In many other countries building can be hundreds, sometimes even several thousands, of years old. My own house in France is one such example (see Figure 14-1). It's been twice extended, but the oldest part of the property is around 350 years old, having been built some time during the mid-1600s.

Figure 14-1. *My own property has some walls two feet thick*

This means that some walls in the house are upward of two feet thick and made from local stone, which is so incredibly hard it's made it difficult to get some work done in the garden that I wanted.

Naturally, the previous owners put the telephone point in this part of the house, and though I've now switched to satellite broadband and consequently moved the main router to a more sensible location, having the router stuck within such huge stone walls made Wi-Fi access elsewhere extremely difficult.

Indeed, I had to invest in a full Mesh Wi-Fi system with various indoor and outdoor repeaters to ensure a good and reliable signal across the property, and large parts of the property and my home office in my gîte, an outhouse common to French countryside properties that itself used to be a barn, are now connected by gigabit Ethernet cable. Some properties are even worse however with homes and workplaces in southern Europe, North Africa, and the Middle East sometimes being a thousand years old or even older.

This is something to bear in mind when a mobile worker complains they can't get a Wi-Fi signal at the place they're visiting, and you probably have to tell them in reply to enjoy the sunshine outside or perhaps go and sit near a window.

Setting your networking and other systems up in a robust way then can prevent problems later on, and being prepared for issues that may arise, such as Wi-Fi and cellular connectivity, can help reduce the volume of support calls. Also, as I wrote in Chapter 5, establishing effective IT training can help mitigate some of these problems as well. You might be surprised how many people would have no idea that thick stone walls can block radio signals, and for the rest I can only quote the late, great Douglas Adams, author of *The Hitchhiker's Guide to the Galaxy* (Pan Books, 1979), who said, *"The problem people face in trying to make something completely foolproof, is that they frequently underestimate the ingenuity of complete fools."*

Configuring Network Settings

Networking is one of those areas of Windows that's been moved wholesale from the Control Panel into Settings. Where it comes to other aspects of the operating system, this is actually a good thing, but networking is different, being complex and sometimes needing advanced configuration. The end result is this is something you want hidden from the end user rather than being available for them to see.

For now, the *Network and Sharing Center* still exists in the Control Panel, and there are no networking tools in Windows Tools. We can no doubt expect this to change in the coming years, so bear this in mind if I reference something you can't later find.

Let's begin with Settings however. Listed in the left panel as *Network & internet*, the main controls are sensibly separated into *WiFi*, *Cellular* (if it's available in your PC's hardware), *Ethernet*, *VPN*, *Mobile Hotspot*, *Flight Mode*, *Proxy* (server), and *Dial-up* for those that still need to use it (see Figure 14-2).

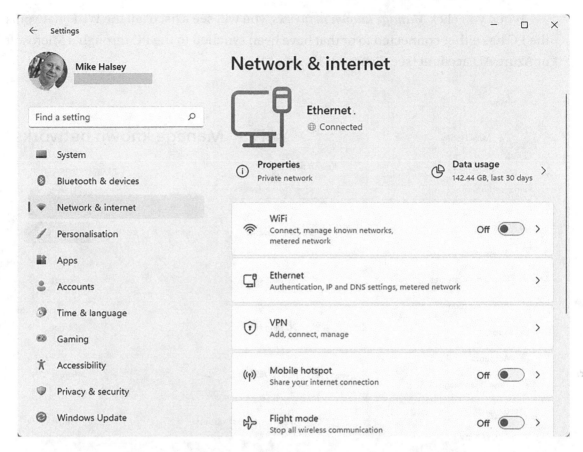

Figure 14-2. *Most networking options have been moved to Settings*

Below these is an *Advanced network settings* option that we'll look at shortly. There are some other things you can do in Settings though that you will find useful.

Wi-Fi Settings

The Wi-Fi settings offer some useful options, not the least of which is a full list of all the stored networks for the PC, but we'll look at that shortly. At its most basic, there is a switch to turn Wi-Fi on or off and an option when you turn Wi-Fi off to turn it back on in one hour, in four hours, the next day, or manually.

The *Random hardware addresses* option can make using your laptop more secure when connected to public Wi-Fi networks. What this feature does is to generate random physical hardware (MAC) addresses for the PC, making it much more difficult for people to track the laptop when scanning networks for hardware and connections.

When you click *Manage known networks*, you will see a list of all the Wi-Fi networks the PC has either connected to or that have been synched to the PC through a Microsoft or Azure AD account (see Figure 14-3).

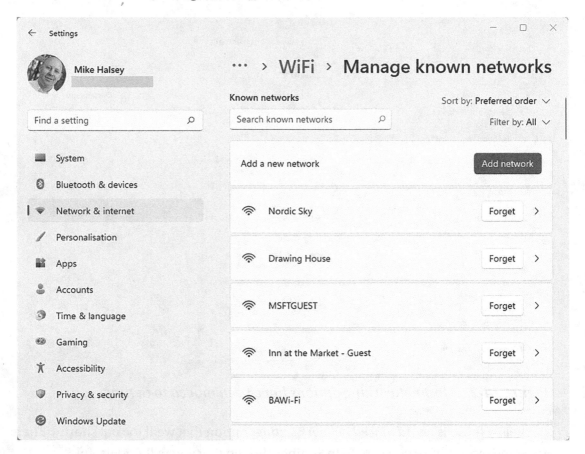

Figure 14-3. *You can view all known Wi-Fi networks in Settings*

Each of these networks has a *Forget* button next to it. This can be useful if the settings for the network have become corrupt, and you need to reconnect to the network with a fresh, rebuilt configuration.

When you click a Wi-Fi network, you will see additional options. These include being able to automatically connect to the network when in range, but also to disable this option. You can also set the network as a metered (cellular) connection (see Figure 14-4), which can be useful if the network is provided by a cellular hotspot device such as a smartphone or cellular modem.

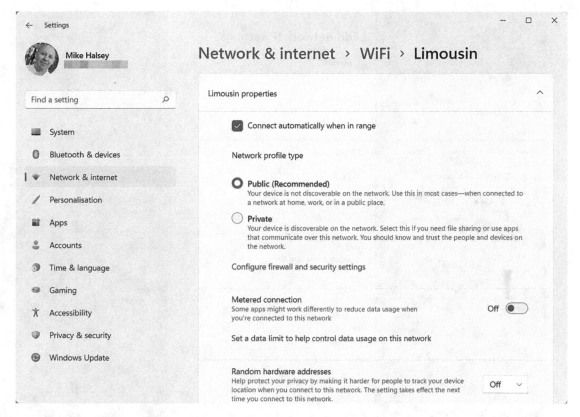

Figure 14-4. *You can set a Wi-Fi connection as cellular*

Again, there's an option to display random MAC addresses for the PC. Below this however are two options that can be very useful for businesses and corporations, being able to manually configure IP and DNS server addresses.

You can set both or either IPv4 or IPv6 addresses for the connection (see Figure 14-5) and also IPv4 and IPv6 DNS addresses. If you have a domain on a local subnet with its own DNS addressing system, this can make sure people can always make a good connection.

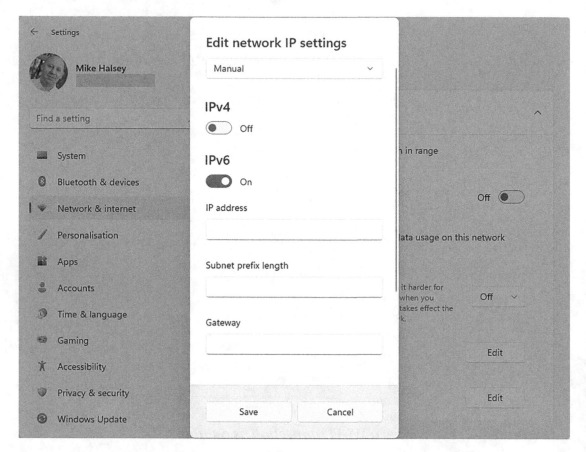

Figure 14-5. *You can set IPv4 and IPv6 IP and DNS addresses in Settings*

Managing Data Usage for Cellular and Other Networks

If you are using a cellular network, and sometimes this is useful for Wi-Fi and wired networks too, you can set data usage. This is because cellular data can be expensive, especially when roaming and visiting a different country.

Tip   It can be wise to advise people to turn on airplane mode or to turn off data roaming when being near a border. People close to the Ireland/Northern Ireland border frequently have issues with their smartphones roaming and running up huge bills. For myself in France, if I get a ferry across the English Channel back to the UK I also need to deactivate roaming as the bills accrued while travelling can be enormous. On modern devices, airplane mode can be activated, and Wi-Fi then turned on safely to avoid roaming charges.

There are a couple of different ways to get to data usage management in Windows 11. From the properties for a particular Wi-Fi network, you can click *Set a data limit to help control data usage on this network* (which is also available in the Cellular and Ethernet settings) or click *Network & internet*, then *Advanced network settings* followed by *Data usage*.

Now it's a misnomer that this is available as an option for individual Wi-Fi and cellular networks as it doesn't actually set data limits for each one individually. What this feature does is set them globally for the PC, though as I mentioned this isn't the only way to manage data usage.

You will see a list of all the apps and software installed on the PC sorted by how large their data usage is. At the top right of the window is a drop-down box where you select the network adapter to set limits for, and below this is an *Enter limit* button that you can click.

Here, you can set the data limit to stop at in either MB or GB and also the date of the month on which this limit will reset, that is, the date each month when a new cellular allowance kicks in if appropriate (see Figure 14-6).

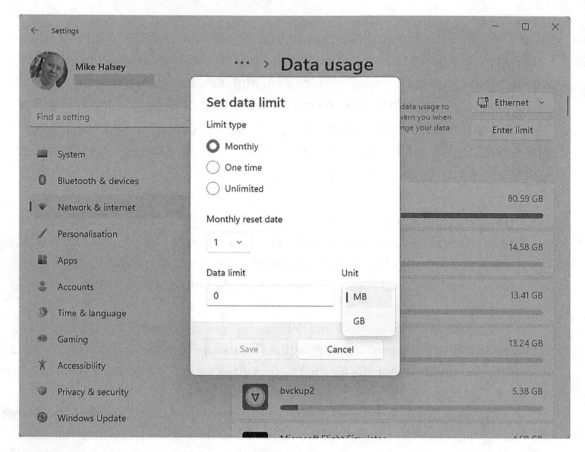

Figure 14-6. *You can set data allowances for any network connection*

Tip   One of the most useful features here, and something many weary travellers wouldn't have the faintest idea even exists, is the *One time* option. Setting this allows you to specify a period for just a short trip of up to a month where the data allowance is limited.

I mentioned that there is more than one way to reduce the amount of data used by a PC when connected to a network. This is to set the connection as *Metered* which I detailed a little while ago. When a connection is set as metered, some services such as automatically downloading Windows Updates, and allowing background apps to search for and download messages and other updates.

Additionally, if you have cellular installed in your PC, either through a physical SIM card slot or by use of an eSIM (Electronic Subscriber Identification Module), there are options in Settings including *Data roaming options* and *Choose apps that can use your cellular data* that can help significantly reduce the cost of data used, especially when roaming.

Managing Advanced Network Settings

When I woke up this morning, sitting in the garden with a friend and a pot of coffee that was, if I'm honest, rather too strong, but at least I know now not to buy it again, I was regaling him with the story of the little unicorn that needed access to his cloud files, but who was being prevented from accessing them by the evil Network Configuration Wizard that had erected the great fire wall.

The little unicorn called on the help of the Network Troubleshooting Wizard who, after a great battle with the Network Configuration Wizard, was able to break through the fire wall, and the unicorn was able to access his cloud files once again... what can I say, it was half seven in the morning and I was still waking up.

Fortunately, you don't need ancient scrolls, the help of sage wizards, and to face long treks across bleak vistas to be able to configure your networks, which is a bit of luck. In Settings, you can click *Network & internet* and then *Advanced network settings* to get access to the tools and configuration options you need.

Each network adapter is listed along with a single button to disable that adapter and an expand arrow to get more information and controls (see Figure 14-7).

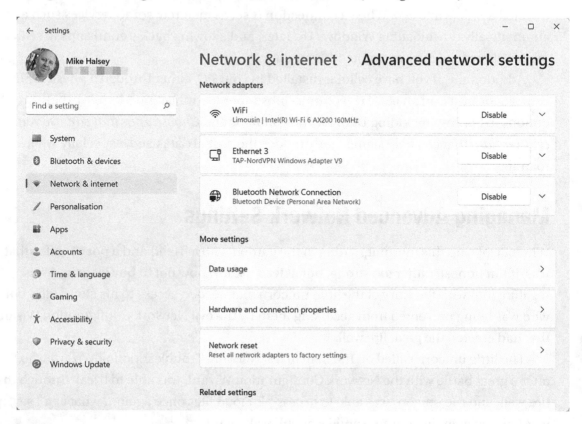

Figure 14-7. *Advanced Network Settings list each adapter*

Expanding the details for an adapter will reveal its current status, the total amount of data sent and received by it, and the total speed of the connection, see Figure 14-8. This can be useful if you're trying to diagnose a gigabit Ethernet line that's only operating at a slow speed because it's been plugged into the wrong socket on the switch panel.

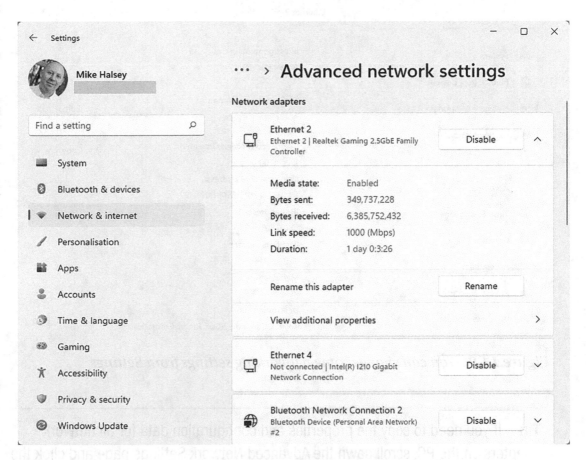

Figure 14-8. *You can check the working status of a network adapter*

Clicking the *View additional properties* link will enable you to change settings for the adapter that you may need, such as the IP address and DNS server assignment, and also to copy its configuration data so it can be pasted into a document or an email and sent to a support person (see Figure 14-9).

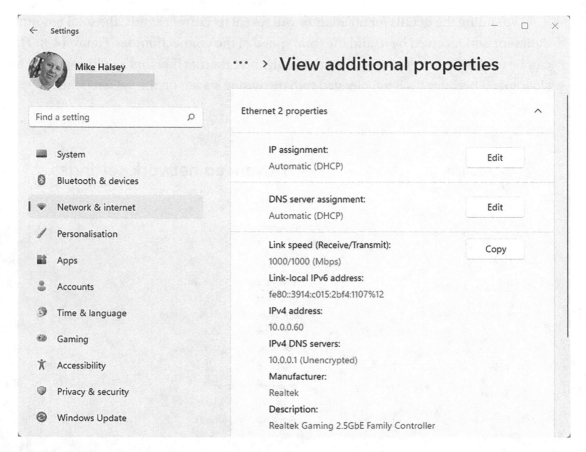

Figure 14-9. You can change some networking settings from Settings

---

Tip   If you need to copy the properties and configuration data for all network adapters on the PC, scroll down the Advanced Network Settings page and click the *Hardware and Connection Properties* option.

Resetting the Network Adapters

The only other option available in the Advanced Network Settings... erm... settings, at least at the time of writing, is a *Network reset* feature. This can be more useful than you might think as, if a user has tried to be helpful by configuring a VPN or a Proxy, or has thought it was a good idea to alter the IP or DNS configuration for the PC themselves, you can undo all of their handiwork with a single click (see Figure 14-10). This will reset all the network adapters in the PC to their default configuration.

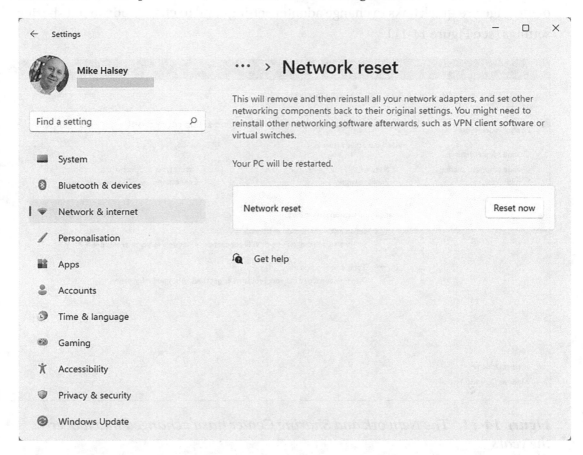

Figure 14-10. *You can easily reset all the network adapters to their default state*

The Network and Sharing Center

I mentioned at the beginning of this chapter that Microsoft is still moving applets out of the Control Panel and into either Settings or Windows Tools. This means that anything from here on is likely to be moved and changed some time in the future. I would imagine though that much of it will be moved to Windows Tools and then left largely as it is so that functionality isn't broken for Microsoft's corporate customers.

The Network and Sharing Center hasn't changed very much over the years. In the main panel are details and a link for the network adapter currently being used for a connection, options to set up a new connection, and a troubleshooting link. On the left of the page are quick links to change adapter settings and to change advanced sharing settings (see Figure 14-11).

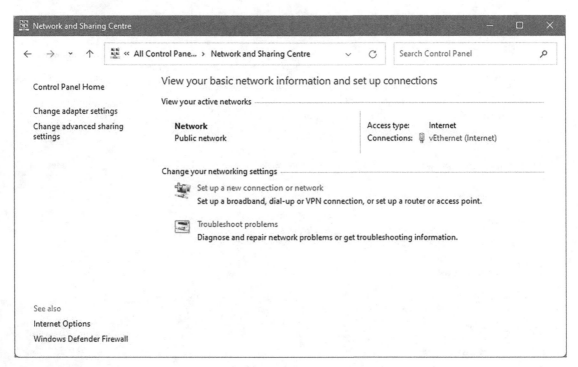

Figure 14-11. *The Network and Sharing Center hasn't changed much over the years*

To be honest, I'd probably ignore the *Set up a new connection or network* options at this stage, as the tools in Settings now provide all you need to a much more friendly interface, especially when it comes to configuring Virtual Private Networks (VPNs) and Proxy servers.

If you click the link for the current network adapter however, a dialog will appear with useful tools (see Figure 14-12).

Figure 14-12. *The network adapter properties dialog can be highly useful*

At the top center of the status dialog is connection information, such as the current uptime and speed of the connection. Additionally, this informs you if the connection is using IPv4 or IPv6. Below this are buttons to access the *Properties* for the adapter, which we'll look at soon, *Disable* it, or *Diagnose* a problem by running the network troubleshooter.

Clicking the *Details* button will display technical data about the adapter and its status. This is very similar to the information provided by the Settings panel except that additional information is available (see Figure 14-13).

Figure 14-13. *You can get technical details about network connections in the Network and Sharing Center*

It's when we dig into the network adapter *Properties* however that we get full controls. The main dialog presents two tabs, *Networking* and *Sharing*. Under the Networking tab are details of all the network services available for that adapter, and the ones that are active are checked (see Figure 14-14).

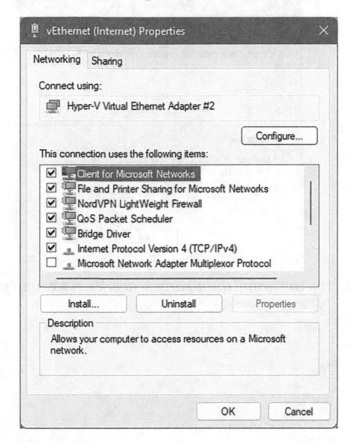

Figure 14-14. *You can see what network services are available to and enabled for the adapter*

You may have a specific Microsoft or third-party service or network protocol you need to install; click the *Install* button, and you will be prompted for a configuration file or driver (see Figure 14-15).

Figure 14-15. *You can install third-party network services and protocols*

Some of the services that are installed and available for an adapter will have configurable properties. Among these will be the IP address options (see Figure 14-16). Though not all network services will be configurable, if you do need to change properties for a service this is where the option resides.

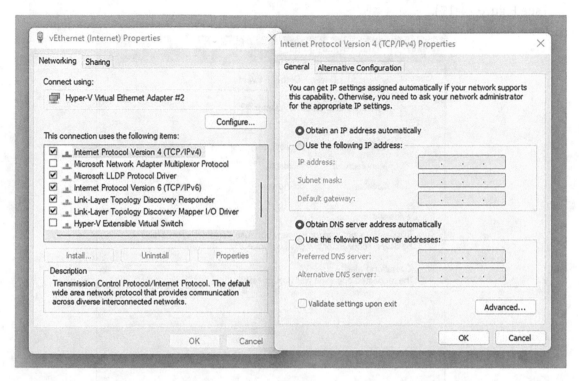

Figure 14-16. *Some network services have options you can configure per adapter*

There are a great deal more options and information available however about the status of network adapters that can be found by clicking the *Configure* button in the adapter properties dialog. The first tab in the new dialog that appears, *General*, can inform you if there is a problem with the adapter or if that adapter is working properly (see Figure 14-17).

Figure 14-17. *The adapter properties can inform you if a problem exists*

If there is an error, you can get further details about it from the *Events* tab, which will pull in data from the full Windows Event Viewer.

We will look at this dialog in much more detail in Chapter 15, but the *Advanced* tab is also where you can find additional configuration options for network adapters. These options will vary greatly from one hardware or software device to another; however, you may find special security, encryption, VPN, or other options here that need to be configured for specific circumstances (see Figure 14-18).

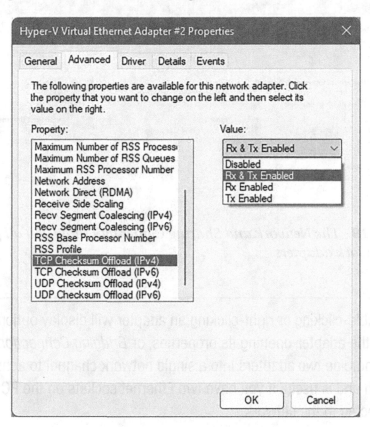

Figure 14-18. *Advanced configuration properties are available for network adapters*

Back in the Network and Sharing Center, you can click the *Change adapter settings* link to see all the installed network adapters on the PC. For many PCs and laptops, this will be just one or two, such as a Wi-Fi adapter, an Ethernet adapter, and your Bluetooth adapter.

Where things can get more complex however is when you have additional networking services installed. On my own office PC, seen in Figure 14-19, I have Microsoft's Hyper-V virtual machine services running, along with having a VPN configured.

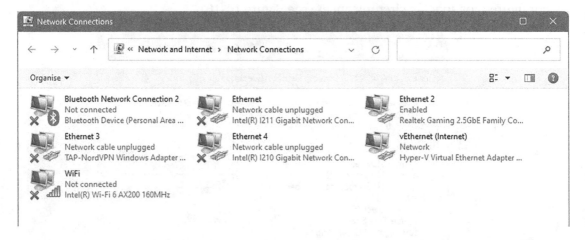

Figure 14-19. *The Network and Sharing Center will show you all physical and virtual network adapters*

Tip   Double-clicking or right-clicking an adapter will display options including disabling the adapter, opening its properties, or *Bridging Connections*. This can be used to combine two adapters into a single network channel to achieve double the bandwidth and is useful if you have two Ethernet sockets on the PC, both of which are connected to the network.

Managing and Troubleshooting Wi-Fi Networks

In this day and age, it's common to find most people connecting to networks via Wi-Fi. This can on occasion cause problems from corrupt networks to forgotten passwords. All of these problems can be solved however. In the first example, a corrupt network, I detailed earlier in this chapter how you can tell Windows 10 to "forget" a network. Should you have a PC that cannot connect to the network it previously connected to perfectly well, this will be your best, quickest, and by far the most effective solution.

Recovering Forgotten Wi-Fi Access Passwords

It's also straightforward to recover forgotten Wi-Fi passwords in Windows, and there are a couple of ways to achieve this. The easiest is from within the Wi-Fi network properties dialog. You will see a *Wireless Properties* button. Click this and another dialog will appear containing connection and security settings for the network.

Under the security tab, in addition to being able to set the security type for the network, there is a *Network security key* box (see Figure 14-20). If you check the *Show characters* box, the password will be displayed.

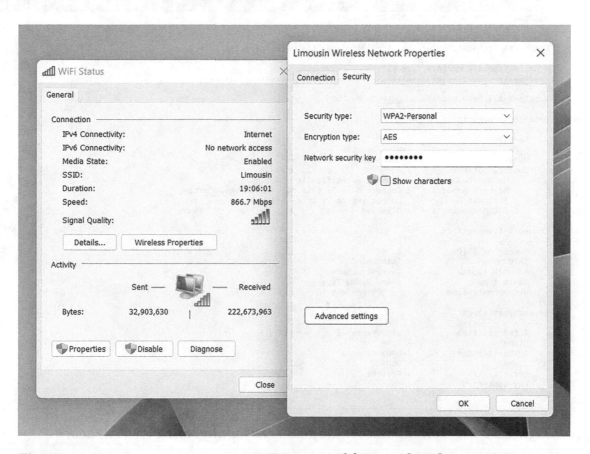

Figure 14-20. *You can recover a Wi-Fi password from within the properties dialog*

This method is only really useful though for getting the password to the currently connected network, so for other networks we need to use scripting within the Command Line or PowerShell (both environments use the same commands). Use the command netsh wlan show profiles to list all the stored Wi-Fi networks on the PC. Once you have the name of the network you need to recover the password for, type netsh wlan show profiles name="network name" key=clear. Technical details for the network will appear, and you will see the password for the network listed in the **Key content** field (see Figure 14-21).

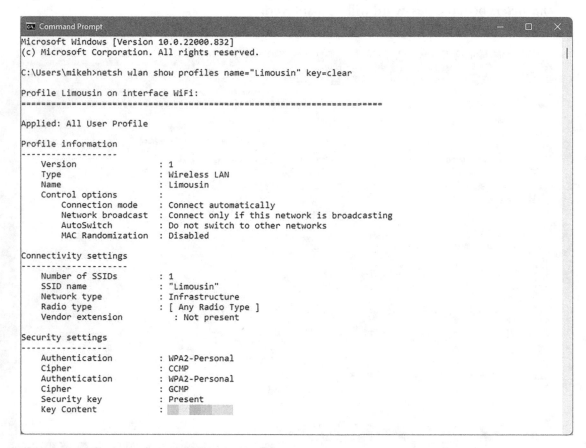

Figure 14-21. *You can recover the password for any stored Wi-Fi network*

Prioritizing Wi-Fi Network Connections

You will be aware that for many Wi-Fi networks your PC or laptop will auto-connect when it detects one you have connected to previously. If you are in a workplace or even a public place where there is more than a single network available, you will want to connect to one specifically and make certain this is always the first network the PC attempts to connect to.

This can be achieved with the command `netsh wlan set profileorder name="network name" priority=1` to set a specific network as the first to connect to, and then you can use the numbers 2, 3, and so on to set other networks' priority if you need to.

Troubleshooting Wi-Fi Networks Using Scripting

I mentioned earlier in this chapter that you can delete the profile for a corrupt Wi-Fi network, so you can reconnect as though it was the first time and rebuild the connection profile (you might want to remember to recover the password before doing this). You can also delete Wi-Fi network profiles using scripting with the command `netsh wlan delete profile name="network name"`.

You can also get a detailed report on Wi-Fi connectivity including any errors and events using the command `netsh wlan show wlanreport`. This will save HTML, XML, and Windows Event files in a folder called **C:\ProgramData\Microsoft\Windows\WlanReport** with the main `wlan-report-latest.html` file containing detailed technical information (see Figure 14-22).

Wireless Sessions

Interface:Intel(R) Wi-Fi 6 AX200 160MHz
Interface GUID: eb664fdd-3b4e-4d94-87da-1ee2b5e476f9
Connection Mode:Automatic connection with a profile
Profile:Limousin
SSID:Limousin
BSS Type:Infrastructure
Session Duration: 0 hours 0 minutes 57 seconds
Disconnect Reason:The network is disconnected by the driver.

Eventid	Time	Message
11004	2022-07-26T15:05:00	[+]Wireless security stopped.
11010	2022-07-26T15:05:00	[+]Wireless security started.
11005	2022-07-26T15:05:00	[+]Wireless security succeeded.
11004	2022-07-26T15:05:01	[+]Wireless security stopped.
11010	2022-07-26T15:05:01	[+]Wireless security started.
11005	2022-07-26T15:05:01	[+]Wireless security succeeded.
11004	2022-07-26T15:05:41	[+]Wireless security stopped.
11010	2022-07-26T15:05:41	[+]Wireless security started.
11005	2022-07-26T15:05:41	[+]Wireless security succeeded.
4003	2022-07-26T15:05:57	[+]WLAN AutoConfig detected limited connectivity, attempting automatic recovery.
11004	2022-07-26T15:05:57	[+]Wireless security stopped.
8003	2022-07-26T15:05:57	[+]WLAN AutoConfig service has successfully disconnected from a wireless network.
1010	2022-07-26T15:05:57	[+]CDE reported an L2 adapter removal
10002	2022-07-26T15:05:58	[+]WLAN Extensibility Module has stopped.
10001	2022-07-26T15:05:58	[+]WLAN Extensibility Module has successfully started.
1009	2022-07-26T15:05:58	[+]CDE reported an L2 adapter arrival

Interface:Intel(R) Wi-Fi 6 AX200 160MHz
Interface GUID: eb664fdd-3b4e-4d94-87da-1ee2b5e476f9
Connection Mode:Automatic connection with a profile
Profile:Limousin
SSID:Limousin
BSS Type:Infrastructure
Session Duration: 66 hours 35 minutes 2 seconds
Disconnect Reason:Unknown

EventId	Time	Message
8000	2022-07-26T15:06:01	[+]WLAN AutoConfig service started a connection to a wireless network.
11000	2022-07-26T15:06:01	[+]Wireless network association started.
11001	2022-07-26T15:06:01	[+]Wireless network association succeeded.
11010	2022-07-26T15:06:01	[+]Wireless security started.

Figure 14-22. *The Wlan report contains detailed technical data*

There is also detailed technical information you can get from using scripting. The command netsh wlan show wirelesscapabilities will display a great deal of technical information about what wireless, security, and other features are supported by your Wi-Fi adapter (see Figure 14-23).

```
Administrator: Command Prompt

Microsoft Windows [Version 10.0.22000.832]
(c) Microsoft Corporation. All rights reserved.

C:\WINDOWS\system32>netsh wlan show wirelesscapabilities

Wireless System Capabilities
----------------------------
    Number of antennas connected to the 802.11 radio (value not available)
    Max number of channels the device can operate on, simultaneously (value not available)
    Co-existence Support                      : Unknown


Wireless Device Capabilities
----------------------------

Interface name: WiFi

    WDI Version (Windows)                     : 0.1.1.12
    WDI Version (IHV)                         : 0.1.1.9
    WiFiCx Version (IHV)                      : WiFiCx Interface Not Supported
    Firmware Version                          : F3.58
    Station                                   : Supported
    Soft AP                                   : Not supported
    Network monitor mode                      : Not supported
    Wi-Fi Direct Device                       : Supported
    Wi-Fi Direct GO                           : Supported
    Wi-Fi Direct Client                       : Supported
    Protected Management Frames               : Supported
    DOT11k neighbor report                    : Supported
    ANQP Service Information Discovery        : Supported
    Action Frame                              : Supported
    Diversity Antenna                         : Supported
    IBSS                                      : Not Supported
    Promiscuous Mode                          : Not Supported
    P2P Device Discovery                      : Supported
```

Figure 14-23. *You can see technical information about security features supported by your Wi-Fi adapter*

Tip   You can display global settings for Wi-Fi network connections using the command `netsh wlan show settings`.

The command `netsh wlan show interfaces` will display information about the currently in use Wi-Fi adapters. Similarly, the command `netsh wlan show drivers` will display technical information about the Wi-Fi driver on the PC (see Figure 14-24). This information goes well beyond the driver date and version number, providing information on how security and encryption are supported and implemented, what legacy Wi-Fi network types it is compatible with, and if the driver also supports wireless display (Wi-Di) technologies.

```
Administrator: Command Prompt

Microsoft Windows [Version 10.0.22000.832]
(c) Microsoft Corporation. All rights reserved.

C:\WINDOWS\system32>netsh wlan show drivers

Interface name: WiFi

    Driver                  : Intel(R) Wi-Fi 6 AX200 160MHz
    Vendor                  : Intel Corporation
    Provider                : Intel
    Date                    : 03 Mar 21
    Version                 : 22.40.0.7
    INF file                : oem22.inf
    Type                    : Native Wi-Fi Driver
    Radio types supported   : 802.11b 802.11g 802.11n 802.11a 802.11ac 802.11ax
    FIPS 140-2 mode supported : Yes
    802.11w Management Frame Protection supported : Yes
    Hosted network supported  : No
    Authentication and cipher supported in infrastructure mode:
                                Open            None
                                Open            WEP-40bit
                                Open            WEP-104bit
                                Open            WEP
                                WPA-Enterprise  TKIP
                                WPA-Enterprise  CCMP
                                WPA-Personal    TKIP
                                WPA-Personal    CCMP
                                WPA2-Enterprise TKIP
                                WPA2-Enterprise CCMP
                                WPA2-Personal   TKIP
```

Figure 14-24. *You can get technical information on the Wi-Fi driver*

Backing Up and Importing Wi-Fi Connection Profiles

I spoke earlier about recovering lost passwords for Wi-Fi connections, but one very useful feature of the **netsh** command is the ability to back up and restore individual Wi-Fi profiles. To do this, you can use the command netsh wlan export profile name="profilename" key=clear folder=E:\Wi-Fi_Backup where **E:\Wi-Fi_Backup** is the destination folder on your hard disk you want the files backed up to; note that this folder must already exist as it won't be created in the export process.

If you want to export all the stored Wi-Fi network profiles on the PC, use the command netsh wlan export profile key=clear folder=E:\Wi-Fi_Backup. These are XML files that open in your browser (see Figure 14-25) and that can then be reimported using the command netsh wlan add profile filename="path-and-

`file-name.xml" interface="interfacename"` where **interface** specifies the network adapter that will be used to connect to this network.

Note   When exporting Wi-Fi connection profiles, be sure to use the `key=clear` switch to also export the password, though bear in mind this will be stored in plain text within the XML file.

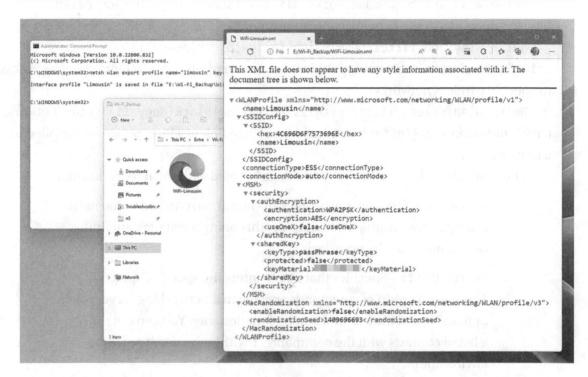

Figure 14-25.   *You can export and reimport Wi-Fi connection profiles*

Tip   You can reset the networking stack in Windows if you have a corruption with the command `netsh int int reset`.

Other Netsh Commands for Managing Networking

There are other commands you can use in the Command Line and PowerShell with `netsh`. The most useful when it comes to diagnosing and troubleshooting problems are as follows:

`Netsh wlan show blocked networks` – To display a list of any networks that are blocked on the PC

`Netsh wlan set blockednetworks display={show|hide}` – To show or hide blocked networks in the network connections panel

`Netsh wlan add filter permission={allow|block|denyall} ssid="networkname" networktype={infrastructure|adhoc}` – To block or allow access to specific wireless networks

`Netsh wlan delete filter permission={allow|block|denyall} ssid="network name" networktype={infrastructure|adhoc}` – To delete a filter previously applied to a network

There are also additional switches that can be used with the **netsh** command:

> `-a <AliasFile>` – Specifies that you should be returned to the netsh prompt after running your alias file, this being a text file containing one or more netsh commands.

> `-c <Context>` – Specifies that netsh enters the specified context. These are a group of commands specific to a networking server role or feature, and they extend netsh's functionality. You can obtain a list of contexts with the command /**?** within the netsh scripting environment.

> `-r <RemoteComputer>` – Specifies a remote computer to connect to on the network.

> `-u <[DomainName\] <UserName>` – Specifies the remote computer you wish to connect to with an optional Domain and User account name.

> `-p <Password | *>` – Specifies the password required for a remote computer that you used with the **-u** switch.

> `{NetshCommand | -f <ScriptFile>}` – Specifies the netsh command you want to run, with the **-f** switch being optionally used to exit netsh after the script you specify has completed.

Ping, TraceRT, and IPConfig

Three more useful Command Line tools are available to help diagnose, troubleshoot, and configure network connections, both wired and wireless. These tools have been available in Windows now for a great many years but have not lost their usefulness.

Ping

The **Ping** command is used to test the connection between your computer and another computer. Use it in the format `Ping 10.0.0.8` or `Ping www.windows.do` to test a connection to a local network or Internet address. It is used with the following switches:

> -t – To continue pinging until manually stopped by pressing **Ctrl + Enter** or **Ctrl + C**.

> -a – To reverse the name resolution for the destination IP address and to display the corresponding hostname.

> /n <count> – To set the number of echo requests to send; the default is four.

> /l <size> – Specifies the length in bytes of the data sent in echo requests; the default is 32; the maximum is 65527.

> /f – Specifies that the echo requests should not be fragmented by servers on path to the destination, useful for troubleshooting Maximum Transmission Unit (MTU) problems.

> /I <TTL> – Specifies the Time to Live (TTL) field in the IP header for echo requests.

> /v <TOS> – Specifies the Type of Service (TOS) field in the IP header for echo requests (IPv4 only).

> /r <count> – Used to record the route taken by the echo request (IPv4 only); you can specify the number of hops between the source and the destination from one to nine.

> /s <count> – Specifies that the Internet Timestamp should be used to record time of arrival for each request and its reply, from a maximum of one to four.

/j <hostlist> – Specifies that requests should use the Loose Source Route option in the IP header with the intermediate destinations specified (IPv4 only) with a maximum of nine addresses specified and separated by spaces.

/k <hostlist> – Specifies that requests should use the Strict Source Route option in the IP header with the intermediate destinations specified (IPv4 only) with a maximum of nine addresses specified and separated by spaces.

/w <timeout> – Determines the amount of time in milliseconds to wait for a reply; the default is 4000 (4 seconds).

/r <srcaddr> – Specifies that a round-trip path is traced (IPv6 only).

/s <compartment> – Specifies the source address to use (IPv6 only).

/c – Specifies a routing compartment identifier.

/p – Ping a Hyper-V network virtualization address.

/4 – Specifies that IPv4 be used to ping.

/6 – Specifies that IPv6 be used to ping.

TraceRT

The Trace Route (**TraceRT**) command is similar to ping but comes with some additional functionality. Whereas Ping will just test the connection, TraceRT will display all the IP addresses, servers, and routes the traffic takes on its journey. This can be especially useful if you are trying to diagnose a bottleneck somewhere on a network path (see Figure 14-26).

```
Command Prompt

Microsoft Windows [Version 10.0.22000.832]
(c) Microsoft Corporation. All rights reserved.

C:\Users\mikeh>tracert windows.do

Tracing route to windows.do [50.31.114.44]
over a maximum of 30 hops:

  1    <1 ms    <1 ms    <1 ms  10.0.0.1
  2     1 ms     1 ms     1 ms  192.168.1.1
  3    56 ms    62 ms    55 ms  100.64.0.1
  4    88 ms    58 ms    73 ms  172.16.249.30
  5    69 ms    67 ms    76 ms  149.19.108.145
  6    78 ms    59 ms    52 ms  de-cix-frankfurt.as13335.net [80.81.194.180]
  7    48 ms    52 ms    53 ms  172.70.248.3
  8    50 ms    43 ms    46 ms  172.70.249.226
  9    55 ms    54 ms    56 ms  172.70.249.18
 10    58 ms    55 ms    55 ms  172.70.249.102
 11     *        *        *     Request timed out.
 12   149 ms   143 ms   146 ms  joe.securedserverspace.com [50.31.114.44]

Trace complete.

C:\Users\mikeh>
```

Figure 14-26. *You can use TraceRT to search for bottlenecks on a network path*

Again, you use it in the format TraceRT 10.0.0.8 or TraceRT www.windows.do to test a connection to a local network or Internet address.

/d – Stops the command from resolving the IP addresses of intermediate routers to their names; this can speed up results.

/h <maxhops> – Specifies the maximum number of hops to the destination; the default is 30.

/j <hostlist> – Specifies that requests should use the Loose Source Route option in the IP header with the intermediate destinations specified (IPv4 only) with a maximum of nine addresses specified and separated by spaces.

/w <timeout> – Determines the amount of time in milliseconds to wait for a reply; the default is 4000 (4 seconds).

/r – Specifies that a round-trip path is traced (IPv6 only).

/s <srcaddr> – Specifies the source address to use (IPv6 only).

/4 – Specifies that IPv4 be used to ping.

/6 – Specifies that IPv6 be used to ping.

IPConfig

You can use the **IPConfig** command to display and configure parameters for the network connections on a PC. You use it with the following switches:

/all – Displays full TCP/IP information for all network adapters in the PC, including virtual adapters created in software or by hypervisors and dial-up connections.

/displaydns – Displays the contents of the local DNS cache, including entries preloaded from the HOSTS file.

/flushdns – Flushes and resets the DNS cache, used to discard erroneous entries from the cache, as well as those which have been added dynamically and that may now be unresolvable.

/registerdns – Starts a dynamic re-registration for all the DNS names and IP addresses configured on the PC and can be used to troubleshoot a failed DNS registration or to repair a problem between the PC and the DNS server without having to restart the PC.

/release <adapter> – Sends a DHCPRELEASE message to the DHCP server to release the current configuration and discard the IP address configuration for all adapters (if no adapter is specified) or a specific adapter.

/release6 <adapter> – Sends a DHCPRELEASE message to the DHCPv6 server to release the current configuration and discard the IP address configuration for all adapters (if no adapter is specified) or a specific adapter.

/renew <adapter> – Renews the DHCP configuration for the specified adapter or for all adapters if none is specified. This can be very useful for resetting network connections without having to restart the PC, though it only works for adapters that are configured to obtain an IP address automatically.

/renew6 <adapter> – Renews the DHCPv6 configuration for the specified adapter or for all adapters if none is specified. This can be very useful for resetting network connections without having to restart the PC, though it only works for adapters that are configured to obtain an IP address automatically.

/setclassid <adapter> [classID] – Configures the DHCP class ID for the specified adapter or all adapters if a wildcard (*) is used. If the classID is not specified, the current one is removed. This switch only works for adapters that are configured to obtain an IP address automatically.

/showclassid <adapter> – Displays the current ClassID for a specified adapter; use an asterisk (*) to display information for all installed adapters. This switch only works for adapters that are configured to obtain an IP address automatically.

Using Microsoft Sysinternals to Troubleshoot Networking

As you might expect, Microsoft's Sysinternals suite comes with a broad range of tools and utilities for configuring and troubleshooting networking and network problems.

ADExplorer

Active Directory Explorer (ADExplorer) allows you to easily view and edit an Active Directory database, including additional functionality not normally available, including making a copy of the database and comparing two AD databases side by side.

ADInsight

ADInsight is a Lightweight Directory Access Protocol (LDAP) real-time monitoring tool that you can use to troubleshoot Active Directory client applications. You can use it to view processes and events that applications make to the Wldap32.dll library.

ADRestore

ADRestore exists to help you undelete "tombstoned" Active Directory objects in a domain. The utility enumerates the deleted objects in a domain and allows to restore the ones you choose.

PsTools

Rather than being a utility, PsTools is actually an extra suite of utilities for administering PC systems remotely. It includes utilities that can remotely execute apps, display information about files and users, kill processes, get detailed information about processes, and shut down and restart the PC. Full details of the tools available and their switches can be found on the Sysinternals website.

PsExec

This command is used to execute processes on a remote PC. Use this in the format **PsExec** \\RemotePC **"C:\\long app name.exe"**.

PsFile

PsFile, also detailed earlier in this chapter, will display a list of files that are currently open on a remote PC. Use this in the format **PsFile [\\RemotePC [-u OptionalUsername [-p UserPassword]]] [[id | PathAndNameOfFile] [-c** ToCloseFile].

PsGetSid

This tool is used to display the Security Identifier (SID) of a remote computer or user. Use it in the format **psgetsid [\\RemotePC[,RemotePC[,...] | @file\] [-u OptionalUsername [-p UserPassword]]] [account|SID]**.

PsInfo

PsInfo can display information about a remote computer. You can use this with the switch **RemotePC** for a specific PC or * to run it on all networked PCs. You can also use it with these switches to get detailed information on **[-h]** installed hotfixes, **[-s]** installed applications, and **[-d]** disk information and use **[-c]** to export the data as a CSV file.

PsPing

PsPing does exactly what you might expect it to: it displays detailed ping information to test network connections. It is a Command Line utility that is much more configurable than Windows 10's standard Ping command. PsPing is used with one of four main switches and then a series of subswitches to test for ICMP (the main protocol used by routers for reporting errors), TCP, latency, and bandwidth. Full details of the switches are available on the Sysinternals website.

PsKill

If you need to kill a running process on a remote PC, then PsKill is the tool to use. Use it in the format **pskill [-] [-t] [\\RemotePC [-OptionalUsername [-p UserPassword]]] <processname | process id>** where **[-]** displays a list of supported options, and **[-t]** kills not just the process but all its dependent processes as well.

PsList

PsList will display detailed information about the processes running on a remote PC. Use it with the switches **[-d]** to display additional details, **[-m]** to show memory usage information, and **[-t]** to show process trees.

PsLoggedOn

This tool will display details of each user currently logged on (signed in) to a remote PC. This can be used with the switch **[-l]** to only show accounts logged in to the PC locally, and not across the network.

PsLogList

This is used to create a dump of event log records from a remote PC. There are quite a few switches and commands for this utility, which you can see in Table 14-1. You use it in the format psloglist [-] **[\\RemotePC[,RemotePC[,...]] | @file [-u OptionalUsername [-p UserPassword]]] [-s [-t delimiter]] [-m #|-n #|-h #|-d #|-w][-c][-x][-r][-a mm/dd/ yy][-b mm/dd/yy][-f filter] [-i ID[,ID[,...] | -e ID[,ID[,...]]] [-o event source[,event source][,..]]] [-q event source[,event source][,..]]] [-l event log file] <eventlog>**.

Table 14-1. *Available switches for PsLogList*

Switch	Description
@file	Executes the command on each of the PCs specified
-a	Exports the records timestamped after the specified date
-b	Exports the records timestamped before the specified date
-c	Clears the event log after displaying its contents
-d	Only displays records from previous *n* days
-e	Excludes events with the specified ID or IDs (up to 10)
-f	Filters event types with a string (e.g., [**-f w]** to filter warnings)
-h	Only displays records from previous *n* hours
-i	Shows only events with the specified ID or IDs (up to 10)
-l	Exports records from the specified event log file
-m	Only displays records from previous *n* minutes
-n	Only displays the number of most recent entries (e.g., **[-n 6]**)
-o	Shows only records from the specified event source
-p	Specifies an optional password for the username. You will be prompted for a password if you omit this
-q	Omits records from the specified event source or sources
-r	SDump log from least recent to most recent
-s	Displays Event Log records one per line, with comma-delimited fields
-t	Changes the delimiter to a specified character
-u	Specifies an optional username for login to a remote computer
-w	Tells PsLogList to wait for new events, exporting them as they generate (on the local PC only)
-x	Dumps extended data
eventlog	Open the event log

PsPasswd

This security tool can be used to change account passwords on a remote PC. Use in the format pspasswd [[\\RemotePC[,RemotePC[,..] | @file [-u Username [-p Password]]] Username [NewPassword].

PsService

This lets you view and control services on a remote PC. Use it in the format **psservice [\\RemotePC [-u OptionalUsername] [-p UserPassword]] <command> <options>** where the options include those listed in Table 14-2.

Table 14-2. *Switches for the PsService command*

Switch	Description
query	Displays the status of a specified service
config	Displays the configuration of a specified service
setconfig	Sets the start type for a specified service (disabled, auto, on-demand)
start	Starts the specified service
stop	Stops the specified service
restart	Stops and then restarts a specified service
pause	Pauses the specified service
cont	Resumes a paused specified service
depend	Lists all of the services that are dependent on the one specified
security	Dumps the specified service's security descriptor
find	Searches the network for the specified service

PsShutdown

PsShutdown can be used to either shut down or restart a remote PC. This can be used with the following useful switches: **[-f]** to force all applications to close immediately rather than giving them time to close on their own; **[-l]** to lock the remote PC; **[-m]** to display a message to appear on the screen for anybody using the PC when the shutdown countdown commences, which can be set with the **[-t xx]** switch, the default being 20 seconds; **[-r]** to restart the PC; and **[-c]** to allow the shutdown to be aborted by somebody still using the remote PC.

PsSuspend

If you need to suspend a process on a remote PC, then this tool will do the job. Use it in the format **pssuspend [-] [-r] [\\RemotePC [-u OptionalUsername] [-p UserPassword]] <process name | process id>** where **[-r]** resumes the suspended processes after they have been previously suspended.

TCPView

The TCPView utility provides information about the endpoint network connections from your PC, including the remote or IP address of the destination and the port used by the PC to make the connection (see Figure 14-27). Using this utility, you can see every running process and service that has an active network connection and the destination they are connected to.

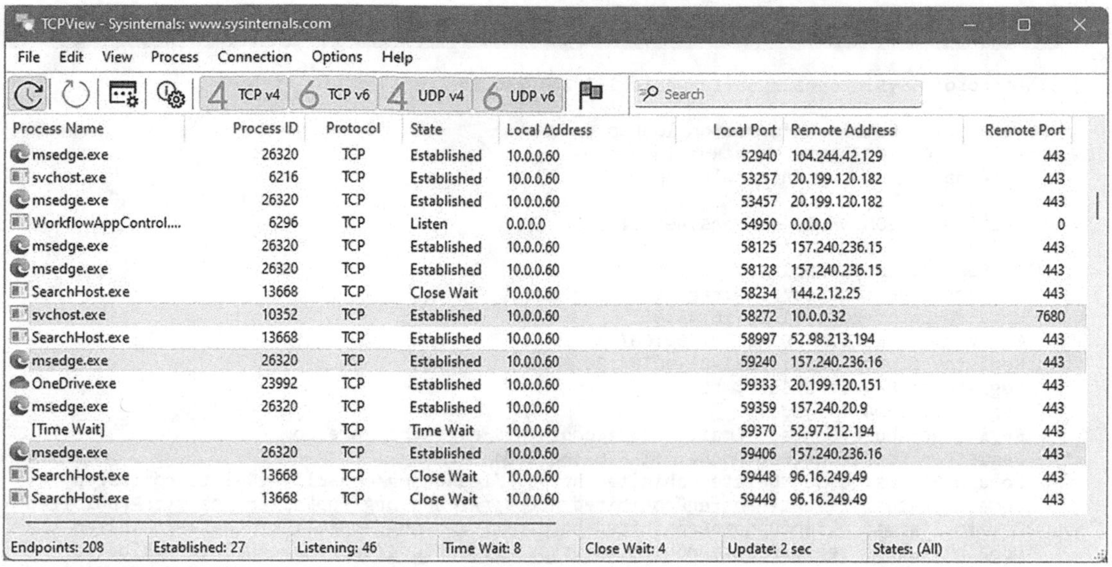
TCPView - Sysinternals: www.sysinternals.com
File Edit View Process Connection Options Help
4 TCP v4 6 TCP v6 4 UDP v4 6 UDP v6
Search
Process Name Process ID Protocol State Local Address Local Port Remote Address Remote Port
msedge.exe 26320 TCP Established 10.0.0.60 52940 104.244.42.129 443
svchost.exe 6216 TCP Established 10.0.0.60 53257 20.199.120.182 443
msedge.exe 26320 TCP Established 10.0.0.60 53457 20.199.120.182 443
WorkflowAppControl.... 6296 TCP Listen 0.0.0.0 54950 0.0.0.0 0
msedge.exe 26320 TCP Established 10.0.0.60 58125 157.240.236.15 443
msedge.exe 26320 TCP Established 10.0.0.60 58128 157.240.236.15 443
SearchHost.exe 13668 TCP Close Wait 10.0.0.60 58234 144.2.12.25 443
svchost.exe 10352 TCP Established 10.0.0.60 58272 10.0.0.32 7680
SearchHost.exe 13668 TCP Established 10.0.0.60 58997 52.98.213.194 443
msedge.exe 26320 TCP Established 10.0.0.60 59240 157.240.236.16 443
OneDrive.exe 23992 TCP Established 10.0.0.60 59333 20.199.120.151 443
msedge.exe 26320 TCP Established 10.0.0.60 59359 157.240.20.9 443
[Time Wait] TCP Time Wait 10.0.0.60 59370 52.97.212.194 443
msedge.exe 26320 TCP Established 10.0.0.60 59406 157.240.236.16 443
SearchHost.exe 13668 TCP Close Wait 10.0.0.60 59448 96.16.249.49 443
SearchHost.exe 13668 TCP Close Wait 10.0.0.60 59449 96.16.249.49 443
Endpoints: 208 Established: 27 Listening: 46 Time Wait: 8 Close Wait: 4 Update: 2 sec States: (All)

Figure 14-27. *TCPView provides useful endpoint information*

You can marry this information with the data you have on IP address ranges within your company, or company VPN, to check for misconfigured network connections or to see where malware or rogue apps might be making connections. You can also save the data as a file to read later or to send to a support technician.

There is also a Command Line version of this tool available in Sysinternals, called **TCPVcon**, which is used in the format **TcpVcon [-a] [-c] [-n] [process name or PID]** where **[-a]** displays all endpoints, **[-n]** doesn't resolve addresses, and **[-c]** outputs the results as a CSV file.

WhoIs

WhoIs is useful for providing information on who owns and maintains domain names or IP addresses to which your PC is connecting. For example, in running TCPView, I spotted that Edge on my PC was connecting to the IP address `157.240.236.16` and wanted to see what company was at the end of this address. A quick search using WhoIs reveals that the IP address is owned by Facebook, and I had the social network open in a browser tab at the time (see Figure 14-28).

```
 C:\ Command Prompt

E:\Microsoft Sysinternals Suite>whois 157.240.236.16

Whois v1.21 - Domain information lookup
Copyright (C) 2005-2019 Mark Russinovich
Sysinternals - www.sysinternals.com

Connecting to COM.whois-servers.net...

WHOIS Server: whois.registrarsafe.com
   Registrar URL: http://www.registrarsafe.com
   Updated Date: 2022-01-26T16:45:06Z
   Creation Date: 1997-03-29T05:00:00Z
   Registry Expiry Date: 2031-03-30T04:00:00Z
   Registrar: RegistrarSafe, LLC
   Registrar IANA ID: 3237
   Registrar Abuse Contact Email: abusecomplaints@registrarsafe.com
   Registrar Abuse Contact Phone: +1-650-308-7004
   Domain Status: clientDeleteProhibited https://icann.org/epp#clientDeleteProhibited
   Domain Status: clientTransferProhibited https://icann.org/epp#clientTransferProhibited
   Domain Status: clientUpdateProhibited https://icann.org/epp#clientUpdateProhibited
   Domain Status: serverDeleteProhibited https://icann.org/epp#serverDeleteProhibited
   Domain Status: serverTransferProhibited https://icann.org/epp#serverTransferProhibited
   Domain Status: serverUpdateProhibited https://icann.org/epp#serverUpdateProhibited
   Name Server: A.NS.FACEBOOK.COM
   Name Server: B.NS.FACEBOOK.COM
   Name Server: C.NS.FACEBOOK.COM
   Name Server: D.NS.FACEBOOK.COM
   DNSSEC: unsigned
   URL of the ICANN Whois Inaccuracy Complaint Form: https://www.icann.org/wicf/
```

Figure 14-28. *WhoIs can provide information on IP addresses you connect to*

Summary

Configuring, diagnosing, troubleshooting, and repairing wired and wireless network connections on a PC is something for which there are a huge number of tools and utilities, and there's something to suit the way anybody wants to work, from GUI interfaces to scripting commands.

In the next chapter, hopefully with our networks working properly, we'll look at hardware devices, including Bluetooth, peripherals, USB systems, and also PC firmware such as UEFI systems, to see how we can troubleshoot problems with everything from printers and wireless headphones to completely unknown devices.

CHAPTER 15

Hardware and Peripherals Troubleshooting

I have some Bluetooth headphones; they were pretty expensive too being high-end Bowers and Wilkins affairs costing almost $400 each (I actually own two of these), and that price was got in a sale. The sound quality from them is astonishing, but as I also purchase 24-bit audio versions of all my favorite albums (digitally pure and uncompressed, unlike 16-bit CD quality), I'd be a bit dim to then try and use cheap headphones to listen to them.

I also purchased a USB high-definition Bluetooth streaming dongle, to ensure the highest bit rate to said headphones, an Avantree Leaf Pro, and the whole affair works brilliantly. The audio is crisp and clear, I can hear all of the high-end and low-end notes, and the overall experience makes paying such a high price for the kit worthwhile.

You can imagine then how frustrating it is to switch on the headphones to discover that something that worked perfectly well the day before suddenly doesn't want to work again. This is, of course, the issue with what has always been a fairly creaky Bluetooth stack in Windows. It's not just Windows of course as Bluetooth can be creaky on any operating system, failing to connect a device that worked perfectly well only the day before.

Bluetooth isn't the only hardware technology that can cause problems though, as we all know. When USB (Universal Serial Bus) first appeared in PCs running Windows 95, it was seen as a revelation. I remember (showing my age now) having to modify the contents of driver .ini files for serial and parallel devices, to tell the PC which port they were plugged into and what BAUD rate they should communicate at, and fighting and struggling for hours sometimes just to get the damn thing to work. I am extremely thankful that I never had to deal with token ring network cables (shudder!). Even USB devices can cause the occasional problem.

© Mike Halsey 2023
M. Halsey, *Troubleshooting and Supporting Windows 11*, https://doi.org/10.1007/978-1-4842-8728-6_15

I remember, when writing my Windows 8 troubleshooting book, having an argument with a senior engineer at Microsoft. I'd written that sometimes when you plugged in a USB device such as a printer, the device wouldn't be recognized, but the solution was to plug it into a different USB port, one on a different bus on the motherboard instead which would force Windows to reload the driver.

Said engineer swore blind this wasn't a thing because Microsoft had never heard of it. I argued that just because Microsoft had never heard of it didn't mean it wasn't a thing and that he should now consider himself informed. Anyway, a couple of versions of Windows later and think the issue got fixed as I've not seen it for a while.

Let's Start with a Top Tip

Seeing then as how much of this chapter will deal with stuff that simply refuses to work, I think we should start on a high note with a top tip. If you've ever had a problem where you've needed to use an old version of a driver, perhaps for stability reasons, perhaps because it's an older piece of hardware and there's only one version of the driver that's actually known to work, then you'll probably have run into the problem that comes with single file drivers.

This is effectively an app that you click to run a driver installer. The alternative and, fortunately, more common approach is for a hardware manufacturer to provide the driver as a folder containing a whole bunch of all the files that constitute the driver.

Well, what can sometimes happen with these single file driver installers is that they can perform a version check on your installed copy of Windows, and if they don't like what they see, they'll just say "No, not doing it!" and the driver installer won't run.

"But," I hear you cry, "I thought this was supposed to be a top tip, not a depressing reality." That single file installer is really just an executable zip file. You might remember back in the early days of ZIP files that you could set the zipped archive to automatically run something or automatically unpack when it was double-clicked. Well, this practice still exists, and it's what these driver files use.

To get around this, you need a third-party archival program such as WinRar, which you can download from `www.winrar.com`, and then use that to open the installer file; note that you will need to tell WinRar to open "All file types" as otherwise it won't see it in the file open dialog.

Here, you will see that the installer is really just a plain ZIP file, and you will be able to see the folder and file structure within (see Figure 15-1). If you then unzip these files and folders to your hard disk, you will be able to completely bypass the Windows version check and manually install the driver from the correct .INF file.

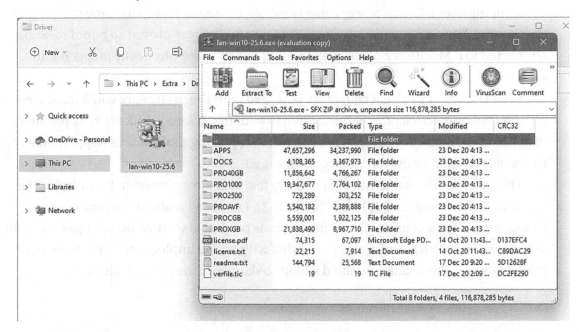

Figure 15-1.   *You can unzip and access sealed single file driver installers*

Caution   Never download any software or ISO file from a general file repository website where there is an official source, as these files can sometimes be injected with malware.

Best Practice for Managing Physical Hardware

So how often have you, or someone you know or worked with, tripped over a cable? This can cause all manner of problems, and it would be remiss of me not to mention how important good cable management is. Plugs and cables can be caught and snagged and often broken.

If you trip over a network or a power cable, the results can be pretty devastating. Not only can you pull and break the cable and the plugs on either end of it, you can damage the sockets the cables are plugged in to. This could include an Ethernet socket on your PC or laptop.

Tripping over a laptop power cable can often cause the laptop to come crashing to the floor, and this is of course why Apple's MagSafe chargers proved so popular, being connected to a MacBook only by magnets and not by being physically plugged into a socket.

Even USB cables can get caught and snagged, and I'm pretty sure you'll have seen a broken USB port on a laptop at some point in your life. It's very difficult to fix problems like this, and sometimes the solution can run to replacing the whole laptop, especially if the case is cracked or the motherboard damaged.

This is, of course, something I personally feel very strongly about. In my book *The Green IT Guide* (Apress, 2022) (see Figure 15-2), I wrote a lot about the problems of ewaste and how currently of the 50 million tons produced worldwide each year, only 20% of it is recycled, with the rest going to landfill with all the unpleasant consequences of the metals and chemicals contained within soaking into the ground and water table.

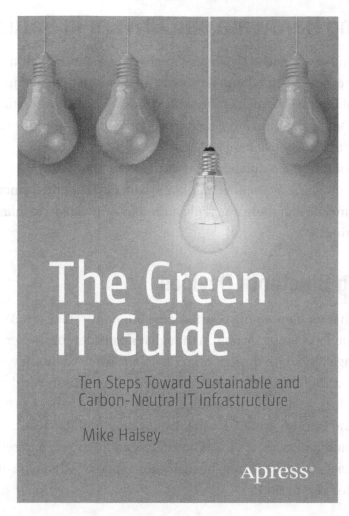

Figure 15-2. *If you want to find out how to make your IT more sustainable, my Green IT Guide can help*

If you've not read the book yet, I would urge you to add it to your reading list as one of my primary motivations for writing it was that I couldn't find a similar book having been written before, not for more than a decade anyway. Oh, and if you happen to know Morgan Freeman, please ask him to narrate the Audible version.

Anyway, there are a huge number of reasons why good cable management is essential. It's a way to save vast volumes of cash on broken equipment and computers, it's a huge time saver as routing and installing new cable and sockets can be enormously time-consuming, and it's also a great way to avoid clumsy Eric from accounts from falling over in the office for the seventh time in a week.

Managing Hardware and Drivers in Settings

If you used Windows 8 and 8.1, then you might remember the Settings "app" (I prefer to call it a panel personally) didn't let you do much more than change the desktop wallpaper. This changed considerably with Windows 10, but when that launched in 2015 if you wanted to do anything more technical than end-user interface stuff, then you had to revert back to the Control Panel.

These days, things are different. I've written a lot about how Settings is slowly getting stuffed (perhaps a little overstuffed in places) with current and former Control Panel applets. This means that there's actually quite a lot you can do to manage devices and drivers in Settings.

Managing Bluetooth Devices

I began this chapter bemoaning how flaky the Bluetooth stack is in Windows. In fairness, it's always been flaky for some reason though it's considerably better than it used to be.

You manage Bluetooth devices from *Bluetooth & devices* funnily enough, and it's a straightforward affair. In fact, this is now the *only* place within Windows 11 to manage Bluetooth devices, as the old Bluetooth applet in Control Panel has been removed, and the Devices and Printers applet doesn't display Bluetooth devices.

With Bluetooth devices, it's a simple affair of adding them and removing them. Click the big *Add device* button and tell the dialog that appears what type of device you're connecting (see Figure 15-3).

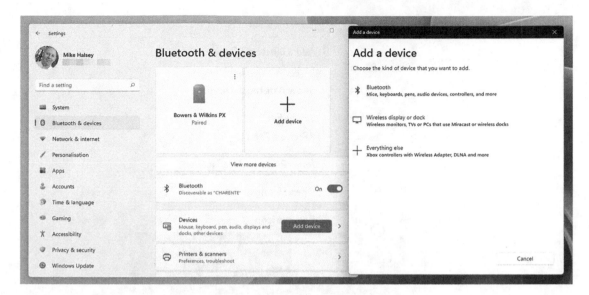

Figure 15-3. *It's simple to add Bluetooth devices to Windows*

You can click the *View more devices* button to see all of the devices connected to the PC, but these sadly are not organized by Bluetooth, USB, etc., but by device class, Input, Audio, and so on.

You can also remove a Bluetooth device by clicking the three dots icon to its right and then clicking *Remove device*, but really that's about it for managing the devices themselves unless you have a Bluetooth device that comes with its own third-party control panel, and this will most likely sit in the System Tray.

Speaking of the System Tray, Windows 11 does also have a Bluetooth icon that resides there, which allows you to perform actions such as adding a Bluetooth device, sending and receiving files from a Bluetooth device, and opening Settings (see Figure 15-4).

Figure 15-4. *You can manage some Bluetooth features from the System Tray*

At the bottom of the *Bluetooth & devices* ➤ *Devices* Settings page are a few additional options. *Show notifications to connect using Swift Pair* can help you connect to discoverable Bluetooth devices when they're in range (see Figure 15-5).

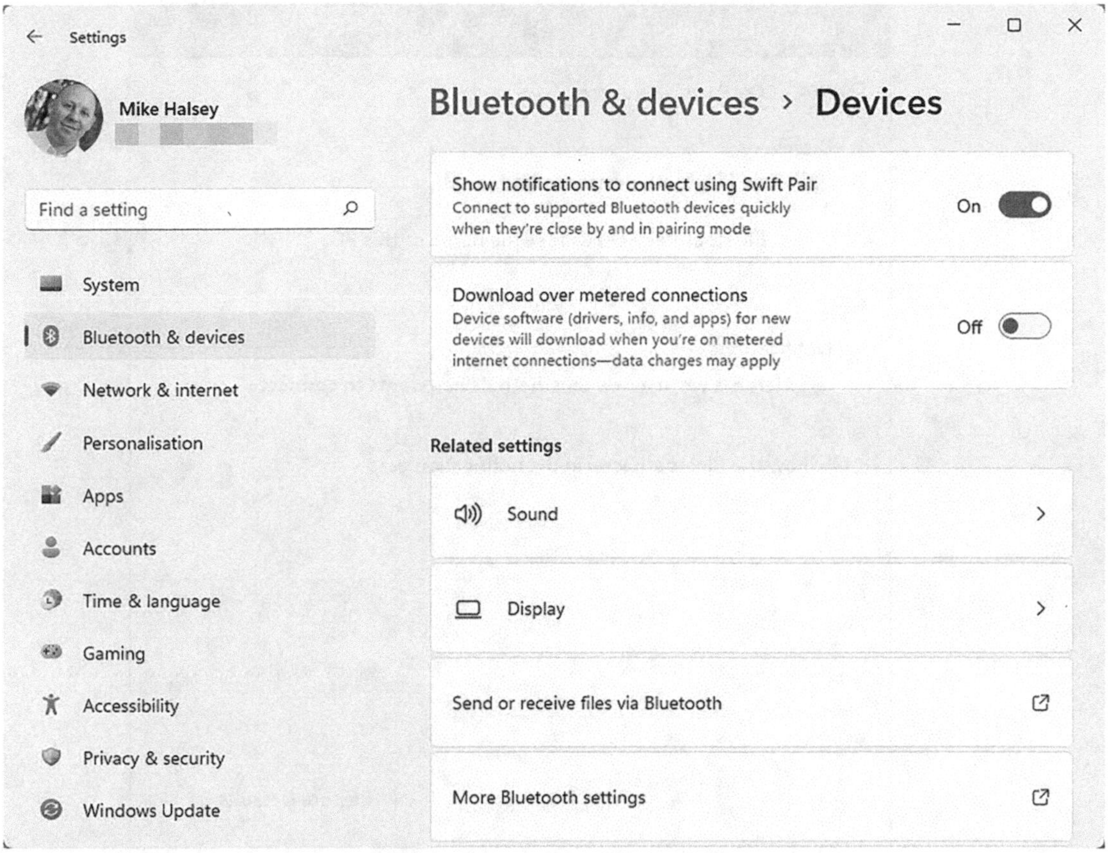

Figure 15-5. *Additional Bluetooth settings are hidden at the bottom of the devices list*

Below this are options to *Send or receive files via Bluetooth* which opens a wizard and which is one of those Windows features like Storage Spaces and File History where I don't know anybody that's ever used it.

Below this is a *More Bluetooth settings* link which, as I write this, pops out a more traditional dialog, but we can probably expect this to be folded more into Settings at some future point. This dialog (see Figure 15-6) has three tabs.

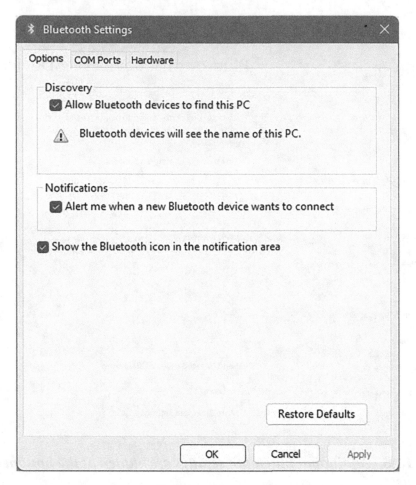

Figure 15-6. *A "few" extra Bluetooth Settings can be found in a pop-out*

The first tab, *Options*, is where you'll find the actual settings. There's not much as you can see from the screenshot, and the *Restore Defaults* button sadly won't reset the Bluetooth stack in the event of a problem, it just unchecks and rechecks some of the boxes.

Some apps and programs, especially older software, require a COM (Serial) port to communicate with a Bluetooth device. This can be especially common for GPS software. You can add and manage virtual Serial ports from the *COM Ports* tab (see Figure 15-7). When you select an outgoing port, you can choose which already installed Bluetooth device will be assigned to it.

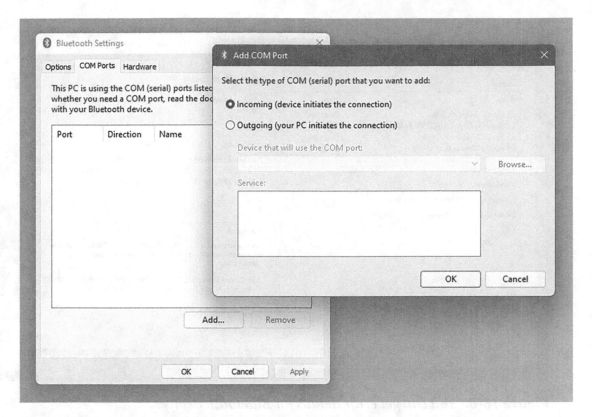

Figure 15-7. *You can add virtual serial ports for software that requires them*

Under the *Hardware* tab, you will see the different Bluetooth hardware and software drivers you have installed. If you are having difficulty with a device, you can select it and click its properties button. Then, under the *Events* tab, you can see any error events that have been pulled from the Event Viewer (see Figure 15-8).

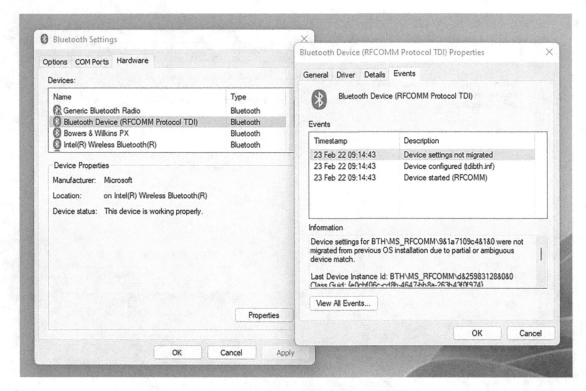

Figure 15-8. *You can get error details for Bluetooth devices*

I am actually having problems with two Bluetooth devices that have been ongoing for a while now, which just goes to show how flaky the Windows Bluetooth stack can still be. One is the error seen in Figure 15-8, and the other is a "Generic Bluetooth Radio" device that I've plugged in just for demonstration. This is a USB Bluetooth 5 dongle that flatly refuses to work no matter what I do with it, but it was a cheap thing from China, so I can hardly expect it to be brilliant when it only cost $5 to begin with.

Managing Printers and Scanners

The term paperless office can be traced back to an article in *Business Week* in 1975. The idea was that office automation would make paper redundant for general tasks like record-keeping. When the desktop computer came into existence, and more documents could be stored electronically, people got very excited about the concept, and this was further fueled when Adobe created the Portable Document Format (PDF) file in 1991.

So that went well then, as printers are still everywhere and trees are still being cut down so that documents that could very well be sent by email or messaging are printed so that Derek in the office can read it once, scrawl on it a bit, and then recycle it (sigh!).

Tip   My top tip for reducing paper usage is to switch to bamboo. It's much more sustainable (i.e., incredibly quick to grow), can be used for any type of paper from printer paper to kitchen roll and toilet paper, and is indistinguishable from paper made from wood... even the loo roll!

If you're interested, in the early days of writing this book, I fed back to Microsoft some suggestions for how to encourage people to use less printer paper. This included separating "Digital Documents" and "Paper Documents" in the Windows and Office *Print* dialogs and adding quick "Print and send digitally" options for messaging services such as Teams. You can read more about this on my website at `https://pcs.tv/3oo7KZD`, and I genuinely hope they build these suggestions into Windows.

It's always a good idea to encourage people to use digital documents anyway, though when I was feeding back my ideas to Microsoft I asked an open question to the attendees at that event, "How many people have had to print a document, so you could sign it, only to scan it in again and email it?" Alas, more than half the people in the room put their hand in the air. For this, I can highly recommend the use of a service such as `www.docusign.com`.

Printing is another of those areas where everything is being shifted into Settings. There's actually not much extra you can do outside of settings now that's worth it, but there are a few administrator-level options you will find useful, and I'll detail these shortly.

Open *Settings* and *Bluetooth & devices*, and you will see a *Printers & scanners* link. This will take you to a page where your physical and digital printers are listed (see Figure 15-9) and where there is an *Add device* button to add a new printer to the PC.

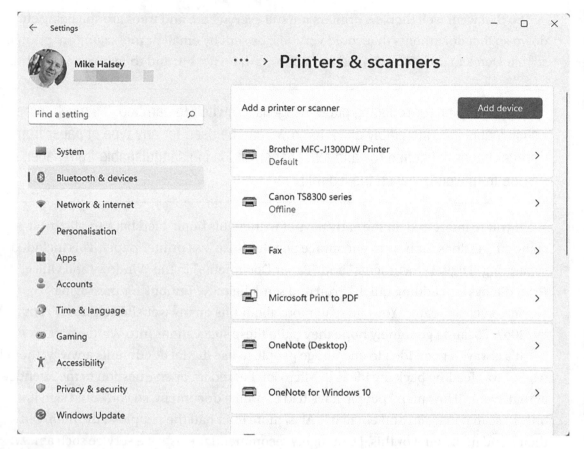

Figure 15-9. *You can manage printers from within Settings*

When you click a printer, there are various options available for it, such as making it the default printer, for the PC. Most of these still currently open older Control Panel applets, but everything is accounted for and available from Settings more easily than it is from the Control Panel itself (see Figure 15-10).

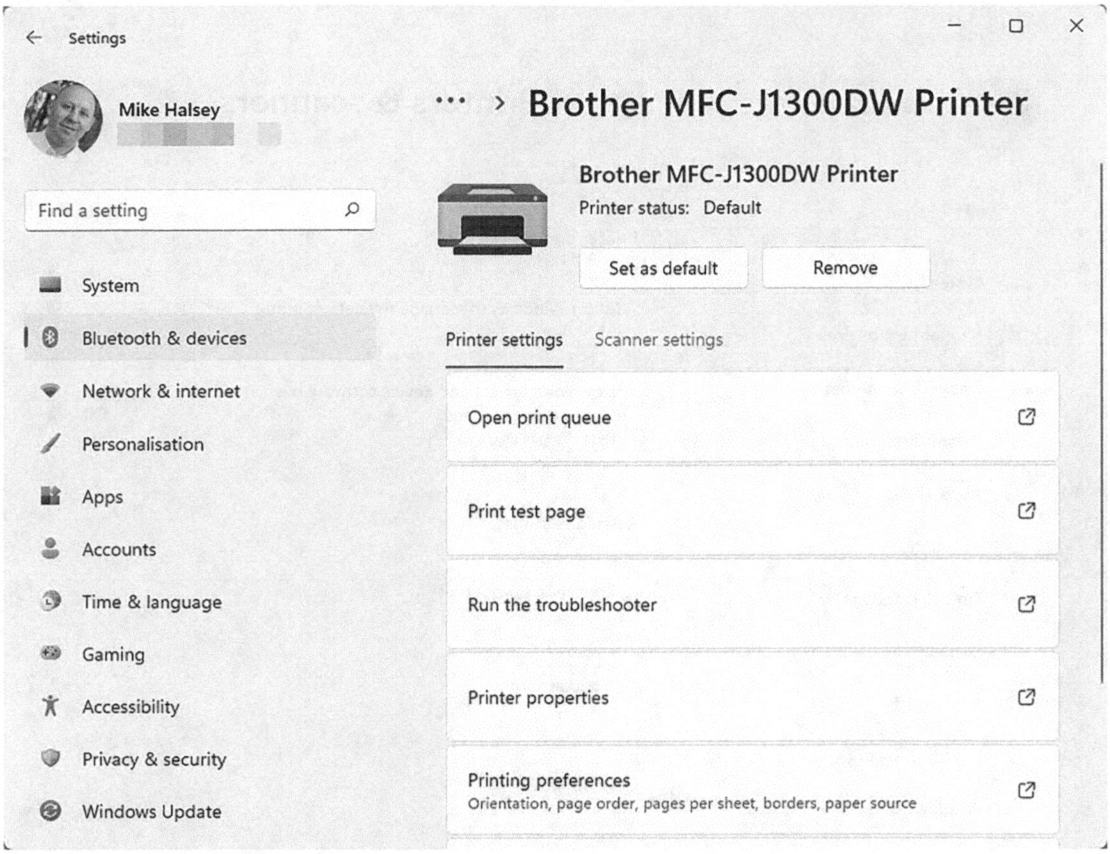

Figure 15-10. You can access all options for printers in Settings

Setting Your Default Printer

While setting your default printer is highly useful for a static, desktop PC where there is only one printer and you don't want Windows to occasionally change it back to send to fax or some other esoteric option, there is also a great way to manage printers.

We're all moving about these days, for as much as international crises allow us to anyway, which means that it's hugely common now for mobile workers to use their laptop between two, three, or even multiple sites. Windows has for some years now included a setting that accommodates this.

In *Settings* under *Printers & scanners* is an option to *Allow Windows to manage my default printer* (see Figure 15-11). With this set, Windows keeps a record of what printer you use at different sites, and it separates them by their different wired or Wi-Fi networks.

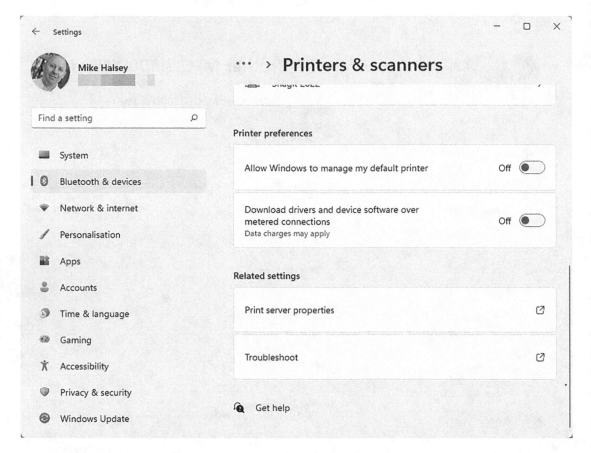

Figure 15-11. *Windows can manage different default printers for different sites*

The upshot of this is that when you move to a different location, the OS *should* remember what printer you used the last time you were there and offer you that when you want to print something next. This is highly effective, but I caveat it with a "should" as we all know what will happen if I were to say "oh yes, it'll *definitely* remember what printer you used last time."

Using Print Servers

You may have a system in your office where a single PC, perhaps an older one, is configured as a file and print server, and the printer is plugged into that PC via USB or perhaps an older connection standard, which I will come to later.

Should this be the case, at the bottom of the *Settings* and *Printers & scanners* page is a *Print server properties* option. Click this and you can manage all aspects of the print server including what printers it manages and what users can have permissions to print documents and manage the printer(s), etc. (see Figure 15-12).

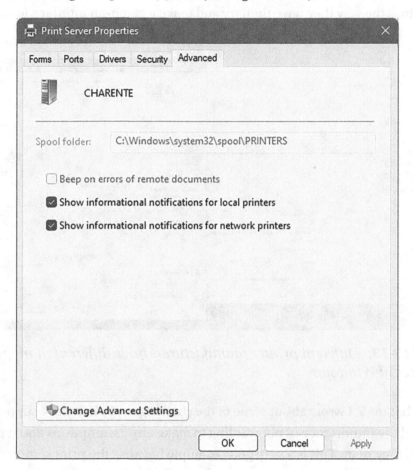

Figure 15-12. *You can run a print server from a Windows 11 PC*

Managing Printing Preferences

The way you choose to print documents on your printers isn't really a subject for troubleshooting. I wanted to cover it though for two reasons. The first of these is to highlight that this is one area of Windows where you will get very different experiences depending on what printer you have installed and the manufacturer of that printer.

Figure 15-13 is a good example of this as I have both Canon and Brother printers on my home/office network. Microsoft has for many years now allowed printer manufacturers to customize their driver interface applets. The reason for this is that different printers support different features, and, frankly, it was just easier for Microsoft to do things the way they have than try and make a catch-all interface for Windows itself.

Figure 15-13. *Different printer manufacturers have different management interfaces in Windows*

In Chapter 5, I wrote about some of the challenges you can have supporting end users and the importance of not wanting to make any assumptions about them or the situation they're in. This is a very good example because the print settings are something an end user might want to and even need to adjust and change from time to time. If you are providing phone support, they may not be able to describe to you what they are seeing, and the end result is that this can be a good time to request remote access, as I detailed in Chapter 6, so you can help them more quickly and effectively.

Managing Printer Properties

Of more use to a system administrator though is the *Printer properties* dialog, again available on a button in Settings when you click a printer. There are various options here that you can set to help make sure printers aren't overused, are only used by the correct people in the correct way, and that you can also use to help save paper and ink as part of your own sustainability policies.

Under the *General* tab, you will see basic information about the printer, such as its IP address on your network, which can be useful for troubleshooting (see Figure 15-14).

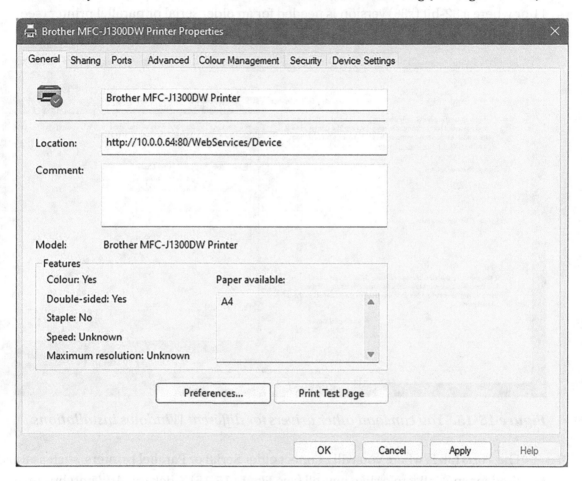

Figure 15-14. *You can get the IP address of a network printer*

Below this is a *Preferences* button. This will display the same *Printing preferences* dialog I detailed just a moment ago, but whereas that is set on a per-user basis, here you can set it globally for all users. This means you can mandate that the default printing settings should be duplex (no both sides of the paper) if your printer supports it, in black and white only, on draft mode to save ink, automatically watermarked with the company logo or message, etc.

The *Sharing* tab will allow you to share a printer that is plugged into a USB port on a PC with other PCs on the network. You can also use this option for PCs already on the network, but let's be honest, why would you want to? You can load additional drivers for the printer too should they be needed, such as those for the ARM version of Windows 11 or where a 32-bit (x86) version is needed for an older serial or parallel printer (see Figure 15-15).

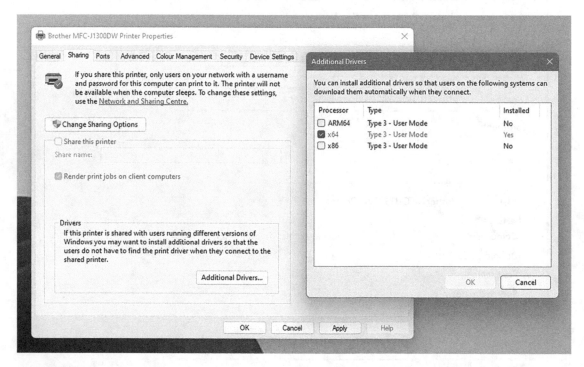

Figure 15-15. *You can load other drivers for different Windows installations*

The *Ports* tab is where you will connect older Serial or Parallel printers, such as those required for specialist roles like payroll (see Figure 15-16). Click the *Add port* button to add a port if it does not automatically appear in the list to add a new port, though this method isn't as filled with options as the one I will detail later in this chapter for adding and managing legacy hardware.

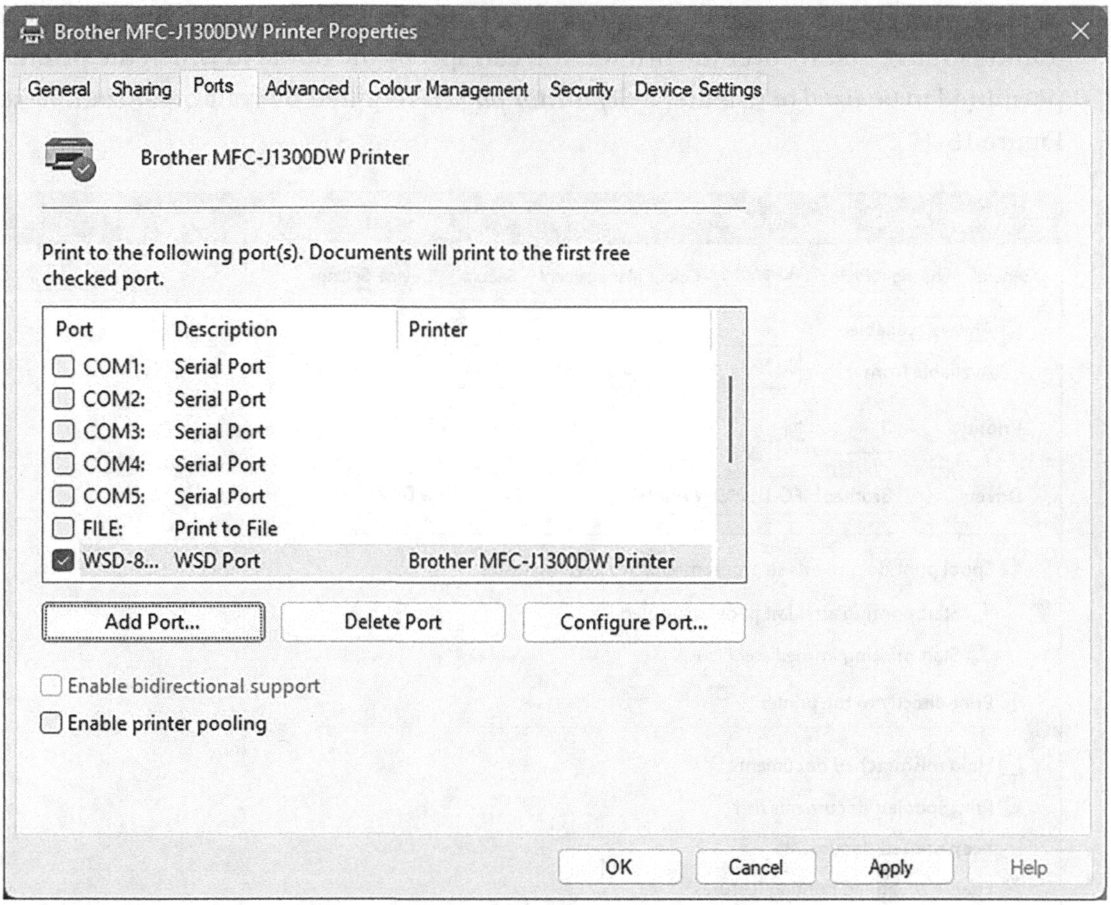

Figure 15-16. *You can assign Serial and Parallel ports to printers*

Tip   Some specialist laptops, especially ruggedized editions such as the
Panasonic Toughbook and Dell Ruggedized ranges, often come with Serial ports
as standard. This is because these are often needed for specialist engineering and
scientific equipment. Serial and Parallel plug-in PCIe cards are also available online
for $20 or so. Additionally, you can also find inexpensive USB to Serial and Parallel
adapters online.

It is with the *Advanced* tab that things begin to get interesting as here you can get full administrative control over the printer. You can specify the hours in which the printer is permitted to be used or whether a *Separator page* is required by your organization (see Figure 15-17).

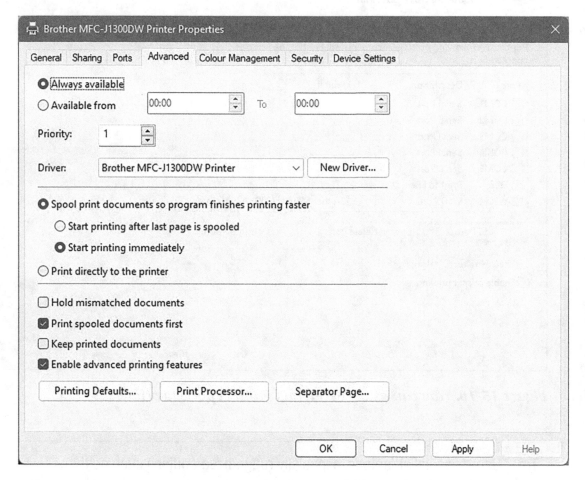

Figure 15-17. *You can specify usage times for printers*

If you work in an environment where color accuracy is of the utmost importance, such as print, advertising, or media, you can load and manage printer (and monitor) color profiles under the *Color Management* tab (see Figure 15-18).

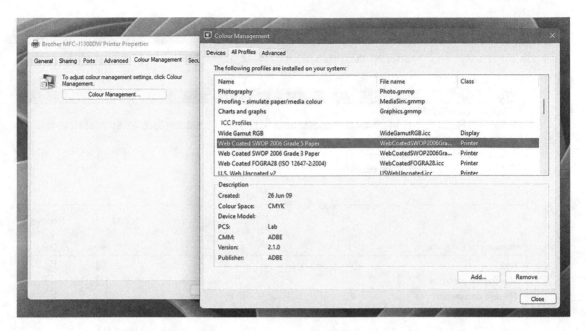

Figure 15-18. *Some specialist use cases require accurate color profiles for screens and printers*

The other tab where you will find administrative options is *Security*. This is where you can specify what different users and user groups can use and configure with printers (see Figure 15-19). You might want to only allow specific groups of users, such as creatives or sales teams, access to color printers, or you might want people in small remote offices to be able to manage printers, where those in larger offices don't have a need. In Chapter 10, I wrote about managing users and groups, and it works exactly the same way with printers.

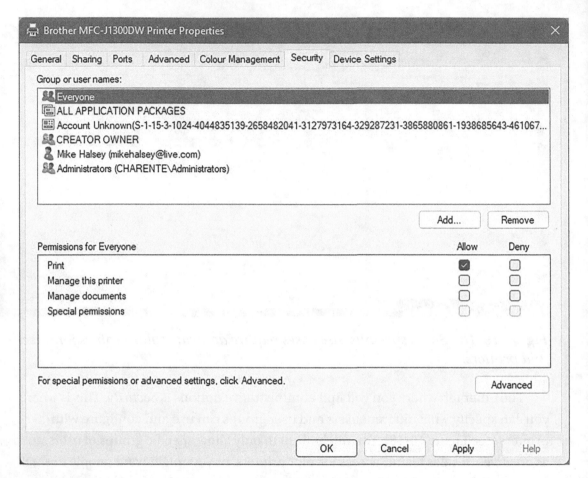

Figure 15-19. *You can specify user and group permissions for printers*

Adding Older and Less-Compatible Printers

Windows 11 is very good at discovering and adding Wi-Fi, networked, and USB printers that it finds and automatically installing the correct driver (an Internet connection is always required for this), but sometimes you have an older or a less-compatible printer you need to install, such as the Serial and Parallel printers I mentioned earlier.

When you click the add printer button in Settings, if no printer is found you will be offered an *Add manually* option. This will allow you to specify where the printer is, by its IP address or name on the network, or if it requires manually installing (see Figure 15-20). We will look more at adding legacy hardware later in this chapter.

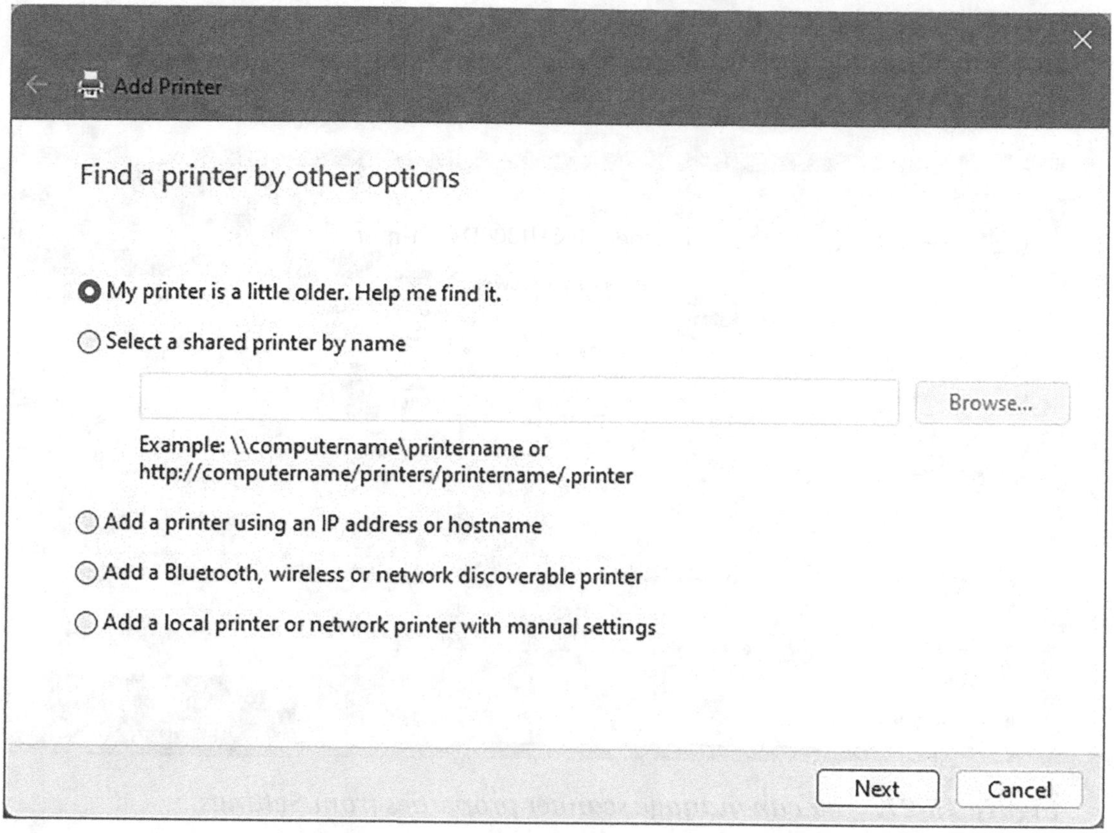

Figure 15-20. *You can manually add a printer to Windows 11*

Tip   If you need more control, and for as long as it remains in Windows 11, opening *Devices and Printers* from the Control Panel has an *Add a printer* button which will also search for a printer but give you quick access to this advanced dialog.

Managing Scanners

This section was called "Managing Printers and Scanners," so we can't let scanners get off without a mention. Scanners are fairly basic machines, so there's not a lot of configuration available for them. If you have a multifunction device as most scanners are nowadays, then you will see a *Scanner settings* tab when you click your printer. This will provide links to download a scanner app, which at the time of writing open a Microsoft Store link to the Windows Scan app, and to access properties for the scanner (see Figure 15-21).

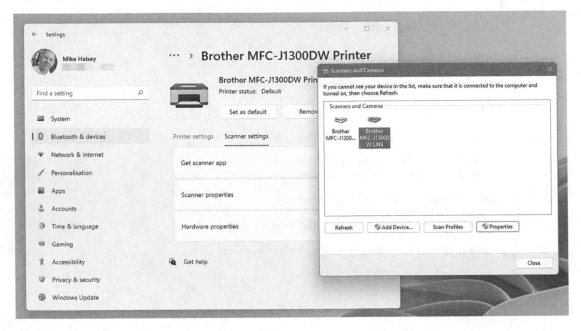

Figure 15-21. *You can manage scanner properties from Settings*

There's really not much here, and a dedicated office document or image scanner will come with its own management and usage applications in any case.

Managing UEFI Systems

You won't find any Windows 11 systems running on a PC with a traditional BIOS firmware. This is because Microsoft specified that the minimum installation requirements for a Windows 11 PC must include a TPM 2.0 (Trusted Platform Module) security and encryption chip, and these can only be found in newer UEFI (Unified Extensible Firmware Interface) firmware.

UEFI is much more secure and robust than BIOS and depending on the motherboard can include useful features such as an automatic dual backup copy of the firmware that the system can boot from if the main copy is corrupt or becomes infected with malware.

There are still some instances however where UEFI can need some attention. This can happen after events such as an update to the UEFI firmware, which will almost always reset it to its default state, and some electrical events like lightning storms can occasionally wreak havoc and cause firmware to reset.

Caution   Some desktop PC systems have a firmware reset button on the back panel that can occasionally and accidentally be pressed when a PC is moved.

There are four main areas that you might need to reconfigure after a UEFI firmware corruption or reset.

The Boot Order

When Windows is installed, the boot system will be set to load the operating system from the *Windows Boot Manager* (see Figure 15-22). Occasionally though, this can become a secondary boot device, and the primary might be set as LAN PXE (Local Area Network Preboot eXecution Environment) which is most commonly used by system administrators when provisioning new PCs on the corporate domain.

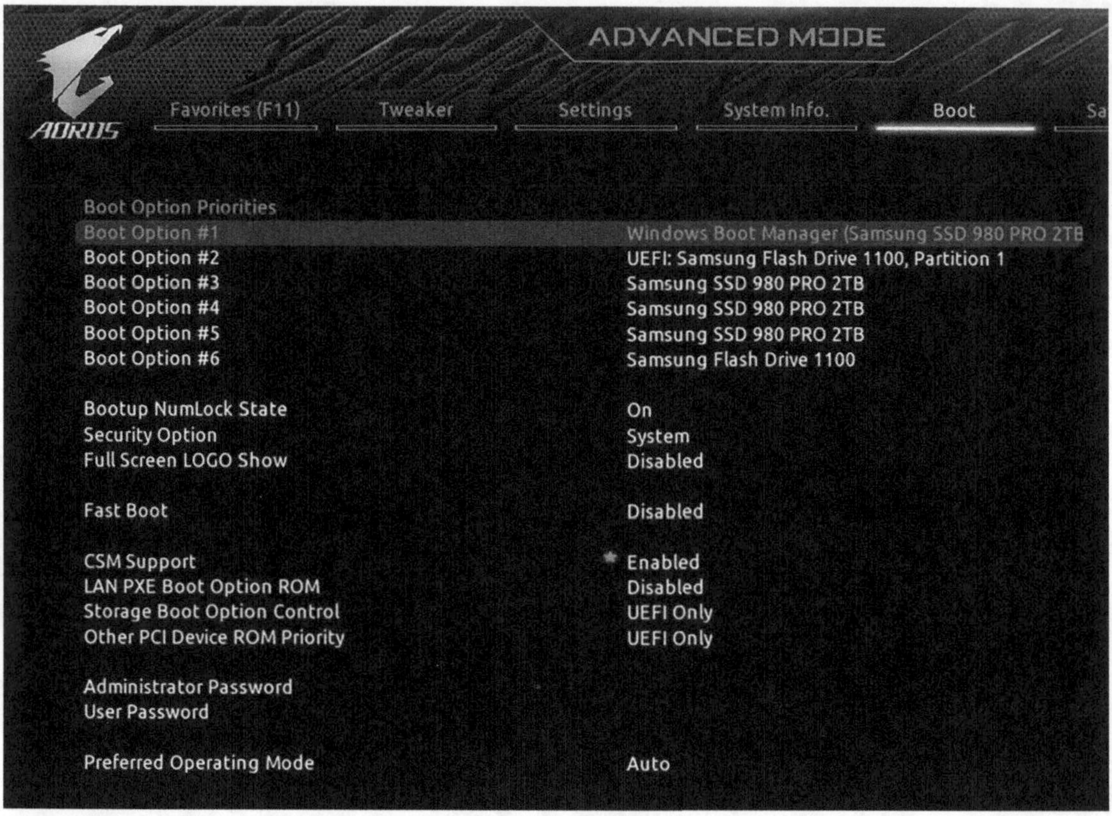

Figure 15-22. You can modify the boot order in the firmware

Bitlocker

It's very common for a TPM chip to be disabled after a firmware reset or upgrade. This doesn't mean the contents of the chip itself will be deleted, though there are circumstances in which this does happen that I will detail, but you will find that you will be nagged at startup for your 50-digit Bitlocker decryption key until you reactivate it.

Where the TPM can become wiped is if you use an fTPM (Firmware TPM) on the PC. This is where the TPM is built into the firmware itself, rather than residing on a separate chip on the motherboard. If you use an fTPM and also use Bitlocker to encrypt the drives in the PC, it is best practice to decrypt the drives *before* upgrading or resetting the firmware.

Your firmware will tell you if you have a physical TPM or a firmware TPM (see Figure 15-23). For my own desktop PC, for which I chose the components and built it myself, the motherboard came with an fTPM but also had a full TPM slot into which I plugged a module. I naturally choose to use the latter so that I don't have to decrypt the drives every time I upgrade the firmware.

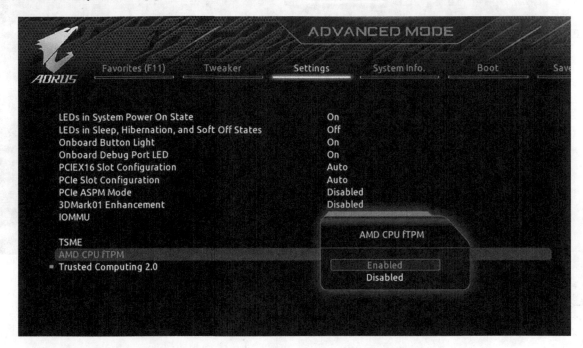

Figure 15-23. *You might need to reenable the TPM or fTPM*

Virtualization

Virtualization works differently in the firmware for Intel and AMD chips. This is because the different chip makers have their own proprietary ways to make virtualization work. With Intel, this is much more smooth, and you will find that a PC running on a Core or Xeon processor will just have virtualization work automatically. On an AMD processor though, you might need to enable their SVM (Secure Virtual Machine) feature in the UEFI firmware (see Figure 15-24).

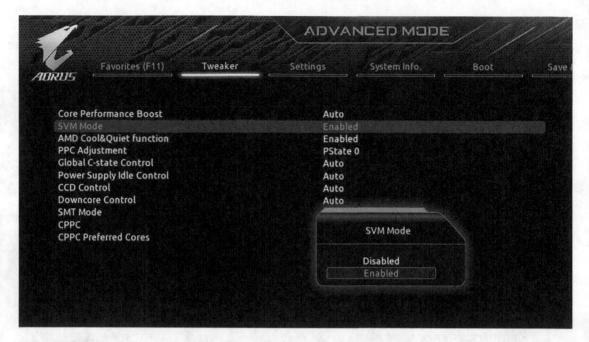

Figure 15-24. *You often need to enable SVM mode on AMD boards to support virtualization*

Fast Boot

Fast Boot is a firmware system that Windows 11 uses to start a PC to the desktop more quickly (see Figure 15-25). What Fast Boot does is save a hibernation snapshot of the PC's status when it is shut down and resumes this at startup. Generally, this is great, but if you have an operation running that requires a full startup operation to run, such as a driver install, Fast Boot can sometimes prevent the operation from running.

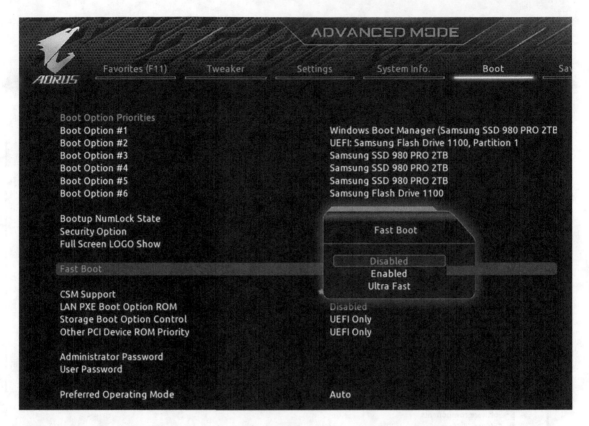

Figure 15-25. *Fast Boot can interfere with some startup operations*

I tend to turn off Fast Boot on my desktop PC as it can prevent you from accessing the UEFI firmware at startup should you need to. If you get stuck in a boot loop where the PC won't start because you need to change something in the firmware, but you can't get into the firmware because Fast Boot keeps bypassing the screen where you can access it, a firmware reset is often the only way out, and that's not an ideal solution just to shave a few seconds of a cold boot time.

Windows Device Manager

Okay, so you were wondering when I was going to get to this, and I've kept you waiting for most of the chapter. Device Manager is currently accessed through the Control Panel, though we can expect this to be moved to Windows Tools during the life of Windows 11.

The default view in Device Manager displays installed hardware according to groups such as *Human Interface Devices, Display Adapters,* and *Network Adapters* (see

Figure 15-26). You click the arrow to the left of a category to see the specific devices contained within it.

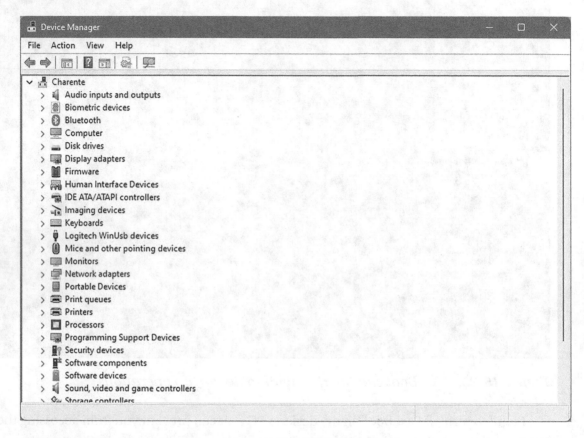

Figure 15-26. *Device Manager groups installed devices by type*

There are other ways to view the devices however, and Windows 11 includes options that weren't available with Windows 10. These include being able to view devices by their driver name (see Figure 15-27). This can help you quickly find and troubleshoot a driver if you have seen its name appear in an event log or a Blue Screen of Death.

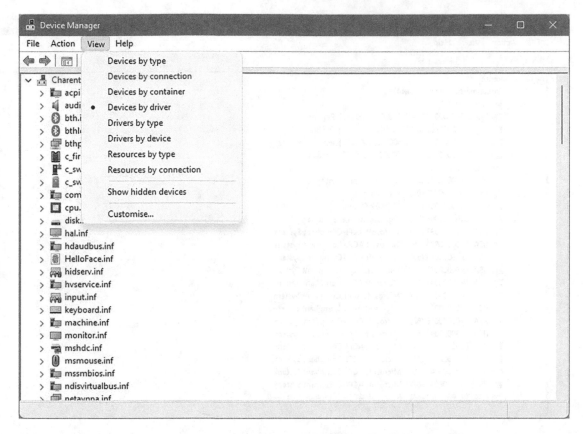

Figure 15-27. *You can view devices by driver name in Windows 11*

Additional views include *Resources by Connection* which lets you view devices sorted according to the memory channels, input/output (I/O) ports they are using, or the processor IRQs (Interrupt Requests) they are using (see Figure 15-28). This can be useful when looking for older devices that are causing conflicts with other devices.

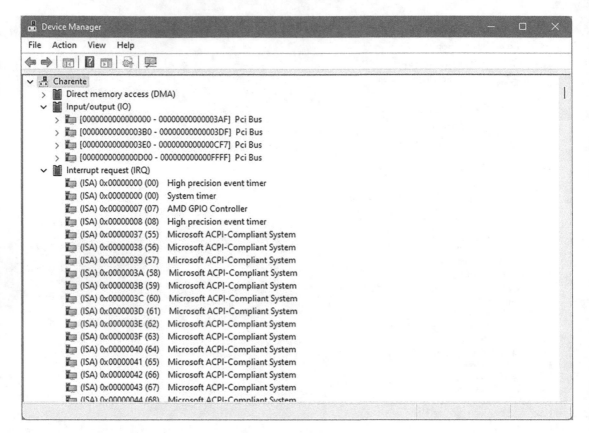

Figure 15-28. *You can view devices by IRQ, I/O Port, or Memory Allocation*

I say older devices here because it's been a long time since IRQ conflicts have caused problems in Windows, but some older drivers may not fully accommodate the way in which Windows 11 assigns IRQ channels.

Note IRQs are a signal sent to the processor that interrupts the current operation and allows a different operation to take place. They were useful for older, single-core processors on which multiple programs had to be run simultaneously. IRQs are still used by Windows but on modern processors are much less of an issue than in the past.

You manage drivers in Device Manager by right-clicking them, and from the menu that appears, you can either *Update* [the] *driver, Disable* [the] *device, Uninstall* [the] *device, Scan for hardware changes,* or open the *Properties* panel for the device (see

Figure 15-29). These options are also available from the *Action* menu at the top of the Device Manager panel.

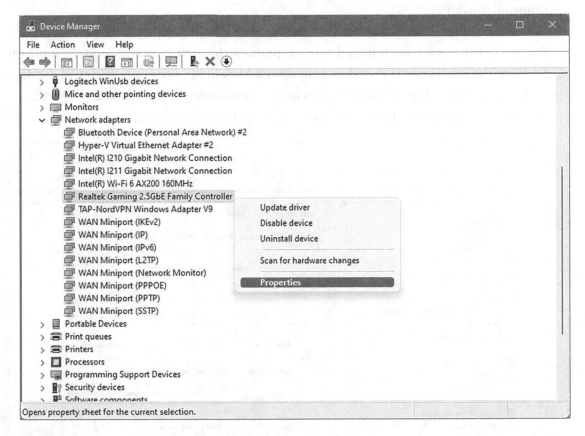

Figure 15-29. *You manage drivers from a right-click*

Managing Device Driver Properties

There are some aspects of the device driver properties panel that we have already covered in this book, such as the *Events* tab where you can view any events logged by Windows pertaining to the device, such as errors and failures, and the *General* tab where any errors will be displayed in the *Device status* box.

Under the *Driver* tab, you can see the name of the driver publisher, the date the driver was written/released, the driver version number (this is especially useful if you know a specific driver version is more stable than the one you may be using), and whether the driver has been digitally signed and by whom.

There are also buttons you can use to get further details about the driver, more on this shortly, update the driver from Windows Update or manually, or disable and uninstall the device.

One especially useful feature is being able to *Roll Back* [the] *Driver* (see Figure 15-30). If you have updated a driver, perhaps through Windows Update, and now find that the new driver is unstable, you can roll back to the previous version of the driver and then pause updates until you find a better, more stable driver to install. Note that this feature requires you to have *System Restore* activated on the PC.

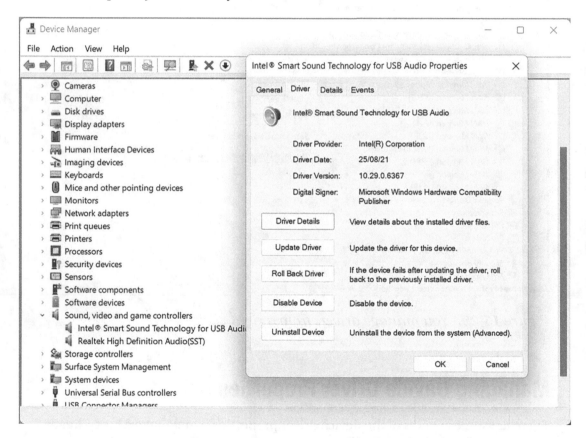

Figure 15-30. *You can update, roll back, and disable a device driver*

Manually Uninstalling/Reinstalling Drivers

One of the problems with drivers, especially with some more specialist hardware, is that you sometimes need an older version of a driver. Windows can prevent this by telling you a "newer version of the driver is already installed." Should this happen, you need to manually remove and reinstall the correct driver version.

In the device properties, you can click the *Driver Details* button. This will display a list of all the files that constitute the driver and in which folder(s) they can be found (see Figure 15-31).

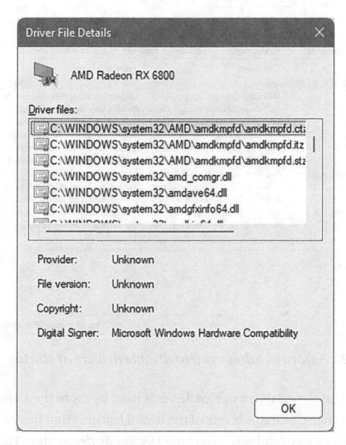

Figure 15-31. *You can view a list of all the files that constitute a driver*

To manually remove the driver, you should **not** at this point delete those driver files from the PC. While it would probably be perfectly fine to do so, you run the risk of creating two bigger problems. The first of these is a raft or pop-up error messages every time you then start to the desktop telling you that the driver cannot be loaded and also that other devices might also malfunction as drivers can sometimes share their files.

This is where you need Microsoft's Sysinternals suite and its *Autoruns* tool. Within Autoruns, click the *Drivers* tab and you will see a long list of all the drivers that start with Windows (see Figure 15-32). You can safely uncheck each one associated with the installed hardware because if you *do* uncheck something that makes the PC unstable, you can run Autoruns again and recheck it.

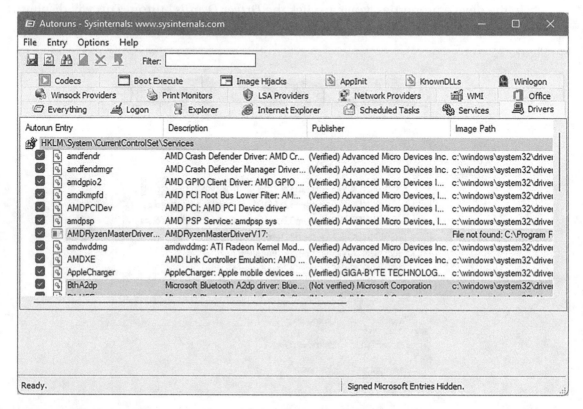

Figure 15-32. *Autoruns allows you to disable drivers at startup*

If you are concerned that a device driver is used by more than one device on the PC, it's possible to check, and this is one of the useful features that has been added since Windows 10. In Device Manager, select the *Devices by driver* view. Here, you can select the driver you are concerned about and see if there is just a single or multiple devices attached to it (see Figure 15-33).

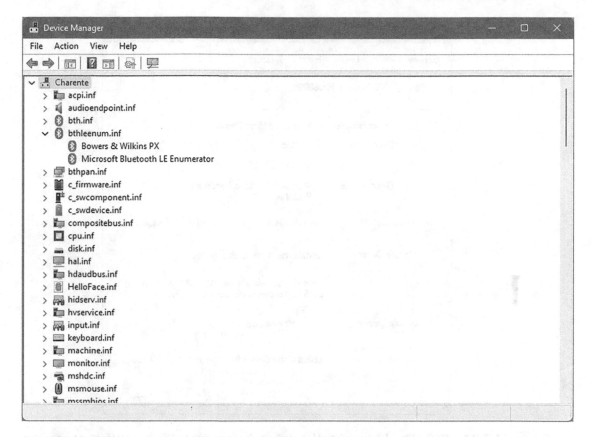

Figure 15-33. *Device Manager can tell you if a driver is used by multiple devices*

Before you restart the PC, you should go back to the driver properties, and from the *Driver* tab, you should *Uninstall* [the] *Device*, or at the very least *Disable* [the] *Device* (see Figure 15-34).

Figure 15-34. *You should uninstall a driver before installing a different version*

When you uninstall a device driver from the PC, you will sometimes, but not always, see an option to *Attempt to remove the driver for this device* (see Figure 15-35). What this will do is delete the driver files so that they cannot be automatically reinstalled. Not all drivers support this option, but it's very useful at the times you need it.

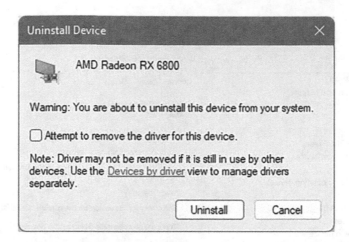

Figure 15-35. *Some drivers will offer to delete driver files*

Tip   At the beginning of this chapter, I detailed how you can bypass the Windows version check for some device driver installers. This can be useful when you need to install an older version of a driver to maintain stability and compatibility.

Identifying Unknown Devices

Sometimes, you will see a device listed in Device Manager as *Unknown*. This is unhelpful as you need to have some idea what the thing is so you can choose the correct driver to install (see Figure 15-36).

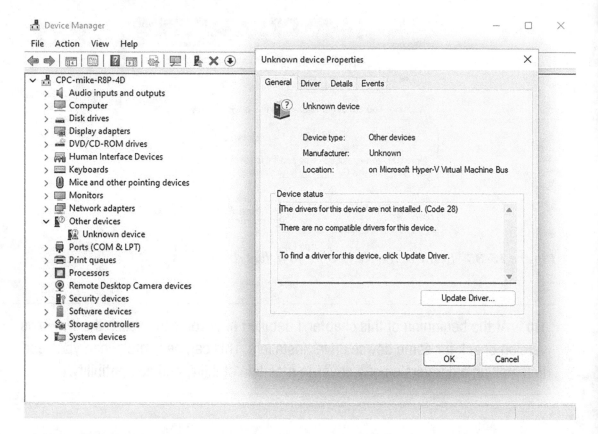

Figure 15-36. *Unknown devices can be annoying, but can still be identified*

This isn't an issue however as it's still possible to identify the device. In its *Properties* panel, open the *Details* tab, and from the *Hardware IDs* option in the drop-down menu, check the codes available. In Figure 15-37, they are VID_0A12&PID_0001&REV_2520. You may also see VEN_ (Vendor) and DEV_ (Device) codes for many devices, and a search online will help you quickly identify the device and, if necessary, download the correct drivers for it.

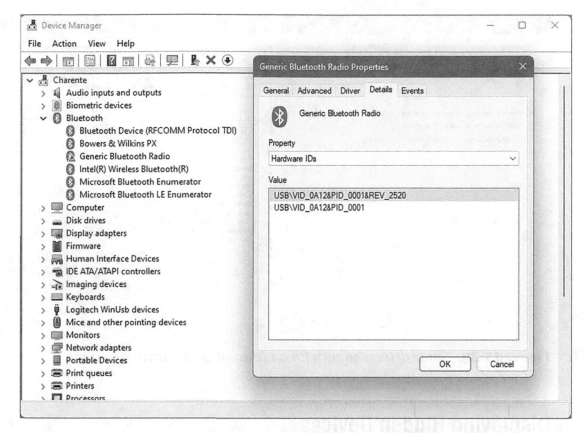

Figure 15-37. *You can identify an unknown device from its Hardware IDs*

Additional Driver Options

Some drivers will come with additional configuration options. This is especially common for network and storage devices and can include options for power management, caching, and advanced security and configuration (see Figure 15-38). These additional options will always appear as extra tabs within the driver properties panel should you need them for specific configuration purposes, such as preventing a device sleeping automatically if it is not waking properly and causing a problem.

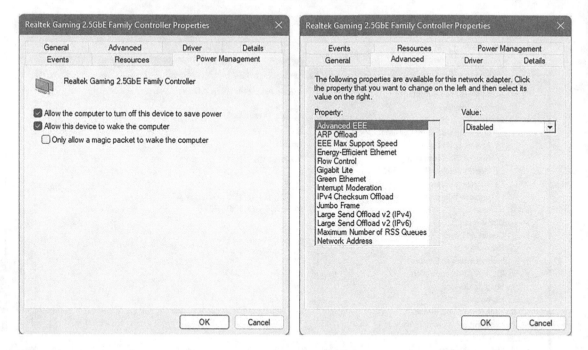

Figure 15-38. *Some drivers come with additional configuration options*

Displaying Hidden Devices

Not all devices on a PC are immediately visible to you in Device Manager, as Windows 11 hides some devices that it believes you don't need to see or interact with. These include devices that are set to be hidden by the vendor, devices that are set to have no overall class, and devices that have been removed but where the Registry entries remain, such as unplugged USB devices.

It is possible to view all these devices though. From the *View* menu in Device Manager, select *Show hidden devices*. These devices will now appear slightly grayed out in Device Manager to help you identify them (see Figure 15-39). This can be useful if, to give one example, a USB device causes Windows to become unresponsive or unstable when it's plugged in.

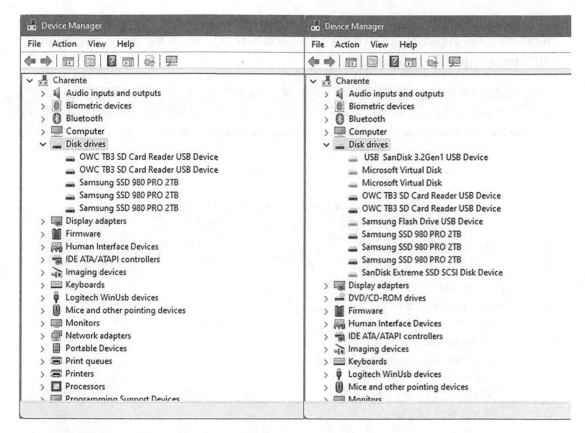

Figure 15-39. *Some devices are hidden in Windows*

Installing Legacy Devices

Earlier in this chapter, I talked about installing legacy printers, such as those on Serial and Parallel ports, and how you can install the ports themselves in Windows. These ports and devices don't have the firmware identification that comes with USB devices, and so all need manual configuration.

There are many other legacy devices that you might need to install in Windows 11 though, from specialist medical and engineering devices to analogue sensors, firewire devices, and dial-up modems. You can install legacy devices from Device Manager by opening the *Action* menu and clicking *Add legacy hardware*.

It's fairly pointless checking the option for Windows to auto-detect the hardware as firstly legacy hardware doesn't tend to be detectable, and also if it could be detected, Windows would have probably done so already.

Windows separates the devices into categories, helping you add and configure the hardware (see Figure 15-40). This is because different types of hardware will require different setup and configuration.

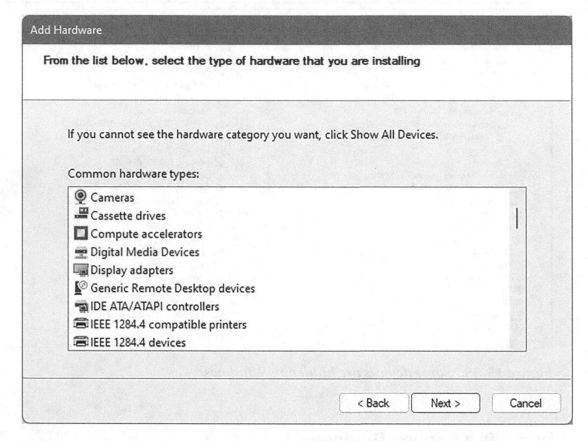

Figure 15-40. *You can add legacy hardware by choosing its device category*

When you select a device type, you will be presented with a list of drivers that are already available within Windows 11. This list isn't anywhere near as long as it has been with previous Windows editions and just includes the main and most common hardware that Windows' telemetry has told Microsoft is used (see Figure 15-41). If you do not see a compatible driver listed and you have the correct driver to hand, click the *Have Disk* button to install it on the PC.

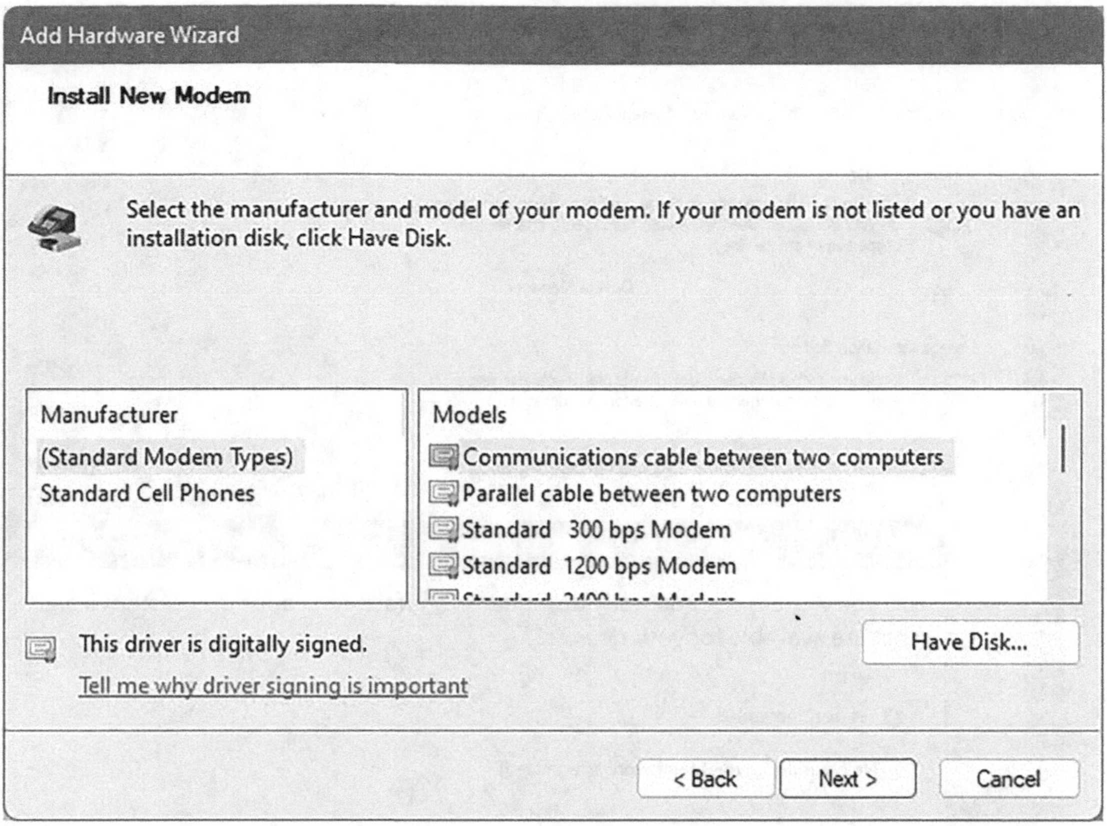

Figure 15-41. *Windows comes with drivers for some legacy hardware types*

Blocking Driver Installs from Windows Update

If you are using a PC that includes specific hardware required for a critical role, you might not want Windows Update to find new versions of drivers and install them automatically, when these new drivers might cause the device to become unstable or unresponsive.

You can disable the automatic installation of new drivers by opening *Settings*, clicking *System* and then *About*, and then clicking the *Advanced system settings* link. This will open a panel where, under the *Hardware* tab, you can click *Device Installation Settings* (it's fairly well hidden then; Ed) and then choose to not automatically install new driver versions on the PC (see Figure 15-42).

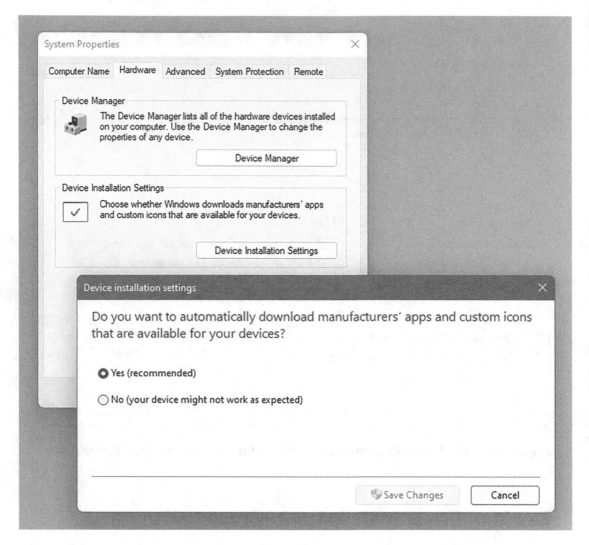

Figure 15-42. *You can choose to not install new drivers from Windows Update*

Backing Up the Driver Store

As you might imagine, all the installed drivers in Windows are placed in a folder on the C: drive. There are two folders involved with this, and both can be copied and backed up should you need them. The advantage of doing so is that, if you need to reinstall Windows on the PC later, you can either just copy everything back from your backup or point Windows to your backup folder and tell it to get on with reinstalling your devices.

These folders can be found at `C:\Windows\System32\DriverStore` and `C:\Windows\System32\Drivers`. It's not always a good idea though to just copy the drivers from the backup back to these two folders in a new installation, as you may be inadvertently overwriting newer versions of drivers that Windows has downloaded or that exist in a newer Windows installer file. As a general way to keep a backup of critical driver files though, these folders can be very helpful.

Summary

Good device driver management on a PC is crucial to ensuring the smooth operation of the PC and especially specialist and legacy hardware. Anybody using a PC in a mission-critical role, such as manufacturing, medicine, or for scientific or engineering work, will tell you just how crucial it is that everything just works, all of the time.

We don't always live in that type of world though, and the interconnectedness of our IT systems, the Internet, cloud services, and communications and electrical infrastructure can create its own problems, especially when you're trying to diagnose and repair PCs.

In the next chapter then, we'll look at this interconnectedness as we progress onto more advanced topics. We'll look at where the kinks in the chain can cause problems, how to identify them, and how climate change can affect our PC use into the future.

PART III

Advanced Troubleshooting Techniques

CHAPTER 16

IT Systems and the Wider World

If you look at the world of PC use and work today compared to just a few short years ago, it's very clear that everything has changed. Indeed, the whole dynamic of the workplace is different, with employees of major corporations now effectively setting policy for attendance, wages, and more. All of this came out of the pandemic of course. Before 2020, businesses around the world had been telling people they *had* to work from the office because that was just the only way to do things and that nobody would get anything done if they didn't.

Then Working from home became not just compulsory but favorable both for employees, who found a better quality of life not having to commute, had more money in their pockets for exactly the same reasons, and businesses that enjoyed plummeting energy bills for workplaces where people weren't in attendance.

Many businesses have tried to return to normal since, generally with mixed success. Apple is a good example of this, being fairly desperate to get people back to the workplace having just spent five billion dollars building the place, and workers who have in some instances taken legal action to prevent their employers from forcing them into the office. This is an action that would have been unthinkable only a few short years ago.

When you're a systems administrator or providing IT support however, this new workplace dynamic throws up all manner of new and unexpected challenges. In Chapters 5, 6, and 7, I wrote about how you can support remote workers, how important it is for both you and them not to make any assumptions about them or their circumstances, and how to make sure you get all your ducks in a row when working in a support environment.

© Mike Halsey 2023
M. Halsey, *Troubleshooting and Supporting Windows 11*, https://doi.org/10.1007/978-1-4842-8728-6_16

It's Not Where You Work, It's the Country You Work In

It's the circumstances workers find themselves in however that I want to look at more in this chapter, and there's no better place to start than off on a foreign trip. Actually, it doesn't even have to be foreign, you might be from New York and sent on a work trip to rural Arkansas, which might seem foreign enough for you. When people are working abroad though, there are challenges they or you might not expect.

Let's begin with architecture. Most of the people who read my books live and work in the USA, though there are many other people right around the world. The USA and Canada tend to build houses and buildings very differently to other countries in the G20, the group of the 20 largest economies in the world.

This is in part because they are the youngest countries in the G20, having both been founded around 1776, but also because they are some of the largest countries in the G20. What I'm talking about here is the fondness for using wood as a construction material for buildings. Wood is used for a variety of reasons, not the least of which is its sheer abundance. I have friends in Vancouver, which is a fairly large metropolitan city on Canada's west coast, but to get to it, I first have to fly over around 3000 miles of forest (see Figure 16-1).

Figure 16-1. *The greenery in Canada stretches for thousands of miles*

The great distances between cities and metropolitan areas also dictate building techniques and the materials used. Unless you have suitable quarries nearby, stone and brick building materials are expensive to transport, so it's much more sensible to use what you already have to hand. It's for these reasons that other large countries in the G20, such as China, Australia, and Brazil, also use wood construction for buildings in rural and remote areas.

The USA and Canada having been formed around 1776 make those countries a little under 250 years old as I write this from my home in central southern France. My home, or at least the oldest part of it, is a full 100 years older than both of those countries, having been built around the mid to late 1600s (see Figure 16-2).

Figure 16-2. *It's not all green fields and blue skies in France, but they certainly help*

The walls in the oldest part of my home are up to two feet thick in places, and while this makes it brilliant for nights loudly playing my vinyl copy of Jeff Wayne's "The War of the Worlds" in front of the fire, it's terrible for my Wi-Fi signal. In fact, the problem when I bought the house was so bad, with the telephone line entering in that part of the house, that I quickly installed Ethernet cable and a mesh Wi-Fi system from Netgear.

I however am the lucky one, as many people live and work in parts of the world where the buildings are a thousand years old, old enough that anything made of wood would have long since disintegrated into dust. Southern European countries like Italy and Greece and most middle-eastern countries have a great many towns built hundreds and hundreds of years ago, and I think you can probably tell where I'm going with this.

When you get the tech support call from the guy from the Boston office that he has a problem with his laptop in that he can't maintain a good Wi-Fi signal, and he's got important meetings that afternoon, you should ask if he's still on that business trip to Medina Azahara in Spain, which was founded in 1560 and is a UNESCO world heritage site.

Indeed, you don't even need to travel to exotic and remote locations with names nobody is able to correctly pronounce to experience these problems. Beijing, China,

Rome in Italy, Mexico City, and Mumbai in India are also UNESCO world heritage cities because of their architecture that dates back hundreds of years. Jerusalem, Israel, is known for being a huge hub for technological development, and the oldest parts of that city are between five and a half and six and a half thousand years old. So when you get the call from the guy, we'll say his name is Jeff for the sake of argument as it's still on my mind, then you should perhaps tell him to go and sit by a window.

Sand, Dust, Water, and Snow Can All Kill Your Laptop

Of course, thick stone walls are just one example of where support calls can come in from remote workers and those on business around the world. Even closer to home, there can be challenges. Back in 2019, we had "the beast from the east" blow over Europe and the UK, bringing with it temperatures as low as –35 Celsius (–31 Fahrenheit). Yours truly was travelling to Microsoft in Seattle during this extreme weather event and wound up in intensive care in Seattle with a bout of pneumonia that damn near killed me.

Now I'm not suggesting that Robin from accounts is going to sit outside a coffee shop in –30 degrees to file her weekly report in a blizzard, but it's a good example of how technology really doesn't like extremes. There are stated tolerances for laptops and tablets of the temperature range in which they will happily operate. While it's far from likely that somebody will ever use a laptop in the extreme cold (unless you're a polar scientist of course; Ed), it works the other way too.

Microsoft doesn't publish the operating tolerances for my Surface Laptop Studio; you usually need to purchase a truly ruggedized laptop to get those figures. Panasonic say the operating tolerances for its Toughbook range are around –29 degrees Celsius (–20 Fahrenheit) to 63 degrees Celsius (145 Fahrenheit). You'll find the usual operating tolerances for an average home or work laptop or tablet will be around –10 degrees Celsius (14 Fahrenheit) to 50 degrees Celsius (122 Fahrenheit). You might think that this could be enough for all uses, but I've learned to never make assumptions. This summer where I live and elsewhere in Europe, we've had record temperatures of 45 degrees Celsius (113 Fahrenheit) with a high of 47 degrees Celsius (117 Fahrenheit) reached in parts of Portugal.

This of course is getting dangerously close to those tolerances, and in some parts of the world such as India and parts of Asia, temperatures in excess of 50 degrees Celsius (122 Fahrenheit) are not uncommon for prolonged periods.

It's unlikely that anybody would be sitting outdoors with their laptop in such heat, though don't discount the foolhardy, but a laptop left sitting in the sun in the garden on a hot summer day can fry its components, screen, and battery all too quickly.

Note   The terms "rugged" and "ruggedized" can often be used to describe laptops that have only been fitted with rubber bumpers to make the device more suitable for a child at school. Equally, there is a big difference between the meanings of the words "water-resistant" and "waterproof."

Then there's water and sand. Many people want to go to the beach for their summer holiday, but sand is as much a killer for technology as water can be. For this, we have the IP (Ingress Protection) rating system you'll be used to seeing for smartphones.

The first number relates to dust and solid ingress, and the second number relates to water ingress, so a smartphone with an IP rating of 65 is protected tightly from dust and from water jets from any angle. You can see how the IP ratings work in Tables 16-1 and 16-2.

Table 16-1. *The IP rating pertaining to dust and solid ingress*

Number/ Letter/ Digit	Description
X	Not tested
0	No protection
1	Protected against a solid object greater than 50mm, such as a hand
2	Protected against a solid object greater than 12.5mm, such as a finger
3	Protected against a solid object greater than 2.5mm, such as a wire
4	Protected against a solid object greater than 1.0mm, such as a strap
5	Dust protected. Prevents ingress of dust sufficient to cause harm
6	Dust tight. No ingress of dust

Table 16-2. *The IP rating system pertaining to water and liquid ingress*

Letter/ Digit	Description
X	Not tested
0	No protection
1	Protection against water drops
2	Protected against water drops at a 15 degree angle
3	Protected against water spray at 60 degree angle
4	Protected against water splashing from any angle
5	Protected against water jets from any angle
6	Protected against powerful water jets and heavy seas
7	Protected against effects of temporary submersion in water (30 minutes at 3 feet)
8	Protected against the effects of permanent submission in water (up to 13 feet)

It is safe to assume that a normal home or workplace laptop or tablet will have an IP rating of 00 (double zero), given that the USB and other ports, the keyboard, and the trackpad will all let in water, and the ports and keyboard will let in dust and particles. Then there are the heat vents to consider which will let in anything at all. A laptop marketed as having a "spill-proof keyboard" will still only be able to cope with small quantities of coffee before the liquid will seep into other parts of the device.

Note The biggest killer of keyboards and laptop keyboards has been for decades now, and continues to be, pizza.

This means that using a laptop on the beach is a bad idea, but what for the people who have no choice? (What? No choice but to work on a beach? Cool!; Ed) I'm talking here about people that work on construction sites or in environments such as desert countries where sand, dust, and perhaps even strong winds are an occupational hazard.

Here, a ruggedized laptop or tablet isn't always an option, as an engineer might, for example, need a powerful GPU to render plans on-site. Ruggedized laptops can be powerful, but rarely are they built to that type of specification.

Note   I want to slip in a note about ruggedized laptops and tablets that conform to MIL-STD (military standards) and MIL-SPEC (military specification) requirements. You should always be careful to choose equipment that has been tested by a third-party laboratory and know exactly what tests it has passed, and not just from a manufacturer that says it's "military grade" or "military grade compatible."

Is the Infrastructure Sound?

We've all heard the story of the guy who called IT support because his computer wouldn't switch on. When asked to reach around the back to check the power cable was plugged in, he replied that he couldn't see it because of the power outage.

When getting calls for support, it's always worth keeping an open mind about the external factors that can affect our IT systems. For example, someone telling you they can't access their online services, Microsoft Azure or Google Workspace, for example, could be down to a permissions or an account error for them, but it's always worth asking if anybody else is having the same problem.

Outages can also be caused by everything from the digger on the construction site next door ripping through a cable to a nationwide outage for a website or service. In this regard, websites such as `isitdownrightnow.com` and `downdetector.com` can be highly useful, but so can searching for the company on Twitter. There you can get an even faster response as it takes just a few seconds for people to start complaining there about outages.

It's here that appropriately logging support calls can help. In Chapter 7, I wrote about how to set up your reporting, logging, and support paperwork and mechanisms in such a way as to make supporting users simpler and quicker. Having a support mechanism that allows you to filter support requests by type, date, and so on can help you to quickly identify if a problem sits with the user's own machine or if it's elsewhere, for example, an external business site has an expired security certificate, and your colleague Theresa has already put the wheels in motion to issue a new one.

A searchable support system can also help identify perhaps more esoteric problems, such as a misconfiguration or a permissions error with a cloud system, by cross-referencing the current call with others that have come in over the previous days and weeks. The more information you have at your disposal, the easier a comprehensive diagnosis can be.

The Hip Bone's Connected to the Leg Bone

You've probably heard the song "The hip bone's connected to the leg bone…" and perhaps sung it as a child in school as a way to help you learn basic human anatomy. It's the same with our IT systems, and sometimes it's all too easy to forget just how far those connections can spread.

In the previous section, I spoke about how an Internet connection can be wiped out by a digger ripping up a cable on the construction site next door, something that's been known to happen quite often if I'm honest. I want to give just two examples from my own life though about how the interconnectedness works.

Let's say I'm using my Windows 365 account. This links to a virtual machine on a server, in a datacenter somewhere in France as I like to keep the connection local purely for reasons of maintaining a speedy connection.

My desktop PC, which is most commonly what I use to connect to Windows 365, is connected via Cat7 Ethernet cable to a small gigabit four-port switch box and then on to my Netgear mesh router system. This in turn plugs into a separate router which is needed as it's connected directly to and controls my Starlink satellite broadband connection.

That router is performing two tasks, one of which is gathering satellite positioning data from Starlink's servers to make sure the dish is always pointed in the right direction. The other is that it's sending my connection request to a satellite in orbit, which is in turn processing it and passing it back to a ground station that will connect via gigabit fiber to the ground telecoms network in France. That network passes the signal through several stops on the ground at interchange stations until it is correctly routed to the Microsoft datacenter in which my virtual machine is running.

We can see in Figure 16-3 that the connection can only be traced so far before it's repeatedly timing out. Now in this particular case, it's happening that way because of the security Microsoft has in place for its server and cloud infrastructure, but using the **TraceRT** command in this way can help diagnose where a dropped connection or a bottleneck for the connection might be taking place, with the last connection being identified as a Microsoft network in Paris (`par21.ntwk.msn.net`) on the IP address `104.44.23.149`.

```
Command Prompt                                                    —    □    ×

Microsoft Windows [Version 10.0.22000.856]
(c) Microsoft Corporation. All rights reserved.

C:\Users\mikeh>tracert 20.111.12.7

Tracing route to 20.111.12.7 over a maximum of 30 hops

  1    <1 ms    <1 ms    <1 ms  10.0.0.1
  2     1 ms     1 ms     1 ms  192.168.1.1
  3    39 ms    39 ms    47 ms  100.64.0.1
  4    52 ms    39 ms    47 ms  172.16.249.30
  5    43 ms    36 ms    39 ms  149.19.108.145
  6    31 ms    31 ms    27 ms  msft-decix-02-fra.ntwk.msn.net [80.81.195.11]
  7    38 ms    31 ms    43 ms  ae24-0.icr02.fra23.ntwk.msn.net [104.44.42.78]
  8    42 ms    40 ms    50 ms  be-102-0.ibr01.fra23.ntwk.msn.net [104.44.20.248]
  9    56 ms    51 ms    35 ms  be-12-0.ibr01.par21.ntwk.msn.net [104.44.17.172]
 10    55 ms    44 ms    59 ms  ae106-0.icr04.par21.ntwk.msn.net [104.44.23.149]
 11     *        *        *     Request timed out.
 12     *        *        *     Request timed out.
 13     *        *        *     Request timed out.
 14     *        *        *     Request timed out.
 15     *        *        *     Request timed out.
 16     *        *        *     Request timed out.
 17     *        *        *     Request timed out.
 18     *        *        *     Request timed out.
 19     *        *        *     Request timed out.
 20     *        *        *     Request timed out.
 21     *        *        *     Request timed out.
 22     *        *        *     Request timed out.
 23     *        *        *     Request timed out.
 24     *        *        *     Request timed out.
 25     *        *        *     Request timed out.
 26     *        *        *     Request timed out.
 27     *        *        *     Request timed out.
 28     *        *        *     Request timed out.
 29     *        *        *     Request timed out.
 30     *        *        *     Request timed out.

Trace complete.

C:\Users\mikeh>
```

Figure 16-3. *The route Internet traffic takes can be long and sometimes problematic*

The systems at that datacenter route the request to the correct server, which in turn routes the request to the correct virtual machine, which performs the request. Then the response is sent back exactly the same way, but possibly with different connection waypoints en route.

The second example is from before I had satellite broadband installed and needed to connect to the Internet via a slow 3.5Mb/s ADSL line over the telephone wire. This connected via an Orange Livebox Wi-Fi router which was plugged into the phone socket and went via a cable to a box on a fairly creaky old wooden telegraph pole in the road that in turn connects to a great many more creaky old wooden telegraph poles that occasionally fall over in the wind (see Figure 16-4). It's not until it gets to the local town where it will connect to a fiber line and out to the rest of the world that things improve.

Figure 16-4. *Not all Internet connections in the world are high-quality fiber*

About a year and a half ago, my ADSL line suddenly went off. I called Orange who ran some tests and could see there was indeed a fault. They sent an engineer who opened the cream box you can see at the top of the pole in the photograph in Figure 16-4 and poked around for 20 minutes in the mess of wires to be found there. Eventually, he found the issue; a wire had come loose from its connection in the wind, and he reinstated it, restoring my ADSL connection.

In the process of doing this however, he moved, disconnected, dislodged (we never really got to the bottom of it) another wire, and took both the phone and Internet connections for my neighbor across the road offline, and offline they stayed for some weeks until Orange finally sent an engineer who could identify the problem.

You can see then that having quick links to the status pages for services, and hopefully your ISP will also provide such a page, can be invaluable. Some of these status pages are linked as follows:

- Microsoft Office 365 – `portal.office.com/servicestatus`

- Microsoft Azure – `status.azure.com`

- Google Workspace – `google.com/appsstatus/dashboard`

- Amazon Web Services (AWS) – `health.aws.amazon.com`

- Zoom – `status.zoom.us`

You should also check if service providers for your business or organization, such as IP telephony and online security, have service status pages.

And for Everything Else...

So we've established that stone walls, dust, sand, water, a strong gust of wind, and even a pizza can be enough to bring down network connections and screw up your laptops and other hardware. Let's not stop there though just when we're enjoying it.

I have two dogs, Robbie and Evan (see Figure 16-5), with the possibility of two Border Collie puppies coming in the next month or so, so I'm very excited. Dog, cat, and other pet hair is well known to be a good cause of problems with electronics, especially when a buildup of hair and fur blocks heat and air vents, and causes increases in temperature for electronic components.

Figure 16-5. *I couldn't resist sneaking a photo of my dogs into this book*

Tip Some problems can be caused by the use of poor-quality cabling. Unshielded twisted pair (UTP) cables are commonly used for networking, as they're cheap. Good-quality shielded cables, however, can prevent many of the problems associated with UTP cables, such as picking up interference from television, radio and cellular signals, microwave ovens, and powerful motors.

Power can also be a problem. You might take a high-quality, stable electricity supply for granted. Here in France though, the electricity supply can be, let's say, a little flaky. This means that sudden and brief power interruptions are common and power cuts can happen from time to time.

Shortly before I first moved to France, and knowing this would be an issue, I purchased uninterruptable power supplies (UPS) for all of my computer, electronics, and home appliances kit. Everything from the TVs to my Rega turntable and amplifier to my desktop PC would be plugged into these boxes which, as they contained their own battery, could smooth out the power interruptions and protect what is many thousands of Euros worth of kit.

Around this time, I read a story in an expat group on Facebook from a man and his partner who had moved from California to France. He was a graphic designer and had brought with him two hugely expensive high-quality monitors for his work. He'd plugged these into a surge protector, as is always the advice with any electronics kit, but within a week both had completely blown and had to be replaced. He was, unsurprisingly, pretty upset, and it's a great example of how you always need to consider the power networks of countries in which you live and work.

Tip Of course, laptops don't need to be plugged into a UPS as their internal battery will perform the same job. A surge protector for them and their power supply though is still always recommended.

Our PCs, the Planet, and Climate Change

As the author of a book about IT and climate change, *The Green IT Guide* (Apress, 2022), just in case I haven't mentioned it before, I couldn't let this conversation about infrastructure pass without bringing in the subject where it's appropriate.

As I write this, Russia is six months into its invasion of Ukraine, an invasion which has thrown the world's energy markets into complete turmoil with electricity and gas prices having risen in the UK by more than 150% so far, and Germany scrambling around to find natural gas and having to pay way over the odds for it, which is pushing up prices (I'm pretty sure it's not all Germany's fault; Ed).

This is in turn causing a huge surge in demand for solar panels on homes and businesses, the cost of which have fallen by 60% or more in recent years. A friend has recently had solar panels fitted at his home, though he had already arranged this before the crisis, and I'll be fitting them too which was always the plan, but something I just hadn't gotten around to yet (so perhaps not the best two examples of your point then; Ed).

Both of us will be fitting batteries. These serve several purposes. The main purpose is to store energy that can be used at night when the solar panels aren't generating any power, so you can still provide power to equipment such as refrigerators without needing to use power from the grid. The second reason, and certainly one where it pertains to this conversation, is that these batteries act as a sort of super-UPS for your house.

Now there's a caveat here, and you will need to research this for your particular solar installers, as not all battery systems kick in immediately on a power interruption. Some take a few seconds to engage, which means you would still need to use UPS boxes on your high value equipment and surge protectors for everything else. There's no doubt though that installing solar panels with a battery backup can be a huge benefit in many ways, not just in reducing the use of fossil fuels.

When you are purchasing cloud and other services for your business or organization, it's worth considering the sustainability policies of the providers. All the main players in the market have clear sustainability policies (though Tencent was a little late to the party), but you'll find that other providers don't yet have their own policy.

This could be because they just haven't gotten around to it yet, and it could be that their services run on top of other services from the big players such as Azure and AWS. It's always a question worth asking however.

Note   Beware of carbon offsetting as a method of becoming more sustainable. This sounds great, but just buying to tree planting and other projects that frankly would have happened anyway is doing absolutely nothing to help the company investing in those projects to reduce its own carbon emissions.

The point to all this is that with the correct environmental and sustainability policies in place, you can actually *reduce* the volume of support calls you receive and make it quicker to fix some of the issues that will arise. Now I can see the confused look on your face, so let me explain. The battery example is just one. Using Internet video and voice telephony for meetings, and using online meeting tools such as collaborative whiteboards instead of flying people around the world, is not just considerably cheaper and a far better use of people's time, but if a problem is encountered, both it and the people reporting it will be much physically closer to you.

Also, adopting a policy of purchasing laptops that are repairable, rather than being glued together as most laptops still are, can not only be much cheaper for you in the long term, but can reduce downtime as it's much faster to swap out a stick of RAM than to have a user wait two weeks for a replacement laptop to arrive.

All in, having one eye on sustainability is not only a great way to convince your bosses and stakeholders that they can save huge volumes of cash, but the right policies implemented in the right way can make your own job much easier too.

Summary

It's very clear that we've come a considerable distance from the days of the stand-alone PC sitting in the corner of the office with a stack of floppy disks sitting next to it. The sheer size and scale of the networks to which our IT equipment is connected, and the number of different types of devices that never existed before such as SonicWalls and virtual machines, can be difficult to comprehend.

It's important therefore to never forget this big wide world exists and to be prepared to think outside of the box when problems arise... especially given the solution to that problem might be outside of the box anyway.

We're going to bring things back down to earth though with a bump in the next chapter and get all serious for a while. The huge networks and the wider world that we connect to can present enormous security problems for your business or organization, and the risks involved in getting something, even the smallest detail, wrong can end up with your name splashed over the national and international media for all the wrong reasons.

So in the next chapter, we'll look in depth at security in Windows 11, completely jettisoning the usual advice of "always keep your antivirus software up to date, and Windows patched" in recognition that the world simply isn't the same place it was a few short years ago and that the way we respond to security, hacking, and malware threats has to change to meet the new and constantly changing nature of those threats.

CHAPTER 17

Security and Encryption Troubleshooting

Security and privacy are a strange thing these days. On the one hand, they're absolutely paramount for the consumer, with social media, advertising, and other corporations wanting to know more and more about us to sell us appropriate advertising. On the other hand, much of that advertising is pretty well targeted, and some would argue that it's so unbearably difficult to keep anything private anymore, especially as many of us put it out on social media willingly, that we're on a hiding to nothing.

For business, it's arguably even more important, not just because of huge fines that governments can issue over data breaches but also because of corporate espionage, entire governments wanting to steal sensitive documents and secret patents, and so on. Indeed, I've written a lot about privacy and security myself over the years (`https://pcs.tv/3Aj9FJp`).

So why when Microsoft launched Windows 11 then with a renewed focus on privacy and security did it cause absolute uproar? Microsoft had decided that in order for a PC to be compatible with Windows 11, it must include a TPM 2.0 chip or an equivalent fTPM (I'll come to what these are in a while). Many Windows 10 PCs both in home and business use don't have one, either because the motherboard never came with one or where there is a socket, one hadn't been fitted.

The upshot of this was that millions of perfectly good Windows 10 PCs, many of which might only be two or three years old when Windows 11 launched, wouldn't be upgradeable and would, when all support ends for Windows 10 in 2025, be resigned to the scrap pile. Now, you might think I, as the author of *The Green IT Guide* (Apress, 2022), have strong thoughts about this. Indeed, I do and I personally petitioned Microsoft to extend support for Windows 10 so as to avoid making the world's growing ewaste pile larger than it needed to be; you can read more about this at `https://pcs.tv/3Oo7KZD`. At the time of writing, nothing has happened yet, and I really can only hope they see sense.

© Mike Halsey 2023
M. Halsey, *Troubleshooting and Supporting Windows 11*, https://doi.org/10.1007/978-1-4842-8728-6_17

As a personal preference, I have for years now always ensured that any new PC I buy, be it a desktop (which is definitely my preferred way of working) or a laptop, comes with a fitted TPM chip. I always use this to fully encrypt the PC using Microsoft's Bitlocker full disk encryption, but this is slightly more complex than it used to be. Let me explain.

TPM vs. fTPM

Let's start with what a TPM (Trusted Platform Module) really is. TPMs are chips that are a hardware encrypted microcontroller that securely stores cryptographic keys that are used to decrypt previously encrypted data. It's used for everything from Windows' Bitlocker full disk encryption to the storage of personal biometric data for Windows Hello and even for the storage of software licenses and to help prevent cheating in some games.

Note   TPMs need to be activated in the UEFI firmware in order for Bitlocker and Windows Hello to work on the PC. In Chapter 15, I detailed how you can find these and activate them.

TPM was adopted as an international standard in 2009, and the more secure 2.0 standard was announced in 2014, so it's been around for a few years already though not everybody adopted it.

You will find that most PCs don't come with a TPM chip as standard. Some business-oriented PCs will come with one, many more will come with a TPM chip as an option, and many more motherboards, especially higher-end boards for enthusiasts and gamers, will come with a slot into which you can insert a TPM module, which is how I've always done it on my desktop PCs.

fTPM is now the much more common standard, but you might not want to use it; allow me to explain. Firmware TPM is a TPM chip that's emulated by the UEFI firmware on a PC's motherboard. Because UEFI firmware already comes with its own encryption and security, it's a more cost-effective way for PC builders to make PCs that are secure and compatible with Windows 11.

There are problems with an fTPM however; chief among them is that if you need to upgrade or reset the UEFI firmware at any time, you will completely wipe all the data stored in the fTPM. This is unlike a separate TPM chip or module where the data is stored completely independently of the motherboard's firmware.

Malware attacks on PCs have become nastier in recent years, something we'll look at in detail in Chapter 18, and so it's important for UEFI firmware to be kept up to date where possible and appropriate, so that it remains secure. The choice of a full TPM chip or module then vs. an fTPM can be a tricky one.

Encryption Is Not Enforced in Windows 11

You might think then, given that TPMs and fTPMs are enforced as part of the Windows 11 minimum specification, that encryption of a PC is also enforced and that all PCs will be fully encrypted and safe from data theft. Sadly, you'd be wrong. While some PCs will come with the disks encrypted by default, most won't so it's something you'll need to do yourself, but don't worry we're going to cover all of that.

The requirement for a TPM (which I shall now use as an umbrella term) is so that PCs can be fully encrypted if the owner chooses to do so, and so that Microsoft's biometric sign-in feature, Windows Hello, can be used on the machine, and again only if it comes with or optionally has compatible hardware such as an infrared webcam, fingerprint reader, or smart card reader, none of which are mandated by the minimum Windows 11 specification.

You can see then that the encryption, TPM, and other security requirements for Windows 11 can be confusing and are not often applied equally or even applied at all.

Windows 11 Home

Things get more complicated with Windows 11 Home. Throughout this book, I have detailed how you can support and troubleshoot problems for the new breed of home and hybrid workers that are using their own computers, some of which are shared with their family and housemates. That's okay, you say, we can encrypt their PCs with Bitlocker and all will be safe. Sadly, if they're using the Home edition of Windows 11 or Windows 10, Bitlocker isn't supported.

Some, and I must stress this, some PCs will support a feature called *Device encryption* which is essentially Bitlocker but managed through a simple switch in *Settings* and then *Privacy & security* (see Figure 17-1), but there's no guarantee that a PC will support the feature as not all of them do.

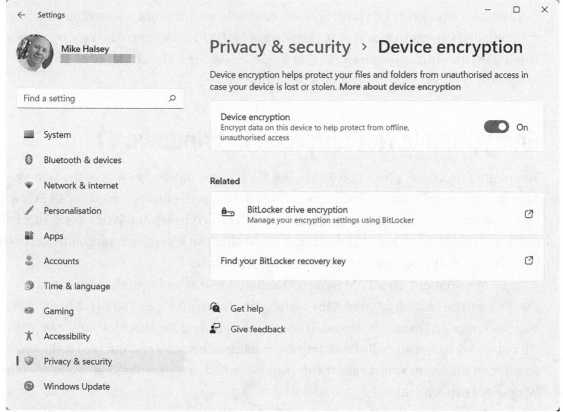

Figure 17-1. *Many, but not all, Windows 11 Home PCs support Device Encryption*

The Complexities of Secure PCs

We end in a situation where the simplicity of purchasing and supporting PCs isn't as simple as it was just a few short years ago. Back in 2015 when Windows 10 launched, or even earlier as Bitlocker first appeared in Windows Vista, you knew that if a PC had a TPM, it would be a chip in hardware and that no Windows Home PCs would support encryption at all, as the Device Encryption feature didn't exist back then. Now it's not a safe assumption that a new PC running Windows 11, or a Windows 10 that's upgradeable to Windows 11, will have the TPM and encryption security you need.

The upshot is that you have to ask a few more questions than before and also try and audit what PCs and hardware your home and hybrid workers are using, so as to maintain the best and most appropriate security for your organization.

Rather than supporting, maintaining, and troubleshooting PCs becoming easier and more straightforward over time, encryption is one area where it's managed to become more complex.

Using Bitlocker on a PC

I have already detailed how to activate Bitlocker on Windows 11 Home. Open *Settings* and then navigate to *Privacy & security* and look for a *Device encryption* option (see Figure 17-2). If you don't see it, it's not supported on the PC. This is a simple on/off switch, and there's no management for it other than that in the Settings interface.

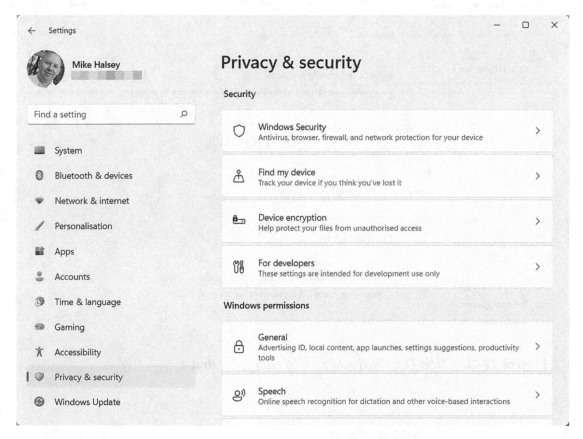

Figure 17-2. *Encryption in Windows 11 Home is found in Settings*

In the Pro, Enterprise, and Education editions of Windows 11, Bitlocker is still, as of the time of writing this, managed from the Control Panel. We can expect it to move to Windows Tools in the future, but there is also a chance it will also appear in Settings as Microsoft takes security more and more seriously.

Note   Only disks formatted using Microsoft's NTFS partition format or their relational file system ReFS can be encrypted with Bitlocker.

Open *Bitlocker Drive Encryption* from the Control Panel, and you will see all of the drives on your PC listed with their encryption status (see Figure 17-3). Encrypting a drive is a simple matter of clicking the *Turn on Bitlocker* link and following the wizard that first checks to see if the drive is compatible (if you have a TPM, almost none aren't).

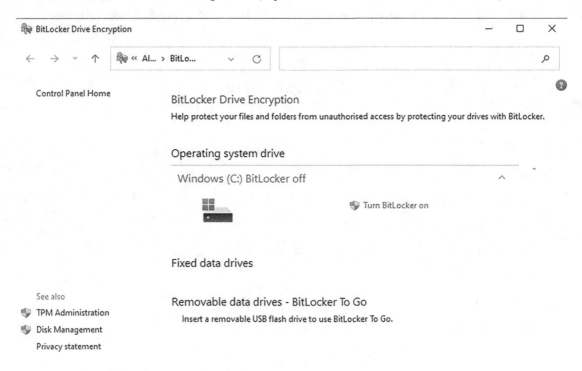

Figure 17-3.   Click Turn Bitlocker on to encrypt a drive

Note   You cannot encrypt any additional disks or partitions in the PC until the Windows disk (C:) has first been encrypted. External (USB) disks can be encrypted at any time.

You will be asked where you want your Bitlocker recovery key to be stored. This is a 50-character decryption key that you *definitely* want to keep a copy of. The reason is that if you need to enter it later, perhaps because of a problem with the PC or the fTPM being reset and you don't have it, you can forget ever getting access to your files and data again. You can store your encryption key in one of several different places:

- **Your Microsoft Account** (more on this shortly)

- **On a printout** (I don't recommend this one for fairly obvious reasons of loss and other people being able to access it)

- **On a USB Flash Drive** (again, I don't recommend this as the file could all too easily be deleted)

- **In an Azure Active Directory Account** if you are using a managed PC in a domain environment

Accessing Your Encryption Key(s) Online

If you choose to back up your encryption key to your Microsoft Account or to an Azure AD account, you need to be able to access them later. Fortunately, this is straightforward. For a Microsoft Account, save the web link `https://account.microsoft.com/devices/recoverykey` into your browser (see Figure 17-4). Note that if you have two-factor (multifactor) authentication set up on your Microsoft Account, which you definitely should have, then you will need to get through that too before you can access the code.

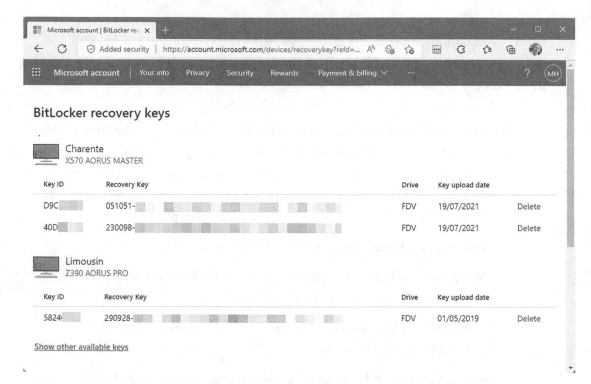

Figure 17-4. *You can access Bitlocker recovery keys from a Microsoft Account via a web browser*

If you are in a managed environment, the Bitlocker encryption keys for PCs, where people are signed in using a Microsoft 365 or Azure AD account, are stored in Endpoint Manager. Open *Endpoint Security* and stored keys are available in the *Disk encryption* section (see Figure 17-5).

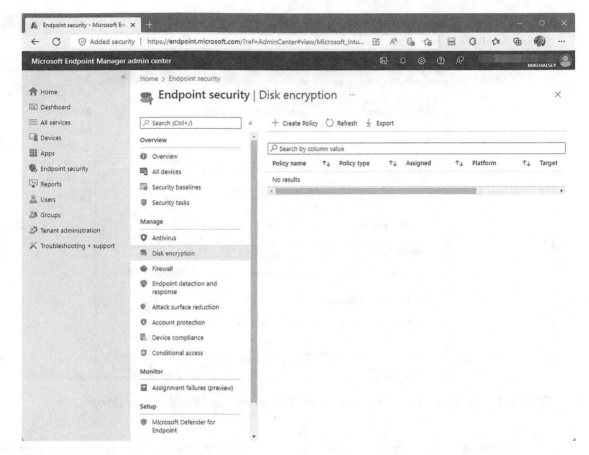

Figure 17-5. *You can find Azure AD Bitlocker keys in Endpoint Manager*

TPM Administration

Sometimes, especially if Bitlocker has been used on the PC previously, you will need to perform administration tasks on the TPM. In the bottom-left corner of the Bitlocker panel is a *TPM Administration* link. Click this and a management console window will open (see Figure 17-6). There's not really much to do with a TPM other than clear it. If the TPM has never been used before however, you might need to click the *Prepare TPM* link to get it ready for its first use.

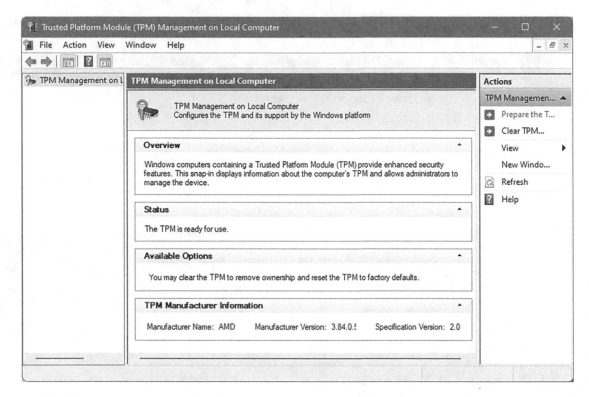

Figure 17-6. *You can administer the TPM from the Windows desktop*

Caution   Clearing a TPM will delete any Bitlocker keys stored and also any saved biometric data for Windows Hello.

Managing Encrypted Disks

I have already mentioned that if you have more than one disk or partition in your PC, such as a D: or E: drive, they cannot be encrypted until after the Windows disk, the C: drive, has first been encrypted. Once disks are encrypted though, there are further options available to you that will appear in the Bitlocker panel (see Figure 17-7).

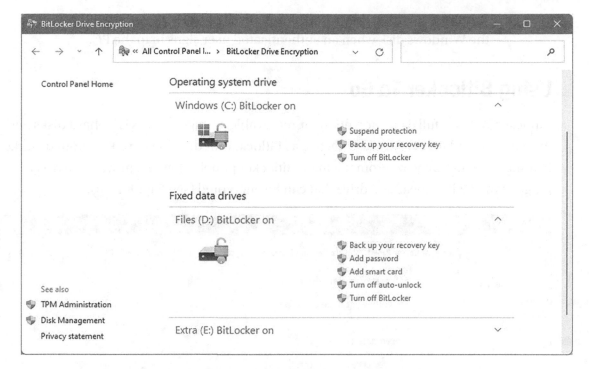

Figure 17-7. *Various options are available for encrypted disks*

The options available to you for encrypted drives are as follows:

- **Suspend protection**, which will temporarily prevent new files written to the disk from being encrypted. They will be encrypted later when protection is reinstated. This is most useful on lower-power machines with slower disks and for when you have intensive work going on that doesn't need to be interrupted.

- **Back up your recovery key** will allow you to create a copy of your recovery key to one of the locations I detailed earlier.

- **Turn off Bitlocker** will deactivate encryption and decrypt the drive. You will need to do this for an fTPM before upgrading or resetting the UEFI firmware.

- **Add password** will allow you to add a separate password that must be typed in to access the disk.

- **Add smart card** will only allow access to the drive when an appropriate smart card is used with the PC.

- **Turn on/off auto-unlock** will automatically unlock drives other than the Windows disk when an authenticated user signs in to the PC.

Using Bitlocker To Go

Bitlocker To Go is full disk encryption for removable storage such as USB hard disks and flash drives, and it's every bit as effective as Bitlocker for disks inside a PC, though works in a slightly different way. From the main Bitlocker panel, when a removable drive is plugged in, it will appear as a drive that can be encrypted (see Figure 17-8).

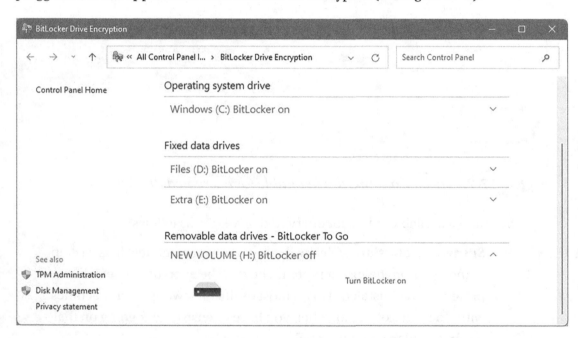

Figure 17-8. *Removal storage can be encrypted with Bitlocker To Go*

Note   Only removable storage formatted using Microsoft's NTFS partition format can be encrypted with Bitlocker and Bitlocker To Go.

The difference with drives inside the PC comes when you go to encrypt the drive, and you are asked how you want to unlock it (see Figure 17-9). There are two choices available, using a smart card or using a password.

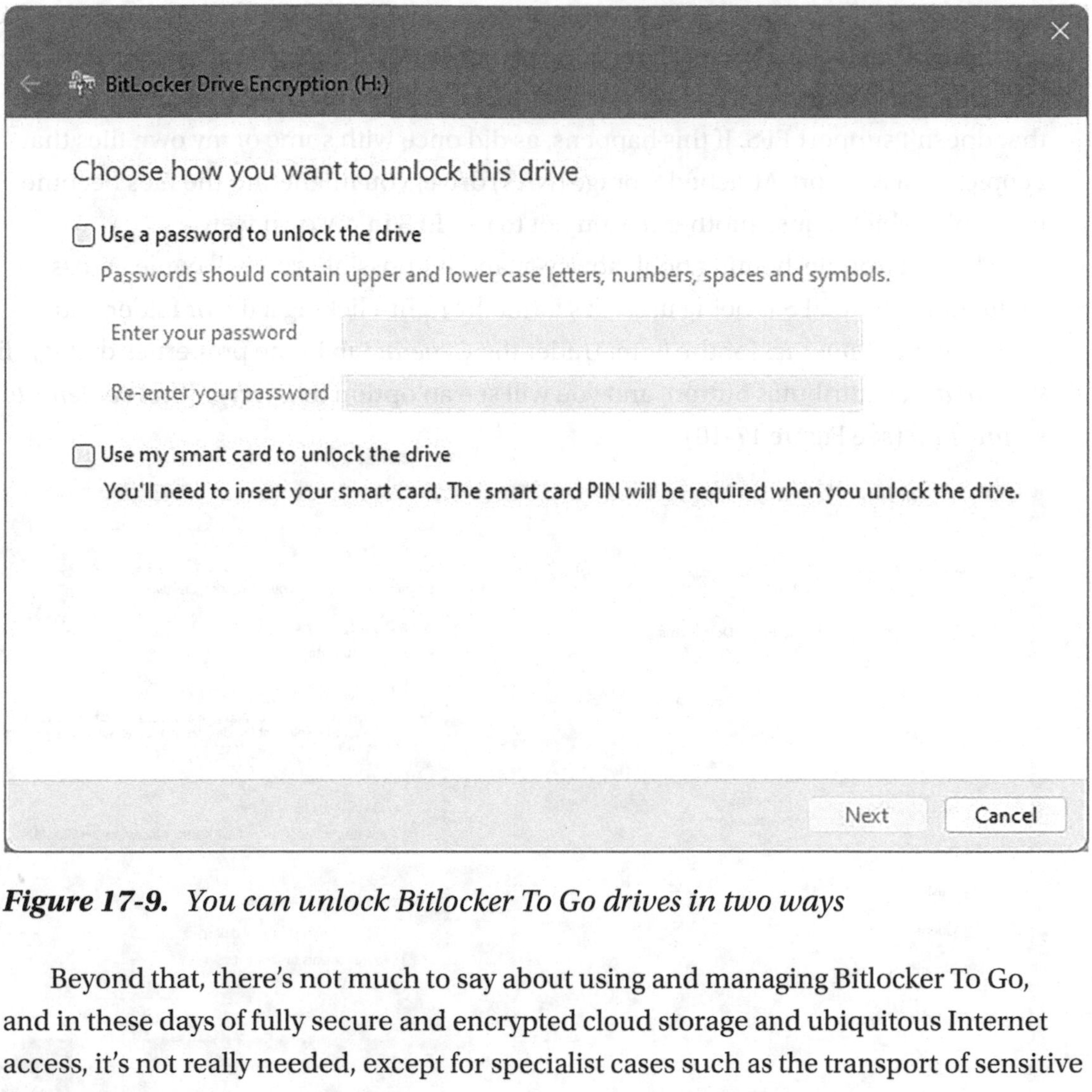

← ⬚ BitLocker Drive Encryption (H:)

✕

Choose how you want to unlock this drive

☐ **Use a password to unlock the drive**
    Passwords should contain upper and lower case letters, numbers, spaces and symbols.

    Enter your password

    Re-enter your password

☐ **Use my smart card to unlock the drive**
    You'll need to insert your smart card. The smart card PIN will be required when you unlock the drive.

| Next | | Cancel |

Figure 17-9. You can unlock Bitlocker To Go drives in two ways

Beyond that, there's not much to say about using and managing Bitlocker To Go, and in these days of fully secure and encrypted cloud storage and ubiquitous Internet access, it's not really needed, except for specialist cases such as the transport of sensitive government secrets by black-ops agents across borders in USB Flash Drives disguised as a ballpoint pen (you watch too many *Mission Impossible* movies; Ed).

Encrypting File System

Speaking of things that are completely obsolete but still around in Windows, the Encrypting File System (EFS) is high up on the list. First introduced with Windows NT 3.0, it's a system for encrypting individual files and folders on a PC, but it doesn't come without its problems, and I really can't recommend that anybody use it when Bitlocker is such a better solution.

EFS differs from Bitlocker in that, because it's not the disk that's encrypted, any files and folders that you encrypt will remain encrypted when copied off the disk. This is fine for general usage, but you can hit problems if those files are copied onto a file system that doesn't support EFS. If this happens, as did once with some of my own files that I copied to a Network Attached Storage (NAS) drive, you might find the files become unusable, which is just another reason not to use EFS in my own view.

This is a troubleshooting book however, and it's possible you will come across a situation where EFS is being used. It's found by right-clicking a file or folder and selecting the *Properties* for the item. Under the *General* tab in the properties dialog, click the *Advanced* attributes button, and you will see an option to *Encrypt* [the] *contents to secure data* (see Figure 17-10).

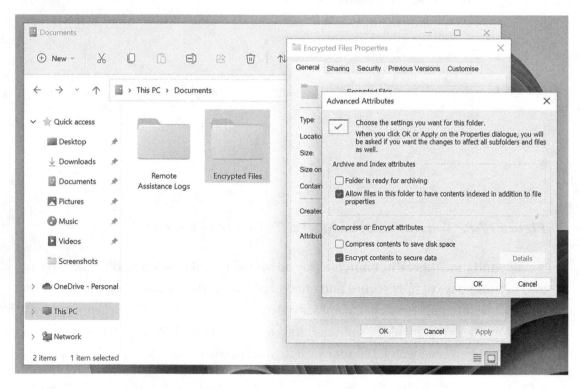

Figure 17-10. *You encrypt files and folders from File Explorer*

With the encryption done, you will be prompted to *Back up your encryption key* (see Figure 17-11), which is essential as otherwise you could lose access to those files forever. The file or folder will then have a padlock icon appear in its top-right corner.

Figure 17-11. *You should always back up your encryption key*

You can back up your encryption certificates at any time however by searching in the Start Menu for *encrypt* and launching *Manage file encryption certificates* when it appears in the search results. This will launch a wizard that will suggest the certificate to back up, and you can view its details to be sure it is the correct one (see Figure 17-12).

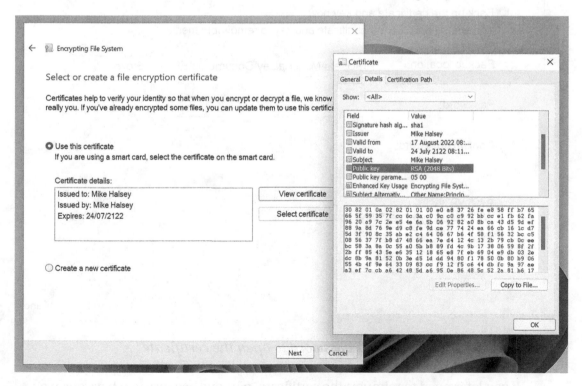

Figure 17-12. *You can back up your certificate(s) at any time*

You will be asked for a save location for the certificate backup and for a password that will be required to unlock it (see Figure 17-13). Under no circumstances should you save this certificate to a folder that is already encrypted with EFS.

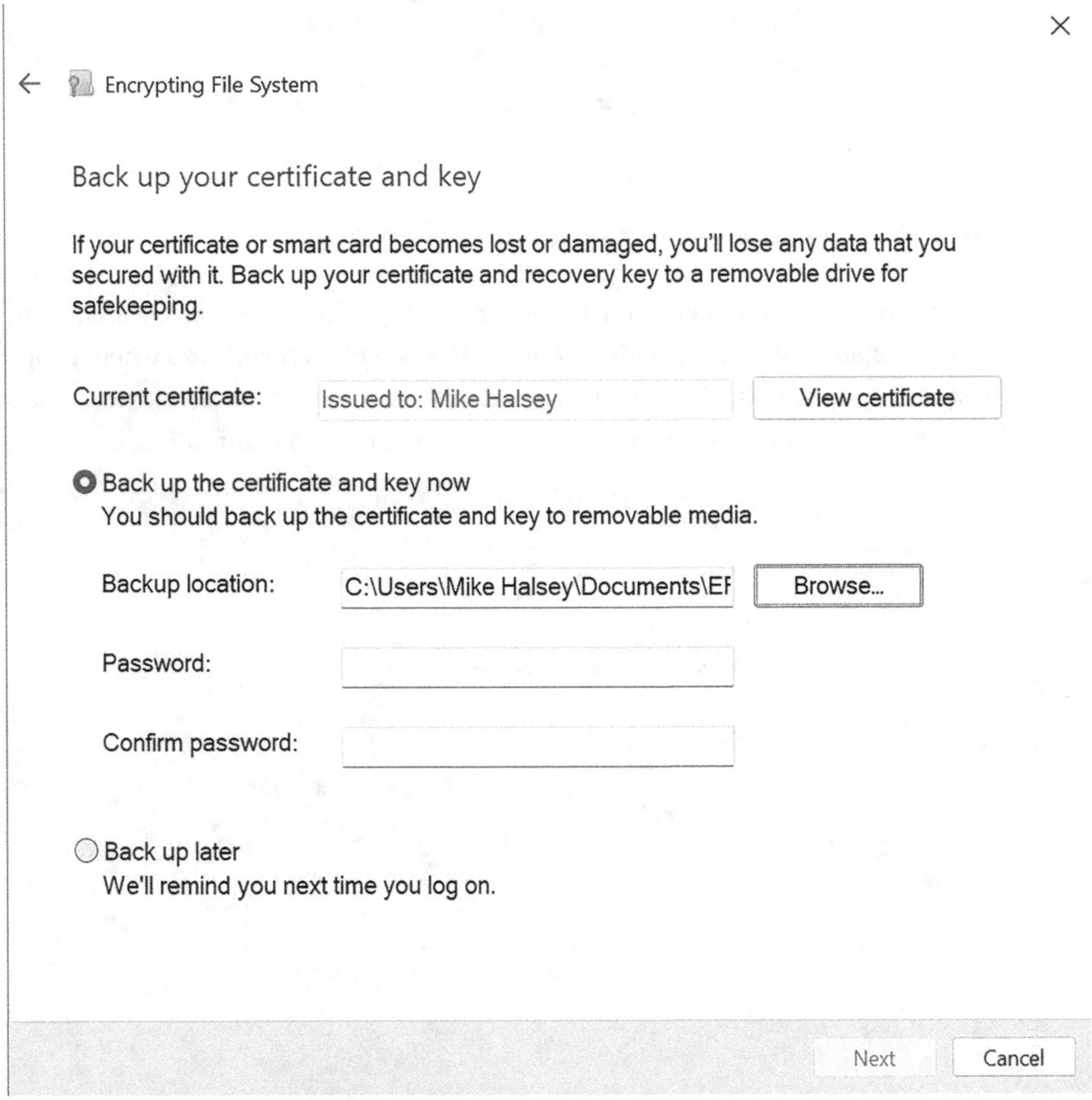

Figure 17-13. *You can set a password to open the certificate*

If you later need to reimport the certificate, perhaps because you have given a copy of the encrypted file(s) to another person, you can do so by double-clicking the certificate file to open it (see Figure 17-14).

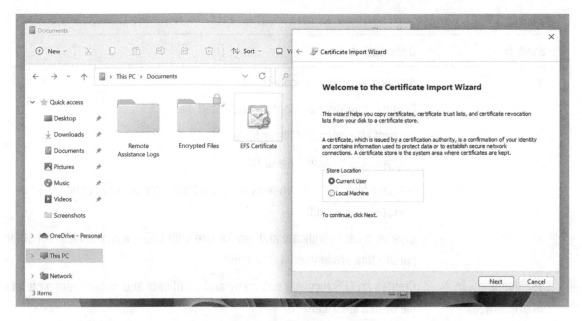

Figure 17-14. *You can reimport certificates by double-clicking them*

Cipher.exe

EFS can also be managed with the Command Line tool **cipher.exe**. This is used with the switches listed in Table 17-1.

Table 17-1. *Cipher.exe command line switches*

Switch	Description
/b	Aborts if an error is encountered
/c	Displays information about an encrypted file
/d	Decrypts the specified file or folder
/e	Encrypts the specified file or folder
/h	Displays files with hidden or system attributes; these are not encrypted or decrypted by default
/k	Creates a new certificate and key for use with EFS encrypted files. All other parameters are ignored if /k is used
/r:<filename> [/smartcard]	Creates an EFS recovery agent key and certificate and writes them as a .pfx file or to a smartcard
/s:<directory>	Performs the specified operation on all subdirectories in the specified directory
/u [/n]	Finds all encrypted files on the local drive(s); if used without /n, it compares the user's file encryption key or the recovery agent's key to the current ones and updates them if they have changed
/w:<directory>	Removes data from available unused disk space on the entire volume; if /w is used, all other parameters are ignored
/x:[efsfile] [<filename>]	Backs up the specified EFS certificate and keys as a .pfx file
/y	Displays the current EFS certificate thumbnail on the local computer
/adduser / certhash:<hash>	Adds a user to the specified file(s) using the SHA1 hash of the valid certificate
/rekey	Updates the specified encrypted files to use the currently configured EFS key
/removeuser / certhash:<hash>	Removes a user from the specified file(s) using the SHA1 hash of the valid certificate

Caution   When you encrypt a file using EFS, Windows first makes a backup copy of the file that is deleted when the file is encrypted. This file might still be recoverable later, and so the /w switch is useful for securely wiping free space on the PC. Note however that it does not work for files less than 1KB in size.

EFSDump

There is also a tool with Microsoft's Sysinternals suite that can be used to help you manage EFS encrypted files. EFSDump can be used to audit which users on a PC have access to encrypted files. It's a simple Command Line tool that is used in the format EFSDump [-s] [-q] <File or Folder> where -s will recurse subdirectories, and -q will suppress errors. If you use it in the format EFSDump -s -q C:*.*, it will detail the users that are authorized to access encrypted files on the C: drive of the PC (see Figure 17-15).

```
Command Prompt - efsdump  -s -q C:\Users\*.*                             —    □    ✕

C:\Users\Mike Halsey\Downloads\Microsoft Sysinternals Suite>efsdump -s -q C:\Use
rs\*.*

EFS Information Dumper v1.02
Copyright (C) 1999 Mark Russinovich
Systems Internals - http://www.sysinternals.com

C:\Users\Mike Halsey\Documents\Encrypted Files\Figure_1-1.jpg:
DDF Entry:
    WINDOWS10VM\Mike Halsey:
        Mike Halsey(Mike Halsey@WINDOWS10VM)
DRF Entry:

C:\Users\Mike Halsey\Documents\Encrypted Files\Figure_1-2.jpg:
DDF Entry:
    WINDOWS10VM\Mike Halsey:
```

Figure 17-15. *EFSDump can report which users have access to encrypted files*

Windows Advanced Firewall

If like me you're old enough to remember the release of Windows XP Service Pack 2, then you'll know just how big a deal it was that Microsoft finally included a firewall with Windows. Before then, and for some time afterward, people including myself had to use a third-party firewall (ZoneAlarm was my personal choice).

These days, if you buy one of the big antivirus and security suites, they'll commonly not ship with a firewall at all. The reason for this is that for many years now the firewall that ships with Windows is really very good indeed.

The Windows Firewall comes with two personalities, the basic and advanced versions. You can find the basic firewall in *Windows Security*, and I detailed how to use it in Chapter 3 so won't repeat any of that here.

In *Windows Tools* however, you will find *Windows Defender Firewall with Advanced Security*, which we can probably expect to be renamed at some point in the future. It's here you can get advanced control over the firewall, such as creating and modifying rules, opening and closing specific ports, and importing and exporting new and existing firewall policies (see Figure 17-16).

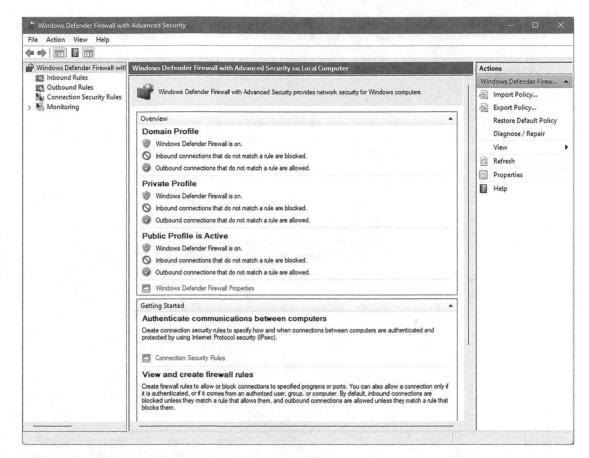

Figure 17-16. *The Advanced Firewall in Windows 11 is very configurable*

You create inbound and outbound rules separately, and a wizard guides you through the process of creating a rule for a specific program on the PC (see Figure 17-17), for a specific port or series of ports, from a predefined list that Windows and server features such as Hyper-V, file sharing, BranchCache, and Remote Desktop, or create a fully custom rule which additionally allows you to create rules for specific installed services.

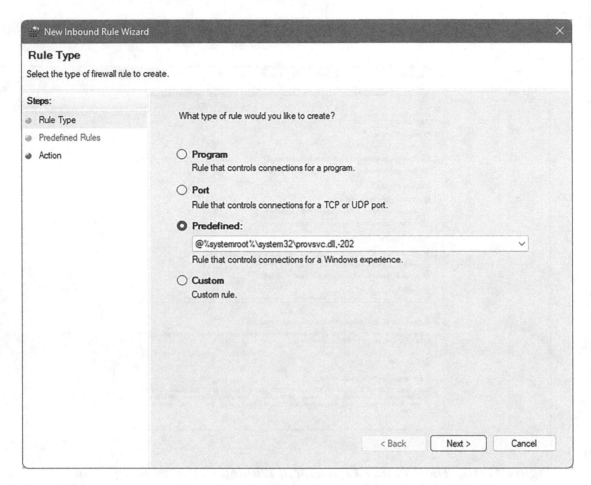

Figure 17-17. *A wizard guides you through the process of creating firewall rules*

Where you will most likely want to use the Advanced Firewall is for managing the security of your workplace connections, especially for workers dialing into your network from around the world. In the left panel, click *Connection Security Rules*, and a *New Rule...* link will then appear in the right side panel.

You can create rules that cover all manner of different security requirements and protocols (see Figure 17-18), authentication, tunnelling, and IP addressing (useful for that spy from earlier in the chapter if they had their secret ballpoint pen/USB Flash Drive stolen, eh?; Ed).

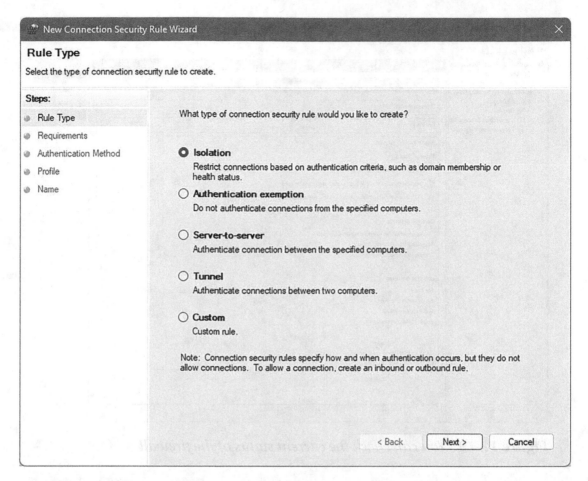

Figure 17-18. All manner of connection security rules can be created

Lastly, if you suspect there could be problems with the firewall configuration or operation, clicking *Monitoring* in the left panel will display current details about the firewall including which of the three profiles (Domain, Private, or Public) is currently in use and whether rules are being implemented (see Figure 17-19).

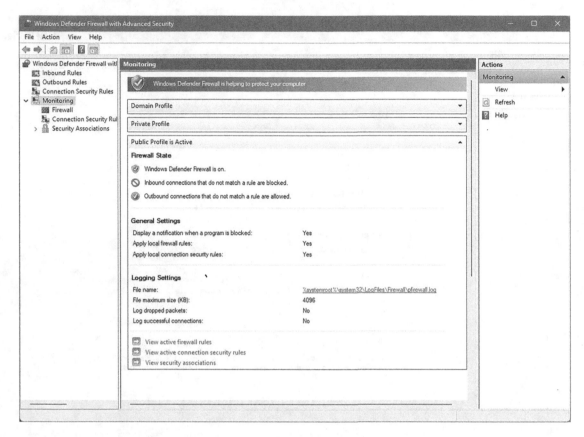

Figure 17-19. *You can check the current status of the firewall*

Tip   If you suspect firewall policies on the PC have become corrupt, click *Windows Defender with Advanced Firewall* in the left panel, then from the *Action* menu click *Restore Default Policy*. This will reset all firewall policies to the state they were in when Windows 11 was installed.

Local Security Policy

I've talked in Chapter 3 how you can use Group Policy to create a secure and robust PC system, though these days many people prefer Mobile Device Management (MDM). In Windows Tools, there is a subset of policies under the heading *Local Security Policy*. This is where you will find not just Group Policy settings related directly to security, such as password policies, but also quick links to other security features within Windows 11 (see Figure 17-20).

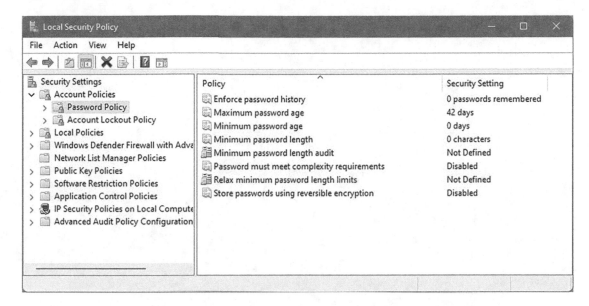

Figure 17-20. Security policies are accessible from within Windows Tools

Summary

Security is clearly hugely important for our PCs, for data privacy, compliance (both corporate and governmental), and for your own peace of mind, especially when it comes to maintaining robust and reliable systems.

We're about to get a crash course though in just how bad things can get in the next chapter when we talk about what can happen with malware and virus infections and how you can both protect a PC from and even manually remove everything from trojans to ransomware.

CHAPTER 18

Virus and Malware Troubleshooting

Long gone are the days when getting a virus on your PC was annoying. As the world has become more connected, and as we're doing more financial and official activities on our PCs, smartphones, and tablets, the risk has increased greatly. When we then factor in home and hybrid workers, and people using their own home PCs for workplace purposes, connecting to cloud services in which sensitive customer data is stored... you take my point.

All of this means that protecting a PC from malware and ransomware is no longer a process of treating it as a stand-alone device, but rather as part of a larger ecosystem of different device types, virtual and physical storage, varying operating systems and how all of this interoperates.

How We Got to Today

It seems appropriate then that we should start with some best practice advice, focused on the world in which we find ourselves today, but in order to understand that, it's important to know where we came from.

When Windows 10 launched in 2015, we hadn't seen the explosion in big data that we have today, although it was slowly underway. The gig economy was just getting started with the launch of apps such as Uber; people were beginning to notice privacy more for their technology, but perhaps one of the biggest technology stories came from Canadian dating website Ashley Madison, where hackers exposed the personal details of 33 million customers.

M. Halsey, *Troubleshooting and Supporting Windows 11*, https://doi.org/10.1007/978-1-4842-8728-6_18

This event was a wake-up call for the industry and for consumers, and where Windows 10 included some basic privacy controls when it launched (see Figure 18-1), these were not really to be found in web browsers because end users and consumers weren't at the time demanding them.

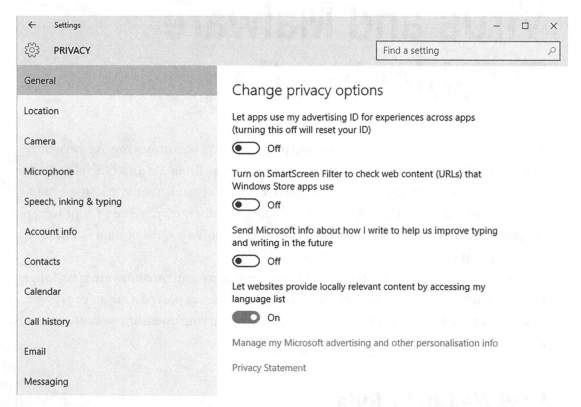

Figure 18-1. *Privacy controls in Windows 10 in 2015 were basic*

Privacy in Windows 10 when it launched was also fairly basic, with few controls and simple on/off switches to manage protections (see Figure 18-2). In October 2015 though, UK ISP TalkTalk suffered a cyber attack that resulted in the theft of 157,000 customers' personal details, including more than 15,600 bank account numbers.

The hackers, teenagers from Staffordshire UK that were hacking for fun, were caught and jailed, with the lead hacker serving four years before starting a no doubt prosperous career in cyber-security.

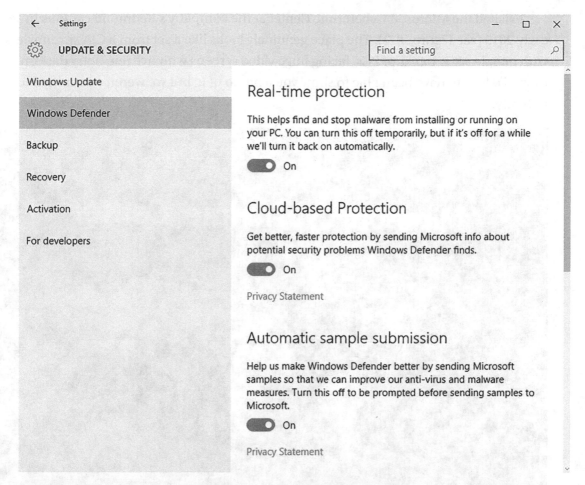

Figure 18-2. *Malware protection was fairly basic in Windows 10 in 2015*

Things have changed significantly in the intervening times sparked in no small part by the WannaCry ransomware that in 2017 infected more than 230,000 computers in over 150 countries, including bringing Britain's National Health Service (NHS) to a standstill. As I write this, another ransomware attack on the NHS just ten days ago is being investigated as it is suspected patient data had been stolen.

Clearly, the threat of malware, ransomware, and hacking is greater than ever, and companies, organizations, governments, and individuals can no longer leave smartphones, computers, and servers unpatched (who remembers web servers running older and unpatched versions of Apache?).

I visited the Microsoft Cybercrime Center at the company's Redmond campus in early 2019 (see Figure 18-3). The place genuinely looks like a set from a CIA spy movie with people sat at banks of PCs, facing huge video screens with live telemetry data on them. I'd love to have been able to show you a photo of it, but we weren't permitted to take any.

Figure 18-3. *The Microsoft Cybercrime Center is fascinating*

In the summer of 2022, I was again at Microsoft, and we received a briefing about the war in Ukraine, detailing the sharp and intense increase in cyber attacks against the country in the two weeks before the invasion by Russia in February of that year.

We were told how Microsoft had been working with partners such as Amazon, Google, the National Security Agency (NSA), Britain's GCHQ security and intelligence center, Ukraine's security and intelligence agencies, and others to thwart the attacks and keep the infrastructure and financial systems of the country operating.

Best Practice for Maintaining Security

So what are my top tips for maintaining good security for your data, your PCs, and your IT ecosystem? Things have clearly moved on, and we're not looking at stand-alone machines sitting in an office any more. This comes with repercussions and potential consequences, not the least of which are hefty fines for the loss of data held by companies that are hacked.

Times have changed so much that when I would have previously listed "Keep your antivirus software and operating system patched and up to date," this no longer appears in the list. Compared to best practice advice these days, it's pretty dumb and obvious.

It's Okay to Be Paranoid Because They Really *Are* Out to Get You

We used to think of people being paranoid as them overreacting to the circumstances they found themselves in. These days, however, things are very different. Every business, every organization, every government, and every individual is a target because all of them can provide hackers and criminals with data, money, and access to other systems.

Taking a paranoid approach to security is not something I would advise against any more as if it helps you maintain proper security, and high levels of protection for your systems, and data, then it'll likely be worth the sleepless nights.

Treat Every System As Being Interconnected with Insecure Systems

As part of the it's okay to be paranoid approach, it's also wise to treat every system as though it can and does connect to other computers and systems that aren't properly secure. This could be a USB Flash Drive the kids brought home from school, or it could be a web service where a vulnerability exists that has not been patched.

This is especially important for home and hybrid workers as their own computers are something you will have little or no control over. Sure, you can use Mobile Device Management (MDM) to enforce strict encryption, updating, and malware protection policies before a computer is allowed to access your network and data, but beyond that, security can be difficult to control.

Encrypt Every Connection

This brings me on to network- and Internet-level encryption. In Chapter 17, I detailed how you can use the Advanced Firewall in Windows 11 to enforce encryption for network and Internet connections. Mandating encryption is crucial for several reasons.

Firstly, there is the mobile worker who likes to sit in their local coffee shop with their laptop or who is travelling on a train or through an airport. Even if the Wi-Fi connection they connect to has password access, this does not mean the laptop can't be seen by other computers connected to that network.

Tip   If you have the budget for it, a mobile worker able to connect their laptop directly to a cellular network with a built-in SIM or eSIM will be more secure than one connecting to public Wi-Fi.

Then there's the sticky subject of home broadband and fiber routers. If you search online for a list of home routers known to have unpatched security vulnerabilities, then you'll get a very unpleasant shock. Sure, in almost every case, a hacker has to be sitting directly outside the property to gain access, but if the data your employee is working on is important enough, that's exactly what they'll be prepared to do.

Sandbox Vulnerable Systems

Hands up everybody that is or that knows somebody using an older version of Windows on a PC, or an older smartphone with an Android or iOS version that's out of support, or that has allowed their smart fridge or living room television to connect to their Wi-Fi network. Yup, that's pretty much everybody.

Sandboxing is no longer about disconnecting a Windows XP or a Windows 7 PC from your network if you have to keep using it. These days, it's more about keeping Internet of Things (IoT) devices in your home on a completely separate Wi-Fi network to the computers you store files and data on and use for banking and work.

If you think the problem with routers is bad, don't search online for IoT devices. The worst part with these devices is that if they do get updated, it always happens quietly in the background, and we have little or no knowledge that it's even happening, let alone what the current security state of the device might be.

Install a Security Appliance

Security appliances are no longer just for companies with complex networks. A small box for the home can sometimes be picked up for under $100, and you can make your own with a Raspberry Pi and open source software for next to nothing.

I use the Netgate 1100 from `www.pfsense.org/products` which is less than $200 and can comfortably protect all the devices in my home and office with its combination of fire-and-forget web filtering, firewall, ad blocking, and traffic monitoring.

This appliance was personally recommended to me by a man who until a few years ago was the Technical Director for Cyber at GCHQ in Cheltenham (UK). In his own words, "For 15 years I was the guy keeping the UK safe from state-initiated cyber threats," so I was inclined to take his advice seriously.

Consider the Implications of Smart Technology

I've already mentioned IoT devices in this list. In my own home and gîte, I have two ovens, two cooker hobs, a fridge freezer, and two washing machines that all want to connect to the Internet, and I will not allow any of them to do so.

A friend told me, "You can turn the washing machine on from an app on your phone," but I pointed out to him that if I wanted to turn the washing machine on, I would very likely have just loaded it, and where would I be standing at that time?

There are also many other types of smart home tech that I will simply never use. Smart door locks are one; I'll never forget the story of the burglar that called through an open window of a home, "Alexa, open the front door," which it dutifully did.

Smart and Internet-connected heating, air conditioning, or other crucial systems are also something I will never allow. If you haven't heard the stories of hackers turning everything off or up to a maximum and then demanding money to release control, then have a search online.

Even something as innocuous as smart lighting is a no-no for me. It might be fun to be able to change the color of the lights in a room for movie night, but when it comes to basic control, I have never found walking two or three steps to a light switch on the wall to be especially difficult.

Create Security Policies That Make Sense to Normal People

People are getting much wiser to the need for data security and privacy controls, but 98% of the population still wouldn't be able to understand the technical language involved or know how to implement these controls in their own lives.

You will set security and encryption policies that will be good for your organization, but making these policies relatable to people's own personal lives will not only help you as it'll hopefully make their own devices and computers more secure, but it'll help them in the process, and a happy employee is always a much more cooperative employee.

The main policy areas I would suggest and how they're sold to employees and stakeholders in your organization include the following.

Use Two-Factor (Multifactor) Authentication

Explaining the importance of two-factor authentication (TFA) to people is the beginning of really tight security. Explaining that they can do this for their own accounts can help protect their email and social media from hackers, but helping them do so will make the process much simpler.

I have my own guide online at `https://pcs.tv/3IBc6tJ` for how TFA can be configured for Microsoft, Google, Amazon, and other services. Once people start using TFA, it's common for them to want to apply it everywhere, and they'll insist you enforce it for the workplace too.

Enforce Encryption Wherever Possible

In Chapter 17, I talked at length about encryption technologies such as Bitlocker and how they are used. Now there are caveats as not every PC is compatible. Multiboot systems as I detailed have problems with Bitlocker encryption, and not all Windows 11 Home laptops and tablets will support it.

Where encryption is available though, it should always be used. People can extend this to their own smartphones and home computers such as laptops that all run the risk of being lost or stolen, and helping people to ensure their personal devices can be and are encrypted will give people greater peace of mind.

Use Biometrics Where Available

All smartphones come with some form of biometric sensor these days, be it a face or retina infrared scanner or a fingerprint reader. Many laptops will include infrared cameras for Windows Hello or a fingerprint reader built into the power button or somewhere else on the keyboard.

If your budget permits, you should always buy equipment that supports Windows Hello, and helping people to understand how better to use biometrics and reassuring them that their personal biometric data is only ever stored locally in an encrypted chip on the device, and is never transmitted over the Internet, can greatly increase their own peace of mind.

Use Password Managers

Many businesses will use password managers, and some will provide the service as a perk for their employees too. Let's face it, if you mandate the use of password managers at work, then when people use their own devices not only will they already be familiar with how they work, but they will also be much more inclined to use one.

Maintain Vigilance over Email, Messaging, and SMS

My late father did at one point in his life know a genuine Nigerian prince, a lovely man whom I met on a couple of occasions when he came to our home. This man had business interests in the UK and worked with my father on construction and financing projects.

Sadly at no point did he say he had $5 million to give us in exchange for a small transfer fee and our bank details. This doesn't stop all the other Nigerian princes though, there seem to be thousands of them, from offering exactly that.

Scams, phishing (where personal data or account access is sought by trickery), and criminal activity by email, private messaging, and by SMS have never been more rife or more varied as it is today. So educating people in the types of things they should look for, and encouraging them to share their own knowledge and experiences with other employees, can not only help secure your own files and data but their personal photos and memories and even their financial accounts.

The Windows Security Center

So with all the good advice out of the way, we have to accept that the basis of good malware protection does indeed start with anti-malware software on the PC. For decades now, it's been common for people to install third-party antivirus software.

These days, however, the anti-malware software written into and included with Windows 10 and Windows 11 is pretty damn good, and there's not that much need for any third-party software. As I write this, I'm checking the latest antivirus test results at `www.av-comparatives.org/comparison` and Microsoft's anti-malware software and ESET at the two highest rated, both having blocked 99% of threats with zero false-positives. Norton by comparison might have blocked 100% of the threats, but scored a huge 50 false-positives, with Trend Micro, another popular package for businesses, having 44 false-positives.

Caution   I always take the view that any additional software installed in an operating system is a potential weak spot for vulnerabilities and bugs. Fortunately, I like using Microsoft's Edge browser and find their anti-malware solution excellent. But either way would probably be using them anyway to avoid installing software on a PC that otherwise might not need to be there.

You can most easily launch Windows Security from its shield icon in the Taskbar, though it's also available in the Start Menu. It's one of the parts of Windows that hasn't yet been fully updated to the Windows 11 look and feel (see Figure 18-4), so we can probably expect it to change somewhat. As regards functionality however, nothing will be removed, though new features might be added over time to meet new threats.

Figure 18-4. *The Windows Security Center*

Note   Windows Security can be managed through Group Policy at *Computer Configuration* ➤ *Administrative Templates* ➤ *Windows Components* ➤ *Microsoft Defender Antivirus* and also through both PowerShell and Mobile Device Manager (MDM); for details of how to use these tools, visit the Microsoft Docs website at `https://pcs.tv/3PLUyxu`.

The main *Virus & threat protection* panel is standard antivirus fare, with a choice of scan types you can perform on the PC, links for the protection history log, and any allowed threats which will likely be older third-party programs that you still use but that might be logged as threats now because of the way they operate.

Tip   Among the scan options is *Microsoft Defender Offline scan*; this will restart the PC and run a full anti-malware scan from the Recovery Console where, hopefully, no malware is able to load and run.

Configuring Windows Virus Protection

You can click the *Manage settings* link in *Virus & threat protection settings* to configure the settings and options for the malware protection (see Figure 18-5). These features should all be switched on, but additional options exist here such as being able to *Submit a* [suspect virus] *sample manually.*

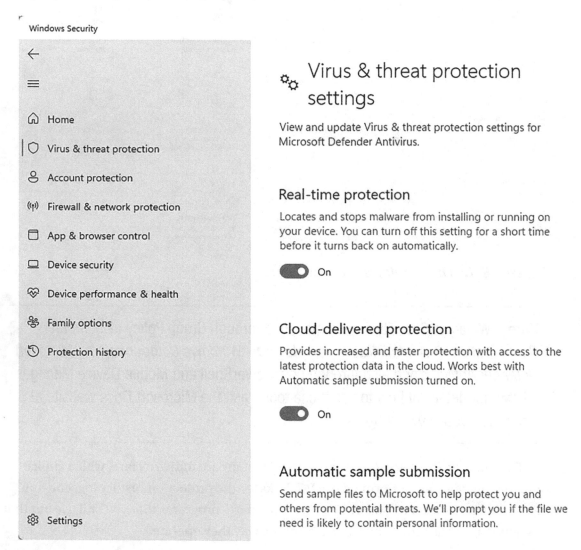

Figure 18-5. *All the parts of Windows malware protection should be activated*

Tip   *Tamper protection* is an important setting to have switched on as while an administrator on the PC can still make changes to the malware protection in the Security Center, this feature will prevent software from making any changes.

Protecting a PC from Ransomware

Windows 11 comes with a feature called *Controlled Folder Access* that can provide effective protection from a ransomware attack. I want to talk about this feature though as it needs to be used carefully to prevent it from causing problems for users of the PC.

Controlled Folder Access is disabled by default on a PC and needs to be manually activated by the administrator. It prevents unauthorized software from making changes to the user folders *Documents, Pictures, Music, Video*, etc. (see Figure 18-6).

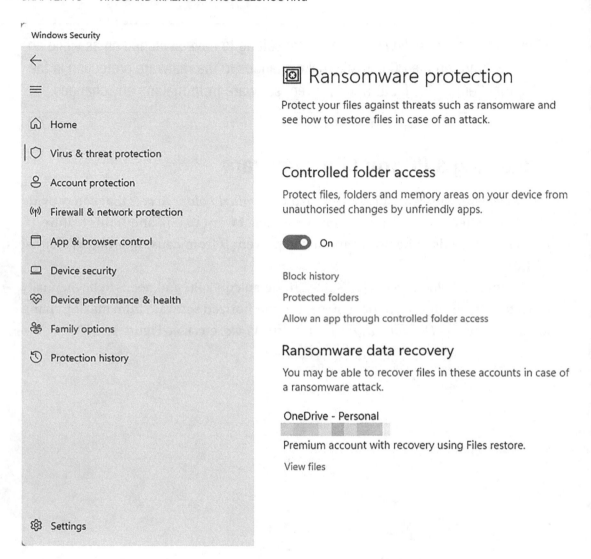

Figure 18-6. *Controlled Folder Access provides effective protection against ransomware*

You can click the *Protected folders* link to add (or to remove) any folders and entire drives from Controlled Folder Access, and in Figure 18-7, you will see that on my desktop PC I have two additional SSDs installed, the E and F drives that I have added for greater security.

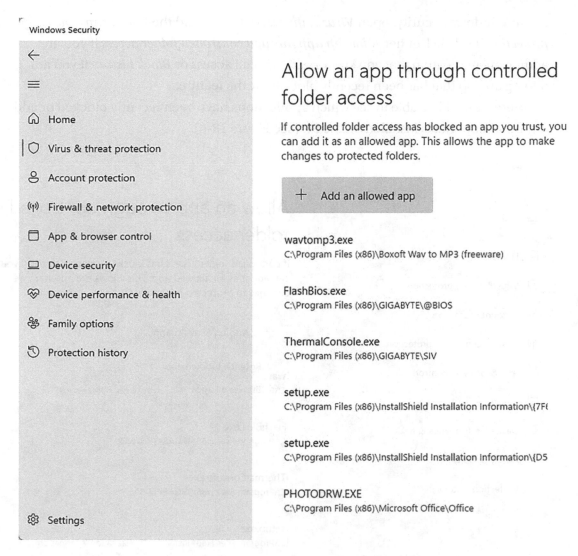

Figure 18-7. *You can add entire drives to Controlled Folder Access*

This is where we get to the tricky part. Some older legacy software and in fact even newer software and especially games can require writing files into the protected folders, usually Documents. If they don't have this access, they will report an error or even fail to work at all.

Sometimes, Windows might display a notification saying **Unauthorized changes blocked**. This message means that Controlled Folder Access has prevented an application from modifying, deleting, or adding a file. When this happens, you will need to manually add the application to the exemption list. There are different ways to achieve this.

In Windows Security, open *Virus & threat protection* and then *Ransomware protection*, and click either *Allow an app through controlled folder access* if you are adding an application that you know needs special access or *Block history* if you are adding an app that has been recently blocked by the feature.

Here, you will be able to see which applications have been recently blocked or add any other app that is installed on the PC (see Figure 18-8).

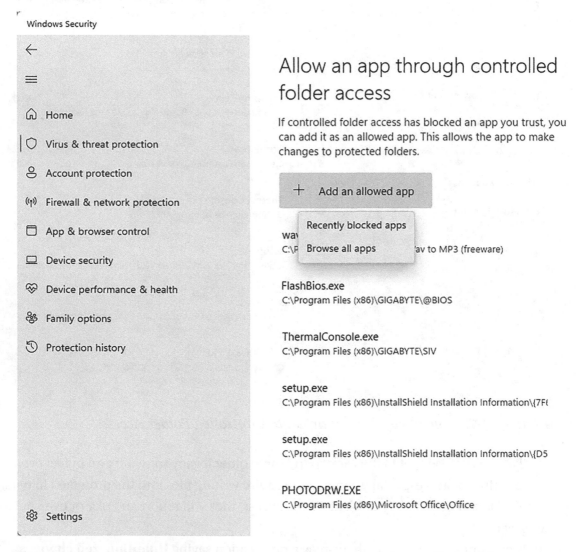

Figure 18-8. *You can add any app as an exemption to Controlled Folder Access*

In Group Policy, navigate to *Computer Configuration* ➤ *Administrative Templates* ➤ *Windows Components* ➤ *Microsoft Defender Antivirus* ➤ *Microsoft Defender Exploit Guard* ➤ *Controlled Folder Access* (see Figure 18-9). Here, you can manage and activate Controlled Folder Access, as well as configure protected folders and allow applications through the feature.

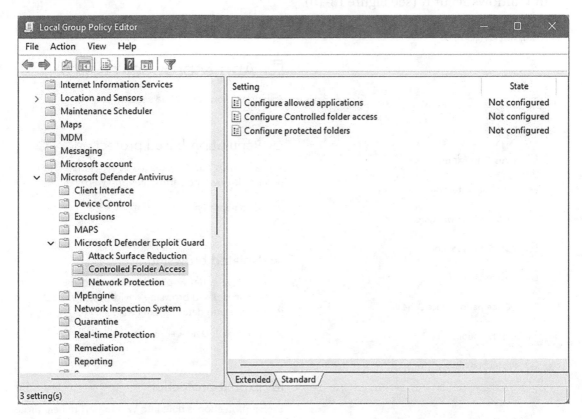

Figure 18-9. *You can manage Controlled Folder Access using Group Policy*

Note   You can also manage Controlled Folder Access and all Windows Security features using both PowerShell and Mobile Device Management (MDM). Full details of how to do this can be found on the Microsoft Docs website at `https://pcs.tv/3PQoIjg`.

App and Browser Control

Windows has for some years now included a feature called *SmartScreen*, which is a tool that, as Microsoft says, "helps protect your device from potentially dangerous apps, files, websites, and downloads." As part of this, you will see an *App & browser control* section in Windows Security (see Figure 18-10).

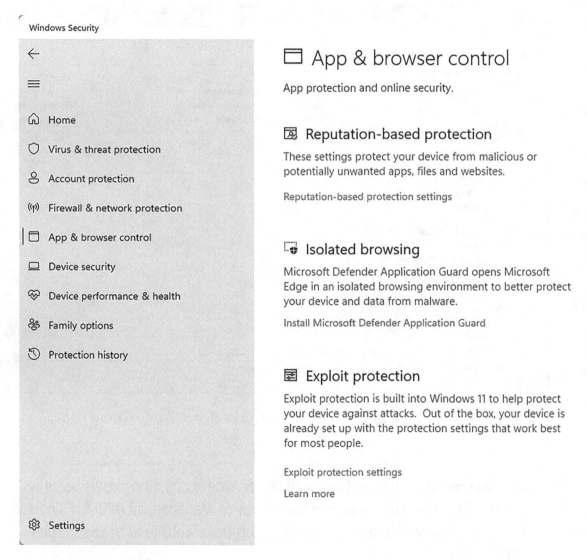

Figure 18-10. *App & browser control is part of Windows SmartScreen*

The *Reputation-based protection* settings here will allow you to control SmartScreen. This can be important in a business environment where you might have false-positives being reported when perfectly legitimate files and documents are shared between employees. If there are any items blocked, you can manage those items through this interface (see Figure 18-11) and also through Group Policy, MDM, and PowerShell as I mentioned previously.

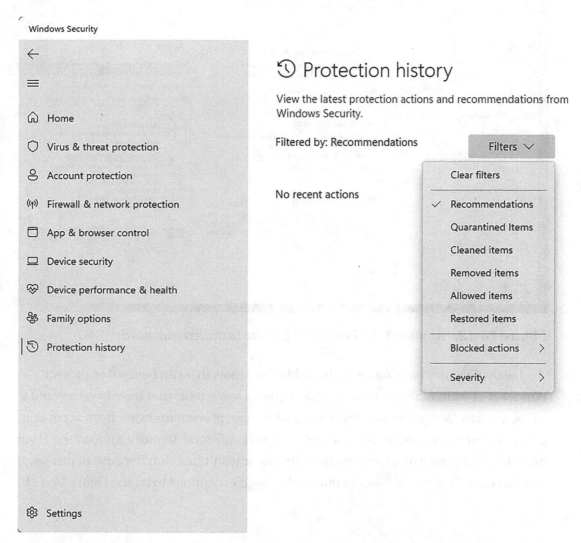

Figure 18-11. *You can manage files, documents, and downloads that have been blocked by SmartScreen*

Isolated browsing is a feature that is not activated by default and that needs to be manually switched on in Windows. This will always launch Microsoft's Edge web browser in an isolated environment to provide better protection when the PC is online (see Figure 18-12).

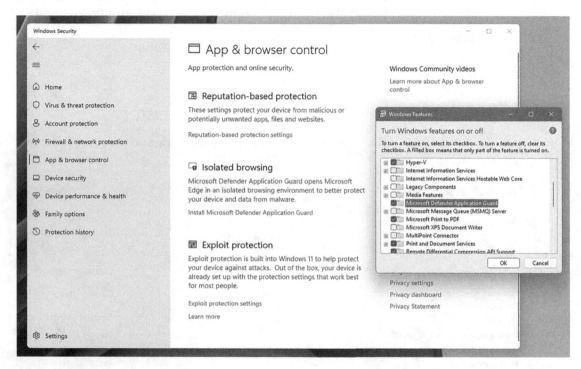

Figure 18-12. *Application Guard needs to be installed manually*

Lastly, *Exploit protection* contains additional tools that can be used to protect Windows 11 from malware attacks. This includes some tools that have been around for years, such as *Data Execution Prevention* which can prevent malware from accessing protected memory, and newer features such as *Randomize Memory Allocations*. If you have an older legacy program that misbehaves or won't function because of this security, you can click *Program Settings* to manually assign exceptions to it (see Figure 18-13).

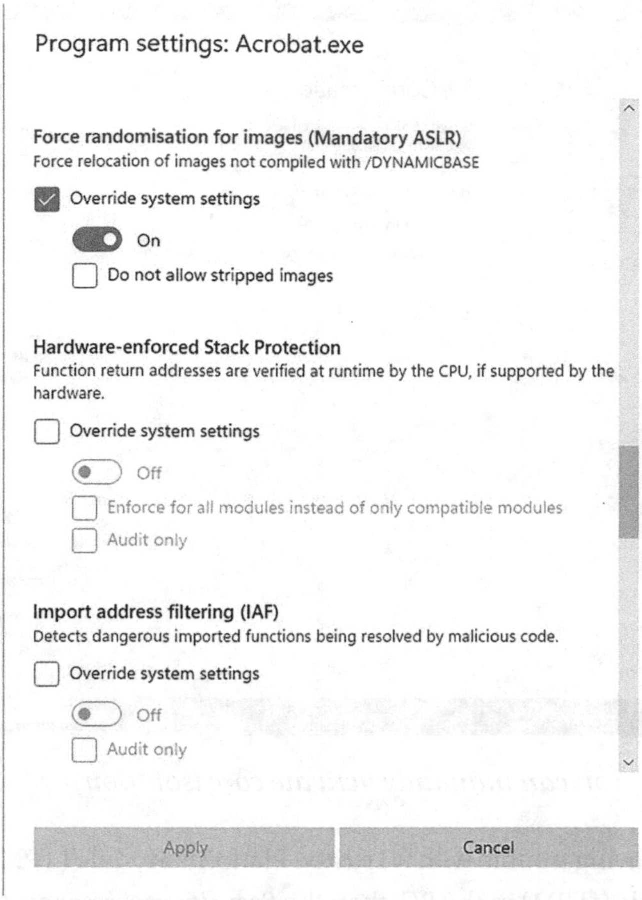

Figure 18-13. *You can change security settings for specific apps that require it*

Device Security

The *Device security* section contains some hardware-focused security options. Core isolation uses virtualization to create a secure area of system memory that is completely isolated from the rest of the operating system. Important system processes are then run inside this memory to prevent them from being tampered with. This feature is disabled by default and has to be manually activated on the PC (see Figure 18-14).

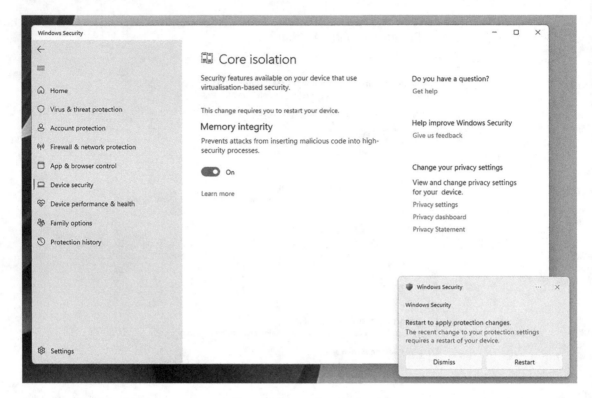

Figure 18-14. *You can manually activate core isolation*

If you are having trouble with a Trusted Platform Module (TPM) or Firmware Trusted Platform Module (fTPM) in the PC, then the *Security processor* section will display any errors that have occurred and offer fixes for the problem where it can (see Figure 18-15).

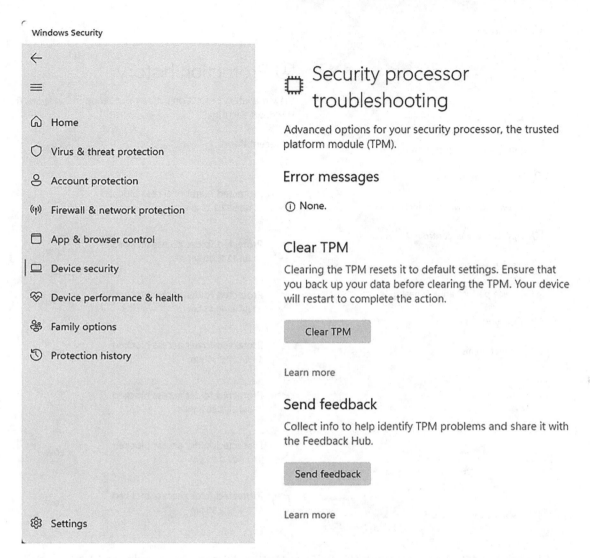

Figure 18-15. You can find TPM-related errors in Windows Security

Protection History

Lastly in Windows Security is a *Protection History* panel. Here, you can view all the notifications from Windows Security going back for around the last 30 days (as long as logs are typically kept by Windows) (see Figure 18-16). This can help you identify a problem, such as an application that's been blocked by a security feature, and fix it.

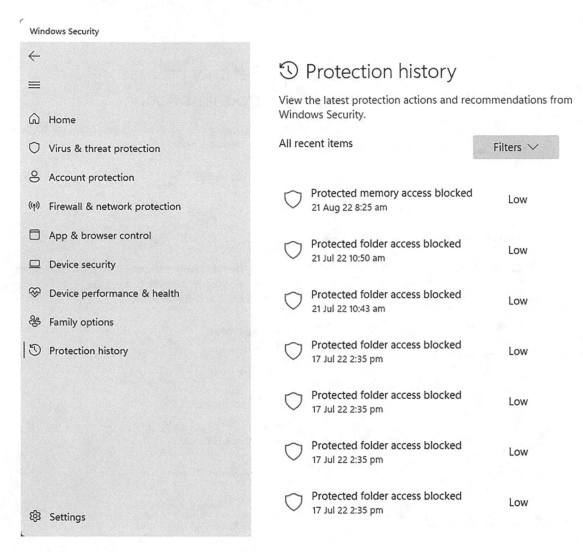

Figure 18-16. *You can view the full protection history in Windows 11*

Safe Mode and Diagnostic Mode

Windows comes with two reduced functionality modes that can, and I stress *can*, help remove infections from a PC, though with malware being as advanced as it is nowadays, it's likely that you will need more advanced tools, which I will talk about shortly.

Everybody that has used Windows over the years will know about Safe Mode. This is a reduced functionality mode of Windows where only basic and essential drivers and services are loaded, and no third-party drivers, services, or apps are loaded (see Figure 18-17).

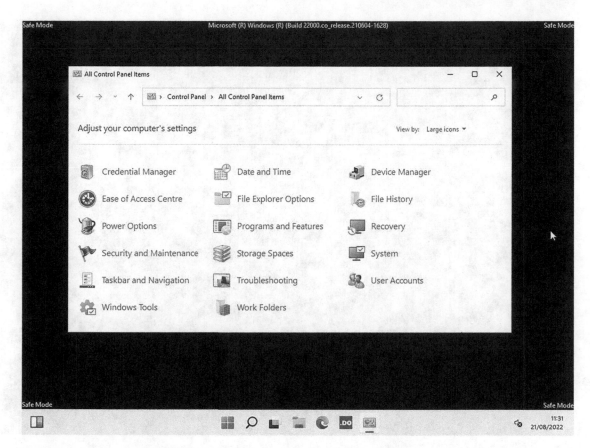

Figure 18-17. *Safe Mode provides a subset of Control Panel items*

You can access Safe Mode from the Recovery Console by clicking *Troubleshoot* ➤ *Advanced Options* ➤ *Startup Settings* and then restarting the PC when a new menu will appear in which you have three Safe Mode options (see Figure 18-18). These are Safe Mode, Safe Mode with networking support, and Safe Mode in a purely Command Line environment.

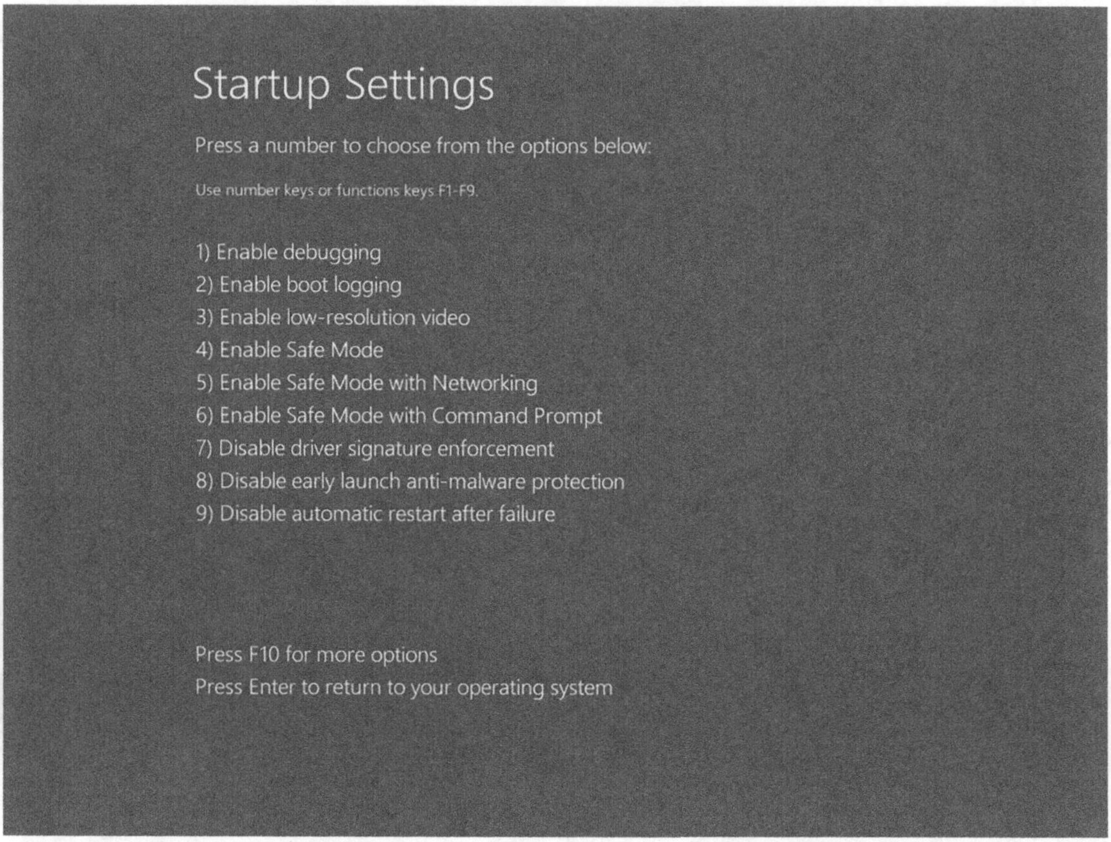

Figure 18-18. *You access Safe Mode from the Recovery Console*

Diagnostic Mode is different as it is accessed from within the Windows desktop environment itself. It's less useful than Safe Mode insofar as more drivers, services, and applications are loaded at startup, but where only a small subset of Control Panel and other administrative options are available in Safe Mode, many more are available in Diagnostic Mode.

You activate Diagnostic Mode by searching in the Start Menu for **msconfig**. This will open a window that older PC users might recognize as where you used to disable Startup programs (see Figure 18-19).

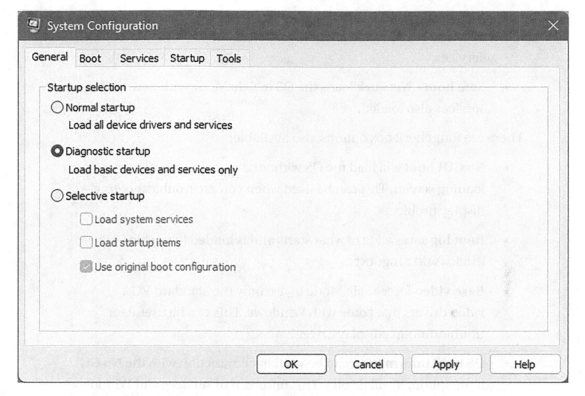

Figure 18-19. *You activate Diagnostic Startup from msconfig*

If you select Diagnostic Startup and then click *Apply*, you will be prompted to restart the PC. When you get to the desktop, everything will appear normal except that Startup programs and some services will not have been loaded.

One thing to note about Diagnostic Startup is that in the same way that you activate it in *msconfig*, you also need to deactivate it the same way, or else you will always start the PC in Diagnostic Mode.

There are also additional options available under the *Boot* tab in msconfig:

- **Safe boot – Minimal** will start the PC in the standard Safe Mode, with no networking support.

- **Safe boot – Alternate shell** will start the PC with a Command Prompt–only interface.

- **Safe boot – Active Directory repair** is an additional option that will also load the Active Directory services, in addition to networking services.

- **Safe boot – Network** loads the OS in Safe Mode with networking services also loaded.

There are four check box options also available:

- **No GUI boot** will load the OS without displaying the Windows loading screen. This can be used when you are troubleshooting display problems.

- **Boot log** saves a log of what starts and is loaded to the file `C:\ Windows\Ntblog.txt`.

- **Base video** forces Safe Mode to use only the standard VGA video drivers that come with Windows. This can be useful for troubleshooting display driver issues.

- **OS boot information** can be used in conjunction with the No GUI boot option. It will display a list onscreen of services and Windows components that are loaded and run, as they are invoked. You may be familiar with Safe Mode displaying this information by default in versions up to Windows XP.

Manually Removing Malware from a PC

You might find that if you get a malware infection, you can manually remove it. This can even include ransomware and might involve a tool you can download from a security website, and I'll detail some of these later in this chapter. There are things you can do from within Windows however, so I'm going to walk through it as, if nothing else, it's a good insight into how malware works.

I will place one caveat on this, however. Microsoft has made great strides with Windows security and proudly proclaimed when they launched Windows 11 that the OS is "the most secure Windows yet." Many people took this with a grain of salt given they saw Windows 11 as just being Windows 10 in a party dress. In truth though, Microsoft has taken advantage of the stricter new installation requirements for Windows 11 to beef up the security, and, try as I might, I simply could not get malware to take hold in my virtual machine test environment at all.

I had test viruses that had been provided to me by security researchers and that were made available to security product vendors so they could test their products. I was also given access to live virus and even ransomware samples, which very clearly I used with great care. I turned off all the security features and antivirus protection in Windows 11 (or at least I thought I had), and still I couldn't get any malware to take hold.

This is great news for us generally, and it really does indicate that when Microsoft said Windows 11 is the most secure version of Windows they've ever produced, they really weren't kidding. As a result, a few of the screenshots in this section will have been taken from a Windows 10 installation a while back, which I *was* able to successfully infect with a test virus.

Windows Defender Offline Scan

I mentioned earlier in this chapter that Windows 11 includes an offline antivirus scanner that works effectively from the Recovery Console. It's not activated from there however. In *Windows Security*, click *Virus & threat protection* and then click the *Scan options* link. Here, you will see an option to run a *Microsoft Defender Offline scan* (see Figure 18-20).

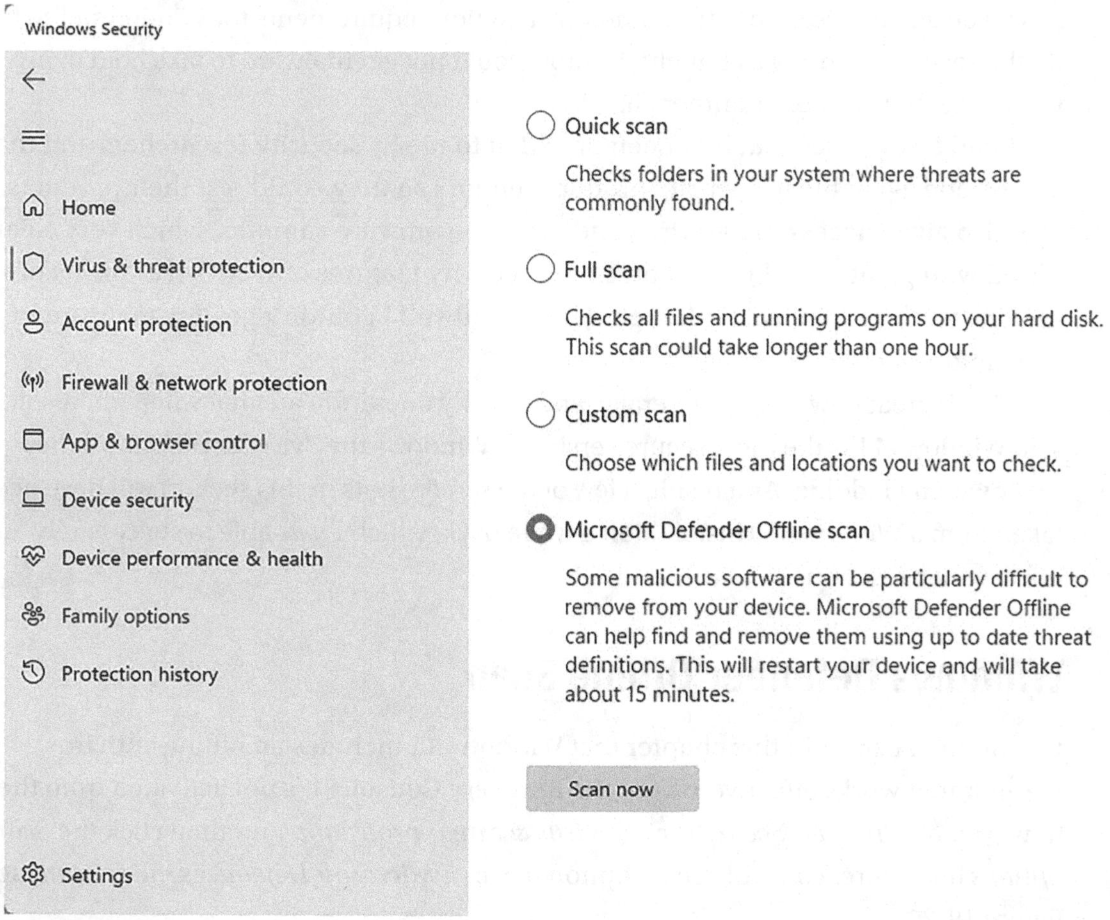

Figure 18-20. *You can run an offline virus scan from Windows Security*

Running this will reboot the PC and then run the scan with the most recently downloaded antivirus scan definitions from a Recovery Console environment where, hopefully, no virus has been able to reside.

Step 1: Isolating the PC

So how do you manually remove malware from a PC? The first step is that you need to completely isolate the PC from your network and the Internet as soon as you have identified an infection. With a network connection, worm viruses can burrow their way through to other PCs and servers on the network.

With an Internet connection, malware can download additional payloads to your PC or upload your files and documents to criminals. The malware can also use your Internet connection to propagate to other machines or even perform actions such as becoming part of a botnet delivering Distributed Denial of Service (DDoS) attacks to companies, organizations, or governments. Isolating the PC also prevents a hacker from taking control of your PC remotely.

If you are using a desktop PC or a laptop that is connected to the network and the Internet via a physical Ethernet cable, then it should be unplugged. If your PC has access to the Wi-Fi, then you should not only disconnect from the network, but you should tell Windows to forget the password to that and any other network within range that it tries to reconnect to (see Figure 18-21).

Figure 18-21. *You should tell Windows to forget any network the PC could connect to*

If your PC connects to the Internet via cellular, then you should remove the SIM card from the PC or delete the eSIM data. These actions will completely isolate the PC from your local network and from the Internet.

Note   If you have open Wi-Fi networks in the vicinity that do not require a password for access, you still have three options available to you. The first is to physically move the PC to a place where it can't see or access those networks. Additionally, some laptops come with a physical switch to deactivate all radio features including Wi-Fi and Bluetooth. Lastly, if you have access to the router for that network, you should be able to block the laptop from the network in the router settings until you have the matter resolved.

Step 2: Identify the Malware Processes

We now need to identify the malware processes, and there will almost always be more than one as they watch one another to make sure they've not been shut down and restart each other if they are. For this, we use *Process Explorer* from the Microsoft Sysinternals suite.

We can see in our screenshot that the malware is highlighted in purple (see Figure 18-22). It has a nonstandard name which is also common for malware processes, but because this is a test virus, it has clearly labelled itself as "Winlogon malware form."

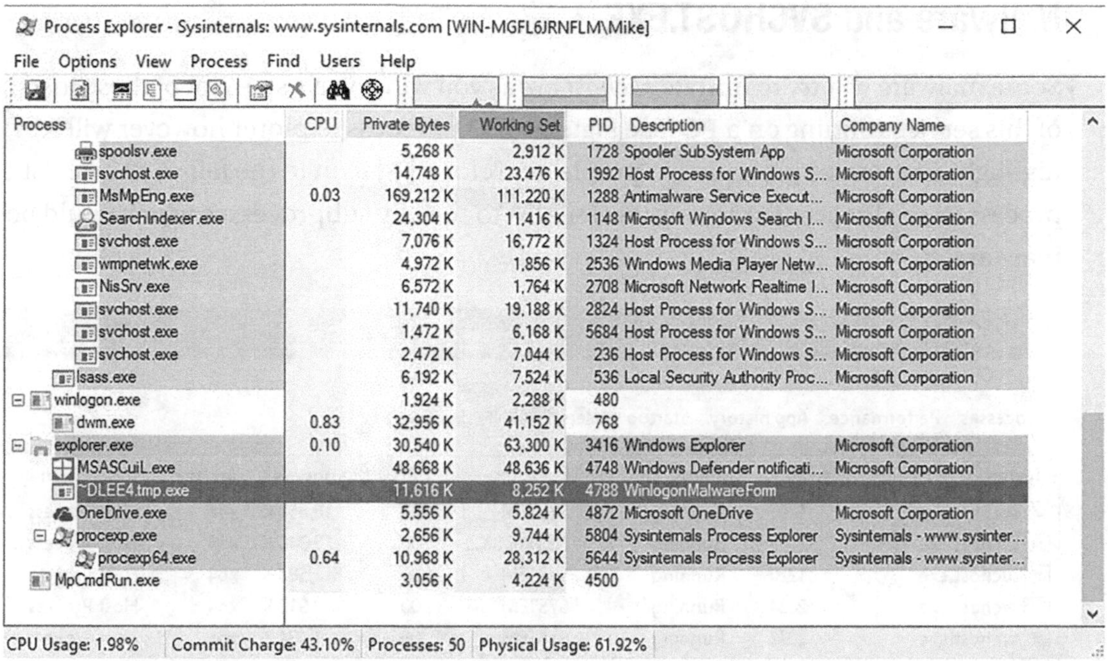
Process Explorer - Sysinternals: www.sysinternals.com [WIN-MGFL6JRNFLM\Mike]
File Options View Process Find Users Help
Process CPU Private Bytes Working Set PID Description Company Name
spoolsv.exe 5,268 K 2,912 K 1728 Spooler SubSystem App Microsoft Corporation
svchost.exe 14,748 K 23,476 K 1992 Host Process for Windows S... Microsoft Corporation
MsMpEng.exe 0.03 169,212 K 111,220 K 1288 Antimalware Service Execut... Microsoft Corporation
SearchIndexer.exe 24,304 K 11,416 K 1148 Microsoft Windows Search I... Microsoft Corporation
svchost.exe 7,076 K 16,772 K 1324 Host Process for Windows S... Microsoft Corporation
wmpnetwk.exe 4,972 K 1,856 K 2536 Windows Media Player Netw... Microsoft Corporation
NisSrv.exe 6,572 K 1,764 K 2708 Microsoft Network Realtime I... Microsoft Corporation
svchost.exe 11,740 K 19,188 K 2824 Host Process for Windows S... Microsoft Corporation
svchost.exe 1,472 K 6,168 K 5684 Host Process for Windows S... Microsoft Corporation
svchost.exe 2,472 K 7,044 K 236 Host Process for Windows S... Microsoft Corporation
lsass.exe 6,192 K 7,524 K 536 Local Security Authority Proc... Microsoft Corporation
winlogon.exe 1,924 K 2,288 K 480
dwm.exe 0.83 32,956 K 41,152 K 768
explorer.exe 0.10 30,540 K 63,300 K 3416 Windows Explorer Microsoft Corporation
MSASCuiL.exe 48,668 K 48,636 K 4748 Windows Defender notificati... Microsoft Corporation
~DLEE4.tmp.exe 11,616 K 8,252 K 4788 WinlogonMalwareForm
OneDrive.exe 5,556 K 5,824 K 4872 Microsoft OneDrive Microsoft Corporation
procexp.exe 2,656 K 9,744 K 5804 Sysinternals Process Explorer Sysinternals - www.sysinter...
procexp64.exe 0.64 10,968 K 28,312 K 5644 Sysinternals Process Explorer Sysinternals - www.sysinter...
MpCmdRun.exe 3,056 K 4,224 K 4500
CPU Usage: 1.98% Commit Charge: 43.10% Processes: 50 Physical Usage: 61.92%

***Figure 18-22.** You can identify malware processes using Process Explorer*

The color coding for processes in Process Explorer works like this:

- **Purple** processes, which in our case include the malware, are files that may be compressed (also called packed), which for legitimate applications can help them to use less memory, but in the case of malware can also help to hide the code from your anti-malware scanner. Looking at the purple-colored files should be your first step.
- **Red** processes are ones that are currently existing (being stopped).
- **Green** processes have been freshly run (also known as spawned).
- **Light blue** processes are those run by the same account that started Process Explorer.
- **Dark blue** processes are ones that have currently been selected by yourself in Process Explorer.
- **Pink** processes are running Services on the PC, such as the common svchost.exe which is a Windows system process that can host one or more other services where they share a process to reduce overall resource usage on a PC.

Malware and SVCHOST.EXE

Some malware will try to imitate *svchost.exe* as you will always see a lot of these instances of this service running on a PC (see Figure 18-23). Process Explorer however will still highlight nonservice processes in purple. Look for a **[+]** icon to the left of an svchost.exe process in the Process Explorer processes list to see any subprocesses which could be malware.

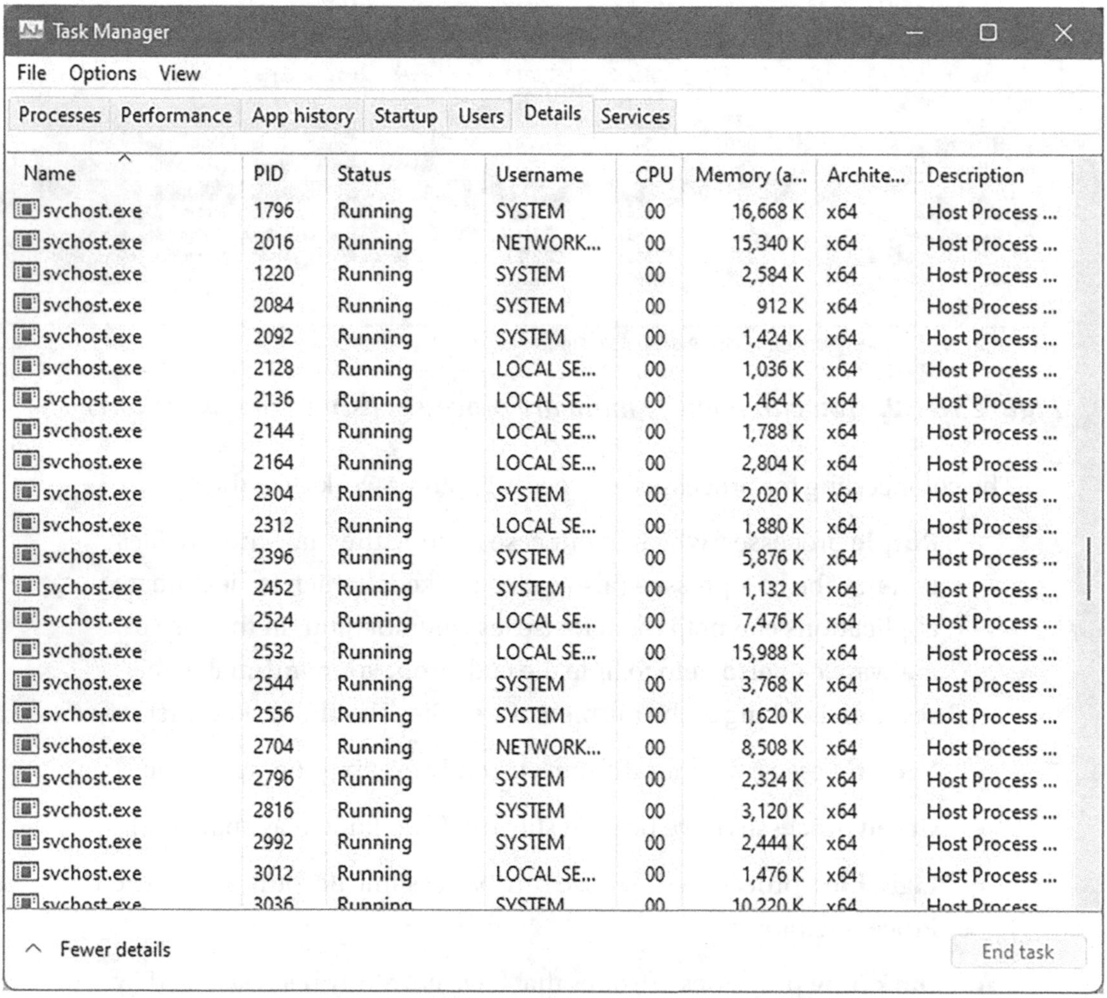

Name	PID	Status	Username	CPU	Memory (a...	Archite...	Description
svchost.exe	1796	Running	SYSTEM	00	16,668 K	x64	Host Process ...
svchost.exe	2016	Running	NETWORK...	00	15,340 K	x64	Host Process ...
svchost.exe	1220	Running	SYSTEM	00	2,584 K	x64	Host Process ...
svchost.exe	2084	Running	SYSTEM	00	912 K	x64	Host Process ...
svchost.exe	2092	Running	SYSTEM	00	1,424 K	x64	Host Process ...
svchost.exe	2128	Running	LOCAL SE...	00	1,036 K	x64	Host Process ...
svchost.exe	2136	Running	LOCAL SE...	00	1,464 K	x64	Host Process ...
svchost.exe	2144	Running	LOCAL SE...	00	1,788 K	x64	Host Process ...
svchost.exe	2164	Running	LOCAL SE...	00	2,804 K	x64	Host Process ...
svchost.exe	2304	Running	SYSTEM	00	2,020 K	x64	Host Process ...
svchost.exe	2312	Running	LOCAL SE...	00	1,880 K	x64	Host Process ...
svchost.exe	2396	Running	SYSTEM	00	5,876 K	x64	Host Process ...
svchost.exe	2452	Running	SYSTEM	00	1,132 K	x64	Host Process ...
svchost.exe	2524	Running	LOCAL SE...	00	7,476 K	x64	Host Process ...
svchost.exe	2532	Running	LOCAL SE...	00	15,988 K	x64	Host Process ...
svchost.exe	2544	Running	SYSTEM	00	3,768 K	x64	Host Process ...
svchost.exe	2556	Running	SYSTEM	00	1,620 K	x64	Host Process ...
svchost.exe	2704	Running	NETWORK...	00	8,508 K	x64	Host Process ...
svchost.exe	2796	Running	SYSTEM	00	2,324 K	x64	Host Process ...
svchost.exe	2816	Running	SYSTEM	00	3,120 K	x64	Host Process ...
svchost.exe	2992	Running	SYSTEM	00	2,444 K	x64	Host Process ...
svchost.exe	3012	Running	LOCAL SE...	00	1,476 K	x64	Host Process ...
svchost.exe	3036	Running	SYSTEM	00	10,220 K	x64	Host Process ...

Figure 18-23. *SVCHOST (Service Host) is a critical component of Windows*

Another thing you can do in Process Explorer is turn on the column to display the user account the processes are running under. Right-click the column headings and click Select columns. Then in the dialog that appears, click *UserName* and then click OK.

All genuine svchost.exe processes will be running under one of these three usernames: **NT AUTHORITY\SYSTEM**, **LOCAL SERVICE**, or **NETWORK SERVICE**. An instance of svchost running under a different username will be malware.

A third way to check if an svchost.exe process is genuine is to right-click it in Process Explorer and examine its Properties. In the Command line field, genuine Windows processes will always start with `C:\Windows\System32\svchost.exe -k` (see Figure 18-24).

Figure 18-24. *You can check if an SVCHOST process is genuine in Process Explorer*

SVCHOST processes can also be checked in Task Manager. At the top of the Properties panel from Process Explorer, you will see the Process Identifier (PID) number for the process, in this case 1796. Open Task Manager, and under the *Details* tab, find the process with this PID. Open its *properties* there, and in the *Digital Signatures* tab, you can check if the process has been digitally signed, and by who (see Figure 18-25).

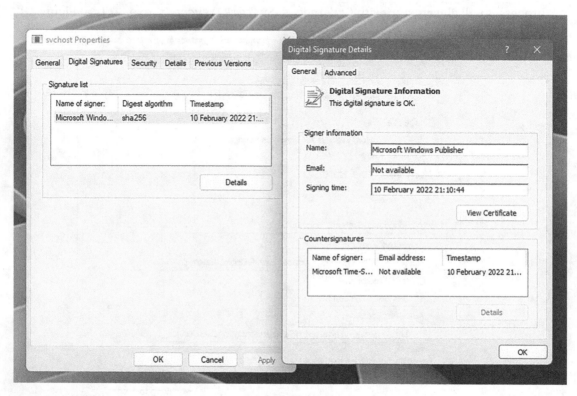

Figure 18-25. *You can check the digital signature of a process*

Step 3: Deactivate the Malware

We are now ready to try and deactivate the malware. If we right-click it and examine its Properties, we will see that this particular piece of malware is being run from the *C:\Windows\Temp folder* (see Figure 18-26). You will need to make a note of both the *Path* and *Autostart Location* parameters.

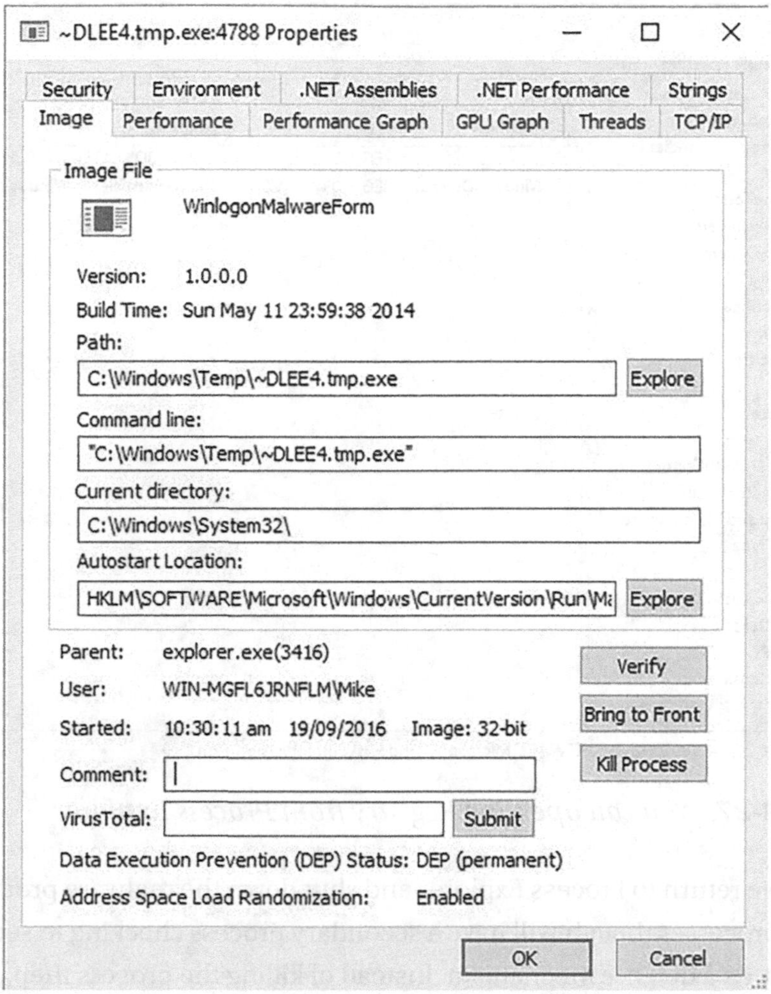

Figure 18-26. *Check the path and autostart parameters to find the malware files*

Open the Registry Editor by clicking the Explore button next to the *Autostart Location* field, and you will be taken directly to that key in the Windows Registry; you should delete this key from the Registry (see Figure 18-27).

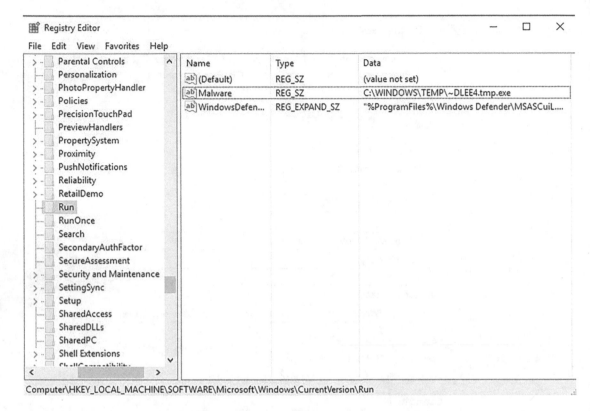

Figure 18-27. *You can open the Registry from Process Explorer*

Now we return to Process Explorer and shut down the malware process. Most malware processes though will have a secondary process checking to see if it is being shut down, as a defense mechanism. Instead of killing the process then, you can right-click the process name and suspend it (see Figure 18-28). This will prevent other malware processes from seeing you are killing the infection.

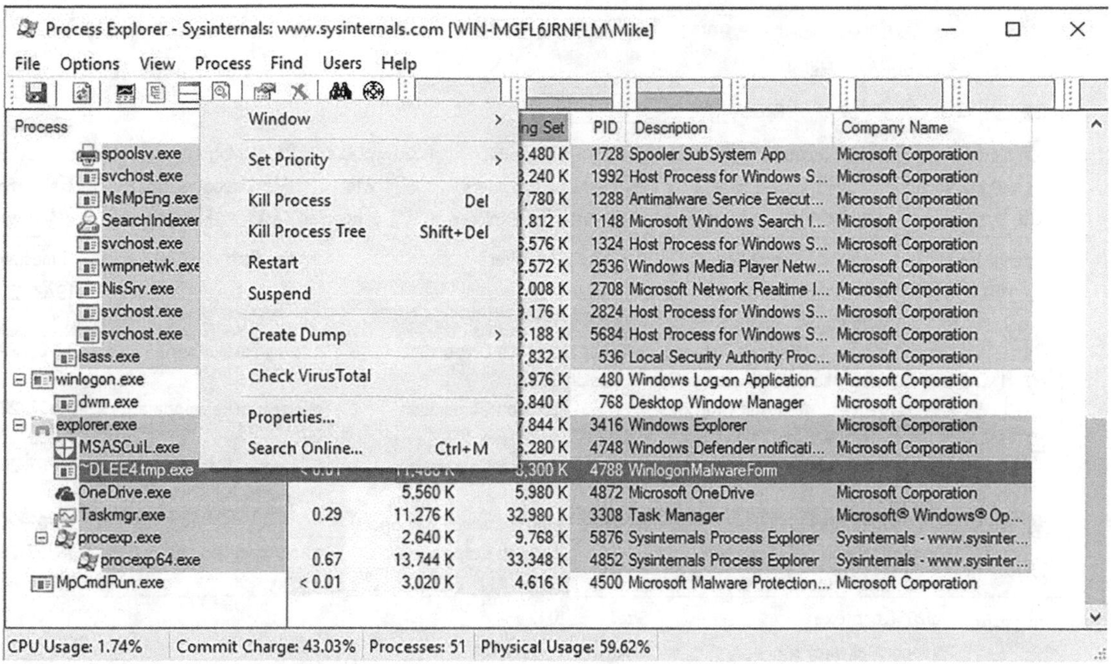

Figure 18-28. *You should suspend processes so they don't think they're being shut down*

Step 4: Test the Results

With the malware possibly disabled, you should restart the PC and then run Process Explorer again as an Administrator to see if the malware process is still running. In this case the malware is still running, so we need to use another Sysinternals tool called *Autoruns* to see if the malware is still running. See if the malware process is listed under the *logon* tab. If it is, uncheck it here to disable it (see Figure 18-29).

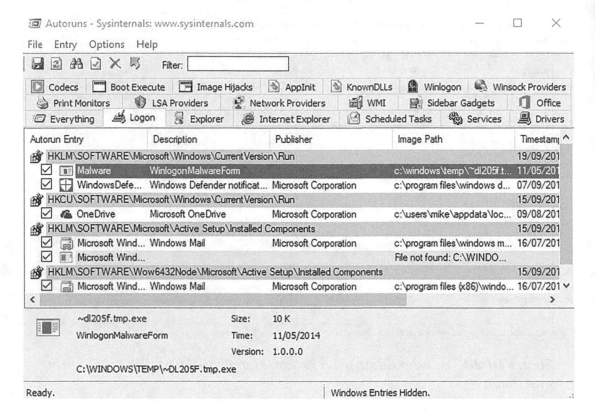

Figure 18-29. *You can check Autoruns to see if malware is still running*

This malware has automatically recreated itself at sign-in, which means there must be something else happening on the PC, so we need to go hunting again. This means that, still in Autoruns, we need to look tab to tab for any processes that are not digitally signed; these will be highlighted in *pink*.

When we look under the *Winlogon* tab, we can see a *SampleCredentialProvider* dll that is highlighted because it's not digitally signed (see Figure 18-30). It might look legitimate, being stored in the C:\Windows\System32 folder having a perfectly normal-sounding name **winlogondll.dll**, but this will be our malware process. We should disable this for now (just in case we're wrong) as we can always reenable it later if we need to. Make a note of the Registry key and the DLL name and folder location.

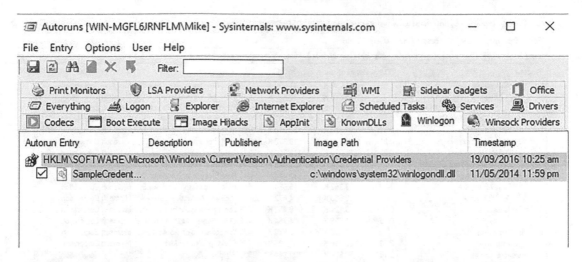

Figure 18-30. *Nondigitally signed startup entries are highlighted in pink in Autoruns*

Step 5: Retest the PC

Now we need to restart the PC again and check once more in Process Explorer for our malware. We can see in Figure 18-31 that we have successfully deactivated it, and it is no longer running on the PC.

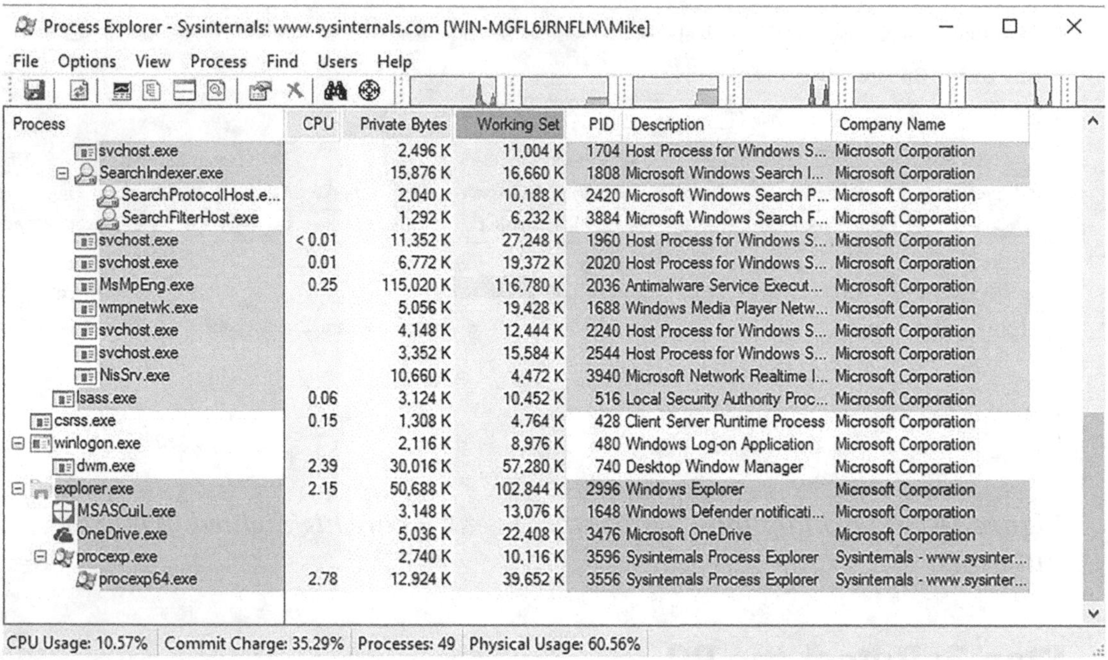

Figure 18-31. *We can see the malware is no longer running on the PC*

Step 6: Clean Up the Malware

The final step in the process is to remove all of the malware files and Registry keys that we found. We know the malware file was in the C:\Windows\Temp folder called **~DLEE4.tmp.exe**, that the malware DLL file was in C:\Windows\System32 and was called **winlogondll.dll**, and that there were a couple of Registry keys associated with the malware too. In Figure 18-32, we can see the startup Registry key that Autoruns highlighted for us and also the malware files itself.

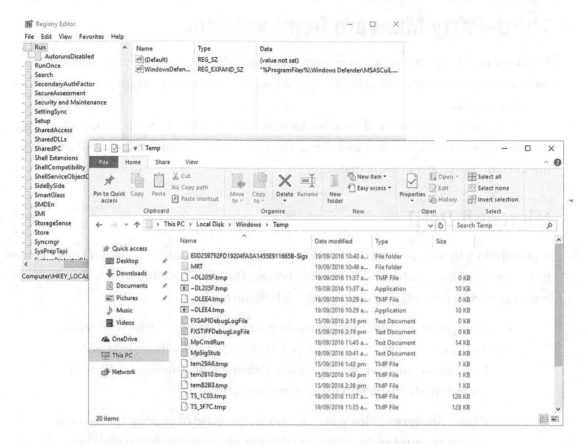

Figure 18-32. *You should delete all traces of the malware*

Of course, the actual malware you're trying to remove will likely be far nastier than the one I have demonstrated here, and the removal process might take some hours of investigation while you track down the multiple processes that are running. You should definitely be prepared to set aside a good amount of time and give this your full concentration.

Note   I want to include a note about rootkit removal. This is much more difficult in Windows 11 than it was in Windows 10 because of the increased security Microsoft built-in. This should make it more difficult for rootkits to infect the PC however. In Chapter 20, I detail how you can rebuild the Boot Configuration Database, which can help remove a rootkit, and how you can use the **BCDEdit** tool to remove unwanted boot entries. For rootkits though, you should always seek out a dedicated removal tool.

Third-Party Malware Removal Tools

Speaking of third-party tools, there are many available, and they vary considerably in functionality with some being highly specialist and others being more general, such as offline scanners.

You should always use the most up-to-date version of these tools, especially if they are antivirus scanners, so they include all the latest virus definition files, and the most up-to-date tools for removing malware.

Microsoft DaRT

If you are in a business using the Enterprise edition of Windows 10, you will have access to Microsoft's Diagnostics and Recovery Toolset (DaRT). This allows you to create recovery media for a PC that includes the following tools:

- **Computer Management console** is the same as on the host Windows 10 PC and allows you to view that PC's event logs, scheduled tasks, local users and user groups, device drivers, autorunning applications, and both Microsoft and third-party services.

- **Crash Analyzer** helps you determine the cause of crashes on the host PC, by examining the contents of the crash memory dump file(s) and having them interpreted for you.

- **Defender** is an offline version of the Windows antivirus package. This can be used to scan a PC for malware and remove it safely without the malware becoming active.

- **Disk Commander** provides tools to help you repair and recover corrupt disks and partitions.

- **Disk Wipe** can be used to delete all data from a hard disk, when you need to wipe a disk completely to eradicate a virus infection, before a reimage.

- **Explorer** is a full version of File Explorer that lets you examine and manipulate the files on the host PC. This can be used when you need to manually remove files as part of malware removal.

- **File Restore** is a file "undeletion" tool to help you recover files that were deleted accidentally or that were too large for the PC's Recycle Bin.

- **File Search** is a general-purpose search tool for locating specific files or file types on the host PC.

- **Hotfix Uninstall** can be used to remove Windows Updates that can be causing the PC to become unstable.

- **Locksmith** lets you change and manage user account passwords for any account on the PC. This can be used if malware has locked you out of your own or the Administrator account.

- **Registry Editor** allows you to access the Registry on the host PC and manually remove any keys placed there by malware.

- **SFC Scan**, the System File Repair Wizard, checks all the Windows OS files on the host PC to determine if any have been changed or have become corrupt. It can then be used with up-to-date installation media to replace any modified or damaged files with the proper ones.

- **Solution Wizard** is a tool that can be used if you are not sure which of the DaRT tools is best to fix your specific problem. It asks a series of questions and will suggest the best way to fix your problem.

- **TCP/IP Config** can be used to manipulate the network settings on the host PC, so that you can access local network resources or the Internet to apply fixes.

ESET Online (and Offline) Scanner

Several companies, including some of those listed in this section, provide online scanners that can scan your PC for viruses through your web browser. ESET provides a scanner that can also be downloaded to use on your PC. This can be useful if you suspect your current antivirus software has missed a virus.

www.eset.com/us/online-scanner/

Norton Bootable Recovery Tool

Many of the following tools all fall into broadly the same category as Windows Defender Offline. Norton is the same in that it allows you to create a bootable DVD or USB Flash Drive that can be used to scan for and remove malware.

`https://norton.com/nbrt`

Sophos Bootable Antivirus

By this point, you might have guessed that the choice of which tool you download and use depends on your personal preference for antivirus vendor. It also needs to work, and not all of these tools will be up to date with the very newest viruses, however. The Sophos tool can only be used to create a bootable CD or DVD, and so it is less suitable for ultrabooks and tablets.

`www.sophos.com/en-us/support/knowledgebase/52011.aspx`

Kaspersky Rescue Disk

Kaspersky Rescue Disk is designed to create a bootable CD or DVD from which to remove malware, though instructions do exist on the website for how you can create a bootable USB Flash Drive.

`https://support.kaspersky.com/viruses/rescuedisk`

Kaspersky Ransomware Decryptor

A suite of free utilities that, while they can't defend against ransomware, will help you remove ransomware from an already infected PC and decrypt any files the ransomware has encrypted. You can download it at

`https://noransom.kaspersky.com`

AVG Rootkit Scanner and Remover

The AVG Rootkit Remover is a tool that you download to an infected PC to scan for malware. If an infection is found, the tool will ask you to restart the PC so that removal and cleanup can take place.

`www.avg.com/en/signal/rootkit-scanner-tool`

F-Secure Online Scanner

This can be used to scan for and remove malware on your PC from a direct download, without having to install a package that could become infected with malware.

www.f-secure.com/en/home/free-tools/online-scanner

McAfee Free Tools

Security firm McAfee provides a selection of free security tools, which include the following tools.

GetSusp will scan for undetected malware on a PC and can be used if you suspect you may have undetected malware on a PC (www.mcafee.com/enterprise/en-us/downloads/free-tools/getsusp.html).

RootkitRemover is a stand-alone utility for detecting and removing complex rootkit attacks (https://pcs.tv/3CE2ewy).

Stinger is used to remove a specific list of supported viruses and is updated regularly with the latest and most common virus definitions (www.mcafee.com/enterprise/en-gb/downloads/free-tools/stinger.html).

D7II

If money is no object, then subscribing to an annual license for D7II can pay dividends. It's a complex suite to use and should not be used unless you're proficient in maintaining and configuring PCs, but it includes a powerful anti-malware suite that includes tools from Kaspersky, Bitdefender, Sophos, McAfee, and more on the unfortunately named domain foolishit (funny; Ed).

www.foolishit.com/d7ii/

RKill

RKill can be used to terminate the running processes that malware is using to keep itself active on a PC. This can be useful if your standard antivirus software is unable to clean the infection. Run RKill first to stop the offending processes, then use your existing antivirus software to clean the infection as per normal.

www.bleepingcomputer.com/download/rkill/

Junkware/Adware Removal Tools

Sometimes, you can have software on your PC called junkware or adware. This isn't actually a virus, but it can be really annoying and slow down your PC. Several companies provide free software for removing junkware including

Malwarebytes Adware Cleaner, `www.malwarebytes.com/adwcleaner`

Adlice RogueKiller, `www.adlice.com/software/roguekiller/`

Xplode AdwCleaner, available by searching online

Summary

Manual antivirus removal can be very difficult, though many tools are created to tackle and remove viruses, especially the biggest and most common threats. This is useful when the malware identifies itself to you. Often, this is the case especially with ransomware as the criminals want you to know who it is that has attacked you. It's not always easy to get the name of the malware however, and this is where researching the malware using Process Explorer and AutoRuns can give you filenames you can search for online to find it.

Anyway, now we have the nasty subject of malware put to bed, in the next chapter we'll take a deep dive into the Windows Registry and look at all aspects of it, its files, values, and keys. We'll examine what's important, what can go wrong with startup entries, and where the entries and keys are that you might want or need on occasion to change can be found. We'll look at how you connect to the Registry files of other users, and other PCs on the network, and we'll examine what all of this has to do with bees.

CHAPTER 19

Registry Troubleshooting

The Registry is what has always set Windows apart from other operating systems; in fact, it's only Windows that does things the Registry way. Whereas Unix-based operating systems such as Linux, Android, and Mac OS use a series of folders such as /etc that contain configuration files for the operating system and installed applications, the Windows Registry consists of a series of binary database files.

You might think that this would make the Registry more secure than the Unix approach, in which many of the configuration files are readable as plain text, with the Registry's "security through obscurity" approach, as said by Q in the *James Bond* movie *Skyfall* (though he wasn't talking about the Registry now was he; Ed) to be more effective.

Sadly, while the base security in Unix systems, where a user does not have administrative privileges, is highly effective, just about anybody can open, read, and even delete a Registry file if they put their mind to it. This means that, as these files are so open in the overall file system, they can be prone to corruption, unauthorized changes, and malware infection. So what is the Registry then, and how can we manage it and troubleshoot problems with it?

Registry Hives

The Registry consists of a series of binary databases, as I have already mentioned, that are stored in different locations on the PC. The main store for Registry files, known as Hives,[1] is the %SYSTEMROOT%\System32\Config folder (see Figure 19-1) in which the following Registry files can be found.

---

[1] When the Registry was being created during the development of Windows NT, the people working in the development team were all fans of bees, so they snuck in as many bee references as they could, calling Registry files "hives" and having Registry data stored in "cells."

© Mike Halsey 2023
M. Halsey, *Troubleshooting and Supporting Windows 11*, https://doi.org/10.1007/978-1-4842-8728-6_19

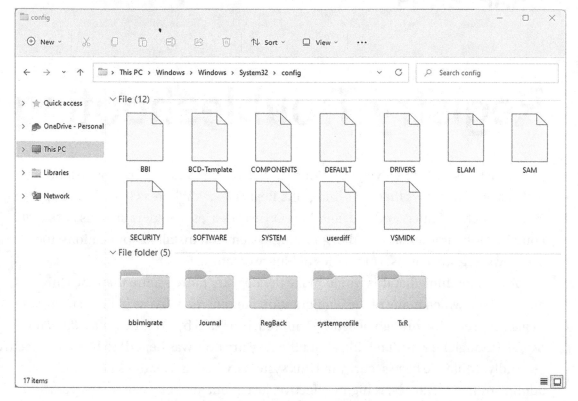

Figure 19-1. *The core Registry files are in the Windows/System32 folder*

- **SAM** – Security Accounts Manager, contains information about network domains the PC is connected to and stores the username, a unique identifier for the domain, the location of the server's Registry hive, and the user's password as a cryptographic hash. SAM appears empty unless the user has appropriate administrative permissions.

- **SECURITY** – Contains security settings and policies when the user is connected to a domain. SECURITY appears empty unless the user has appropriate administrative permissions.

- **SOFTWARE** – Contains keys for the current Windows installation and installed software and apps. Keys are organized by vendor name.

- **SYSTEM** – Contains keys related to Windows setup, settings, the default configuration, and details of any currently mounted and attached hardware devices and drives.

- **DEFAULT** – Contains the default system configuration information and keys.

- **HARDWARE** – Is not stored as a file, but is created each time the PC starts, and is discarded when the PC is switched off.

- **DRIVERS** – Is also created when the PC starts and discarded at shutdown.

- **Userdiff** (only used when the OS is being upgraded).

In addition to these Registry files, there are two more that are unique to each user account, with each user account having them:

- **%USERPROFILE%\ntuser.dat** – Contains user profile, customization, and configuration settings and options

- **%USERPROFILE%\AppData\Local\Microsoft\Windows\UsrClass. dat** – Contains additional user settings such as user-specific file associations

Registry Keys and Values

Database entries within each hive are called keys and values (clearly, the developers ran out of appropriate bee-related words by this point). There are five main sections within a Registry file containing these.

HKEY_CLASSES_ROOT (HKCR)

Keys and values for installed applications are stored here, including file associations. If a key is added or modified here that is also found in HKEY_CURRENT_USER, then HKCU is used as the master.

HKEY_CURRENT_USER (HKCU)

This contains configuration options for the currently signed-in user, including locations for User Shell Folders (Documents, Pictures, etc.), Control Panel, and other settings, and application configuration options. It pulls its data from the Registry files in the %USERPROFILE% folder.

HKEY_LOCAL_MACHINE (HKLM)

This is where most Registry changes made by administrators and end users are made. Here are the keys for Windows, drivers, and installed applications. These are generic keys and values for all users on the PC. In this section are loaded the following Registry hives:

- **SAM**
- **SECURITY**
- **SYSTEM**
- **SOFTWARE**
- **HARDWARE**
- **DRIVERS**

HKEY_USERS (HKU)

This contains settings and options for the currently signed-in user that are pulled from the NTUser.dat Registry hive.

HKEY_CURRENT_CONFIG (HKCC)

This contains information gathered at PC startup and that is only relevant to the current working session. It is discarded when the PC is shut down.

HKEY_PERFORMANCE_DATA

This is hidden in the Registry and contains performance data provided by the Windows kernel (the core OS files), drivers, installed applications, and services. This data only relates to the current session, and it is discarded when the PC is switched off.

Registry Value Types

Within these key areas (bad joke there, but I get it; Ed) are different types of Registry value. These are as follows:

- **REG_BINARY** keys store raw binary data.

- **REG_DWORD** are variable-length 32-bit integers.

- **DWORDS** are commonly used to define parameters for strings, settings, drivers, and configuration options.

- **REG_SZ** are field-length string values.

- **REG_EXPAND** are expandable length string values, also used to contain environment variables.

- **REG_MULTI_SZ** are multiple string arrays that can contain a list of values, normally separated by a comma or space.

- **REG_RESOURCE_LIST** is a list of resources in a nested array; these are used by device drivers.

- **REG_RESOURCE_REQUIREMENTS_LIST** is an array list of hardware resources that is used by device drivers.

- **REG_FULL_RESOURCE_DESCRIPTOR** are nested arrays used to store resource lists for physical hardware.

- **REG_LINK** are symbolic links to other Registry keys. They specify both the root and target key.

- **REG_NONE** is data that does not have a specific type.

- **REG_QWORD** are variable-length 64-bit integers.

Important Registry Locations

Having access to the Registry and being able to create, modify, and delete individual keys is useful, but locating what you're actually looking for in such a large database can seem daunting. There are a few common areas however that you will find yourself in where the most important and relevant Registry keys will always be found:

- **HKEY_CURRENT_USER ➤ Control Panel** – Is where you will find Control Panel Registry values related to input, accessibility, and desktop appearance

- **HKEY_CURRENT_USER ➤ Software** – Is the location for installed apps (normally win32) settings and configuration

- **HKEY_CURRENT_USER ➤ Software ➤ Microsoft ➤ Windows ➤ CurrentVersion** – Is where you will find settings related to Windows

- **HKEY_CURRENT_USER ➤ Software ➤ Microsoft ➤ Windows ➤ CurrentVersion ➤ Explorer** – Is the location for desktop configuration options for the current user including the all-important User Shell Folders

The Registry Editor

Windows includes a tool for managing and editing the Registry snappily called the Registry Editor (see Figure 19-2). You can find it by searching for it in the Start Menu or launching **regedit.exe** from the command line (which also works from the Windows Recovery Environment).

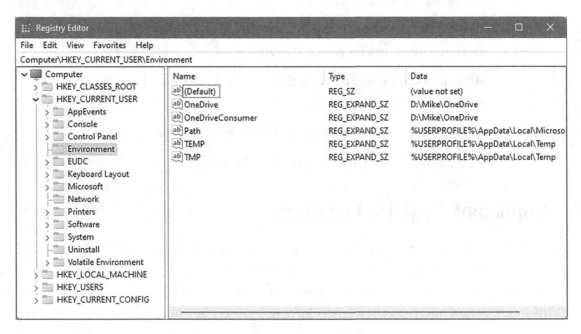

Figure 19-2. *You can manage the Registry using the Registry Editor*

Here, the different Registry hives and keys are organized in a tree hierarchy, with right and down clickable arrows to the left of items that allow you to expand and close individual Registry sections.

From the **Edit** menu, you can copy Registry key names and search the Registry. You can also create new keys which can also be done by right-clicking in either the left or right panels of the editor.

Backing Up and Restoring Registry Hives

You can create backups of Registry hives, specific keys, or the entire Registry at any time, and it is always good practice to do so before making any changes to the Registry. This is done from the **File** menu using the **Export** and **Import** options when you have clicked, to highlight, a part of the Registry you want to back up.

To back up the entire Registry, click **Computer** at the top of the left panel and then choose **Export** from the **File** menu. When you import a Registry key, you do not need to have anything selected in the left panel, as the location of where and in which hive the key is stored will be within the file you are importing.

Working the .REG Files

Registry hives might be binary databases, but when you export a key, or even the entire Registry, it is saved in plain text as a .REG file (see Figure 19-3). This enables you to modify keys easily for implementation on multiple PCs or to check and perhaps edit keys that you have been sent or have downloaded from the Internet. This can be useful for reasons of maintaining basic security.

Figure 19-3. *.REG files contain plain text versions of the Registry*

Creating and Modifying Registry Keys

As I have already mentioned, you can create new Registry keys and values by right-clicking in the left or right panels of the Registry Editor (see Figure 19-4). When you do so, I would imagine that you will be following specific instructions from a software or hardware vendor, or from a reputable website, as frankly there's little reason to start creating keys randomly as they won't do anything.

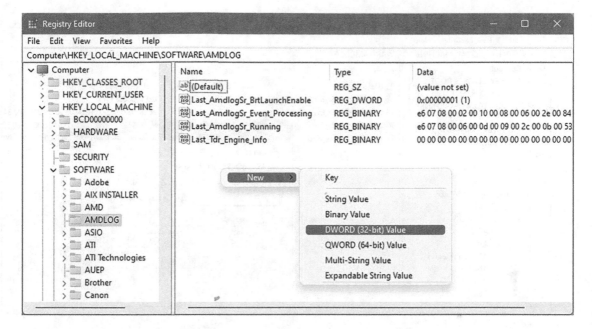

Figure 19-4. *You can create new Registry keys*

You also need to be sure you are creating the right type of key, as I detailed on the "Registry Value Types" section earlier in this chapter. When you right-click and select *New* from the context menu, a fly-out submenu will appear where you can choose the right key value type.

You can modify a value by either right-clicking it and selecting *Modify* or by double-clicking the value. This will display a dialog where you can change the value (see Figure 19-5), but you can also modify the raw binary data should that be a requirement for the change you need to make.

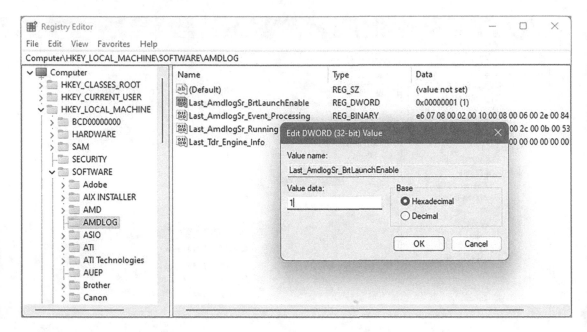

Figure 19-5. *You can modify Registry values*

Editing Hives for Other Users on the PC

If you need to edit the Registry for a user on the PC who is not currently signed in, perhaps because you are fixing a configuration error with their user account, you can load their Registry hive into the Registry Editor.

With **HKEY_LOCAL_MACHINE** or **HKEY_USERS** selected in the left panel, open the **File** menu and a *Load Hive* option will be available. You will need to have *Hidden files* visible in File Explorer to see the hive file. You will then be asked for a name for the Hive, and this is the name under which it will appear in the Registry Editor (see Figure 19-6), where I have loaded the hive for a user on the PC called "Jake."

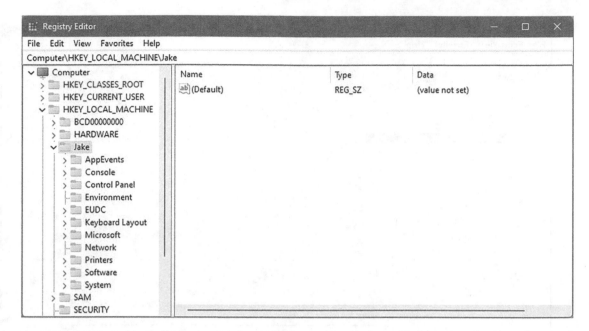

Figure 19-6. *You can load the hives for other users on the PC*

With that hive selected in the left panel, you can then select *Unload Hive* from the **File** menu when you are finished and want to close the hive.

Editing Hives on Other PCs on the Network

If you need to edit the Registry hive for a different PC on your network, or for a specific user on one of those PCs, you can select *Connect Network Registry* from the File Menu (see Figure 19-7). This will enable you to connect to the PC remotely as has been described earlier in the "Editing Hives for Other Users on the PC" section.

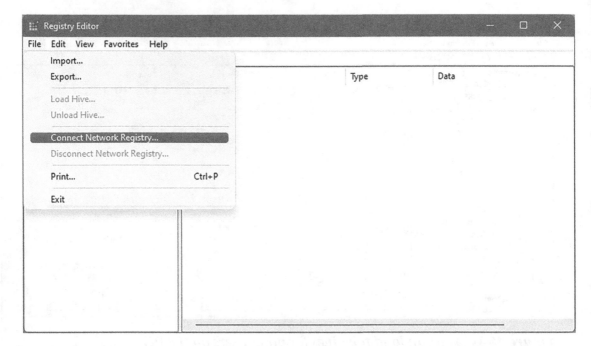

Figure 19-7. *You can connect to the Registries of other PCs on your network*

Enabling Remote Administration on Networked PCs

In order for you to be able to connect to the Registries on networked PCs, you have to do a few things first. In the Group Policy Editor, search for **gpedit** in the Start Menu, and navigate to *Computer Configuration* ➤ *Administrative Templates* ➤ *Network* ➤ *Network Connections* ➤ *Windows Defender Firewall* and then either the *Standard* or *Domain* profile as required.

Once there, look for the *Windows Defender Firewall: Allow inbound remote administration* rule and enable it on all the PCs you want remote access to (see Figure 19-8).

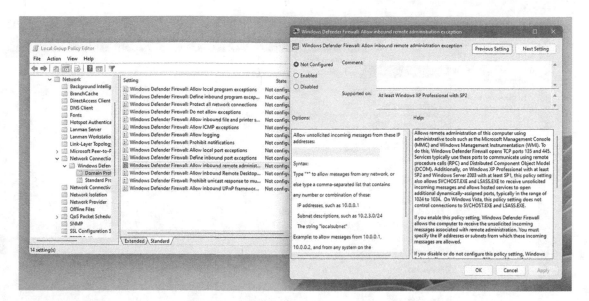

Figure 19-8. *You need to change the Allow Remote Administration Group Policy rule*

Tip   You can also enable or disable the Remote Administration policy from the Command Prompt by using the command `netsh firewall set service type = remoteadmin mode = [mode]` where `[mode]` is either enable or disable.

Next, you need to open Ports 135 and 445 in the Windows Firewall. Search in the Start Menu for **firewall** and open *Windows Defender Firewall with Advanced Security*. Click inbound rules, and from the option in the top right of the window, create a new rule in which you can allow access through these two ports (see Figure 19-9).

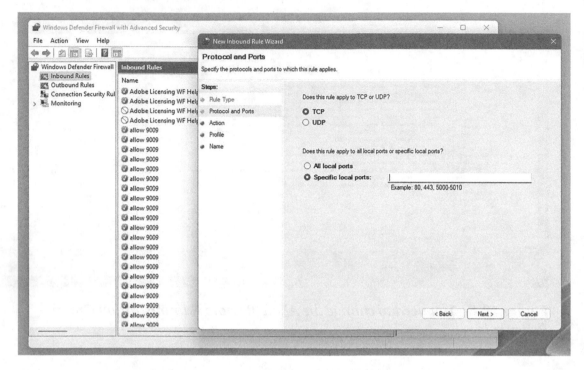

Figure 19-9. *You need to open two ports in the Windows Firewall*

The last thing to do is to enable the Remote Registry service. Search in the Start Menu for **services**, and when you have the Services panel open, scroll down the list until you get to *Remote Registry*. You need to set the status of this service to Automatic and then to start it (see Figure 19-10).

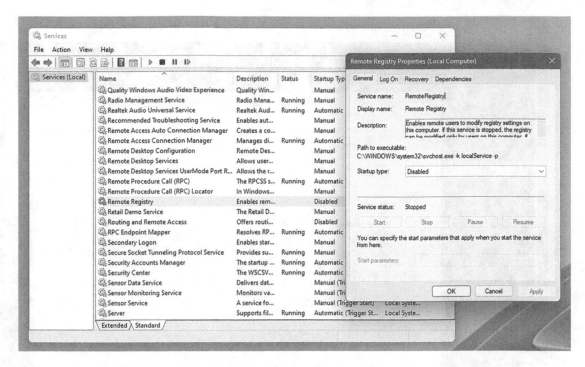

Figure 19-10. *You need to activate the Remote Registry service on PCs you wish to administer*

Tip   You can also enable the Remote Registry service from the Command Prompt by typing `sc start RemoteRegistry` or by typing `sc config RemoteRegistry start = auto` to have the service start automatically every time Windows starts.

Using the Registry Editor from the Recovery Console

As I mentioned earlier in this chapter, the Registry Editor can be run from the Windows Recovery Console. Select *Troubleshoot*, then *Advanced Options*, and lastly *Command Prompt*. When the Command Line interface appears, type **regedit** and press Enter (see Figure 19-11).

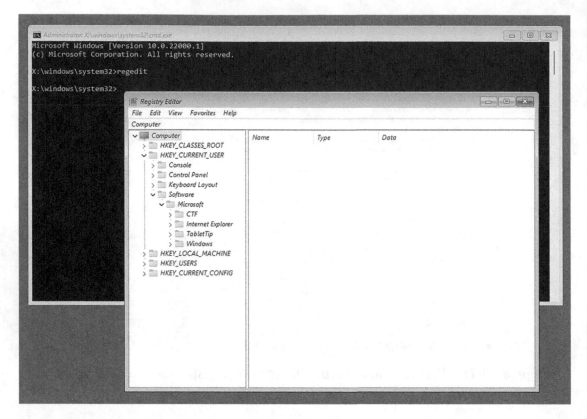

Figure 19-11. *You can edit the Registry from the Recovery Console*

The thing to bear in mind when doing this is that you're actually editing the Registry hives for the Recovery Console itself, and not for the PC. This means you will need to click **HKEY_LOCAL_MACHINE** or **HKEY_USERS** and then select *Load Hive* from the **File** menu to load a Registry hive for the host PC.

Note   You cannot use *Connect Network Registry* from the Recovery Console as there is no networking support available.

REG.EXE and REGINI.EXE

As with everything in Windows, the Registry can be edited and managed using scripting. There's PowerShell of course, which we'll talk about shortly, but also the Command Line tools **reg.exe** and **regini.exe**. These tools do the same thing as each other with the sole exception being regini's ability to run scripts.

REG.EXE

There are 11 commands you can use with Reg.exe to manipulate and edit the Windows Registry files:

- **REG ADD** to add an entry to the Registry.

- **REG COMPARE** to compare two different Registry entries, perhaps in HKCR and HKCU.

- **REG COPY** is used to copy a Registry key to a new location on a local or a remote PC.

- **REG DELETE** to delete a Registry key.

- **REG EXPORT** to export a key, a hive, or the whole Registry.

- **REG IMPORT** to import a key, a hive, or the whole Registry from a backup.

- **REG LOAD** to load a Registry hive.

- **REG QUERY** will return a list of subkeys and entries located at a specified place in the Registry.

- **REG RESTORE** will write saved subkeys back into the Registry.

- **REG SAVE** to save a copy of specified keys to a .reg file.

- **REG UNLOAD** to unload a Registry hive that has previously been loaded.

Unlike other Command Line tools, each of these is its own command, meaning that each Reg.exe command has different switches to the others. Rather than list them all here and take up the next ten pages when you're much more likely to use the Registry Editor or PowerShell anyway, you can follow this link to full details on the Microsoft Docs website `https://pcs.tv/3K7vWOu`.

REGINI.EXE

Regini works with text files containing the commands I detailed earlier for Reg.exe, and it has its own command structure. Use Regini.exe in the format

```
regini [-m \\pcname | -h hivefile hiveroot][-i n] [-o outputWidth][-b]
textFiles...
```

where the following switches are used:

> **-m \\pcname** specifies the name of a remote computer to connect to.
>
> **-h <hivefile hiveroot>** specifies the local Registry hive to modify and the root of the hive to use.
>
> **-i <n>** specifies the level of indentation to use for the tree structure of the Registry keys in the command.
>
> **-o <outputwidth>** specifies the width of the command output in characters; the default value is 240 character.s
>
> **-b** specifies that regini.exe be compatible with older versions of regini.exe and older scripts.
>
> **textFiles** specifies the names of the text files in ANSI or Unicode format that contain the commands.

You can find further information about Regini on the Microsoft Docs website at `https://pcs.tv/3wksjzb`.

Editing the Registry with PowerShell

As you might expect, the amount of control and the number of available commands you can get with PowerShell to manage and edit the Windows Registry is pretty large, with literally dozens of commands available to manipulate the Registry files on the local or on remote PCs.

You can find the full list of available commands on the Microsoft Docs website at `https://pcs.tv/3wjyjrQ`, with all their syntax and other requirements.

Tip   To make sure PowerShell works as you expect it to, you need to check the command execution policy. You can do this in the PowerShell interface with the command **Get-ExecutionPolicy**, and you may find it is set to Restricted. You should then use the command **Set-ExecutionPolicy** Unrestricted so that your commands will run.

Third-Party Registry Utilities

There are also some very useful third-party utilities that exist that can be used to manage, edit, and manipulate the Windows Registry. These tools can also be highly useful in troubleshooting, especially if the PC is unbootable. These all work in various ways, but the best tools available are

- **PCRegEdit** – Found by searching online

- **Hiren's Boot CD** – www.hiren.info/pages/bootcd

- **Lazesoft Recovery Suite Home, Recovery CD** – www.lazesoft.com/lazesoft-recovery-suite-free.html

- **UBCD4Win** – ubcd4win.org

- **Microsoft Desktop Optimization Pack (DaRT)** – Available through Software Assurance

Comparing Registry Files

In addition to third-party Registry editors and utilities, there are also third-party tools you can use to compare two Registry files. You might want to do this to compare the Registry files of a PC containing software or a hardware driver that is causing problems and cannot be cleanly uninstalled with the Registry files on a similar PC on which this is not installed. Some of the tools you can use for this include

- **InstallWatch Pro** – http://installwatch-pro.en.lo4d.com/

- **Process Monitor (Windows Sysinternals)** – http://technet.microsoft.com/sysinternals/bb896645.aspx

- **Regshot** – www.aplusfreeware.com/categories/util/registry.html

- **Tiny Watcher** – http://kubicle.dcmembers.com/watcher/

- **Total Commander** – http://ghisler.com/

- **What Changed** – www.majorgeeks.com/files/details/what_changed.html

- **WinDiff** – www.grigsoft.com/download-windiff.htm

- **WinMerge** – http://winmerge.org

Troubleshooting the Registry with Sysinternals

There are a couple of highly useful tools available as part of the Microsoft Sysinternals suite that you can use to help you manage and troubleshoot the Windows Registry.

RegJump

RegJump is a Command Line tool that has one very simple job. RegJump will open the Windows Registry Editor at a specific path in a hive. Use it in the format **Regjump <<path>> | -c** where **<<path>>** is a pathname in the format **HKLM\Software\Microsoft\Windows** and the **-c** switch copies the path from the Windows clipboard.

AutoRuns

So what happens when you have a program, such as a startup entry where an essential Registry key is missing, incorrect, or corrupt? Well, if it's a program that you're launching from the Start Menu, Taskbar, or from a shortcut on the desktop, you can find out what error has occurred by using the Event Viewer, which will tell you which key cannot be found or loaded.

With Startup programs, services, drivers, and other essential parts of the operating system, it can be much more difficult. This is where Microsoft's Sysinternals program **AutoRuns** comes in handy.

When you use AutoRuns, you will see a great many tabs along the top of the window for everything from codecs to drivers, to logon scripts, and scheduled tasks. Anything that is not found however is automatically highlighted in yellow (see Figure 19-12).

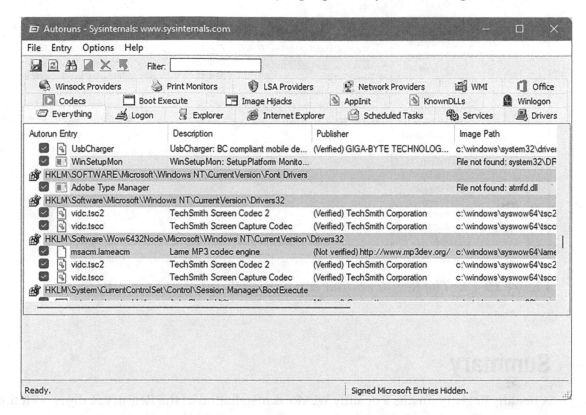

Figure 19-12. *Startup items that cannot be found are highlighted in yellow in AutoRuns*

This can make it very straightforward to find startup items on the PC that are causing or reporting errors. You can then simply uncheck the item to leave it in the Windows startup items, but mark it as inactive, or you can delete it entirely from a right-click.

If the item that is not found is a program, or another non-Registry element such as a DLL, you can right-click it, and from the context menu that appears, select *Jump to entry*. This will open the Registry editor at and highlighting the Registry entry for the offending item (see Figure 19-13). It is then a simple process of correcting the Registry entry or deleting it if it is no longer required.

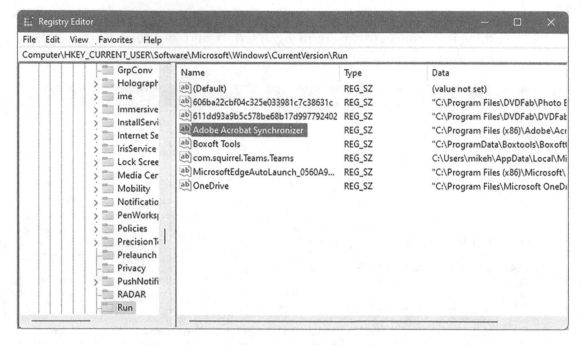

Figure 19-13. *The Registry Editor can be directly invoked from AutoRuns*

Summary

A healthy Registry means a healthy Windows installation as the Registry really is both the brain and the nervous system that makes everything work, properly and reliably. There really is nothing worse than pop-up error messages telling you that X or Y won't start or won't load because Z Registry key cannot be found and then having to troubleshoot that.

Speaking of startup, there is nothing worse than a PC that won't boot to the desktop. All is not lost however, and it's not the case that you will automatically have to reimage the PC or reinstall a fresh copy of Windows 11. In the next chapter, we'll look in depth at startup troubleshooting and what you can do to fix problems that arise.

CHAPTER 20

Startup and Repair Troubleshooting

Nothing is more annoying than a PC that won't start to the desktop, but this is a fate that can sometimes befall a PC. The common solution is to reinstall Windows from scratch or to reimage the PC. I always argue these aren't good solutions. If you reimage the PC from an image created using software from a company such as Symantec or Acronis, which have always been popular among IT Pros for the creation of image backups, then you will have to update every installed application that requires it, reinstall any new applications that have been installed since the image snapshot was taken, and then run Windows Update for possibly a long period to get the operating system up to date.

If you reimage Windows from a Reset image created by the operating system itself, then you will be up to date, well up until 30 days before anyway, on Windows Updates, but you'll have to reinstall and configure every single application on the PC.

And yes, I know that both Acronis and Symantec offerings allow you to create rolling backup images, but there's always a risk with these that any errors or problems could have crept into those as well.

For these reasons, I always suggest trying to repair the Windows installation first, partly because it's often the best solution, but mostly because on most occasions it really isn't that hard to do.

Quickly Repairing a Nonbooting PC

There are a few things you can do to quickly repair a nonbootable PC, assuming of course that it's a problem with the software and not a hardware issue, which I'll come to in a moment. So what are my top tips for repairing Windows Startup?

© Mike Halsey 2023
M. Halsey, *Troubleshooting and Supporting Windows 11*, https://doi.org/10.1007/978-1-4842-8728-6_20

Check Cables and Plugs

Clearly, the first thing to check if a PC won't start is all the cables and plugs. I know I'm preaching to the converted here, but you need to remember the people you will be supporting, most of whom will not be technically minded at all.

It was Douglas Adams, author of *The Hitchhiker's Guide to the Galaxy*, that said, "The problem people face in trying to make something completely foolproof, is that they frequently underestimate the ingenuity of complete fools." So asking a user to check the cable to the monitor (unless it's a laptop or all-in-one), the power cable, and even if the socket is switched on or if there's a power cut (oh yes, this does happen!) is always wise.

Hardware Failure

There's always the possibility with a nonbootable PC that the problem resides in the hardware. If it's a laptop or a tablet, you can plug it in to check if the battery is still holding a charge, as batteries will eventually die if they've been used for long enough and charged enough times.

For a desktop PC, the most common culprit is the power supply (PSU). These work similar to the engine in an automobile in that, as they get older, they don't deliver as much power as they used to. A vehicle that delivered 250 horsepower when it was new might only deliver half of that after 15 years and even less when it gets to the end of its useful life.

Tip   For my own PCs, I always purchase power supplies that are larger than I need. This might seem counterintuitive for a guy who wrote a climate change and IT book, but a more powerful PSU will not use more power than a less powerful PSU in general usage, but there's far more headroom for power delivery as it gets older, helping to reduce cost for replacements and ewaste when the PSU eventually dies.

Fans can also cause problems for both desktop PCs and especially for laptops, where they are significantly more difficult to replace. All PCs will include temperature sensors on the hardware. If the processor or another component overheats, the firmware will automatically cut the power, allowing the PC to cool. Power will not be restored until after the component has cooled to an appropriate level.

Startup Repair

If Windows won't boot to the desktop, the first thing to try is Startup Repair. This is a system that will run automatically if the operating system fails to start two or three times, but you can force it to run by starting the PC and forcing shutdown when the startup logo appears, usually the Windows logo, but many OEMs place their own logo there instead. Do this twice and Startup Repair will then run.

If you are in the Recovery Console, you can run Startup Repair manually from *Troubleshooting* ➤ *Advanced Options* ➤ *Start-up Repair*. Startup Repair works by resetting Windows startup components to their default state, in the same way that the built-in Troubleshooters do for other system components. If it can't fix the problem though, it will tell you (see Figure 20-1).

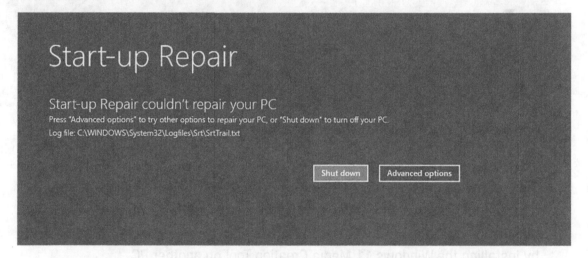

Figure 20-1. Startup Repair can attempt to fix straightforward problems

Using a USB Recovery Drive

Back in Chapter 3, I detailed how you can create a USB Recovery Drive for your PC, but sometimes PCs boot so quickly that actually starting the PC from one can be a challenge. If you need to use a USB Recovery Drive, perhaps because you suspect some of the boot files in Windows are corrupt, but you are in the Recovery Console already, click *Use a device* and a list of any available USB Flash Drives plugged into the PC (see Figure 20-2). Make sure these are plugged into the body of the PC itself and not an external module such as a desktop dock for which drivers will need to be loaded before USB devices can be seen.

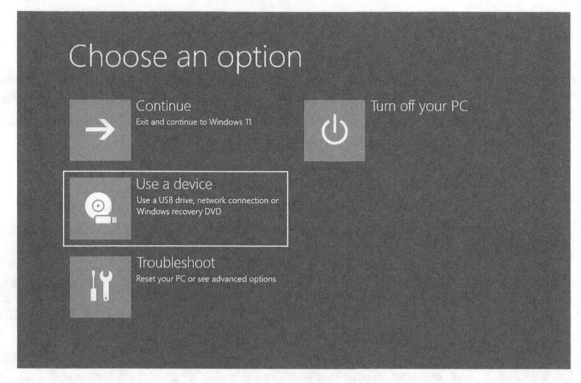

Figure 20-2. *You can choose a device to recover your PC from*

Tip   If you do not have a USB Recovery Drive or installation media, you can download a Windows 10 ISO file, which you can burn to DVD, or create USB installation media at `www.microsoft.com/software-download/windows11` by installing the Windows 11 Media Creation Tool on another PC.

System Restore

It's almost impossible for a PC to suddenly start misbehaving unless something has changed, and often this can be the installation of a driver, a Windows Update, or an application. Should this happen, you can run System Restore from the Recovery Console to roll back the most recent changes.

Tip   If a Windows Update has caused problems, when you boot to the desktop again remember to open Windows Update in Settings and pause updates for a while, so that the problems can be rectified and don't automatically repeat themselves.

Select *Troubleshoot* and then *Advanced Options* to find System Restore, which will search for any restore points on the PC (see Figure 20-3).

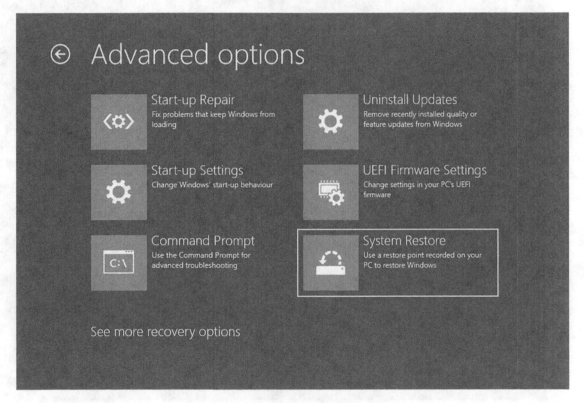

Figure 20-3.   *System Restore can roll back changes to a PC*

Tip   Additionally to System Restore, there is an option in the Recovery Console called *Uninstall Updates*. This is useful if an annual Feature Update has been installed and is causing problems, but while this will allow you to remove Feature and Quality updates, it will not remove Security, Stability, and many driver updates in the way System Restore will.

Safe Mode

The venerable old Safe Mode still exists in Windows, but is now accessible from the Recovery Console. Click *Troubleshoot* and then *Advanced Options* and *Start-up Settings*, and you will be prompted to restart the PC. The traditional boot menu that you might remember from the days prior to Windows Vista will appear in which you can start the PC into Safe Mode (see Figure 20-4).

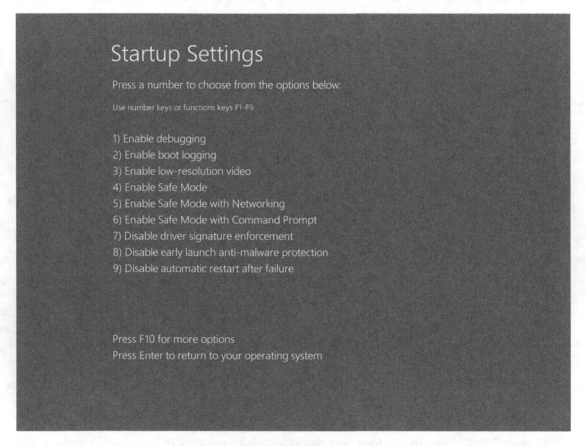

Figure 20-4. *Safe Mode can be useful for rolling back unwanted changes*

Safe Mode is a reduced functionality mode in Windows in which only essential Microsoft services and drivers are loaded. Anything from third parties such as display drivers, startup applications, and third-party services and DLLs won't be loaded.

There are also fewer features and tools available in Safe Mode. In Figure 20-5, you can see that only a subset of the Control Panel items are available, and although everything in Settings looks like it's there, in reality if you try and use something that isn't loaded, Settings will just exit.

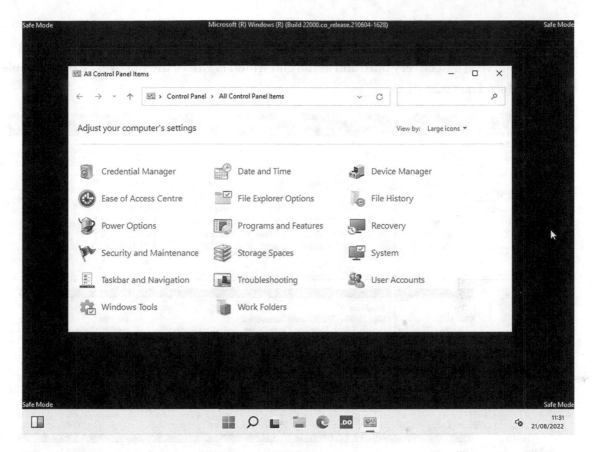

Figure 20-5. *Safe Mode still exists in Windows*

All of this makes Safe Mode useful for rolling back changes that would otherwise be blocked. This can happen if you're trying to remove the display driver or a third-party application that won't install properly because some of the services it installed are still running.

Repairing the Windows Boot Partitions

Windows has a reasonably complex startup partition structure in no small part because on older BIOS systems it was all too easy for malware to infect the single boot partition and either wipe it completely (some even wiped the BIOS itself) or inject itself into the boot partition, making it significantly more difficult to remove.

If you open the Windows disk and partitioning tool, you will see that on your installation disk (Disk 0) you have a 100MB EFI boot partition and then your Windows partition, with a Recovery partition at the end which is where the Recovery Console tools reside (see Figure 20-6).

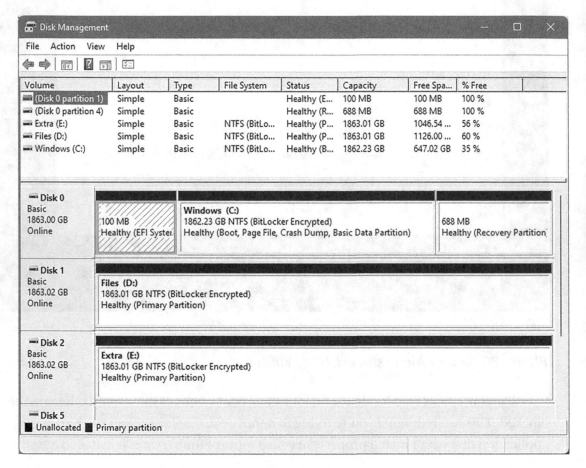

Figure 20-6. *Windows looks like it has one boot partition and one recovery partition*

In truth, what Windows is doing is deliberately hiding the important stuff to make sure malware can't access and infect it. Booting the same PC from a portable Linux drive shows a very different story. In Figure 20-7, you will see there are two boot partitions ahead of the Windows partition, the EFI system partition that Windows is happy to show you and a hidden *Microsoft Reserved Partition* of about 16MB in size.

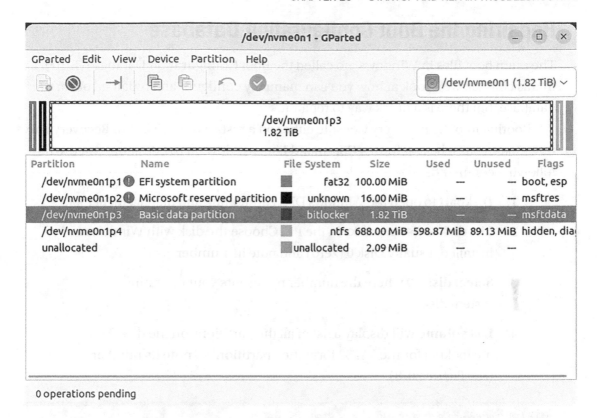

Figure 20-7. *Booting from Linux shows the true extent of the Windows boot system*

The main EFI security tools are hidden in this partition, and it's from here that Microsoft aims to make the Windows boot system more secure and inaccessible to malware and hackers.

Note   The sizes and locations of the Windows boot partitions might vary from one PC to another, such as a PC upgraded from Windows 10 or even Windows 8.1 to Windows 11. The partitions could be in different positions on the disk or of different sizes.

Repairing the Boot Configuration Database

The main boot files in Windows are called the Boot Configuration Database (BCD). Later in this chapter, we'll look at how you can manually configure and repair errors in the database, but there is a quick way to repair it.

Booting into the Recovery Console either on a restart or from a USB Recovery Drive, note this can also be run from a Command Line window on the desktop, you use the following commands:

1. **Diskpart** to open the Windows Disk Partitioning and management tool.

2. **List disk** to list the disks in the PC. Choose the disk with Windows installed, usually Disk 0 (zero) and note its number.

3. **Select disk=0** where the number represents your operating system disk.

4. **List volume** will display a list of all the partitions on the disk. You are looking for the FAT32 formatted partition, so note its number (see Figure 20-8).

```
Administrator: X:\windows\system32\cmd.exe - diskpart
Microsoft Windows [Version 10.0.22000.1]
(c) Microsoft Corporation. All rights reserved.

X:\windows\system32>diskpart

Microsoft DiskPart version 10.0.22000.1

Copyright (C) Microsoft Corporation.
On computer: MININT-DLKUMP3

DISKPART> select disk=0

Disk 0 is now the selected disk.

DISKPART> list volume

  Volume ###  Ltr  Label        Fs     Type        Size     Status     Info
  ----------  ---  -----------  -----  ----------  -------  ---------  --------
  Volume 0     D                       DVD-ROM        0 B   No Media
  Volume 1     C                NTFS   Partition   126 GB   Healthy
  Volume 2     E    Recovery    NTFS   Partition   529 MB   Healthy    Hidden
  Volume 3                      FAT32  Partition    99 MB   Healthy    Hidden

DISKPART>
```

Figure 20-8. *You are looking for the FAT32 formatted partition*

5. **Select volume=3** where the number you choose is the FAT32 formatted partition.

6. **Assign letter=F** to assign it a driver letter so you can make changes on it.

7. **Exit** to exit the Diskpart utility.

8. **F:** to switch to the FAT32 drive.

9. **CD .\EFI\Microsoft\Boot** to access the boot folder. Note on your PC this could be called **\Boot** or **\ESD\Windows\EFI\ Microsoft\Boot**.

10. **Ren BCD BCD.old** to rename the Boot Configuration Database while not deleting it, just in case you need it again.

11. **BootRec /RebuildBCD** to force Windows to build a new version of the Boot Configuration Database. You will be prompted to add the discovered Windows installation; press **Y** at this point.

12. Lastly, repeat the first few steps, but instead of assigning a drive letter to the FAT32 partition, type **Remove letter=F** to make certain it does not appear in File Explorer when you restart the PC.

We will look in more detail at the Boot Configuration Database and BootRec and other tools later in this chapter, but for now there are also a few useful commands you can use to help repair the boot system from the Command Line:

- **Bootrec /FixMBR** creates a new Master Boot Record for the disk and should be used if the MBR file is corrupt.

- **Bootrec /FixBoot** writes a new boot sector to the disk and should be used if the disk boot sector is corrupt.

- **Bootrec /ScanOS** can be used if your Windows 10 installation is not found. This command searches for operating system installations and reports what it finds.

- **BcdBoot C:\Windows /s F: /f ALL** is used if the **Bootrec /
  RebuildBCD** command does not repair your boot files. This
  command creates completely new boot files by copying the necessary
  files from your Windows installation (which should be on C: at
  this point, but you can check in Diskpart by viewing the disks and
  volumes as I detailed earlier). The **/s** switch designates the boot drive
  and the letter you gave it, in this case **F:**, and the **/f** switch specifies
  the firmware type to create a boot system for. This should be UEFI,
  but as it's a legacy tool, it also supports BIOS and ALL.

Recreating or Moving the Boot Partition

So let's now look at the most extreme of circumstances. You have a PC that is absolutely
crucial in its role, but it won't boot. Configuration is complex, so you would prefer not to
have to reinstall Windows; what do you do?

In a less critical example, you have a PC with more than one disk installed, and you
have performed a fresh installation of Windows 11. Unfortunately, an error has been
made, and Windows 11 has been installed on Disk 1 on the PC, and the installer has
placed all the boot and system partitions on Disk 0. Disk 1 however is where you keep all
your files, and you now find that your system image backup software won't work without
also including the partition with all your files on it.

This is clearly a less than favorable circumstance as you know restoring that image
backup will also restore your old versions of your files. So in this circumstance, what the
hell can you do? Well, you can move the boot partition from Disk 0 to Disk 1 and still
have the PC boot, but the process is slightly complex, so I'll talk you through it.

Caution   Moving the boot partition will completely break the functionality of the
Windows Reset backup system, the Recovery Console, and the USB Recovery Drive
creation tool, so be certain you have created a USB Recovery Drive and a backup
before proceeding.

Step 1a: Create a New Boot Partition (Command Prompt)

The first step involves creating a new partition on which the boot system can reside. You can do this from the Disk Management Console on the desktop, but I will show you how to action this from the Command Line when you start the PC from a USB Recovery Drive or Windows 11 installation media, as it's most likely that you're doing this because you can't start the PC. I will include side instructions though on how to achieve this from the desktop. At the Command Prompt (Admin) (accessed using the method I described in the "Manually Repairing Windows Startup" section), type the following commands:

1. **Diskpart**, to enter the Disk Partitioning and Management tool.

2. **List Disk**, and make a note of the disk on which Windows 11 is installed.

3. **Select Disk=0**, where the number is the number of the disk on which Windows 10 resides.

4. **List Volume**, to list all the volumes and partitions on the disk.

5. **Select Volume=4**, where the number represents the final or largest partition on the disk. I say largest because sometimes a UEFI install can place hidden partitions at the end of the disk.

6. **Shrink desired=500**, to shrink the partition by 500MB. This will create blank space at the end of the partition.

7. **Create Partition Primary Size=500**, to create a new partition in the available space.

8. **List Volume**, to check the number for the newly created partition; it will be listed as having a RAW filesystem.

9. **Select Volume=5**, where the number represents the number of the new partition.

10. **Format FS=NTFS LABEL="Boot" Quick**, to format the disk.

11. **Assign Letter=F**, to assign a drive letter to the partition temporarily. This should be a letter that is not currently showing as being in use in List Volume for any installed disk.

12. **Exit**, to leave the Diskpart tool.

Step 1b: Create a New Boot Partition (Disk Management Console)

If you can get to the desktop, perhaps because the boot folders were placed on the wrong disk during the installation of Windows 10, follow these instructions:

1. Press Windows key + X to open the Administration menu.

2. Click *Disk Management* to open the Disk Management Console. You can also open this by searching for **diskmgmt.msc** in the Start Menu.

3. Right-click the last or largest partition on the disk on which Windows 11 is installed (I say largest because sometimes, as in the example in Figure 20-9, the Windows installer places boot partitions at the end of the disk, not giving us space to create a new partition).

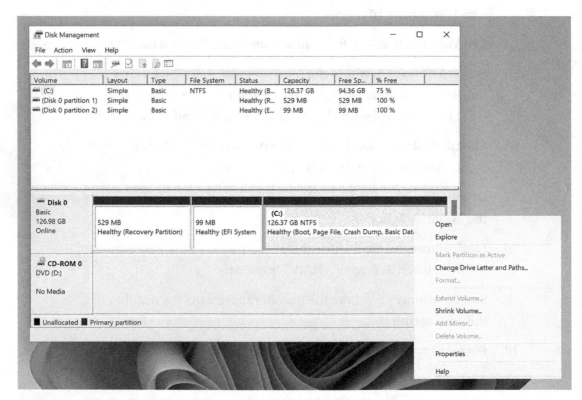

Figure 20-9.   *You need to create space for a new boot partition*

4.   Click *Shrink Volume* in the menu that appears.

5.   In the dialog that appears, set the Enter the amount of space to shrink in MB figure to 500 (see Figure 20-10), and click *Shrink*.

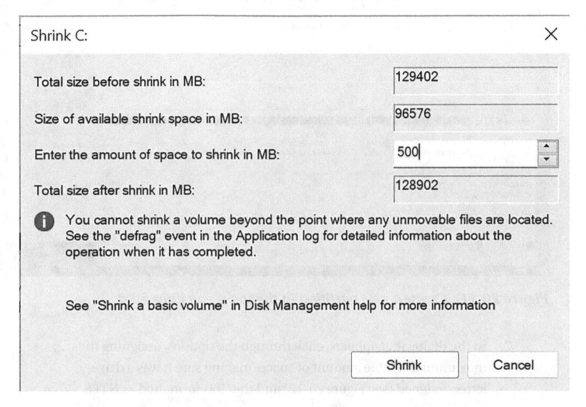

Figure 20-10. *You need a 500MB space at the end of the disk*

6.   In the blank partition space that is created, right-click and select Create Simple Volume from the menu that appears (see Figure 20-11).

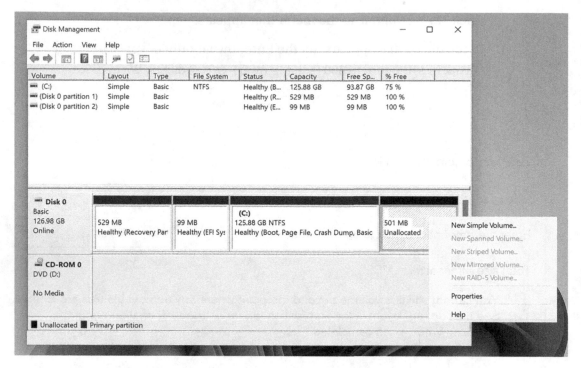

Figure 20-11. *Create a new partition in the space you have freed*

7. In the dialog that appears, click through the options, assigning the maximum available amount of space, making sure it was a drive letter assigned (see Figure 20-12) and that it is formatted as NTFS with the volume name "Boot."

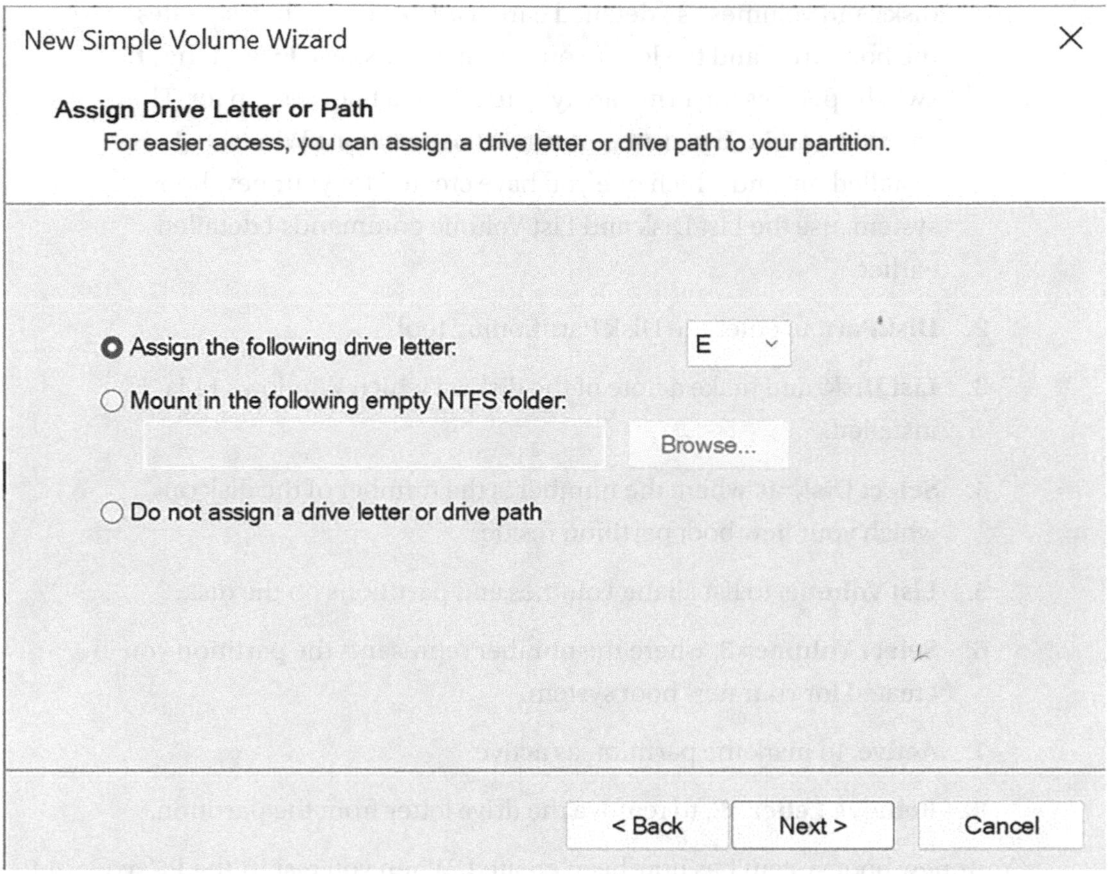

New Simple Volume Wizard   ✕

Assign Drive Letter or Path
    For easier access, you can assign a drive letter or drive path to your partition.

⦿ Assign the following drive letter: E ▾

◯ Mount in the following empty NTFS folder:

                                                              Browse...

◯ Do not assign a drive letter or drive path

                                    < Back   Next >   Cancel

Figure 20-12. *You need to temporarily assign a drive letter to the new partition*

Step 2: Create the New Boot Files

Once your new boot partition has been created, either from the desktop or the Command Prompt, you need to move the boot files across to it. To do this, you must be at the Command Prompt. This can be done either from the recovery environment or from the desktop. Should you be doing this from the desktop, run the Command Prompt as an Administrator; the option for this is in the **Win + X** menu. Next, type the following commands:

1. **BcdBoot C:\Windows /s E: /f UEFI**, used if the Bootrec / RebuildBCD command does not repair your boot files. This command creates completely new boot files by coping the necessary files from your Windows installation (which should be on C: at this point, but you can check in Diskpart by viewing the

disks and volumes as I detailed earlier). The **/s** switch designates the boot drive and the letter you gave it, in this case **E:**, and the **/f** switch specifies the firmware type to create a boot system for. This should be UEFI. If you are not sure what partitions Windows 11 is installed on, and which one you have created for your new boot system, use the List Disk and List Volume commands I detailed earlier.

2. **DiskPart**, to enter the Disk Partitioning tool.

3. **List Disk**, and make a note of the disk on which Windows 11 is installed.

4. **Select Disk=0**, where the number is the number of the disk on which your new boot partition resides.

5. **List Volume**, to list all the volumes and partitions on the disk.

6. **Select Volume=5**, where the number represents the partition you created for your new boot system.

7. **Active**, to mark the partition as active.

8. **Remove Letter=E**, to remove the drive letter from the partition.

Your new boot system has now been created. When you restart the PC, your old boot partitions will no longer be used. Bear in mind the caution earlier, however, that performing this task will completely break some parts of the recovery environment, the Reset backup image, and the USB Recovery Drive creator utility. If these are important to you, perhaps a better alternative is to physically unplug all but the hard disk on which you want Windows 11 installed and perform a clean install, wiping out all your existing partitions on the Windows drive first. I will show you how to do this in Chapter 22.

Manually Editing the Boot Configuration Database

I mentioned earlier in this chapter that the boot system for Windows is stored in something called the Boot Configuration Database (BCD). This is editable in Windows 11, but why might you want to do so? There are circumstances such as when you have a dual-boot configuration, which I'll talk about later in the chapter, or when something in the database has changed or become corrupt.

To edit the database, open the Command Line or Windows Terminal as an Administrator and type the command **BCDEdit**. This will display the current configuration in the database (see Figure 20-13).

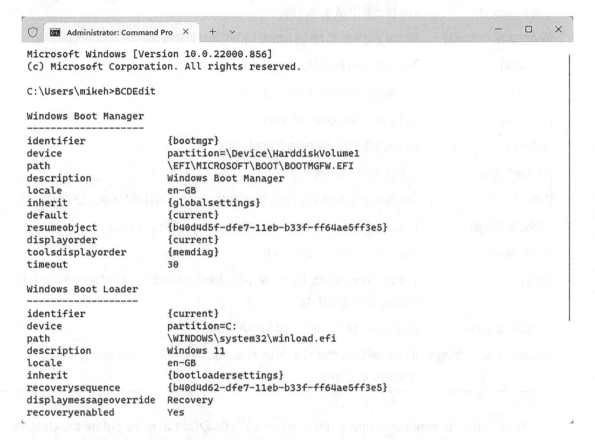

Figure 20-13. *You can display the contents of the Boot Configuration Database*

Each entry in the database begins with its *Identifier*. This could be a technical name, a text string, or even a hexadecimal GUID (General Unique Identifier). These come in the format {xxxxxxxx-xxxx-xxxx-xxxx-xxxxxxxxxxxx}. A full list of identifiers is shown in Table 20-1.

Table 20-1. *Identifiers used by the BCDEdit command*

Identifier	Description
{badmemory}	The global RAM defect list
{bootloadersettings}	Global settings to be inherited by all boot loader entries
{bootmgr}	The Windows Boot Manager
{current}	The main operating system on the PC
{dbgsettings}	The global debugger settings
{default}	An identifier for the default boot entry
{emssettings}	The global EMS settings
{fwbootmgr}	The firmware boot manager boot entry; stored in NVRAM on UEFI systems
{globalsettings}	Global settings that should be inherited by all boot entries
{memdiag}	The memory diagnostic utility
{ntldr}	The Windows legacy loader, NTLDR; used for versions of Windows released prior to Windows Vista
{ramdiskoptions}	Additional options required for RAM disks
{resumeloadersettings}	Global settings that should be inherited by all Windows resume-from-hibernation entries

There are different commands you can use with BCDEdit to manipulate the database contents:

- **bcdedit [/store filename] /bootdebug [id] { ON | OFF }** is used to enable or disable the debugger for the specified boot entry. The debug log is stored in the file specified in the command. This might be used in the format *bcdedit /store C:\BootDebugLog /bootdebug {current} ON*.

- **bcdedit [/store filename] /bootsequence id [...] [/addfirst | / addlast | /remove]** specifies the boot sequence for a one-time boot. This might be used in the format *bcdedit /bootsequence { e397815a-15a9-11e5-9622-fc025c6ab93c } {current} {ntldr}*.

- **bcdedit [/store filename] /copy id /d description** creates a copy of the specified boot entry. This might be used in the format *bcdedit /copy { e397815a-15a9-11e5-9622-fc025c6ab93c } /d "Copy of Windows 11"*.

- **bcdedit [/store filename] /create [id] /d description [/ application apptype | /inherit [apptype] | /inherit DEVICE | /device]** creates a new boot entry with the specified ID. The supported application types are *BOOTSECTOR, OSLOADER,* and *RESUME*, and the supported inherit types are *BOOTMGR, BOOTSECTOR, FWBOOTMGR, MEMDIAG, NTLDR, ORLOADER,* and *RESUME*. This might be used in the format *bcdedit /create {ntldr} /d "Compatibility OS"*.

- **bcdedit [/store filename] /debug [id] { ON | OFF }** enables or disables the kernel debugger for the specified boot entry. This might be used in the format *bcdedit /debug ON*.

- **bcdedit [/store filename] /default id** sets the default boot entry for the PC. This might be used in the format *bcdedit /default { e397815a-15a9-11e5-9622-fc025c6ab93c }*.

- **bcdedit [/store filename] /delete id [/f] [/cleanup | /nocleanup]** deletes the specified boot entry and optionally cleans it from the display order. This might be used in the format *bcdedit /delete {cbd971bf-b7b8-4885-951a-fa03044f5d71} /cleanup*.

- **bcdedit [/store filename] /deletevalue [id] datatype** deletes an element or value from a boot entry. This might be used in the format *bcdedit /deletevalue {bootmgr} bootsequence*.

- **bcdedit [/store filename] /displayorder id [...] [/addfirst | /addlast | /remove]** sets the boot manager's display order. This might be used in the format *bcdedit /displayorder { e397815a-15a9-11e5-9622-fc025c6ab93c } /addlast*.

- **bcdedit [/store filename] /enum [type | id] [/v]** lists all the boot entries in the specified BCD store. This can be used with the enum types *ACTIVE, ALL, BOOTAPP, BOOTMGR, FIRMWARE, INHERIT, OSLOADER,* and *RESUME*. It may be used in the format *bcdedit /enum OSLOADER*.

- **bcdedit /export filename** creates a backup copy of the BCD store to the specified file. It might be used in the format *bcdedit /export "C:\BCD Backup"*.

- **bcdedit /import [/clean] filename** imports the contents of an exported BCD backup. It might be used in the same format as the export command. The */clean* switch is used only on UEFI systems, and it forces the firmware to delete all its existing NVRAM boot entries that are used with Secure Boot.

- **bcdedit [/store filename] /set [id] datatype value [/addfirst | / addlast | /remove]** creates or modifies an element in a boot entry. It might be used in the format *bcdedit /set { e397815a-15a9-11e5-9622-fc025c6ab93c } path \windows\system32\winload.exe*.

- **bcdedit /sysstore partition** specifies the partition used for the BCD store. This switch is used only on UEFI systems and might be used in the format *bcdedit /sysstore C:*.

- **bcdedit [/store filename] /timeout timeout** specifies how long the boot loader should wait at the OS loader menu before selecting the default entry. It might be used in the format *bcdedit /timeout 30*, where the number is a representation of seconds.

You will have seen that each BCDEdit command is used with data fields such as ID. The different types of data used with the command are shown in Table 20-2.

Table 20-2. *BCDEdit data formats*

Data Format	Description
boolean	A Boolean value that can be set to TRUE or FALSE. You can also use the values TRUE or FALSE, as well as 1 and 0, and YES and NO
device	A device data type that can be one of BOOT, PARTITION=drive, FILE=[parent]path, or RAMDISK=[parent]path,optionsid
enum	The data type that takes a value from a list
id	The identifier for a boot entry, known as its GUID
integer	A 64-bit integer, 32-bit variables are not supported
list	A boot entry identifier list that contains one or more boot entry identifiers separated by spaces. This list type does not use quotation marks
string	A string variable. It should be surrounded by quotation marks ("") if it contains spaces

An excellent and full reference document for the BCDEdit command is available to download from the Microsoft website `http://pcs.tv/1MBUbPu`.

How BCDEdit Is Used in Practice

While you can edit and manipulate the contents of the Boot Configuration Database, it might be unclear as to how you might want to do so in the real world. Let's step through some examples then of what you might want to use the BCDEdit command for:

1. To change the default operating system, the one that appears first in the OS choices list and that will load automatically if no option is selected there, use the command **BCDEdit /default {id}**.

2. If an operating system has the incorrect disk or partition associated with it, this can be rectified with the command **BCDEdit /set {id} device partition=X:**, where X: represents the disk or partition on which the operating system is installed. You must then also use the command **BCDEdit /set {id} osdevice partition=X:**.

3. To manually add a legacy operating system that isn't appearing in the list, use these commands with the new custom ID {legacy}:

    a. BCDEdit /create {legacy} /d "Legacy OS Name"

    b. BCDEdit /set {legacy} device partition=D: or the letter of the partition where the legacy OS is installed

    c. BCDEdit /set {legacy} path /ntldr

    d. BCDEdit /displayorder {legacy} /addlast

4. If you are adding a Linux installation to the boot menu, follow these instructions:

    a. Boot into Linux and launch a Terminal session with root privileges.

    b. Find which partition Linux is installed on with the command **fdisk -l (lowercase "L")**. The Linux installation will be on a partition labelled as /dev/sda1 or /dev/hda1.

    c. Install a GRUB (Grand Unified Boot Loader) boot manager on that partition with the command **grub-install /dev/sda1**.

    d. Copy the Linux boot sector with the command **dd if=/dev/sda1 of /tmp/ linux.bin bs=512 count=1**.

    e. Copy the file *linux.bin* to a USB Flash Drive as a backup.

    f. Install Windows 11 on your PC.

    g. Press *Win + X* to open the Administration menu and run Command Prompt (Admin) or Windows Terminal (Admin).

    h. Type **diskpart** to enter the disk management utility.

    i. Type **select disk=0**, which is more than likely where your boot partition is located.

    j. Type **list volume** and look for the active or System partition; see Figure 20-14.

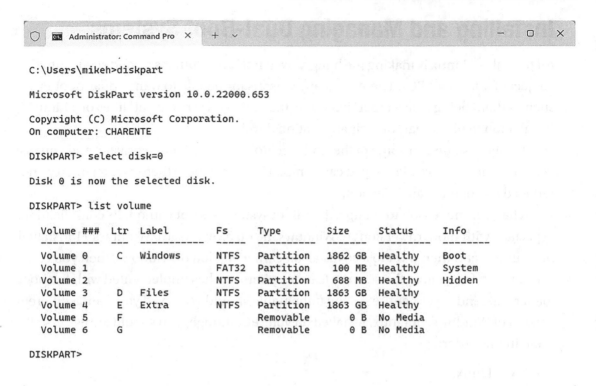

Figure 20-14. *You are looking for the "System" partition on the disk*

k. You need to temporarily assign a drive letter to the System partition. Type **assign letter=n** and use the next available drive letter.

l. Copy your *linux.bin* backup file from your USB Flash Drive to the root (active) partition.

m. Type **remove letter=n** to remove the drive letter.

n. Create a GRUB entry with the command **BCDEdit /create /d "GRUB" /application BOOTSECTOR**. This will return a unique ID: make a note of it. For the remainder of this example, I will call it *{linuxid}*.

o. Type **BCDEdit /set {linuxid}** device boot.

p. Type **BCDEdit /set {linuxid} PATH /linux.bin**.

q. Type **BCDEdit /displayorder {linuxid} /addlast**.

Installing and Managing Dual-Boot Systems

All this talk of Linux is making me hungry, well not really, but it's a good segue into the subject of dual-boot PCs. There are many reasons for people to want a dual-boot PC, such as them being a developer that wants the tools and scripting abilities of a Linux installation to use as part of their application development work.

It could also be that some of the work you do is extraordinarily private, and you just want a separate OS you know you can completely trust where there's no telemetry and a reduced risk of malware infection.

Whatever the reason to set up a dual-boot system, it's not without its complications, especially with modern versions of Windows. If you already have Windows 11 installed on your PC, and then want to also install an earlier version of Windows, then you can pretty much forget it, as the security features Microsoft has implemented with the boot loader will render your entire system unbootable should you try. If you want a different version of Windows, or Linux, installed on your PC, though, you should always install them in this order:

- Linux

- Legacy Windows OS

- Windows 10

- Windows 11

Caution   I want to slip in a note here about end-of-support dates for Windows versions. By the time you read this, all versions of Windows before Windows 10 will be completely out of support, with the paid-for extended support for Windows 7 having ended in January 2022, Windows 8.1 support having ended in January 2023, and support for Windows XP and Vista having ended in 2014 and 2017, respectively. Windows 10 support ends in October 2025, and as I write this, there's no word on whether additional paid-for support will be offered. Extended support for Windows 11 is expected to end around 2031.

Bitlocker and Secure Boot

With Windows 11, Microsoft has enforced strict installation requirements, such as UEFI firmware and a TPM 2.0 security chip or fTPM in the firmware. There is strong encouragement from the company to keep PCs secure through the use of Bitlocker encryption, biometric sign-in, and enhanced security.

Not all operating systems though are compatible with security features such as Intel's Secure Boot (also known as Trusted Boot). This is built into UEFI firmware and is designed to prevent the execution of any code at the PC's startup that is not digitally signed, such as rootkits and malware.

Any version of Windows prior to Windows 8.1 will not support secure boot and will not install if it is enabled on the PC. Given the security implications of running a non-supported operating system however, I would always recommend running them in a virtual machine instead. You should also check that a Linux distro that you want to install is compatible with Secure Boot. While almost all are, there are a few distros that still do not support it.

Additionally, Bitlocker is known to be famously incompatible with dual-boot systems. Should you try and use it, each time you switch to your alternate operating system and then back again you will be prompted for your 50-character Bitlocker decryption key. This is less than desirable, so be aware you won't be able to encrypt your drives in this way.

Summary

There is always a strong temptation to just wipe a Windows installation and start again with a fresh one when a problem with the boot system arises. While a very rare circumstance, it's hideously irritating, but surprising to many just how many tools and methods there are to repair the system and get it working again.

This complexity doesn't just exist with the Windows boot system however, as it extends into every aspect of a PC, from the core OS files to installed applications, drivers, physical hardware, and so on.

Over the course of this book, we've looked at all of those subjects, but PCs are so complex, and with every single PC having a unique combination of hardware and software, it's impossible to predict every type of problem that can arise. For this reason, in the next chapter we'll take a deep dive into everything else and look at how you go about researching and troubleshooting the most difficult problems on a PC.

CHAPTER 21

Researching and Troubleshooting Difficult Problems

Sometimes, you hit a problem on a PC that you know fully well doesn't require a reinstall or reimaging, but is so frustrating and knotty that it drives you nuts. This type of scenario can occur regularly, and you end up searching online trying to find the answer only to find either that there's no answer, but that a ton of other people have experienced the same problem, or that there's no mention of it at all, at least not that you can find.

So how do you go about researching these problems and finding solutions? So far in this book, we've dealt with and covered all the biggest problem areas including reliability and updating, user accounts and file access, apps and compatibility, processes and services, networking and Internet access, hardware and peripherals, security and encryption, malware and ransomware, the Windows Registry, and startup and repair. It seems appropriate then to bring this all together in a chapter that could very reasonably be called "AAARRGGH!"

Reading Windows Log and BSOD Files

In Chapter 8, I talked about how you can use the Event Viewer to get information on practically any event on the PC. Each of these produces a log or a dump file (depending on the type of event it is) that resides on the PC for up to 30 days, after which time it is deleted to free up space. But where do these logs reside, and how can you open and read them?

© Mike Halsey 2023
M. Halsey, *Troubleshooting and Supporting Windows 11*, https://doi.org/10.1007/978-1-4842-8728-6_21

Log Text Files

The Windows\Debug log files contain audit (installation, deletion, update, etc.) operation details and app crash details in plain text file formats (see Figure 21-1). The files you will find in this folder will vary and are entirely dependent on what's been happening on the specific machine. In Figure 21-1, we can see that there are logs for the wiatrace file.

Figure 21-1. *Windows\Debug files are stored in plain text format*

You will see that some log files contain links either to previous versions of the file still stored on the PC or to website links. You can copy and paste these into your PC to get more information where it's made available to you.

Reading .xml and .etl Files

The Windows\Logs folder is where the main Windows logs are stored. They are separated into subfolders, most of which are sensibly named, such as RecoveryDrive and SystemRestore (see Figure 21-2). The log files are stored either as plain text (.txt) files, which can be opened in Notepad; as Extensible Markup Language (.xml) files, which can be opened and read in a web browser, such as Edge or Chrome; or as Event Trace Log (.etl) files.

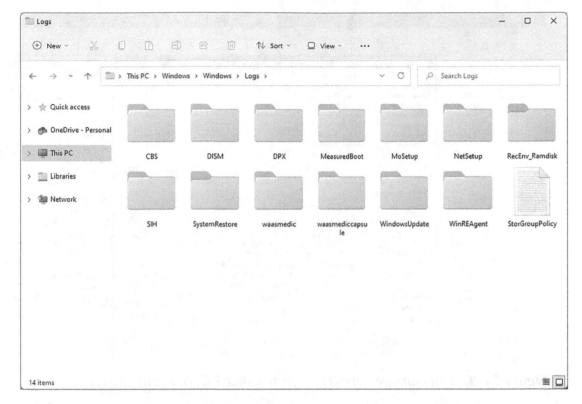

Figure 21-2. *The Windows\Logs folder contains the main Windows log files*

Event Trace Log (.etl) files will also all be available to view in the Windows Event Viewer, as this is the file extension primarily associated with that utility. If you are opening .etl files from another PC however, they can be opened from the Event Viewer *Action* menu by selecting *Open Saved Log*. When open, the log files will appear in the left panel of Event Viewer in a *Saved Logs* section (see Figure 21-3).

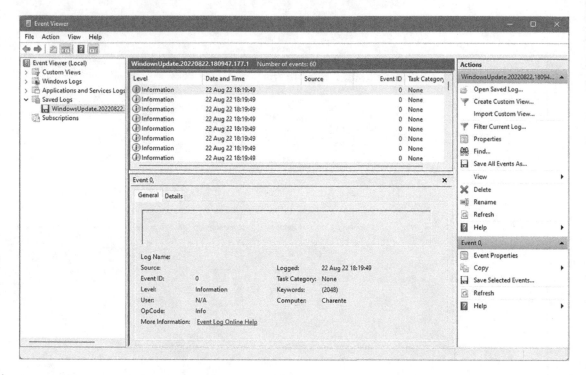

Figure 21-3. *You can open event logs from other PCs in Event Viewer*

Reading .dmp Files

The Windows\MiniDump folder is where you will find critical error log files, such as those associated with a Blue Screen of Death (BSOD). These files are stored in a .dmp format and cannot be opened natively in Windows. There are several ways to open them, however. If you have access to Microsoft Visual Studio, you can download the Windows Driver Kit (WDK) or Windows Software Development Kit (SDK). Both of these will allow you to open, and read, the contents of the .dmp file.

Perhaps a preferable option for many people will be the third-party utility BlueScreenView. You can download this from www.nirsoft.net/utils/blue_screen_view.html, and it will automatically display the contents of all the .dmp files located in your Windows\MiniDump folder (see Figure 21-4).

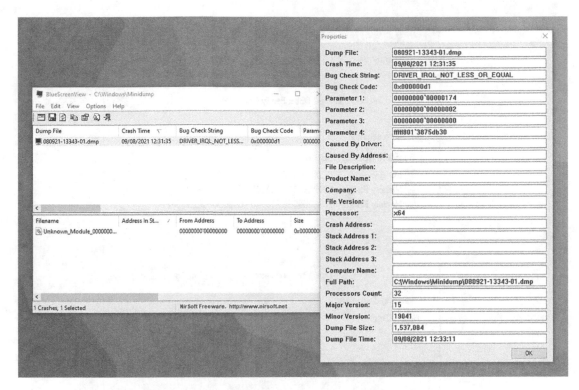

***Figure 21-4.** BlueScreenView is a great utility for reading .dmp files*

So what is it you're looking for within a .dmp file that can tell you why a Blue Screen occurred? There are plenty of pieces of useful information to be contained in the log, including the verbose text of the Bug Check String and the Windows standard error code in Bug Check Code. These come in the format 0x000... and can be searched for online to discover the cause of the problem and hopefully a solution.

You can see in Figure 21-4 a critical error that occurred completely out of the blue on my own PC just the other day. The description is DRIVER_IRQL_NOT_LESS_OR_EQUAL and the Windows error code is 0x000000d1. A quick search online reveals useful information about this error, which dates back several versions of Windows. It could be caused by a variety of things including an incompatible or corrupt device driver or an Interrupt Request (IRQ) conflict. While the latter is extremely rare in Windows since the introduction of the Windows Side-by-Side (**WinSxS**) folder, it's a legacy problem that can appear occasionally, and for many drivers, you can check in their Resources tab in the Properties inspector for the driver to see what IRQs they use and if any conflicts exist (see Figure 21-5).

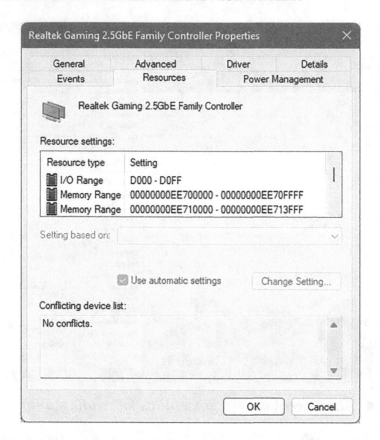

Figure 21-5. *You can check the properties of a driver to see if there are error and conflicts*

Searching Online for Solutions

There are many resources you can use on the Internet to help you find solutions to problems. These range from a simple web search to specialist online resources. You want to be able to find the information you need quickly though, so where can you look and what are the best ways to find information quickly?

Search Engines

So you're searching online for the solution to the problem you're facing, and you're hitting a wall. Is there a way you can better leverage the results you're getting? All

Internet search engines allow you to use what's called "operators" to refine your searches and find specific information.

Note   Not all searches produce quality results. If you ask Amazon's Alexa, "Who is Mike Halsey?", it will tell you that I've written a few more books than I really have. This isn't especially helpful, but it's always good for a laugh at parties.

Google is probably going to be your first port of call, being by far the web's biggest search engine, and, for as much as I personally can't stand Google's "we'll harvest all your data and sell it to advertisers" approach, they do produce the best search results.

There are plenty of operators you can use with Google search; these are detailed in Table 21-1.

Table 21-1. *Google search operators*

Operator	Description
@[Name]	To search on social media, e.g., @Twitter
$[Num]	To search for a price, e.g., Keyboard $200
#[Hashtag]	To search for a hashtag, e.g., #WindowsDo
-[Word]	To exclude a word from results, e.g., Gaming -Playstation
"[Term]"	To search for an exact word or phrase, e.g., "Microsoft Azure" or "Mike Halsey MVP"
[Num]…[Num]	To search within a range of numbers, e.g., $10…$50
[Term] or [Term]	To combine two different searches in one set of results
site:Windows.do	To search for results from a specific website
related:Windows.do	To search for websites related to your search term
cache:Windows.do	To search Google's website cache

Microsoft's Bing search engine also includes specific search operators you can use. These can be seen in Table 21-2.

Table 21-2. *Microsoft Bing search operators*

Operator	Description
+[Term]	To force inclusion of a term in your search results, can be used with ""
"[Term]"	To search for exact words or a phrase, can be used with +
()	Excludes results containing a group of words
[Term] AND [Term]	Search for results containing both of the terms
[Term] OR or | [Term]	Search for results containing either term
NOT or –[Term]	Exclude a term from results, can be used with ""

While it's perhaps less useful for searching for answers to IT and technical queries, WolframAlpha.com is a powerful search engine that produces high-quality results. Its operators are, as you might expect, more complex than those for Google and Microsoft. You can find them detailed at https://pcs.tv/3RnblIm.

Note   I want to slip in a note about the websites I am about to reference. The companies behind them do revamp and improve them from time to time, so it's possible that not everything I describe will be exactly where I said it was when you come to look at the website yourself.

Microsoft Docs

Back in the day when I was writing troubleshooting books for earlier versions of Windows, the support and documentation websites provided by Microsoft were somewhat fragmented. We had Visual Studio websites, Microsoft's MSDN (Microsoft Developer Network) and TechNet websites, Microsoft Support, and more. Now these documentation and support websites are well on their way to being improved and streamlined with most of the documents and technical information ending up at docs. microsoft.com.

This website is organized by the different products and the different product areas (cloud, client) that Microsoft covers (see Figure 21-6). One of the issues currently with Microsoft Docs is that search might be more powerful, something that I and other MVPs (Microsoft Most Valuable Professional awardees) have fed back to Microsoft, so hopefully it'll be improved.

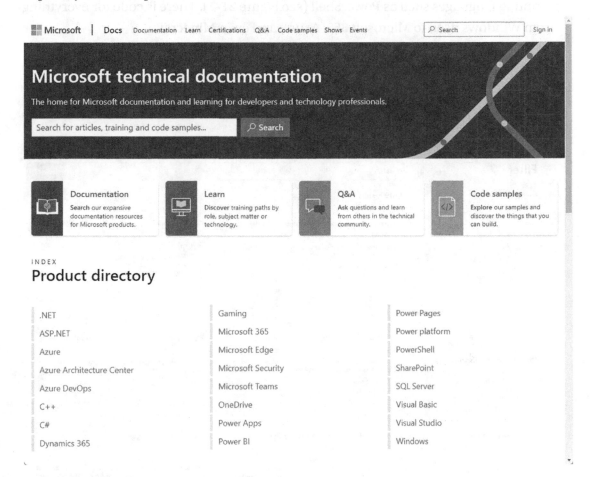

Figure 21-6. *Microsoft Docs contains many thousands of documentation and support articles*

The upshot of this is that sometimes you can find it easier to use Google or Bing to search for articles on Microsoft Docs, rather than by searching inside Microsoft Docs itself.

Microsoft Docs Code Samples

One of the best features of the Microsoft Docs website is its *Code Samples* section, accessible from the menu that runs across the top of the screen. This part of the website contains code you can download and run for every Microsoft product that includes scripting languages such as PowerShell (see Figure 21-7). There is code for everything from Windows itself to Microsoft 365, Azure, and even Minecraft.

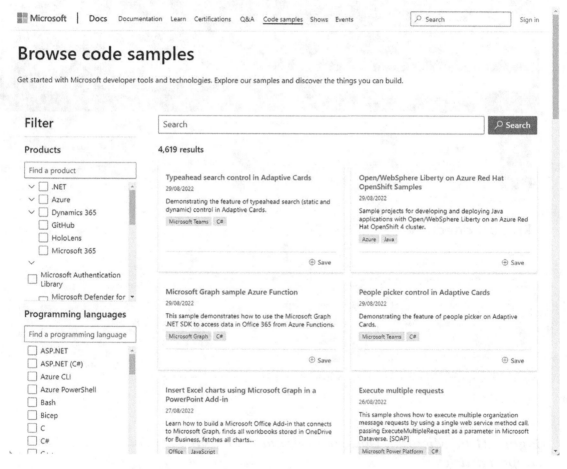

Figure 21-7. *Microsoft Docs contains a repository of downloadable code you can use*

GitHub

`GitHub.com` is a code sharing website and repository that became hugely popular after it launched in 2008, and even though it is primarily a resource for open source code, it remained hugely popular after Microsoft purchased it in 2018, largely because the company left it alone.

You can find code from just about every developer on the Planet at GitHub, including Microsoft that maintains repositories there including a large repository of PowerShell scripts (see Figure 21-8). If you are looking to get started with PowerShell, or looking for specific scripts to help you manage and troubleshoot Windows, this is a great place to start looking.

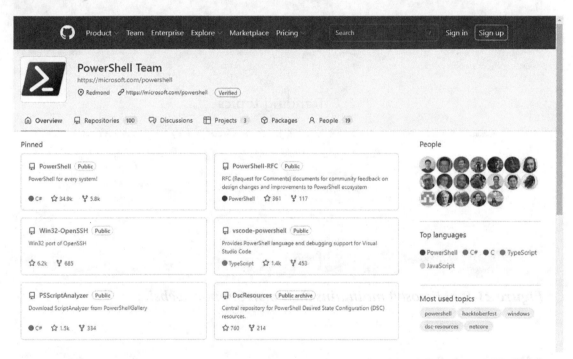

Figure 21-8. *Microsoft maintains a PowerShell script repository on GitHub*

Microsoft Support

The main Microsoft support website remains at `support.microsoft.com` and contains help and support articles for all of Microsoft's products (see Figure 21-9). The articles published on the Microsoft Support website are all easy to read and well laid out. This makes them accessible to a wide range of people, as opposed to many third-party websites where sadly accessibility isn't a consideration.

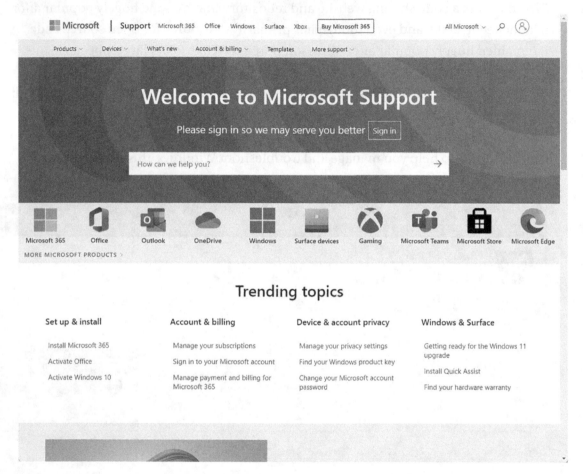

Figure 21-9. *Microsoft maintains their own Support website*

Microsoft Answers

This is sort of a subset of the Microsoft Support website, but is available on its own from answers.microsoft.com. This website is more interactive and is where Microsoft support agents, MVPs, and Microsoft partners can respond to and answer technical questions from the community of users of all Microsoft products (see Figure 21-10).

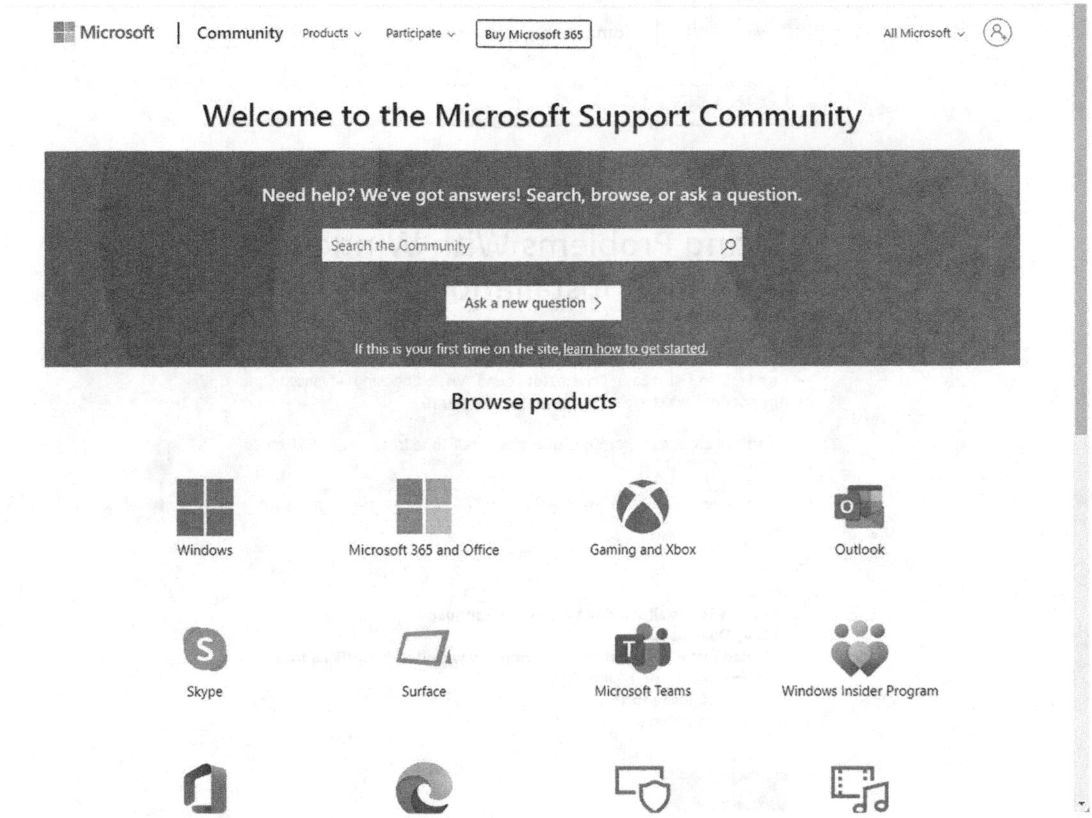

Figure 21-10. *Microsoft Answers is where you can get interactive help from experts*

People who reply and answer your questions will be clearly labelled as *Microsoft Agent, MVP*, or *Independent Agent,* among other titles. You can see this in Figure 21-11 when, while looking for a suitable answer I could take a screenshot of for this book, I saw a question I thought I might be able to help with.

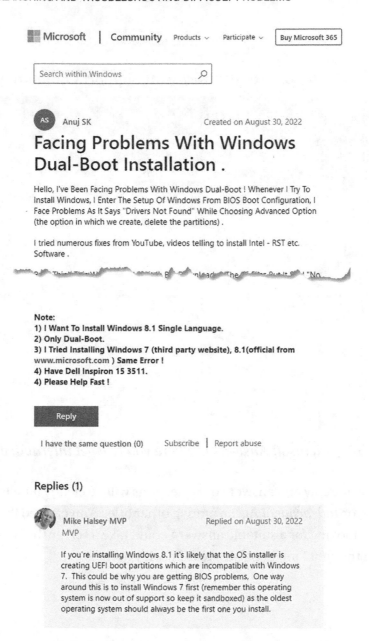

Figure 21-11. *Responders at Microsoft Answers are clearly labelled as to who they are*

Other Microsoft and Third-Party Support Sites

There are a great many excellent-quality support websites provided by third parties. The best of these are as follows:

- Annoyances.org – `www.annoyances.org`

- Computing.net – `www.computing.net`

- How-To Geek – `www.howtogeek.com`

- Microsoft Download Center – `www.microsoft.com/download`

- Tom's Hardware – `www.tomshardware.co.uk`

Windows.do

Of course at this point, it would be completely remiss of me not to mention my own website which you can find at `windows.do` (see Figure 21-12). I have hundreds of help, how-to, and support articles there with a new article almost every single day. I focus on keeping articles short, just three paragraphs usually, as speaking strictly for myself, if somebody wants to write a help article that's two thousand words long, I certainly don't want to read it.

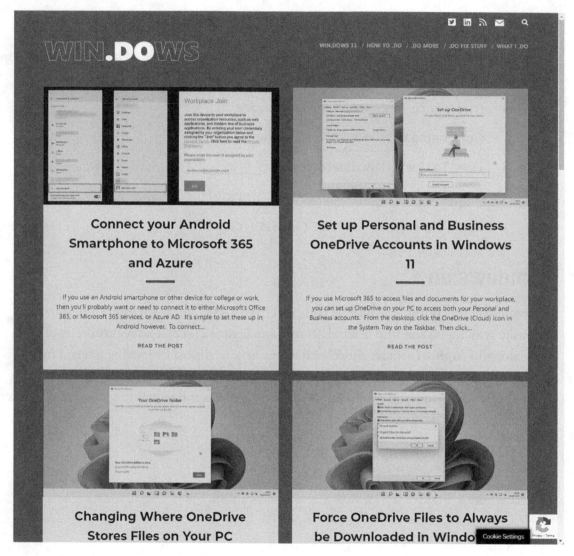

Figure 21-12. *My own website Windows.do contains hundreds of help, how-to, and support articles*

You can also follow me on Twitter at @MikeHalsey where I am always happy to respond to questions submitted by private messages.

Hardware Driver and Support Sites

I always recommend that you download hardware drivers directly from the manufacturer's website. These websites will also have forums in which you can post questions and get answers directly from technical staff at the company:

- Acer – www.acer.com/support

- Asus – www.asus.com/support

- AMD – support.amd.com

- Dell – www.dell.com/support

- HP – support.hp.com

- Intel – downloadcenter.intel.com

- Lenovo – support.lenovo.com

- Microsoft Surface Support – www.microsoft.com/surface/support

- Nvidia – www.nvidia.com/page/support.html

- Samsung – www.samsung.com/support

Third-Party Support Tools

Additionally, there are many excellent third-party help, information, and support tools that are favored by IT Pros; these are in addition to the Microsoft Sysinternals suite that I detailed in Chapter 22:

- Aida64 – www.aida64.com

- CCleaner – www.piriform.com/ccleaner

- Disk Digger – www.diskdigger.org

- GRC – www.grc.com

- Hiren's Boot CD – www.hiren.info/pages/bootcd

- Sandra Utilities – www.sisoftware.eu

- TeamViewer – www.teamviewer.com

- Ultimate Boot CD – `www.ultimatebootcd.com`

- WhoCrashed – `www.resplendence.com/whocrashed`

Other Useful Microsoft Tools

Throughout this book, I have detailed all the tools and utilities in Windows 11 that can be used to help you diagnose and troubleshoot problems on a PC. This is all but four of them, and there are some tools that are very useful, but very specific for what they do and, as such, really didn't fit neatly into any other chapter.

DXDiag

DXDiag can be found by a search in the Start Menu and not any other way, as it's pretty well hidden. It's been in Windows since Vista and is a diagnostics tool that tests the DirectX functionality of graphics, audio, and USB hardware on the PC. DirectX is an API (Application Programming Interface) framework for handling multimedia tasks.

When you run DXDiag, the utility will run its tests and then present the results as a series of tabs across its window (see Figure 21-13). If it finds any problems or errors, they will appear in the *Notes* section of the appropriate tab.

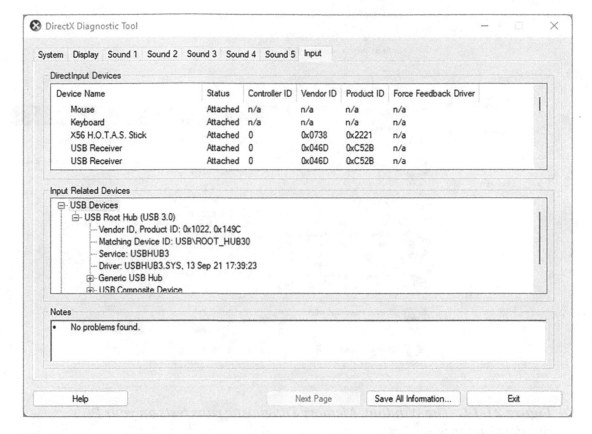

Figure 21-13. *DXDiag runs diagnostics on multimedia hardware in Windows*

Windows Memory Diagnostic

One utility you can find in *Windows Tools* is the *Windows Memory Diagnostic* (see Figure 21-14). This will prompt you to restart your PC where, from the Recovery Console, it will run a series of tests on the physical memory installed in the PC to see if it can determine if any errors exist. This can be useful if you are getting random application or other crashes, an unidentifiable Blue Screen of Death.

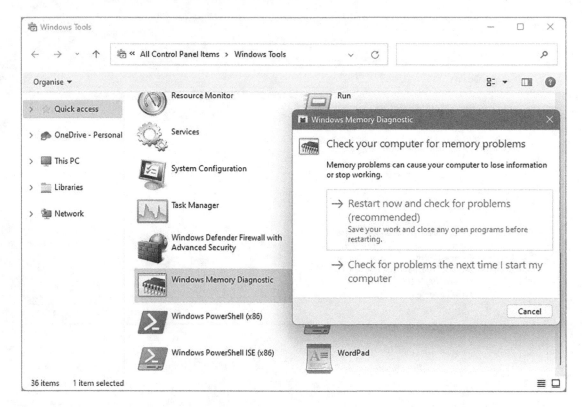

Figure 21-14. *The Windows Memory Diagnostic runs tests on your PC's physical memory*

Note   Windows Memory Diagnostic used to be available in the Windows Recovery Environment, though it has been removed with Windows 11.

When the PC restarts, you will get a great blast from the past as an old-style DOS window will fill your screen running the memory diagnostic tool (see Figure 21-15). This has a progress bar and will restart the PC automatically when it is finished.

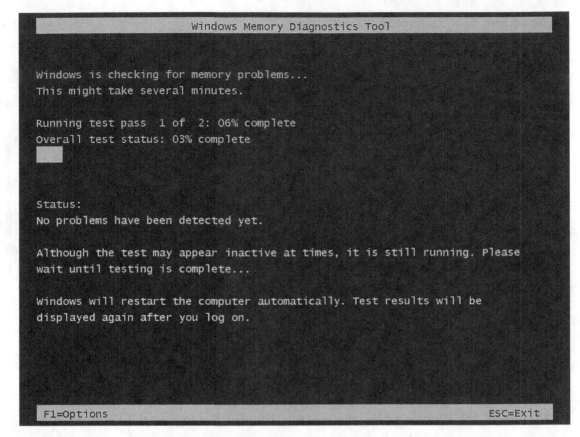

Figure 21-15. *The Windows Memory Diagnostic is a proper old-style DOS tool*

You can at any time press the **F1** key on your keyboard (assuming your keyboard has one that is) and change the settings for the diagnostic, such as to tell it to run a more detailed and thorough test. When the Memory Diagnostic has run and the PC restarted, you can access the logs it created in *Event Viewer*.

You can find the test results under *Windows Logs* and then *System*. Click the *Action* menu and select *Filter Current Log*. In the dialog that appears, in the *Event sources* drop-down menu, select *MemoryDiagnostics-Results* and click OK. The results of the memory diagnostic will then become available to you (see Figure 21-16).

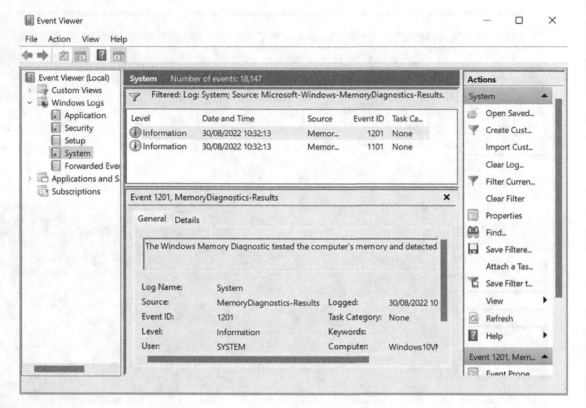

Figure 21-16. *You can view the memory diagnostics logs in the Event Viewer*

Windows Sandbox

If you are using the Pro or Enterprise version of Windows 11 and have virtualization support on your PC's processor, you will have access to a feature called *Windows Sandbox*. This needs to be activated on most PCs, so in the Start Menu search for **features** and select *Turn Windows features on or off* from the search results.

You will see *Windows Sandbox* at the bottom of the list in the dialog that appears (see Figure 21-17), though you will have to also activate some other virtualization features such as the *Hyper-V Management Tools*. After restarting the PC, *Windows Sandbox* will then appear as an app in the Start Menu.

Figure 21-17. *You need to activate Windows Sandbox on many PCs*

Where Windows Sandbox is most useful is for testing things that might cause a PC or an installation to become unstable, such as a new piece of software or a file that you suspect might have a malicious Visual Basic (VB) script contained within it that you need to remove.

Sandbox will appear full screen on your desktop though it can be resized into a window (see Figure 21-18). It is a fully containerized, isolated Windows 11 desktop. Each instance is created new when Sandbox is run and completely discarded when the instance is closed, making it highly secure for testing.

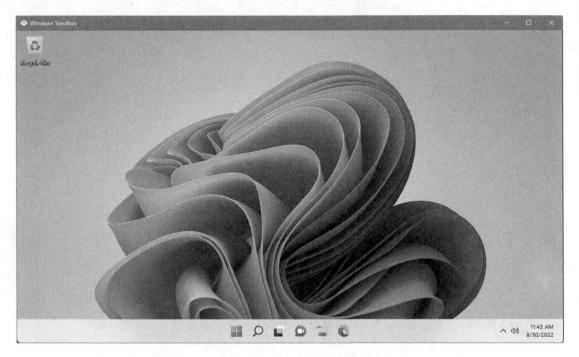

Figure 21-18. *Windows Sandbox is excellent for testing things that might cause instabilities*

Windows Subsystem for Linux

In Figure 21-17, you might have noticed a little optional feature called the *Windows Subsystem for Linux*. This allows a full Linux kernel to be run virtually within Windows 11. If you activate this feature, you will then be able to install a wide variety of Linux distros from the Microsoft Store app (see Figure 21-19).

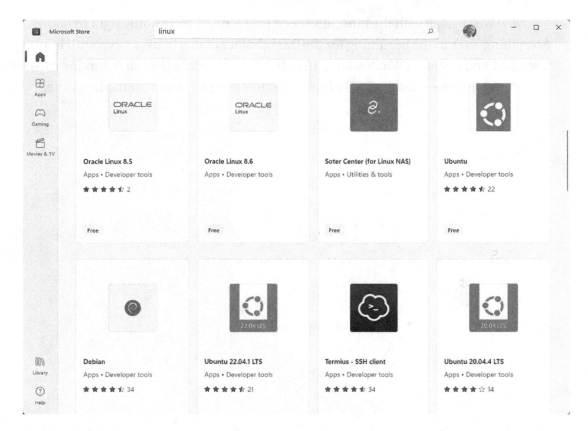

Figure 21-19. *The Windows Subsystem for Linux lets you run Linux as part of your Windows 11 system*

The biggest advantage here is that it gives you access to Linux scripting environments such as BASH (one of the very few "acronyms" in tech that doesn't actually stand for anything at all). While BASH is primarily used in Windows for application development, there are some administrative tools you can use for Windows from within Linux itself, and with new tools being added periodically by third parties, you might find scripting tools here that are useful to you.

Summary

If you can't get the solution to a problem from within the Windows 11 tools and utilities, there are always other places you can look for solutions and different ways in which you can use those tools to get the results you need to troubleshoot and repair problems.

Now we've dealt with the most advanced problems, it seems only right to take everything back to the beginning for the final chapter of this book, where we'll look at installing and restoring Windows 11, including how you can reinstall it nondestructively, and configure a new installation before a user has even signed in for the first time.

CHAPTER 22

Installing and Restoring Windows 11

It's becoming increasingly rare that anybody installs a copy of Windows these days. The largest number of installs will be corporations upgrading their desktop machines from Windows 10, but even that's not a clean install, it's an upgrade. IT departments reimaging a PC after a problem isn't a clean installation either, it's restoring a backup image. For consumers and the rest of society, Windows 11 will come preinstalled on a new PC or laptop, and those moving from Windows 10 to Windows 11 will perform an in-place upgrade that's rolled out through Windows Update, so that's not a clean installation either.

I performed a clean installation of Windows 11, but I'm weird, when I built myself a new workstation/work/gaming desktop PC in 2021; a beast of a machine running an, at the time, top of the line unlocked AMD Ryzen 9 processor with burst speeds up to 4.9GHz, 64GB DDR4 RAM, itself running at 4GHz, three 2TB Samsung PCIe 4 M.2 SSDs with speeds up to 7000MB/s, and an ASUS Radeon RX6800 graphics card with 16GB RAM and a clock speed of 1980MHz (see Figure 22-1).

© Mike Halsey 2023
M. Halsey, *Troubleshooting and Supporting Windows 11*, https://doi.org/10.1007/978-1-4842-8728-6_22

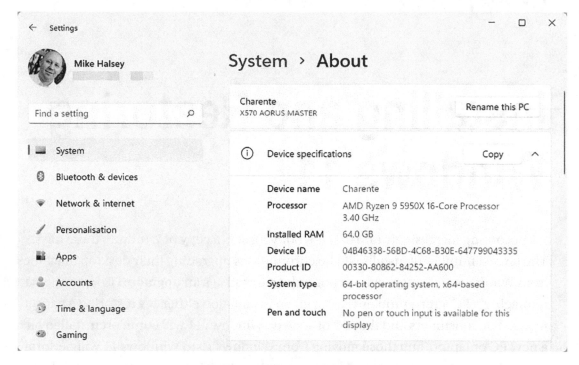

Figure 22-1. *I'm weird because I still clean install Windows*

All of this is running on a Gigabyte X570 Aorus Master motherboard with a Corsair RMx 1000 Watt PSU, in a Be quiet! Silent Base 802 case on a sesame seed bun (you made the last bit up!; Ed).

It's a beast of a machine that's hardly taxed by my writing this book in Microsoft Word, recording a video course in Camtasia, or even pootling[1] around the galaxy in *Elite Dangerous* (Cmdr Travers if you're a fellow player), so you might wonder why I bothered spending more than $4000 on the thing. Actually, I address this in my book *The Green IT Guide* (Apress, 2022)... yes, you knew I was going to get in one last plug for it before this book was finished!

The reasoning I use in that book though is to purchase the fastest, most powerful computer you can afford. The reason is that it will last you much longer than a cheaper PC, reducing the amount of chemicals, metals, and plastics going to landfill and polluting the environment. Choosing a 1000 Watt PSU over a more reasonable 600 Watt unit which would work nicely is also part of this idea. Power supplies lose some of their power over the years, just as a car engine does, so purchasing a more powerful one to

---

[1] Poo-tle (verb, British informal), to move or travel in a leisurely manner.

begin with will also reduce the amount of tech going to landfill (ah, so that's why you said you want an Aston Martin!; Ed).

I always build my own desktop PCs as I've found getting one from any system builder, even one with a great online configurator, inevitably means making compromises. Usually, the storage is slower, or the motherboard doesn't support the new superfast storage technology you want, or the case is lacking a front-mounted USB-C port, etc. When this happens, you have no choice but to install Windows 11 yourself after building the thing, which is always tremendous fun. This leads me neatly into the first subject of this chapter...

Obtaining Up-to-Date Windows Installation Media

So where can you go to download fresh installation media for Windows that isn't horribly out of date and will require 30,000 Windows Updates? One place you should certainly never download a Windows ISO from, or anything else for that matter, is a website or torrent site, as it's all too easy for malware to be injected into the ISO file that's installed right along with Windows.

If you have a volume licensing subscription to Microsoft, or a `my.visualstudio.com` account, then you can download an up-to-date ISO file from there, but you get better options from `www.microsoft.com/software-download`. This website will allow you to download ISO files for the currently supported versions of Windows, but it will also allow you to create a bootable USB Flash Drive from which Windows can be installed (see Figure 22-2).

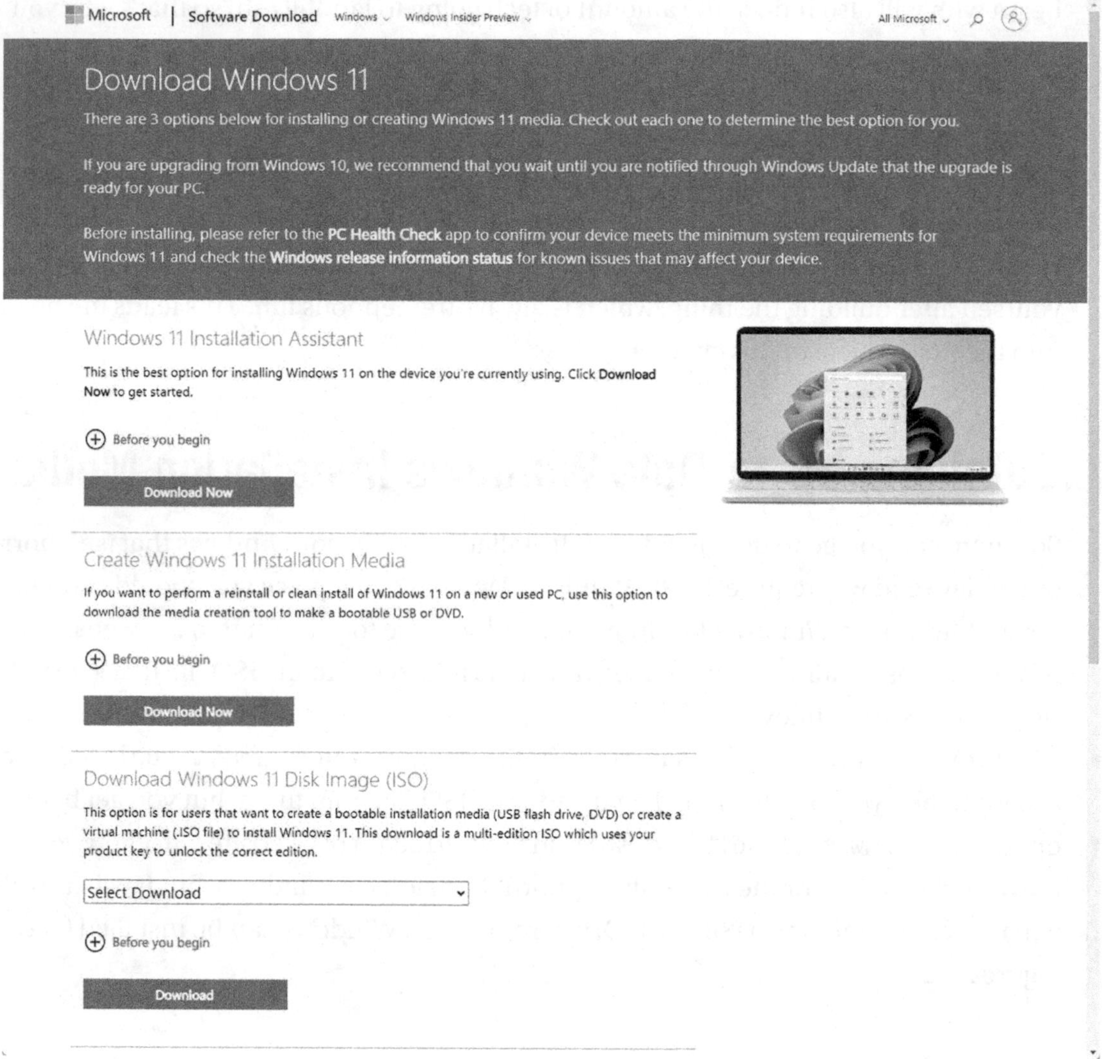

Figure 22-2. *The Microsoft Windows Download website is the best place to get Windows 11*

Any ISO file you download from this website, or any installer USB Flash Drive you create, will be the latest version of Windows 11, so there will be much fewer Windows Updates to install later on. If you need to purchase a license to install Windows 11, you can do so on the following links:

- **Windows 11 Home** – https://pcs.tv/3AKu8ae

- **Windows 11 Pro** – https://pcs.tv/3q6XF8N

- **Windows 11 Pro for Workstations** – https://pcs.tv/3AFCOJZ

- **Windows Volume Licensing** – https://pcs.tv/3wKzgto

Tip   It is often much cheaper to purchase a valid license for Windows from a reputable PC magazine, where these sometimes resell discounted licenses, or from an in-store or online retailer during the Black Friday or end-of-year sales.

As is always the case, you should be very careful when purchasing a Windows license that you get it from a reputable source and not just some third-party reseller on Amazon or eBay. These can often be scams, selling a product key that has already been used or that isn't valid at all.

Tip   If you have a Windows 10 product key that's no longer in use on a PC, you ought to be able to use that product key during the Windows 11 installation process. If that doesn't work, which it should frankly, then you can install Windows 10 from the download link I mentioned earlier and upgrade it to Windows 11 in-place after activating it.

Managing Windows Activation and Changing Your Product Key

If you need to activate your copy of Windows, add a product key, or perhaps change your product key because, for example, you are upgrading from Windows 11 Home to Windows 11 Pro, you can do so in Settings under *System* and *Activation* (see Figure 22-3).

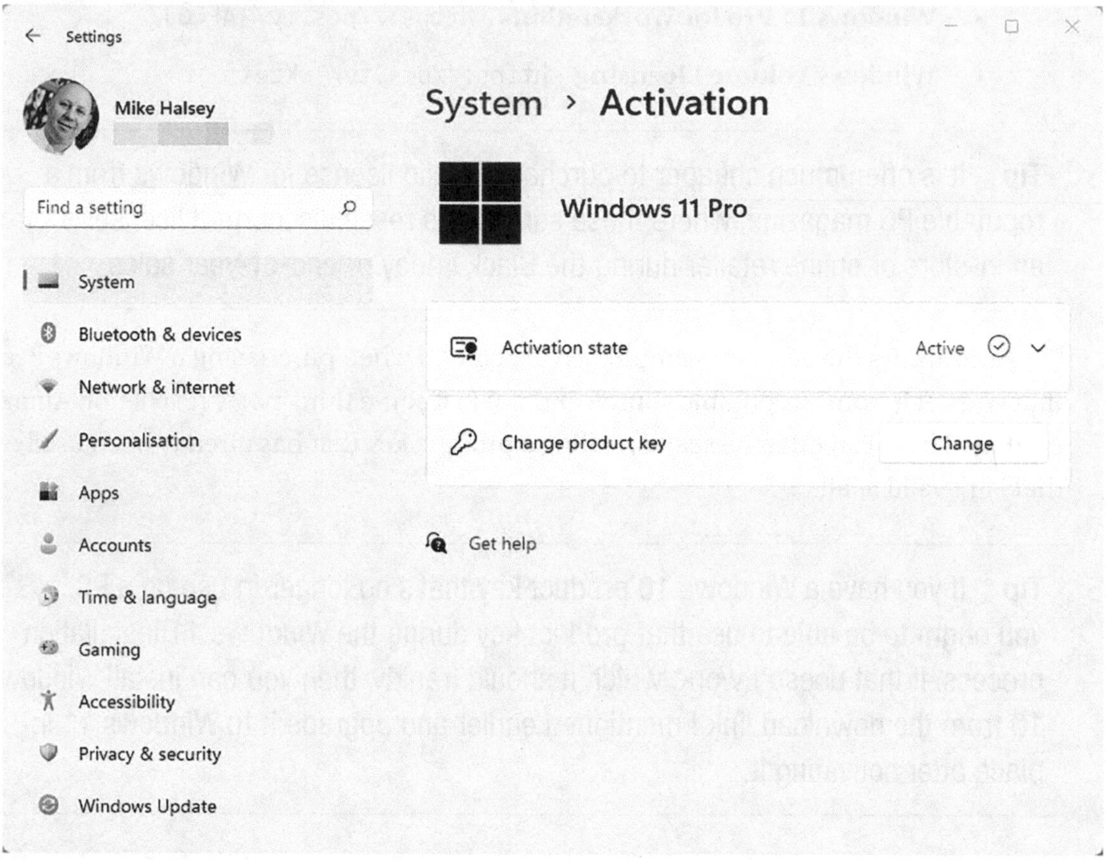

Figure 22-3. *You can activate Windows and change your product key in Settings*

Nondestructively Reinstalling Windows 11

Let's say that everything's gone horribly wrong, you don't have a backup image of your installation, but you also need to reinstall the operating system without harming all of the files on the PC (accounts and applications will sadly have to be redone in the worst cases).

It is possible to nondestructively reinstall Windows however. You first need to boot your PC from your installation media, which is most likely the USB Flash Drive you created from the media creation tool on the Microsoft download website I detailed earlier in this chapter.

At the install screen, choose your language and country options and then click the *Install now* button, enter your product key, or if you already have a valid license on the PC that's tied to your Microsoft Account, click *I don't have a product key*. When you are prompted to choose how you want to install Windows, you will see an option to *Upgrade: Install Windows and keep files, settings and applications* (see Figure 22-4). This won't work when booting from the installation media, but will reinstall Windows over the top of your existing installation, effectively refreshing the OS if you are able to run it from the desktop.

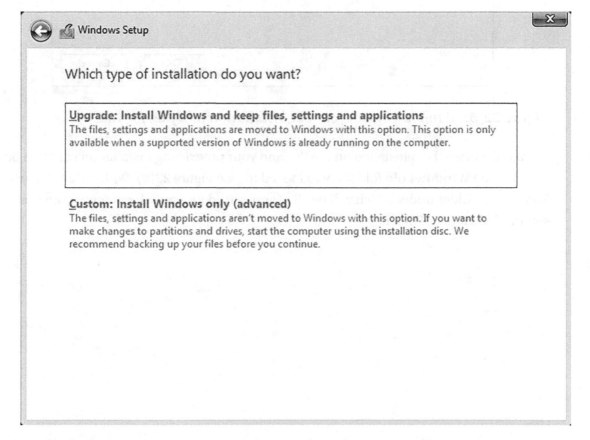

Figure 22-4. The Windows installer allows you to upgrade your installation

If you can't boot to the desktop, perhaps because the existing installation has become too corrupt in some way. In this case, and again booting the PC from your Windows 11 installation media, click the *Custom: Install Windows only (advanced)* option.

When you choose this option, you will be presented with a dialog telling you that a previous installation of Windows has been found and that it will be moved to a **Windows.old** folder (see Figure 22-5).

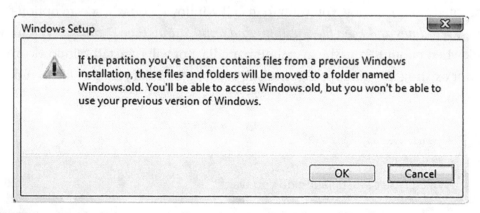

Figure 22-5.   *Windows moves your old installation and files for you*

Windows will be reinstalled on the PC, and your preexisting installation can then be found in the **Windows.old** folder it was moved to (see Figure 22-6). Within this, you will find a *Users* folder under which will be all of your saved files and documents from the standard Shell User Folders.

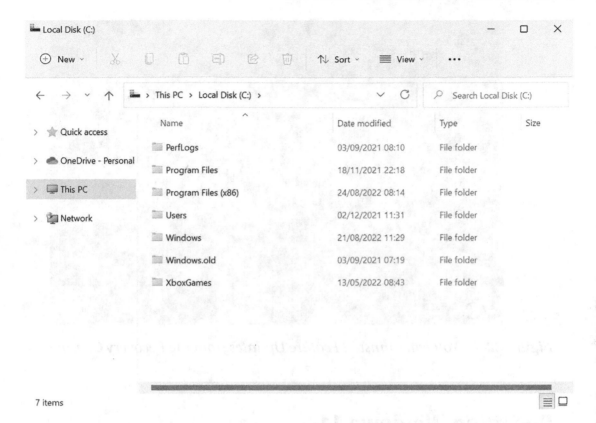

Figure 22-6. *Your preexisting Windows installation will be found in the Windows.old folder*

Caution   Note that any files, documents, and folders not stored in the shell user folders, but stored elsewhere on the Windows drive, will be wiped during the reinstallation.

Uninstalling Problematic Feature Updates

If it's an annual "Feature Update," what we used to call a Service Pack that's caused Windows to go all screwy, you can boot the PC into the Recovery Console from pressing *Shift + Restart* at the Lock Screen or in the Start Menu or from a USB Recovery Drive and select *Troubleshoot ➤ Advanced options ➤ Uninstall Updates* and then click *Uninstall the latest feature update* (see Figure 22-7).

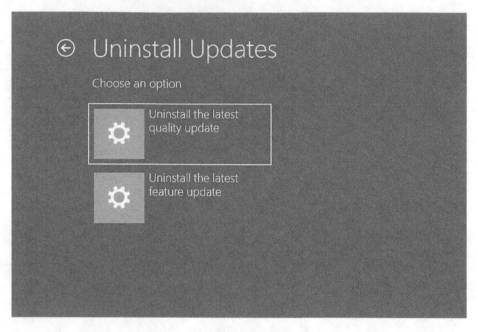

Figure 22-7. You can uninstall Feature Updates from the Recovery Console

Resetting Windows 11

Alternatively, if that's not working for you, select *Troubleshoot* ➤ *Reset this PC*, and then click *Keep my files*. This will reinstall Windows from the backup image it keeps of itself that's 30 days old, which will hopefully be before the Feature Update or other screwy Windows Update will have been installed (see Figure 22-8).

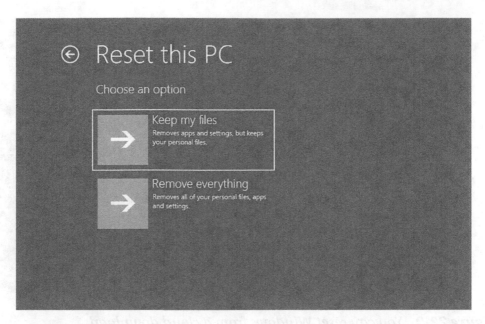

Figure 22-8. *You can reset Windows from the Recovery Console*

When you reset your Windows installation, you will be asked if you want to use the local image on the PC, this being the one that Windows creates itself and maintains. This is always 30 days old, the reason being that if the PC has worked perfectly well for the last 30 days, then that will be a stable position to reinstall to.

Alternatively, you can choose *Cloud download* (see Figure 22-9). This will download a fresh installation image of Windows from Microsoft's servers and use that to reinstall the OS. This is most useful when the local image has become corrupt and can't be reinstalled.

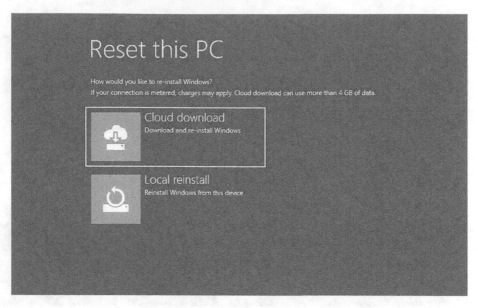

Figure 22-9. *You can reset Windows from a cloud download*

> **Caution**   Not all laptops and tablets are compatible with cloud download. The
> PC has to include Wi-Fi drivers that work with the feature, so when you purchase
> new PCs, it's worth asking the vendor if they provide these. As an alternative,
> connecting the PC to the Internet via an Ethernet cable, perhaps through a dongle
> in a USB-A port as Thunderbolt ports may also not be supported, will enable you to
> download a cloud image.

Creating Custom Installation Media for Windows 11

When you deploy a new operating system across an organization, it's very common to
preinject that OS image with the software and settings you need, as it's considerably
simpler to do this than to deploy a standard Windows 11 installation and then have to
manually configure each PC afterward.

Microsoft provides a whole range of tools for its volume licensing customers which
you can find on the Microsoft Docs website at https://pcs.tv/3TCoMpP. These include

tutorials on how the whole process works, how to plan your deployment and rollout of Windows 11, and the various tools the company provides such as their Autopilot system.

This is fine for those with a Volume Licensing subscription, but what about everybody else? Well, one of the best third-party solutions on the Internet is the software called NTLite (see Figure 22-10), which you can download from www.ntlite.com. This is a full image creation tool that allows you to manage your different Windows images, install and remove language packs and Windows features, configure Registry keys and set Group and Security policies, install drivers and applications, and deploy these images using an unattended setup process.

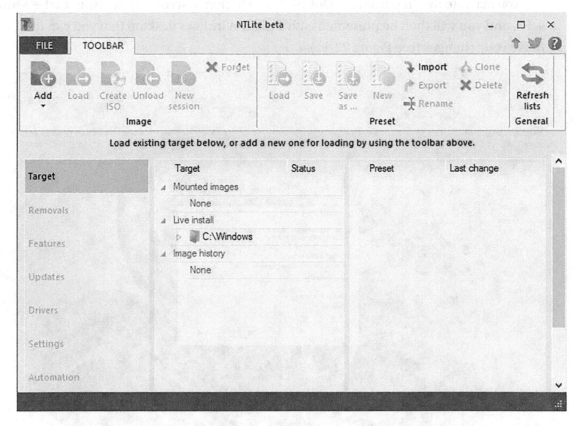

Figure 22-10. *NTLite can be used to create custom installation images*

Windows OOBE

No, it's not a Roy Orbison song, but the Windows Out-of-Box Experience, otherwise known as SysPrep. After Windows 11 has been installed, this can be used to change settings, install software, and install drivers. This is for changes made on a whole computer level and not a per-user level, so it can't be used to pre-create user accounts. This is because OOBE bypasses the Windows Out-of-Box installer, where a user is guided through signing into the operating system and setting their preferences for Windows features, such as OneDrive, and for privacy.

You activate SysPrep from the Out-of-Box Experience screen by pressing **Ctrl + Shift + F3**, and you will then be presented with a plain Windows desktop that you can use to make your changes (see Figure 22-11).

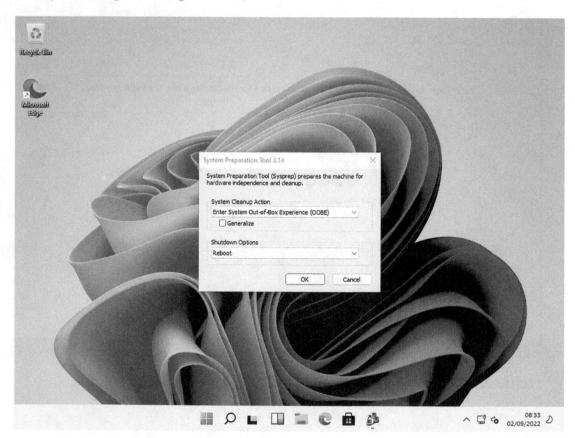

Figure 22-11. *SysPrep can make changes to a new PC that affect all users*

Tip   If the PC does not have an F3 key, you can run SysPrep from the `C:\`
`Windows\System32\Sysprep` folder, but you will first need to have created an
account on the PC to reach this so it's not ideal.

SysPrep is most useful when you have a new PC or laptop that is being given to a
friend, family member, or employee where a few changes need to be made that aren't or
haven't already been rolled out in a custom installation image for the operating system.

You should leave the SysPrep window open on your desktop, as you will need it when
you are finished, but if you do accidentally close it, it can be run from the `C:\Windows\`
`System32\Sysprep` folder.

When you have made the changes you want to make and want to lock down the
changes you have made to Windows, in the SysPrep window check the *Generalize* option
and either *Restart* or *Shutdown* the PC (see Figure 22-12).

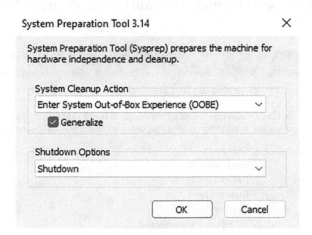

Figure 22-12. *Any changes you "generalize" in SysPrep will apply to all new users
on the PC*

Now, when anybody creates themselves a new account from the Out-of-Box
Experience, any changes you have made will automatically apply to the account(s)
they create.

Installing Windows 11 in a Virtual Machine

Many people will want to install Windows 11 in a virtual machine environment, perhaps for testing or perhaps to give you a clean installation to reference. I have used Windows 11 virtual machines extensively for screenshots throughout this book.

Because the minimum installation requirements for Windows 11 have changed from Windows 10, you can't simply install Windows 11, you first have to set some specific options. I will show you how to do this in Hyper-V because as you're reading this it's very likely you'll be using a Windows PC anyway, but you will need to set the same options in whatever virtual machine software you're using.

Hyper-V first needs to be activated on your PC, and for this, you will need the Pro or Enterprise version of Windows, as the feature does not exist in the Home edition. In the Start Menu, search for **features** and select *Turn Windows features on or off* from the search results.

In the dialog that appears, make sure you have both Hyper-V options checked (see Figure 22-13).

Figure 22-13. *You need to have Hyper-V activated on your PC*

Note that if you are using an AMD processor on your PC, you will need to make sure that SVM (Secure Virtual Machine) mode is enabled in the firmware (see Figure 22-14).

This is often disabled by default and will prevent Hyper-V or other virtual machine software from running on the PC. If you are using an Intel processor and don't have virtualization enabled, you should enable VT-x in your UEFI firmware.

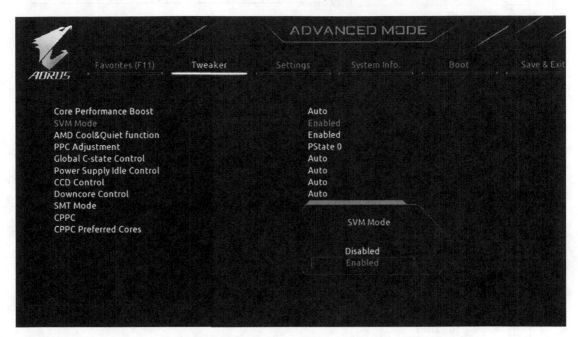

Figure 22-14. *AMD processors need SVM mode enabled in the firmware*

When you are creating your virtual machine in Hyper-V, there are two changes you need to make. The first is in the *Security* settings for the virtual machine. Check the box for *Enable Trusted Platform Module* (see Figure 22-15).

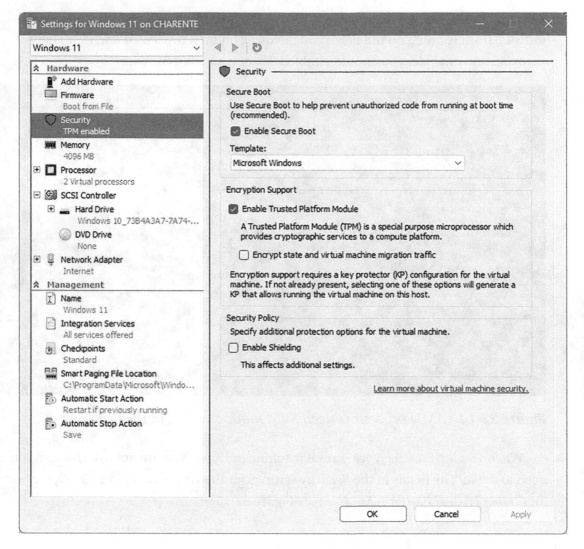

Figure 22-15. *You need to enable a virtual TPM for the virtual machine*

The second change you need to make is in the *Processor* settings. Here, you need to change the *Number of virtual processors* to at least **two** (see Figure 22-16). With these changes made, Windows 11 will happily install in the virtual machine.

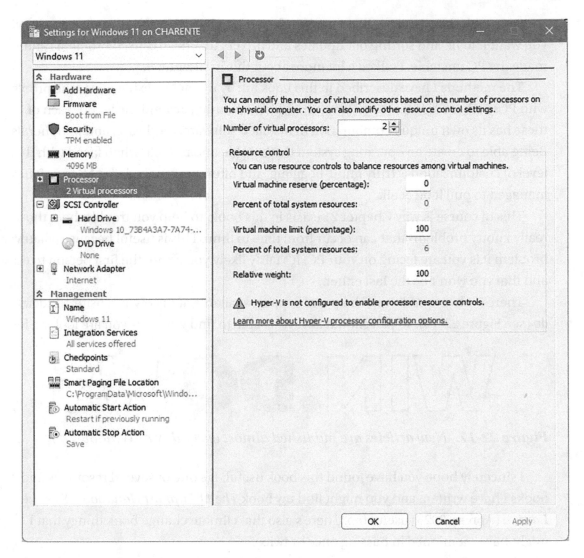

Figure 22-16. *Windows 11 requires a dual-core processor to install*

Summary

It's actually very difficult to break a Windows install these days. I tried it a few years ago for my Windows 10 troubleshooting books, repeatedly switching a machine off while the "Don't switch off your PC" message was on screen, and Windows successfully recovered every single time. You can also get details about Windows installation and upgrading errors on the Microsoft Docs website at https://pcs.tv/3AJOwba.

So troubleshooting installation in Windows 11 really is just about configuring how you want it to be and sorting out updates and drivers that have caused problems and made the PC unstable. I talked a lot more about this in Chapter 9.

The methods I have described in this book are by no means exhaustive. The problem with PCs is that while there are around a billion operating around the world, each of these has its own unique combination of installed software, hardware, and peripherals. Being able to create an operating system that's stable and reliable when faced with that level of customization is truly mind-boggling, and often I'm amazed that Microsoft has managed to pull it off at all.

This of course is why Chapter 21 exists in this book, to help you troubleshoot those really knotty problems that can occur from time to time. This is useful because whatever problem it is you are facing on your PC, it's fairly likely you're not the first person to do so and that you won't be the last either.

There is always additional help and support available at my own website, `Windows.do` (see Figure 22-17), so you should always be able to find what it is you are looking for.

Figure 22-17. *New articles are published almost every day at Windows.do*

I sincerely hope you have found this book useful. It's one of several resources and books I have written, and you might find my book *The IT Support Handbook, Second Edition* (Apress, 2023) useful too. There's also that climate change book thingy that I might have mentioned in passing once or twice.

If you have any questions or would like to get in touch, I encourage you to do so through Twitter where you can find me at *@MikeHalsey*, and I'm available to answer questions if you ever get stuck on a problem, which hopefully now won't happen.

Index

A

Accessibility
    benefits, 171, 172
    hardware, 172
    tools, 172
Active Directory Explorer
    (ADExplorer), 425
ADInsight, 425
Administrative privileges, 304
Administrator-elevated Command
    Prompt, 237
Administrator privileges, 304
ADRestore, 426
Advanced windows processes and
    services management, 361–363
Amazon Appstore, 321, 356
AMD, 236, 666, 667
American Express card (AMEX), 77
Analyze offline system, 378
Android apps, 322
Antivirus scanner, 80
Antivirus software, 500
App and browser control, 544–546
Apple, 4, 116, 485
Apple Mac computers, 322
Apple Macintosh, 364
Apple's MagSafe chargers, 436
Application environment, 323
Astro Slide, 351, 352
AutoRuns, 377–379, 469, 565, 574, 594–596
Avantree Leaf Pro, 433

Azure AD account, 508
Azure AD Bitlocker keys, 509
Azure Cloud services, 49, 356

B

Base video, 554
BASH, 25, 322, 649
Battery, 22, 30, 379, 490, 497–499, 598
BCDEdit command, 618–621
BCDEdit data formats, 619
Biometrics, 535
    Fido, 79
    flavors, 78
    smartphone set up, 78
    vs. TFA, 75
    Windows Hello, 78
BIOS firmware, 458
Bitlocker, 460, 461, 623
    accessing encryption key(s) online,
        507, 508
    Bitlocker drive encryption, 506
    Bitlocker To Go, 512, 513
    encrypted disks management, 510–512
    encryption key storing, 507
    privacy & security option, 505
    recovery key, 507
    TPM Administration, 509, 510
    Windows 11, 506
Bitlocker To Go, 512, 513
Blizzard, 489

671

H

I, J

Printed in the United States
by Baker & Taylor Publisher Services